Lecture Notes in Computer Science 13465

More information about this series at https://link.springer.com/bookseries/558

Sergiy Bogomolov · David Parker (Eds.)

Formal Modeling and Analysis of Timed Systems

20th International Conference, FORMATS 2022
Warsaw, Poland, September 13–15, 2022
Proceedings

Springer

Editors
Sergiy Bogomolov ⓘ
Newcastle University
Newcastle upon Tyne, UK

David Parker ⓘ
University of Birmingham
Birmingham, UK

ISSN 0302-9743   ISSN 1611-3349 (electronic)
Lecture Notes in Computer Science
ISBN 978-3-031-15838-4   ISBN 978-3-031-15839-1 (eBook)
https://doi.org/10.1007/978-3-031-15839-1

This Springer imprint is published by the registered company Springer Nature Switzerland AG
The registered company address is: Gewerbestrasse 11, 6330 Cham, Switzerland

Preface

This volume contains the proceedings of the 20th International Conference on Formal Modeling and Analysis of Timed Systems (FORMATS 2022), held in Warsaw, Poland, during September 13–15, 2022. The conference was co-located with three others, CONCUR, QEST and FMICS, held together as part of the CONFEST 2022 event.

FORMATS is an annual conference which aims to promote the study of fundamental and practical aspects of timed systems, and to bring together researchers from different disciplines that share interests in the modeling, design, and analysis of timed computational systems. The conference aims to attract researchers interested in real-time issues in hardware design, performance analysis, real-time software, scheduling, semantics, and verification of real-timed, hybrid, and probabilistic systems.

In total, 30 paper submissions were received and distributed for review amongst a Program Committee comprising 32 members. All papers received at least three reviews and were then discussed amongst committee members. Ultimately, 14 papers (46%) were accepted for inclusion in the scientific program, including 12 full-length papers and two short papers. The conference had specifically solicited papers for a featured track on "Learning-based and data-driven systems". Five of the accepted papers fell within this category and were split across two sessions of the program.

New to FORMATS this year, authors of accepted papers that included computational results or tools were invited to submit accompanying artifacts for evaluation. This was to allow independent reproduction of the results stated in the papers, thereby strengthening the quality of the published papers. Nine artifacts were submitted (representing over 60% of all accepted papers), which were evaluated by a separate artifact evaluation committee, comprising 17 members. All artifacts received three reviews and all but one passed the acceptance criteria. The corresponding papers display an "Artifact Evaluated" badge in this proceedings.

FORMATS 2022 also included two invited talks from Thao Dang (CNRS and VERIMAG, Université Grenoble Alpes, France) and Jöel Ouaknine (Max Planck Institute for Software Systems, Germany). The abstract for the former and an accompanying paper for the latter are included in this proceedings. Separately, to celebrate the 20th anniversary of the FORMATS conference series, a special session was organized, including presentations from some of the founding members of the community: Patricia Bouyer (CNRS, LMF, France), Thomas A. Henzinger (IST Austria) and Kim Guldstrand Larsen (Aalborg University, Denmark). The first and third of these also contributed a corresponding paper, which can be found in this proceedings.

Finally, we would like to thanks all those who have contributed to FORMATS 2022, including the Program Committee, the artifact evaluation committee, the steering committee, in particular the chair Martin Fränzle, and the organizational committee behind CONFEST 2022. We would also like to thank DENSO and MathWorks for their generous sponsorship of FORMATS, Springer for their support with publishing the proceedings, and EasyChair for providing the paper submission and review system.

July 2022

Sergiy Bogomolov\
David Parker

Organization

Program Committee Chairs

Sergiy Bogomolov   Newcastle University, UK
David Parker   University of Birmingham, UK

Artifact Evaluation Committee Chairs

Akshay Rajhans   MathWorks, USA
Paolo Zuliani   Newcastle University, UK

Publicity Chair

Gethin Norman   University of Glasgow, UK

Special Track Chair

Alessandro Abate   University of Oxford, UK

Webmaster

Kostiantyn Potomkin   Newcastle University, UK

Steering Committee

Rajeev Alur   University of Pennsylvania, USA
Eugene Asarin   Paris Cité University, France
Martin Fränzle (Chair)   Universität Oldenburg, Germany
Thomas A. Henzinger   IST Austria, Austria
Joost-Pieter Katoen   RWTH Aachen University, Germany
Kim G. Larsen   Aalborg University, Denmark
Oded Maler (Founding Chair,   CNRS, France
   1957–2018)
Pavithra Prabhakar   Kansas State University, USA
Mariëlle Stoelinga   University of Twente, The Netherlands
Wang Yi   Uppsala University, Sweden

Program Committee

Alessandro Abate	University of Oxford, UK
Parosh Aziz Abdulla	Uppsala University, Denmark
Erika Abraham	RWTH Aachen University, Germany
Bernhard K. Aichernig	Graz University of Technology, Austria
Nicolas Basset	Université Grenoble Alpes, France
Nathalie Bertrand	Inria, France
Sergiy Bogomolov	Newcastle University, UK
Lei Bu	Nanjing University, China
Milan Ceska	Brno University of Technology, Czech Rebublic
Thao Dang	CNRS and Verimag, France
Catalin Dima	LACL, Université Paris-Est Créteil, France
Rayna Dimitrova	CISPA Helmholtz Center for Information Security, Germany
Mirco Giacobbe	University of Birmingham, UK
Radu Grosu	Stony Brook University, USA
Arnd Hartmanns	University of Twente, The Netherlands
Hsi-Ming Ho	University of Sussex, UK
Peter Gjøl Jensen	Aalborg University, Denmark
Taylor T. Johnson	Vanderbilt University, USA
Sebastian Junges	Radboud University, The Netherlands
Joost-Pieter Katoen	RWTH Aachen University, Germany
Sophia Knight	University of Minnesota Duluth, USA
Matthieu Martel	Université de Perpignan Via Domitia, France
Gethin Norman	University of Glasgow, UK
Miroslav Pajic	Duke University, USA
David Parker	University of Birmingham, UK
Igor Potapov	University of Liverpool, UK
Christian Schilling	Aalborg University, Denmark
Ana Sokolova	University of Salzburg, Austria
Sadegh Soudjani	Newcastle University, UK
Stavros Tripakis	Northeastern University, USA
Jana Tumova	KTH Royal Institute of Technology, Sweden
Naijun Zhan	Institute of Software, Chinese Academy of Sciences, China

Additional Reviewers

Zahra Babaiee	Patrick Musau
Dorra Ben Khalifa	Neelanjana Pal
Axel Brunnbauer	Adam Rogalewicz
Alec Edwards	Licio Romao

Nathaniel Hamilton
Abdelrahman Hekal
Chung-Hao Huang
Xiangyu Jin
Bram Kohlen

Jiri Srba
Paulius Stankaitis
Masaki Waga
Tengshun Yang
Hengjun Zhao

Artifact Evaluation Committee

Roman Andriushchenko	Brno University of Technology, Czech Republic
Shenghua Feng	Institute of Computing Technology, Chinese Academy of Sciences, China
Daniel Fentham	University of Birmingham, UK
Romulo Meira Goes	Carnegie Mellon University, USA
Andrea Pferscher	Graz University of Technology, Austria
Chung-Hao Huang	National Taiwan University, Taiwan
Dorra Ben Khalifa	Université de Perpignan Via Domitia, France
Bram Kohlen	University of Twente, The Netherlands
Alexis Linard	KTH Royal Institute of Technology, Sweden
Khushraj Madnani	IIT Bombay, India
Enrico Magnago	University of Trento and FBK, Italy
Neelanjana Pal	Vanderbilt University, USA
Kostiantyn Potomkin	Newcastle University, UK
Fedor Shmarov	University of Manchester, UK
Morten Konggaard Schou	Aalborg University, Denmark

Sponsors

Abstracts

A Behaviour-Based Approach to Quantitative Validation of Cyber-Physical Systems

Thao Dang

CNRS and VERIMAG, Université Grenoble Alpes, France
thao.dang@univ-grenoble-alpes.fr

Abstract. In this talk we describe a behaviour-based approach to quantitative property validation of Cyber-Physical Systems (CPS). The heterogeneity and complexity of industrial CPS make a behaviour-based approach very desirable since it is widely recognized that it is hard or impossible to derive sound mathematical models for such systems. Quantitative validation means providing, instead of a Boolean answer about property satisfaction, quality measures, such as confidence interval, robustness bound, coverage of the set of tested behaviours over the set of all possible behaviours, etc.

We first discuss the problem of encoding and measuring CPS signal spaces with respect to some approximation quality measures. In particular, we consider signal spaces subject to temporal constraints, namely they must satisfy given timing assumptions or properties. For a set of (usually uncountably many) signals representing CPS behaviours of interest, an approximation quality measure reflects how well a finite set of signals sampled from the original set can replace the original set in terms of property validation. We discuss a number of measures for sets of temporal behaviours: uniformity, epsilon-entropy and discrepancy measures. We then describe methods for generating CPS signals with good approximation quality, by combining sampling (as in Monte Carlo and quasi-Monte Carlo methods) and optimisation. The approach is finally illustrated on CPS benchmarks in particular in automative control.

A Personal History of Formal Modeling and Analysis of Timed Systems Before There was FORMATS

Thomas A. Henzinger

IST Austria, Austria
tah@ist.ac.at

Abstract. The 1990s were a time of much activity in developing formal models and analysis techniques for timed systems. I will give a personal view of some of the early developments in which I was involved, including freeze quantifiers and event clocks; location invariants and time divergence; symbolic region algebras and fixpoints; hybrid automata and timed games.

Contents

Invited Papers

Algebraic Model Checking for Discrete Linear Dynamical Systems   3
  Florian Luca, Joël Ouaknine, and James Worrell

Zone-Based Verification of Timed Automata: Extrapolations, Simulations
and What Next? 16
  *Patricia Bouyer, Paul Gastin, Frédéric Herbreteau, Ocan Sankur,
  and B. Srivathsan*

Monitoring Timed Properties (Revisited) 43
  *Thomas Møller Grosen, Sean Kauffman, Kim Guldstrand Larsen,
  and Martin Zimmermann*

Probabilistic and Timed Systems

Bounded Delay Timed Channel Coding 65
  Bernardo Jacobo Inclán, Aldric Degorre, and Eugene Asarin

Robustly Complete Finite-State Abstractions for Verification of Stochastic
Systems 80
  Yiming Meng and Jun Liu

Model Checking for Entanglement Swapping 98
  Surya Sai Teja Desu, Anubhav Srivastava, and M. V. Panduranga Rao

Temporal Logic

An STL-Based Formulation of Resilience in Cyber-Physical Systems 117
  Hongkai Chen, Shan Lin, Scott A. Smolka, and Nicola Paoletti

MITL Verification Under Timing Uncertainty 136
  Daniel Selvaratnam, Michael Cantoni, J. M. Davoren, and Iman Shames

Classification of Driving Behaviors Using STL Formulas: A Comparative
Study 153
  Ruya Karagulle, Nikos Aréchiga, Jonathan DeCastro, and Necmiye Ozay

Timed Automata and Games

Timed Games with Bounded Window Parity Objectives 165
  James C. A. Main, Mickael Randour, and Jeremy Sproston

Non-blind Strategies in Timed Network Congestion Games 183
  Aline Goeminne, Nicolas Markey, and Ocan Sankur

Efficient Convex Zone Merging in Parametric Timed Automata 200
  Étienne André, Dylan Marinho, Laure Petrucci, and Jaco van de Pol

Neural Networks

Neural Network Repair with Reachability Analysis 221
  Xiaodong Yang, Tom Yamaguchi, Hoang-Dung Tran, Bardh Hoxha,
  Taylor T. Johnson, and Danil Prokhorov

On Neural Network Equivalence Checking Using SMT Solvers 237
  Charis Eleftheriadis, Nikolaos Kekatos, Panagiotis Katsaros,
  and Stavros Tripakis

Reachability Analysis of a General Class of Neural Ordinary Differential
Equations 258
  Diego Manzanas Lopez, Patrick Musau, Nathaniel P. Hamilton,
  and Taylor T. Johnson

Reinforcement Learning

Robust Event-Driven Interactions in Cooperative Multi-agent Learning 281
  Daniel Jarne Ornia and Manuel Mazo Jr.

Learning that Grid-Convenience Does Not Hurt Resilience in the Presence
of Uncertainty 298
  Mathis Niehage and Anne Remke

Author Index 307

Invited Papers

Algebraic Model Checking for Discrete Linear Dynamical Systems

Florian Luca[1], Joël Ouaknine[2(✉)], and James Worrell[3]

[1] School of Mathematics, University of the Witwatersrand,
Johannesburg, South Africa
[2] Max Planck Institute for Software Systems, Saarland Informatics Campus,
Saarbrücken, Germany
joel@mpi-sws.org
[3] Department of Computer Science, Oxford University, Oxford, UK

Abstract. Model checking infinite-state systems is one of the central
challenges in automated verification. In this survey we focus on an important and fundamental subclass of infinite-state systems, namely discrete
linear dynamical systems. While such systems are ubiquitous in mathematics, physics, engineering, etc., in the present context our motivation
stems from their relevance to the formal analysis and verification of program loops, weighted automata, hybrid systems, and control systems,
amongst many others. Our main object of study is the problem of model
checking temporal properties on the infinite orbit of a linear dynamical
system, and our principal contribution is to show that for a rich class
of properties this problem can be reduced to certain classical decision
problems on linear recurrence sequences, notably the Skolem Problem.
This leads us to discuss recent advances on the latter and to highlight
the prospects for further progress on charting the algorithmic landscape
of linear recurrence sequences and linear dynamical systems.

Keywords: Discrete Linear Dynamical Systems · Linear Recurrence
Sequences · Model Checking · Orbit Problem · Skolem Problem

1 Introduction

Dynamical systems are a fundamental modelling paradigm in many branches
of science, and have been the subject of extensive research for many decades.
A *(rational) discrete linear dynamical system (LDS)* in ambient space $\mathbb{R}^d$ is

F. Luca—Also affiliated with: the Research Group in Algebraic Structures and Applications, King Abdulaziz University, Jeddah, Saudi Arabia; the Centro de Ciencias
Matemáticas UNAM, Morelia, Mexico; and the Max Planck Institute for Software Systems, Saarland Informatics Campus, Germany.
J. Ouaknine—Also affiliated with Keble College, Oxford as emmy.network Fellow, and
supported by DFG grant 389792660 as part of TRR 248 (see https://perspicuous-
computing.science).

S. Bogomolov and D. Parker (Eds.): FORMATS 2022, LNCS 13465, pp. 3–15, 2022.
https://doi.org/10.1007/978-3-031-15839-1_1

given by a square $d \times d$ matrix M with rational entries, together with a starting point $x \in \mathbb{Q}^d$. The *orbit* of (M, x) is the infinite trajectory $\mathcal{O}(M, x) := \langle x, Mx, M^2x, \ldots \rangle$. An example of a two-dimensional LDS is given in Fig. 1. A central concern in the computational theory of dynamical systems is the task of devising algorithms enabling one to decide various kinds of assertions on dynamical-system orbits.

$$M \stackrel{\text{def}}{=} \begin{pmatrix} 1 & 1 \\ 1 & 0 \end{pmatrix} \qquad x \stackrel{\text{def}}{=} \begin{pmatrix} 1 \\ 0 \end{pmatrix}$$

Fig. 1. A two-dimensional discrete linear dynamical system.

One of the most natural and fundamental computational questions concerning linear dynamical systems is the *Point-to-Point Reachability Problem*, also known as the *Kannan-Lipton Orbit Problem*: given a d-dimensional LDS (M, x) together with a point target $y \in \mathbb{Q}^d$, does the orbit of the LDS ever hit the target? The decidability of this question was settled affirmatively in the 1980s in the seminal work of Kannan and Lipton [28, 29]. In fact, Kannan and Lipton showed that this problem is solvable in polynomial time, answering an earlier open problem of Harrison from the 1960s on reachability for linear sequential machines [26].

Interestingly, one of Kannan and Lipton's motivations was to propose a line of attack to the well-known *Skolem Problem*, which had itself been famously open since the 1930s. The Skolem Problem remains unsolved to this day, although substantial advances have recently been made—more on this shortly. Phrased in the language of linear dynamical systems, the Skolem Problem asks whether it is decidable, given (M, x) as above, together with a $(d - 1)$-dimensional subspace H of $\mathbb{R}^d$, to determine if the orbit of (M, x) ever hits H. Kannan and Lipton suggested that, in ambient space $\mathbb{R}^d$ of arbitrary dimension, the problem of hitting a low-dimensional subspace might be decidable. Indeed, this was eventually substantiated by Chonev *et al.* for linear subspaces of dimension at most 3 [17, 19].

Subsequent research focussed on the decidability of hitting targets of increasing complexity, such as half-spaces [25, 33, 36–38], polytopes [3, 18, 42], and semi-algebraic sets [4, 5]. It is also worth noting that discrete linear dynamical systems can equivalently be viewed as linear (or affine) simple, branching-free while loops, where reachability corresponds to loop termination. There is a voluminous literature on the topic, albeit largely focussing on heuristics and semi-algorithms (via spectral methods or the synthesis of ranking functions), rather than exact decidability results. Relevant papers include [6–9, 13, 14, 16, 21, 27, 40, 41, 44]. Several of these approaches have moreover been implemented in software verification tools, such as Microsoft's Terminator [22, 23].

In recent years, motivated in part by verification problems for stochastic systems and linear loops, researchers have begun investigating more sophisticated specification formalisms than mere reachability: for example, the paper [1] studies approximate LTL model checking of Markov chains (which themselves can be viewed as particular kinds of linear dynamical systems), whereas [32] focuses on LTL model checking of low-dimensional linear dynamical systems with semi-algebraic predicates.[1] In [2], the authors solve the semialgebraic model-checking problem for diagonalisable linear dynamical systems in arbitrary dimension against prefix-independent MSO[2] properties, whereas [31] investigates semialge-braic MSO model checking of linear dynamical systems in which the dimensions of predicates are constrained. For a comprehensive survey of the state of the art on model checking for linear dynamical systems, we refer the reader to [30].

There is an intimate connection between linear dynamical systems and linear recurrence sequences. A *(rational) linear recurrence sequence (LRS)* $u = \langle u_n \rangle_{n=0}^{\infty}$ is an infinite sequence of rational numbers satisfying

$$u_{n+d} = c_1 u_{n+d-1} + \cdots + c_{d-1} u_{n+1} + c_d u_n \tag{1}$$

for all $n \in \mathbb{N}$, where the coefficients $c_1, \ldots, c_d$ are rational numbers and $c_d \neq 0$. We say that the above recurrence has *order* d. We moreover say that an LRS is *simple* if the characteristic polynomial[3] of its minimal-order recurrence has no repeated roots. The sequence of Fibonacci numbers $\langle f_n \rangle_{n=0}^{\infty} = \langle 0, 1, 1, 2, 3, 5, \ldots \rangle$, which obeys the recurrence $f_{n+2} = f_{n+1} + f_n$, is perhaps the most emblematic LRS, and also happens to be simple. It is a straightforward exercise to show that the orbit $\langle x, Mx, M^2x, \ldots \rangle$ of the LDS from Fig. 1 consists precisely of successive pairs of consecutive Fibonacci numbers:

$$\langle x, Mx, M^2x, \ldots \rangle = \left\langle \begin{pmatrix} 1 \\ 0 \end{pmatrix}, \begin{pmatrix} 1 \\ 1 \end{pmatrix}, \begin{pmatrix} 2 \\ 1 \end{pmatrix}, \ldots \right\rangle = \left\langle \begin{pmatrix} f_1 \\ f_0 \end{pmatrix}, \begin{pmatrix} f_2 \\ f_1 \end{pmatrix}, \begin{pmatrix} f_3 \\ f_2 \end{pmatrix}, \ldots \right\rangle. \tag{2}$$

Let us now define the following two bivariate predicates:

$$P(y, z) \stackrel{\text{def}}{=} \left(y^2 - yz - z^2 - 1 = 0 \right) \tag{3}$$

$$Q(y, z) \stackrel{\text{def}}{=} \left(y^2 - yz - z^2 + 1 = 0 \right). \tag{4}$$

Identifying P and Q with the respective subsets of $\mathbb{R}^2$ that they represent, one can straightforwardly show that the orbit of (M, x) visits P precisely at even-valued indices, and Q at odd-valued indices (where the first element of the orbit is understood to have index 0). In other words, the LDS (M, x) satisfies the following LTL specification:

$$P \wedge \neg Q \wedge \mathbf{G}(P \Rightarrow \mathbf{X}Q) \wedge \mathbf{G}(Q \Rightarrow \mathbf{X}P). \tag{5}$$

Of course, the general task of determining algorithmically whether a given LDS (in arbitrary dimension) meets a given specification would appear to be

---

[1] Semialgebraic predicates are Boolean combinations of polynomial equalities and inequalities.

[2] Monadic Second-Order Logic (MSO) is a highly expressive specification formalism that subsumes the vast majority of temporal logics employed in the field of auto-mated verification, such as Linear Temporal Logic (LTL).

[3] The characteristic polynomial associated with recurrence (1) is $X^d - c_1 X^{d-1} - \ldots - c_d$.

highly challenging. The principal goal of this paper is to delineate the extent to which this can be achieved automatically when the predicates are built from *algebraic* sets[4] and the specification formalism is either MSO, or its prefix-independent fragment. Before stating our key results, we need to take a brief detour through the Skolem landscape.

1.1   Skolem Oracles

The celebrated theorem of Skolem, Mahler, and Lech (see [24]) describes the structure of the set $\{n \in \mathbb{N} : u_n = 0\}$ of zero terms of an LRS as follows:

Theorem 1. *Given a linear recurrence sequence $\boldsymbol{u} = \langle u_n \rangle_{n=0}^{\infty}$, its set of zero terms is a semilinear set, i.e., it consists of a union of finitely many full arithmetic progressions,[5] together with a finite set.*

As shown by Berstel and Mignotte [10], in the above one can effectively extract all of the arithmetic progressions; we refer herein to the corresponding procedure as the 'Berstel-Mignotte algorithm'. Nevertheless, how to compute the leftover finite set of zeros remains open, and is easily seen to be equivalent to the *Skolem Problem*: given an LRS $\boldsymbol{u}$, does $\boldsymbol{u}$ contain a zero term?

Let us therefore introduce the notion of a *Skolem oracle*: given an LRS $\boldsymbol{u} = \langle u_n \rangle_{n=0}^{\infty}$, such an oracle returns the finite set of indices of zeros of $\boldsymbol{u}$ that do not already belong to some infinite arithmetic progression of zeros. Likewise, a *Simple-Skolem oracle* is a Skolem oracle restricted to simple LRS.

As mentioned earlier, the decidability of the Skolem Problem is a longstanding open question [24,39], with a positive answer for LRS of order at most 4 known since the mid-1980s [43,45]. Very recently, two major conditional advances on the Skolem Problem have been made, achieving decidability subject to certain classical number-theoretic conjectures: in [34], Lipton *et al.* established decidability for LRS of order 5 assuming the *Skolem Conjecture* (also known as the *Exponential Local-Global Principle*); and in [11], Bilu *et al.* showed decidability for simple LRS of arbitrary order, subject to both the Skolem Conjecture and the *p-adic Schanuel Conjecture*. It is interesting to note that in both cases, the procedures in question rely on the conjectures *only* for termination; correctness is unconditional. In fact, these procedures are *certifying algorithms* (in the sense of [35]) in that, upon termination, they produce an independent certificate (or witness) that their output is correct. Such a certificate can be checked algorithmically by a third party with no reliance on any unproven conjectures. The authors of [11] have implemented their algorithm within the SKOLEM tool, available online.[6]

In view of the above, Simple-Skolem oracles *can* be implemented with unconditional correctness, and guaranteed termination subject to the Skolem and p-adic Schanuel conjectures. Whether full Skolem oracles can be devised is the

---

[4] Algebraic sets correpond to positive Boolean combinations of polynomial equalities.

[5] A full arithmetic progression is a set of non-negative integers of the form $\{a + bm : m \in \mathbb{N}\}$, with $a, b \in \mathbb{N}$.

[6] https://skolem.mpi-sws.org/.

subject of active research; at the time of writing, to the best of our knowledge, no putative procedure is even conjectured in the general (non-simple) case.

To illustrate the applicability of Skolem oracles to model checking linear dynamical systems, let us return to our running example involving the LDS (M, x) from Fig. 1. Recall predicate $P(y, z)$ from Eq. (3), and identify it with the polynomial it implicitly represents, namely $P(y, z) = y^2 - yz - z^2 - 1$. In view of Eq. (2), we can write the orbit of (M, x) as follows:

$$\langle M^n x \rangle_{n=0}^{\infty} = \left\langle \begin{pmatrix} y_n \\ z_n \end{pmatrix} \right\rangle_{n=0}^{\infty} = \left\langle \begin{pmatrix} f_{n+1} \\ f_n \end{pmatrix} \right\rangle_{n=0}^{\infty},$$

where the reader will recall that $\langle f_n \rangle_{n=0}^{\infty}$ is the LRS of Fibonacci numbers. Evaluating the polynomial $P(y, z)$ at each point of the orbit therefore yields the sequence $\langle f_{n+1}^2 - f_{n+1} f_n - f_n^2 - 1 \rangle_{n=0}^{\infty}$. Given that LRS (resp. simple LRS) are closed under addition and multiplication, the resulting sequence is immediately seen to be a (simple) LRS. Therefore the Berstel-Mignotte algorithm, together with a (Simple-)Skolem oracle, enable us to compute the set of zeros of this LRS as a semilinear set. In turn, this set is precisely the sequence of indices at which the predicate P holds, i.e., at which the orbit of the LDS (M, x) visits the set represented by P. Since one-dimensional semilinear sets are ultimately periodic, and since every step along the way was effective (assuming the existence of (Simple-)Skolem oracles), evaluating the predicate P on the orbit of (M, x) gives rise to an *effectively ultimately periodic word*. As already noted, this word is indeed in fact $\langle TRUE, FALSE, TRUE, FALSE, TRUE, FALSE, TRUE, \ldots \rangle$.

One can of course repeat the procedure with the predicate Q, so that both P and Q are effectively ultimately periodic. Since MSO over effectively ultimately periodic words is decidable, we have just outlined a general algorithmic process by which one can decide algebraic MSO specifications (such as (5)) on orbits of linear dynamical systems, assuming the existence of Skolem or Simple-Skolem oracles.

Remark 2. As hinted above, it is a general fact that the sequence of values obtained by evaluating a multivariate polynomial on the successive points of the orbit of an LDS is always an LRS; moreoever, whenever the LDS is diagonalis-able[7], the corresponding LRS is always simple. We provide sketch justifications of these facts in Sect. 2.

1.2 Main Results

We require one final ingredient in order to state the main contributions of this paper. Fix the ambient space to be $\mathbb{R}^d$, and define the collection $\mathcal{C}$ of subsets of $\mathbb{R}^d$ to be the smallest set containing all algebraic subsets of $\mathbb{R}^d$, and which is closed under finite union, finite intersection, and complement. In algebraic geometry, $\mathcal{C}$ is usually referred to as the collection of *constructible* subsets of $\mathbb{R}^d$.

---

[7] An LDS (M, x) is *diagonalisable* provided the matrix M is diagonalisable over the complex numbers.

We refer to MSO formulas over predicates from $\mathcal{C}$ as *algebraic MSO*, and the corresponding model-checking problem as *algebraic model checking*.

Our main results are as follows (precise definitions and statements can be found in Sect. 2):

1. The algebraic model-checking problem for LDS is decidable in arbitrary dimension, subject to the existence of a Skolem oracle.
2. The algebraic model-checking problem for diagonalisable LDS is decidable in arbitrary dimension, subject to the existence of a Simple-Skolem oracle.
   - As an immediate corollary, decidability holds subject to the Skolem and p-adic Schanuel conjectures; moreover, correctness of the model-checking procedure is unconditional, and independent correctness certificates can always be produced upon termination.
3. The algebraic model-checking problem for LDS against prefix-independent specifications is (unconditionally) decidable.

Item 3 above follows from the fact that prefix-independent assertions depend only upon the ultimately periodic components of predicates (see, e.g., [2]), and the latter can be effectively extracted via the Berstel-Mignotte algorithm.

Three further remarks are in order: (i) in ambient space $\mathbb{R}^3$, algebraic and even semialgebraic model checking for LDS become unconditionally decidable; this follows immediately from the results of [31], since every predicate in $\mathbb{R}^3$ belongs to a 3-dimensional subspace (namely $\mathbb{R}^3$). However: (ii) in ambient space $\mathbb{R}^4$, unconditional decidability of algebraic model checking in not known to hold even for diagonalisable LDS, as one can establish hardness for the Skolem Problem at order 5; see [18] for details. (iii) For simplicity, all our results are stated in terms of *rational* linear dynamical systems, living in ambient space $\mathbb{R}^d$. Nevertheless, it is a straightforward corollary that we can extend our entire framework to *complex-algebraic*[8] linear dynamical systems, replacing the ambient space $\mathbb{R}^d$ by $\mathbb{C}^d$, $\mathbb{Q}^d$ by $\overline{\mathbb{Q}}^d$, and real constructible sets by complex constructible sets.[9] As we sketch in Sect. 2, our main results (as listed above) carry over easily to this more general complex setting. In this extension, it is noteworthy that our Skolem oracles however remain unchanged, i.e., are maintained to apply only to *rational* (rather than complex-algebraic) linear recurrence sequences.

Lastly, it is interesting to note that the algebraic model-checking problem for LDS subsumes not only the original Point-to-Point Reachability Problem, but also the Subspace Reachability Problem suggested by Kannan and Lipton [29] (along with its affine variants), as well as reachability for the *glued vector spaces* of [20].

---

[8] We are referring here to the field of complex algebraic numbers, denoted $\overline{\mathbb{Q}}$.

[9] Complex constructible sets play a central rôle in algebraic geometry; moreover, since the first-order theory of algebraically closed fields admits quantifier elimination, the constructible subsets of $\mathbb{C}^d$ are exactly the subsets of $\mathbb{C}^d$ that are first-order definable over $\mathbb{C}$.

In the next section, we present a slightly more formal treatment of our framework and results, along with justifications for some of our unsupported assertions. Section 3 concludes with a brief summary and directions for further research.

2   Algebraic Model Checking

Throughout this section, we assume familiarity with the elementary theory of linear recurrence sequences as well as the rudiments of Monadic Second-Order Logic (MSO); there are many excellent references for both topics, such as [24] and [12].

Let us work in fixed ambient space $\mathbb{R}^d$, and consider a d-dimensional LDS (M, x) (i.e., $M \in \mathbb{Q}^{d \times d}$ and $x \in \mathbb{Q}^d$). Recall that the orbit $\mathcal{O} = \mathcal{O}(M, x)$ of our LDS is the infinite sequence $\langle x, Mx, M^2x, \ldots \rangle$ in $\mathbb{Q}^d$. Let us write $\mathcal{O}[n]$ for the nth term of the orbit, and, for $1 \leq i \leq d$, $\mathcal{O}[n]_i$ for the ith entry of the point $\mathcal{O}[n] \in \mathbb{Q}^d$.

Lemma 3. *Let (M, x) be as above. For any fixed $i \in \{1, \ldots, d\}$, the sequence $\langle \mathcal{O}[n]_i \rangle_{n=0}^{\infty}$ is an LRS whose characteristic polynomial divides the minimal polynomial of M.*

Proof. The fact that the minimal polynomial of M is associated with a recurrence satisfied by the sequence $\langle \mathcal{O}[n]_i \rangle_{n=0}^{\infty}$ is a straightforward linear-algebraic calculation. It follows that sequence $\langle \mathcal{O}[n]_i \rangle_{n=0}^{\infty}$ is indeed an LRS having characteristic roots among the eigenvalues of M, with the multiplicity of each characteristic root at most the algebraic multiplicity of the corresponding eigenvalue. The result then immediately follows.   □

Corollary 4. *Let (M, x) be as above. If M is diagonalisable, then for each fixed $i \in \{1, \ldots, d\}$, the LRS $\langle \mathcal{O}[n]_i \rangle_{n=0}^{\infty}$ is simple.*

Proof. This follows immediately from the well-known fact that a square matrix M is diagonalisable if and only if its minimal polynomial is a product of distinct linear factors (over $\mathbb{C}$).   □

A set $A \subseteq \mathbb{R}^d$ is *algebraic* if A can be written as a finite positive Boolean combination of polynomial equalities, where all polynomials involved have integer coefficients. The collection $\mathcal{C} \subseteq 2^{\mathbb{R}^d}$ of *constructible* subsets of $\mathbb{R}^d$ is the smallest set that includes all algebraic sets and is closed under finite Boolean combinations (including complementation). Any constructible set $C \in \mathcal{C}$ can therefore be represented in conjunctive normal form, i.e., as an expression of the form $C = \bigcap_{i=1}^{a} \bigcup_{j=1}^{b} B_{i,j}$, where each $B_{i,j}$ is either an algebraic set or the complement of one.

Let $\mathbf{C} = \{C_1, \ldots, C_\ell\}$ be a finite list of constructible sets (not necessarily disjoint), giving rise to an alphabet $\Sigma \stackrel{\text{def}}{=} 2^{\mathbf{C}}$. The orbit $\mathcal{O}$ of our LDS (M, x) then naturally gives rise to an infinite *characteristic word* $w \in \Sigma^\omega$, as follows: writing $w[n]$ for the nth letter of w, we have $C_i \in w[n]$ iff $M^n x \in C_i$.

Proposition 5. *Characteristic words over constructible predicates are ultimately periodic.*

Proof. Let us write $\mathcal{O} = \langle x_n \rangle_{n=0}^{\infty}$ to denote the orbit of our LDS (M, x), and let us further write each x_n as $(x_n^{(1)}, \ldots, x_n^{(d)})^T$. Fix a polynomial $f \in \mathbb{Z}[X_1, \ldots, X_d]$, and consider the sequence $\langle f(x_n) \rangle_{n=0}^{\infty}$. Since sums and products of LRS are LRS, by Lemma 3 the sequence $\langle f(x_n) \rangle_{n=0}^{\infty}$ is an LRS, and by the Skolem-Mahler-Lech theorem its set of zeros is therefore semilinear, hence ultimately periodic. Since pointwise Boolean combinations (including complementation) of ultimately periodic words are ultimately periodic, and taking account of the fact that any constructible set is a finite Boolean combination of algebraic sets, the result immediately follows.   □

We say that a word is *effectively* ultimately periodic if one can compute an integer threshold beyond which the word in question becomes periodic. Stringing everything together:

Corollary 6.

1. *Assume the existence of a Skolem oracle. Then characteristic words over constructible predicates are effectively ultimately periodic.*
2. *Suppose (M, x) is a diagonalisable LDS, and assume the existence of a Simple-Skolem oracle. Then any characteristic word associated with the orbit of (M, x) over constructible predicates is effectively ultimately periodic.*

Proof. The first item follows directly from Proposition 5, together with the Berstel-Mignotte algorithm. So does the second item, invoking in addition Corollary 4, and taking account of the fact that simple LRS are closed under sums and products, along with the fact that constant sequences are themselves simple LRS.   □

Let (M, x) and C be as above, and let φ be an MSO formula with atomic predicates drawn from C—we refer to such formulas as *algebraic MSO specifications*. The question of whether the characteristic word w associated with the orbit of (M, x) satisfies specification φ—which is usually written as $(M, x) \vDash \varphi$—is the *algebraic model-checking problem* for discrete linear dynamical systems.

In addition, we say that φ is *prefix-independent* if the infinite words that satisfy it are closed under the operations of insertion and deletion of finitely many letters. Prefix-independent properties can be used to describe asymptotic behaviours (e.g., "does the orbit enter C_1 infinitely often?"), but not reachability.

We are now ready to formally state our main results:

Theorem 7.

1. *The algebraic model-checking problem for LDS is decidable, subject to the existence of a Skolem oracle.*
2. *The algebraic model-checking problem for diagonalisable LDS is decidable, subject to the existence of a Simple-Skolem oracle.*

3. *The algebraic model-checking problem for LDS against prefix-independent specifications is (unconditionally) decidable.*

Proof. Item 1 is an immediate consequence of Büchi's seminal work [15] establishing the decidability of MSO, together with Corollary 6(1) and the observation that effectively ultimately periodic predicates can be algorithmically translated to ordinary MSO by encoding the predicates as formulas.

The same holds for Item 2, invoking Corollary 6(2) in lieu of Corollary 6(1).

Finally, Item 3 follows from the fact that prefix-independent assertions depend only upon the ultimately periodic components of predicates (see, e.g., [2]), and the latter can be effectively extracted via the Berstel-Mignotte algorithm.   □

As noted earlier, since Simple-Skolem oracles can be implemented into provably correct certifying procedures which terminate subject to classical number-theoretic conjectures [11], we have:

Corollary 8. *The algebraic model-checking problem for diagonalisable LDS is decidable, assuming the Skolem Conjecture and the p-adic Schanuel Conjecture. Moreover, correctness of the attendant procedure is unconditional, and independent correctness certificates can be produced upon termination.*

Corollary 8 is arguably our most consequential and interesting contribution. Given that promising experimental results are reported in [11] regarding the implementation of a Simple-Skolem algorithm, it appears rather plausible that one could likewise build an efficient and practical model checker for diagonalisable LDS against algebraic specifications.

Finally, let us record, as already noted in the Introduction, that both Theorem 7 and Corollary 8 can be extended *mutatis mutandis* to *complex-algebraic* linear dynamical systems, whilst only invoking Skolem oracles for *rational* linear recurrence sequences. We sketch a short justification of this claim below.

Let (M, x) be a complex-algebraic LDS in ambient space $\mathbb{C}^d$, i.e., $M \in \overline{\mathbb{Q}}^{d \times d}$ and $x \in \overline{\mathbb{Q}}^d$, and let $f \in \overline{\mathbb{Q}}[X_1, \ldots, X_d]$ be an arbitrary polynomial with complex-algebraic coefficients. Let $Z \overset{\text{def}}{=} \{n \in \mathbb{N} : f(M^n x) = 0\}$ be the set of indices at which the orbit of (M, x) lies in the algebraic set $f^{-1}(0)$. The crux of our claim boils down to the following lemma:

Lemma 9. *Let (M, x), f, and Z be as above. Then one can effectively construct a rational LRS $u = \langle u_n \rangle_{n=0}^{\infty}$ such that Z is precisely the zero set of u. Moreover, if M is diagonalisable, then u is a simple rational LRS.*

Proof. Let $\mathbb{K} \subset \overline{\mathbb{Q}}$ be the smallest number field containing all the entries of M and x, as well as all the coefficients of f. As in the proof of Proposition 5, one easily shows that the sequence $v = \langle f(M^n(x)) \rangle_{n=0}^{\infty}$ is an LRS lying entirely in $\mathbb{K}$.

Recall the notion of *norm* $\mathcal{N}_{\mathbb{K}} : \mathbb{K} \to \mathbb{Q}$ from algebraic number theory, defined as $\mathcal{N}_{\mathbb{K}}(x) = \prod_{\sigma : \mathbb{K} \to \mathbb{C}} \sigma(x)$, where the product is indexed by the collection of field embeddings of $\mathbb{K}$ into $\mathbb{C}$. Since v is an LRS, then so is $\sigma(v) = \langle \sigma(v_n) \rangle_{n=0}^{\infty}$ for any embedding $\sigma : \mathbb{K} \to \mathbb{C}$, and moreover such applications will also preserve simplicity of LRS (this can be seen by inspecting the effect of σ on the exponential-polynomial closed-form representation of v). Write $u \stackrel{\text{def}}{=} \mathcal{N}_{\mathbb{K}}(v) = \langle \mathcal{N}_{\mathbb{K}}(v_n) \rangle_{n=0}^{\infty}$. Since products of (simple) LRS are again (simple) LRS, we have that u is a (simple) LRS lying entirely in $\mathbb{Q}$. Moreover, since field embeddings fix 0, u and v have precisely the same zero set, as required. $\square$

3   Conclusion

This paper has demonstrated that solving the Skolem Problem is key to model checking a rich class of algebraic properties on linear dynamical systems. We have formulated our results in terms of the existence of oracles for the Skolem Problem and a special subcase, the Simple-Skolem Problem. Implementing such oracles is the subject of ongoing research. As remarked earlier, we have recently devised an algorithm for the Simple-Skolem Problem whose output comes with an easily checkable correctness certificate (namely a set of zeros of the given sequence and a certificate that the remaining terms of the sequence are non-zero) and which terminates subject to certain classical number-theoretic conjectures. We are currently investigating whether a similar approach can be devised in the general (non-simple) case.

In this note we have concentrated on logical specifications built over constructible predicates, that is, those that are defined by Boolean combinations of polynomial equalities. In many applications, one is also interested in the more general class of *semialgebraic* predicates, that is, those defined by Boolean combinations of polynomial *inequalities*. The task of model checking MSO formulas over such predicates appears vastly more complex. Already the question of whether the orbit of an LDS remains within a prescribed halfspace—or equivalently whether all terms of an LRS are non-negative, known as the *Positivity Problem*—is highly challenging: decidability is known only for sequences of order at most 5, whereas for sequences of order 6 a solution to the Positivity Problem would entail major breakthroughs in number theory [37,39].

References

1. Agrawal, M., Akshay, S., Genest, B., Thiagarajan, P.S.: Approximate verification of the symbolic dynamics of Markov chains. J. ACM **62**(1), 2:1–2:34 (2015)
2. Almagor, S., Karimov, T., Kelmendi, E., Ouaknine, J., Worrell, J.: Deciding ω-regular properties on linear recurrence sequences. Proc. ACM Program. Lang. 5(POPL), 1–24 (2021)
3. Almagor, S., Ouaknine, J., Worrell, J.: The polytope-collision problem. In: 44th International Colloquium on Automata, Languages, and Programming, ICALP 2017. LIPIcs, vol. 80, pp. 24:1–24:14. Schloss Dagstuhl - Leibniz-Zentrum für Informatik (2017)
4. Almagor, S., Ouaknine, J., Worrell, J.: The semialgebraic orbit problem. In: 36th International Symposium on Theoretical Aspects of Computer Science, STACS 2019. LIPIcs, vol. 126, pp. 6:1–6:15. Schloss Dagstuhl - Leibniz-Zentrum für Informatik (2019)

5. Almagor, S., Ouaknine, J., Worrell, J.: First-order orbit queries. Theory Comput. Syst. **65**(4), 638–661 (2021)
6. Ben-Amram, A.M., Doménech, J.J., Genaim, S.: Multiphase-linear ranking functions and their relation to recurrent sets. In: Chang, B.-Y.E. (ed.) SAS 2019. LNCS, vol. 11822, pp. 459–480. Springer, Cham (2019). https://doi.org/10.1007/978-3-030-32304-2_22
7. Ben-Amram, A.M., Genaim, S.: On the linear ranking problem for integer linear-constraint loops. In: The 40th Annual ACM SIGPLAN-SIGACT Symposium on Principles of Programming Languages, POPL 2013, pp. 51–62. ACM (2013)
8. Ben-Amram, A.M., Genaim, S.: Ranking functions for linear-constraint loops. J. ACM **61**(4), 26:1–26:55 (2014)
9. Ben-Amram, A.M., Genaim, S.: On multiphase-linear ranking functions. In: Majumdar, R., Kunčak, V. (eds.) CAV 2017. LNCS, vol. 10427, pp. 601–620. Springer, Cham (2017). https://doi.org/10.1007/978-3-319-63390-9_32
10. Berstel, J., Mignotte, M.: Deux propriétés décidables des suites récurrentes linéaires. Bull. Soc. Math. France **104**, 175–184 (1976)
11. Bilu, Y., Luca, F., Nieuwveld, J., Ouaknine, J., Purser, D., Worrell, J.: Skolem meets Schanuel. In: Szeider, S., Ganian, R., Silva, A. (eds.) 47th International Symposium on Mathematical Foundations of Computer Science, MFCS 2022, 22–26 August 2022, Vienna, Austria. LIPIcs, vol. 241, pp. 62:1–62:15. Schloss Dagstuhl - Leibniz-Zentrum für Informatik (2022)
12. Börger, E., Grädel, E., Gurevich, Y.: The Classical Decision Problem. Perspectives in Mathematical Logic, Springer, Heidelberg (1997)
13. Bradley, A.R., Manna, Z., Sipma, H.B.: Termination analysis of integer linear loops. In: Abadi, M., de Alfaro, L. (eds.) CONCUR 2005. LNCS, vol. 3653, pp. 488–502. Springer, Heidelberg (2005). https://doi.org/10.1007/11539452_37
14. Braverman, M.: Termination of integer linear programs. In: Ball, T., Jones, R.B. (eds.) CAV 2006. LNCS, vol. 4144, pp. 372–385. Springer, Heidelberg (2006). https://doi.org/10.1007/11817963_34
15. Büchi, J.R.: Weak second order arithmetic and finite automata. Zeit. für Math. Logik und Grund. der Math. **6**(1–6), 66–92 (1960)
16. Chen, H.Y., Flur, S., Mukhopadhyay, S.: Termination proofs for linear simple loops. Int. J. Softw. Tools Technol. Transfer **17**(1), 47–57 (2013). https://doi.org/10.1007/s10009-013-0288-8
17. Chonev, V., Ouaknine, J., Worrell, J.: The orbit problem in higher dimensions. In: Symposium on Theory of Computing Conference, STOC 2013, pp. 941–950. ACM (2013)
18. Chonev, V., Ouaknine, J., Worrell, J.: The polyhedron-hitting problem. In: Proceedings of the Twenty-Sixth Annual ACM-SIAM Symposium on Discrete Algorithms, SODA 2015, pp. 940–956. SIAM (2015)
19. Chonev, V., Ouaknine, J., Worrell, J.: On the complexity of the Orbit Problem. J. ACM **63**(3), 23:1–23:18 (2016)
20. Colcombet, T., Petrişan, D.: Automata in the category of glued vector spaces. In: Larsen, K.G., Bodlaender, H.L., Raskin, J. (eds.) 42nd International Symposium on Mathematical Foundations of Computer Science, MFCS 2017, 21–25 August 2017, Aalborg, Denmark. LIPIcs, vol. 83, pp. 52:1–52:14. Schloss Dagstuhl - Leibniz-Zentrum für Informatik (2017)
21. Colón, M.A., Sipma, H.B.: Synthesis of linear ranking functions. In: Margaria, T., Yi, W. (eds.) TACAS 2001. LNCS, vol. 2031, pp. 67–81. Springer, Heidelberg (2001). https://doi.org/10.1007/3-540-45319-9_6

22. Cook, B., Podelski, A., Rybalchenko, A.: Termination proofs for systems code. In: Proceedings of the ACM SIGPLAN 2006 Conference on Programming Language Design and Implementation, pp. 415–426. ACM (2006)
23. Cook, B., Podelski, A., Rybalchenko, A.: TERMINATOR: beyond safety. In: Ball, T., Jones, R.B. (eds.) CAV 2006. LNCS, vol. 4144, pp. 415–418. Springer, Heidelberg (2006). https://doi.org/10.1007/11817963_37
24. Everest, G., van der Poorten, A.J., Shparlinski, I.E., Ward, T.: Recurrence Sequences. Mathematical Surveys and Monographs, vol. 104. American Mathematical Society (2003)
25. Halava, V., Harju, T., Hirvensalo, M.: Positivity of second order linear recurrent sequences. Discret. Appl. Math. **154**(3), 447–451 (2006)
26. Harrison, M.A.: Lectures on Linear Sequential Machines. Academic Press, New York (1969)
27. Hosseini, M., Ouaknine, J., Worrell, J.: Termination of linear loops over the integers. In: 46th International Colloquium on Automata, Languages, and Programming, ICALP 2019. LIPIcs, vol. 132, pp. 118:1–118:13. Schloss Dagstuhl - Leibniz-Zentrum für Informatik (2019)
28. Kannan, R., Lipton, R.J.: The orbit problem is decidable. In: Proceedings of the 12th Annual ACM Symposium on Theory of Computing 1980, pp. 252–261. ACM (1980)
29. Kannan, R., Lipton, R.J.: Polynomial-time algorithm for the orbit problem. J. ACM **33**(4), 808–821 (1986)
30. Karimov, T., Kelmendi, E., Ouaknine, J., Worrell, J.: What's decidable about discrete linear dynamical systems? CoRR **abs/2206.11412** (2022). https://doi.org/10.48550/arXiv.2206.11412
31. Karimov, T., et al.: What's decidable about linear loops? Proc. ACM Program. Lang. **6**(POPL), 1–25 (2022)
32. Karimov, T., Ouaknine, J., Worrell, J.: On LTL model checking for low-dimensional discrete linear dynamical systems. In: 45th International Symposium on Mathematical Foundations of Computer Science, MFCS 2020. LIPIcs, vol. 170, pp. 54:1–54:14. Schloss Dagstuhl - Leibniz-Zentrum für Informatik (2020)
33. Laohakosol, V., Tangsupphathawat, P.: Positivity of third order linear recurrence sequences. Discret. Appl. Math. **157**(15), 3239–3248 (2009)
34. Lipton, R.J., Luca, F., Nieuwveld, J., Ouaknine, J., Worrell, D.P.J.: On the skolem problem and the skolem conjecture. In: 37th Annual ACM/IEEE Symposium on Logic in Computer Science, LICS 2022, Haifa, Israel, 2 August–5 August 2022. ACM (2022)
35. McConnell, R.M., Mehlhorn, K., Näher, S., Schweitzer, P.: Certifying algorithms. Comput. Sci. Rev. **5**(2), 119–161 (2011)
36. Ouaknine, J., Worrell, J.: On the positivity problem for simple linear recurrence sequences'. In: Esparza, J., Fraigniaud, P., Husfeldt, T., Koutsoupias, E. (eds.) ICALP 2014. LNCS, vol. 8573, pp. 318–329. Springer, Heidelberg (2014). https://doi.org/10.1007/978-3-662-43951-7_27
37. Ouaknine, J., Worrell, J.: Positivity problems for low-order linear recurrence sequences. In: Proceedings of the Twenty-Fifth Annual ACM-SIAM Symposium on Discrete Algorithms, SODA 2014, pp. 366–379. SIAM (2014)
38. Ouaknine, J., Worrell, J.: Ultimate positivity is decidable for simple linear recurrence sequences. In: Esparza, J., Fraigniaud, P., Husfeldt, T., Koutsoupias, E. (eds.) ICALP 2014. LNCS, vol. 8573, pp. 330–341. Springer, Heidelberg (2014). https://doi.org/10.1007/978-3-662-43951-7_28

39. Ouaknine, J., Worrell, J.: On linear recurrence sequences and loop termination. ACM SIGLOG News **2**(2), 4–13 (2015)
40. Podelski, A., Rybalchenko, A.: A complete method for the synthesis of linear ranking functions. In: Steffen, B., Levi, G. (eds.) VMCAI 2004. LNCS, vol. 2937, pp. 239–251. Springer, Heidelberg (2004). https://doi.org/10.1007/978-3-540-24622-0_20
41. Podelski, A., Rybalchenko, A.: Transition invariants. In: 19th IEEE Symposium on Logic in Computer Science (LICS 2004), pp. 32–41. IEEE Computer Society (2004)
42. Tarasov, S., Vyalyi, M.: Orbits of linear maps and regular languages. In: Kulikov, A., Vereshchagin, N. (eds.) CSR 2011. LNCS, vol. 6651, pp. 305–316. Springer, Heidelberg (2011). https://doi.org/10.1007/978-3-642-20712-9_24
43. Tijdeman, R., Mignotte, M., Shorey, T.N.: The distance between terms of an algebraic recurrence sequence. Journal für die reine und angewandte Mathematik **349**, 63–76 (1984)
44. Tiwari, A.: Termination of linear programs. In: Alur, R., Peled, D.A. (eds.) CAV 2004. LNCS, vol. 3114, pp. 70–82. Springer, Heidelberg (2004). https://doi.org/10.1007/978-3-540-27813-9_6
45. Vereshchagin, N.: The problem of appearance of a zero in a linear recurrence sequence. Mat. Zametki **38**(2), 609–615 (1985)

Zone-Based Verification of Timed Automata: Extrapolations, Simulations and What Next?

Patricia Bouyer[1]([✉]) [ID], Paul Gastin[1,5] [ID], Frédéric Herbreteau[2] [ID],
Ocan Sankur[3] [ID], and B. Srivathsan[4,5] [ID]

[1] Université Paris-Saclay, CNRS, ENS Paris-Saclay, Laboratoire Méthodes Formelles,
Gif-sur-Yvette 91190, France
bouyer@lsv.fr
[2] Univ. Bordeaux, CNRS, Bordeaux INP, LaBRI, UMR5800, Talence 33400, France
[3] Univ Rennes, Inria, CNRS, Irisa, Rennes, France
[4] Chennai Mathematical Institute, Chennai, India
[5] CNRS IRL 2000, ReLaX, Chennai, India

Abstract. Timed automata have been introduced by Rajeev Alur and David Dill in the early 90's. In the last decades, timed automata have become the *de facto* model for the verification of real-time systems. Algorithms for timed automata are based on the traversal of their state-space using zones as a symbolic representation. Since the state-space is infinite, termination relies on finite abstractions that yield a finite representation of the reachable states.

The first solution to get finite abstractions was based on extrapolations of zones, and has been implemented in the industry-strength tool UPPAAL. A different approach based on simulations between zones has emerged in the last ten years, and has been implemented in the fully open source tool TCHECKER. The simulation-based approach has led to new efficient algorithms for reachability and liveness in timed automata, and has also been extended to richer models like weighted timed automata, and timed automata with diagonal constraints and updates.

In this article, we survey the extrapolation and simulation techniques, and discuss some open challenges for the future.

Keywords: Timed automata · Verification algorithms · Zones · Finite abstractions

1 Introduction

Timed automata have been defined in the early 1990's [4,5] as a formal model for representing systems in which timing constraints play an important role. A timed automaton is a finite automaton that can manipulate variables. These variables have very specific behaviours: they increase synchronously with time,

---

This work was partially funded by ANR project Ticktac (ANR-18-CE40-0015).

S. Bogomolov and D. Parker (Eds.): FORMATS 2022, LNCS 13465, pp. 16–42, 2022.
https://doi.org/10.1007/978-3-031-15839-1_2

they can be constrained (for instance, compared to a constant), and they can be updated (most often, reset to 0). The number of states of a timed automaton is infinite, and hence no properties of standard finite automata can trivially be transferred to timed automata. However, a finite-state abstraction, called the *region automaton*, can be constructed that allows us to check for reachability properties, ω-regular properties, some branching-time timed temporal logics, *etc.* An extensive literature has been written on this model since the original paper [4]. Research on timed automata since then has resulted in a rich theory, and in more practice-guided developments. In this paper we focus on the latter, and present algorithmic issues, which we believe are the important ones.

There are two main families of symbolic approaches to analyze reachability properties: the backward and the forward analysis. Backward analysis consists in computing iteratively (symbolic) predecessors of the target state, until hitting the initial configuration or until no new symbolic state can be computed. By chance, such a symbolic computation, when applied to timed automata, always terminates and therefore provides a symbolic algorithm for the verification of reachability properties. Unfortunately it is not really adequate to analyse models with discrete structures (like discrete variables) and does not extend very well to other properties. On the other hand, forward analysis consists in computing iteratively (symbolic) successors of the initial configuration, until hitting the target or until some stopping criterion. The exact forward computation does not terminate in general, and so there is a need for some theoretical developments to ensure termination of the computation and prove the correctness of the approach. We focus on the forward analysis algorithm here, and primarily restrict to reachability properties.

The key advantage in timed automata verification is the fact that the reachable symbolic states can be represented using simple constraints over the variables, called zones. Zones can be efficiently manipulated, and therefore the computation of successors is quick. The main challenge is to get a stopping criterion for the forward analysis that can ensure, as soon as possible, that all reachable states have been visited. The first approach to stop the forward analysis makes use of an extrapolation operation on zones. Extrapolation of a zone gives a bigger zone picked from a finite range, thereby automatically ensuring termination. Starting from the late 90's, extrapolations have been studied in depth, leading to the development of efficient tools [14,35] and several fundamental observations about what extrapolations can do and cannot do [11,12,22,23]. With the aim of circumventing the limitations of the extrapolation-based approach, an alternative solution has been pioneered in [62,64]. This approach keeps the zones as they are, and makes use of simulations between them to stop the computation. In addition to overcoming the limitations of the extrapolation-based approach, the simulation-based approach has paved the way for several remarkable advances in timed automata verification, in particular: dynamic abstractions for reachability checking [63,84], refinement-based verification of liveness properties [64], simulation-based finite abstractions for weighted timed automata [26], for automata with diagonal constraints and more general updates than plain resets [49,50,52], for pushdown timed automata [2] and for event-clock automata [1]. Some of these techniques have been implemented in the tool TCHECKER [59], and experiments have shown significant gains with respect to previous approaches.

The goal of this survey is to present the extrapolation-based and the simulation-based approaches, which have been instrumental in the success of timed automata verification. We also include a discussion on "what next?", where we throw light on some of the current challenges in timed automata verification that cannot be tackled just by using extrapolations or simulations. The plan of the paper is the following. In Sect. 2, we briefly recall the model of timed automata and its semantics. In Sect. 3, we explain the symbolic approach to the forward analysis of timed automata, by presenting zones, generic forward schemes to enforce termination of the forward computation while preserving completeness and soundness, and finally DBMs as a useful representation of zones. In Sect. 4, we present the extrapolation-based approach. In Sect. 5, we present the simulation-based approach. In Sect. 6, we discuss two extensions, one concerning the model, and one concerning the properties to be checked. There have been multiple tools which have been developed to verify timed automata; in Sect. 7 we present UPPAAL, the most successful model-checker, whose development started in 1995 [18] and is based algorithmically on the extrapolation approach, and TCHECKER, an open-source model-checker under development [59], which implements the most recent algorithms based on simulation. In Sect. 8 we discuss the next challenges which occur as a natural follow-up to the theory and practice that has been built so far.

2   Birth of Timed Automata for Verification: The Early 90's

2.1   Preliminaries

We consider a finite set X of variables, called *clocks*. A *(clock) valuation* over X is a mapping $v\colon X \to \mathbb{R}_+$ which assigns to each clock a non-negative real, which denotes a time value. The set of all clock valuations over X is denoted $\mathbb{R}_+^X$, and $\mathbf{0}$ denotes the valuation assigning 0 to every clock $x \in X$. Let $v \in \mathbb{R}_+^X$ be a valuation and $\delta \in \mathbb{R}_+$, the valuation $v + \delta$ is defined by $(v + \delta)(x) = v(x) + \delta$ for every $x \in X$. For $Y \subseteq X$, we denote by $[Y]v$ the valuation such that for every $x \in Y$, $([Y]v)(x) = 0$ and for every $x \in X \setminus Y$, $([Y]v)(x) = v(x)$.

Given a finite set of clocks X, we introduce two sets of *clock constraints over* X. The most general one, denoted $\mathcal{C}(X)$, is defined by the grammar:

$$g ::= x \bowtie c \mid x - y \bowtie c \mid g \wedge g \mid true$$
$$\text{where } x, y \in X, \ c \in \mathbb{Z} \text{ and } \bowtie \in \{<, \leq, =, \geq, >\}.$$

A clock constraint of the form $x - y \bowtie c$ is said to be a *diagonal* constraint. Next we also use the proper subset of *diagonal-free* clock constraints where diagonal constraints are not allowed. This set is denoted $\mathcal{C}_{df}(X)$.

If $v \in \mathbb{R}_+^X$ is a clock valuation, we write $v \models g$ when v satisfies the clock constraint g, and we say that v satisfies $x \bowtie c$ (resp. $x - y \bowtie c$) whenever $v(x) \bowtie c$ (resp. $v(x) - v(y) \bowtie c$). If g is a clock constraint, we write $\llbracket g \rrbracket$ for the set of clock valuations $\{v \in \mathbb{R}_+^X \mid v \models g\}$.

2.2   The Timed Automaton Model [4,5]

A *timed automaton* is a tuple $\mathcal{A} = (Q, X, q_0, T, F)$ where Q is a finite set of states, X is a finite set of clocks, $q_0 \in Q$ is the initial state, $T \subseteq Q \times \mathcal{C}(X) \times 2^X \times Q$ is a finite set of transitions, and $F \subseteq Q$ is a set of final states. A timed automaton is said to be diagonal free if $\mathcal{C}(X)$ is replaced by $\mathcal{C}_{df}(X)$ in the definition of the transition relation.

A *configuration* of a timed automaton $\mathcal{A}$ is a pair (q, v) where $q \in Q$ is a state of the automaton and $v \in \mathbb{R}_+^X$ is a valuation. The semantics of $\mathcal{A}$ is given as a transition system over its configurations. The initial node is $(q_0, \mathbf{0})$ consisting of the initial state q_0 and the initial valuation $\mathbf{0}$. There are two kinds of transitions:

time elapse $(q, v) \xrightarrow{\delta} (q, v + \delta)$ for every $\delta \in \mathbb{R}_+$,

discrete transition $(q, v) \xrightarrow{t} (q_1, v_1)$ if there exists a transition $t = (q, g, R, q_1) \in T$ such that $v \models g$ and $v_1 = [R]v$.

A run of $\mathcal{A}$ is a (finite or infinite) alternating sequence of time elapses and discrete transitions starting from the initial configuration: $(q_0, \mathbf{0}) \xrightarrow{\delta_1} (q_0, \mathbf{0} + \delta_1) \xrightarrow{t_1} (q_1, v_1) \xrightarrow{\delta_2} (q_1, v_1 + \delta_2) \xrightarrow{t_2} \ldots$.

In the following we will be interested in the verification of reachability properties: given a timed automaton $\mathcal{A}$ and a control state q, does there exist a (finite) run that leads to a configuration of the form (q, v)? This problem was shown to be PSPACE-complete in the paper introducing timed automata [4]. The first algorithm for reachability made use of a finite partition of the set of valuations into *regions*, and then using it to construct a region automaton. There are exponentially many regions and hence this solution is not useful in practice.

3   A Symbolic Approach to the Verification of Timed Automata

The original decidability result which uses regions is not suited for implementation, and symbolic approaches exploring the set of reachable states (forward or backward), and based on so-called *zones* [3,58] are preferred. In this survey we focus on forward computations, which compute iteratively successors of the initial configuration, until hitting the target set (a configuration whose state is in F), or (hopefully) until getting a certificate (e.g., an invariant) showing that it cannot be hit. We fix for this section a timed automaton $\mathcal{A} = (Q, X, q_0, T, F)$.

3.1   Zones and Symbolic Forward Computation

A *zone* over X is a set of clock valuations defined by a general clock constraint of $\mathcal{C}(X)$. Figure 1(a) gives an example of a zone Z over $X = \{x_1, x_2\}$. Given a set of valuations W (over X), we define the following operations:

- *Intersection of W and W'*: $W \cap W' = \{v \in \mathbb{R}_+^X \mid v \in W \text{ and } v \in W'\}$;

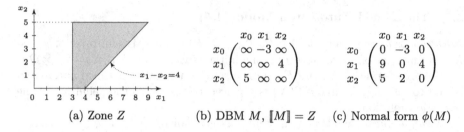

(a) Zone Z (b) DBM M, $[\![M]\!] = Z$ (c) Normal form $\phi(M)$

Fig. 1. Representations of zone Z defined by $((x_1 \geq 3) \land (x_2 \leq 5) \land (x_1 - x_2 \leq 4))$.

– *Reset to zero of W w.r.t. $Y \subseteq X$*: $[Y]W = \{[Y]v \in \mathbb{R}_+^X \mid v \in W\}$;
– *Future of W*: $\overrightarrow{W} = \{v + \delta \in \mathbb{R}_+^X \mid v \in W$ and $\delta \in \mathbb{R}_+\}$.

One can see that those operations transform a zone into another zone. Furthermore, if $t = (q, g, Y, q') \in T$ is a transition of $\mathcal{A}$, then the operator Post_t defined by $\mathsf{Post}_t(W) := \{v' \in \mathbb{R}_+^X \mid \exists v \in W, \exists \delta \in \mathbb{R}_+$ s.t. $v \models g$ and $v' = [Y]v + \delta\}$ can be computed symbolically as $\mathsf{Post}_t(W) = \overrightarrow{[Y](W \cap [\![g]\!])}$. In particular, if Z is a zone, then so is $\mathsf{Post}_t(Z)$.

A *symbolic state* is a pair (q, Z) where $q \in Q$ is a state and Z is a nonempty zone. The *initial* symbolic state is $s_0 = (q_0, Z_0)$ where $Z_0 = \overrightarrow{\{0_X\}}$. The set $\mathcal{S}$ of *reachable* symbolic states of $\mathcal{A}$ is the least fixed point of the following rules:

$$\frac{}{s_0 \in \mathcal{S}} \; \text{Init}$$

$$\frac{(q, Z) \in \mathcal{S} \qquad t = (q, g, Y, q') \in T \qquad Z' = \mathsf{Post}_t(Z) \neq \emptyset}{(q', Z') \in \mathcal{S}} \; \text{Trans}$$

What is called the *forward analysis* is a saturation computation of the set of reachable states using the above deduction rules. For the analysis of this basic forward analysis, details of the implementation are not very important, but they might be crucial in practice (see for instance [16]). Note that we assume future-closed zones, since it allows to prove optimality of some of the abstractions, see [86, App. A]. First, this symbolic forward analysis is sound and complete for control-state reachability:

Soundness. If $(q, Z) \in \mathcal{S}$, then there exists $v \in Z$ s.t. (q, v) is reachable in $\mathcal{A}$, i.e., there is a run of $\mathcal{A}$ from its initial configuration $(q_0, \mathbf{0})$ to (q, v).
Completeness. If a configuration (q, v) is reachable in $\mathcal{A}$ then there is some $(q, Z) \in \mathcal{S}$ with $v \in Z$.

The problem with this approach is that the set $\mathcal{S}$ may be infinite, in which case any implementation of this forward analysis will not terminate on some instances. There are two main approaches to overcome this problem: *extrapolation* and *simulation*.

Extrapolation. The extrapolation approach defines an idempotent operator extra on symbolic states: if (q, Z) is a symbolic state then $\mathsf{extra}\big((q, Z)\big)$ is a symbolic state (q, Z') with $Z \subseteq Z'$. This approach changes the Trans rule as follows:

$$\frac{(q, Z) \in \mathcal{S}_{\mathsf{extra}} \quad t = (q, g, Y, q') \in T \quad (q', Z') = \mathsf{extra}\,((q', \mathsf{Post}_t(Z))) \neq \emptyset \quad \text{and there are no } (q', Z'') \in \mathcal{S}_{\mathsf{extra}} \text{ with } Z' \subseteq Z''}{\mathsf{add}\ (q', Z') \text{ to } \mathcal{S}_{\mathsf{extra}}}\ \text{extra-Trans}$$

We say that an operator extra is finite if for every $q \in Q$, for all infinite sequences $Z_1, Z_2, \ldots$ of zones, we find $1 \leq i < j$ with $\mathsf{extra}\big((q, Z_j)\big) \subseteq \mathsf{extra}\big((q, Z_i)\big)$. An easy way to ensure finiteness of operator extra is to ensure that its range is finite. If extra is finite then any forward analysis induced by the rule extra-Trans always terminates. Note that the set $\mathcal{S}_{\mathsf{extra}}$ which is computed may depend on the order in which the extra-Trans rule is applied. Optimized search strategies can be used to efficiently compute $\mathcal{S}_{\mathsf{extra}}$ [65]. Since Post_t is monotone, it is easy to see that for all $(q, Z) \in \mathcal{S}$, there is some $(q, Z') \in \mathcal{S}_{\mathsf{extra}}$ with $Z \subseteq Z'$. We deduce that completeness is preserved by extrapolation. We discuss in Sect. 4 extrapolation operators which are finite and also preserve soundness. The corresponding forward analysis will therefore be an algorithm for control-state reachability.

Simulation. The simulation approach considers a preorder relation $\preceq$ between symbolic states of $\mathcal{A}$ and restricts the application of the Trans rule as follows:

$$\frac{(q, Z) \in \mathcal{S}_{\preceq} \quad t = (q, g, Y, q') \in T \quad Z' = \mathsf{Post}_t(Z) \neq \emptyset \quad \text{and there are no } (q', Z'') \in \mathcal{S}_{\preceq} \text{ with } (q', Z') \preceq (q', Z'')}{\mathsf{add}\ (q', Z') \text{ to } \mathcal{S}_{\preceq}}\ \preceq\text{-Trans}$$

where $\mathcal{S}_{\preceq}$ is the new set of symbolic states.

We say that $\preceq$ is *finite* if for all infinite sequences $(q, Z_1), (q, Z_2), \ldots$ of symbolic states of $\mathcal{A}$, we find $1 \leq i < j$ with $(q, Z_j) \preceq (q, Z_i)$. If $\preceq$ is finite then the induced forward analysis always terminates. Note that the set $\mathcal{S}_{\preceq}$ which is computed may depend on the order in which we apply the $\preceq$-Trans rule (the optimized search strategy in [65] can also be applied in this settings). In all cases, we have $\mathcal{S}_{\preceq} \subseteq \mathcal{S}$, so soundness is preserved. Now, if $\preceq$ is a *simulation* (defined in Sect. 5) then completeness is also preserved and the corresponding forward analysis will therefore be an algorithm for control-state reachability.

Remark 1. A stronger version of the soundness property is satisfied by the exact forward computation based on the Trans rule: if $(q, Z) \in \mathcal{S}$, then *for all* $v \in Z$, the configuration (q, v) is reachable in $\mathcal{A}$. This also holds for the variant based on simulation ($\preceq$-Trans rule), but not for the variant based on extrapolation (extra-Trans rule).

The efficiency of the forward analysis crucially depends on the complexity of applying the Trans rule. We will see below how this is implemented in practice.

3.2   Difference Bounded Matrices (DBMs)

The most common data structure for representing zones is the so-called DBM data structure. This data structure has been first introduced in [20] and then set in the framework of timed automata in [46]. Several presentations of this data structure can be found in the literature, for example in [19,23,41].

A *difference bounded matrix* (DBM in short) for a set $X = \{x_1, \ldots, x_n\}$ of n clocks is an $(n+1)$-square matrix of pairs

$$(\lhd, m) \in \mathbb{V} := (\{<, \leq\} \times \mathbb{Z}) \cup \{(<, \infty)\}.$$

A DBM $M = ((\lhd_{i,j}, m_{i,j}))_{0 \leq i,j \leq n}$ defines the zone:

$$\llbracket M \rrbracket := \{v \colon X \to \mathbb{R}_+ \mid \forall\, 0 \leq i,j \leq n,\ \overline{v}(x_i) - \overline{v}(x_j) \lhd_{i,j} m_{i,j}\}$$

where $\overline{v} \in \mathbb{R}_+^{\{x_0\} \cup X}$ is such that $\overline{v}_{|X} = v$ and $\overline{v}(x_0) = 0$, and where $\gamma < \infty$ simply means that $\gamma \in \mathbb{R}_+$. To simplify the notations, we assume from now on that all constraints are non-strict (except $(<, \infty)$), so that coefficients of DBMs can simply be seen as elements of $\mathbb{Z} \cup \{\infty\}$. With this convention, the zone Z of Fig. 1(a) can be represented by the DBM of Fig. 1(b).

A zone can have several representations using DBMs. For example, the previous zone can equivalently be represented by the DBM given in Fig. 1(c). This DBM contains constraints that were implicit in the former representation: for instance, the constraint $x_1 - x_0 \leq 9$ encoded in the DBM is implied by $x_1 - x_2 \leq 4$ and $x_2 - x_0 \leq 5$.

With every DBM M we associate its adjacency graph G_M, and when there is no negative cycle in G_M, we let $\phi(M)$ be the DBM obtained by computing the shortest paths in G_M (for instance using the Floyd-Warshall algorithm). Then $\phi(M)$ is the smallest[1] DBM representing the same zone as M. It is called the *normal form* of M and the computation of $\phi(M)$ from M is called *normalization*. We can then notice the following:

- $\llbracket M \rrbracket \subseteq \llbracket M' \rrbracket$ iff $\phi(M) \leq M'$ iff $\phi(M) \leq \phi(M')$;
- $\llbracket M \rrbracket = \emptyset$ iff there is a negative cycle in G_M.

The first point says that inclusion of zones can be checked efficiently, i.e., in time $\mathcal{O}(|X|^2)$, on normal forms of DBMs. The second point says that emptiness can be checked in time $\mathcal{O}(|X|^3)$; this check will never be used as is, and emptiness is detected while computing the various operations (keeping DBMs in normal form).

Finally, the various operations on zones that we need for forward analysis can be done efficiently on DBMs:

- *Intersection of M and M':* $\min(M, M')$. The complexity is $\mathcal{O}(|X|^2)$. But notice that, even if we start with DBMs M, M' in normal form, the resulting DBM $\min(M, M')$ is not necessarily in normal form. To get the result in normal form, we need normalization which takes time $\mathcal{O}(|X|^3)$.

---

[1] For the partial order $\leq$ defined pointwise.

- *Intersection of M with an atomic constraint g of the form $x_i - x_j \leq c$:* assuming $M = \phi(M)$ is in normal form, the normal form M' of $M \cap g$ is defined by $m'_{k,\ell} = \min(m_{k,\ell}, m_{k,i} + c + m_{j,\ell})$ and can be computed in time $\mathcal{O}(|X|^2)$. When g is an arbitrary constraint, we repeat the above operation with every atomic constraints in g. The complexity is $\mathcal{O}(|X|^2 \cdot |g|)$.
- *Reset x_i to zero in M:* as $x_i = x_0$ after the reset, this is achieved on $\phi(M)$ as follows: for all j, set $m_{i,j}$ to $m_{0,j}$, and set $m_{j,i}$ to $m_{j,0}$. The resulting DBM is still in normal form. The complexity is $\mathcal{O}(|X|)$.

  Resetting a set Y of clocks in M amounts to repeat the above operation for all $x_i \in Y$. The complexity is $\mathcal{O}(|X| \cdot |Y|)$.
- *Future of M:* on $\phi(M)$, relax (i.e., set to ∞) all upper-bound constraints $x_i - x_0$ with $i \neq 0$ (that is, all coefficients on column x_0 except the first one). The resulting DBM is still in normal form. The complexity is $\mathcal{O}(|X|)$.

3.3   Efficiency of the Forward Analysis

Let us discuss the complexity of applying the Trans rule. First, given a transition $t = (q, g, Y, q')$ and a zone Z represented by a DBM M in normal form, we compute a DBM M' in normal form for the zone $\mathsf{Post}_t(Z)$. To do so, we intersect M with g, then we reset clocks in Y and finally we let time elapse (future). As explained above, this is computed in time $\mathcal{O}(|X|^2 \cdot |t|)$.

We will define in Sect. 4 extrapolation operators $\mathsf{extra}(q, Z) = (q, Z')$ which are finite and sound for diagonal-free timed automata. When Z is represented by a DBM M in normal form, we compute a DBM M' for Z' in time $\mathcal{O}(|X|^2)$. But M' is not in normal form, so we need normalization, which takes time $\mathcal{O}(|X|^3)$. We saw above that the inclusion test $Z' \subseteq Z''$ required by the extra-Trans rule can be performed in time $\mathcal{O}(|X|^2)$ when the DBM for Z' is in normal form. Hence, we may also apply the extra-Trans rule efficiently.

In Sect. 5, we will define a preorder $\preceq$ which is a finite simulation relation, for all timed automata, even those using diagonal constraints. Moreover, the test $(q, Z) \preceq (q, Z')$ can be checked in time $\mathcal{O}(|X|^2)$ when the timed automaton is diagonal-free. Hence, we may apply the $\preceq$-Trans rule of the forward analysis efficiently. If diagonal constraints are allowed, checking the simulation $(q, Z) \preceq (q, Z')$ is an NP-complete problem.

Notice that, when applying the extra-Trans rule (resp. the $\preceq$-Trans rule), we need to check inclusion $Z' \subseteq Z''$ (resp. simulation $(q', Z') \preceq (q', Z'')$) against all already computed zones Z'' with the same state. Hence, checking simulation (resp. inclusion) is the dominant operation when applying the Trans rule.

4   Extrapolation: A First Solution

4.1   The First Extrapolation Operator

We discuss here the first extrapolation operator which has been defined [45] to ensure good properties of the forward analysis, and which has been prevalent in the timed systems verification community until the early 2010's.

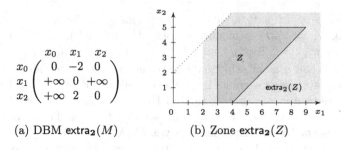

$$
\begin{array}{c c}
& \begin{array}{ccc} x_0 & x_1 & x_2 \end{array} \\
\begin{array}{c} x_0 \\ x_1 \\ x_2 \end{array} & \left(\begin{array}{ccc} 0 & -2 & 0 \\ +\infty & 0 & +\infty \\ +\infty & 2 & 0 \end{array} \right)
\end{array}
$$

(a) DBM $\mathsf{extra_2}(M)$ (b) Zone $\mathsf{extra_2}(Z)$

Fig. 2. Illustration of the extrapolation operator

Let $K \in \mathbb{N}^X$ be a tuple of integers. A K-bounded clock constraint is a clock constraint where clock x is only compared to constants between $-K_x$ and $+K_x$, and the difference $x - y$ is compared to constants between $-K_y$ and $+K_x$. By extension, a K-bounded zone is a zone which can be defined by a K-bounded clock constraint. If (q, Z) is a symbolic state, the K-extrapolation $\mathsf{extra}_K\big((q, Z)\big)$ of (q, Z) is the pair (q, Z') such that Z' is the smallest K-bounded zone which contains Z. Intuitively, this operator relaxes constraints bounding clock x where constants are larger than K.

This operation is well-defined on DBMs: if M is a DBM in normal form representing Z, a DBM representing the zone Z' such that $(q, Z') = \mathsf{extra}_K\big((q, Z)\big)$ is M' (denoted $\mathsf{extra}_K(M)$) such that:

$$
(\lhd'_{i,j}; m'_{i,j}) := \begin{cases} (<; \infty) & \text{if } m_{i,j} > K_{x_i} \\ (<; -K_{x_j}) & \text{if } m_{i,j} < -K_{x_j} \\ (\lhd_{i,j}, m_{i,j}) & \text{otherwise} \end{cases}
$$

Considering the zone given in Fig. 1, its extrapolation w.r.t. $\mathsf{extra_2}$ (where **2** denotes the tuples associating 2 to every clock) is the DBM of Fig. 2(a) (which is not in normal form) and is depicted in Fig. 2(b).

Obviously, extra_K is finite (since its range is finite), hence any forward analysis using the K-extrapolation will terminate. Thus only soundness requires some careful proof, and will actually not hold in general. The first complete proof of soundness was given in [22,23], and was done in the more general context of updatable timed automata. It requires to show that the extrapolation is a *simulation-based abstraction*, that is, there is some simulation relation (in a sense that we will make clear in the next section) such that any configuration which is computed in $\mathcal{S}_{\mathsf{extra}}$ can be simulated by some configuration in $\mathcal{S}$.

Theorem 1. *Let $K \in \mathbb{N}^X$ be a tuple of integers and let $\mathcal{A}$ be a K-bounded[2] and diagonal-free timed automaton. Then, the forward analysis which computes $\mathcal{S}_{\mathsf{extra}_K}$ terminates, and is sound and complete.*

---

[2] For every $x \in X$, for every constraint $x \bowtie c$ appearing in $\mathcal{A}$, $K_x \geq c$.

4.2   Two Refinements of This Approach

State-Dependent Constants. The extrapolation operator is parametrized using a tuple $K \in \mathbb{N}^X$. This can actually be refined and made state-dependent, by considering one constant per state and per clock (i.e., a tuple $K \in \mathbb{N}_\infty^{X \times Q}$, with $\mathbb{N}_\infty = \mathbb{N} \cup \{+\infty\}$), taking only into account constraints which have an impact on the current state: for instance, if x is compared to constant c and then reset before reaching state q, then constant c is not taken into account (this limited propagation idea will be presented in the context of $\mathcal{G}$-simulation in Sect. 5). This refined extrapolation was proven sound for forward analysis in [10].

Note that the notion of active and inactive clocks of [45] can be recovered from this refined extrapolation: a clock x is inactive at state q whenever the constant $K_{x,q}$ is $+\infty$, in which case it can be ignored at state q.

Distinguishing Lower and Upper Bounds. Another refinement, developed in [11], consists in distinguishing lower-bounding and upper-bounding constraints of clocks: instead of having one constant per clock, we consider two constants $L, U \in \mathbb{N}_\infty^X$. An LU-bounded zone is one where x is compared to constants between $-U_x$ and $+L_x$, and the difference $x - y$ is compared to constants between $-U_y$ and $+L_x$. Then the LU-extrapolation $\mathsf{extra}_{LU}((q, Z))$ of (q, Z) is the pair (q, Z') such that Z' is the smallest LU-bounded zone that contains Z.

This operation can be better understood on DBMs: if M is a DBM in normal form representing Z, a DBM representing the zone Z' such that $(q, Z') = \mathsf{extra}_{LU}((q, Z))$ is M' (denoted $\mathsf{extra}_{LU}(M)$) such that:

$$(\triangleleft'_{i,j}; m'_{i,j}) := \begin{cases} (<; \infty) & \text{if } m_{i,j} > L_{x_i} \\ (<; -U_{x_j}) & \text{if } m_{i,j} < -U_{x_j} \\ (\triangleleft_{i,j}, , m_{i,j}) & \text{otherwise} \end{cases}$$

Obviously, extra_{LU} is finite (since its range is finite), hence any forward analysis using the LU-extrapolation will terminate. Only soundness requires some careful proof, see [11]. It uses a LU-simulation, which is a technical notion that we do not discuss here, since a refinement will be discussed in Sect. 5.

Theorem 2. *Let $L, U \in \mathbb{N}^X$ be tuples of integers and let $\mathcal{A}$ be a diagonal-free and LU-bounded[3] timed automaton. Then the forward analysis which computes $\mathcal{S}_{\mathsf{extra}_{LU}}$ terminates, and is sound and complete.*

Further refinements can be made, see [11], but will not be discussed here.

4.3   Problems with Diagonal Clock Constraints

Surprisingly, the approach using extrapolation is not appropriate to analyze general timed automata, which may use diagonal clock constraints, and until

---

[3] For every $x \in X$, for every constraint $x < c$ or $x \leq c$ (resp. $x > d$ or $x \geq d$) appearing in $\mathcal{A}$, $U_x \geq c$ (resp. $L_x \geq d$).

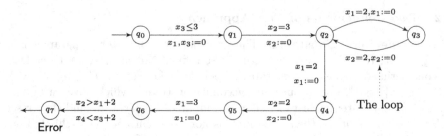

Fig. 3. Automaton $\mathcal{A}_{\text{bug}}$, with diagonal constraints, which cannot be analyzed by any algorithm using a zone extrapolation

recent advances presented in Sect. 5, there was no really satisfactory solution for analyzing general timed automata, see [31].

Indeed, consider the timed automaton $\mathcal{A}_{\text{bug}}$ depicted on Fig. 3. Then it is proven in [23] that it cannot be analyzed using a forward analysis computation using any finite-ranged extrapolation (like those we have described before).

Proposition 1. *There is no extrapolation operator* extra *with finite range, for which the forward analysis which computes* $\mathcal{S}_{\text{extra}}$ *is sound on* $\mathcal{A}_{\text{bug}}$. *This obviously applies to operators* extra$_K$ *and* extra$_{LU}$ *that we have discussed before.*

Let us explain what happens in this timed automaton. If the loop is taken α times, the zone which is reachable at q_6 is Z_α, defined by the constraint

$$(1 \le x_2 - x_1 \le 3) \wedge (1 \le x_4 - x_3 \le 3) \wedge (x_4 - x_2 = x_3 - x_1 = 2\alpha + 5).$$

If we apply an extrapolation operator, extra$_K$ or extra$_{LU}$, to this zone when α is large, we will lose the property that $x_2 - x_1 = x_4 - x_3$ in Z_α (this implicit constraint prevents the transition $q_6 \to q_7$ to be taken). The saturation algorithm which computes $\mathcal{S}_{\text{extra}}$ will then add some symbolic state of the form (q_7, Z) to $\mathcal{S}_{\text{extra}}$, even though control-state q_7 is not reachable!

5   Simulation: An Alternative Solution

The extrapolation approach is lucrative as it allows to work with zones and efficient operations over them. There are two main shortcomings: the approach does not work when diagonal constraints are present, and secondly even for diagonal-free automata, it does not use the coarsest known abstraction of zones, which was proposed in [11]. An LU-simulation relation $v \preccurlyeq_{LU} v'$ between valuations was defined in [11]. In principle, one could consider an extrapolation extra$(Z) = \{v \in \mathbb{R}_+^X \mid \exists v' \in Z \text{ with } v \preccurlyeq_{LU} v'\}$, which is simply the downward closure of Z with respect to the LU-simulation. However, there are zones for which this downward closure is not even convex. Hence the LU-simulation cannot be used with the extrapolation approach. The coarser the abstraction, the smaller is the number of zones enumerated and therefore it is motivating to look for ways to use coarser abstractions. These two questions have been the driving force of research in this area over the last decade.

The central idea is to use simulations between zones, instead of extrapolating them. Extrapolations need to store abstracted zones explicitly. This is a bottleneck for the usage of non-convex abstractions. The simulation approach, in principle, eliminates this problem. The missing piece is an efficient simulation test between zones. This was settled in [62] for diagonal-free automata where it was shown that $Z \preccurlyeq_{LU} Z'$ (the inclusion up to LU-simulation, more precisely $\forall v \in Z, \exists v' \in Z'$ s.t. $v \preccurlyeq_{LU} v'$) can be done in time quadratic in the number of clocks, as efficient as a plain inclusion $Z \subseteq Z'$. Later, a new simulation, known as the $\mathcal{G}$-simulation, was developed for automata with diagonal constraints [50]. It is based on a map $\mathcal{G}$ associating sets of constraints to states of the timed automaton. It was not as pretty a picture as in the diagonal-free case since the corresponding simulation test was shown to be NP-complete ([51] and [78, Section 4.4]). In spite of this, the $\mathcal{G}$-simulation approach is promising: (1) when restricted to diagonal-free automata, the $\mathcal{G}$-simulation is coarser than the LU-simulation and the simulation test remains quadratic [51] (see [78, Section 4.2] for a more elaborate exposition), (2) in the general case when diagonals are present, heuristics have been proposed to get a fast test in practice and have been shown to work well in experiments and (3) the approach can be extended seamlessly for automata with updates. Previous approaches for dealing with diagonals had to eliminate the diagonal constraints explicitly and therefore resulted in a blow-up in space. Here the difficulty gets absorbed into the time to do the simulation test. For automata with updates, no zone based solution was available previously.

In this section, we present the $\mathcal{G}$-simulation framework. Recall from Sect. 3 that the simulation approach makes use of a preorder $\preceq$ to prune the saturation computation of the symbolic states. More specifically, the $\preceq$-Trans rule adds a new symbolic state (q', Z') if there are no existing symbolic states (q', Z'') with $(q', Z') \preceq (q', Z'')$. The idea is that if $(q', Z') \preceq (q', Z'')$ then every control state reachable from (q', Z') should be reachable from (q', Z'') and therefore it is not necessary to explore further from (q', Z'). This idea is neatly captured by simulation relations. For the rest of this section, we fix a timed automaton $\mathcal{A}$.

Definition 1 (Simulation). *A preorder relation $\preceq$ between configurations of $\mathcal{A}$ having the same control state is said to be a simulation if for every $(q, v) \preceq (q, v')$, two properties are satisfied:*

(1) (time elapse): for every $\delta \in \mathbb{R}_+$, we have $(q, v + \delta) \preceq (q, v' + \delta)$, and

(2) (discrete transition): for every $(q, v) \xrightarrow{t} (q_1, v_1)$ with t a transition of $\mathcal{A}$, there exists $(q, v') \xrightarrow{t} (q_1, v_1')$ with $(q_1, v_1) \preceq (q_1, v_1')$.

We extend $\preceq$ to zones by defining $(q, Z) \preceq (q, Z')$ if for every $v \in Z$ there exists $v' \in Z'$ such that $(q, v) \preceq (q, v')$.

Notice that if $(q, v) \preceq (q, v')$ and there is a run from (q, v) to (q_1, v_1) alternating time elapses and discrete transitions, then there is a run from (q, v') to some (q_1, v_1') using the same sequence of time elapses and discrete transitions.

The relation as defined above is known as a strong-timed simulation in literature [89] since we require the same δ from (q, v') in condition (1). When we relax (1) to say that we have $(q, v + \delta) \preceq (q, v' + \delta')$ for some $\delta' \in \mathbb{R}_+$, the relation is called a time-abstract simulation. The concrete relations that we know so far turn out to be strong-timed simulations and so we restrict to the above definition. Our goal is to now find a concrete simulation relation.

From condition (2) of Definition 1, it is clear that the guards of the automaton play a crucial role in coming up with a simulation relation. So, as a first step, we collect a set of *relevant* constraints at each state of the automaton. Clearly, the guards from the outgoing transitions of a state q are relevant at q. Now, consider a transition $q \xrightarrow{t} q_1$ of the automaton. A constraint that is relevant at q_1 needs to be propagated in some form to q depending on the resets at t. Otherwise, there is no means to achieve the forward propagation of the simulation (condition (2)). The next definition formalizes this idea through a fixpoint characterization.

Definition 2 (Constraint map, [50,78]). *The constraint map $\mathcal{G}$ of $\mathcal{A}$ associates a set $\mathcal{G}(q)$ of constraints to every state $q \in Q$. It is obtained as the least fixpoint of the following system of equations:*

$$\mathcal{G}(q) = \bigcup_{(q,g,Y,q') \in T} \left(\{ \text{ atomic constraints of } g \} \cup \bigcup_{\varphi \in \mathcal{G}(q')} \text{pre}(\varphi, Y) \right)$$

where $\text{pre}(x \bowtie c, Y)$ *is* $\{x \bowtie c\}$ *if* $x \notin Y$ *and is the empty set when* $x \in Y$, *and* $\text{pre}(x - y \bowtie c)$ *is* $\{x \bowtie c\}$ *if* $x \notin Y, y \in Y$; *is* $\{-y \bowtie c\}$ *if* $x \in Y, y \notin Y$; *is* $\{x - y \bowtie c\}$ *when* $x, y \notin Y$, *and is the empty set when both* $x, y \in Y$.

For the automaton $\mathcal{A}_{\text{bug}}$ in Fig. 3, we have $\mathcal{G}(q_6) = \{x_2 - x_1 > 2, x_4 - x_3 < 2\}$, $\mathcal{G}(q_2) = \{x_1 = 2, x_2 = 2, x_4 - x_3 < 2\}$ and $\mathcal{G}(q_0) = \{x_3 \leq 3, x_2 = 3, x_4 < 2\}$. To see why $\mathcal{G}(q_0)$ is this set of constraints, notice that $x_3 \leq 3$ appears in the guard out of q_0. Since x_1 and x_3 are reset in $q_0 \to q_1$, constraints on these clocks which appear later are not relevant at q_0 (and will be made empty set by the pre operator). Since x_2 is reset in $q_1 \to q_2$, only the $x_2 = 3$ propagates to q_0. Finally, the constraint $x_4 - x_3 < 2$ in $q_6 \to q_7$ propagates all the way back to q_1 as it is, and due to the reset of x_3 in $q_0 \to q_1$, we get $\text{pre}(x_4 - x_3 < 2, \{x_1, x_3\}) = \{x_4 < 2\}$ and hence we have $x_4 < 2$ in $\mathcal{G}(q_0)$.

The computation of the constraint map of a timed automaton is in the same spirit as the local computation of constants proposed for the extrapolation operator in [10] (mentioned in Sect. 4.2), although now we deal with constraint sets instead of constants. We now have the parameters for the simulation ready. Our next definition gives a relation between configurations that is based on these computed constraints.

Definition 3 ($\mathcal{G}$-preorder, [50,78]). *Let $\mathcal{G}$ be the associated constraint map to $\mathcal{A}$. We define $(q, v) \preceq_{\mathcal{G}} (q, v')$ if for all $\delta \in \mathbb{R}_+$ and all $\varphi \in \mathcal{G}(q)$, $v + \delta \models \varphi$ implies $v' + \delta \models \varphi$.*

Thanks to its definition, it is not difficult to show that the $\mathcal{G}$-preorder $\preceq_\mathcal{G}$ is a simulation relation. Showing finiteness is more involved. Let Z be a zone and q be a state of $\mathcal{A}$. We write $\downarrow_{q,\mathcal{G}} Z = \{v \in \mathbb{R}_+^X \mid \exists v' \in Z \text{ s.t. } (q,v) \preceq_\mathcal{G} (q,v')\}$. Let M be the maximum constant appearing in $\mathcal{G}(q)$. From M, one can construct a finite partition of the space of valuations and show that $\downarrow_{q,\mathcal{G}}$ is a union of its classes. Therefore, the set $\{\downarrow_{q,\mathcal{G}} Z \mid Z \text{ is a zone}\}$ is finite, which implies that the simulation $\preceq_\mathcal{G}$ is finite [51], [78, Section 4.1].

Theorem 3 ([51,78]). *Let $\mathcal{A}$ be a timed automaton possibly with diagonal constraints. The relation $\preceq_\mathcal{G}$ is a finite simulation relation. Moreover the forward analysis which computes $\mathcal{S}_{\preceq_\mathcal{G}}$ terminates, and is sound and complete.*

Coming back to the example $\mathcal{A}_{\text{bug}}$, let us see how the simulation approach works here. Since no new valuations are added (in contrast to the extrapolation approach), soundness is always guaranteed and q_7 would be unreachable. The question is about termination. Due to the loop, there are potentially infinitely many zones appearing at state q_6. As seen in Sect. 4.3, the zone Z_α reached at q_6 after α iterations of the loop satisfies $x_4 - x_2 = x_3 - x_1 = 2\alpha + 5$ and $1 \leq x_4 - x_3 = x_2 - x_1 \leq 3$. We claim that $(q_6, Z_\alpha) \preceq_\mathcal{G} (q_6, Z_\beta)$ for all $\alpha, \beta \geq 0$. Indeed, from $v \in Z_\alpha$ we define v' by $v'(x_1) = v(x_1)$, $v'(x_2) = v(x_2)$, $v'(x_3) = v(x_3) + 2(\beta - \alpha)$ and $v'(x_4) = v(x_4) + 2(\beta - \alpha)$. Intuitively, v' is obtained by taking the loop β times instead of α times and keeping the other delays unchanged. We can check that $v' \in Z_\beta$. Moreover, $v'(x_2) - v'(x_1) = v(x_2) - v(x_1)$ and $v'(x_4) - v'(x_3) = v(x_4) - v(x_3)$. As we have seen above, $\mathcal{G}(q_6) = \{x_2 - x_1 > 2, x_4 - x_3 < 2\}$. We deduce that $(q_6, v) \preceq (q_6, v')$. Hence the zone enumeration will stop at the second zone appearing at q_6, due to the simulation. An analogous situation happens at other states q_2, q_3, q_4 and q_5.

When $\mathcal{G}(q)$ contains no diagonal constraints, the test $(q, Z) \preceq_\mathcal{G} (q, Z')$ can be done in time quadratic in the number of clocks [51], [78, Section 4.2]. The main idea is that this test can be broken into tests of the form $Z \preceq_{\{x \lhd c, y \rhd d\}} Z'$ where $x \lhd c$ with $\lhd \in \{<, \leq\}$ is an upper bound constraint and $y \rhd d$ with $\rhd \in \{>, \geq\}$ is a lower bound constraint in $\mathcal{G}(q)$. When $\mathcal{G}(q)$ contains diagonal constraints, the test is NP-complete [51],[78, Section 4.4]. More precisely, the test is exponential in the number of diagonals present in the set $\mathcal{G}(q)$. An algorithm to compute this test in the general case appears in [50]. The algorithm essentially reduces $(q, Z) \preceq_\mathcal{G} (q, Z')$ to several (exponentially many in the worst case) simulation checks over non-diagonal constraints. It employs heuristics which can reduce this number in practice.

Dealing with Updates. The reset operation can be extended with updates to clocks. An update up to the set of clocks X is a function which maps each clock x to an expression $x := c$ or $x := y + d$ where $c \in \mathbb{N}$, $y \in X$ (which could as well be x) and $d \in \mathbb{Z}$. Automata with such update functions are known as updatable timed automata [27]. Due to the presence of updates $x := x + 1$ and $x := x - 1$, reachability becomes undecidable, even with 0 time elapse. Several decidable subclasses have been studied by constructing a finite region equivalence.

The zone based simulation method can be extended to updatable timed automata [50], just by changing one definition: in Definition 2, replace transition (q, g, R, q') with (q, g, up, q') and the the operator $\text{pre}(\varphi, R)$ with an operation $\text{pre}(\varphi, up)$ that is defined as follows. Define up_x to be c (resp. $y + d$) if up maps x to $x := c$ (resp. $x := y + d$). The constraint $\text{pre}(\varphi, up)$ is obtained by replacing occurrence of x in φ with up_x. For example $\text{pre}(x - y \le 5, x := z - 2)$ is $\{z - y \le 7\}$. The least fixpoint of the equations in Definition 2 may not be finite. When it is finite, the constraint map $\mathcal{G}$ and the $\mathcal{G}$-preorder can be used to get a finite simulation as before. An algorithm to detect termination of the fixpoint computation is provided. For all decidable subclasses tabulated in [27], the constraint map $\mathcal{G}$ is finite. A refined version of the constraint map computation that uses an operator $\text{pre}(\varphi, g, up)$ taking the guard g into consideration gives finite constraint maps for a larger class of automata, including timed automata with bounded subtraction that has been used to model preemptive scheduling [48].

6   Beyond Reachability

6.1   Weighted Timed Automata

Timed automata do not offer the possibility to model other quantities than time (or durations). It may however be useful to also model other quantities. The more general model of hybrid automata is unfortunately not adequate for automatic verification, since it is undecidable in general [57]. In 2001, the model of weighted timed automata (also called priced timed automata at that time) has been proposed [7,15]: on top of a standard timed automaton, a weight is associated with every state (where it is a rate) and with every transition (where it is a discrete change). Let $\mathsf{wgt} \colon Q \cup T \to \mathbb{Z}$ be such a weight function. It allows to give a *cost* value to time elapse $(q, v) \xrightarrow{\delta} (q, v + \delta)$ (with $\delta \in \mathbb{R}_+$) as $\delta \cdot \mathsf{wgt}(q)$, and to discrete transition $(q, v) \xrightarrow{t} (q_1, v_1)$ as $\mathsf{wgt}(t)$. The cost is then defined on a finite run by summing up the costs of all single steps (time elapses or discrete transitions) along it. This cost function, defined on every finite run, represents the evolution of an observer variable which is piecewise-linear w.r.t. time elapsing, and it can be used for various purposes: ensure that it remains within given bounds [28,30,32]; or optimize its value while ensuring to reach some state [7,15,24]. The model is discussed in the survey [29]. Here, we focus on this last problem, assuming that the weight function is nonnegative.

Decidability and complexity for this model were proven in the early papers [7, 15,24], making use of a refinement of the region construction (called corner-point abstraction later in [25]). Already in [70], a symbolic solution built on zones has been proposed, based on so-called *priced zones*. The idea is to store information on the cost function on top of a zone as a pair (Z, ζ), where ζ is an affine function of the clocks, the meaning being that valuation $v \in Z$ can be reached from the initial configuration, and the minimal cost to do that is given by $\zeta(v)$. Similar to zones, priced zones can be efficiently represented by a DBM, an offset cost and an affine coefficient for each clock, see Fig. 4. All operations needed for a forward

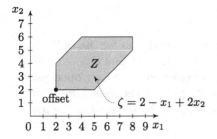

Priced zone (Z, ζ) is represented as a standard DBM for Z, plus the offset cost $+4$ (i.e. cost at the lowest point of the zone, here point $(2, 2)$), plus the rate (-1) for x and the rate for y $(+2)$.

$$\zeta = 2 - x_1 + 2x_2$$

Fig. 4. A priced zone (Z, ζ).

exploration can be done using this data structure. Only termination of the computation has remained open until [26]. Indeed, there is *a priori* no possible sound extrapolation in this context, but the development of the simulation approach (as presented in Sect. 5) for timed automata proved extremely useful and could be extended in some sense to weighted timed automata as well [26].

6.2 Liveness Properties

Liveness properties amount to checking whether some good event may happen infinitely often, and are captured using Büchi conditions: given a timed automaton $\mathcal{A}$ and a state q, does there exist an infinite run of $\mathcal{A}$ that visits q infinitely often? To solve this problem using zones, one crucial modification needs to be done in both the extrapolation and the simulation approaches. In the extra-Trans rule, the inclusion $Z' \subseteq Z''$ is replaced with $Z' = Z''$ [69, 74]. In the $\preceq$-Trans rule, in addition to $(q', Z') \preceq (q', Z'')$, we add $(q', Z'') \preceq (q', Z')$ which is a simulation in the other direction as well [60, 61] (simulation is replaced with a bisimulation).

This seemingly simple change results in a huge difference in performance. It has been noticed in experiments that the number of zones enumerated for liveness properties is substantially higher than for reachability properties. This has led to a close study of the role of inclusion/simulation (collectively called subsumptions), as opposed to equality/bisimulation, in pruning zones. Suppose we call the transition system over symbolic states computed using subsumptions as a subsumption graph. Reachability problems can be solved in polynomial time if the subsumption graph is given as input. However, it has been shown that deciding liveness is PSPACE-complete even if both the automaton and a subsumption graph are given as input [61]. This is evidence to the power of subsumptions in reducing the number of symbolic states. Unfortunately, we cannot use the full power of subsumptions for liveness.

It is however possible to restrict subsumption in such a way that no spurious Büchi run is created. Algorithms that can use restricted subsumption for the liveness problem have been studied [60, 61, 69], with good performances in practice.

7 Tools

Since the nineties, several tools have implemented algorithms for the verification of timed automata, in particular: KRONOS [35], UPPAAL [14] and RED [91] to cite a few. In the last years we have started the development of a new open-source tool TCHECKER [59]. In this section, we shortly present the tools UPPAAL and TCHECKER which are both based on the zone approach presented in the paper.

7.1 A Tool for Verifying Timed Automata: UPPAAL

UPPAAL is the state-of-the-art tool for timed automata verification. Models consist of a network of timed automata that communicate through handshaking and shared variables. Specifications are expressed in a subset of the TCTL logic that allows to express reachability properties as well as a restricted subset of liveness properties. Adding extra processes to the system allows to check richer specifications. The tool UPPAAL implements model-checking algorithms. Extensions of the tool have been proposed for statistical model-checking [37] and two player concurrent safety and reachability games [12].

UPPAAL has played a tremendous role in the adoption of the timed automata formalism in the industry. Numerous case studies have been successfully achieved using UPPAAL: Philips Audio Protocol [73], Bang&Olufsen Audio/Video Protocol [56], Commercial Fieldbus Protocol [44], Schedulability analysis [77], Web Services Business Activity [83], and SCADA Attacks Detection [76] to cite a few. Several of these case studies have allowed to detect flaws in the systems under study, leading to safer real-time systems.

Both the DBM library and the parser of UPPAAL are open-source. However, the remaining parts of its source code are not publicly available.

7.2 The Tool TCHECKER

In the last years we have started the development of a fully open-source verification tool for timed automata. TCHECKER [59] consists of a set of libraries and tools. It can be used both as a model-checker, and as a framework to develop new verification algorithms.

TCHECKER models consist in networks of timed automata that communicate through multiprocess synchronisations and shared variables. Its companion tool UPPAAL-TO-TCHECKER [82] can be used to automatically translate a subset of UPPAAL input language into TCHECKER models. Properties are encoded by adding observers to the model. Reachability and liveness algorithms can be applied to detect if specific states of the observers can be reached (repeatedly).

The TCHECKER library is implemented in C++ and provides various classes that allow to manipulate models, to represent and manipulate zones using DBMs, to compute zone graphs using various semantics and extrapolations, and to represent and compute the state-space of a model using verification algorithms. The TCHECKER library and input language can easily be extended to support new data structures and verification algorithms, as well as extensions of timed automata such as weighted timed automata or timed games. A tutorial on how to implement verification algorithms using TCHECKER libraries is available from the website [59].

TCHECKER also comes with a set of tools to perform syntactic verification of models (`tck-syntax`), simulation (`tck-simulate`), reachability verification (`tck-reach`) and liveness verification (`tck-liveness`). These tools can be used online on TCHECKER demonstration webpage [81]. The TCHECKER libraries and tools implement most of the approaches described in this paper, although some of them are not implemented yet and will be available in future releases of TCHECKER. Several research teams are currently using TCHECKER to implement and test their verification algorithms: Irisa (Rennes, France), LaBRI (Bordeaux, France), LIF (Marseille, France) and CMI (Chennai, India).

8 What Next?

Over the years, timed automata verification has been successfully used in many case studies, e.g. [44, 56, 72, 76]. In several instances complex bugs have been discovered and fixed, leading to safer real-time systems. Efficient verification algorithms and tools are crucial for practical applications. Timed automata verification algorithms heavily rely on finite abstractions for termination. As we have discussed in this article, this has been achieved by means of extrapolations or simulations. Both extrapolations and simulations serve to keep the number of zones Z per control state q firstly finite, and secondly as small as possible. This is the motivation behind finding coarser extrapolations/simulations, and this endeavour has been largely successful. Based on our experience with experiments, we find that by applying extrapolation/simulation the number of zones per control state is usually small. The major bottleneck is the large number of control states q appearing in the forward computation. In untimed systems, this explosion is handled using SAT-based methods or partial-order reduction. Lifting these techniques to the timed setting has not been straightforward. We conclude this article by first discussing some attempts in this direction and then finish with some other open challenges.

8.1 BDD and SAT Based Methods

In [84], abstract reachability algorithms were given where zones were overapproximated by a set of clock constraint predicates. This generalizes the zone-based exploration algorithm but requires a counter-example guided refinement loop to ensure soundness and completeness. A similar idea was considered in [88], which is based on using lazy abstractions when exploring the zones, and refining them using interpolants to ensure that the exploration is sound and complete.

[84] also gives a variant of the algorithm based on binary decision diagrams (BDDs), where the abstract zone-based semantics was encoded using Boolean functions. A similar but more efficient way of using predicate abstractions for analyzing timed automata was given in [39] based on the use of the IC3 algorithm

[36] combined with implicit abstractions [40]. Thanks to the implicit abstraction method, one does not need to build the abstract transition relation, but
rather guesses, at each step, an abstract transition and its corresponding witness concrete transition. This enables the use of SAT-based algorithms, including IC3. The nuXmv model checker was extended with a syntax to describe
timed automata, and provides a powerful alternative to zone-based algorithms
for timed automata models with large discrete state spaces.

There have been previous propositions for applying IC3 to timed automata
without abstractions, such as [67] where zones were used to backpropagate counterexamples to inductions.

There have been other attempts at combining timed automata semantics
with symbolic approaches for handling large discrete state spaces. An algorithm
encoding the region automaton using BDDs was given in [66] along with an
extension of the SMV language for specifying timed automata. In the past, several works attempted at extending binary decision diagrams to represent information on the clocks such as [21,47,90], while some of these only consider discrete time [79,87]. In [42], an extension of the *and-inverter graph* data structure
with predicates was considered in order to represent the state space of linear
hybrid automata. These can represent possible non-convex polyhedra extended
by Boolean variables.

Bounded model checking was applied to timed automata in [9,85] and [66];
see also [75] specifically for the partial-order semantics.

The above works conclude on the complementarity of the zone-based enumerative algorithms and various symbolic approaches either based on (variants
of) BDDs or SAT/SMT solvers. This is, in fact, also observed for finite-state
models where enumerative and symbolic model checkers are both useful in different contexts. We thus believe that it is important that both zone-based model
checkers such as UPPAAL and TCHECKER, and SAT-based ones such as NUXMV
are available. A practical verification tool box should in fact contain various
algorithms since a single algorithm may not succeed in verifying all types of
models.

8.2   The Local-Time Semantics and Partial-Order Reduction

Verification of very large networks with multiple timed processes is currently
out of reach of the existing methods. Enumerative model-checkers for untimed
systems have immensely benefitted from partial-order reduction methods that
exploit the concurrency in the network representation of the model. Roughly,
two actions a and b are independent if there is no component of the network
containing both these actions. For such actions, doing ab or ba from a global state
leads to the same global state (popularly known as the diamond property). This
property allows to pick one of either ab or ba for further exploration. In general,
given a set of independent actions, partial-order methods aim to pick one path
out of the several possible interleavings of the independent actions. This leads
to exponential reduction in the number of states enumerated. Unfortunately,
for (networks of) timed automata, partial-order reduction is not straightforward

due to the lack of a diamond property: for instance, suppose that x is reset at a and y is reset at b, then ab and ba lead to different zones keeping track of the different order of resets. There is an implicit synchronization due to the global nature of time.

In the last few years, there has been some work in making use of a local-time semantics for networks of timed automata [17] to obtain a symbolic computation that contains diamonds. The nice aspect of the local-time semantics is the presence of diamonds, but unfortunately, getting finite abstractions is not immediate. A first solution has been proposed in [53], but it is not compatible with partial-order reduction. It has later been shown that there is no finite abstraction for the local-time semantics [54] that is compatible with partial-order reduction, although some subclasses of timed automata admit such a finite abstraction. The next challenge is to define a partial-order reduction technique which works well in the timed setting, as well as to detect subclasses of timed automata for which partial-order reduction and finite abstractions can be combined. Other works on partial-order reduction which do not go via the local-time semantics also work on restricted settings: applying the reduction only to parts of the network where independent actions occur in zero time, [71], or discovering independent actions in the standard global-time semantics, either statically [43] or dynamically [55].

8.3 Domain-Specific Algorithms

For some applications that can be modelled as timed automata, standard algorithms for generic timed automata might be quite slow. We therefore believe that it would be beneficial to develop domain-specific verification algorithms. As an example, the model of funnel automata has been developed to model some robotics systems [33,34]: funnel automata are timed automata with few clocks (three clocks) but a large discrete state-space. While small instances could be verified using tool TIAMO [26] (a precursor of TCHECKER implemented in OCaml), larger instances could not be verified due to the state-explosion problem. Techniques mixing BDDs and zones could possibly be developed for this specific application.

8.4 Richer Models

Another interesting direction is to investigate the extent to which the advances in timed automata can help in the algorithmics for richer models. There has been some progress already in this direction. Apart from updatable timed automata and weighted timed automata, the simulation approach has been extended to pushdown timed automata [2] and event-clock automata [1]. It remains to be seen whether this approach can be lifted to the context of parametric timed automata [6,8], probabilistic timed automata [68,80] and controller synthesis for timed games [13,38].

References

1. Akshay, S., Gastin, P., Govind, R., Srivathsan, B.: Simulations for event-clock automata. In: Proceedings of 33th International Conference on Concurrency Theory (CONCUR 2022). Lecture Notes in Computer Science, Springer, Cham (2022, to appear)
2. Akshay, S., Gastin, P., Prakash, K.R.: Fast zone-based algorithms for reachability in pushdown timed automata. In: Silva, A., Leino, K.R.M. (eds.) CAV 2021. LNCS, vol. 12759, pp. 619–642. Springer, Cham (2021). https://doi.org/10.1007/978-3-030-81685-8_30
3. Alur, R., Courcoubetis, C., Dill, D.L., Halbwachs, N., Wong-Toi, H.: An implementation of three algorithms for timing verification based on automata emptiness. In: Proceedings of 13th IEEE Real-Time Systems Symposium (RTSS 1992), pp. 157–166. IEEE Computer Society Press (1992)
4. Alur, R., Dill, D.: Automata for modeling real-time systems. In: Paterson, M.S. (ed.) ICALP 1990. LNCS, vol. 443, pp. 322–335. Springer, Heidelberg (1990). https://doi.org/10.1007/BFb0032042
5. Alur, R., Dill, D.L.: A theory of timed automata. Theoret. Comput. Sci. **126**(2), 183–235 (1994)
6. Alur, R., Henzinger, T.A., Vardi, M.Y.: Parametric real-time reasoning. In: Proceedings of 25th Annual ACM Symposium on the Theory of Computing (STOC 1993), pp. 592–601. ACM (1993)
7. Alur, R., La Torre, S., Pappas, G.J.: Optimal paths in weighted timed automata. In: Di Benedetto, M.D., Sangiovanni-Vincentelli, A. (eds.) HSCC 2001. LNCS, vol. 2034, pp. 49–62. Springer, Heidelberg (2001). https://doi.org/10.1007/3-540-45351-2_8
8. André, É.: IMITATOR 3: synthesis of timing parameters beyond decidability. In: Silva, A., Leino, K.R.M. (eds.) CAV 2021. LNCS, vol. 12759, pp. 552–565. Springer, Cham (2021). https://doi.org/10.1007/978-3-030-81685-8_26
9. Audemard, G., Cimatti, A., Kornilowicz, A., Sebastiani, R.: Bounded model checking for timed systems. In: Peled, D.A., Vardi, M.Y. (eds.) FORTE 2002. LNCS, vol. 2529, pp. 243–259. Springer, Heidelberg (2002). https://doi.org/10.1007/3-540-36135-9_16
10. Behrmann, G., Bouyer, P., Fleury, E., Larsen, K.G.: Static guard analysis in timed automata verification. In: Garavel, H., Hatcliff, J. (eds.) TACAS 2003. LNCS, vol. 2619, pp. 254–270. Springer, Heidelberg (2003). https://doi.org/10.1007/3-540-36577-X_18
11. Behrmann, G., Bouyer, P., Larsen, K.G., Pelánek, R.: Lower and upper bounds in zone based abstractions of timed automata. In: Jensen, K., Podelski, A. (eds.) TACAS 2004. LNCS, vol. 2988, pp. 312–326. Springer, Heidelberg (2004). https://doi.org/10.1007/978-3-540-24730-2_25
12. Behrmann, G., Bouyer, P., Larsen, K.G., Pelànek, R.: Zone based abstractions for timed automata exploiting lower and upper bounds. Int. J. Softw. Tools Technol. Transf. **8**(3), 204–215 (2005)
13. Behrmann, G., Cougnard, A., David, A., Fleury, E., Larsen, K.G., Lime, D.: UPPAAL-TIGA: time for playing games! In: Damm, W., Hermanns, H. (eds.) CAV 2007. LNCS, vol. 4590, pp. 121–125. Springer, Heidelberg (2007). https://doi.org/10.1007/978-3-540-73368-3_14

14. Behrmann, G., et al.: Uppaal 4.0. In: Proceedings of 3rd International Conference on Quantitative Evaluation of Systems (QEST 2006), pp. 125–126. IEEE Computer Society Press (2006)
15. Behrmann, G., et al.: Minimum-cost reachability for priced time automata. In: Di Benedetto, M.D., Sangiovanni-Vincentelli, A. (eds.) HSCC 2001. LNCS, vol. 2034, pp. 147–161. Springer, Heidelberg (2001). https://doi.org/10.1007/3-540-45351-2_15
16. Behrmann, G., Hune, T., Vaandrager, F.: Distributing timed model checking — how the search order matters. In: Emerson, E.A., Sistla, A.P. (eds.) CAV 2000. LNCS, vol. 1855, pp. 216–231. Springer, Heidelberg (2000). https://doi.org/10.1007/10722167_19
17. Bengtsson, J., Jonsson, B., Lilius, J., Yi, W.: Partial order reductions for timed systems. In: Sangiorgi, D., de Simone, R. (eds.) CONCUR 1998. LNCS, vol. 1466, pp. 485–500. Springer, Heidelberg (1998). https://doi.org/10.1007/BFb0055643
18. Bengtsson, J., Larsen, K., Larsson, F., Pettersson, P., Yi, W.: UPPAAL — a tool suite for automatic verification of real-time systems. In: Alur, R., Henzinger, T.A., Sontag, E.D. (eds.) HS 1995. LNCS, vol. 1066, pp. 232–243. Springer, Heidelberg (1996). https://doi.org/10.1007/BFb0020949
19. Bengtsson, J., Yi, W.: Timed automata: semantics, algorithms and tools. In: Desel, J., Reisig, W., Rozenberg, G. (eds.) ACPN 2003. LNCS, vol. 3098, pp. 87–124. Springer, Heidelberg (2004). https://doi.org/10.1007/978-3-540-27755-2_3
20. Berthomieu, B., Menasche, M.: An enumerative approach for analyzing time Petri nets. In: Proceedings of IFIP 9th World Computer Congress. Information Processing, vol. 83, pp. 41–46. North-Holland/ IFIP (1983)
21. Beyer, D., Lewerentz, C., Noack, A.: Rabbit: a tool for BDD-based verification of real-time systems. In: Hunt, W.A., Somenzi, F. (eds.) CAV 2003. LNCS, vol. 2725, pp. 122–125. Springer, Heidelberg (2003). https://doi.org/10.1007/978-3-540-45069-6_13
22. Bouyer, P.: Untameable timed automata! In: Alt, H., Habib, M. (eds.) STACS 2003. LNCS, vol. 2607, pp. 620–631. Springer, Heidelberg (2003). https://doi.org/10.1007/3-540-36494-3_54
23. Bouyer, P.: Forward analysis of updatable timed automata. Formal Methods Syst. Des. **24**(3), 281–320 (2004)
24. Bouyer, P., Brihaye, T., Bruyère, V., Raskin, J.F.: On the optimal reachability problem. Formal Methods Syst. Des. **31**(2), 135–175 (2007)
25. Bouyer, P., Brinksma, E., Larsen, K.G.: Optimal infinite scheduling for multi-priced timed automata. Formal Methods Syst. Des. **32**(1), 2–23 (2008)
26. Bouyer, P., Colange, M., Markey, N.: Symbolic optimal reachability in weighted timed automata. In: Chaudhuri, S., Farzan, A. (eds.) CAV 2016. LNCS, vol. 9779, pp. 513–530. Springer, Cham (2016). https://doi.org/10.1007/978-3-319-41528-4_28
27. Bouyer, P., Dufourd, C., Fleury, E., Petit, A.: Updatable timed automata. Theoret. Comput. Sci. **321**(2–3), 291–345 (2004)
28. Bouyer, P., Fahrenberg, U., Larsen, K.G., Markey, N.: Timed automata with observers under energy constraints. In: Proceedings of 13th International Conference on Hybrid Systems: Computation and Control (HSCC 2010), pp. 61–70. ACM Press (2010)
29. Bouyer, P., Fahrenberg, U., Larsen, K.G., Markey, N.: Quantitative analysis of real-time systems using priced timed automata. Commun. ACM **54**(9), 78–87 (2011)

30. Bouyer, P., Fahrenberg, U., Larsen, K.G., Markey, N., Srba, J.: Infinite runs in weighted timed automata with energy constraints. In: Cassez, F., Jard, C. (eds.) FORMATS 2008. LNCS, vol. 5215, pp. 33–47. Springer, Heidelberg (2008). https://doi.org/10.1007/978-3-540-85778-5_4

31. Bouyer, P., Laroussinie, F., Reynier, P.-A.: Diagonal constraints in timed automata: forward analysis of timed systems. In: Pettersson, P., Yi, W. (eds.) FORMATS 2005. LNCS, vol. 3829, pp. 112–126. Springer, Heidelberg (2005). https://doi.org/10.1007/11603009_10

32. Bouyer, P., Larsen, K.G., Markey, N.: Lower-bound constrained runs in weighted timed automata. In: Proceedings of 9th International Conference on Quantitative Evaluation of Systems (QEST 2012), pp. 128–137. IEEE Computer Society Press (2012)

33. Bouyer, P., Markey, N., Perrin, N., Schlehuber-Caissier, P.: Timed-automata abstraction of switched dynamical systems using control funnels. In: Sankaranarayanan, S., Vicario, E. (eds.) FORMATS 2015. LNCS, vol. 9268, pp. 60–75. Springer, Cham (2015). https://doi.org/10.1007/978-3-319-22975-1_5

34. Bouyer, P., Markey, N., Perrin, N., Schlehuber-Caissier, P.: Timed-automata abstraction of switched dynamical systems using control invariants. Real-Time Syst. **53**(3), 327–353 (2017). https://doi.org/10.1007/s11241-016-9262-3

35. Bozga, M., Daws, C., Maler, O., Olivero, A., Tripakis, S., Yovine, S.: Kronos: a model-checking tool for real-time systems. In: Hu, A.J., Vardi, M.Y. (eds.) CAV 1998. LNCS, vol. 1427, pp. 546–550. Springer, Heidelberg (1998). https://doi.org/10.1007/BFb0028779

36. Bradley, A.R.: SAT-based model checking without unrolling. In: Jhala, R., Schmidt, D. (eds.) VMCAI 2011. LNCS, vol. 6538, pp. 70–87. Springer, Heidelberg (2011). https://doi.org/10.1007/978-3-642-18275-4_7

37. Bulychev, P.E., et al.: UPPAAL-SMC: statistical model checking for priced timed automata. In: Proceedings of 10th Workshop on Quantitative Aspects of Programming Languages (QAPL 2012). Electronic Proceedings in Theoretical Computer Science, vol. 85, pp. 1–16 (2012). https://doi.org/10.4204/EPTCS.85.1

38. Cassez, F., David, A., Fleury, E., Larsen, K.G., Lime, D.: Efficient on-the-fly algorithms for the analysis of timed games. In: Abadi, M., de Alfaro, L. (eds.) CONCUR 2005. LNCS, vol. 3653, pp. 66–80. Springer, Heidelberg (2005). https://doi.org/10.1007/11539452_9

39. Cimatti, A., Griggio, A., Magnago, E., Roveri, M., Tonetta, S.: Extending nuXmv with timed transition systems and timed temporal properties. In: Dillig, I., Tasiran, S. (eds.) CAV 2019. LNCS, vol. 11561, pp. 376–386. Springer, Cham (2019). https://doi.org/10.1007/978-3-030-25540-4_21

40. Cimatti, A., Griggio, A., Mover, S., Tonetta, S.: IC3 modulo theories via implicit predicate abstraction. In: Ábrahám, E., Havelund, K. (eds.) TACAS 2014. LNCS, vol. 8413, pp. 46–61. Springer, Heidelberg (2014). https://doi.org/10.1007/978-3-642-54862-8_4

41. Clarke, E., Grumberg, O., Peled, D.: Model-Checking. MIT Press, Cambridge (1999)

42. Damm, W., et al.: Exact and fully symbolic verification of linear hybrid automata with large discrete state spaces. Sci. Comput. Program. **77**(10), 1122–1150 (2012). https://doi.org/10.1016/j.scico.2011.07.006, https://www.sciencedirect.com/science/article/pii/S0167642311001523

43. Dams, D., Gerth, R., Knaack, B., Kuiper, R.: Partial-order reduction techniques for real-time model checking. Formal Aspects Comput. **10**(5–6), 469–482 (1998). https://doi.org/10.1007/s001650050028

44. David, A., Yi, W.: Modelling and analysis of a commercial field bus protocol. In: Proceedings of 12th Euromicro Conference on Real-Time Systems (ECRTS 2000), pp. 165–172. IEEE Computer Society Press (2000). https://doi.org/10.1109/EMRTS.2000.854004

45. Daws, C., Tripakis, S.: Model checking of real-time reachability properties using abstractions. In: Steffen, B. (ed.) TACAS 1998. LNCS, vol. 1384, pp. 313–329. Springer, Heidelberg (1998). https://doi.org/10.1007/BFb0054180

46. Dill, D.L.: Timing assumptions and verification of finite-state concurrent systems. In: Sifakis, J. (ed.) CAV 1989. LNCS, vol. 407, pp. 197–212. Springer, Heidelberg (1990). https://doi.org/10.1007/3-540-52148-8_17

47. Ehlers, R., Fass, D., Gerke, M., Peter, H.J.: Fully symbolic timed model checking using constraint matrix diagrams. In: Proceedings of 31th IEEE Real-Time Systems Symposium (RTSS 2010), pp. 360–371. IEEE Computer Society Press (2010). https://doi.org/10.1109/RTSS.2010.36

48. Fersman, E., Krcal, P., Pettersson, P., Yi, W.: Task automata: schedulability, decidability and undecidability. Inf. Comput. 205(8), 1149–1172 (2007)

49. Gastin, P., Mukherjee, S., Srivathsan, B.: Reachability in timed automata with diagonal constraints. In: Proceedings of 29th International Conference on Concurrency Theory (CONCUR 2018). LIPIcs, vol. 118, pp. 28:1–28:17. Leibniz-Zentrum für Informatik (2018)

50. Gastin, P., Mukherjee, S., Srivathsan, B.: Fast algorithms for handling diagonal constraints in timed automata. In: Dillig, I., Tasiran, S. (eds.) CAV 2019. LNCS, vol. 11561, pp. 41–59. Springer, Cham (2019). https://doi.org/10.1007/978-3-030-25540-4_3

51. Gastin, P., Mukherjee, S., Srivathsan, B.: Fast algorithms for handling diagonal constraints in timed automata. CoRR abs/1904.08590 (2019). http://arxiv.org/abs/1904.08590

52. Gastin, P., Mukherjee, S., Srivathsan, B.: Reachability for updatable timed automata made faster and more effective. In: Proceedings of 40th IARCS Annual Conference on Foundations of Software Technology and Theoretical Computer Science (FSTTCS 2020). LIPIcs, vol. 118, pp. 47:1–47:17. Leibniz-Zentrum für Informatik (2020)

53. Govind, R., Herbreteau, F., Srivathsan, B., Walukiewicz, I.: Revisiting local time semantics for networks of timed automata. In: Proceedings of 30th International Conference on Concurrency Theory (CONCUR 2019). LIPIcs, vol. 140, pp. 16:1–16:15. Leibniz-Zentrum für Informatik (2019)

54. Govind, R., Herbreteau, F., Srivathsan, B., Walukiewicz, I.: abstractions for the local-time semantics of timed automata: a foundation for partial-order methods. Accepted at LICS (2022)

55. Hansen, H., Lin, S.-W., Liu, Y., Nguyen, T.K., Sun, J.: Diamonds are a girl's best friend: partial order reduction for timed automata with abstractions. In: Biere, A., Bloem, R. (eds.) CAV 2014. LNCS, vol. 8559, pp. 391–406. Springer, Cham (2014). https://doi.org/10.1007/978-3-319-08867-9_26

56. Havelund, K., Skou, A., Larsen, K.G., Lund, K.: Formal modeling and analysis of an audio/video protocol: an industrial case study using UPPAAL. In: Proceedings of 18th IEEE Real-Time Systems Symposium (RTSS 1997), pp. 2–13. IEEE Computer Society Press (1997)

57. Henzinger, Th.A., Kopke, P.W., Puri, A., Varaiya, P.: What's decidable about hybrid automata? In: Proceedings of 27th Annual ACM Symposium on the Theory of Computing (STOC 1995), pp. 373–382. ACM (1995)

58. Henzinger, T.A., Nicollin, X., Sifakis, J., Yovine, S.: Symbolic model-checking for real-time systems. Inf. Comput. **111**(2), 193–244 (1994)
59. Herbreteau, F., Point, G.: The TChecker tool and librairies. https://github.com/ticktac-project/tchecker
60. Herbreteau, F., Srivathsan, B., Tran, T.T., Walukiewicz, I.: Why liveness for timed automata is hard, and what we can do about it. In: Proceedings of 36th IARCS Annual Conference on Foundations of Software Technology and Theoretical Computer Science (FSTTCS 2016). LIPIcs, vol. 65, pp. 48:1–48:14. Leibniz-Zentrum für Informatik (2016)
61. Herbreteau, F., Srivathsan, B., Tran, T.T., Walukiewicz, I.: Why liveness for timed automata is hard, and what we can do about it. ACM Trans. Comput. Logic **21**(3), 17:1-17:28 (2020)
62. Herbreteau, F., Srivathsan, B., Walukiewicz, I.: Better abstractions for timed automata. In: Proceedings of 27th Annual Symposium on Logic in Computer Science (LICS 2012), pp. 375–384. IEEE Computer Society Press (2012)
63. Herbreteau, F., Srivathsan, B., Walukiewicz, I.: Lazy abstractions for timed automata. In: Sharygina, N., Veith, H. (eds.) CAV 2013. LNCS, vol. 8044, pp. 990–1005. Springer, Heidelberg (2013). https://doi.org/10.1007/978-3-642-39799-8_71
64. Herbreteau, F., Srivathsan, B., Walukiewicz, I.: Better abstractions for timed automata. Inf. Comput. **251**, 67–90 (2016)
65. Herbreteau, F., Tran, T.-T.: Improving search order for reachability testing in timed automata. In: Sankaranarayanan, S., Vicario, E. (eds.) FORMATS 2015. LNCS, vol. 9268, pp. 124–139. Springer, Cham (2015). https://doi.org/10.1007/978-3-319-22975-1_9
66. Kindermann, R., Junttila, T., Niemela, I.: Modeling for symbolic analysis of safety instrumented systems with clocks. In: Proceedings of 11th International Conference on Application of Concurrency to System Design (ACSD 2011), pp. 185–194. IEEE Computer Society Press (2011). https://doi.org/10.1109/ACSD.2011.29
67. Kindermann, R., Junttila, T., Niemelä, I.: SMT-based induction methods for timed systems. In: Jurdziński, M., Ničković, D. (eds.) FORMATS 2012. LNCS, vol. 7595, pp. 171–187. Springer, Heidelberg (2012). https://doi.org/10.1007/978-3-642-33365-1_13
68. Kwiatkowska, M., Norman, G., Parker, D.: PRISM 4.0: verification of probabilistic real-time systems. In: Gopalakrishnan, G., Qadeer, S. (eds.) CAV 2011. LNCS, vol. 6806, pp. 585–591. Springer, Heidelberg (2011). https://doi.org/10.1007/978-3-642-22110-1_47
69. Laarman, A., Olesen, M.C., Dalsgaard, A.E., Larsen, K.G., van de Pol, J.: Multicore emptiness checking of timed Büchi automata using inclusion abstraction. In: Sharygina, N., Veith, H. (eds.) CAV 2013. LNCS, vol. 8044, pp. 968–983. Springer, Heidelberg (2013). https://doi.org/10.1007/978-3-642-39799-8_69
70. Larsen, K.G., et al.: As cheap as possible: efficient cost-optimal reachability for priced timed automata. In: Proceedings of 13th International Conference on Computer Aided Verification (CAV 2001). Lecture Notes in Computer Science, vol. 2102, pp. 493–505. Springer (2001)
71. Larsen, K.G., Mikučionis, M., Muñiz, M., Srba, J.: Urgent partial order reduction for extended timed automata. In: Hung, D.V., Sokolsky, O. (eds.) ATVA 2020. LNCS, vol. 12302, pp. 179–195. Springer, Cham (2020). https://doi.org/10.1007/978-3-030-59152-6_10

72. Larsen, K.G., Pettersson, P., Yi, W.: Compositional and symbolic model-checking of real-time systems. In: Proceedings of 16th IEEE Real-Time Systems Symposium (RTSS 1995), pp. 76–89. IEEE Computer Society Press (1995)

73. Laxsen, K.G., Pettersson, P., Yi, W.: Diagnostic model-checking for real-time systems. In: Alur, R., Henzinger, T.A., Sontag, E.D. (eds.) HS 1995. LNCS, vol. 1066, pp. 575–586. Springer, Heidelberg (1996). https://doi.org/10.1007/BFb0020977

74. Li, G.: Checking timed Büchi automata emptiness using LU-abstractions. In: Ouaknine, J., Vaandrager, F.W. (eds.) FORMATS 2009. LNCS, vol. 5813, pp. 228–242. Springer, Heidelberg (2009). https://doi.org/10.1007/978-3-642-04368-0_18

75. Malinowski, J., Niebert, P.: SAT based bounded model checking with partial order semantics for timed automata. In: Esparza, J., Majumdar, R. (eds.) TACAS 2010. LNCS, vol. 6015, pp. 405–419. Springer, Heidelberg (2010). https://doi.org/10.1007/978-3-642-12002-2_34

76. Mercaldo, F., Martinelli, F., Santone, A.: Real-time SCADA attack detection by means of formal methods. In: Proceedings of 28th IEEE International Conference on Enabling Technologies: Infrastructure for Collaborative Enterprises (WETICE 2019), pp. 231–236. IEEE Computer Society Press (2019). https://doi.org/10.1109/WETICE.2019.00057

77. Mikučionis, M., et al.: Schedulability analysis using UPPAAL: Herschel-Planck case study. In: Margaria, T., Steffen, B. (eds.) ISoLA 2010. LNCS, vol. 6416, pp. 175–190. Springer, Heidelberg (2010). https://doi.org/10.1007/978-3-642-16561-0_21

78. Mukherjee, S.: Reachability in timed automata with diagonal constraints and updates. Ph.D. thesis, Chennai Mathematical Institute, India (2022)

79. Nguyen, T.K., Sun, J., Liu, Y., Dong, J.S., Liu, Y.: Improved BDD-based discrete analysis of timed systems. In: Giannakopoulou, D., Méry, D. (eds.) FM 2012. LNCS, vol. 7436, pp. 326–340. Springer, Heidelberg (2012). https://doi.org/10.1007/978-3-642-32759-9_28

80. Norman, G., Parker, D., Sproston, J.: Model checking for probabilistic timed automata. Formal Methods Syst. Des. **43**(2), 164–190 (2013)

81. Point, G.: TChecker online demonstration. https://tchecker.labri.fr/

82. Point, G.: UPPAAL-to-TChecker: a tool to translate UPPAAL models into TChecker models. https://github.com/ticktac-project/uppaal-to-tchecker

83. Ravn, A.P., Srba, J., Vighio, S.: Modelling and verification of web services business activity protocol. In: Abdulla, P.A., Leino, K.R.M. (eds.) TACAS 2011. LNCS, vol. 6605, pp. 357–371. Springer, Heidelberg (2011). https://doi.org/10.1007/978-3-642-19835-9_32

84. Roussanaly, V., Sankur, O., Markey, N.: Abstraction refinement algorithms for timed automata. In: Dillig, I., Tasiran, S. (eds.) CAV 2019. LNCS, vol. 11561, pp. 22–40. Springer, Cham (2019). https://doi.org/10.1007/978-3-030-25540-4_2

85. Sorea, M.: Bounded model checking for timed automata. Electron. Notes Theoret. Comput. Sci. **68**(5), 116–134 (2003)

86. Srivathsan, B.: Abstractions for timed automata. Ph.D. thesis, University of Bordeaux (2012)

87. Thierry-Mieg, Y.: Symbolic model-checking using ITS-tools. In: Baier, C., Tinelli, C. (eds.) TACAS 2015. LNCS, vol. 9035, pp. 231–237. Springer, Heidelberg (2015). https://doi.org/10.1007/978-3-662-46681-0_20

88. Tóth, T., Majzik, I.: Lazy reachability checking for timed automata using interpolants. In: Abate, A., Geeraerts, G. (eds.) FORMATS 2017. LNCS, vol. 10419, pp. 264–280. Springer, Cham (2017). https://doi.org/10.1007/978-3-319-65765-3_15

89. Tripakis, S., Yovine, S.: Analysis of timed systems using time-abstracting bisimu-lations. Formal Methods Syst. Des. **18**(1), 25–68 (2001)
90. Wang, F.: Symbolic verification of complex real-time systems with clock-restriction diagram. In: Kim, M., Chin, B., Kang, S., Lee, D. (eds.) FORTE 2001. IIFIP, vol. 69, pp. 235–250. Springer, Boston (2002). https://doi.org/10.1007/0-306-47003-9_15
91. Wang, F.: REDLIB for the formal verification of embedded systems. In: Proceedings of 2nd International Symposium on Leveraging Applications of Formal Methods (ISoLA 2006), pp. 341–346. IEEE Computer Society Press (2006)

Monitoring Timed Properties (Revisited)

Thomas Møller Grosen, Sean Kauffman, Kim Guldstrand Larsen[(✉)], and Martin Zimmermann[(✉)]

Aalborg University, Aalborg, Denmark
{tmgr,seank,kgl,mzi}@cs.aau.dk

Abstract. In this paper we revisit monitoring real-time systems with respect to properties expressed either in Metric Interval Temporal Logic or as Timed Büchi Automata. We offer efficient symbolic online monitoring algorithms in a number of settings, exploiting so-called zones well-known from efficient model checking of Timed Automata. The settings considered include new, much simplified treatment of time divergence, monitoring under timing uncertainty, and, extension of monitoring to offer minimum time estimates before conclusive verdicts can be made.

Keywords: Monitoring · Timed Automata · Metric Temporal Logic

1 Introduction

Runtime monitoring has gained acceptance as a method for formally verifying the correctness of executing systems. Monitoring means to test a sequence of observations of a system against a specification, often written in a formal logic. Monitoring contrasts with static verification methods, like model checking, in that it is computationally easier due to only testing a single system execution. Runtime monitoring may also be applied to black-box systems where details about the environment and design of the monitored system are not required to be known in advance.

Many systems have so-called "extra-functional" requirements that must be expressed with respect to time. These systems, generally called real-time systems, are pervasive in modern life as the controllers of cyber-physical systems. To express requirements with time components, logics such as Metric Temporal Logic (MTL) and derivatives like Metric Interval Temporal Logic (MITL) have been developed that extend the more classical Linear Temporal Logic (LTL) with timing constraints [2,22]. Finite Automata have also been extended with time to form Timed Automata [1]. These formalisms allow the expression of notions such as that "a response should occur within 20 ms of a request."

Monitoring timed properties is possible and several solutions have been proposed, each with their own advantages and drawbacks. In this work, we introduce an efficient solution to the online monitoring problem for timed properties

This paper was partly sponsored by the S4OS Villum Investigator Grant and DIREC Digital Research Center Denmark.

S. Bogomolov and D. Parker (Eds.): FORMATS 2022, LNCS 13465, pp. 43–62, 2022.
https://doi.org/10.1007/978-3-031-15839-1_3

under time divergence. Given a property expressed in MITL and a finite timed sequence, our method determines if the property is guaranteed to be satisfied or violated by any continuation of that finite sequence. Additionally, the eventual satisfaction or violation of a property considers that any future timing constraints will eventually be settled. Note that online monitoring here contrasts with offline monitoring, where the system is assumed to have terminated and timed properties are interpreted with finite semantics. In online monitoring, liveness properties (e.g., "eventually, plaid shirts will be popular") cannot be violated since there will always be more symbols, while they can be violated in offline monitoring, since the entire sequence is known.

In this paper we revisit the monitoring of real-time properties expressed in the logic MITL. In particular, we offer efficient symbolic online monitoring algorithms for a number of settings. The symbolic approach exploits the fact that properties in MITL may be translated into Timed Büchi Automata (TBA) [9] under a point-wise semantics. Our symbolic approach exploits so-called zones[1], which are used for efficient model checking of Timed Automata [8]. In fact, zones have been exploited in the tool UPPAAL TRON [23] for on-line testing that the behavior of a real-time system conforms to a Timed Automata specification.

In the first setting, we offer a new much simplified way of dealing with time divergence. Time divergence means that during the infinite behavior of a realtime system time progresses beyond any finite bound. Time divergence is stated as an assumption by most works in the area because it reflects reality. However, the algorithmic support for time divergence in earlier work seems somewhat underdeveloped.

To understand how time divergence impacts monitor verdicts, consider the property "nothing should be observed after an hour". It should be clear that time divergence guarantees that no infinite sequence will satisfy this property. Because we are interested in online monitoring of properties over infinite timed sequences, the language of the property is empty, and its monitor should evaluate any finite prefix to be in violation of it. Conversely, a monitor that does not compensate for time divergence will register an *unknown* verdict for finite prefixes that do not include observations past the hour mark.

In a second setting, we extend our algorithmic method for monitoring to the setting of timing uncertainty, i.e. a setting where the real-valued time-points of events can only be observed up to a given precision. Finally, in a third and final setting, we refine the algorithmic monitor to offer guaranteed minimum time estimates that must pass until a conclusive verdict can be made.

2   Related Work

Many techniques to monitor timed properties have focused on monitoring logics with finite-word semantics. The first work to introduce timed property monitoring is by Roşu et al. focusing on discrete-time finite-word Metric Temporal

---

[1] Also known as DBMs: Difference Bounded Matrices.

Logic (MTL) [31]. Basin et al. proposed algorithms for monitoring real-time finite-word properties in [5] and compared the differences between different time models. Ulus et al. described monitoring Timed Regular Expressions (TREs) for finite words using a union of two-dimensional zones [32,33].

The most closely related work to ours is that by Bauer et al. in which the authors introduced the classical Three-value LTL (LTL_3) monitor construction and then showed how a similar construction could be used for Timed LTL (TLTL) [6]. Their method transforms a TLTL formula to event-clock automata which are strictly less expressive than Timed Büchi Automata (TBAs), which we support. Their algorithm also differs from ours in being based on the so-called region automata. Though this construction *does* provide a principle monitoring algorithm the performance of zone-based monitoring algorithms provide an order of magnitude improvement. Finally, their monitoring algorithm does not readily seem to support time divergence. Two more recent works have proposed solutions to the problem of monitoring timed languages specified in MTL. Baldor et al. showed how to construct a monitor for a dense-time MITL formula by constructing a tree of timed transducers [3]. They showed how subsets of MITL could be used to limit the complexity of their technique which requires linear space in the size of the input for the full fragment. Ho et al. split unbounded and bounded parts of a dense-time MITL formula for monitoring, using traditional LTL monitoring for the unbounded parts and permitting a simpler construction for the (finite-word) bounded parts [18]. Unlike the work by Baldor et al., their method is size independent of the input. However, it does require non-elementary blowup of the formula to ensure no unbounded operators appear in the context of a bounded operator. They also monitor bounded parts using a dynamic programming formulation that relies on a maximum bound for the number of events in a time span. Neither the solution by Baldor et al. or Ho et al. address time-divergence.

Crucially, none of the previously mentioned works implement their solutions. On the other hand, some tools have been released for monitoring other timed logics. Basin et al. implemented MonPoly, which can monitor an expressive finite-word (safety) fragment of Metric First-Order Temporal Logic (MFOTL) using discrete time semantics [4]. Bulychev et al. implemented a rewrite-based monitoring algorithm similar to the one proposed in [31] for Weighted MTL in the Uppaal SMC tool [11]. R2U2 is a tool for generating monitors for Field Programmable Gate Arrays (FPGAs) developed by Moosbrugger et al. that supports finite-word MITL properties [26]. Much more recently, Chattopadhyay and Mamouras presented a verified monitor for discrete, past-time (finite word) MITL with quantitative semantics [13]. Some tools also exist to convert timed logics to automata which we will cover in the next section.

3   Preliminaries

We first define some notation used throughout the paper. The set of natural numbers (including zero) is $\mathbb{N}$. The set of real numbers is $\mathbb{R}$ and the set of non-negative real numbers is $\mathbb{R}_{\geq 0}$. The set of Boolean values is $\mathbb{B}$ and the three-valued set of monitor verdicts is $\mathbb{B}_3 = \{\top, ?, \bot\}$. We shall assume that $\mathbb{B}_3$ is equipped with a partial order where $? \sqsubseteq \top$ and $? \sqsubseteq \bot$. Given a set S the set of all its subsets is denoted 2^S. The cross product of two sets S and T is $S \times T$. Given a sequence σ, σ_i denotes the element at the ith position of σ (where one is the first position) and σ^i denotes the suffix of σ starting at index i. Given two sequences s and t, we write $s \cdot t$ to denote their concatenation.

A timed word over a finite alphabet Σ is a pair $\rho = (\sigma, \tau)$ where σ is a non-empty word over Σ and τ is a sequence of strictly increasing non-negative real numbers of the same length as σ. Timed words may be finite or infinite where the type of finite timed words is $T\Sigma^*$ and the type of infinite timed words is $T\Sigma^\omega$. We also represent a timed word as a sequence of pairs $(\sigma_1, \tau_1), (\sigma_2, \tau_2), \ldots$. If $\rho = (\sigma_1, \tau_1), (\sigma_2, \tau_2), \ldots (\sigma_n, \tau_n)$ is a finite timed word, we denote by $\tau(\rho)$ the total time duration of ρ, i.e. τ_n.

Metric Temporal Logic. We use the Metric Interval Temporal Logic, MITL, in this work to formalize examples because we can translate it into the TBAs that we use in our monitoring algorithm. Brihaye et al. developed the tool MightyL to translate MITL formulas to TBAs in a compositional manner [9]. Some earlier work implemented algorithms to translate subsets of MITL to TBAs as well. Li et al. proposed and implemented Casaal, a tool to construct deterministic approximations of TBAs from $\text{MTL}_{0,\infty}$ formulas [10,24]. Geilen and Dams implemented an algorithm to produce a deterministic Timed Automaton (TA) for dense-time $\text{MITL}_\leq$ (a subset of $\text{MTL}_{0,\infty}$) using an on-the-fly tableau construction that discretizes the time domain and only supports an upper bound [17]. Note that some other works exist that provide algorithms for the translation of MITL or related logics to TBAs, but without providing implementations [16,27].

Let Σ be a finite alphabet. The syntax of MITL formulas over Σ is given by the following grammar:

$$\varphi ::= p \mid \neg\varphi \mid \varphi \vee \varphi \mid X_I\varphi \mid \varphi \, U_I\varphi$$

where $p \in \Sigma$, and I is a non-singular interval over $\mathbb{R}_{\geq 0}$ with endpoints in $\mathbb{N} \cup \{+\infty\}$. Note that we often write $\sim n$ for $I = \{d \in \mathbb{R} : d \sim n\}$ where $\sim \in \{<, \leq, \geq, >\}$, and $n \in \mathbb{N}$.

The semantics of MITL is defined over infinite timed words. Given such a timed word $\rho = (\sigma_1, \tau_1), (\sigma_2, \tau_2), \ldots \in T\Sigma^\omega$, a position $i \geq 1$, and an MITL formula φ, we inductively define the satisfaction relation $\rho, i \models \varphi$ as follows:

$$
\begin{array}{llll}
\rho, i \models & p & \text{if} & p = \sigma_i \\
\rho, i \models & \neg\varphi & \text{if} & \rho, i \not\models \varphi \\
\rho, i \models & \varphi \vee \psi & \text{if} & \rho, i \models \varphi \text{ or } \rho, i \models \psi \\
\rho, i \models & X_I\varphi & \text{if} & \rho, (i+1) \models \varphi \text{ and } \tau_{i+1} - \tau_i \in I \\
\rho, i \models & \varphi \, U_I\psi & \text{if} & \exists k \geq i. \, \rho, k \models \psi, \tau_k - \tau_{i-1} \in I \text{ and } \forall j. \, 1 \leq j < k. \, \rho, j \models \varphi
\end{array}
$$

where $\tau_0 = 0$. We write $\rho \models \varphi$ whenever $\rho, 1 \models \varphi$. We also define the standard syntactic sugar: $true = p \vee \neg p$, $false = \neg true$, $\varphi \wedge \psi = \neg(\neg\varphi \vee \neg\psi)$, $\varphi \rightarrow \psi = \neg\varphi \vee \psi$, $F_I\varphi = true \, U_I\varphi$, and $G_I\varphi = \neg F_I\neg\varphi$. Given an MITL formula φ, its language $\mathcal{L}(\varphi)$ is the set of all infinite timed words that satisfy φ.

Timed Automata. A TBA $\mathcal{A}$ is a six-tuple $(Q, Q_0, \Sigma, C, \Delta, \mathcal{F})$, where Σ is a finite alphabet, Q is a finite set of locations, $Q_0 \subseteq Q$ is a set of initial locations, C is a finite set of clocks, $\Delta \subseteq Q \times Q \times \Sigma \times 2^C \times G(C)$ is a finite set of transitions with $G(C)$ being the type of constraints over C, and $\mathcal{F} \subseteq Q$ is a set of accepting locations. A transition $(q, q', \alpha, \lambda, g)$ is an edge from q to q' on input symbol α where λ is the set of clocks to reset and g is a clock constraint over C. A clock constraint is a conjunction of atomic constraints of the form $c \sim n$, where c is a clock, $n \in \mathbb{N}$, and $\sim \in \{<, \leq, =, \geq, >\}$. A state of a TBA is a pair (q, v) where q is a location in Q and $v : C \to \mathbb{R}_{\geq 0}$ is a valuation mapping clocks to their values. We say that for any $d \in \mathbb{R}_{\geq 0}$, $v + d$ is the valuation where d is added to all clock values in v.

A run of $\mathcal{A}$ from a starting state (q_0, v_0) is a sequence of steps over a timed word (σ, τ) of the form

$$(q_0, v_0) \xrightarrow{(\sigma_1, t_1)} (q_1, v_1) \xrightarrow{(\sigma_2, t_2)} (q_2, v_2) \xrightarrow{(\sigma_3, t_3)} \cdots$$

where for all $i \geq 1$ there is a transition $(q_{i-1}, q_i, \sigma_i, \lambda_i, g_i)$ such that $v_i(c) = 0$ for all c in λ_i and $v_{i-1}(c) - (t_i - t_{i-1})$ otherwise, and g is satisfied by the valuation $v_{i-1} + (t_i - t_{i-1})$. Given a run r, we denote the set of locations visited infinitely many times by r as $inf(r)$. A run r of $\mathcal{A}$ is accepting if $inf(r) \cap \mathcal{F} \neq \varnothing$. The language of $\mathcal{A}$ from a starting state (q, v), denoted $\mathcal{L}(\mathcal{A}, (q, v))$, is the set of all timed words with an accepting run in $\mathcal{A}$ starting from (q, v). We define the language of $\mathcal{A}$, written $\mathcal{L}(\mathcal{A})$, to be $\bigcup_q \mathcal{L}(\mathcal{A}, (q, v_0))$, where q ranges over all locations in Q_0 and where $v_0(c) = 0$ for all $c \in C$.

Given two TBAs $\mathcal{A} = (Q, Q_0, \Sigma, C, \Delta, \mathcal{F})$ and $\mathcal{A}' = (Q', Q_0', \Sigma, C', \Delta', \mathcal{F}')$, their intersection is denoted $\mathcal{A} \otimes \mathcal{A}' = (Q^\otimes, Q_0^\otimes, \Sigma, C^\otimes, \Delta^\otimes, \mathcal{F}^\otimes)$, where

- $Q_\otimes = Q \times Q' \times \{1, 2\}$,
- $Q_0^\otimes = Q_0 \times Q_0' \times \{1\}$,
- $C^\otimes = C \cup C'$ (we assume they are disjoint),
- $\Delta^\otimes = \Delta_1^\otimes \cup \Delta_2^\otimes$ with
  $\Delta_1^\otimes = \{((q_1, q_1', 1), (q_2, q_2', i), \alpha, \lambda \cup \lambda', g \wedge g') : (q_1, q_2, \alpha, \lambda, g) \in \Delta$ and $(q_1', q_2', \alpha, \lambda', g') \in \Delta'$ and $i = 2$ if $q_1 \in \mathcal{F}$ else $i = 1\}$ and
  $\Delta_2^\otimes = \{((q_1, q_1', 2), (q_2, q_2', i), \alpha, \lambda \cup \lambda', g \wedge g') : (q_1, q_2, \alpha, \lambda, g) \in \Delta$ and $(q_1', q_2', \alpha, \lambda', g') \in \Delta'$ and $i = 1$ if $q_1' \in \mathcal{F}'$ else $i = 2\}$,
- and $\mathcal{F}^\otimes = (\mathcal{F} \times Q' \times \{1\}) \cup (Q \times \mathcal{F}' \times \{2\})$.

We note that $\mathcal{L}(\mathcal{A} \otimes \mathcal{A}') = \mathcal{L}(\mathcal{A}) \cap \mathcal{L}(\mathcal{A}')$.

4   Monitoring in a Timed Setting

In this section, we describe monitoring and show how it applies in the timed setting. We first, briefly, introduce monitoring in the untimed case and then extend it to the timed case.

Traditionally in Runtime Verification (RV), properties are specified using a temporal logic such as LTL and a monitor is constructed from those properties.

A monitor is a kind of program that takes a finite word as an input and returns a *verdict* depending on the relationship between the input and the property from which the monitor is constructed. Verdicts are usually of the form *accept* ($\top$), *reject* ($\bot$), or *unknown* (*?*), although larger verdict domains exist to provide more information.

In online monitoring (our interest), the properties specify behaviors over infinite sequences of symbols, or words, while the monitor must interpret those specifications over an ever-growing finite prefix of such an infinite word. The most prevalent solution to this problem is to use a monitor semantics where acceptance or rejection means that the finite word *determines* the property and no future suffix can alter the verdict. In the case where the finite prefix does not determine the property, the monitor outputs an *unknown* verdict and continues.

Monitoring languages of timed infinite words works in much the same way as in the untimed setting. A finite prefix of an infinite timed word is checked to see if it determines the property. If all possible infinite extensions of the prefix result in a word that is included in the monitored property, then the monitor returns the $\top$ verdict. If no possible infinite extensions lead to a word that is included in the monitored property, then the monitor returns the $\bot$ verdict. If extensions exist that could lead to either outcome, then the monitor returns *?* and continues monitoring.

Definition 1 (Monitor verdicts for timed languages). *Given a language of infinite timed words $\phi \subseteq T\Sigma^\omega$ and a finite timed word $\rho \in T\Sigma^*$, the function $\mathcal{V} : 2^{T\Sigma^\omega} \to T\Sigma^* \to \mathbb{B}_3$ evaluates to a verdict with the following definition:*

$$\mathcal{V}(\phi)(\rho) = \begin{cases} \top & \text{if } \rho \cdot \mu \in \phi \text{ for all } \mu \in T\Sigma^\omega, \\ \bot & \text{if } \rho \cdot \mu \notin \phi \text{ for all } \mu \in T\Sigma^\omega, \\ ? & \text{otherwise.} \end{cases}$$

Example 1. Consider the bounded response property "whenever a is observed, b should be observed within 30 time units" that is specified by the MITL formula $\varphi = G(a \to F_{\leq 30}b)$ where $\Sigma = \{a, b, c\}$. This property corresponds to the TBA shown in Fig. 1. This type of time-bounded leadsto property is very common for real-time systems [25]. It states that some trigger a is followed by a reaction b before the deadline elapses. Note we draw the "sink" state q_3 here for illustrative purposes as we will return to this example later in the paper, but it can be omitted without changing the language of the automaton.

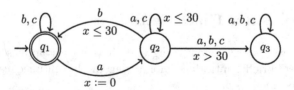

Fig. 1. TBA corresponding to $G(a \to F_{\leq 30}b)$

Now consider the finite timed prefix $\rho_{ok} = (a, 10), (b, 20)$. The verdict in this case is $\mathcal{V}(\mathcal{L}(\varphi))(\rho_{ok}) = \text{?}$, since there are infinite extensions of the prefix that satisfy the property and those that violate it. For example, if the pattern of ρ_{ok} was repeated infinitely many times, the resulting infinite timed word $\rho_{ok}^{\omega} = ((a, 10 \cdot i), (b, 20 \cdot i))^{i \geq 1}$ would satisfy φ. Now suppose the prefix $\rho_{bad} = (a, 10), (b, 50)$. In this case, the prefix only has infinite extensions that violate the property, so $\mathcal{V}(\mathcal{L}(\varphi))(\rho_{bad}) = \bot$.

This property demonstrates a way in which timed monitoring differs from the untimed setting. If we remove the time constraint and consider the (unbounded) response property $G(a \rightarrow Fb)$, no finite prefix could ever determine the property and so the only possible verdict would be ?. This is a classic example of what is called an *unmonitorable* property [7,21,29].

5   Time Divergence

Note that Definition 1 does not take time divergence into account, i.e., a verdict can be based on convergent extensions of a given prefix. As we will see in Example 2, this leads to invalid verdicts. In this section, we consider the monitoring problem in the presence of time divergence and show how it affects the verdicts from monitors for timed languages. Time divergence entails that time will always progress beyond any given time-bound.

We begin by defining the type of infinite time divergent words. These are the only timed words that will occur in practice, since time always diverges. Mathematically, however, the type $T\Sigma^{\omega}$ includes words that are not time divergent, e.g., $(\alpha, \frac{1}{2}), (\alpha, \frac{3}{4}), (\alpha, \frac{7}{8}), \ldots$. The definition states that time divergent words are those where the time sequence is unbounded. Note that we do not consider *finite* timed words either divergent or convergent even though their time sequences technically converge.

Definition 2. *The set of all time divergent words* $\mathbb{T}\Sigma^{\omega} \subseteq T\Sigma^{\omega}$ *is the set of all timed words* $(\sigma_1, \tau_1), (\sigma_2, \tau_2) \ldots$ *such that* $\lim_{i \to \infty} \tau_i = +\infty$.

We now use the set of time divergent words to define a verdict function that accounts for time divergence. Crucially, the properties that we monitor may include non-time divergent words. In that case, the verdict returned by the evaluation function under time divergence $\mathcal{V}_D$ may differ from the verdict returned by $\mathcal{V}$.

Definition 3 (Monitor verdicts under time divergence). *Given a language of infinite timed words* $\phi \subseteq T\Sigma^{\omega}$ *and a finite timed word* $\rho \in T\Sigma^*$, *the function* $\mathcal{V}_D : 2^{T\Sigma^{\omega}} \rightarrow T\Sigma^* \rightarrow \mathbb{B}_3$ *evaluates to a verdict with the following definition:*

$$\mathcal{V}_D(\phi)(\rho) = \begin{cases} \top & \text{if } \rho \cdot \mu \in \phi \text{ for all } \mu \in \mathbb{T}\Sigma^{\omega}, \\ \bot & \text{if } \rho \cdot \mu \notin \phi \text{ for all } \mu \in \mathbb{T}\Sigma^{\omega}, \\ ? & \text{otherwise.} \end{cases}$$

Example 2. Consider the property "the system will continue past 20 time units" represented by the MITL formula $\varphi = F_{\geq 20}a$, where $\Sigma = \{a\}$. This property corresponds to the TBA shown in Fig. 2.

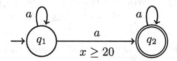

Fig. 2. TBA corresponding to $F_{\geq 20}a$

If this property is monitored, the verdict may change depending on whether time divergence is accounted for. Under time divergence, this property is clearly a tautology since all infinite time divergent words must eventually reach time 20 and location q_2. However, if time divergence is not assumed as in Definition 1, then it is possible for an infinite timed word to never pass time 20 and therefore stay in location q_1.

Suppose, for example, the finite timed prefix $\rho = (a, 10)$. Since φ is a tautology under time divergence, $\mathcal{V}_D(\mathcal{L}(\varphi))(\rho) = \top$. However, $\mathcal{V}(\mathcal{L}(\varphi))(\rho) = ?$, since $T\Sigma^\omega$ contains time-convergent suffixes to ρ that are in not in the language of φ.

To ensure that verdicts are correct for all properties, we monitor an intersection of the given automata with a special TBA that only accepts time divergent words. This TBA, which we will call $\mathcal{A}_D$, is shown in Fig. 3. The automaton must visit the left location infinitely often to accept and it can only visit this state once time has passed a threshold of one time unit. Note that the exact threshold is arbitrary and could be any number; the purpose is ensure that the language of the automaton is exactly the language of time divergent words.

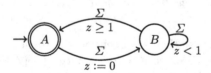

Fig. 3. TBA $\mathcal{A}_D$ to model divergence

Theorem 1. *The language of $\mathcal{A}_D$ is exactly the set of all time divergent words.*

Example 3. We now consider the complement property to Example 2 that is accepted by the MITL formula $\bar{\varphi} = G_{\geq 20}false$. Note that, since we use symbols in our MITL formulas and not propositions, we cannot write $\neg a$ here but must use its complement $\Sigma \setminus \{a\} = \varnothing$ which is equivalent to *false* in our MITL syntax. The TBA for $\bar{\varphi}$ is shown in Fig. 4.

Fig. 4. TBA corresponding to $G_{\geq 20}false$

Now we want to intersect this TBA with $\mathcal{A}_D$ to restrict its language to only time divergent words. The result of this operation is shown in Fig. 5. Note that we are intentionally showing a trivial example to simplify the presentation; a two state automaton like that in Fig. 1 intersected with $\mathcal{A}_D$ has eight locations and, in that case, 23 transitions.

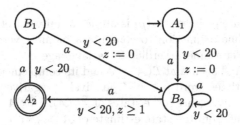

Fig. 5. TBA corresponding to $G_{\geq 20}false$ intersected with $\mathcal{A}_D$

In this TBA, an accepting run must visit location A_2 infinitely many times. However, it should be clear that this is not possible, since the run must include fewer than 20 combinations of the transition from B_1 to B_2 (which resets the z clock) and the transition from B_2 to A_2, which requires that it passes 1. The reason is that the latter transition also requires the clock y to stay below 20 and y is never reset. The result is that the automaton has an empty language.

6   A Symbolic Method for Monitoring

In this section, we describe an algorithm to monitor languages of infinite timed words that correctly accounts for time divergence. Our algorithm is loosely based on the classical construction for monitoring LTL_3 by Bauer et al. [6], but with alterations to address the many differences between the timed and untimed domains.

Our solution requires that properties are specified as two TBAs - one for the property and one for its complement. Although non-deterministic TBAs are not closed under complementation, we consider this requirement to not be too much of a limitation. This is because we expect a property to be expressed by a user in MITL, which, along with its negation, can be converted to a TBAs using one of the methods described in Sect. 3.

Before we address the monitoring algorithm, we first introduce the notions of states of a TBA with a non-empty language and state estimates. Given a TBA

$\mathcal{A}$, a state (q, v) has a non-empty language when it has an accepting run starting in (q, v).

Definition 4. *Given a TBA* $\mathcal{A} = (Q, Q_0, \Sigma, C, \Delta, \mathcal{F})$, *the set of states with non-empty language is* $S_{\mathcal{A}}^{ne} = \{(q, v) : q \in Q, v \in C \to \mathbb{R}_{\geq 0} . \mathcal{L}(\mathcal{A}, (q, v)) \neq \varnothing\}$.

In the following definition, we write $(q_0, v_0) \xrightarrow{\rho}_{\mathcal{A}} (q, v)$ to denote a run that takes $\mathcal{A}$ from (q_0, v_0) to (q, v) processing the input ρ.

Definition 5. *Given a TBA* $\mathcal{A}$ *and a finite timed word* $\rho \in T\Sigma^*$, *the set of possible states a run over* ρ *starting from initial states of* $\mathcal{A}$ *can end in is given by* $\mathcal{T}_{\mathcal{A}}(\rho) = \{(q, v) : (q_0, v_0) \xrightarrow{\rho}_{\mathcal{A}} (q, v)$ *where* (q_0, v_0) *is an initial state of* $\mathcal{A}\}$. *We call this the state estimate of* $\mathcal{A}$ *over* ρ.

Note that the state estimate $\mathcal{T}_{\mathcal{A}}(\rho)$ is always a finite set of states of $\mathcal{A}$.

We can now define a function to compute a monitor verdict using Definitions 4 and 5. To determine a verdict for a language $\phi \subseteq T\Sigma^\omega$, the function requires both a TBA $\mathcal{A}$ such that $\mathcal{L}(\mathcal{A}) = \phi$ and its complement, $\overline{\mathcal{A}}$. Definition 6 states that a finite timed word $\rho \in T\Sigma^*$ positively (negatively) determines the property under time divergence if the states of $\overline{\mathcal{A}} \otimes \mathcal{A}_D$ ($\mathcal{A} \otimes \mathcal{A}_D$) with non-empty languages are disjoint from the state estimate of $\overline{\mathcal{A}} \otimes \mathcal{A}_D$ ($\mathcal{A} \otimes \mathcal{A}_D$) over ρ.

Definition 6 (Monitoring TBAs under time divergence). *Given a TBA* $\mathcal{A}$, *its complement* $\overline{\mathcal{A}}$ ($\mathcal{L}(\overline{\mathcal{A}}) = T\Sigma^\omega \setminus \mathcal{L}(\mathcal{A})$), *the automaton* $\mathcal{A}_D$ *such that* $\mathcal{L}(\mathcal{A}_D) = T\!b\Sigma^\omega$, *and a finite timed word* $\rho \in T\Sigma^*$, $\mathcal{M} : \mathbb{A} \times \mathbb{A} \to T\Sigma^* \to \mathbb{B}_3$ *computes a verdict with the following definition.*

$$\mathcal{M}(\mathcal{A}, \overline{\mathcal{A}})(\rho) = \begin{cases} \top & \text{if } \mathcal{T}_{\overline{\mathcal{A}} \otimes \mathcal{A}_D}(\rho) \cap S_{\overline{\mathcal{A}} \otimes \mathcal{A}_D}^{ne} = \varnothing \\ \bot & \text{if } \mathcal{T}_{\mathcal{A} \otimes \mathcal{A}_D}(\rho) \cap S_{\mathcal{A} \otimes \mathcal{A}_D}^{ne} = \varnothing \\ ? & \text{otherwise} \end{cases}$$

Theorem 2. $\mathcal{M}(\mathcal{A}, \overline{\mathcal{A}})(\rho) = \mathcal{V}_D(\mathcal{L}(\mathcal{A}))(\rho)$ *for all* $\rho \in T\Sigma^*$.

So far, this construction is very similar to the classical procedure for monitoring LTL_3 with the addition of $\mathcal{A}_D$ to account for time divergence. However, the set of states with non-empty languages of a TBA is likely to be infinite, and its state estimate over a symbolic trace (see Sect. 7) may be as well. We now present a symbolic online algorithm to compute these infinite sets and their intersections in an efficient manner.

Monitoring Algorithm. We assume that the language we will monitor ϕ and its complement $\overline{\phi}$ are given as TBAs $\mathcal{A}_\phi$ and $\mathcal{A}_{\overline{\phi}}$, where $\mathcal{L}(\mathcal{A}_\phi) = \phi$ and $\mathcal{L}(\mathcal{A}_{\overline{\phi}}) = \overline{\phi}$. We begin by computing the intersection of both automata with $\mathcal{A}_D$ (we hereafter refer to these intersection automata as $\mathcal{A}$ and $\overline{\mathcal{A}}$). We continue by finding the states of the automata with non-empty languages, also called the non-empty states from Definition 4. We then compute the intersection of the non-empty states with the state estimate (from Definition 5) of $\mathcal{A}$ and $\overline{\mathcal{A}}$ over ρ. If one of the intersections is empty, then we can output $\top$ or $\bot$, otherwise, we output $?$.

We can calculate the set $S_{\mathcal{A}}^{ne}$ as a fixpoint using a backwards reachability algorithm. In order to practically work with the states of a TBA we use a symbolic representation of the clock valuations, namely zones. A symbolic state (q, Z) is a pair of a location and a zone. A zone is a finite conjunction of lower and upper bound integer constraints on clocks and clock differences, and may be efficiently represented using so-called Difference Bounded Matrices (DBMs) [8]. We say that $(q, v) \in (q, Z)$ or $v \in Z$ iff $v \models Z$, such that the clock values in v satisfies all constraints in Z. Similarly we say that $v(x) \models Z$ if the value $v(x)$ satisfies the bounds on x in Z. We now define several zone operations, that we will need.

Definition 7. *Given two zones Z and Z' over a set C of clocks, a set of clocks $\lambda \subseteq C$, a positive real number t and an interval $I = [t_1, t_2]$ between two positive real numbers, we define the following operations on zones:*

- $\mathit{free}_\lambda(Z) = \{v : \forall x \in C . \ v(x) \models Z \text{ if } x \notin \lambda\}$
- $Z_{\mathit{free}} = \mathit{free}_C(Z)$
- $Z[\lambda] = \{v : \exists v' \in Z \ \forall x \in C . \ v(x) = 0 \text{ if } x \in \lambda \text{ otherwise } v(x) = v'(x)\}$
- $Z^\nearrow = \{v : \exists v' \in Z . \ v = v' + d \text{ for some } d \in \mathbb{R}_{\geq 0}\}$
- $Z^\searrow = \{v : \exists v' \in Z . \ v = v' - d \text{ for some } d \in \mathbb{R}_{\geq 0}\}$
- $Z^{\nearrow I} = \{v : \exists v' \in Z \ \forall x \in C . \ v'(x) + t_1 \leq v(x) \leq v'(x) + t_2\}$
- $Z \wedge Z' = \{v : v \models Z \text{ and } v \models Z'\}$
- $Z_0 = \{v : \forall x \in C . \ v(x) = 0\}$

All of the above operations on zones may be efficiently implemented using the DBM data-structure [8]. We now proceed to develop the online zone-based procedure we use to monitor real-time properties specified by TBAs.

$Pred_{\mathcal{A}}(q, Z)$ (described in Algorithm 1) is the set of symbolic states that can, by a single transition and delay, reach the state (q, Z) of $\mathcal{A}$.

Algorithm 1. Find the predecessors (single transition) of a state

---

Input: a TBA $\mathcal{A} = (Q, Q_0, \Sigma, C, \Delta, \mathcal{F})$ and a symbolic state (q, Z)
Output: $Pred_{\mathcal{A}}(q, Z)$

$\quad Predecessors \leftarrow \varnothing$
$\quad \textbf{for } (q', q, \alpha, \lambda, g) \in \Delta \ \textbf{do}$
$\quad\quad Z' = \mathit{free}_\lambda(Z^\searrow \wedge \{x = 0 : x \in \lambda\} \wedge g)$
$\quad\quad Predecessors \leftarrow Predecessors \cup \{(q', Z')\}$
$\quad \textbf{end for}$
$\quad \textbf{return } Predecessors$

$Reach_{\mathcal{A}}(S)$ (described in Algorithm 2) is the set of symbolic states that can, by at least one transition, reach a state in S.

$Reach_{\mathcal{A}}^\infty(Q')$ (described in Algorithm 3) is the set of states that can infinitely many times reach a location in Q'. We can use this to calculate the set of states,

Algorithm 2. Compute the states that can reach the given states with at least one transition

---

Input: a TBA $\mathcal{A}$ and a set of symbolic states S
Output: $Reach_{\mathcal{A}}(S)$

  $Waiting \leftarrow \varnothing$
  $Passed \leftarrow \varnothing$
  for $s \in S$ **do**
    $Waiting \leftarrow Waiting \cup Pred_{\mathcal{A}}(s)$
  end for
  while $Waiting \neq \varnothing$ **do**
    select and remove s from $Waiting$
    $Waiting \leftarrow Waiting \cup Pred_{\mathcal{A}}(s)$
    $Passed \leftarrow Passed \cup \{s\}$
  end while
  return $Passed$

Algorithm 3. Calculate the set of states that can infinitely often reach a location in Q

Input: a TBA $\mathcal{A}$ and a set of locations Q'
Output: $Reach_{\mathcal{A}}^{\infty}(Q')$

  $S_{Q'} \leftarrow \varnothing$
  for $q \in Q'$ **do**
    $S_{Q'} \leftarrow S_{Q'} \cup \{(q, Z_{free})\}$
  end for
  $S_a \leftarrow S_{Q'}$
  $S_b \leftarrow \varnothing$
  while $S_a \neq S_b$ **do**
    $S_b \leftarrow S_a$
    $S_a \leftarrow Reach_{\mathcal{A}}(S_a \cap S_{Q'})$
  end while
  return S_a

---

from which there is a possible accepting run: Given a TBA $\mathcal{A}$ we write $Reach_{\mathcal{A}}^{\infty}$ as a shorthand for $Reach_{\mathcal{A}}^{\infty}(\mathcal{F})$, where $\mathcal{F}$ is the set of accepting locations of $\mathcal{A}$.

Theorem 3. *Given a TBA $\mathcal{A}$. Then $Reach_{\mathcal{A}}^{\infty} = S_{\mathcal{A}}^{ne}$.*

Using this fixpoint, we can do online monitoring given $\mathcal{A}$ and $\overline{\mathcal{A}}$ by storing the state estimate given by a finite timed word over $\mathcal{A}$ and $\overline{\mathcal{A}}$, while continuously checking if the state estimates still overlap with $S_{\mathcal{A}}^{ne}$ and $S_{\overline{\mathcal{A}}}^{ne}$ respectively. If both state estimates still have non-empty languages, then the verdict is $?$, but if all the states in the state estimate of $\mathcal{A}$ have empty languages, then the verdict is $\bot$ ($\top$ for $\overline{\mathcal{A}}$).

Given the procedure $Succ_{\mathcal{A}}$ described in Algorithm 4 we can compute the state estimate of $\mathcal{A}$ over a finite timed word $\rho \in T\Sigma^*$ of length n iteratively. If S_0 is the set of initial states then $S_n = Succ_{\mathcal{A}}^{S_{n-1}}(\alpha_n, t_n) = \mathcal{T}_{\mathcal{A}}(\rho)$ is the state estimate after ρ.

Algorithm 4. Get the set of possible successor states from S after an input (α, t)

Input: a TBA $\mathcal{A} = (Q, Q_0, \Sigma, C, \Delta, \mathcal{F})$, a set of symbolic states S and a timed input $(\alpha, t) \in \Sigma \times \mathbb{R}_{\geq 0}$
Output: $Succ_{\mathcal{A}}^{S}(\alpha, t)$
    $Successors \leftarrow \varnothing$
    for $(q, Z) \in S$ **do**
        for $(q, q', \alpha, \lambda, g) \in \Delta$ **do**
            if $Z^{\nearrow [t,t]} \models g$ **then**
                $Successors \leftarrow Successors \cup \{(q', (Z^{\nearrow [t,t]} \wedge g)[\lambda])\}$
            end if
        end for
    end for
    return $Successors$

An overview of the online monitoring procedure (see Algorithm 5) with $\mathcal{A}_{\phi}$ and $\mathcal{A}_{\bar{\phi}}$ is as follows. First we define $\mathcal{A}$ and $\overline{\mathcal{A}}$ as the intersection of each input automaton $\mathcal{A}_D$. We then use the backwards reachability algorithm to compute the set of states that have a non-empty language (in each TBA). While continuously receiving inputs, we compute the symbolic successor states from the initial states. After each input, we check if there is an overlap between the states with a non-empty language, and the state estimates and output a verdict. The verdict is either $\top$ or $\bot$ when one of the state estimates falls outside the set of states with a non-empty language and $?$ otherwise.

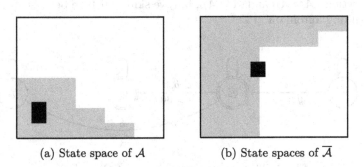

(a) State space of $\mathcal{A}$ (b) State spaces of $\overline{\mathcal{A}}$

Fig. 6. Illustration of the state spaces in Algorithm 5 given a timed word ρ. The grey areas are the states with a non-empty language $Reach_{\mathcal{A}}^{\infty}$ and $Reach_{\overline{\mathcal{A}}}^{\infty}$. The black areas are the state-estimates after ρ, i.e. $\mathcal{T}_{\mathcal{A}}(\rho)$ and $\mathcal{T}_{\overline{\mathcal{A}}}(\rho)$.

Figure 6 shows an example of the state space, with the non-empty states marked as grey and the current state estimates marked as black. In this example the verdict would be $?$, since both state estimates overlap with the set of states with a non-empty language.

Algorithm 5. Online monitoring procedure given $\mathcal{A}_\phi$ and $\mathcal{A}_{\overline{\phi}}$. Gives a verdict $\top$, $\bot$ or **?** after each input

---

$time \leftarrow 0$
$A \leftarrow \mathcal{A}_\phi \otimes \mathcal{A}_D$
$\overline{A} \leftarrow \mathcal{A}_{\overline{\phi}} \otimes \mathcal{A}_D$
$S \leftarrow \{(q, Z_0) : q$ is an initial location of $A\}$
$\overline{S} \leftarrow \{(q, Z_0) : q$ is an initial location of $\overline{A}\}$
loop
    Receive new input: $(\alpha, t) \in \Sigma \times \mathbb{R}_{\geq 0}$
    $S \leftarrow Succ_A^S(\alpha, t - time)$ // Update state estimate
    $\overline{S} \leftarrow Succ_{\overline{A}}^{\overline{S}}(\alpha, t - time)$
    $time \leftarrow t$
    if $S \cap Reach_A^\infty = \emptyset$ **then**
        output $\bot$
    else if $\overline{S} \cap Reach_{\overline{A}}^\infty = \emptyset$ **then**
        output $\top$
    else
        output **?**
    end if
end loop

Example 4. Consider the MITL formula $\varphi = G(a \rightarrow F_{\leq 30} b)$ from Example 1. We are given the TBA $\mathcal{A}$ in Fig. 1 and its complement $\overline{\mathcal{A}}$, the TBA for $\overline{\varphi} = F(a \wedge G_{\leq 30} \neg b)$ shown in Fig. 7. As before, we draw the sink state $\overline{q_4}$ here for illustrative purposes. If we were to monitor $\mathcal{L}(\varphi)$, the first step would be to take the intersections $\mathcal{A} \otimes \mathcal{A}_D$ and $\overline{\mathcal{A}} \otimes \mathcal{A}_D$, but we skip that here because of the size of the resulting automata.

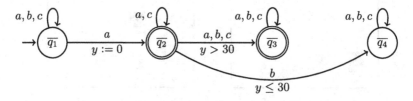

Fig. 7. TBA corresponding to $F(a \wedge G_{\leq 30} \neg b)$

Now suppose the finite prefix $\rho_{ok} = (a, 10), (b, 20)$ as seen in Example 1. We compute the state estimate for $\mathcal{A}$ as $\mathcal{T}_\mathcal{A}(\rho_{ok}) = \{ (q_1, \{x = 10\}) \}$ and for $\overline{\mathcal{A}}$ as $\mathcal{T}_{\overline{\mathcal{A}}}(\rho_{ok}) = \{ (\overline{q_1}, \{y = 20\}), (\overline{q_4}, \{y = 10\}) \}$ where $\{c = v\}$ represents the symbolic constraints on the clocks of the TBAs. Although the algorithm uses a symbolic representation for the state estimates, for a concrete input the clock constraints are equalities. Note that, for $\overline{\mathcal{A}}$, there are two possible states for ρ_{ok} since

$\overline{A}$ is non-deterministic. For the other Example 1 prefix, $\rho_{\text{bad}} = (a, 10), (b, 50)$, $\mathcal{T}_A(\rho_{\text{bad}}) = \{(q_3, \{x = 40\})\}$ and $\mathcal{T}_{\overline{A}}(\rho_{\text{bad}}) = \{(\overline{q_1}, \{y = 50\}), (\overline{q_3}, \{y = 40\})\}$.

7 Time Uncertainty

So far, we have assumed that we can measure the real-valued time-points τ_i appearing in a finite timed word with arbitrary mathematical precision. Given that our monitor has to be implemented as an algorithm, this cannot necessarily be achieved. To ensure implementability, we rather assume that the time-points are observed with a certain precision. More precisely, we assume that we observe some integer-bounded interval I_i containing τ_i, e.g. $[\lfloor \tau \rfloor, \lceil \tau \rceil]$. In related settings, concrete timing information may be missing for many reasons, particularly when monitoring distributed systems [19,28,30]. The problem we consider is also closely related to the robustness of TA [15] as well as work on monitoring over unreliable channels [20,21].

We assume that during monitoring, we observe a *symbolic* timed word of the form $\rho_s = (\sigma, \upsilon)$, where σ is a finite word over the symbol alphabet Σ and υ is a sequence of time intervals $I_1, I_2, \ldots, I_n$ of the same length as σ. Each time interval I_i is a pair of natural numbers $[l_i, u_i]$ $(l_i < u_i)$ representing a lower and upper bound of the real-valued time-point, when the symbol σ_i occurred. The set of finite symbolic timed words is denoted $\mathcal{B}\Sigma^*$. We limit bounds in symbolic timed words to natural numbers which is equivalent to supporting rationals with a fixed granularity.

Semantically a symbolic timed word $\rho_s = (\sigma, I_1, I_2, \ldots, I_n)$ covers all timed words (σ, τ) where $\tau_i \in I_i$. We write $\rho \sqsubseteq \rho_s$. Also, whenever $\rho_s = (\sigma, I_1, I_2, \ldots, I_n)$ and $\rho'_s = (\sigma, J_1, J_2, \ldots, J_n)$ are two symbolic timed words, we write $\rho_s \sqsubseteq \rho'_s$ if $I_i \subseteq J_i$ for all $i = 1 \ldots n$.

Now monitoring a language of timed infinite words in the setting of timing uncertainty refines timed monitoring in the following way. Given a finite symbolic prefix, it is checked whether all concrete realization of this prefix determine the property. That is whether all possible infinite extensions of such a concrete realization are included in the monitored property. More formally:

Definition 8 (Monitoring with timing uncertainty). *Given a language of infinite timed words* $\phi \subseteq T\Sigma^\omega$ *and a finite symbolic timed word* $\rho_s \in \mathcal{B}\Sigma^*$, *the function* $\mathcal{V}_U : 2^{T\Sigma^\omega} \to \mathcal{B}\Sigma^* \to \mathbb{B}_3$ *evaluates to a verdict with the following definition:*

$$\mathcal{V}_U(\phi)(\rho_s) = \begin{cases} \top & \text{if } \rho \cdot \mu \in \phi \text{ for all } \rho \sqsubseteq \rho_s \text{ and all } \mu \in \mathcal{B}\Sigma^\omega, \\ \bot & \text{if } \rho \cdot \mu \notin \phi \text{ for all } \rho \sqsubseteq \rho_s \text{ and all } \mu \in \mathcal{B}\Sigma^\omega, \\ \text{?} & \text{otherwise.} \end{cases}$$

We note that if $\rho_s \sqsubseteq \rho'_s$ then $\mathcal{V}_U(\phi)(\rho_s) \sqsubseteq \mathcal{V}_U(\phi)(\rho'_s)$.

Example 5. Consider the MITL property $F_{[5,6]}a$, and the concrete timed word $\rho = (b, 1.2), (a, 5.4), (c, 7.3)$. Assume that we observe time-points as integer-bounded intervals of length 1 respectively 2 reflected by the following two symbolic timed words $\rho_s^1 = (b, [1,2]), (a, [5,6]), (c, [7,8])$ and $\rho_s^2 = (b, [1,3]), (a, [5,7]), (c, [7,9])$. Now $\mathcal{V}(F_{[5,6]}a)(\rho) = \top$ and $\mathcal{V}_U(F_{[5,6]}a)(\rho_s^1) = \top$ whereas $\mathcal{V}_U(F_{[5,6]}a)(\rho_s^2) = \bot$.

To obtain a monitoring algorithm for monitoring under timing uncertainty it merely requires that the symbolic successor computation of Algorithm 4 is extended to pairs (α, I) where I is an integer-bounded interval. Thus Algorithm 5 can easily be extended to support time uncertainty.

8   Time Predictive Monitoring

In the timed setting studied in this paper, we want to refine the rather uninformative verdict $?$ that occurs during monitoring to provide guaranteed minimum times before a positive or negative verdict can be made.

Example 6. Consider the MITL property $F_{[20,40]}b$. Monitoring the finite timed word $\rho = (a, 5.1), (c, 21.0), (c, 30.4), (b, 35.1), (a, 40.2)$ will result in three $?$ verdicts followed by the verdict $\top$ when $(b, 35.1)$ is read. However, we may offer significantly more information, e.g. when reading $(a, 5.1)$ it is clear that at least 14.9 time-units must elapse before we can claim that the property holds, and at least 34.9 time-units must elaps before we can claim that it does not hold.

Definition 9 (Time Predictive Monitor Verdicts). *Given a language of infinite timed words $\phi \subseteq T\Sigma^\omega$ and a finite timed word $\rho \in T\Sigma^*$, the function $\mathcal{V}_T : 2^{T\Sigma^\omega} \to T\Sigma^* \to \mathbb{R}_{\geq 0}^2$ evaluates to the verdict $\mathcal{V}_T(\phi)(\rho) = (D_\phi^\rho, D_{\bar{\phi}}^\rho)$, where:*

$$D_\phi^\rho = \inf \left\{ \tau(\rho') : \rho' \in T\Sigma^* \text{ such that } \forall \mu \in T\!b\Sigma^\omega \,.\, \rho \cdot \rho' \cdot \mu \in \phi \right\}$$

$$D_{\bar{\phi}}^\rho = \inf \left\{ \tau(\rho') : \rho' \in T\Sigma^* \text{ such that } \forall \mu \in T\!b\Sigma^\omega \,.\, \rho \cdot \rho' \cdot \mu \notin \phi \right\}$$

where $\tau(\rho')$ denotes the time duration of ρ'.

The intuition behind Definition 9 is illustrated in Fig. 8. We note that when $\mathcal{V}(\phi)(\rho) = \top$ then $\mathcal{V}_T(\phi)(\rho) = (0, +\infty)$. Dually, when $\mathcal{V}(\phi)(\rho) = \bot$ then $\mathcal{V}_T(\phi)(\rho) = (+\infty, 0)$. We note however, that the opposite implications do not hold. As an example consider the property $F_{\geq 5}b$ and the finite timed word $\rho = (c, 6)$. Then clearly $\mathcal{V}_T(\phi)(\rho) = (0, +\infty)$ but $\mathcal{V}(\phi)(\rho) \neq \top$.

To make steps toward a time predicting monitoring algorithm, we assume that the property ϕ (as well as $\bar{\phi}$) can be captured by a TBA $\mathcal{A}$. During monitoring, we constantly check whether the state estimate $\mathcal{T}_\mathcal{A}(\rho)$ of the current prefix word ρ intersects the set of states with non-empty language, i.e. $Reach_\mathcal{A}^\infty$. Now $R_\mathcal{A} = Reach_\mathcal{A}(\overline{Reach_\mathcal{A}^\infty})$ describes the set of states that can reach a state with an empty language. By extending the TBA $\mathcal{A}$ with a fresh clock z, the extended set $R_\mathcal{A}^z = Reach_{\mathcal{A}^z}(\overline{Reach_{\mathcal{A}^z}^\infty} \wedge (z = 0))$ captures in a symbolic way the time required to reach a state with an empty language[2]. In particular $d_\mathcal{A}(q, v) = \inf\{v_z : (q, v, v_z) \in R_\mathcal{A}^z\}$ is the infimum reachability time for a

---

[2] Similar to a method in [12] for time-optimal strategies.

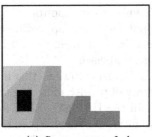 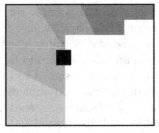

(a) State space of $\mathcal{A}$ (b) State space of $\overline{\mathcal{A}}$

Fig. 8. Illustration of the state spaces while monitoring given the inputs $\mathcal{A}$ and $\overline{\mathcal{A}}$ and a timed word ρ. This figure is a refinement of Fig. 6. In particular the states with a non-empty language, e.g. $Reach_{\mathcal{A}}^{\infty}$, has been divided into two subsets: the set of states that can reach outside $Reach_{\mathcal{A}}^{\infty}$ (darker grey indicating larger infimum reachability time) and the states that cannot (darkest grey). The black areas are the state-estimates after ρ, i.e. $\mathcal{T}_{\mathcal{A}}(\rho)$ and $\mathcal{T}_{\overline{\mathcal{A}}}(\rho)$.

state $(q, v) \in R_{\mathcal{A}}$. For S a set of states, we define $d_{\mathcal{A}}(S)$ to be the supremum of $d_{\mathcal{A}}(q, v)$ over all $(q, v) \in S$. Now we claim the following Theorem, pointing to an effective way of providing guaranteed minimum time predictions of positive and negative verdicts during monitoring.

Theorem 4. *Let* $\phi \subseteq T\Sigma^{\omega}$ *be a language of infinite timed words. Assume that* ϕ *is accepted by a TBA* $\mathcal{A}_{\phi}$ *and the complement* $\overline{\phi}$ *is accepted by a TBA* $\mathcal{A}_{\overline{\phi}}$. *Then the following holds:*

$$d_{\mathcal{A}_{\phi}}(\mathcal{T}_{\mathcal{A}_{\phi}}(\rho)) \leq D_{\phi}^{\rho} \quad and \quad d_{\mathcal{A}_{\overline{\phi}}}(\mathcal{T}_{\mathcal{A}_{\overline{\phi}}}(\rho)) \leq D_{\overline{\phi}}^{\rho}$$

Moreover, if $\mathcal{A}_{\phi}$ *(*$\mathcal{A}_{\overline{\phi}}$*) is deterministic the first (second) inequality is an equality.*

9   Conclusion

In this work, we have revisited the online monitoring problem for timed properties. We presented an efficient online monitoring algorithm for languages of infinite timed words. We require the language and its complement to be expressed as TBAs, a requirement that is, for example, satisfied for languages specified in the logic MITL. Hence our method is applicable in many realistic scenarios.

We showed how to account for time divergence which prior work did not readily seem to support. We also introduced two extensions to our method: support for time uncertainty in the time sequence observed by the monitor, and time predictions that refine the unknown verdict. By supporting time uncertainty in the observed input, we account for real-world systems where the real-valued time-points of events can only be observed up to a given precision. This limits the soundness of verdicts from monitors that support only concrete timed traces. Time predictions refine the mostly unhelpful unknown verdict to provide extra information on the possible time-to-failure of the monitored system. For nondeterministic TBAs we show how to compute an under-approximation which is exact in the case of deterministic automata. In the future, we will investigate the existence of an exact algorithm for the general case.

While our work was designed to facilitate implementation, this has not yet been completed. Our planned implementation will be distributed in the form of a C++ library with facilities to read TBAs in the UPPAAL XML format [23] that is output by tools like Casaal [24] and MightyL [9]. We also plan to integrate the tool into UPPAAL SMC [14] to replace the current rewrite-based Weighted MTL implementation [11].

Further improvements to our monitoring algorithm include improved support for uncertainties in the input and additional analysis of timed properties. One direction in which we plan to extend the work is to support unobservable symbols in the monitor alphabet. This can be logically extended to consider arbitrary mutations to an input sequence modeled in the form of a TA. We also plan to provide a method to compute the monitorability of a timed property.

References

1. Alur, R., Dill, D.L.: A theory of timed automata. Theoret. Comput. Sci. **126**(2), 183–235 (1994). https://doi.org/10.1016/0304-3975(94)90010-8
2. Alur, R., Feder, T., Henzinger, T.A.: The benefits of relaxing punctuality. J. ACM **43**(1), 116–146 (1996)
3. Baldor, K., Niu, J.: Monitoring dense-time, continuous-semantics, metric temporal logic. In: Qadeer, S., Tasiran, S. (eds.) RV 2012. LNCS, vol. 7687, pp. 245–259. Springer, Heidelberg (2013). https://doi.org/10.1007/978-3-642-35632-2_24
4. Basin, D., Klaedtke, F., Müller, S., Pfitzmann, B.: Runtime monitoring of metric first-order temporal properties. In: IARCS Annual Conference on Foundations of Software Technology and Theoretical Computer Science. LIPIcs, vol. 2, pp. 49–60. Schloss Dagstuhl (2008). https://doi.org/10.4230/LIPIcs.FSTTCS.2008.1740
5. Basin, D., Klaedtke, F., Zălinescu, E.: Algorithms for monitoring real-time properties. In: Khurshid, S., Sen, K. (eds.) RV 2011. LNCS, vol. 7186, pp. 260–275. Springer, Heidelberg (2012). https://doi.org/10.1007/978-3-642-29860-8_20
6. Bauer, A., Leucker, M., Schallhart, C.: Monitoring of real-time properties. In: Arun-Kumar, S., Garg, N. (eds.) FSTTCS 2006. LNCS, vol. 4337, pp. 260–272. Springer, Heidelberg (2006). https://doi.org/10.1007/11944836_25
7. Bauer, A., Leucker, M., Schallhart, C.: Runtime verification for LTL and TLTL. ACM Trans. Softw. Eng. Methodol. (TOSEM) **20**(4), 14:1–14:64 (2011). https://doi.org/10.1145/2000799.2000800
8. Bengtsson, J., Yi, W.: Timed automata: semantics, algorithms and tools. In: Desel, J., Reisig, W., Rozenberg, G. (eds.) ACPN 2003. LNCS, vol. 3098, pp. 87–124. Springer, Heidelberg (2004). https://doi.org/10.1007/978-3-540-27755-2_3
9. Brihaye, T., Geeraerts, G., Ho, H.-M., Monmege, B.: MightyL: a compositional translation from MITL to timed automata. In: Majumdar, R., Kunčak, V. (eds.) CAV 2017. LNCS, vol. 10426, pp. 421–440. Springer, Cham (2017). https://doi.org/10.1007/978-3-319-63387-9_21

10. Bulychev, P., et al.: Monitor-based statistical model checking for weighted metric temporal logic. In: Bjørner, N., Voronkov, A. (eds.) LPAR 2012. LNCS, vol. 7180, pp. 168–182. Springer, Heidelberg (2012). https://doi.org/10.1007/978-3-642-28717-6_15

11. Bulychev, P., David, A., Larsen, K.G., Legay, A., Li, G., Poulsen, D.B.: Rewrite-based statistical model checking of WMTL. In: Qadeer, S., Tasiran, S. (eds.) RV 2012. LNCS, vol. 7687, pp. 260–275. Springer, Heidelberg (2013). https://doi.org/10.1007/978-3-642-35632-2_25

12. Cassez, F., David, A., Fleury, E., Larsen, K.G., Lime, D.: Efficient on-the-fly algorithms for the analysis of timed games. In: Abadi, M., de Alfaro, L. (eds.) CONCUR 2005. LNCS, vol. 3653, pp. 66–80. Springer, Heidelberg (2005). https://doi.org/10.1007/11539452_9

13. Chattopadhyay, A., Mamouras, K.: A verified online monitor for metric temporal logic with quantitative semantics. In: Deshmukh, J., Ničković, D. (eds.) RV 2020. LNCS, vol. 12399, pp. 383–403. Springer, Cham (2020). https://doi.org/10.1007/978-3-030-60508-7_21

14. David, A., Larsen, K.G., Legay, A., Mikučionis, M., Wang, Z.: Time for statistical model checking of real-time systems. In: Gopalakrishnan, G., Qadeer, S. (eds.) CAV 2011. LNCS, vol. 6806, pp. 349–355. Springer, Heidelberg (2011). https://doi.org/10.1007/978-3-642-22110-1_27

15. De Wulf, M., Doyen, L., Markey, N., Raskin, J.F.: Robust safety of timed automata. Formal Methods Syst. Des. 33(1), 45–84 (2008). https://doi.org/10.1007/s10703-008-0056-7

16. Finkbeiner, B., Kuhtz, L.: Monitor circuits for LTL with bounded and unbounded future. In: Bensalem, S., Peled, D.A. (eds.) RV 2009. LNCS, vol. 5779, pp. 60–75. Springer, Heidelberg (2009). https://doi.org/10.1007/978-3-642-04694-0_5

17. Geilen, M., Dams, D.: An on-the-fly tableau construction for a real-time temporal logic. In: Joseph, M. (ed.) FTRTFT 2000. LNCS, vol. 1926, pp. 276–290. Springer, Heidelberg (2000). https://doi.org/10.1007/3-540-45352-0_23

18. Ho, H.-M., Ouaknine, J., Worrell, J.: Online monitoring of metric temporal logic. In: Bonakdarpour, B., Smolka, S.A. (eds.) RV 2014. LNCS, vol. 8734, pp. 178–192. Springer, Cham (2014). https://doi.org/10.1007/978-3-319-11164-3_15

19. Jahanian, F., Rajkumar, R., Raju, S.C.V.: Runtime monitoring of timing constraints in distributed real-time systems. Real-Time Syst. 7(3), 247–273 (1994). https://doi.org/10.1007/BF01088521

20. Kauffman, S., Havelund, K., Fischmeister, S.: Monitorability over unreliable channels. In: Finkbeiner, B., Mariani, L. (eds.) RV 2019. LNCS, vol. 11757, pp. 256–272. Springer, Cham (2019). https://doi.org/10.1007/978-3-030-32079-9_15

21. Kauffman, S., Havelund, K., Fischmeister, S.: What can we monitor over unreliable channels? Int. J. Softw. Tools Technol. Transfer 23(4), 579–600 (2021). https://doi.org/10.1007/s10009-021-00625-z

22. Koymans, R.: Specifying real-time properties with metric temporal logic. Real-Time Syst. 2(4), 255–299 (1990). https://doi.org/10.1007/BF01995674

23. Larsen, K.G., Mikucionis, M., Nielsen, B.: Online testing of real-time systems using UPPAAL. In: Grabowski, J., Nielsen, B. (eds.) FATES 2004. LNCS, vol. 3395, pp. 79–94. Springer, Heidelberg (2005). https://doi.org/10.1007/978-3-540-31848-4_6

24. Li, G., Jensen, P.G., Larsen, K.G., Legay, A., Poulsen, D.B.: Practical controller synthesis for $mtl_{0,\infty}$. In: International SPIN Symposium on Model Checking of Software, SPIN 2017, pp. 102–111. ACM (2017). https://doi.org/10.1145/3092282.3092303

25. Lindahl, M., Pettersson, P., Yi, W.: Formal design and analysis of a gear controller. In: Steffen, B. (ed.) TACAS 1998. LNCS, vol. 1384, pp. 281–297. Springer, Heidelberg (1998). https://doi.org/10.1007/BFb0054178
26. Moosbrugger, P., Rozier, K.Y., Schumann, J.: R2U2: monitoring and diagnosis of security threats for unmanned aerial systems. Formal Methods Syst. Des. **51**(1), 31–61 (2017). https://doi.org/10.1007/s10703-017-0275-x
27. Ničković, D., Piterman, N.: From MTL to deterministic timed automata. In: Chatterjee, K., Henzinger, T.A. (eds.) FORMATS 2010. LNCS, vol. 6246, pp. 152–167. Springer, Heidelberg (2010). https://doi.org/10.1007/978-3-642-15297-9_13
28. Pike, L.: A note on inconsistent axioms in Rushby's "systematic formal verification for fault-tolerant time-triggered algorithms. IEEE Trans. Softw. Eng. **32**(5), 347–348 (2006)
29. Pnueli, A., Zaks, A.: PSL model checking and run-time verification via testers. In: Misra, J., Nipkow, T., Sekerinski, E. (eds.) FM 2006. LNCS, vol. 4085, pp. 573–586. Springer, Heidelberg (2006). https://doi.org/10.1007/11813040_38
30. Rushby, J.: Systematic formal verification for fault-tolerant time-triggered algorithms. IEEE Trans. Software Eng. **25**(5), 651–660 (1999). https://doi.org/10.1109/32.815324
31. Thati, P., Rou, G.: Monitoring algorithms for metric temporal logic specifications. Electron. Notes Theor. Comput. Sci. **113**, 145–162 (2005). https://doi.org/10.1016/j.entcs.2004.01.029. Proceedings of the Fourth Workshop on Runtime Verification (RV 2004)
32. Ulus, D., Ferrère, T., Asarin, E., Maler, O.: Timed pattern matching. In: Legay, A., Bozga, M. (eds.) FORMATS 2014. LNCS, vol. 8711, pp. 222–236. Springer, Cham (2014). https://doi.org/10.1007/978-3-319-10512-3_16
33. Ulus, D., Ferrère, T., Asarin, E., Maler, O.: Online timed pattern matching using derivatives. In: Chechik, M., Raskin, J.-F. (eds.) TACAS 2016. LNCS, vol. 9636, pp. 736–751. Springer, Heidelberg (2016). https://doi.org/10.1007/978-3-662-49674-9_47

Probabilistic and Timed Systems

Bounded Delay Timed Channel Coding

Bernardo Jacobo Inclán, Aldric Degorre⊙, and Eugene Asarin$^{(\boxtimes)}$⊙

Université Paris Cité, CNRS, IRIF, 75013 Paris, France
asarin@irif.fr

Abstract. We consider the problem of timed channel coding: given two
timed languages, can we transmit the information produced by the first,
used as information source, as words of the second, used as communication channel? More precisely, we look at coding with bounded delay:
having a uniform bound between the timed length of any word from the
source and its encoding on the channel. Moreover, we consider approximated coding satisfying the following property: whenever the channel
word is observed with precision ε', then the original word can be recovered with precision ε.

Our solution is based on the new notion of ε-bandwidth of a timed language, which characterises the quantity of information in its words, in bits
per time unit, when these words are observed with precision ε. We present
basic properties of ε-bandwidth of timed regular languages, and establish a necessary, and a sufficient simple condition for existence of bounded
delay coding in terms of bandwidths of the source and the channel.

1 Introduction

This paper is about lifting the classical theory of constrained-channel coding to
timed languages. As such, it can be seen as a follow-up of [2], although coding
is now constrained by real time instead of the number of discrete events.

Given a *source* from which messages are issued, and a *channel* through which
they should be transmitted, many questions may arise:

- Can any source-generated message be transmitted via the channel?
- With what speed?
- If so, how should it be encoded?
- How should it be decoded after the transmission?

Coding theory offers a framework for answering such questions. The source
and the channel are represented by languages: S, the words that can be generated
by the source, and C the words that can pass through the channel.

The goal of coding theory is then to establish which conditions are to be
expected on S and C for the possibility of transmitting a message. With that
purpose, for each language L, its *entropy* $h(L)$ is computed. The entropy is a

This work was funded by ANR project MAVeriQ ANR-CE25-0012.

S. Bogomolov and D. Parker (Eds.): FORMATS 2022, LNCS 13465, pp. 65–79, 2022.
https://doi.org/10.1007/978-3-031-15839-1_4

real, non-negative value characterizing the quantity of information in a language (usually written in bits per symbol). The main results from coding theory are the following:

- a necessary condition for the transmission of information (from S onto C) in real-time is that $h(S) \leq h(C)$ – and for transmission with speed α, the condition is $\alpha h(S) \leq h(C)$;
- a sufficient condition for the transmission of information is $h(S) < h(C)$ – respectively, $\alpha h(S) < h(C)$, note that these inequalities are strict;
- whenever this second condition is verified, an encoding and decoding can be given by a finite-state transducer.

Usually the case where $h(S) = h(C)$ is more involved.

An important example is EFMPlus code [6], its source being the language with all possible binary words $\{0,1\}^*$ (entropy 1), and its channel being a DVD admitting all the words without factors 11, 101 and 011 (entropy 0.5418), (in this case, the rate is almost optimal: $\alpha = \frac{1}{2}$, see [4]).

Classical theory of channel coding deals with sequences of discrete events. However, (cyber-)physical appliances typically transmit more than that: indeed, delays between events can vary, either by design (music scores, Morse code, event logs with timestamps etc.) or because of implementation contingencies (side-channels in supposedly pure discrete systems, such as microprocessors subject to Meltdown [11] and Spectre [7] vulnerabilities, disclosed in 2018). When the delay variations occur in the source language, they contain information which can (or sometimes should) be encoded. When they occur in the channel, if the channel operator can control them, then they can be used to transmit information. Both for source and channel, this fact represents well known security issues if delay variations were not a design choice (i.e. the source leaks information which can be exploited through timing attacks [8]; or the channel contains a timed covert channel). Be it for assessing the seriousness of a security threat or just measuring the efficiency of a communication system, it is anyway useful to know how much information the source produces or a channel transmits thanks to delays.

Coding for the case where both source and channel are modelled by timed languages has already been studied in [2], the starting point for this research. That work defined a notion of coding between a (timed) source and a (timed or discrete) channel and established necessary and sufficient conditions for the existence of a coding when the languages are regular. However, this notion of coding and the notion of volumic entropy (as defined in [10]) which is used in these conditions, correspond to "information per event". Hence, they only allow to issue statements such as: any given timed word of n events from the source can be encoded as a channel word of n' events or more; but they cannot relate the durations and respective timings of a source word and its coded image (the events in the channel word can arrive before those in the source, or much later). Hence this approach is more relevant to offline processing of timed data (compression etc.), than to real-time applications.

In the current paper we develop a coding theory for timed languages that considers "information per time unit". We introduce a new notion of coding more in accordance with practical real-time expectations: the encoded message should be bounded on time w.r.t. the source word, and one should be able to decode it with some positive precision. As the key tool, we define and use entropic and capacitive bandwidths, which characterize asymptotics with respect to time of, resp., ε-entropy and ε-capacity (as defined by Kolmogorov and Tikhomirov [9]). Then, using these notions, we establish conditions for the existence of a coding.

The paper is structured as follows. In Sect. 2, we recall some background notions, and describe a simple construction of timed factor language. In Sect. 3 we introduce and study the two notions of bandwidth of a timed language. In Sect. 4 we finally come up with the notion of bounded delay channel coding, and establish a necessary and a sufficient conditions for the existence of such a coding. We discuss the perspectives of this work in concluding Sect. 5.

2 Preliminary Work

2.1 Timed Languages and Timed Automata

Given Σ, a finite alphabet of discrete events, a *timed word* over Σ is an element of $(\Sigma \times \mathbb{R}_+)^*$ of the form $w = (a_1, t_1) \ldots (a_n, t_n)$, such that $0 \leq t_1 \leq t_2 \cdots \leq t_n$. Each real number component should be interpreted as the *date* at which the associated discrete event happens. A *timed language* over Σ is a set of timed words over Σ.

For any word $w = (a_1, t_1) \ldots (a_n, t_n)$, we denote its *discrete length* as $|u| =_{def} n$ and its *timed length* or *duration* as $\tau(u) =_{def} t_n$.

Regular timed languages are the timed languages recognized by timed automata, as introduced in [1]:

Definition 1 (Timed automaton)
For a set of variables Ξ, let G_Ξ be the set of constraints expressible as finite conjunctions of inequalities of the form $\xi \sim b$ with $\xi \in \Xi$, $\sim \in \{<, \leq, >, \geq\}$ and $b \in \mathbb{N}$.

A timed automaton (TA) is a tuple $(Q, X, \Sigma, \Delta, I, F)$ where

- *Q is the finite set of discrete locations;*
- *X is the finite set of clocks;*
- *Σ is a finite alphabet;*
- *$I : Q \rightarrow G_X$ defines the initial clock values for each location;*
- *$F : Q \rightarrow G_X$ defines the accepting clock values for each location;*
- *$\Delta \subseteq Q \times Q \times \Sigma \times G_X \times 2^X$ is the transition relation.*

For any $\delta \in \Delta$ we also define the projections src_δ (source), dst_δ (destination), lbl_δ (label), $\mathfrak{g}_\delta$ (guard) and $\mathfrak{r}_\delta$ (set of reset clocks) such that $\delta = (src_\delta, dst_\delta, lbl_\delta, \mathfrak{g}_\delta, \mathfrak{r}_\delta)$.

We define two operations that can be applied to any clock vector $x \in \mathbb{R}_+^X$: first, given a non-negative real number t, we denote by $x + t \in \mathbb{R}_+^X$ the clock vector such that for all clock c, $(x + t)_c = x_c + t$; second, given a set of clocks

$\mathfrak{r} \in X$, then $x[\mathfrak{r}] \in \mathbb{R}_+^X$ is the clock vector such that $x[\mathfrak{r}]_c = 0$ whenever $c \in \mathfrak{r}$ and $x[\mathfrak{r}]_c = x_c$ otherwise.

A timed automaton A defines a timed language L_A: a timed word $w = (a_1, t_1) \ldots (a_n, t_n)$ belongs to L_A iff there is a sequence of edges of the form (for $i \in 1..n$) $\delta_i = (q_{i-1}, q_i, a_i, \mathfrak{g}_i, \mathfrak{r}_i) \in \Delta$ and a sequence of clock vectors $x_0 \ldots x_n \in \mathbb{R}_+^X$ such that $x_0 \vDash I(q_0)$, $x_n \vDash F(q_n)$ and, for all $i \in 1..n$, $x_{i-1} + (t_i - t_{i-1}) \vDash \mathfrak{g}_i$ and $x_i = (x_{i-1} + (t_i - t_{i-1}))[\mathfrak{r}_i]$. Said in English: state (q_0, x_0) is initial, state (q_n, x_n) is accepting and, for all i, between the two states (q_{i-1}, x_{i-1}) and (q_i, x_i), there is a transition along the edge δ_i consisting in waiting $t_i - t_{i-1}$ units of time and reading the letter a_i.

In the following, we only consider Deterministic Timed Automata. A timed automaton is *deterministic* when, for any two edges δ and $\delta' \in \Delta$, it holds that $[src_\delta = src_{\delta'} \wedge lbl_\delta = lbl_{\delta'} \wedge ((\mathfrak{g}_\delta \wedge \mathfrak{g}_{\delta'}) \neq \bot)] \implies \delta = \delta'$.

2.2   Entropy and Capacity

Now we address the question of determining the quantity of information contained in a language. Intuitively, when only words that are very close to one another can be observed, then one may not be able to distinguish many different words, thus little information may be conveyed. On the contrary, if there are many words that are set sufficiently far apart one from another, the fact of choosing among them conveys a large amount of information.

A second point of view is how many words are necessary to approximate the language up to some precision.

Both points of view, of course, depend on the precision with which we observe, as is apparent with the following definition, taken from [9]:

Definition 2. *Let (R, d) be a pseudo-metric space and $A, B \subseteq R$, then:*

- *$M \subseteq A$ is an ε-separated set if $\forall x, y \in M, d(x, y) \leq \varepsilon \Rightarrow x = y$;*
- *$N \subseteq B$ is an ε-net of A in B if $\forall y \in A, \exists s \in N$ s.t. $d(y, s) \leq \varepsilon$.*

On one hand, an ε-separated subset of A contains elements of A all distant from each other of at least ε, hence all distinguishable with this precision. On the other hand, an ε-net of A allows to approximate every element of A with precision ε. Hence the following definitions, as measures of the information content of a set:

Definition 3. *For (R, d) a pseudo-metric space and $A, B \subseteq R$ we define*

- *ε-capacity of A: $C_\varepsilon(A) =_{def} \log(\max_{M:\varepsilon\text{-separated set}} \#M)$*
- *ε-entropy of A w.r.t. B: $\mathcal{H}_\varepsilon^B(A) =_{def} \log(\min_{N:\varepsilon\text{-net of} A in B} \#N)$.*
  When the superscript B is omitted, we assume $B = R$.

The following inequality is known to hold for any A subset of R:

Proposition 1
$$C_{2\varepsilon}(A) \leq \mathcal{H}_\varepsilon(A) \leq C_\varepsilon(A).$$

In the developments thereafter, R and B will typically be U_Σ, the universal timed language on the working alphabet Σ, while different regular timed languages on Σ will play the role of A. The pseudo-metric will be the one we describe next.

2.3   Pseudo-Distance on Timed Languages

To give a meaningful interpretation to capacity and entropy, an appropriate metric, modelling the ability of the observer, is required. We need to explicit what it takes to distinguish between two words. To this purpose, we imagine an observer that reads the discrete letters of the word exactly (they can determine whether or not a letter has occurred) but with some imprecision w.r.t. time, so they cannot determine -if two letters are very close- which one came before the other, and not even how many times a letter was repeated within a short interval.

Hence, we use the following pseudo-distance:

Definition 4 (Pseudo-distance on timed words [3]). *For two timed words* $w = (a_1, t_1) \ldots (a_n, t_n)$ *and* $v = (b_1, s_1) \ldots (b_m, s_m)$ *we define:*

$$\overrightarrow{d}(w, v) =_{def} \max_{i \in \{1, \ldots, n\}} \min_{j \in \{1, \ldots, n\}} \{|t_i - s_j| : a_i = b_j\};$$

$$d(w, v) =_{def} \max(\overrightarrow{d}(w, v), \overrightarrow{d}(v, w)).$$

We can understand $\overrightarrow{d}(w, v)$ as follows: for every occurrence of a letter in w, we search for the closest occurrence of the same letter in v (hence the timing is approximated while the nature of the event it kept identical), then $\overrightarrow{d}(w, v)$ is the worst distance between any letter occurrence in v and its closest match in w.

This definition however is not symmetrical w.r.t. v and w, so we define d as a symmetrized version of $\overrightarrow{d}$.

Remark that d is defined very similarly to the Hausdorff distance between two subsets of a metric space. However, in contrary to the latter, because timed words may have simultaneous letters, d does not satisfy the axiom of separation $(d(x, y) = 0 \not\Rightarrow x = y)$. For this reason, it is not a distance but only a pseudo-distance.

2.4   The Factor Language $\tilde{L}$

We now introduce the closure by factors of timed languages, because, as we will see, factor closed languages behave in a more regular way with respect to bandwidth.

The intuition is as follows: given a language, we are interested in what can happen for a given duration at any point in time, independently of what happened before and what will happen after. For instance, we may want to know what may happen when we take 5 s in a language, not necessarily at the beginning, but anywhere. For this purpose, we have the following definition:

Definition 5. *For any timed word* $u = (a_1, t_1) \ldots (a_n, t_n)$, *its timed factors are all the words* w *of the form* $(a_i, t_i - x) \ldots (a_j, t_j - x)$ *where* $1 \leq i \leq j \leq n$ *and* $t_{i-1} < x \leq t_i$ *(with* $t_0 = 0$*).*
    Then the closure of L *by time factors is*

$$\tilde{L} =_{def} \{w \mid \exists u \in L \text{ s.t. } w \text{ is a timed factor of } u\}.$$

A language L *is timed factor closed whenever* $\tilde{L} = L$.

Extracting a factor from a word u, consists in "erasing" two parts: a prefix and a suffix. Let us note two things. First, this operation does not modify the inner structure of a word, that is, the delays between two letters are never modified. Second, for regular languages it is possible to prove that, in the automaton recognizing the language, we can go from the initial state to any reachable state (and from any co-reachable state to an accepting state) in a bounded amount of time and with a bounded number of transitions, and these bounds depend only on the automaton. Hence, we expect that, for typical automata, L and $\tilde{L}$ have closely related bandwidths. For this reason and because $\tilde{L}$ is easier to study, some of the results below will be stated on $\tilde{L}$ rather than L.

3   Bandwidth

We now introduce bandwidth, the main tool to characterize the ability for a language to produce or convey information *per time unit* in the long run. Like the previous notions introduced in Sect. 2.2 (ε-net versus ε-separated, ε-entropy versus ε-capacity), bandwidths come in two versions, depending on whether it is about producing or transmitting information. Bandwidths are asymptotics with respect to time, of the growth rate of the previous notions, which finally yield quantities expressed in bits per second.

3.1   Definitions

First remark that the entropy of a time bounded language is finite. Indeed, as we will see in the first example below, the entropy and capacity of the universal language restricted to a bounded duration are finite. Conversely, time-unbounded languages contain an infinite sequence of words $u_1, \ldots u_k, \ldots$ such that $\forall k \geq 1, \tau(u_k) + \varepsilon < \tau(u_{k+1})$. This sequence is an infinite ε-separated subset. Moreover, no finite $\varepsilon/2$-net can cover this sequence (each element of any $\varepsilon/2$-net can be close to only one element of the sequence).

    Thus, it makes sense to consider the entropy and capacity of time-bounded languages only and, for unbounded ones, look at the asymptotics of its time-bounded "slices". Hence, the following definitions:

Definition 6. *Given a timed language* L *and a time* $T \geq 0$, *its timed slice at* T *is* $L_T =_{def} \{w : w \in L, \tau(w) \leq T\}$.

Fig. 1. Universal Automaton On Alphabet $\{a\}$

Definition 7 (ε-entropic and ε-capacitive bandwidths).

$$\mathcal{BH}_\varepsilon(L) =_{def} \limsup_{T\to\infty} \frac{\mathcal{H}_\varepsilon(L_T)}{T};$$

$$\mathcal{BC}_\varepsilon(L) =_{def} \limsup_{T\to\infty} \frac{\mathcal{C}_\varepsilon(L_T)}{T}.$$

3.2 Examples

Now, let us check on examples that these two definitions correspond to the intuitive notion of "information per time unit".

Let L^1 be the language recognized by the automaton depicted on Fig. 1.

We fix time T.

The set $A_T^1 = \{(a,t_1)\ldots(a,t_n)|\forall i \in \{1,n\}, t_i \in \varepsilon\mathbb{N}, t_n \leq T\}$ is ε-separated in L_T^1, its size is $\#A_T^1 = 2^{\lfloor \frac{T}{\varepsilon}+1\rfloor}$. It is of maximal cardinality: given an ε-separated set E, we take for every word $w = (a,t_1)\ldots(a,t_n) \in E$ the word $v = (a,t_1')\ldots(a,t_n')$ where $t_i' = \lfloor \frac{t_i}{\varepsilon}\rfloor\varepsilon$. We obtain an ε-separated set contained in A_T^1.

Hence, we deduce $\mathcal{BC}_\varepsilon(L^1) = \limsup_{T\to\infty} \frac{1}{T}\log(2^{\lfloor \frac{T}{\varepsilon}+1\rfloor}) = \frac{1}{\varepsilon}$.

We reason in a similar manner for the entropy and we obtain $\mathcal{BH}_\varepsilon(L^1) = \frac{1}{2\varepsilon}$.

These two results concerning the bandwidth of L^1 can be interpreted as follows. A word in the universal language can have an a at any date and arbitrarily many times within any one time unit interval. However, as stated before, we consider an imperfect observer, with a limited precision. Within a given ε seconds interval, the observer can only distinguish whether there was at least an a or not; during one second, they can do that $\frac{1}{\varepsilon}$ times.

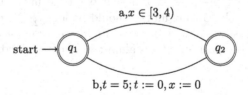

Fig. 2. Automaton with "non-vanishing" choice. The width of the interval within which the transition labelled by a may be fired does not depend on the past.

Consider now the language L^2 accepted by the automaton on Fig. 2; an equivalent characterization would be: $L^2 = \{(a_1,t_1)\ldots(a_n,t_n) : \forall i \in \{1, \lfloor n/2\rfloor\}, a_{2i} = b, a_{2i-1} = a, t_{2i} = 5i, t_{2i-1} \in [5i-2, 5i-1]\}$.

Below, we only compute the bandwidth of this language for values of ε smaller than 1. Practically, this corresponds to the reasonable context where the time precision of sensors is an order of magnitude smaller than the time scale of the observed system.

Let us briefly explain the separated sets we consider for computing the capacitive bandwidth (the reasoning for the entropic one being quite similar).

First recall that for two words to be distant of at least ε, it is enough that one has a letter occurrence such that every occurrence of the same letter in the other word is distant of at least ε time units from it.

In L^2, starting at time 0, every 5 time units the same is repeated: there is a between 3 and 4 and b at 5, then, at the end of the pattern, exactly 5 units of time after its start, there is a b. Because the position of the bs for a word of a given length is fixed, only the position of the as can convey information. Hence, we need to reason on the timings of the as only.

To that purpose, within a step (of 5 time units), we partition the interval $[3; 4)$ into $k =_{def} \lceil 1/\varepsilon \rceil$ subintervals, all having length ε except possibly the last one whose length is $\delta \leq \varepsilon$. For $i = 1..k$, for each subinterval $[l_i, u_i)$, we select a witness date inside the interval: $t_i =_{def} l_i + \frac{i}{k+1}\delta$. The set of witnesses is a maximal ε-separated subset of $[3, 4)$. Thus, for each i, we consider the word $w_i =_{def} (a, t_i)(b, 5) \in L_5^2$. The language of words consisting in, every 5 time units until time T, choosing $i \in 1..k$ and playing w_i is a ε-separated subset of L_T^2. Observe it is maximal: indeed, allowing only one more possibility for placing a between two consecutive b's would produce two words having occurrences of a distant of ε or less.

The cardinality of this set is $\lceil \frac{1}{\varepsilon} \rceil^n$, but, for the ε-net of L_T^2, we need to consider all words of length $\leq T$, so this means to make the union of the above for all values of n smaller than $T/5$ and also, for every word given by the construction, consider the same word with the final b removed. Notice we still obtain a maximal ε-separated subset.

The latter has the following total word amount: $2\sum_{n=1}^{t} \lceil \frac{1}{\varepsilon} \rceil^n = 2 \cdot \frac{1 - \lceil \frac{1}{\varepsilon} \rceil^t}{1 - \lceil \frac{1}{\varepsilon} \rceil}$. Going to the limit, we obtain: $\mathcal{BC}_\varepsilon(L^2) = \frac{1}{5}\log(\lceil \frac{1}{\varepsilon} \rceil)$. For the entropy, following a similar reasoning, the result is $\mathcal{BH}_\varepsilon(L^2) = \frac{1}{5}\log(\lceil \frac{1}{2\varepsilon} \rceil)$.

If the bandwidth represents information per time unit, then the quantity of information per cycle (5 time units), should be $\log(\lceil \frac{1}{2\varepsilon} \rceil)$. Intuitively, in this example, it is the position of a that transmits information, as a has freedom of movement whereas the position of b is almost fully determined.

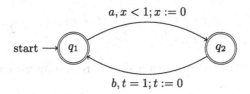

$$a, x < 1; x := 0$$

start $\rightarrow q_1 \qquad q_2$

$$b, t = 1; t := 0$$

Fig. 3. Automaton with "vanishing choice". In any given trace, the delay between any b and the next a must become smaller and smaller.

Our last example concerns the language accepted by the automaton on Fig. 3. Once again, let us give an informal explanation. This automaton, produces or reads a b every time unit. Within any time unit, it also produces or reads an a. The exact date of a is not fully determined, however, between any a and the next one, there is at most one time unit. This means that the distance between each b and its successor (an a) is decreasing, which constrains more and more the position of each a.

Let us compute the capacitive bandwidth for $0 < \varepsilon < \frac{1}{2}$. We look separately at each execution of the cycle $(q_1, t = 0), a, (q_2, x = 0), b, (q_1, t = 0)$. Because, as before, the position of a is the only variable in the execution of a cycle, we also divide the interval of dates in which a can be triggered, into $\lceil \frac{1}{\varepsilon} \rceil$ small intervals of size at most ε; we select an ε-separated set of witness dates and deduce a ε-separated subset of L_T^3. Now we need to know the size of this set. To this purpose, we index the intervals in increasing order with respect to date. Every time the cycle is repeated, to trigger a new a, the new interval that will be chosen must have an index that is smaller or equal to that of the previous one (remark the previous example did not have this restriction). For k iterations of the cycle where $k \in \mathbb{N}$, as to count the number of choices, let's decompose the sequence choice as several steps:

1. first, we choose j, the number of interval indexes that will be used to trigger a a during the whole execution;
2. then, given j, we choose which actual indices are going to be used (that is a subset of $1..\lceil \frac{1}{\varepsilon} \rceil$ of size j);
3. finally, also given j, we choose at which iteration we decrease from an index to the next one (that is choosing j indices within $1..k$).

Hence, there are $\sum_{j=1}^{\lceil \frac{1}{\varepsilon} \rceil} \binom{\lceil \frac{1}{\varepsilon} \rceil}{j} \binom{k}{j}$ choices.

So, we know the size of the maximal ε-separated subset for $\{w \in L^3 | \tau(w) = 5k\}$ for any natural number k. This can be generalized to a maximal ε-separated subset of L_{5k}^3 by adding one more index, smaller than all the others, to code the fact that the word has already ended, hence also accounting for all words of length $t < 5k$.

To obtain a maximal ε-separated subset of L_T^3 for any T, just use the same subset and add, for each of its words, the same word without the final b. The cardinality of this set is:

$$2 \sum_{j=1}^{\lceil \frac{1}{\varepsilon} \rceil + 1} \binom{\lceil \frac{1}{\varepsilon} \rceil + 1}{j} \binom{T}{j} \sim 2 \sum_{j=1}^{\lceil \frac{1}{\varepsilon} \rceil + 1} \binom{\lceil \frac{1}{\varepsilon} \rceil + 1}{j} t^j \sim 2 t^{\lceil \frac{1}{\varepsilon} \rceil + 1}.$$

This gives us $\mathcal{BC}_\varepsilon(L^3) = 0$ and with a similar reasoning we have $\mathcal{BH}_\varepsilon(L^3) = 0$ as well.

In these three examples, the ε-separated subsets have sizes that grow to infinity when ε becomes small, confirming the intuition that exact characterization of a timed word requires infinite information. Nonetheless, it is interesting to observe the different possible dependencies in ε of the bandwidth.

3.3   Existence of Limits

Previously, we defined the bandwidth as a lim sup. As we will see now, for any regular timed language L, the entropic bandwidth of its closure by factors $\tilde{L}$ is actually a limit.

To that aim, first we define the functions $h_\varepsilon : T \mapsto \mathcal{H}_\varepsilon(L_T)$ and $\tilde{h}_\varepsilon : T \mapsto \mathcal{H}_\varepsilon(\tilde{L}_T)$, then we prove the following result:

Lemma 1. $\tilde{h}$ *is sub-additive.*

And we obtain its direct corollary (according to Fekete's lemma [5]):

Theorem 1. $\lim_{T \to \infty} \tilde{h}/T$ *exists.*

Proof (of Lemma 1). Given a time T, we take T_1 and T_2 two time values such that $T_1 + T_2 = T$. Let h_1 and h_2 be minimal ε-nets for $\tilde{L}_{T_1}$ and $\tilde{L}_{T_2}$ (and we force the first one to only have letters between 0 and $T_1 - \varepsilon/2$, by simply moving backwards any letter appearing afterwards; remark it is still a minimal ε-net).

Let us consider the set

$$h_1 *_{T_1} h_2 =_{def} \{(a_1, t_1) \ldots (a_n, t_n), (b_1, s_1 + T_1) \ldots (b_m, s_m + T_1) :$$
$$(a_1, t_1) \ldots (a_n, t_n) \in h_1, (b_1, s_1) \ldots (b_m, s_m) \in h_2\},$$

obtained by concatenating a word from h_1 at 0 and a word of h_2 at T_1

We prove that it is an ε-net for $\tilde{L}_T$. Let us take any timed word $w = (a_1, t_1) \ldots (a_n, t_n)$ in $\tilde{L}_T$, let $c = \max_{i:t_i < T_1}(i)$, then we have that $w_1 := (a_1, t_1) \ldots (a_c, t_c) \in \tilde{L}_{T_1}$ and $w_2 := (a_{c+1}, t_{c+1} - T_1) \ldots (a_n, t_n - T_1) \in \tilde{L}_{T_2}$ (w_2 is the empty word whenever $\tau(w) < T_1$, which belongs to $\tilde{L}_{T_2}$ if it is the case). There are elements $v_1 \in h_1$ and $v_2 \in h_2$ such that $d(w_1, v_1) < \varepsilon$ and $d(w_2, v_2) < \varepsilon$ (we note that if the same delay is applied to all letters in w_2 and in v_2, the distance between the two words does not change). We consider the concatenation between v_1 and v_2 at time T_1 and we denote it by $v = v_1 *_{T_1} v_2$. We easily verify that $d(w, v) < \varepsilon$. This proves that $h_1 *_{T_1} h_2$ is an ε-net of $\tilde{L}_T$. Now we only have to evaluate the cardinality of $h_1 *_{T_1} h_2$, its value is $\#(h_1 *_{T_1} h_2) = \#h_1 \cdot \#h_2$ (we are sure that the letters of v_1 and v_2 cannot overlap, as letters in v_1 arrive before T_1 and letters in v_2 after -once we have delayed it-, so we do not risk counting the same word twice). The cardinality of a minimal net is obviously smaller, the size of minimal nets being sub-multiplicative, the entropy is sub-additive, which is exactly the expected result.   □

As for capacitive bandwidth, we show, under an additional hypothesis on reachability that it is also a limit: we require that between any two states of the automaton there exists a "shortcut run" of some constant duration.

Definition 8 (Shortcut property). *A timed automaton satisfies the* shortcut property *if there exists $\Delta > 0$ such that, for any two states (q_1, x_1) and (q_2, x_2), there is a run r of duration Δ such that $(q_1, x_1) \xrightarrow{r} (q_2, x_2')$, where (q_2, x_2) and (q_2, x_2') are equivalent in the sense that the same words are accepted starting from both states.*

Hence the condition only requires that an equivalent state can be reached, through a run of fixed duration. Note that only an equivalent state is required because, in general, $|x_2|$ could be unbounded. Just remark that replacing x_2 by the same clock vector where clocks values greater than $M + 1$ (with M the largest integer constant appearing in the automaton) become $M + 1$ does not change the accepted suffixes.

Theorem 2. *If L is the language of a timed automaton with shortcut property, then $\lim_{T \to \infty} \frac{1}{T} \mathcal{C}_\varepsilon(\tilde{L}_T)$ exists.*

The proof below is based on super-additivity of $\mathcal{C}_\varepsilon(\tilde{L}_T)$, which in its turn is established by combining separated sets in $\tilde{L}_{T_1}$ and $\tilde{L}_{T_2}$ through shortcuts introduced in Definition 8. We do not know yet if the shortcut property is necessary.

Proof. First, fix optimal ε-separated subsets S_1 and S_2 for $\tilde{L}_{T_1}$ and $\tilde{L}_{T_2}$, where $T_1 > \varepsilon$ and $T_2 > \varepsilon$.

Because of shortcut property, there is $\Delta > 0$ such that, for any state (q_1, x_1) that can be reached after a run of duration T_1, and any state (q_2, x_2) from which a run of length T_2 can be read, there is a run of length Δ going from (q_1, x_1) to (q_2, x_2'), where (q_2, x_2) and (q_2, x_2') are equivalent. Let A be the language of the labels of such runs.

Then:

- Following the construction above, you can choose any pair of words in $\tilde{L}_{T_1}$ and $\tilde{L}_{T_2}$, then some word in A such that their concatenation corresponds to an existing run of maximal duration $T =_{def} T_1 + \Delta + T_2$ in the automaton, i.e. the concatenation is a word of $\tilde{L}_T$.
- We partition S_1 according to the set of discrete events occurring between $T_1 - \varepsilon$ and T_1 in a word. The largest class of equivalence has cardinality at least $\#S_1/2^{\#\Sigma}$. Let's call it S_1'. Remark that for any pair of words in S_1', there exists a letter from one of the two that is unmatched in the other and such that its date is $t < T_1 - \varepsilon$ (indeed: for later dates, by definition of S_1', the same set of letters exists in this interval of length ε).
- We also define S_2' in a similar way (subset of S_2 having the same letters between time 0 and ε). Here too, any pair of words is distinguishable thanks to an event occurring after ε and this set has size at least $\#S_2/2^{\#\Sigma}$.

– So, if we extract from $(S_1 A S_2) \cap \tilde{L}_T$ one word for each choice from S_1' and S_2' (by construction, we can), we obtain an ε-separated set S: indeed, each pair of words $u, v \in S$ differs at least by either the chosen prefix in S_1' or suffix in S_2'; if their prefixes are different, then u (or v) has an event of date $t < T_1 - \varepsilon$ that cannot be matched to an event in $[t - \varepsilon, t + \varepsilon]$ from v (or u), be it from the prefix in S_1' or the suffix in AS_2' (the added events have dates after T_1). The same goes if the suffixes are different.

The above proves that $\tilde{L}_T$ contains an ε-separated subset of size at least $\#S_1 \#S_2 / 2^{2\#\Sigma}$, hence capacity is super-additive (up to an additive constant).

Finally, we use Fekete's lemma and conclude that capacitive bandwidth actually is a limit.   □

4 Encodings

4.1 Definition

In order to study the transmission of information between a source and a channel, we need to define its characteristics. First, we want the difference in duration between any word from S and its translation as a word of C to be bounded uniformly with respect to the source. Moreover, when two words from the source are distinguishable, we want their translations to be distinguishable as well: that is, when the distance between two words is greater than the source precision parameter, then the distance between their images should be greater than the channel precision parameter. Now that these two requirements have been stated, we propose the following definition.

Definition 9. *A (S,C)-encoding with precision $\varepsilon - \varepsilon'$, delay δ and rate α is a function $\phi : S \to C$ such that:*

– *ϕ preserves time with delay δ and rate α: $\alpha\tau(\phi(w)) \leq \tau(w) + \delta$;*
– *ϕ is $\varepsilon - \varepsilon'$-injective: $d(\phi(w), \phi(w')) \leq \varepsilon' \Rightarrow d(w, w') \leq \varepsilon$.*

α can be understood as the speed at which the transmission of information is done. If the quantity of information per time unit is greater in S, then for transmitting it through C, S will have to be slowed down.

4.2 Necessary Condition

The notion of encoding being defined, we can proceed to stating the necessary condition for such an encoding to exist. Unsurprisingly, this condition is expressed as inequalities between capacities and entropies of the source and the channel. Intuitively, whenever the amount of information the channel can describe is smaller than that which the source can produce, it is impossible to encode the latter into the former without losing some information in the process.

The condition is as follows:

Theorem 3 (Necessary conditions of encoding). *For an (S, C)-encoding with precision $(\varepsilon, \varepsilon')$ and rate α to exist, the following inequality must hold:*

$$\alpha \mathcal{BC}_\varepsilon(S) \leq \mathcal{BC}_{\varepsilon'}(C);$$

Also, the additional condition below is a direct corollary:

$$\alpha \mathcal{BH}_\varepsilon(S) \leq \mathcal{BC}_{\varepsilon'}(C).$$

Proof. Let us assume that such an encoding exists, we denote it by ϕ and we denote by δ its delay. Let us take $T > 0$. For $w \in S$ such that $\tau(w) \leq T$, it holds that $\tau(\phi(w)) \leq \frac{1}{\alpha}(T + \delta)$. Let us define $T' = T + \delta$. We take M a maximal ε-separated set of S_T. For each $x \in S_T$, we have $\phi(x) \in C_{\frac{1}{\alpha}T'}$ and that the $\phi(x)$ form an ε'-separated set of $C_{\frac{1}{\alpha}T'}$. We can deduce that $\mathcal{C}_{\varepsilon'}(C_{\frac{1}{\alpha}T'}) \geq \mathcal{C}_\varepsilon(S_T)$ and then $\frac{\alpha}{T'}\mathcal{C}_{\varepsilon'}(C_{\frac{1}{\alpha}T'}) \geq \frac{\alpha}{T'}\mathcal{C}_\varepsilon(S_T)$, and, as $T \sim_{T \to \infty} T'$,

$$\limsup_{T \to \infty} \frac{\alpha}{T'}\mathcal{C}_{\varepsilon'}(C_{\frac{1}{\alpha}T'}) \geq \limsup_{T \to \infty} \frac{\alpha}{T'}\mathcal{C}_\varepsilon(S_T),$$

and finally

$$\alpha \mathcal{BC}_\varepsilon(S) \leq \mathcal{BC}_{\varepsilon'}(C).$$

$\square$

As is common with similar works [2], the necessary condition is not a strict inequality but, as we will see, the sufficient condition will be one (the case of entropy equality is usually more involved).

4.3 Sufficient Condition

After the necessary condition, naturally we proceed to stating a sufficient one. We established such a condition for encoding with rate 1, under an additional hypothesis:

Theorem 4. *Assuming that $c : T \mapsto \mathcal{C}_{\varepsilon'}(C_T)$ is super-additive and that $\mathcal{BH}_\varepsilon(S)$ is a limit, then, if $\mathcal{BH}_\varepsilon(S) < \mathcal{BC}_{\varepsilon'}(C)$, there exists an (S, C)-encoding with precision $(\varepsilon, \varepsilon')$ and rate 1.*

Let us recall that ε-entropy can be seen as the minimal information necessary to describe any word, taken from the language, with precision ε, while ε-capacity can be interpreted as the maximal information that can be conveyed through distinguishable words of a language. In an encoding, we try to describe every word in S and to encode them in C in such a way that they are distinguishable. So, the proposition states that whenever the channel makes it possible to distinguish as many words as it is necessary to describe any word from the source, an encoding exists.

Proof. We first note that both bandwidths are actual limits. Let A and B be their values ($A < B$) and $\xi = \frac{A+B}{2}$.

There is a Δ such that $\frac{\mathcal{C}_{\varepsilon'}(C_\Delta)}{\Delta} > \xi$ (and we can choose Δ big enough so that $(2^{\xi\Delta} - 1) > 1$). Capacity C being super-additive, we have for all T that $\mathcal{C}_{\varepsilon'}(C_{T+\Delta+\varepsilon'}) > \mathcal{C}_{\varepsilon'}(C_{T+\varepsilon'}) + \xi\Delta$.

Let m be the function giving a maximal ε'-separated set of a given set, and n the one giving a minimal ε-net. Then $m(C_{T+\Delta+\varepsilon'}) \cap \{w|\tau(w) \le T + \varepsilon'\}$ is ε'-separated and included in $C_{T+\varepsilon'}$, its cardinality is smaller or equal than $\#m(C_{T+\varepsilon'})$, then

$$\#m(C_{T+\Delta+\varepsilon'}) > \#m(C_{T+\varepsilon'}) \cdot 2^{\xi\Delta};$$
$$\#(m(C_{T+\Delta+\varepsilon'}) \cap \{w|\tau(w) > T + \varepsilon'\}) > \#m(C_{T+\varepsilon'}) \cdot (2^{\xi\Delta} - 1);$$
$$\#(m(C_{T+\Delta+\varepsilon'}) \cap \{w|\tau(w) > T + \varepsilon'\}) > \#n(S_T) \cdot (2^{\xi\Delta} - 1) > \#n(S_T).$$

We choose T so that $\#m(C_T) > \#n(S_T)$. We consider ε'-separated sets and ε-nets, we enumerate them (they will be denoted $c_1, \ldots c_m$ and $h_1, \ldots h_n$, $n < m$, the notation is a little heavy but it bears little significance in the following). We construct the encoding of words of length at most T as follows: given a word, we take the first h_i word being ε-near to it and we take its image to be c_i.

We the n consider a step $t > \Delta$. We will look at times in $T + \mathbb{N}t$. For each T_i such time, $m(C_{T_i+\Delta+\varepsilon'} \backslash C_{T_i+\varepsilon'}) > n(S_T)$. This allows us to consider an ε-net of S_T, and an ε'-separated set of $C_{T_i+\Delta+\varepsilon'} \backslash C_{T_i+\varepsilon'}$ and encode the missing words of S_T as was done before (the new c_j are all distanced by at least ε' with the previous ones). Once we've done this, there is an encoding for all words of time at most T_i. As t is constant, by repeating this manoeuvre, all words in S will have an encoding (by induction). It is easy to verify that the defined function is an (S, C)-encoding.

5   Conclusion and Further Work

Information and coding theory for timed languages is in its early stages. In [2] its groundwork has been laid, with information measured in bits per event, and codings preserving the number of events. In the current paper, we took a new angle, more relevant to real-time applications, to tackle the notion of quantity of information by unit of the time. We defined the bandwidth of a timed language and characterized the possibility of coding in terms of bandwidth comparison.

At this stage of the research, many important questions are still unsettled. It would be interesting to know more on the properties of the bandwidth, e.g. prove Theorems 1–2 without stringent hypotheses. Computability of the (numerical) value of the bandwidth of a timed regular language and, if applicable, complexity for computing it, as well as practical algorithms to that aim, are to be explored. They constitute the subject of an ongoing work.

The necessary condition for existence of a timed code is satisfactory: if the bandwidth inequality does not hold, it is impossible to code. But the sufficient condition in its current form only states theoretical feasibility, without describing a practical method for coding, other than an unrealistic enumeration-based one. We believe that the identification of a relevant class of timed transducers, allowing for a definition of coding and synthesis of codes based on it, is an important challenge.

Last but not least, practical applications of timed coding are to be identified and realized.

References

1. Alur, R., Dill, D.L.: A theory of timed automata. Theor. Comput. Sci. **126**(2), 183–235 (1994). https://doi.org/10.1016/0304-3975(94)90010-8
2. Asarin, E., Basset, N., Béal, M.-P., Degorre, A., Perrin, D.: Toward a timed theory of channel coding. In: Jurdziński, M., Ničković, D. (eds.) FORMATS 2012. LNCS, vol. 7595, pp. 27–42. Springer, Heidelberg (2012). https://doi.org/10.1007/978-3-642-33365-1_4
3. Asarin, E., Basset, N., Degorre, A.: Distance on timed words and applications. In: Jansen, D.N., Prabhakar, P. (eds.) FORMATS 2018. LNCS, vol. 11022, pp. 199–214. Springer, Cham (2018). https://doi.org/10.1007/978-3-030-00151-3_12
4. Blahut, R.E.: Digital Transmission of Information. Addison Wesley, Boston (1990)
5. Fekete, M.: Über die Verteilung der Wurzeln bei gewissen algebraischen Gleichungen mit ganzzahligen Koeffizienten. Math. Z. **17**, 228–249 (1923). https://doi.org/10.1007/BF01504345
6. Immink, K.: EFMPlus: the coding format of the multimedia compact disc. IEEE Trans. Consum. Electron. **41**(3), 491–497 (1995). https://doi.org/10.1109/30.468040
7. Kocher, P., et al.: Spectre attacks: exploiting speculative execution. In: IEEE Symposium on Security and Privacy (S&P 2019) (2019). https://doi.org/10.1109/SP.2019.00002
8. Kocher, P.C.: Timing attacks on implementations of Diffie-Hellman, RSA, DSS, and other systems. In: Koblitz, N. (ed.) CRYPTO 1996. LNCS, vol. 1109, pp. 104–113. Springer, Heidelberg (1996). https://doi.org/10.1007/3-540-68697-5_9
9. Kolmogorov, A.N., Tikhomirov, V.M.: ε-entropy and ε-capacity of sets in function spaces. Uspekhi Matematicheskikh Nauk **14**(2), 3–86 (1959). https://doi.org/10.1007/978-94-017-2973-4_7. http://mi.mathnet.ru/eng/umn7289
10. Lind, D., Marcus, B.: An Introduction to Symbolic Dynamics and Coding. Cambridge University Press, Cambridge (1995)
11. Lipp, M., et al.: Meltdown: reading kernel memory from user space. Commun. ACM **63**(6), 46–56 (2020). https://doi.org/10.1145/3357033

Robustly Complete Finite-State Abstractions for Verification of Stochastic Systems

Yiming Meng$^{(\boxtimes)}$ and Jun Liu$^{(\boxtimes)}$

University of Waterloo, Waterloo, ON N2L 3G1, Canada
{yiming.meng,j.liu}@uwaterloo.ca

Abstract. In this paper, we focus on discrete-time stochastic systems modelled by nonlinear stochastic difference equations and propose robust abstractions for verifying probabilistic linear temporal specifications. The current literature focuses on developing sound abstraction techniques for stochastic dynamics without perturbations. However, soundness thus far has only been shown for preserving the satisfaction probability of certain types of temporal-logic specification. We present constructive finite-state abstractions for verifying probabilistic satisfaction of general ω-regular linear-time properties of more general nonlinear stochastic systems. Instead of imposing stability assumptions, we analyze the probabilistic properties from the topological view of metrizable space of probability measures. Such abstractions are both sound and approximately complete. That is, given a concrete discrete-time stochastic system and an arbitrarily small $\mathcal{L}_1$-perturbation of this system, there exists a family of finite-state Markov chains whose set of satisfaction probabilities contains that of the original system and meanwhile is contained by that of the slightly perturbed system. A direct consequence is that, given a probabilistic linear-time specification, initializing within the winning/losing region of the abstraction system can guarantee a satisfaction/dissatisfaction for the original system. We make an interesting observation that, unlike the deterministic case, point-mass (Dirac) perturbations cannot fulfill the purpose of robust completeness.

Keywords: Verification of stochastic systems · Finite-state abstraction · Robustness · Soundness · Completeness · $\mathcal{L}_1$-perturbation · Linear temporal logic · Metrizable space of probability measures

1 Introduction

Formal verification is a rigorous mathematical technique for verifying system properties using formal analysis or model checking [4]. So far, abstraction-based formal verification for deterministic systems has gained its maturity [5]. Whilst bisimilar (equivalent) symbolic models exist for linear (control) systems [17,30], sound and approximately complete finite abstractions can be achieved via stability assumptions [14,25] or robustness (in terms of Dirac perturbations) [19–21].

© Springer Nature Switzerland AG 2022
S. Bogomolov and D. Parker (Eds.): FORMATS 2022, LNCS 13465, pp. 80–97, 2022.
https://doi.org/10.1007/978-3-031-15839-1_5

There is a recent surge of interest in studying formal verification for stochastic systems. The verification of temporal logics for discrete-state homogeneous Markov chains can be solved by existing tools [4,6,9,24].

In terms of verification for general discrete-time continuous-state Markov systems, a common theme is to construct abstractions to approximate the probability of satisfaction in proper ways. First attempts [2,3,26,28,29] were to relate the verification of fundamental probabilistic computation tree logic (PCTL) formulas to the computation of corresponding value functions. The authors [31,32] developed alternative techniques to deal with the potential error blow-up in infinite-horizon problems. The same authors [34] investigated the necessity of absorbing sets on the uniqueness of the solutions of corresponding Bellman equations. The related PCTL verification problem can be then precisely captured by finite-horizon ones. They also proposed abstractions for verifying general bounded linear-time (LT) properties [33], and extended them to infinite-horizon reach-avoid and repeated reachability problems [33,35].

Markov set-chains are also constructive to be abstractions. The authors [1] showed that the error is finite under strong assumptions on stability (ergodicity). A closely related approach is to apply interval-valued Markov chains (IMCs), a family of finite-state Markov chains with uncertain transitions, as abstractions for the continuous-state Markov systems with certain transition kernel. The authors [18] argued without proof that for every PCTL formula, the probability of (path) satisfaction of the IMC abstractions forms a compact interval, which contains the real probability of the original system. They further developed 'O'-maximizing/minimizing algorithms based on [15,38] to obtain the upper/lower bound of the satisfaction probability of 'next', 'bounded until', and 'until' properties. The algorithm provides a fundamental view of computing the bounds of satisfaction probability given IMCs. However, the intuitive reasoning for soundness seems inaccurate based on our observation (readers who are interested in the details are referred to Remark 6 of this paper). Inspired by [18], the work in [7] formulated IMC abstraction for verifying bounded-LTL specifications; the work in [11,12] constructed IMC abstractions for verifying general ω-regular properties of mixed-monotone systems, and provided a novel automata-based approach in obtaining the bounds of satisfaction probability. Both [11,12, Fact 1] and [10] claimed the soundness of verifying general ω-regular properties using IMC abstractions, but a proof is not provided.

Motivated by these issues, our first contribution is to provide a formal mathematical proof of the soundness of IMC abstractions for verifying ω-regular linear-time properties. We show that, for any discrete-time stochastic dynamical systems modelled by a stochastic difference equation and any linear-time property, an IMC abstraction returns a compact interval of probability of (path) satisfaction which contains the satisfaction probability of the original system. A direct consequence is that starting within the winning/losing region computed by the abstraction can guarantee a satisfaction/dissatisfaction for the original system. The second contribution of this paper is to deal with stochastic systems with extra uncertain perturbations (due to, e.g., measurement errors or modeling uncertainties). Under mild assumptions, we show that, in verifying probabilistic satisfaction of general ω-regular linear-time properties, IMC abstractions that are both sound and approximately complete are constructible for nonlinear stochastic systems. That is, given a concrete discrete-time continuous-state Markov system $\mathbb{X}$, and an arbitrarily small $\mathcal{L}_1$-bounded perturbation of this system, there exists an IMC abstraction whose set of satisfaction probability contains that of $\mathbb{X}$, and meanwhile is contained by that of the slightly perturbed system. We argue in Sect. 4 that to make the IMC abstraction robustly complete, the perturbation is generally necessary to be $\mathcal{L}_1$-bounded rather than only bounded in terms of point mass. We analyze the probabilistic properties based on the topology of metrizable space of (uncertain) probability measures, and show that the technique proves more powerful than purely discussing the value of probabilities. We also would like to clarify that the main purpose of this paper is not on providing more efficient algorithms for computing abstractions. We aim to provide a theoretical foundation of IMC abstractions for verifying continuous-state stochastic systems with perturbations and hope to shed some light on designing more powerful robust verification algorithms.

The rest of the paper is organized as follows. Section 2 presents some preliminaries on probability spaces and Markov systems. Section 3 presents the soundness of abstractions in verifying ω-regular linear-time properties for discrete-time nonlinear stochastic systems. Section 4 presents the constructive robust abstractions with soundness and approximate completeness guarantees. We discuss the differences of robustness between deterministic and stochastic systems. The paper is concluded in Sect. 5.

Notation: We denote by $\prod$ the product of ordinary sets, spaces, or function values. Denote by $\otimes$ the product of collections of sets, or sigma algebras, or measures. The n-times repeated product of any kind is denoted by $(\cdot)^n$ for simplification. Denote by $\pi_j : \prod_{i=0}^{\infty}(\cdot)_i \to (\cdot)_j$ the projection to the jth component. We denote by $\mathscr{B}(\cdot)$ the Borel σ-algebra of a set.

Let $|\cdot|$ denote the infinity norm in $\mathbb{R}^n$, and let $\mathbb{B} := \{x \in \mathbb{R}^n : |x| \le 1\}$. We denote by $\|\cdot\|_1 := \mathcal{E}|\cdot|$ the $\mathcal{L}_1$-norm for $\mathbb{R}^n$-valued random variables, and let $\mathbb{B}_1 := \{X : \mathbb{R}^n$-valued random variable with $\|X\|_1 \le 1\}$. Given a matrix M, we denote by M_i its ith row and by M_{ij} its entry at i^{th} row and j^{th} column.

Given a general state space $\mathcal{X}$, we denote by $\mathfrak{P}(\mathcal{X})$ the space of probability measures. The space of bounded and continuous functions on $\mathcal{X}$ is denoted by $C_b(\mathcal{X})$. For any stochastic processes $\{X_t\}_{t \ge 0}$, we use the shorthand notation $X := \{X_t\}_{t \ge 0}$. For any stopped process $\{X_{t \wedge \tau}\}_{t \ge 0}$, where τ is a stopping time, we use the shorthand notation X^τ.

2   Preliminaries

We consider $\mathbb{N} = \{0, 1, \cdots\}$ as the discrete time index set, and a general Polish (complete and separable metric) space $\mathcal{X}$ as the state space. For any discrete-time $\mathcal{X}^\infty$-valued stochastic process X, we introduce some standard concepts.

2.1 Canonical Sample Space

Given a stochastic process X defined on some (most likely unknown) probability space $(\Omega^\dagger, \mathscr{F}^\dagger, \mathbb{P}^\dagger)$. Since we only care about the probabilistic behavior of trajectories in the state space, we prefer to work on the canonical probability spaces $(\Omega, \mathcal{F}, \mathcal{P}) := (\mathcal{X}^\infty, \mathscr{B}(\mathcal{X}^\infty), \mathbb{P}^\dagger \circ X^{-1})$ and regard events as sets of sample paths (see details in [23, Section 2.1]). We denote by $\mathcal{E}$ the associated expectation. In the context of discrete state spaces $\mathcal{X}$, we specifically use the boldface notation $(\mathbf{\Omega}, \mathbf{F}, \mathbf{P})$ for the canonical spaces of some discrete-state processes.

Remark 1. *We usually denote by ν_i the marginal distribution of $\mathcal{P}$ at some $i \in \mathbb{N}$. We can informally write the n-dimensional distribution (on n-dimensional cylinder set) as $\mathcal{P}(\cdot) = \otimes_{i=1}^n \nu_i(\cdot)$ regardless of the dependence.*

2.2 Markov Transition Systems

For any discrete-time stochastic process X, we set $\mathcal{F}_t = \sigma\{X_0, X_1, \cdots, X_t\}$ to be the natural filtration.

Definition 1 (Markov process). *A stochastic process X is said to be a Markov process if each X_t is $\mathcal{F}_t$-adapted and, for any $\Gamma \in \mathscr{B}(\mathcal{X})$ and $t > s$, we have*

$$\mathcal{P}[X_t \in \Gamma \mid \mathcal{F}_s] = \mathcal{P}[X_t \in \Gamma \mid \sigma\{X_s\}], \quad a.s. \tag{1}$$

Correspondingly, for every t, we define the transition probability as

$$\Theta_t(x, \Gamma) := \mathcal{P}[X_{t+1} \in \Gamma \mid X_t = x], \quad \Gamma \in \mathscr{B}(\mathcal{X}). \tag{2}$$

We denote $\Theta_t := \{\Theta_t(x, \Gamma) : x \in \mathcal{X}, \Gamma \in \mathscr{B}(\mathcal{X})\}$ as the family of transition probabilities at time t. Note that homogeneous Markov processes are special cases such that $\Theta_t = \Theta_s$ for all $t, s \in \mathbb{N}$.

We are interested in Markov processes with discrete observations of states, which is done by assigning abstract labels over a finite set of atomic propositions. We define an abstract family of labelled Markov processes as follows.

Definition 2 (Markov system). *A Markov system is a tuple $\mathbb{X} = (\mathcal{X}, [\![\Theta]\!], \Pi, L)$, where*

- *$\mathcal{X} = \mathcal{W} \cup \Delta$, where $\mathcal{W}$ is a bounded working space, $\Delta := \mathcal{W}^c$ represents all the out-of-domain states;*
- *$[\![\Theta]\!]$ is a collection of transition probabilities from which Θ_t is chosen for every t;*
- *Π is the finite set of atomic propositions;*
- *$L : \mathcal{X} \to 2^\Pi$ is the (Borel-measurable) labelling function.*

For $X \in \mathbb{X}$ with $X_0 = x_0$ a.s., we denote by $\mathcal{P}_X^{x_0}$ the law, and $\{\mathcal{P}_X^{x_0}\}_{X \in \mathbb{X}}$ by its collection. Similarly, for any initial distribution $\nu_0 \in \mathfrak{P}(\mathcal{X})$, we define the law by $\mathcal{P}_X^{\nu_0}(\cdot) = \int_{\mathcal{X}} \mathcal{P}_X^x(\cdot) \nu_0(dx)$, and denote $\{\mathcal{P}_X^{\nu_0}\}_{X \in \mathbb{X}}$ by its collection. We denote by $\{\mathcal{P}_n^{q_0}\}_{n=0}^\infty$ (resp. $\{\mathcal{P}_n^{\nu_0}\}_{n=0}^\infty$) a sequence of $\{\mathcal{P}_X^{x_0}\}_{X \in \mathbb{X}}$ (resp. $\{\mathcal{P}_X^{\nu_0}\}_{X \in \mathbb{X}}$). We simply use $\mathcal{P}_X$ (resp. $\{\mathcal{P}_X\}_{X \in \mathbb{X}}$) if we do not emphasize the initial condition.

For a path $\varpi := \varpi_0 \varpi_1 \varpi_2 \cdots \in \Omega$, define by $L_\varpi := L(\varpi_0)L(\varpi_1)L(\varpi_2) \cdots$ its trace. The space of infinite words is denoted by

$$(2^\Pi)^\omega = \{A_0 A_1 A_2 \cdots : A_i \in 2^\Pi, \ i = 0, 1, 2 \cdots \}.$$

A linear-time (LT) property is a subset of $(2^\Pi)^\omega$. We are only interested in LT properties Ψ such that $\Psi \in \mathscr{B}((2^\Pi)^\omega)$, i.e., those are Borel-measurable.

Remark 2. *Note that, by [35] and [36, Proposition 2.3], any ω-regular language of labelled Markov processes is measurable. It follows that, for any Markov process X of the given $\mathbb{X}$, the traces L_ϖ generated by measurable labelling functions are also measurable. For each $\Psi \in \mathscr{B}((2^\Pi)^\omega)$, we have the event $L_\varpi^{-1}(\Psi) \in \mathcal{F}$.*

A particular subclass of LT properties can be specified by linear temporal logic (LTL)[1]. To connect with LTL specifications, we introduce the semantics of path satisfaction as well as probabilistic satisfaction as follows.

Definition 3. *For the syntax of LTL formulae Ψ and the semantics of satisfaction of Ψ on infinite words, we refer readers to [20, Section 2.4].*

For a given labelled Markov process X from $\mathbb{X}$ with initial distribution ν_0, we formulate the canonical space $(\Omega, \mathcal{F}, \mathcal{P}_X^{\nu_0})$. For a path $\varpi \in \Omega$, we define the path satisfaction as

$$\varpi \vDash \Psi \iff L_\varpi \vDash \Psi.$$

We denote by $\{X \vDash \Psi\} := \{\varpi : \varpi \vDash \Psi\} \in \mathcal{F}$ the events of path satisfaction. Given a specified probability $\rho \in [0,1]$, we define the probabilistic satisfaction of Ψ as

$$X \vDash \mathcal{P}_{\bowtie \rho}^{\nu_0}[\Psi] \iff \mathcal{P}_X^{\nu_0}\{X \vDash \Psi\} \bowtie \rho,$$

where $\bowtie \in \{\leq, <, \geq, >\}$.

2.3 Weak Convergence and Prokhorov's Theorem

We consider the set of possible uncertain measures within the topological space of probability measures. The following concepts are frequently used later.

Definition 4 (Tightness of set of measures). *Let $\mathcal{X}$ be any topological state space and $M \subseteq \mathfrak{P}(\mathcal{X})$ be a set of probability measures on $\mathcal{X}$. We say that M is tight if, for every $\varepsilon > 0$ there exists a compact set $K \subset \mathcal{X}$ such that $\mu(K) \geq 1 - \varepsilon$ for every $\mu \in M$.*

Definition 5 (Weak convergence). *A sequence $\{\mu_n\}_{n=0}^\infty \subseteq \mathfrak{P}(\mathcal{X})$ is said to converge weakly to a probability measure μ, denoted by $\mu_n \Rightarrow \mu$, if*

$$\int_\mathcal{X} h(x)\mu_n(dx) \to \int_\mathcal{X} h(x)\mu(dx), \quad \forall h \in C_b(\mathcal{X}). \tag{3}$$

We frequently use the following alternative condition [8, Proposition 2.2]:

$$\mu_n(A) \to \mu(A), \quad \forall A \in \mathscr{B}(\mathcal{X}) \ s.t. \ \mu(\partial A) = 0. \tag{4}$$

---

[1] While we consider LTL due to our interest, it can be easily seen that all results of this paper in fact hold for any measurable LT property, including ω-regular specifications.

It is straightforward from Definition 5 that weak convergence of measures also describes the convergence of probabilistic properties. We refer readers to [27] and [23, Remark 3] for more details on the weak topology.

Theorem 1 (Prokhorov). *Let $\mathcal{X}$ be a complete separable metric space. A family $\Lambda \subseteq \mathfrak{P}(\mathcal{X})$ is relatively compact if and only if it is tight. Consequently, for each sequence $\{\mu_n\}$ of tight Λ, there exists a $\mu \in \bar{\Lambda}$ and a subsequence $\{\mu_{n_k}\}$ such that $\mu_{n_k} \Rightarrow \mu$.*

Remark 3. *The first part of Prokhorov's theorem provides an alternative criterion for verifying the compactness of family of measures w.r.t. the corresponding metric space using tightness. On a compact metric space $\mathcal{X}$, every family of probability measures is tight.*

2.4 Discrete-Time Continuous-State Stochastic Systems

We define Markov processes determined by the difference equation

$$X_{t+1} = f(X_t) + b(X_t)w_t + \vartheta \xi_t \tag{5}$$

where the state $X_t(\varpi) \in \mathcal{X} \subseteq \mathbb{R}^n$ for all $t \in \mathbb{N}$, the stochastic inputs $\{w_t\}_{t \in \mathbb{N}}$ are i.i.d. Gaussian random variables with covariance $I_{k \times k}$ without loss of generality. Mappings $f : \mathbb{R}^n \to \mathbb{R}^n$ and $b : \mathbb{R}^n \to \mathbb{R}^{n \times k}$ are locally Lipschitz continuous. The memoryless perturbation $\xi_t \in \mathbb{B}_1$ are independent random variables with intensity $\vartheta \geq 0$ and unknown distributions.

For $\vartheta \neq 0$, (5) defines a family $\mathbb{X}$ of Markov processes X. A special case of (5) is such that ξ has Dirac (point-mass) distributions $\{\delta_x : x \in \mathbb{B}\}$ centered at some uncertain points within a unit ball.

Remark 4. *Gaussian random variables are naturally selected to simulate Brownian motions at discrete times. Note that in [11], random variables are used with known unimodal symmetric density with an interval as the support. Their choice is in favor of the mixed-monotone models to provide a more accurate approximation of transition probabilities. Other than the precision issue, such a choice does not bring us more of the other $\mathcal{L}_1$ properties. Since we focus on formal analysis based on $\mathcal{L}_1$ properties rather than providing accurate approximation, using Gaussian randomnesses as a realization does not lose any generality.*

We only care about the behaviors in the bounded working space $\mathcal{W}$. By defining stopping time $\tau := \inf\{t \in \mathbb{N} : X \notin \mathcal{W}\}$ for each X, we are able to study the probability law of the corresponding stopped (killed) process X^τ for any initial condition x_0 (resp. ν_0), which coincides with $\mathcal{P}_X^{x_0}$ (resp. $\mathcal{P}_X^{\nu_0}$) on $\mathcal{W}$. To avoid any complexity, we use the same notation X and $\mathcal{P}_X^{x_0}$ (resp. $\mathcal{P}_X^{\nu_0}$) to denote the stopped processes and the associated laws. Such processes driven by (5) can be written as a Markov system

$$\mathbb{X} = (\mathcal{X}, \llbracket T \rrbracket, \Pi, L), \tag{6}$$

where for all $x \in \mathcal{X} \setminus W$, the transition probability should satisfy $\mathcal{T}(x, \Gamma) = 0$ for all $\Gamma \cap W \neq \emptyset$; $\llbracket \mathcal{T} \rrbracket$ is the collection of transition probabilities. For ξ having Dirac distributions, the transition $\mathcal{T}$ is of the following form:

$$\mathcal{T}(x, \cdot) \in \begin{cases} \{\mu \sim \mathcal{N}(f(x) + \vartheta\xi, \ b(x)b^T(x)), \ \xi \in \mathbb{B}\}, \ \forall x \in W, \\ \{\mu : \mu(\Gamma) = 0, \ \forall \Gamma \cap W \neq \emptyset\}, \ \forall x \in \mathcal{X} \setminus W. \end{cases} \quad (7)$$

Assumption 1. *We assume that $in \in L(x)$ for any $x \notin \Delta$ and $in \notin L(\Delta)$. We can also include 'always (in)' in the specifications to observe sample paths for 'inside-domain' behaviors, which is equivalent to verifying $\{\tau = \infty\}$.*

2.5 Robust Abstractions

We define a notion of abstraction between continuous-state and finite-state Markov systems via state-level relations and measure-level relations.

Definition 6. *A (binary) relation γ from A to B is a subset of $A \times B$ satisfying (i) for each $a \in A$, $\gamma(a) := \{b \in B : (a, b) \in \gamma\}$; (ii) for each $b \in B$, $\gamma^{-1}(b) := \{a \in A : (a, b) \in \gamma\}$; (iii) for $A' \subseteq A$, $\gamma(A') = \cup_{a \in A'} \gamma(a)$; (iv) and for $B' \subseteq B$, $\gamma^{-1}(B') = \cup_{b \in B'} \gamma^{-1}(b)$.*

Definition 7. *Given a continuous-state Markov system*

$$\mathbb{X} = (\mathcal{X}, \llbracket \mathcal{T} \rrbracket, \Pi, L)$$

and a finite-state Markov system

$$\mathbb{I} = (\mathcal{Q}, \llbracket \Theta \rrbracket, \Pi, L_{\mathbb{I}}),$$

where $\mathcal{Q} = (q_1, \cdots, q_n)^T$ and $\llbracket \Theta \rrbracket$ stands for a collection of $n \times n$ stochastic matrices. A state-level relation $\alpha \subseteq \mathcal{X} \times \mathcal{Q}$ is said to be an abstraction from $\mathbb{X}$ to $\mathbb{I}$ if (i) for all $x \in \mathcal{X}$, there exists $q \in \mathcal{Q}$ such that $(x, q) \in \alpha$; (ii) for all $(x, q) \in \alpha$, $L_{\mathbb{I}}(q) = L(x)$.

A measure-level relation $\gamma_\alpha \subseteq \mathfrak{P}(\mathcal{X}) \times \mathfrak{P}(\mathcal{Q})$ is said to be an abstraction from $\mathbb{X}$ to $\mathbb{I}$ if for all $i \in \{1, 2, \cdots, n\}$, all $\mathcal{T} \in \llbracket \mathcal{T} \rrbracket$ and all $x \in \alpha^{-1}(q_i)$, there exists $\Theta \in \llbracket \Theta \rrbracket$ such that $(\mathcal{T}(x, \cdot), \Theta_i) \in \gamma_\alpha$ and that $\mathcal{T}(x, \alpha^{-1}(q_j)) = \Theta_{ij}$ for all $j \in \{1, 2, \cdots, n\}$.

Similarly, $\gamma_\alpha \subseteq \mathfrak{P}(\mathcal{Q}) \times \mathfrak{P}(\mathcal{X})$ is said to be an abstraction from $\mathbb{I}$ to $\mathbb{X}$ if for all $i \in \{1, 2, \cdots, n\}$, all $\Theta \in \llbracket \Theta \rrbracket$ and all $x \in \alpha^{-1}(q_i)$, there exists $\mathcal{T} \in \llbracket \mathcal{T} \rrbracket$ such that $(\Theta_i, \mathcal{T}(x, \cdot)) \in \gamma_\alpha$ and that $\mathcal{T}(x, \alpha^{-1}(q_j)) = \Theta_{ij}$ for all $j \in \{1, 2, \cdots, n\}$.

If such relations α and γ_α exist, we say that $\mathbb{I}$ abstracts $\mathbb{X}$ (resp. $\mathbb{X}$ abstracts $\mathbb{I}$) and write $\mathbb{X} \preceq_{\gamma_\alpha} \mathbb{I}$ (resp. $\mathbb{I} \preceq_{\gamma_\alpha} \mathbb{X}$).

Assumption 2. *Without loss of generality, we assume that the labelling function is amenable to a rectangular partition[2]. In other words, a state-level abstraction can be obtained from a rectangular partition.*

---

[2] See e.g. [11, Definition 1].

3 Soundness of Robust IMC Abstractions

IMCs[3] are quasi-Markov systems on a discrete state space with upper/under approximations $(\hat{\Theta}/\check{\Theta})$ of the real transition matrices. To abstract the transition probabilities of continuous-state Markov systems (6), $\hat{\Theta}$ and $\check{\Theta}$ are obtained from over/under approximations of $\mathcal{T}$ based on the state space partition. Throughout this section, we assume that $\hat{\Theta}$ and $\check{\Theta}$ have been correspondingly constructed.

Given an IMC, we recast it to a true finite-state Markov system

$$\mathbb{I} = (\mathcal{Q}, [\![\Theta]\!], \Pi, L_{\mathbb{I}}),\tag{8}$$

where

- $\mathcal{Q}$ is the finite state-space partition with dimension $N+1$ containing $\{\Delta\}$, i.e., $\mathcal{Q} = (q_1, q_2, \cdots, q_N, \Delta)^T$;
- $[\![\Theta]\!]^4$ is a set of stochastic matrices satisfying

$$[\![\Theta]\!] = \{\Theta : \text{stochastic matrices with } \check{\Theta} \leq \Theta \leq \hat{\Theta} \text{ componentwisely}\};\tag{9}$$

- $\Pi, L_{\mathbb{I}}$ are as before.

To make $\mathbb{I}$ an abstraction for (8), we need the approximation to be such that $\check{\Theta}_{ij} \leq \int_{q_j} \mathcal{T}(x, dy) \leq \hat{\Theta}_{ij}$ for all $x \in q_i$ and $i, j = 1, \cdots, N$, as well as $\Theta_{N+1} = (0, 0, \cdots, 1)$. We further require that the partition should respect the boundaries induced by the labeling function, i.e., for any $q \in \mathcal{Q}$,

$$L_{\mathbb{I}}(q) := L(x), \ \forall x \in q.$$

Clearly, the above connections on the state and transition probabilities satisfy Definition 7.

The Markov system $\mathbb{I}$ is understood as a family of 'perturbed' Markov chains generated by the uncertain choice of Θ for each t. The n-step transition matrices are derived based on $[\![\Theta]\!]$ as

$$[\![\Theta^{(2)}]\!] = \{\Theta_0 \Theta_1 : \ \Theta_0, \Theta_1 \in [\![\Theta]\!]\},$$
$$\cdots$$
$$[\![\Theta^{(n)}]\!] = \{\Theta_0 \Theta_1 \cdots \Theta_n : \ \Theta_i \in [\![\Theta]\!], \ i = 0, 1, \cdots, n\}.$$

Given an initial distribution $\mu_0 \in \mathfrak{P}(\mathcal{Q})$, the marginal probability measure at each t forms a set

$$\mathfrak{P}(\mathcal{Q}) \supseteq \mathcal{M}_t^{\mu_0} := \{\mu_t = (\Theta^{(t)})^T \mu_0 : \ \Theta^{(t)} \in [\![\Theta^{(t)}]\!]\}.\tag{10}$$

If we do not emphasize the initial distribution μ_0, we also use $\mathcal{M}_t$ to denote the marginals for short.

We aim to show the soundness of robust IMC abstractions in this section. The proofs in this section are completed in [23].

---

[3] We omit the definition from this paper due to the limitation of space. For a formal definition see e.g. [18, Definition 3].

[4] This is a necessary step to guarantee proper probability measures in (10). Algorithms can be found in [16] or [18, Section V-A].

3.1 Weak Compactness of Marginal Space $\mathscr{M}_t$ of Probabilities

The following lemma is rephrased from [37, Theorem 2] and shows the structure of the $\mathscr{M}_t$ for each $t \in \mathbb{N}$ and any initial distribution μ_0.

Lemma 1. *Let $\mathbb{I}$ be a Markov system of the form (8) that is derived from an IMC. Then the set $\mathscr{M}_t$ of all possible probability measures at each time $t \in \mathbb{N}$ is a convex polytope, and immediately is compact. The vertices of $\mathscr{M}_t$ are of the form*

$$(V_{i_t})^T \cdots (V_{i_2})^T (V_{i_1})^T \mu_0 \tag{11}$$

for some vertices V_{i_j} of $[\![\Theta]\!]$.

An illustrative example is provided in [23, Example 1]. Now we introduce the total variation distance $\| \cdot \|_{\mathrm{TV}}$ and see how $(\mathscr{M}_t, \| \cdot \|_{\mathrm{TV}})$ (at each t) implies the weak topology.

Definition 8 (Total variation distance). *Given two probability measures μ and ν on $\mathcal{X}$, the total variation distance is defined as*

$$\|\mu - \nu\|_{TV} = 2 \sup_{\Gamma \in \mathscr{B}(\mathcal{X})} |\mu(\Gamma) - \nu(\Gamma)|. \tag{12}$$

In particular, if $\mathcal{X}$ is a discrete space, $\|\mu - \nu\|_{TV} = \sum_{q \in \mathcal{X}} |\mu(q) - \nu(q)|$ (1-norm).

Corollary 1. *Let $\mathbb{I}$ be a Markov system of the form (8) that is derived from an IMC. Then at each time $t \in \mathbb{N}$, for each $\{\mu_n\} \subseteq \mathscr{M}_t$, there exists a $\mu \in \mathscr{M}_t$ and a subsequence $\{\mu_{n_k}\}$ such that $\mu_{n_k} \Rightarrow \mu$. In addition, for each $h \in C_b(\mathcal{X})$ and $t \in \mathbb{N}$, the set $H = \{\sum_{\mathcal{X}} h(x)\mu(x), \ \mu \in \mathscr{M}_t\}$ forms a convex and compact subset in $\mathbb{R}$.*

Remark 5. *Note that since $\mathcal{Q}$ is bounded and finite, any metrizable family of measures on $\mathcal{Q}$ is compact. However, the convexity does not hold in general (see [23, Remark 6] for details).*

3.2 Weak Compactness of Probability Laws of $\mathbb{I}$ on Infinite Horizon

We focus on the case where $I_0 = q_0$ a.s. for any $q_0 \in \mathcal{Q} \setminus \{\Delta\}$. The cases for arbitrary initial distribution should be similar. We formally denote $\mathscr{M}^{q_0} := \{\mathbf{P}_I^{q_0}\}_{I \in \mathbb{I}}$ by the set of probability laws of every discrete-state Markov processes $I \in \mathbb{I}$ with initial state $q_0 \in \mathcal{Q}$. We denote $\mathscr{M}_t^{q_0}$ by the set of marginals at t.

Proposition 1. *For any $q_0 \in \mathcal{Q}$, every sequence $\{\mathbf{P}_n^{q_0}\}_{n=0}^{\infty}$ of $\mathscr{M}^{q_0}$ has a weakly convergent subsequence.*

The above property is an extension of the marginal weak compactness relying on the (countable) product topology. The following result demonstrates the probabilistic regularity of general IMC abstractions.

Theorem 2. *Let $\mathbb{I}$ be a Markov system of the form (8) that is derived from an IMC. Then for any LTL formula Ψ, the set $S^{q_0} = \{\mathbf{P}_I^{q_0}(I \vDash \Psi)\}_{I \in \mathbb{I}}$ is a convex and compact subset in $\mathbb{R}$, i.e., a compact interval.*

3.3 Soundness of IMC Abstractions

Proposition 2. *Let $\mathbb{X}$ be a Markov system driven by (6). Then every sequence $\{\mathcal{P}_n^{x_0}\}_{n=0}^{\infty}$ of $\{\mathcal{P}_X^{x_0}\}_{X \in \mathbb{X}}$ has a weakly convergent subsequence. Consequently, for any LTL formula Ψ, the set $\{\mathcal{P}_X^{x_0}(X \vDash \Psi)\}_{X \in \mathbb{X}}$ is a compact subset in $\mathbb{R}$.*

Lemma 2. *Let $X \in \mathbb{X}$ be any Markov process driven by (6) and $\mathbb{I}$ be the finite-state IMC abstraction of $\mathbb{X}$. Suppose the initial distribution ν_0 of X is such that $\nu_0(q_0) = 1$. Then, there exists a unique law $\mathbf{P}_I^{q_0}$ of some $I \in \mathbb{I}$ such that, for any LTL formula Ψ,*

$$\mathcal{P}_X^{\nu_0}(X \vDash \Psi) = \mathbf{P}_I^{q_0}(I \vDash \Psi).$$

Theorem 3. *Assume the settings in Lemma 2. For any LTL formula Ψ, we have*

$$\mathcal{P}_X^{\nu_0}(X \vDash \Psi) \in \{\mathbf{P}_I^{q_0}(I \vDash \Psi)\}_{I \in \mathbb{I}},$$

Proof. The conclusion is obtained by combining Lemma 2 and Theorem 2. ∎

Corollary 2. *Let $\mathbb{X}$, its IMC abstraction $\mathbb{I}$, an LTL formula Ψ, and a constant $\rho \in [0, 1]$ be given. Suppose $I \vDash \mathbf{P}_{\bowtie \rho}^{q_0}[\Psi]$ for all $I \in \mathbb{I}$, we have $X \vDash \mathcal{P}_{\bowtie \rho}^{\nu_0}[\Psi]$ for all $X \in \mathbb{X}$ with $\nu_0(q_0) = 1$.*

Remark 6. *Note that we do not have $\mathcal{P}_X^{\nu_0} \in \{\mathbf{P}_I^{q_0}\}_{I \in \mathbb{I}}$ since each $\mathbf{P}_I^{q_0}$ is a discrete measure whereas $\mathcal{P}_X^{\nu_0}$ is not. They only coincide when measuring Borel subset of $\mathbf{F}$ (recall notation in Sect. 2.1). It would be more accurate to state that $\mathcal{P}_X^{\nu_0}(X \vDash \Psi)$ is a member of $\{\mathbf{P}_I^{q_0}(I \vDash \Psi)\}_{I \in \mathbb{I}}$ rather than say "the true distribution (the law as what we usually call) of the original system is a member of the distribution set represented by the abstraction model" [18].*

Proposition 3. *Let $\varepsilon := \max_i \|\hat{\Theta}_i - \check{\Theta}_i\|_{TV}$. Then for each LTL formula Ψ, as $\varepsilon \to 0$, the length $\lambda(S^{q_0}) \to 0$.*

By Lemma 2, for each $X \in \mathbb{X}$, there exists exactly one $\mathbf{P}_I$ of some $I \in \mathbb{I}$ by which satisfaction probability equals to that of X. The precision of $\hat{\Theta}$ and $\check{\Theta}$ determines the size of S^{q_0}. Once we are able to calculate the exact law of X, the S^{q_0} becomes a singleton by Proposition 3. Special cases are provided in [23, Remark 10].

4 Robust Completeness of IMC Abstractions

In this section, we are given a Markov system $\mathbb{X}_1$ driven by (5) with point-mass perturbations of strength $\vartheta_1 \geq 0$. Based on $\mathbb{X}_1$, we first construct an IMC abstraction $\mathbb{I}$. We then show that $\mathbb{I}$ can be abstracted by a system $\mathbb{X}_2$ with more general $\mathcal{L}_1$-bounded noise of any arbitrary strength $\vartheta_2 > \vartheta_1$.

Recalling the soundness analysis of IMC abstractions in Sect. 3, the relation of satisfaction probability is induced by a relation between the continuous and discrete transitions. To capture the probabilistic properties of stochastic processes, reachable set of probability measures is the analogue of the reachable set in deterministic cases. We rely on a similar technique in this section to discuss how transition probabilities of different uncertain Markov systems are related. To metricize sets of Gaussian measures and to connect them with discrete measures, we prefer to use Wasserstein metric.

Definition 9. *Let $\mu, \nu \in \mathfrak{P}(\mathcal{X})$ for $(\mathcal{X}, |\cdot|)$, the Wasserstein distance[5] is defined by $\|\mu - \nu\|_W = \inf \mathcal{E}|X - Y|$, where the infimum is taken over all joint distributions of the random variables X and Y with marginals μ and ν respectively. We frequently use the following duality form of definition[6],*

$$\|\mu - \nu\|_W := \sup \left\{ \left| \int_{\mathcal{X}} h(x) d\mu(x) - \int_{\mathcal{X}} h(x) d\nu(x) \right|, \ h \in C(\mathcal{X}), \mathrm{Lip}(h) \le 1 \right\}.$$

The discrete case, $\|\cdot\|_W^d$, is nothing but to change the integral to summation. Let $\mathbb{B}_W = \{\mu \in \mathfrak{P}(\mathcal{X}) : \|\mu - \delta_0\|_W \le 1\}$. Given a set $\mathfrak{G} \subseteq \mathfrak{P}(\mathcal{X})$, we denote $\|\mu\|_{\mathfrak{G}} = \inf_{\nu \in \mathfrak{G}} \|\mu - \nu\|_W$ by the distance from μ to $\mathfrak{G}$, and $\mathfrak{G} + r\mathbb{B}_W := \{\mu : \|\mu\|_{\mathfrak{G}} \le r\}$[7] by the r-neighborhood of $\mathfrak{G}$.

Note that $\mathbb{B}_W$ is dual to $\mathbb{B}_1$. For any $\mu \in \mathbb{B}_W$, the associated random variable X should satisfy $\mathcal{E}|X| \le 1$, and vice versa. The following well-known result estimates the Wasserstein distance between two Gaussians.

Proposition 4. *Let $\mu \sim \mathcal{N}(m_1, \Sigma_1)$ and $\nu \sim \mathcal{N}(m_2, \Sigma_2)$ be two Gaussian measures on $\mathbb{R}^n$. Then*

$$|m_1 - m_2| \le \|\mu - \nu\|_W \le \left(\|m_1 - m_2\|_2^2 + \|\Sigma_1^{1/2} - \Sigma_2^{1/2}\|_F^2 \right)^{1/2}, \tag{13}$$

where $\|\cdot\|_F$ is the Frobenius norm.

Proposition 5. *[13] For any μ, ν on some discrete and finite space $\mathcal{Q}$, we have*

$$\|\mu - \nu\|_W^d \le \mathrm{diam}(\mathcal{Q}) \cdot \|\mu - \nu\|_{TV}. \tag{14}$$

Before proceeding, we define the set of transition probabilities of $\mathbb{X}_i$ from any box $[x] \subseteq \mathbb{R}^n$ as

$$\mathbb{T}_i([x]) = \{\mathcal{T}(x, \cdot) : \ \mathcal{T} \in [\![T]\!]_i, \ x \in [x]\}, \ i = 1, 2,$$

and use the following lemma to approximate $\mathbb{T}_1([x])$.

Lemma 3. *Fix any $\varepsilon > 0$, any box $[x] \subseteq \mathbb{R}^n$. For all $\kappa > 0$, there exists a finitely terminated algorithm to compute an over-approximation of the set of (Gaussian) transition probabilities from $[x]$, such that*

$$\mathbb{T}_1([x]) \subseteq \widehat{\mathbb{T}_1([x])} \subseteq \mathbb{T}_1([x]) + \kappa \mathbb{B}_W,$$

where $\widehat{\mathbb{T}_1([x])}$ is the computed over-approximation set of Gaussian measures.

---

[5] This is formally termed as 1st-Wasserstein metric. We choose 1st-Wasserstein metric due to the convexity and nice property of test functions.

[6] $\mathrm{Lip}(h)$ is the Lipschitz constant of h such that $|h(x_2) - h(x_1)| \le \mathrm{Lip}(h)|x_2 - x_1|$.

[7] This is valid by definition.

Remark 7. *The lemma renders the inclusions with larger Wasserstein distance to ensure no missing information about the covariances. The proof is provided in [23].*

Definition 10. *For $i = 1, 2$, we introduce the modified transition probabilities for $\mathbb{X}_i = (\mathcal{X}, [\![T]\!]_i, x_0, \Pi, L)$ based on (7). For all $T_i \in [\![T]\!]_i$, let*

$$\tilde{T}_i(x, \Gamma) = \begin{cases} T_i(x, \Gamma), & \forall \Gamma \subseteq W, \ \forall x \in W, \\ T_i(x, W^c), & \Gamma = \partial W, \ \forall x \in W, \\ 1, & \Gamma = \partial W, \ x \in \partial W. \end{cases} \qquad (15)$$

Correspondingly, let $[\![\tilde{T}]\!]$ denote the collection. Likewise, we also use $(\tilde{\cdot})$ to denote the induced quantities of any other types w.r.t. such a modification.

Remark 8. *We introduce the concept only for analysis. The above modification does not affect the law of the stopped processes since we do not care about the 'out-of-domain' transitions. We use a weighted point mass to represent the measures at the boundary, and the mean should remain the same. It can be easily shown that the Wasserstein distance between any two measures in $[\![\tilde{T}]\!](x, \cdot)$ is upper bounded by that of the non-modified ones.*

Theorem 4. *For any $0 \le \vartheta_1 < \vartheta_2$, we set $\mathbb{X}_i = (\mathcal{X}, [\![\tilde{T}]\!]_i, x_0, \Pi, L)$, $i = 1, 2$, where $\mathbb{X}_1$ is perturbed by point masses with intensity ϑ_1, and $\mathbb{X}_2$ is perturbed by general L_1-perturbation with intensity ϑ_2. Then, under Assumption 2, there exists a rectangular partition $\mathcal{Q}$ (state-level relation $\alpha \subseteq \mathcal{X} \times \mathcal{Q}$), a measure-level relation γ_α and a collection of transition matrices $[\![\Theta]\!]$, such that the system $\mathbb{I} = (\mathcal{Q}, [\![\Theta]\!], q_0, \Pi, L)$ abstracts $\mathbb{X}_1$ and is abstracted by $\mathbb{X}_2$ by the following relation:*

$$\mathbb{X}_1 \preceq_{\gamma_\alpha} \mathbb{I}, \quad \mathbb{I} \preceq_{\gamma_\alpha^{-1}} \mathbb{X}_2. \qquad (16)$$

Proof. We construct a finite-state IMC with partition $\mathcal{Q}$ and an inclusion of transition matrices $[\![\Theta]\!]$ as follows. By Assumption 2, we use uniform rectangular partition on W and set $\alpha = \{(x, q) : q = \eta \lfloor \frac{x}{\eta} \rfloor\} \cup \{(\Delta, \Delta)\}$, where $\lfloor \cdot \rfloor$ is the floor function and η is to be chosen later. Denote the number of discrete nodes by $N + 1$.

Note that any family of (modified) Gaussian measures $[\![\tilde{T}]\!]_1$ is induced from $[\![T]\!]_1$ and should contain its information. For any $\tilde{T} \in [\![\tilde{T}]\!]_1$ and $q \in \mathcal{Q}$,

(i) for all $\tilde{\nu} \sim \tilde{\mathcal{N}}(m, s^2) \in \tilde{\mathbb{T}}_1(\alpha^{-1}(q), \cdot)$, store $\{(m_l, \Sigma_l) = (\eta \lfloor \frac{m}{\eta} \rfloor, \eta^2 \lfloor \frac{s^2}{\eta^2} \rfloor)\}_l$;

(ii) for each l, define $\tilde{\nu}_l^{\text{ref}} \sim \tilde{\mathcal{N}}(m_l, \Sigma_l)$ (implicitly, we need to compute $\nu_l^{\text{ref}}(\Delta)$); compute $\tilde{\nu}_l^{\text{ref}}(\alpha^{-1}(q_j))$ for each $q_j \in \mathcal{Q} \setminus \Delta$;

(iii) for each l, define $\mu_l^{\text{ref}} = [\tilde{\nu}_l^{\text{ref}}(\alpha^{-1}(q_1)), \cdots, \tilde{\nu}_l^{\text{ref}}(\alpha^{-1}(q_N)), \tilde{\nu}_l^{\text{ref}}(\Delta)]$;

(iv) compute $\mathbf{ws} := (\sqrt{2N} + 2)\eta$ and $\mathbf{tv} := N\eta \cdot \mathbf{ws}$;

(v) construct $[\![\mu]\!] = \bigcup_l \{\mu : \|\mu - \mu_l^{\text{ref}}\|_{\text{TV}} \le \mathbf{tv}(\eta), \ \mu(\Delta) + \sum_j^N \mu(q_j) = 1\}$;

(vi) Let $\gamma_\alpha = \{(\tilde{\nu}, \mu), \ \mu \in [\![\mu]\!]\}$ be a relation between $\tilde{\nu} \in \tilde{\mathbb{T}}(\alpha^{-1}(q))$ and the generated $[\![\mu]\!]$.

Repeat the above step for all q, the relation γ_α is obtained. The rest of the proof falls in the following steps. For $i \leq N$, we simply denote $\mathfrak{G}_i := \tilde{\mathbb{T}}_1(\alpha^{-1}(q_i))$ and $\hat{\mathfrak{G}}_i := \widetilde{\tilde{\mathbb{T}}_1(\alpha^{-1}(q_i))}$.

Claim 1: For $i \leq N$, let $[\![\Theta_i]\!] = \gamma_\alpha(\hat{\mathfrak{G}}_i)$. Then the finite-state IMC $\mathbb{I}$ with transition collection $[\![\Theta]\!]$ abstracts $\mathbb{X}_1$.

Indeed, for each $i = 1, \cdots, N$ and each $\tilde{\mathcal{T}}$, we have $\gamma_\alpha(\mathfrak{G}_i) \subseteq \gamma_\alpha(\hat{\mathfrak{G}}_i)$. We pick any modified Gaussian $\tilde{\nu} \in \hat{\mathfrak{G}}_i$, there exists a $\tilde{\nu}^{\mathrm{ref}}$ such that (by Proposition 4) $\|\tilde{\nu} - \tilde{\nu}^{\mathrm{ref}}\|_W \leq \|\nu - \nu^{\mathrm{ref}}\|_W \leq \sqrt{2N}\eta$. We aim to find all discrete measures μ induced from $\tilde{\nu}$ (such that their probabilities match on discrete nodes as requirement by Definition 7). All such μ should satisfy[8],

$$\|\mu - \mu^{\mathrm{ref}}\|_W^d = \|\mu - \mu^{\mathrm{ref}}\|_W$$
$$\leq \|\mu - \tilde{\nu}\|_W + \|\tilde{\nu} - \tilde{\nu}^{\mathrm{ref}}\|_W + \|\tilde{\nu}^{\mathrm{ref}} - \mu^{\mathrm{ref}}\|_W \quad (17)$$
$$\leq (2 + \sqrt{2N})\eta,$$

where the first term of line 2 is bounded by,

$$\|\mu - \tilde{\nu}\|_W = \sup_{h \in C(\mathcal{X}), \mathrm{Lip}(h) \leq 1} \left| \int_\mathcal{X} h(x) d\mu(x) - \int_\mathcal{X} h(x) d\tilde{\nu}(x) \right|$$
$$\leq \sup_{h \in C(\mathcal{X}), \mathrm{Lip}(h) \leq 1} \sum_{j=1}^n \int_{\alpha^{-1}(q_j)} |h(x) - h(q_j)| d\tilde{\nu}(x) \quad (18)$$
$$\leq \eta \sum_{j=1}^n \int_{\alpha^{-1}(q_j)} d\tilde{\nu}(x) \leq \eta,$$

and the third term of line 2 is bounded in a similar way. By step (v)(vi) and Proposition 5, all possible discrete measures μ induced from $\tilde{\nu}$ should be included in $\gamma_\alpha(\hat{\mathfrak{G}}_i)$. Combining the above, for any $\tilde{\nu} \in \mathfrak{G}_i$ and hence in $\hat{\mathfrak{G}}_i$, there exists a discrete measures in $\Theta_i \in \gamma_\alpha(\hat{\mathfrak{G}}_i)$ such that for all q_j we have $\tilde{\nu}(\alpha^{-1}(q_j)) = \Theta_{ij}$. This satisfies the definition of abstraction.

Claim 2: $\gamma_\alpha^{-1}(\gamma_\alpha(\mathfrak{G}_i)) \subseteq \mathfrak{G}_i + (2\eta + N\eta \cdot \mathbf{tv}(\eta)) \cdot \mathbb{B}_W$. This is to recover all possible (modified) measures $\tilde{\nu}$ from the constructed $\gamma_\alpha(\mathfrak{G}_i)$, such that their discrete probabilities coincide. Note that, the 'ref' information is recorded when computing $\gamma_\alpha(\mathfrak{G}_i)$ in the inner parentheses. Therefore, for any $\mu \in \gamma_\alpha(\mathfrak{G}_i)$ there exists a μ^{ref} within a total variation radius $\mathbf{tv}(\eta)$. We aim to find corresponding measure $\tilde{\nu}$ that matches μ by their probabilities on discrete nodes. All such $\tilde{\nu}$ should satisfy,

$$\|\tilde{\nu} - \tilde{\nu}^{\mathrm{ref}}\|_W \leq \|\tilde{\nu} - \mu\|_W + \|\mu - \mu^{\mathrm{ref}}\|_W^d + \|\mu^{\mathrm{ref}} - \tilde{\nu}^{\mathrm{ref}}\|_W \quad (19)$$
$$\leq 2\eta + N\eta \cdot \mathbf{tv}(\eta),$$

---

[8] Note that we also have $\|\mu - \mu^{\mathrm{ref}}\|_W^d \leq \|\mu - \tilde{\nu}\|_W^d + \|\tilde{\nu} - \tilde{\nu}^{\mathrm{ref}}\|_W^d + \|\tilde{\nu}^{\mathrm{ref}} - \mu^{\mathrm{ref}}\|_W^d = \|\tilde{\nu} - \tilde{\nu}^{\mathrm{ref}}\|_W^d$, but it is hard to connect $\|\tilde{\nu} - \tilde{\nu}^{\mathrm{ref}}\|_W^d$ with $\|\tilde{\nu} - \tilde{\nu}^{\mathrm{ref}}\|_W$ for general measures. This connection can be done if we only compare Dirac or discrete measures.

where the bounds for the first and third terms are obtained in the same way as (18). The second term is again by a rough comparison in Proposition 5. Note that $\tilde{\nu}^{\text{ref}}$ is already recorded in $\mathfrak{G}_i$. The inequality in (19) provides an upper bound of Wasserstein deviation between any possible satisfactory measure and some $\tilde{\nu}^{\text{ref}} \in \mathfrak{G}_i$.

Claim 3: If we can choose η and κ sufficiently small such that $2\eta + N\eta \cdot \mathbf{tv}(\eta) + \kappa \leq \vartheta_2 - \vartheta_1$, then $\mathbb{I} \preceq_{\gamma_\alpha^{-1}} \mathbb{X}_2$. Indeed, the $[\![\Theta]\!]$ is obtained by $\gamma_\alpha(\hat{\mathfrak{G}}_i)$ for each i. By Claim 2 and Lemma 3, we have that for each i

$$\gamma_\alpha^{-1}(\gamma_\alpha(\hat{\mathfrak{G}}_i)) \subseteq \hat{\mathfrak{G}}_i + (2\eta + N\eta \cdot \mathbf{tv}(\eta)) \cdot \mathbb{B}_W \subseteq \mathfrak{G}_i + (2\eta + N\eta \cdot \mathbf{tv}(\eta) + \kappa) \cdot \mathbb{B}_W.$$

By the construction, we can verify that $\tilde{\mathbb{T}}_2(\alpha^{-1}(q_i)) = \mathfrak{G}_i + (\vartheta_2 - \vartheta_1) \cdot \mathbb{B}_W$. The selection of η makes $\gamma_\alpha^{-1}(\gamma_\alpha(\hat{\mathfrak{G}}_i)) \subseteq \tilde{\mathbb{T}}_2(\alpha^{-1}(q_i))$, which completes the proof. ∎

Remark 9. *The relation γ_α (resp. γ_α^{-1}) provides a procedure to include all proper (continuous, discrete) measures that connect with the discrete probabilities. The key point is to record $\tilde{\nu}^{ref}$, μ^{ref}, and the corresponding radius. These are nothing but finite coverings of the space of measures. This also explains the reason why we use 'finite-state' rather than 'finite' abstraction. The latter has a meaning of using finite numbers of representative measures to be the abstraction.*

To guarantee a sufficient inclusion, conservative estimations are made. These estimations can be done more accurately given more assumptions (see details in [23, Remark 14]).

Remark 10. *To guarantee the second abstraction based on γ_α^{-1}, we search all possible measures that has the same discrete probabilities as $\mu \in \gamma_\alpha(\hat{\mathfrak{G}}_i)$, not only those Gaussians with the same covariances as $\mathfrak{G}_i$ (or $\hat{\mathfrak{G}}_i$). Such a set of measures provide a convex set w.r.t. Wasserstein distance. Recall that in the forward step of creating $\mathbb{I}$, we have used both Wasserstein and total variation distance to find a convex inclusion of all Gaussian or Gaussian related measures. There ought to be some measures that are 'non-recoverable' to Gaussians, unless we extract some 'Gaussian recoverable' discrete measures in $[\![\Theta_i]\!]$, but this loses the point of over-approximation. In this view, IMC abstractions provide unnecessarily larger inclusions than needed.*

For the deterministic case [20], the above mentioned 'extraction' is possible, since the transition measures do not have diffusion, the convex inclusion becomes a collection of vertices themselves (also see [23, Remark 6]). Based on these vertices, we are able to use γ_α to find the δ measures within a convex ball w.r.t. Wasserstein distance. In contrast to this special case [20], where the uncertainties are bounded w.r.t. the infinity norm, for stochastic systems, we can only guarantee the approximated completeness via a robust $\mathcal{L}_1$-bounded perturbation with strictly larger intensity than the original point-mass perturbation. However, this indeed describes a general type of uncertainties for the stochastic systems to guarantee $\mathcal{L}_1$-related properties, including probabilistic properties. Unless higher-moment specifications are of interests, uncertain $\mathcal{L}_1$-random variables are what we need to be the analogue of perturbations in [20].

Corollary 3. *Given an LTL formula* Ψ, *let* $S_i^{\nu_0} = \{\mathcal{P}_X^{\nu_0}(X \vDash \Psi)\}_{X \in \mathbb{X}_i}$ $(i = 1, 2)$ *and* $S_{\mathbb{I}}^{q_0} = \{\mathbf{P}_I^{q_0}(I \vDash \Psi)\}_{I \in \mathbb{I}}$, *where the initial conditions are such that* $\nu_0(\alpha^{-1}(q_0)) = 1$. *Then all the above sets are compact and* $S_1^{\nu_0} \subseteq S_{\mathbb{I}}^{q_0} \subseteq S_2^{\nu_0}$.

The proof is shown in [23].

5   Conclusion

In this paper, we constructed an IMC abstraction for continuous-state stochastic systems with possibly bounded point-mass (Dirac) perturbations. We showed that such abstractions are not only sound, in the sense that the set of satisfaction probability of linear-time properties contains that of the original system, but also approximately complete in the sense that the constructed IMC can be abstracted by another system with stronger but more general $\mathcal{L}_1$-bounded perturbations. Consequently, the winning set of the probabilistic specifications for a more perturbed continuous-state stochastic system contains that of the less Dirac perturbed system. Similar to most of the existing converse theorems, e.g. converse Lyapunov functions, the purpose is not to provide an efficient approach for finding them, but rather to characterize the theoretical possibilities of having such existence.

It is interesting to compare with robust deterministic systems, where no random variables are involved. In [20], both perturbed systems are w.r.t. bounded point masses. More heavily perturbed systems abstract less perturbed ones and hence preserve robust satisfaction of linear-time properties. However, when we try to obtain the approximated completeness via uncertainties in stochastic system, the uncertainties should be modelled by more general $\mathcal{L}_1$ random variables. Note that the probabilistic properties is dual to the weak topology of measures, we study the laws of processes instead of the state space *per se*. The state-space topology is not sufficient to quantify the regularity of IMC abstractions. In contrast, $\mathcal{L}_1$ uncertain random variables are perfect analogue of the uncertain point masses (in $|\cdot|$) for deterministic systems. If we insist on using point masses as the only type of uncertainties for stochastic systems, the IMC type abstractions would possibly fail to guarantee the completeness. For example, suppose the point-mass perturbations represent less precision of deterministic control inputs [22, Definition 2.3], the winning set decided by the ϑ_2-precision stationary policies is not enough to cover that of the IMC abstraction, which fails to ensure an approximated bi-similarity of IMCs compared to [20].

For future work, it would be useful to extend the current approach to robust stochastic control systems. It would be interesting to design algorithms to construct IMC (resp. bounded-parameter Markov decision processes) abstractions for more general robust stochastic (resp. control) systems with $\mathcal{L}_1$ perturbations based on metrizable space of measures and weak topology. The size of state discretization can be refined given more specific assumptions on system dynamics and linear-time objectives. For verification or control synthesis w.r.t. probabilistic safety or reachability problems, comparisons can be made with stochastic Lyapunov-barrier function approaches.

References

1. Abate, A., D'Innocenzo, A., Di Benedetto, M.D., Sastry, S.S.: Markov set-chains as abstractions of stochastic hybrid systems. In: Egerstedt, M., Mishra, B. (eds.) HSCC 2008. LNCS, vol. 4981, pp. 1–15. Springer, Heidelberg (2008). https://doi.org/10.1007/978-3-540-78929-1_1
2. Abate, A., Katoen, J.P., Mereacre, A.: Quantitative automata model checking of autonomous stochastic hybrid systems. In: Proceedings of Hybrid Systems: Computation and Control (HSCC), pp. 83–92 (2011)
3. Abate, A., Prandini, M., Lygeros, J., Sastry, S.: Probabilistic reachability and safety for controlled discrete time stochastic hybrid systems. Automatica 44(11), 2724–2734 (2008)
4. Baier, C., Katoen, J.P.: Principles of Model Checking. MIT Press, Cambridge (2008)
5. Belta, C., Yordanov, B., Aydin Gol, E.: Formal Methods for Discrete-Time Dynamical Systems. SSDC, vol. 89. Springer, Cham (2017). https://doi.org/10.1007/978-3-319-50763-7
6. Bustan, D., Rubin, S., Vardi, M.Y.: Verifying ω-regular properties of Markov chains. In: Alur, R., Peled, D.A. (eds.) CAV 2004. LNCS, vol. 3114, pp. 189–201. Springer, Heidelberg (2004). https://doi.org/10.1007/978-3-540-27813-9_15
7. Cauchi, N., Laurenti, L., Lahijanian, M., Abate, A., Kwiatkowska, M., Cardelli, L.: Efficiency through uncertainty: scalable formal synthesis for stochastic hybrid systems. In: Proceedings of Hybrid Systems: Computation and Control (HSCC), pp. 240–251 (2019)
8. Da Prato, G., Zabczyk, J.: Stochastic Equations in Infinite Dimensions. Cambridge University Press, Cambridge (2014)
9. Dehnert, C., Junges, S., Katoen, J.-P., Volk, M.: A storm is coming: a modern probabilistic model checker. In: Majumdar, R., Kunčak, V. (eds.) CAV 2017. LNCS, vol. 10427, pp. 592–600. Springer, Cham (2017). https://doi.org/10.1007/978-3-319-63390-9_31
10. Delimpaltadakis, G., Laurenti, L., Mazo Jr., M.: Abstracting the sampling behaviour of stochastic linear periodic event-triggered control systems. arXiv preprint arXiv:2103.13839 (2021)
11. Dutreix, M., Coogan, S.: Specification-guided verification and abstraction refinement of mixed monotone stochastic systems. IEEE Trans. Autom. Control 66(7), 2975–2990 (2020)
12. Dutreix, M.D.H.: Verification and synthesis for stochastic systems with temporal logic specifications. Ph.D. thesis, Georgia Institute of Technology (2020)
13. Gibbs, A.L., Su, F.E.: On choosing and bounding probability metrics. Int. Stat. Rev. 70(3), 419–435 (2002)
14. Girard, A., Pola, G., Tabuada, P.: Approximately bisimilar symbolic models for incrementally stable switched systems. IEEE Trans. Autom. Control 55(1), 116–126 (2009)
15. Givan, R., Leach, S., Dean, T.: Bounded-parameter Markov decision processes. Artif. Intell. 122(1–2), 71–109 (2000)

16. Hartfiel, D.J.: Markov Set-Chains. Springer, Heidelberg (2006)
17. Kloetzer, M., Belta, C.: A fully automated framework for control of linear systems from temporal logic specifications. IEEE Trans. Autom. Control **53**(1), 287–297 (2008)
18. Lahijanian, M., Andersson, S.B., Belta, C.: Formal verification and synthesis for discrete-time stochastic systems. IEEE Trans. Autom. Control **60**(8), 2031–2045 (2015)
19. Li, Y., Liu, J.: Robustly complete synthesis of memoryless controllers for nonlinear systems with reach-and-stay specifications. IEEE Trans. Autom. Control **66**(3), 1199–1206 (2020)
20. Liu, J.: Robust abstractions for control synthesis: completeness via robustness for linear-time properties. In: Proceedings of Hybrid Systems: Computation and Control (HSCC), pp. 101–110 (2017)
21. Liu, J.: Closing the gap between discrete abstractions and continuous control: completeness via robustness and controllability. In: Dima, C., Shirmohammadi, M. (eds.) FORMATS 2021. LNCS, vol. 12860, pp. 67–83. Springer, Cham (2021). https://doi.org/10.1007/978-3-030-85037-1_5
22. Majumdar, R., Mallik, K., Soudjani, S.: Symbolic controller synthesis for büchi specifications on stochastic systems. In: Proceedings of the 23rd International Conference on Hybrid Systems: Computation and Control, pp. 1–11 (2020)
23. Meng, Y., Liu, J.: Robustly complete finite-state abstractions for verification of stochastic systems. arXiv preprint arXiv:2205.01854 (2022)
24. Parker, D.: Verification of probabilistic real-time systems. In: Proceedings of 2013 Real-Time Systems Summer School (ETR 2013) (2013)
25. Pola, G., Girard, A., Tabuada, P.: Approximately bisimilar symbolic models for nonlinear control systems. Automatica **44**(10), 2508–2516 (2008)
26. Ramponi, F., Chatterjee, D., Summers, S., Lygeros, J.: On the connections between PCTL and dynamic programming. In: Proceedings of Hybrid Systems: Computation and Control (HSCC), pp. 253–262 (2010)
27. Rogers, L.C.G., Williams, D.: Diffusions, Markov Processes and Martingales, Volume 1: Foundations. Cambridge Mathematical Library (2000)
28. Soudjani, S.E.Z., Abate, A.: Adaptive gridding for abstraction and verification of stochastic hybrid systems. In: 2011 Eighth International Conference on Quantitative Evaluation of SysTems, pp. 59–68. IEEE (2011)
29. Summers, S., Lygeros, J.: Verification of discrete time stochastic hybrid systems: a stochastic reach-avoid decision problem. Automatica **46**(12), 1951–1961 (2010)
30. Tabuada, P., Pappas, G.J.: Linear time logic control of discrete-time linear systems. IEEE Trans. Autom. Control **51**(12), 1862–1877 (2006)
31. Tkachev, I., Abate, A.: On infinite-horizon probabilistic properties and stochastic bisimulation functions. In: 2011 50th IEEE Conference on Decision and Control and European Control Conference, pp. 526–531. IEEE (2011)
32. Tkachev, I., Abate, A.: Regularization of bellman equations for infinite-horizon probabilistic properties. In: Proceedings of Hybrid Systems: Computation and Control (HSCC), pp. 227–236 (2012)
33. Tkachev, I., Abate, A.: Formula-free finite abstractions for linear temporal verification of stochastic hybrid systems. In: Proceedings of Hybrid Systems: Computation and Control (HSCC), pp. 283–292 (2013)
34. Tkachev, I., Abate, A.: Characterization and computation of infinite-horizon specifications over Markov processes. Theoret. Comput. Sci. **515**, 1–18 (2014)
35. Tkachev, I., Mereacre, A., Katoen, J.P., Abate, A.: Quantitative model-checking of controlled discrete-time Markov processes. Inf. Comput. **253**, 1–35 (2017)

36. Vardi, M.Y.: Automatic verification of probabilistic concurrent finite state programs. In: 26th Annual Symposium on Foundations of Computer Science (FOCS), pp. 327–338. IEEE (1985)
37. Vassiliou, P.C.: Non-homogeneous Markov set systems. Mathematics **9**(5), 471 (2021)
38. Wu, D., Koutsoukos, X.: Reachability analysis of uncertain systems using bounded-parameter Markov decision processes. Artif. Intell. **172**(8–9), 945–954 (2008)

Model Checking for Entanglement Swapping

Surya Sai Teja Desu, Anubhav Srivastava, and M. V. Panduranga Rao$^{(\boxtimes)}$

Indian Institute of Technology Hyderabad,
Sangareddy, India
{cs17b21m000002,cs21mtech02001,mvp}@iith.ac.in

Abstract. Entanglement swapping is a basic primitive in long distance quantum communications. The stochastic nature of various operations like entanglement generation and BSMs makes the entanglement swapping primitive failure prone. It is difficult to predict whether or not an entanglement swapping operation will succeed within a stipulated time. In this paper, we use Probabilistic Timed Automata (PTA) to model the experiment and analyze it through model checking. We report a proof-of-concept mechanism, opening way for the analysis of large scale quantum networks through formal methods. We also report supporting results on a quantum simulator.

Keywords: Entanglement Swapping · Quantum Networks · Probabilistic Timed Automata · Quantum Network Simulators

1 Introduction

A major application of quantum information lies in secure communications. Beginning with the famous BB84 protocol for Quantum Key Distribution [4], the area has seen rapid advances in both theory and implementation. While BB84 in its original form was concerned with point-to-point distribution of secret keys through transmission of qubits, it proved difficult to transmit qubits across long distances. Unlike in classical communications, the fragility of qubits and inability to clone qubits necessitated paradigmatic changes in designing *quantum* repeaters.

Entanglement is a phenomenon unique to quantum physics [9, 24]. In this work, we are interested in the maximally entangled pair of qubits called an EPR pair (named after Einstein, Podolsky and Rosen). If two quantum communication nodes share an EPR pair, several interesting applications like quantum teleportation and secure key distribution can be achieved. Quantum teleportation transfers quantum information (that is, a quantum state) with no communication channel other than the shared EPR pair [6, 8]. Thus, for such applications, it is essential that the quantum nodes share an EPR pair. Again, it is not straightforward to distribute EPR pairs between distant quantum nodes.

To solve this problem, the so-called *entanglement swapping* protocol was proposed [30]. Consider three quantum nodes a, b and c. The protocol converts shared EPR pairs between a and b, and b and c, to a shared EPR pair between

S. Bogomolov and D. Parker (Eds.): FORMATS 2022, LNCS 13465, pp. 98–114, 2022.
https://doi.org/10.1007/978-3-031-15839-1_6

a and c. Theoretically, this process can be lifted to an arbitrarily long sequence of quantum nodes, where intermediate nodes act as *quantum repeaters*. The protocol results in shared entanglement between the two end quantum nodes of the sequence.

It is easy to see that entanglement swapping will play a major role in quantum communications in the future [26,27]. However, implementing this protocol poses practical problems. Firstly, qubits and quantum memory are fragile and current technology limits their longevity. Secondly, implementation of unitary transformations and measurements are error prone. Techniques like entanglement distillation, and use of quantum error correction are being explored to mitigate these problems [5,7,13].

Under these circumstances, it is crucial to be able to estimate the success of a given implementation with accuracy, given individual device parameters. For example, in the case of a line graph of quantum nodes, what is the probability that an EPR pair will be shared between the end nodes within a stipulated time? Ability to answer this query for a set of parameters would help in making design decisions.

An important model for analyzing probabilistic timed systems is the Probabilistic Timed Automaton (PTA) [22,25].

In this work, we model the components of an entanglement swapping protocol using PTA. We abstract away various device parameters like success probabilities of entanglement generation and other quantum operations and expected lifetimes of an EPR pair, to build the PTA model. We use the PRISM model checker [20] for model checking. Drawing parallels from PTA modeling of (task-graph) scheduling problems [1,2,25], we estimate the probability of success of EPR sharing between a and c for a three node linear network.

At the moment, quantum device technology is mature only for a small number of quantum repeater nodes. For "experiments" at a larger scale, several quantum network simulators have been developed [10–12,28]. In the absence of quantum hardware, these software simulators are an important tool in testing and validating protocols at scale.

We "validate" our model using one such discrete event simulator called SeQUeNCe [28]. We report results for analogous set of parameters in the PTA model as well as the simulator. Quantum communications, and indeed quantum computing are time-critical applications. We believe that this work opens up the area of using (probabilistic) timed automata for analyzing quantum systems.

There is a body of work in the last two decades towards analysis of quantum systems through formal methods, particularly model checking. These range from formal methods for quantum programs [18,23] to model checking systems like quantum Markov chains [29]. There also have been efforts to analyze quantum protocols like Quantum Key Distribution [14,17], superdense coding, quantum teleportation, and quantum error correction [15], through probabilistic model checking using PRISM. Very recently, Khatri [19] has proposed a theoretical analysis of near-term quantum networks using Markov Decision Processes.

To the best of our knowledge, this work is the first effort in the direction of using formal methods and model checking to study time critical quantum systems. We find that the model checking and simulation results match well enough to be of practical use in designing quantum communication technology solutions. For example, given two different quantum system designs, this approach can be used to check which one has higher success probability. The source code for this work is available at https://github.com/suryadesu/artifact.

We report results on linear topologies. Even in a general quantum network, the entanglement swapping protocol between two nodes works on the linear path that is fixed by a routing algorithm. Therefore, a study of entanglement swapping on linear topologies is sufficient. Moreover, we find that for even linear topologies, the simulator takes an inordinate amount of time; even the model checker slows down as the number of nodes increases. Therefore, we focus on understanding the problem for a three node set up as an initial step.

The rest of the paper is arranged as follows. Section 2 gives a quick introduction to important ideas needed for reading this paper – quantum entanglement swapping and probabilistic timed automata. In Sect. 3, we develop the PTA model and discuss the SeQUeNCe simulator setup. Section 4 details the experimental setup. Section 5 discusses the results and we conclude in Sect. 6 with a discussion of future directions.

2   Preliminaries

In this section we briefly discuss some ideas that are prerequisite for reading the rest of the paper. We assume a basic knowledge of quantum computing, in particular, the fundamental postulates of quantum mechanics – the state, evolution and measurement postulates [24].

Of particular interest for this paper, is the maximally entangled Bell state $\frac{|00\rangle+|11\rangle}{\sqrt{2}}$. A pair of particles (or qubits) entangled thus, is called an EPR pair.

Consider a linear arrangement of three quantum nodes a, b and c, where a and b share a direct quantum link, and so do b and c. The purpose of entanglement swapping is to convert EPR pairs shared between neighboring nodes a, b and b, c into EPR pairs shared between a and c. This process can be lifted to a line graph of any number of quantum nodes. The objective then is to have shared entanglement between the end nodes of the line graph.

The Entanglement swapping protocol uses two important "subroutines".

1. Generation of EPR pairs between neighboring nodes a, b (and, b, c):
   Node a (without loss of generality – this can be done by b as well, or even a third party) takes two qubits set to $|00\rangle$ and applies a Hadamard transformation on the first qubit, followed by a $controlled-NOT$ gate with the first qubit as control and the second as target:

$$\underbrace{\frac{1}{\sqrt{2}}\begin{bmatrix}1\\0\\0\\1\end{bmatrix}}_{\text{EPR pair}} = \underbrace{\frac{1}{\sqrt{2}}\begin{bmatrix}1&0&0&0\\0&1&0&0\\0&0&0&1\\0&0&1&0\end{bmatrix}}_{\text{CNOT}} \underbrace{\begin{bmatrix}1&0&1&0\\0&1&0&1\\1&0&-1&0\\0&1&0&-1\end{bmatrix}}_{\text{Hadamard on first qubit}} \underbrace{\begin{bmatrix}1\\0\\0\\0\end{bmatrix}}_{\text{Initial quantum state }|00\rangle}$$

Node a then sends one qubit to node b. At this point, node a and b are said to share an EPR pair. It is natural to denote this pair as $\frac{|0_a 0_b\rangle + |1_a 1_b\rangle}{\sqrt{2}}$.

2. Bell State Measurement:

When an EPR pair is shared between a and b and one between b and c, the joint state can be written as: $\frac{(|0_a 0_b\rangle + |1_a 1_b\rangle)(|0_b 0_c\rangle + |1_b 1_c\rangle)}{2}$. At this point b performs, on the two qubits that it has received (from a and c) a measurement in the Bell basis: $\{\frac{|00\rangle + |11\rangle}{\sqrt{2}}, \frac{|01\rangle + |10\rangle}{\sqrt{2}}, \frac{|01\rangle - |10\rangle}{\sqrt{2}}, \frac{|00\rangle - |11\rangle}{\sqrt{2}}\}$. Such a measurement is called a "Bell State Measurement" (BSM). The outcome of the measurement is transmitted classically to one of a or c, which then performs local unitary transformation on its qubit to yield an EPR pair $\frac{|0_a 0_c\rangle + |1_a 1_c\rangle}{\sqrt{2}}$ shared between a and c.

In practice, both these procedures are error prone. Further, the EPR pairs have a limited life time before they have be used (for applications like teleportation). This makes the entanglement swapping a very time critical process.

2.1 Probabilistic Timed Automata

We briefly discuss the syntax and semantics of Probabilistic Timed Automata. A large and excellent body of research and expository literature exists for Timed Automata and Probabilisitic Timed Automata, to which we refer the reader [3, 22, 25]. Of particular relevance is the paper by Norman et al. [25], given the parallels of our problem with task-graph scheduling and since we use the PRISM model checker in this work.

A popular approach for modeling reactive systems are *Kripke structures* – finite automata augmented with a finite set *Act* of *action symbols* and a finite set *AP* of *atomic propositions*. A *labeling function* specifies which atomic propositions from *AP* are *true* on which locations.

Similarly, Timed Automata are finite automata augmented with *clock* variables, and are used to model real time systems [3]. Clock variables take values from $\mathcal{R}_{\geq 0}$, and as the name suggests, increase at the same rate as time. We denote the set of clock variables employed by a timed automaton $\mathcal{M}$ by $\mathcal{C}$. For such a set $\mathcal{C}$, it is possible to define a set CC of clock constraints through the following grammar:

$$\xi = true \mid x \leq d \mid c \geq x \mid x + c \leq y + d \mid \neg \xi \mid \xi \wedge \xi$$

where $x, y \in \mathcal{C}$ and c and d are natural numbers. To be able to model and analyze stochastic timed systems, the probabilistic timed automata were introduced [22].

A Probabilistic Timed Automaton $\mathcal{M}$ is a tuple $\langle L, l_0, \mathcal{C}, Act, inv, enab, \mathcal{P}, \mathcal{L} \rangle$ defined as follows:

- L is a finite set of *locations*.
- l_0 is an initial location.
- $\mathcal{C}$ is a finite set of clocks.
- Act is a finite set of action symbols.

- $inv : L \to CC(\mathcal{C})$ is an invariant condition.
- $enab : L \times Act \to CC(\mathcal{C})$ is an enabling condition.
- $\mathcal{P} : L \times Act \to Dist(2^{\mathcal{C}} \times L)$ is a probabilistic transition function.
- $\mathcal{L} \to 2^{AP}$ is a labeling function.

For example, in Fig. 2, $ab = 0$, 1, 2, 3, and 4 are locations, $ab = 0$ is the initial location. $clock\_ab$ is a clock, while Act contains action symbols like $ab\_assigned\_to\_1$, $op\_done\_in\_1$, $op\_failed\_in\_1$, etc. Further, $(clock\_ab \leq \tau_{a,b})$ in state $ab = 3$ is an example invariant condition. Transitions from one state to another, like $ab = 1$ to $ab = 3$ synchronized by action symbol $ab\_done\_to\_1$ and $clock\_ab$ is reset to 0 are enabled by the $enab$ function. It is noteworthy that some of the features may not be needed in some applications. By default, all the transitions are of probability 1. For example, in our work, we do not need an explicit set of atomic propositions (AP) – just the set of location names suffices.

We now informally discuss the semantics. The automaton is initially in the location l_0. While in a location, time passes. The inv condition for a location $l \in L$ specifies that the automaton can remain in the location as long as the corresponding clock constraints are satisfied. The conditions $enab$ and $prob$ define the inter-location dynamics of the automaton. The automaton probabilistically transits from one location to another when an action is enabled, some clock conditions are satisfied, and the transition is accompanied by the resetting of a subset of clocks: An action $a \in Act$ is $enabled$ at location l if the values of the clocks satisfy clock conditions specified by $enab(l, a)$. For such an enabled action, the next state and the subset of clocks to be reset are chosen as per the probability distribution $\mathcal{P}(l, a)$. The labeling function $\mathcal{L}$ assigns to each location $l \in L$ a subset of atomic propositions from AP which are said to be $true$ at l.

It is possible to compose several (probabilistic) timed automata that synchronize on action symbols [3, 25]. This enables a modular design for large systems.

The Query Language. The requirements are modeled using a probabilistic variant of either Timed Computational Tree Logic (TCTL) [20, 25] or CTL [16]. Without going into the details of PCTL [16], we mention the query that is used in this paper, in PRISM syntax:

$$Pmax_{=?}[\text{F} \leq \mu \quad \text{is\_success} = 1]$$

This query asks for the maximum probability that an EPR pair is generated between end nodes within time μ. Since there is no bound on the number of failures of EPR pair generations and BSM, the minimum probability of successful establishment of EPR pairs between two nodes is zero-this happens when the number of failures are too many, given the time limit for success. On the other hand, given a reasonable time limit, the success probability is bounded away from 1, since the EPR pair generations and BSM fail with a non-zero probability. Practically speaking, a hardware configuration with a higher maximum success probability (say 0.9) would be preferable to one with a lower maximum success probability (say 0.3). Therefore, we choose to evaluate the maximum probability of success.

3   Modeling and Validation

3.1   The PTA Model

We now describe the Probabilistic Timed Automata model for entanglement swapping of three nodes.

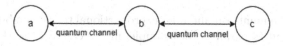

Fig. 1. In a linear topology between three nodes a, b and c, a and b share a quantum channel, and thus adjacent to each other. Similarly, b and c are adjacent to each other.

Consider three nodes a, b and c arranged linearly (Fig. 1), where a is adjacent to b and b is adjacent to c. The objective is to generate an EPR pair between a and c, within a stipulated time.

In an ideal scenario, the protocol proceeds as follows. EPR pairs are generated between nodes a and b and between b and c simultaneously. Then, a BSM is performed at node b, causing an EPR pair to be established between a and c. However, the system deviates from ideal behaviour in the following ways. Generation of EPR pairs is error prone. Secondly, every EPR pair has a small lifetime, after which it expires and cannot be used. Finally, BSM is also error prone. If a failure occurs in EPR generation, or an EPR pair expires, it has to be generated again. If a Bell Statement Measurement at node b fails, the EPR pairs shared between a and b and between b and c are rendered useless, and have to be generated again. All these deviations are probabilistic in nature.

The PTA model that we use is essentially an extension to the task-graph scheduler of Norman et al. [25], modified to suit our requirements. What essentially distinguish the current problem from the task-graph scheduling are (i) the possibility of re-trials of entanglement generation after failure and (ii) modeling the life times of EPR pairs. If an EPR pair expires, another is generated again, to ensure the end-to-end entanglement is achieved within the stipulated time.

Before we describe the model in detail, we will first identify the parameters involved to capture the deviations.

- Time limit (μ) : If an EPR pair is shared between node a and node c before μ, the objective is achieved.
- Processing time (t_{op}) : Time taken to perform an operation – either entanglement generation or BSM.
- Probability of success for an operation (p_{op}): Probability of success of an operation considering the error parameters of the system.
- Lifetime ($\tau_{a,b}$) : This is the (expected) life time of an EPR pair formed between nodes a and b.

We will now describe the PTA model in detail. The model is a composition of several PTA modules. For entanglement swapping in three nodes, the operations that need to be performed are primarily (i) EPR pair generation between nodes a and b (ii) and b and c (iii) a BSM at node b. (i) and (ii) may be performed simultaneously, but (iii) starts only after the successful completion of (i) and (ii). As such, we use two PTA modules, named QuantumOp1 and QuantumOp2. Each of these modules model both operations – entanglement generation as well as BSM.

In general, the number of modules is proportional to the number of tasks that can be carried out in parallel. For example, in our case, we use three modules – two for modeling the simultaneous operations, and one for overall scheduling.

We now discuss these modules in detail. For ease of understanding, we explain the scheduler module using state diagram per operation.

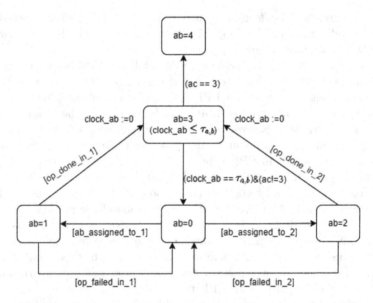

Fig. 2. The state diagram for EPR pair generation operation between nodes a and b.

In Fig. 2 we show how EPR pair generation between a and b is modeled. Starting from the initial state $ab = 0$, there are two possible scenarios. Either the operation is assigned to QuantumOp1 or QuantumOp2. These are synchronized using the action symbols $ab\_assigned\_to\_1$ and $ab\_assigned\_to\_2$ respectively and the transition from state $ab = 0$ to $ab = 1$ or $ab = 2$ takes place accordingly.

Without loss of generality, ab is assigned to QuantumOp1. The case when the EPR pair between a and b is generated successfully is synchronized by QuantumOp1 using $op\_done\_in\_1$ and the transition takes place from $ab = 1$ to $ab = 3$. Therefore, $ab = 3$ is the state where an EPR pair between a and b exists. On the other hand, if the EPR pair generation has failed, QuantumOp1 module synchronizes this using *op_failed_in_1* in which case transition takes place to $ab = 0$. The case when ab is assigned to QuantumOp2 is symmetric.

In state $ab = 3$, we use the clock variable *clock_ab* for modeling the life time of the EPR pair between a and b. For this, we start the clock by resetting it to 0 before entering $ab = 3$. Invariant $(clock\_ab \leq \tau_{a,b})$ in state $ab = 3$ ensures that the clock never goes beyond the life time of EPR pair between a and b. We note that the EPR pair will survive until the BSM operation at node b is complete. Hence, if the clock elapses $\tau_{a,b}$ units and if BSM at b is not complete (i.e., when $ac! = 3$), we return to the initial state $ab = 0$.

However, once an EPR pair is formed between a and c, we no longer need to track time for the EPR pair between a and b. Thus, we assign it to a dead state $ab = 4$ to reflect the fact that the success of the our objective is no longer dependent on the EPR pair between a and b.

This modeling approach can be generalized to the EPR pair generation between nodes b and c. We will now discuss modeling a BSM task, given in Fig. 3.

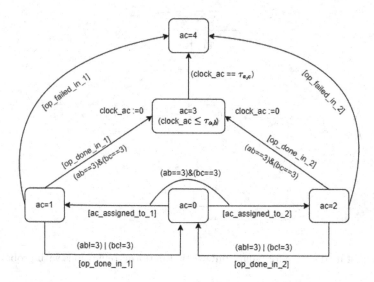

Fig. 3. The state diagram for modeling the operation ac of BSM at b to form an EPR pair between nodes a and c.

Similarly, the BSM operation starts from state $ac = 0$ and can be assigned to either QuantumOp1 or QuantumOp2. However, since the BSM operation is dependent on existence of EPR pairs being formed between nodes a and b and between nodes b and c, these transitions have the guard condition $(ab = 3)\&(bc = 3)$.

The success of the BSM operation is synchronized using *op_done_in_1* or *op_done_in_2*. After the BSM operation is assigned, there is a possibility that either EPR pair between a and b or between b and c or both failed to survive. To model this scenario, we add the guard condition to check if both the EPR pairs are surviving, that is, $(ab == 3)\&(bc == 3)$ by the time the BSM operation succeeds. Only then we consider the operation to be successful and transit to $ac = 3$. If either of the pairs failed to survive, we return to $ac = 0$.

If either the BSM operation fails or if the EPR pair formed between a and c after BSM hit its life time, then the intermediate EPR pairs between a and b and between b and c need to be generated again. To make the model simpler, we stop the process and consider that attempt to be a failure in such scenarios. This is modeled by transitions synchronized by $op\_failed\_in\_1$ and $op\_failed\_in\_2$ to state $ac = 4$, and the transition from $ac = 3$ to $ac = 4$ when $clock\_ac = \tau_{a,c}$. Here $ac = 4$ is considered a dead state.

Let us now discuss how to model the QuantumOp modules. Since both QuantumOp1 and QuantumOp2 are similar in structure, we detail the structure of the QuantumOp1 module only.

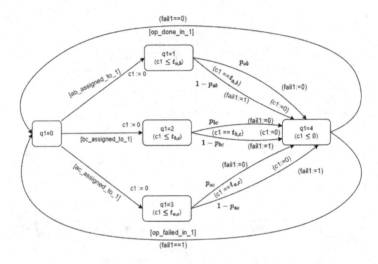

Fig. 4. The state diagram for QuantumOp1 that performs operations with probabilistic success.

QuantumOp1 (Fig. 4) starts from the initial state $q1 = 0$. From here, there are three possible transitions, one for each operation. These are synchronized with their corresponding action symbols. For instance, EPR pair generation between a and b being assigned to QuantumOp1 using action symbol $ab\_assigned\_to\_1$ and the automaton transits from $q1 = 0$ to $q1 = 1$.

We use clock $c1$ to track processing times of the operations. For this, $c1$ gets reset on reaching the states $q1 = 1$ or 2 or 3. In these states, the time elapses to mimic the processing time t_{op} for the corresponding operation. Invariants are added to each of the states $1, 2$ and 3 so that the clock never elapses more than

t_{op}. Then, we have probabilistic transitions to state $q1 = 4$ from each of the states $1, 2$ and 3 to model the success probability p_{op}.

Let us consider EPR generation between a and b as an example. From state $q1 = 1$ there are two probabilistic transitions to the state $q1 = 4$–one with probability p_{ab} which assigns a value 0 to $fail1$ denoting success, while the other with probability $1 - p_{ab}$ assigns a value 1 to $fail1$ denoting failure. Both the transitions have guard conditions to check if the clock elapsed $t_{a,b}$.

To get rid of any delay, the clock $c1$ is reset to 0 before reaching the state $q1 = 4$. In the state $q1 = 4$, an invariant $c1 <= 0$ ensures that the next transition happens as soon $q1 = 4$ is reached. The next transitions to the state $q1 = 0$ are conditioned on the value of $fail1$. These transitions flag the scheduler module with the result of assigned operation using action symbols $op\_done\_in\_1$ and $op\_failed\_in\_1$. Reaching the initial state $q1 = 0$, the QuantumOp1 is now idle and can be assigned to any further operations.

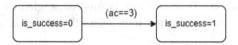

Fig. 5. $is\_success = 1$ is the final state which deems the whole process a success.

Finally, the end result of the process is modeled using the state $is\_success$. Initially $is\_success$ is 0 and the transition to state $is\_success = 1$ happens when the objective is achieved which in our case, an EPR pair is generated between nodes a and c ($ac = 3$). Note that this can also be achieved by checking the property $[F \leq \mu \ ac = 3]$ as well.

3.2   Validation Through Simulations

We use an open source discrete event simulator called SeQUeNCe [28] for our simulations. SeQUeNCe has a dedicated hardware layer that aims at realistic simulation of various physical components required for entanglement distribution such as quantum memory, light source, detectors etc. Additionally, it also has the capability to perform EPR pair generation and BSM operation via its Entanglement Management module. To perform our simulations we make the following modifications to SeQUeNCe:

– *Counting entanglement generation and BSM operations:*
  We make use of the global timeline instance to store our auxiliary variables. One of these is a two dimensional list that stores the number of generation attempts made between any two neighboring nodes. We increment this value upon each EPR pair generation attempt.
– *Mapping the time used in model to the time used by the simulator:*
  For our experimental parameters, we find the average time taken by the simulator to perform entanglement generation t_{gen}^{simul}. This time should be equal

to the generation time taken by the model t_{gen}, thus providing us with a conversion factor: $\frac{t_{gen}^{simul}}{t_{gen}}$. This factor is important for converting values such as coherence time of quantum memory (life time of a EPR pair) from model units to the simulator compatible units.

– *Configurable generation and BSM success probabilities:*
EPR pair generation and BSM being probabilistic processes, we need to be able to specify the success probabilities of both operations. SeQUeNCe provides BSM success probability parameter, however for generation, the probabilities depend on the physical devices. We change this by adding a success probability check directly in generation protocol. If successful, we pick an entangled state with the fidelity computed by the physical devices, otherwise we mark this operation as failed.

– *Stop rule execution after final entanglements are generated:*
We do not want any generations to happen after the final entanglements between a and c have been shared. To ensure this, we create a global state variable that is set to *True* as soon as final entanglements are created. We add a check in the rule execution unit where if this flag is *True*, rules will not be executed.

– *Handling BSM failures:*
We assume an iteration has failed upon the occurrence of first BSM failure. To ensure this, we maintain a global flag which is raised to *True* on a BSM failure and we terminate the current iteration. We use this flag to mark current iteration as Success/Fail during final probability calculation.

– *Computing total execution time of an iteration:*
Total execution time is computed using the counts of generation (n_{gen}), BSM operations (n_{bsm}) and their individual execution times by using:
$$t_{iteration} = n_{gen}t_{gen} + n_{bsm}t_{bsm}.$$

– *Overall probability computation:*
We classify each run as either Success or Fail depending on whether end-to-end entanglement has been distributed between a and c. This is tracked with the help of stop_rules flag. If it is true, we count the current entanglement as successful. To calculate overall success probability, we find ratio of successful $n_{success}$ to total iterations n_{total}:
$$P_{output} = \frac{n_{success}}{n_{total}}$$

4   Experimental Setup

We use the following quantum channel attributes for a linear topology of three nodes ($a - b - c$), for all the experiments that we report:

```
length of quantum channel between neighbor nodes = 50 km
attenuation of quantum channel = 0.2 dB/km
classical channel delay between a and b, b and c = 1 ms
classical channel delay between a and c = 2 ms
quantum channel frequency =  100 GHz.
```

As a consequence of the discussion in Sect. 3.2, changing these attributes does not result in a significant deviation in the overall success probability.

We define an iteration as one simulation run for a given set of parameters. We perform multiple such iterations per scenario and classify each of them as Success/Fail depending upon whether entanglement was created between a and c. Results in the next section is obtained for 2000 iterations per scenario.

For each iteration we create a request from a to c for one EPR pair using the network manager's request module. We obtain the status of the current iteration inside the Success/Fail method of BSM protocol and we raise the flag accordingly. We finally compute the overall probability as described above and exit the simulation, reporting the calculated values.

For the time related parameters, we report the values used in the model (in time units). As given in Sect. 3.2, the values for the simulator is $\frac{0.002}{t_{gen}}$ s × the values used for model checking.

Considering the constraints of the simulator, we made the following assumptions which shall help to understand the correctness of the modeling approach without vastly differing from the entanglement swapping protocol in real life applications.

- All the parameters except probabilities are integers.
- Lifetimes of all EPR pairs are equal ($=\tau$).
- Success probability for all EPR pair generation operations between adjacent nodes are equal ($=p_{gen}$).
- Success probability for all BSM operations are equal ($=p_{bsm}$).
- Processing time for all EPR pair generation operations between adjacent nodes are equal ($=t_{gen}$).
- Processing time for all BSM operations are equal ($=t_{bsm}$).

We would like to point out that these are not strict assumptions for the model; it can model different lifetimes per EPR pair and different processing times per operation.

5   Results

In this section we use our modeling approach to evaluate the impact of different parameters on the probability that an EPR pair is formed between nodes a and c within a stipulated time. We use the digital clocks engine in the PRISM model checker [21] for analyzing our PTA model and compare the results using SeQUeNCe simulator [28].

To better understand the impact of the parameters, we vary one parameter at a time while keeping the other parameters fixed. The results are summarized in Fig. 6. For rest of the parameters that are fixed, values are assigned such that these parameters have very little impact on the overall success probability. The fixed values of these parameters are detailed as captions to the plots. We will now discuss each of the plots in detail.

1. *Maximum success probability vs Life time of an EPR pair* (τ) (Fig. 6a)
   Increasing the lifetime of EPR pairs allows them to survive longer. This will help in case any other operations get delayed due to errors. As a result, we can see that the overall success probability increases steeply with increase in the lifetimes. However, it is never greater than 0.5. This can be observed from the figure–increasing the lifetime to more than 15 time units has very little effect on the overall success probability. This is because p_{gen} and p_{bsm} are fixed at 0.5.

2. *Maximum success probability vs Time limit* (μ) (Fig. 6b)
   An increase in the time limit allows for more number of EPR pair generation failures. Thus, the overall success probability increases with μ. However, for the same reason as in the case of τ, the maximum probability does not go beyond 0.5 and this can be observed from $\mu > 50$.

3. *Maximum success probability vs Probability of EPR pair generation* (p_{gen}) (Fig. 6c)
   As the probability p_{gen} increases, it is easy to see that with higher chance, the EPR pairs between a and b and between b and c are formed. As a result, the overall success probability increases. However, since the overall entanglment swapping process ends with the BSM operation at node b whose success probability $p_{bsm} = 0.5$, we can observe that increasing p_{gen} beyond 0.5 has little effect on the overall success probability.

4. *Maximum success probability vs Probability of BSM* (p_{bsm}) (Fig. 6d)
   As we increase p_{bsm}, the BSM is successful with high probability, thereby increasing the overall success probability. It is interesting to note that the maximum success probability is continuously increasing but does not flatten out unlike the other scenarios. This can be because of the following reasons. μ, τ are higher compared to per EPR pair generation time t_{gen}. Thus, even in cases of failures in EPR pair generations between a and b and between b and c, the operations can be repeated within the stipulated time limit μ. As a result, with high probability the final BSM operation occurs. At this point, the only contributing factor is p_{bsm}. Hence, the maximum success probability increases monotonically with p_{bsm}.

5. *Maximum success probability vs Processing time of EPR pair generation* (t_{gen}) (Fig. 6e)
   For a fixed μ, a higher delay t_{gen} in the generation of EPR pairs results in a lesser overall success probability, since it allows for lesser number of EPR pair generation failures. We can see similar trends in the simulator as well; however the success probability reduces to 0 when $t_{gen} \geq 30$. This is because in the simulator we consider a-b and b-c generations independently and count both of them towards total time irrespective of any temporal overlap between them. This does not affect the results for low values of t_{gen} but it becomes an important factor when t_{gen} approaches μ.

6. *Maximum success probability vs Processing time of BSM* (t_{bsm}) (Fig. 6f)
   The maximum success probability reduces only marginally with an increase in t_{bsm}. The slight reduction is likely caused by a lower number of BSMs completing within μ with increasing t_{bsm}. However, this reduction is not very

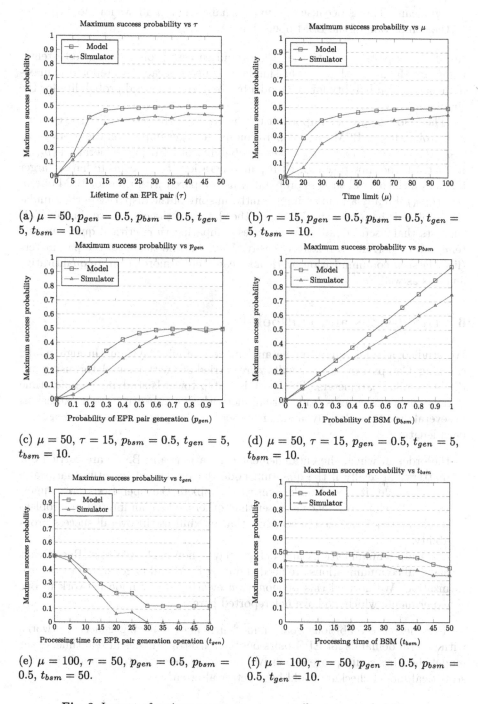

(a) $\mu = 50$, $p_{gen} = 0.5$, $p_{bsm} = 0.5$, $t_{gen} = 5$, $t_{bsm} = 10$.

(b) $\tau = 15$, $p_{gen} = 0.5$, $p_{bsm} = 0.5$, $t_{gen} = 5$, $t_{bsm} = 10$.

(c) $\mu = 50$, $\tau = 15$, $p_{bsm} = 0.5$, $t_{gen} = 5$, $t_{bsm} = 10$.

(d) $\mu = 50$, $\tau = 15$, $p_{gen} = 0.5$, $t_{gen} = 5$, $t_{bsm} = 10$.

(e) $\mu = 100$, $\tau = 50$, $p_{gen} = 0.5$, $p_{bsm} = 0.5$, $t_{bsm} = 50$.

(f) $\mu = 100$, $\tau = 50$, $p_{gen} = 0.5$, $p_{bsm} = 0.5$, $t_{gen} = 10$.

Fig. 6. Impact of various parameters on overall success probability

significant. This is because t_{gen} much smaller than μ allows for more time for the completion of the BSM operation.

In all of the plots, we note that the overall success probability is consistently higher for the model than for the simulator. This is because we report the maximum success probability for the model but only the expected probability for the simulator.

The following are the important takeaways from the results. Firstly, the success probability of BSM (p_{bsm}) operation has a larger impact on the overall success probability compared to success probability of EPR pair generation (p_{gen}). In contrast, the time taken for EPR pair generation (t_{gen}) seems to have a larger impact on the overall success probability as compared with time for BSM operation (t_{bsm}). Finally and most importantly, in spite of the disparity in the simulation tool and the model checking tool, the shapes of the curves are similar. This suggests that useful qualitative analyses comparing time critical quantum systems can be performed relatively easily. A careful fine tuning of the parameters (like classical communication overheads) can yield a more accurate quantitative analysis as well.

6   Discussions and Outlook

We studied a small quantum entanglement swapping system through model checking. Comparison of the results were carried out with a simulator, using justifiably similar parameters. This work is a step towards studying complex time critical quantum systems using formal methods. We are carrying out extensions in several directions, largely arising from scaling the quantum network. For large path lengths:

- the order in which the entanglement generations and BSMs are carried out matters, especially if the quantum nodes have different quantum hardware. For example, it would make sense to complete the operations on a quantum node whose resilience is lesser than others. Then, an interesting problem would be to synthesize the schedule that maximizes the overall success probability.
- classical communications and delays play a non-negligible role. Recall that classical communications are needed during BSM and in general, for synchronization. We noticed this phenomenon even in a four node network in our experiments which we have not reported here.

For the more ambitious goal of modeling and analyzing generic networks with several demands for EPR pairs between arbitrary nodes in real time, exact model checking could prove expensive. For such systems, other approaches like statistical model checking could be a better alternative.

References

1. Abdeddaim, Y., Kerbaa, A., Maler, O.: Task graph scheduling using timed automata. In: Proceedings International Parallel and Distributed Processing Symposium, p. 237 (2003)
2. Abdeddaïm, Y., Asarin, E., Maler, O.: Scheduling with timed automata. Theor. Comput. Sci. **354**, 272–300 (2006)
3. Baier, C., Katoen, J.P.: Principles of Model Checking (Representation and Mind Series). The MIT Press, Cambridge (2008)
4. Bennett, C.H., Brassard, G.: Quantum cryptography: public key distribution and coin tossing. In: Proceedings of IEEE International Conference on Computers, Systems, and Signal Processing, p. 175. India (1984)
5. Bennett, C.H., Bernstein, H.J., Popescu, S., Schumacher, B.: Concentrating partial entanglement by local operations. Phys. Rev. A **53**, 2046–2052 (1996)
6. Bennett, C.H., Brassard, G., Crépeau, C., Jozsa, R., Peres, A., Wootters, W.K.: Teleporting an unknown quantum state via dual classical and Einstein-Podolsk-rosen channels. Phys. Rev. Lett. **70**, 1895–1899 (1993)
7. Bennett, C.H., Brassard, G., Popescu, S., Schumacher, B., Smolin, J.A., Wootters, W.K.: Purification of noisy entanglement and faithful teleportation via noisy channels. Phys. Rev. Lett. **76**, 722–725 (1996)
8. Bouwmeester, D., Pan, J.W., Mattle, K., Eibl, M., Weinfurter, H., Zeilinger, A.: Experimental quantum teleportation. Nature **390**(6660), 575–579 (1997)
9. Coecke, B.: The logic of entanglement. In: van Breugel, F., Kashefi, E., Palamidessi, C., Rutten, J. (eds.) Horizons of the Mind. A Tribute to Prakash Panangaden. LNCS, vol. 8464, pp. 250–267. Springer, Cham (2014). https://doi.org/10.1007/978-3-319-06880-0_13
10. Coopmans, T., et al.: NetSquid, a network simulator for quantum information using discrete events. Commun. Phys. **4**(1), 164 (2021)
11. Dahlberg, A., Wehner, S.: Simulaqron-a simulator for developing quantum internet software. Quan. Sci. Technol. **4**(1) (2018)
12. Diadamo, S., Nötzel, J., Zanger, B., Beşe, M.M.: Qunetsim: a software framework for quantum networks. IEEE Trans. Quant. Eng. **2**, 1–12 (2021)
13. Dür, W., Briegel, H.J.: Entanglement purification and quantum error correction. Rep. Progr. Phys. **70**(8), 1381–1424 (2007)
14. Elboukhari, M., Azizi, M., Azizi, A.: Analysis of the security of bb84 by model checking. Int. J. Netw. Secur. Appl. **2** (2010)
15. Gay, S., Nagarajan, R., Papanikolaou, N.: Probabilistic model-checking of quantum protocols (2005). https://arxiv.org/abs/quant-ph/0504007
16. Hansson, H., Jonsson, B.: A logic for reasoning about time and reliability. Form. Asp. Comput. **6**(5), 512–535 (1994)
17. Huang, B., Huang, Y., Kong, J., Huang, X.: Model checking quantum key distribution protocols. In: 2016 8th International Conference on Information Technology in Medicine and Education (ITME), pp. 611–615 (2016)
18. Kakutani, Y.: A logic for formal verification of quantum programs. In: Datta, A. (ed.) ASIAN 2009. LNCS, vol. 5913, pp. 79–93. Springer, Heidelberg (2009). https://doi.org/10.1007/978-3-642-10622-4_7
19. Khatri, S.: On the design and analysis of near-term quantum network protocols using Markov decision processes (2022). https://arxiv.org/abs/2207.03403

20. Kwiatkowska, M., Norman, G., Parker, D.: PRISM 4.0: verification of probabilistic real-time systems. In: Gopalakrishnan, G., Qadeer, S. (eds.) CAV 2011. LNCS, vol. 6806, pp. 585–591. Springer, Heidelberg (2011). https://doi.org/10.1007/978-3-642-22110-1_47

21. Kwiatkowska, M., Norman, G., Parker, D., Sproston, J.: Performance analysis of probabilistic timed automata using digital clocks. Form. Methods Syst. Des. **29**, 33–78 (2006)

22. Kwiatkowska, M., Norman, G., Segala, R., Sproston, J.: Automatic verification of real-time systems with discrete probability distributions. In: Katoen, J.-P. (ed.) ARTS 1999. LNCS, vol. 1601, pp. 75–95. Springer, Heidelberg (1999). https://doi.org/10.1007/3-540-48778-6_5

23. Liu, J., et al.: Formal verification of quantum algorithms using quantum Hoare logic. In: Dillig, I., Tasiran, S. (eds.) CAV 2019. LNCS, vol. 11562, pp. 187–207. Springer, Cham (2019). https://doi.org/10.1007/978-3-030-25543-5_12

24. Nielsen, M.A., Chuang, I.L.: Quantum Computation and Quantum Information: 10th Anniversary Edition, 10th edn. Cambridge University Press, USA (2011)

25. Norman, G., Parker, D., Sproston, J.: Model checking for probabilistic timed automata. Form. Methods Syst. Des. **43**(2), 164–190 (2013)

26. Nötzel, J., DiAdamo, S.: Entanglement-enhanced communication networks. In: 2020 IEEE International Conference on Quantum Computing and Engineering (QCE), pp. 242–248 (2020)

27. Pu, Y.E., et al.: Experimental demonstration of memory-enhanced scaling for entanglement connection of quantum repeater segments. Nat. Phot. **15**(5), 374–378 (2021)

28. Wu, X., et al.: SeQUeNCe: a customizable discrete-event simulator of quantum networks. Quantum Sci. Technol. **6** (2020)

29. Ying, M., Feng, Y.: Model Checking Quantum Systems: Principles and Algorithms. Cambridge University Press, Cambridge (2021)

30. Žukowski, M., Zeilinger, A., Horne, M.A., Ekert, A.K.: "Event-ready-detector" bell experiment via entanglement swapping. Phys. Rev. Lett. **71**, 4287–4290 (1993)

Temporal Logic

An STL-Based Formulation of Resilience in Cyber-Physical Systems

Hongkai Chen[1]([envelope]) [iD], Shan Lin[1] [iD], Scott A. Smolka[1], and Nicola Paoletti[2] [iD]

[1] Stony Brook University, Stony Brook, USA
{hongkai.chen,shan.x.lin}@stonybrook.edu, sas@cs.stonybrook.edu
[2] Royal Holloway, University of London, Egham, UK
nicola.paoletti@rhul.ac.uk

Abstract. Resiliency is the ability to quickly recover from a violation and avoid future violations for as long as possible. Such a property is of fundamental importance for Cyber-Physical Systems (CPS), and yet, to date, there is no widely agreed-upon formal treatment of CPS resiliency. We present an STL-based framework for reasoning about resiliency in CPS in which resiliency has a syntactic characterization in the form of an *STL-based Resiliency Specification* (SRS). Given an arbitrary STL formula φ, time bounds α and β, the SRS of φ, $R_{\alpha,\beta}(\varphi)$, is the STL formula $\neg\varphi \mathbf{U}_{[0,\alpha]} \mathbf{G}_{[0,\beta)}\varphi$, specifying that recovery from a violation of φ occur within time α (*recoverability*), and subsequently that φ be maintained for duration β (*durability*). These R-expressions, which are atoms in our SRS logic, can be combined using STL operators, allowing one to express composite resiliency specifications, e.g., multiple SRSs must hold simultaneously, or the system must eventually be resilient. We define a quantitative semantics for SRSs in the form of a *Resilience Satisfaction Value* (ReSV) function r and prove its soundness and completeness w.r.t. STL's Boolean semantics. The r-value for $R_{\alpha,\beta}(\varphi)$ atoms is a singleton set containing a pair quantifying recoverability and durability. The r-value for a composite SRS formula results in a set of non-dominated recoverability-durability pairs, given that the ReSVs of subformulas might not be directly comparable (e.g., one subformula has superior durability but worse recoverability than another). To the best of our knowledge, this is the first *multi-dimensional* quantitative semantics for an STL-based logic. Two case studies demonstrate the practical utility of our approach.

1 Introduction

Resiliency (*syn.* resilience) is defined as the ability to recover from or adjust easily to adversity or change [20]. Resiliency is of fundamental importance in Cyber-Physical Systems (CPS), which are expected to exhibit safety- or mission-critical behavior even in the presence of internal faults or external disturbances. Consider for example the *lane keeping* problem for autonomous vehicles (AVs), which requires a vehicle to stay within the marked boundaries of the lane it is driving in at all times. The standard temporal-logic-based notion of safety is not

© Springer Nature Switzerland AG 2022
S. Bogomolov and D. Parker (Eds.): FORMATS 2022, LNCS 13465, pp. 117–135, 2022.
https://doi.org/10.1007/978-3-031-15839-1_7

ideally suited for specifying the AV's behavior when it comes to lane keeping. This is because AV technology is not perfect and driving conditions (e.g., being crowded by a neighboring vehicle) and other external disturbances may require occasional or even intermittent violations of lane keeping. Rather, the AV should behave resiliently in the presence of a lane violation, recovering from the violation in a timely fashion, and avoiding future lane departures for as long as possible. Unfortunately, there is no widely agreed notion of resiliency within the CPS community, despite several efforts to settle the issue (see Sect. 5).

Our Contributions. In this paper, we present an STL-based framework for reasoning about resiliency in Cyber-Physical Systems. In our approach, resiliency has a syntactic characterization in the form of an *STL-based Resiliency Specification* (SRS). Given an arbitrary STL formula φ, time bounds α and β, the SRS of φ, $R_{\alpha,\beta}(\varphi)$, is the STL formula $\neg\varphi\mathbf{U}_{[0,\alpha]}\mathbf{G}_{[0,\beta)}\varphi$, which specifies that recovery from a violation of φ occur within time α, and subsequently φ be maintained for duration β at least. The SRS of φ captures the requirement that a system quickly recovers from a violation of φ (*recoverability*) and then satisfy φ for an extended period of time (*durability*). The $R_{\alpha,\beta}(\varphi)$ expressions, which are atoms in our SRS logic, can be inductively combined using STL operators, allowing one to express composite resiliency specifications; e.g., multiple SRSs must hold simultaneously $(R_{\alpha_1,\beta_1}(\varphi_1) \wedge R_{\alpha_2,\beta_2}(\varphi_2))$, or that the system must eventually be resilient $(\mathbf{F}_I R_{\alpha,\beta}(\varphi))$.

We define a quantitative semantics for SRSs in the form of a *Resilience Satisfaction Value* (ReSV) function r. Our semantics for $R_{\alpha,\beta}(\varphi)$ atoms is a singleton set of the form $\{(rec, dur)\}$, where *rec* quantifies how early before bound α recovery occurs, and *dur* indicates for how long after bound β property φ is maintained. To the best of our knowledge, this is the first *multi-dimensional* quantitative semantics for STL.

Our approach does not make any simplifying assumption as to which of the two requirements (recoverability and durability) to prioritize or how to combine the two values. This decision can lead to a semantic structure involving two or more non-dominated (rec, dur) pairs. In such situations, we choose to retain *all* non-dominated pairs so as to provide a comprehensive, assumption-free, characterization of CPS resiliency. Thus, our semantics is a set of non-dominated (rec, dur) pairs, which is derived inductively from subformulas using Pareto optimization.

For example, consider the SRS $\psi_1 \vee \psi_2$, where the ReSV of ψ_1 (over a given signal at a particular time) is $\{(2,5)\}$ and, similarly, the ReSV of ψ_2 is $\{(3,3)\}$. The semantics of $\psi_1 \vee \psi_2$ should choose the dominant pair, but the two are non-dominated: $(3,3)$ has better recoverability, while $(2,5)$ has better durability. So we include both. We prove that our semantics is sound and complete with respect to the classic STL Boolean semantics by (essentially) showing that an SRS ψ has at least one non-dominated pair with *rec*, *dur* > 0 iff ψ is true.

We perform an extensive experimental evaluation of our framework centered around two case studies: UAV package delivery and multi-agent flocking. In both cases, we formulate mission requirements in STL, and evaluate their ReSV values in the context of various SRS specifications. Our results clearly demonstrate the expressive power of our framework.

2 Preliminaries

In this section, we introduce the syntax and semantics of Signal Temporal Logic (STL) [12,17]. STL is a formal specification language for real-valued signals. We consider n-dimensional discrete-time signals $\xi : \mathbb{T} \to \mathbb{R}^n$ where $\mathbb{T} = \mathbb{Z}_{\geq 0}$ is the (discrete) time domain.[1] $\mathbb{T}$ is the interval $[0, |\xi|]$, where $|\xi| > 0$ is the length of the signal. If $|\xi| < \infty$, we call ξ bounded. We use the words signal and trajectory interchangeably. An STL atomic predicate $p \in AP$ is defined over signals and is of the form $p \equiv \mu(\xi(t)) \geq c$, $t \in \mathbb{T}$, $c \in \mathbb{R}$, and $\mu : \mathbb{R}^n \to \mathbb{R}$. STL formulas φ are defined recursively according to the following grammar [12]:

$$\varphi ::= p \mid \neg\varphi \mid \varphi_1 \wedge \varphi_2 \mid \varphi_1 \mathbf{U}_I \varphi_2$$

where $\mathbf{U}$ is the *until* operator and I is an interval on $\mathbb{T}$. Logical disjunction is derived from $\wedge$ and $\neg$ as usual, and operators *eventually* and *always* are derived from $\mathbf{U}$ as usual: $\mathbf{F}_I \varphi = \top \mathbf{U}_I \varphi$ and $\mathbf{G}_I \varphi = \neg(\mathbf{F}_I \neg \varphi)$. The satisfaction relation $(\xi, t) \models \varphi$, indicating ξ satisfies φ at time t, is defined as follows:[2]

$$(\xi, t) \models p \quad\Leftrightarrow\quad \mu(\xi(t)) \geq c$$
$$(\xi, t) \models \neg\varphi \quad\Leftrightarrow\quad \neg((\xi, t) \models \varphi)$$
$$(\xi, t) \models \varphi_1 \wedge \varphi_2 \quad\Leftrightarrow\quad (\xi, t) \models \varphi_1 \wedge (\xi, t) \models \varphi_2$$
$$(\xi, t) \models \varphi_1 \mathbf{U}_I \varphi_2 \quad\Leftrightarrow\quad \exists\, t' \in t + I \text{ s.t. } (\xi, t') \models \varphi_2 \wedge \forall\, t'' \in [t, t'),\ (\xi, t'') \models \varphi_1$$

We call an STL formula φ *bounded-time* if all of its temporal operators are bounded (i.e., their intervals have finite upper bounds) and $|\xi|$ is large enough to determine satisfiability at time 0; i.e., $|\xi|$ is greater than the maximum over the sums of all the nested upper bounds on the temporal operators [26]. For example, if φ is $\varphi_1 \mathbf{U}_{[0,5]} \mathbf{G}_{[1,2]} \varphi_2 \wedge \mathbf{F}_{[0,10]} \mathbf{G}_{[1,6]} \varphi_2$, then a trajectory with length $N \geq \max(5 + 2, 10 + 6) = 16$ is sufficient to determine whether φ holds. In this paper, we only consider bounded-time STL formulas as in its original definition [17].

STL admits a quantitative semantics given by a real-valued function ρ such that $\rho(\varphi, \xi, t) > 0 \Rightarrow (\xi, t) \models \varphi$, and defined as follows [12]:

$$\rho(\mu(\xi(t)) \geq c, \xi, t) = \mu(\xi(t)) - c$$
$$\rho(\neg\varphi, \xi, t) = -\rho(\varphi, \xi, t)$$
$$\rho(\varphi_1 \wedge \varphi_2, \xi, t) = \min(\rho(\varphi_1, \xi, t), \rho(\varphi_2, \xi, t))$$
$$\rho(\varphi_1 \mathbf{U}_I \varphi_2, \xi, t) = \max_{t' \in t + I} \min(\rho(\varphi_2, \xi, t'), \min_{t'' \in [t, t+t')} \rho(\varphi_1, \xi, t''))$$

A ρ-value, called the *robustness satisfaction value* (RSV), can be interpreted as the extent to which ξ satisfies φ at time t. Its absolute value can be viewed as the distance of ξ from the set of trajectories satisfying or violating φ, with positive values indicating satisfaction and negative values indicating violation.

---

[1] Discrete-time signals over an arbitrary time step can always be mapped to signals over a unit time step.

[2] Given $t \in \mathbb{T}$ and interval I on $\mathbb{T}$, $t + I$ is used to denote the set $\{t + t' \mid t' \in I\}$.

3 Specifying Resilience in STL

In this section, we introduce our STL-based resiliency specification formalism and its quantitative semantics in terms of non-dominated recoverability-durability pairs.

3.1 Resiliency Specification Language

We introduce an STL-based temporal logic to reason about resiliency of STL formulas. Given an STL specification φ, there are two properties that characterize its resilience w.r.t. a signal ξ, namely, *recoverability* and *durability*: the ability to (1) recover from a violation of φ within time α, and (2) subsequently maintain φ for at least time β.

Example 1. Consider an STL specification $\varphi = (2 \leq y \leq 4)$, where y is a signal. In Fig. 1(a), signals ξ_1 and ξ_2 violate φ at time t_1. Given recovery deadline α, we see that only ξ_1 satisfies recoverability of φ w.r.t. α because φ becomes true before $t_1 + \alpha$. In the case of ξ_2, φ becomes true only after $t_1 + \alpha$. In Fig. 1(b), signals ξ_3 and ξ_4 recover to satisfy φ at time t_2. Given durability bound β, we observe that only ξ_3 is durable w.r.t. β.

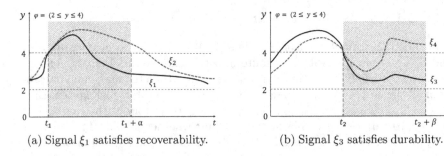

(a) Signal ξ_1 satisfies recoverability.   (b) Signal ξ_3 satisfies durability.

Fig. 1. Resilience w.r.t. an STL formula $\varphi = (2 \leq y \leq 4)$

Resilience of an STL formula φ relative to a signal should be determined by the joint satisfaction of recoverability and durability of φ. We can formalize this notion using the STL formula $R_{\alpha,\beta}(\varphi) \equiv \neg\varphi\,\mathbf{U}_{[0,\alpha]}\mathbf{G}_{[0,\beta)}\varphi$, which captures the requirement that the system recovers from a violation of φ within bound α and subsequently maintains φ for bound β. In what follows, we introduce SRS, an STL-based resiliency specification language that allows one to combine multiple $R_{\alpha,\beta}(\varphi)$ expressions using Boolean and temporal operators.

Definition 1 (STL-based Resiliency Specification). *The STL-based resiliency specification (SRS) language is defined by the following grammar:*

$$\psi ::= R_{\alpha,\beta}(\varphi) \mid \neg\psi \mid \psi_1 \wedge \psi_2 \mid \psi_1 \mathbf{U}_I \psi_2$$

where φ is an STL formula, $R_{\alpha,\beta}(\varphi) \equiv \neg\varphi\,\mathbf{U}_{[0,\alpha]}\mathbf{G}_{[0,\beta)}\varphi$, $\alpha, \beta \in \mathbb{T}$, $\beta > 0$.

We use a semi-closed interval in the $\mathbf{G}$ operator, reflecting our requirement that φ stays true for a time interval of duration β, and may be false at the end of the interval. The piece-wise constant interpretation of discrete-time signals implies that properties between two consecutive steps remain unchanged (see Remark 5). SRS formulas are also restricted to bounded-time intervals as those in STL formulas. Boolean satisfiability of an SRS formula ψ reduces to the satisfiability of the corresponding STL formula obtained by replacing every atom $R_{\alpha,\beta}(\varphi)$ with $\neg\varphi\mathbf{U}_{[0,\alpha]}\mathbf{G}_{[0,\beta)}\varphi$. Note that satisfiability of an $R_{\alpha,\beta}(\varphi)$ atom involves satisfying the recoverability and durability requirements for φ highlighted in Example 1.

Remark 1 (Why a new logic? (1/2)). We note that SRS is equivalent to STL in the sense that any STL formula φ is equivalent to the SRS atom $R_{0,1}(\varphi)$ and, conversely, any SRS formula is an STL formula. *Then why would we introduce a new logic?* The SRS logic is explicitly designed to express specifications that combine resiliency requirements with Boolean and temporal operators. Most importantly, as we will see, our semantics for SRS is defined inductively starting from $R_{\alpha,\beta}(\varphi)$ atoms, and not from STL atomic predicates. The former are more expressive than the latter (an STL atomic predicate can be expressed via an SRS atom, but not vice versa).

Remark 2 (Resilience vs. safety, liveness, and stability). We stress that safety properties $\mathbf{G}_I\varphi$ are not sufficient to capture resilience, as they do not allow for occasional, short-lived violations. Among the liveness properties, reachability properties $\mathbf{F}_I\varphi$ do not capture the requirement that we want to satisfy φ in a durable manner. Similarly, progress properties, summarized by the template $\mathbf{G}_{I_1}(\neg\varphi \rightarrow \mathbf{F}_{I_2}\varphi)$, do not require the signal to satisfy φ for extended time periods (but they "infinitely" often lead to φ).

Thus, one might be tempted to combine safety and liveness and express resilience as a $\mathbf{F}_{[0,\alpha]}\mathbf{G}_{[0,\beta)}\varphi$, a template often called *stability* or stabilization [10]. There is a subtle but important difference between stability and our definition $\neg\varphi\mathbf{U}_{[0,\alpha]}\mathbf{G}_{[0,\beta)}\varphi$ of resilience: there could be multiple recovery episodes occurring in a trajectory, i.e., time steps where φ transitions from false to true. Stability is satisfied by *any* recovery episode within time $[0,\alpha]$ provided that φ stays true for at least time β. On the contrary, resilience is satisfied by only the *first* recovery episode, provided that φ is not violated for longer than α and stays true for at least β. This is an important difference because our resiliency semantics is defined as a recoverability-durability pair, roughly corresponding to the time it takes to recover from a violation of φ and the time for which φ subsequently remains true (see Definition 4). Since the stability pattern matches multiple recovery episodes, it is not clear which episode to use in the computation of our resiliency semantics. Our definition solves this ambiguity by considering the first episode. We remark that SRS allows us to express properties like $\mathbf{G}_I R_{\alpha,\beta}(\varphi)$ (or $\mathbf{F}_I R_{\alpha,\beta}(\varphi)$), which can be understood as enforcing the resiliency requirement $R_{\alpha,\beta}(\varphi)$ for each (for some) recovery episode within I, and whose semantics can be interpreted as the worst- (best-) case recovery episode within I.

Remark 3 (Why a new logic? (2/2)). The reader might wonder why we would be interested in using temporal operators to reason about a resiliency atom of the form $R_{\alpha,\beta}(\varphi)$ as opposed to pushing these operators into $R_{\alpha,\beta}(\varphi)$. For example, why would we consider (1) $\mathbf{G}_I R_{\alpha,\beta}(\varphi)$ instead of (2) $R_{\alpha,\beta}(\mathbf{G}_I \varphi)$ for an STL formula φ? The two expressions are fundamentally different: (1) states that the resiliency specification holds for all φ-related recovery episodes occurring in interval I; (2) states that the resiliency specification must hold in the first recovery episode relative to $\mathbf{G}_I \varphi$ (i.e., the first time $\mathbf{G}_I \varphi$ switches from false to true). Arguably, (1) is more useful than (2), even though both are reasonable SRS expressions (compound and atomic, respectively).

3.2   Semantics of Resiliency Specifications

We provide a quantitative semantics for SRS specifications in the form of a *resilience satisfaction value* (ReSV). Intuitively, an ReSV value quantifies the extent to which recoverability and durability are satisfied. More precisely, it produces a non-dominated set of pairs $(x_r, x_d) \in \mathbb{Z}^2$, where (in the atomic case) x_r quantifies how early before bound α the system recovers, and x_d quantifies how long after bound β the property is maintained. We further demonstrate the soundness of the ReSV-based semantics w.r.t. the STL Boolean interpretation of resiliency specifications. The first step is to establish when one recoverability-durability pair is better than another.

A *set $S \subseteq \mathbb{R}^n$ of non-dominated tuples* is one where no two tuples x and y can be found in S such that x *Pareto-dominates* y, denoted by $x \succ y$. We have that $x \succ y$ if $x_i \geq y_i$, $1 \leq i \leq n$, and $x_i > y_i$ for at least one such i, under the usual ordering $>$.

We define a novel notion of "resilience dominance" captured by the relation $\succ_{re}$ in $\mathbb{Z}^2$. This is needed because using the standard Pareto-dominance relation $\succ$ (induced by the canonical $>$ order) would result in an ordering of ReSV pairs that is inconsistent with the Boolean satisfiability viewpoint. Consider the pairs $(-2, 3)$ and $(1, 1)$. By Pareto-dominance, $(-2, 3)$ and $(1, 1)$ are mutually non-dominated, but an ReSV of $(-2, 3)$ indicates that the system doesn't satisfy recoverability; namely it recovers two time units too late. On the other hand, an ReSV of $(1, 1)$ implies satisfaction of both recoverability and durability bounds, and thus should be preferred to $(-2, 3)$. We formalize this intuition next.

Definition 2 (Resiliency Binary Relations).   *We define binary relations $\succ_{re}$, $=_{re}$, and $\prec_{re}$ in $\mathbb{Z}^2$. Let $x, y \in \mathbb{Z}^2$ with $x = (x_r, x_d)$, $y = (y_r, y_d)$, and sign is the signum function. We have that $x \succ_{re} y$ if either of the following conditions holds:*

1. $sign(x_r) + sign(x_d) > sign(y_r) + sign(y_d)$.
2. $sign(x_r) + sign(x_d) = sign(y_r) + sign(y_d)$, and $x \succ y$.

We say that x and y are mutually non-dominated, denoted $x =_{re} y$, if $sign(x_r) + sign(x_d) = sign(y_r) + sign(y_d)$ and neither $x \succ y$ nor $x \prec y$. Under this ordering, a non-dominated set S is such that $x =_{re} y$ for every choice of $x, y \in S$. We denote by $\prec_{re}$ the dual of $\succ_{re}$.

It is easy to see that $\succ_{re}$, $\prec_{re}$ and $=_{re}$ are mutually exclusive, and in particular, they collectively form a partition of $\mathbb{Z}^2 \times \mathbb{Z}^2$. This tells us that for any $x, y \in \mathbb{Z}^2$, either x dominates y (i.e., $x \succ_{re} y$), x is dominated by y (i.e., $x \prec_{re} y$), or the two are mutually non-dominated (i.e., $x =_{re} y$).

Lemma 1. *Relations $\succ_{re}$ and $\prec_{re}$ are strict partial orders.*

A proof can be found in Appendix C in [8].

Definition 3 (Maximum and Minimum Resilience Sets). *Given $P \subseteq \mathbb{Z}^2$, with $P \neq \emptyset$, the* maximum resilience set *of P, denoted $\max_{re}(P)$, is the largest subset $S \subseteq P$ such that $\forall x \in S$, $\forall y \in P$, $x \succ_{re} y$ or $x =_{re} y$. The* minimum resilience set *of P, denoted $\min_{re}(P)$, is the largest subset $S \subseteq P$ such that $\forall x \in S$, $\forall y \in P$, $x \prec_{re} y$ or $x =_{re} y$.*

Corollary 1. *Maximum and minimum resilience sets are non-empty and non-dominated sets.*

A proof can be found in Appendix A in [8].

Example 2. Let $P = \{(-1, 2), (1, -2), (2, -1)\}$. Then, we have $\max_{re}(P) = \{(-1, 2), (2, -1)\}$ because $(-1, 2) =_{re} y$ for all $y \in P$ and $(2, -1) \succ_{re} (1, -2)$, $(2, -1) =_{re} (1, -2)$, and $(2, -1) =_{re} (2, -1)$. In contrast, $(1, -2)$ is not in $\max_{re}(P)$ because $(1, -2) \prec_{re} (2, -1)$. Similarly, we have $\min_{re}(P) = \{(-1, 2), (1, -2)\}$. We also note that (as per Corollary 1) the elements of $\max_{re}(P)$ and $\min_{re}(P)$ are mutually non-dominated, i.e., $(-1, 2) =_{re} (2, -1)$ and $(-1, 2) =_{re} (1, -2)$, respectively.

Now we are ready to introduce the semantics for our SRS logic. Its definition makes use of maximum and minimum resilience sets in the same way as the traditional STL robustness semantics (see Sect. 2) uses max and min operators in compound formulas. Hence, by Corollary 1, our semantics produces non-dominated sets, which implies that all pairs in such a set are equivalent from a Boolean satisfiability standpoint. This is because $x_r > 0$ ($x_d > 0$) in Definition 2 implies Boolean satisfaction of the recoverability (durability) portion of an $R_{\alpha,\beta}(\varphi)$ expression. This property will be useful in Theorem 1, where we show that our semantics is sound with respect to the Boolean semantics of STL.

Definition 4 (Resilience Satisfaction Value). *Let ψ be an SRS specification and $\xi : \mathbb{T} \to \mathbb{R}^n$ a signal. We define $r(\psi, \xi, t) \subseteq \mathbb{Z}^2$, the* resilience satisfaction value *(ReSV) of ψ with respect to ξ at time t, as follows.*

– *For ψ an SRS atom of the form $R_{\alpha,\beta}(\varphi)$, φ an STL formula,*

$$r(\psi, \xi, t) = \{(-t_{rec}(\varphi, \xi, t) + \alpha, t_{dur}(\varphi, \xi, t) - \beta)\} \tag{1}$$

where

$$t_{rec}(\varphi, \xi, t) = \min(\{d \in \mathbb{T} \mid (\xi, t + d) \models \varphi\} \cup \{|\xi| - t\}) \tag{2}$$

$$t_{dur}(\varphi, \xi, t) = \min(\{d \in \mathbb{T} \mid (\xi, t' + d) \models \neg\varphi\} \cup \{|\xi| - t'\}),$$

$$t' = t + t_{rec}(\varphi, \xi, t) \tag{3}$$

- *The ReSV of a composite SRS formula is defined inductively as follows.*

$$r(\neg\psi,\xi,t) = \{(-x,-y) : (x,y) \in r(\psi,\xi,t)\}$$
$$r(\psi_1 \wedge \psi_2,\xi,t) = \min{}_{re}(r(\psi_1,\xi,t) \cup r(\psi_2,\xi,t))$$
$$r(\psi_1 \vee \psi_2,\xi,t) = \max{}_{re}(r(\psi_1,\xi,t) \cup r(\psi_2,\xi,t))$$
$$r(\mathbf{G}_I\psi,\xi,t) = \min{}_{re}(\cup_{t'\in t+I}\, r(\psi,\xi,t'))$$
$$r(\mathbf{F}_I\psi,\xi,t) = \max{}_{re}(\cup_{t'\in t+I}\, r(\psi,\xi,t'))$$
$$r(\psi_1\mathbf{U}_I\psi_2,\xi,t) = \max{}_{re} \cup_{t'\in t+I} \min{}_{re}(r(\psi_2,\xi,t') \cup$$
$$\min{}_{re} \cup_{t''\in[t,t+t')} r(\psi_1,\xi,t''))$$

In the base case, $t' = t + t_{rec}(\varphi,\xi,t)$ is the first time φ becomes true starting from and including t. If recovery does not occur along ξ (and so the first set in Eq. (2) is empty), then $t' = |\xi|$ (the length of the trajectory). Similarly, $t' + t_{dur}(\varphi,\xi,t)$ is the first time φ is violated after t'. Thus $t_{dur}(\varphi,\xi,t)$ quantifies the maximum time duration φ remains true after recovery at time t'. If φ is true for the entire duration of ξ, then $t_{rec}(\varphi,\xi,t) = 0$ and $t_{dur}(\varphi,\xi,t) = |\xi| - t$. If φ is false for the duration of ξ, then $t_{rec}(\varphi,\xi,t) = |\xi| - t$; therefore $t' = |\xi|$ and $t_{dur}(\varphi,\xi,t) = 0$.

Therefore, the semantics for an SRS atom $R_{\alpha,\beta}(\varphi)$ is a singleton set $\{(x_r, x_d)\}$, where x_r quantifies how early before time bound α recovery occurs, and x_d indicates for how long after time bound β the property is maintained. Thus, x_r and x_d quantifies the satisfaction extent (in time) of recoverability and durability, respectively. An important property follows from this observation: similar to traditional STL robustness, a positive (pair-wise) ReSV value indicates satisfaction of recoverability or durability, a negative ReSV value indicates violation, and larger ReSV values indicate better resiliency, i.e., shorter recovery times and longer durability.

The ReSV semantics for composite SRS formulas is derived by computing sets of maximum/minimum recoverability-durability pairs in a similar fashion to STL robustness: for the $\wedge$ and $\mathbf{G}$ operators, we consider the minimum set over the ReSV pairs resulting from the semantics of the subformulas; for $\vee$ and $\mathbf{F}$, we consider the maximum set. We remark that our semantics induces sets of pairs (rather than unique values); our $\succ_{re}$ and $\prec_{re}$ relations used to compute maximum and minimum resilience sets are therefore partial in nature. This is to be expected because any reasonable ordering on multi-dimensional data is partial by nature. For example, given pairs $(2,5)$ and $(3,3)$, there is no way to establish which pair dominates the other: the two are indeed non-dominated and, in particular, the first pair has better durability but worse recoverability than the second pair. In such a situation, our semantics would retain both pairs.

Algorithm for Computing the ReSV Function r. The algorithm to compute r is a faithful implementation of Definition 4. It takes an SRS formula ψ, signal ξ, and time t, produces a syntax tree representing ψ, and computes the r-values of the subformulas of ψ in a bottom-up fashion starting with the SRS atomic R-expressions at the leaves. Each leaf-node computation amounts to evaluating satisfaction of the corresponding STL formula. The complexity of this operation is $O(|\xi|^{2l})$, for a trajectory ξ and an STL formula with at most l nested *until* operators [12,15]. Let m be the number of R-expressions in ψ. Given that we need to evaluate the R-expressions at each time point along ξ, the time needed to compute the r-values of all SRS atoms in ψ is $O(m|\xi|^{2l+1})$.

Every node v of the tree has an associated result set P_v of (rec, dur) pairs. When v is an interior node of the tree, P_v is determined, using Definition 4, by computing the maximum or minimum resilience set of the result set(s) of v's children. The complexity for computing P_v can thus be shown to be quadratic in the size of its input. In particular, the size of the input at the root of ψ's syntax tree is bounded by $O(|\xi|^{2L})$, where L is the maximum number of nested *until* operators in ψ.[3] Furthermore, the ReSV of the *until* operator can be computed in a manner similar to how STL robustness is computed for the *until* operator. Therefore, the complexity of computing the root node's ReSV is $O((|\xi|^{2L})^2 + |\xi|^{2L})$. Consequently, the total complexity of computing the ReSV of ψ is $O(m|\xi|^{2l+1} + |\xi|^{4L})$.

Remark 4 (Bounded-time SRS formulas). We say that an SRS formula is *bounded-time* if all of its temporal operators are bounded and the STL formulas serving as SRS atoms are bounded-time. When a bounded signal ξ is not long enough to evaluate a bounded-time formula, we extend it to the required length simply by repeating its terminal value $\xi(T)$. For example, let $\varphi = \mathbf{G}_{[0,10]} (2 \leq y \leq 4)$ and consider ξ_3 from Fig. 1(b), where $|\xi_3| = t_2 + \beta$. We extend $|\xi_3|$ to $t_2 + \beta + 10$, the required length to determine if $(\xi_3, t + \beta) \models \varphi$ (it does). Note that the signal extension might result in an overestimate of recoverability or durability.

Remark 5 (Relation to time robustness). A notion of (right) time robustness of an STL atomic proposition p on a trajectory ξ at time t is given by [12,23]:

$$\theta^+(p,\xi,t) = \chi(p,\xi,t) \cdot \max\{d \geq 0 \; s.t. \; \forall t' \in [t, t+d], \chi(p,\xi,t') = \chi(p,\xi,t)\}$$

where $\chi(p,\xi,t) = +1$ if $(\xi,t) \models p$, and -1 otherwise. Intuitively, $|\theta^+(p,\xi,t)|$ measures how long after t property p (or $\neg p$) remains satisfied. One might be tempted to use θ^+ in our definition $t_{rec}(\varphi,\xi,t)$ by setting it to $\max\{0, \theta^+(\neg\varphi,\xi,t)\}$, i.e., the maximum time duration for which φ is violated (or 0 if φ holds at t). This, however, implies that $t' = t + t_{rec}(\varphi,\xi,t)$ now represents the last time point for which φ is false. In our definition, we want instead t' to be the first time point φ becomes true. This difference is important, especially for discrete-time signals where the distance between two consecutive time points is non-negligible.

Moreover, time robustness may not quite handle some common corner cases. Consider a proposition p, and two signals ξ_1 and ξ_2 such that $(\xi_1, t) \models p$ and $(\xi_1, t') \not\models p$, $t' > t$, and $(\xi_2, t) \not\models p$ and $(\xi_2, t') \models p$, $t' > t$. The two signals have opposite behaviors in terms of satisfying p. In discrete-time settings (where

---

[3] This is because the size of an interior node v's input is bounded (in the case of the *until* operator) by $|\xi|^2$ times the sum of the sizes of the result sets of v's children. The size of the root node's input is thus $O(|\xi|^{2L})$.

a discrete-time signal is interpreted in the continuous domain as a piece-wise constant function), we have that ξ_1 (ξ_2) satisfies p ($\neg p$) throughout the interval $[t, t+1)$ (i.e., for "almost" 1 time unit). However, time robustness cannot distinguish between the two signals, namely, $\theta^+(p, \xi_1, t) = \theta^+(p, \xi_2, t) = 0$. Thus, if we used θ^+ to define t_{rec} it would be impossible to disambiguate between the first case (where no violation occurs at t) and the second case (where a violation occurs at t followed by a recovery episode at the next step). Our definition of t_{rec} in Eq. (2) correctly assign a value of 0 to ξ_1 (p is already satisfied, no recovery at t) and a value of 1 to ξ_2 (from t, it takes 1 time unit for p to become true).

Remark 6. We focus on discrete-times signals, thus a discrete-time SRS framework and discrete-time ReSV semantics. However, we expect that our approach can be extended to continuous time in a straightforward manner, because STL is well-defined over continuous-time signals. We leave this extension for future work.

Example 3. In Fig. 2, we consider a (one-dimensional) signal x (Fig. 2(a) top) and the proposition $x > 0$ (whose Boolean satisfaction value w.r.t. x is plotted on top of x). Consider the SRS formula $\psi_1 = \mathbf{G}_{[0,20]} R_{\alpha,\beta}(x > 0)$ with $\alpha = 1$, $\beta = 2$. Following Definition 4, the ReSV of ψ_1 can be written as:

$$r(\psi_1, x, 0) = \min_{re} \left(\cup_{t' \in [0,20]} r(R_{\alpha,\beta}(x > 0), x, t') \right)$$

where $r(R_{\alpha,\beta}(x > 0), x, t') = \{(-t_{rec}(x > 0, x, t') + \alpha, t_{dur}(x > 0, x, t') - \beta)\}$. Figure 2(a) bottom shows how the $-t_{rec}$ and the t_{dur} values evolve over time. These values are also displayed in Fig. 2(b) on a recoverability-durability plane, to better identify the Pareto-optimal values that constitute the ReSV of ψ_1, i.e., the elements of the minimum resilience set in the RHS of the above equation.

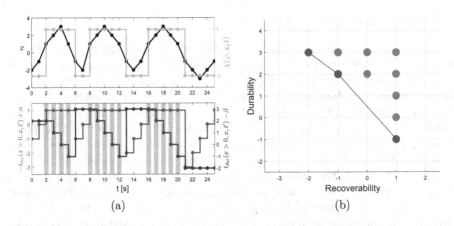

Fig. 2. (a) Signal x and its Boolean semantics w.r.t. $x > 0$ (top). Recoverability (red) and durability (blue) values for $x > 0$ over signal x (bottom). Green bars indicate $x > 0$. (b) Red dots represent the Pareto front for the recoverability-durability pairs of $R_{\alpha,\beta}(x > 0)$ over time interval $[0, 20]$. (Color figure online)

This is equal to $\{(-1,2),(1,-1),(-2,3)\}$, representing the recoverability and durability values of x w.r.t. $R_{\alpha,\beta}(x > 0)$ at times $t' = 0, 5, 13$.

On the other hand, we obtain a different ReSV if we consider the SRS formula $\psi_2 = R_{\alpha,\beta}(\mathbf{G}_{[0,20]}x > 0)$, where the $\mathbf{G}$ temporal operator is pushed inside the resiliency atom. Since x never satisfies $\mathbf{G}_{[0,20]}x > 0$ (thus, it violates the property at time 0 and never recovers), we have $t_{rec}(\mathbf{G}_{[0,20]}x > 0, x, 0) = |x| = 25$ and $t_{dur}(\mathbf{G}_{[0,20]}x > 0, x, 0) = 0$, resulting in $r(\psi_2) = \{(-24, -2)\}$.

Proposition 1. *The ReSV $r(\psi, \xi, t)$ of an SRS formula ψ w.r.t. a signal ξ at time t is a non-dominated set.*

A simple proof is given in Appendix B in [8], showing that any ReSV is either a maximum or minimum resilience set and thus, a non-dominated set as per Corollary 1. We are now ready to state the main theorem of our work, which establishes the soundness and completeness of SRS logic; i.e., our semantics is consistent from a Boolean satisfiability standpoint.

Theorem 1 (Soundness and Completeness of SRS Semantics). *Let ξ be a signal and ψ an SRS specification. The following results at time t hold:*
1) $\exists\, x \in r(\psi, \xi, t)$ s.t. $x \succ_{re} \mathbf{0} \implies (\xi, t) \models \psi$
2) $\exists\, x \in r(\psi, \xi, t)$ s.t. $x \prec_{re} \mathbf{0} \implies (\xi, t) \models \neg\psi$
3) $(\xi, t) \models \psi \implies \exists\, x \in r(\psi, \xi, t)$ s.t. $x \succ_{re} \mathbf{0}$ or $x =_{re} \mathbf{0}$
4) $(\xi, t) \models \neg\psi \implies \exists\, x \in r(\psi, \xi, t)$ s.t. $x \prec_{re} \mathbf{0}$ or $x =_{re} \mathbf{0}$

A proof is given in Appendix D in [8]. Since every ReSV $r(\psi, \xi, t)$ is a non-dominated set, then $\exists\, x \in r(\psi, \xi, t)$ s.t. $x \succ_{re} \mathbf{0}$ implies that $x \succ_{re} \mathbf{0}$ holds for all $x \in r(\psi, \xi, t)$ (see the proof of Theorem 1 for further details).

4   Case Study

In this section, we demonstrate the utility of our SRS logic and ReSV semantics on two case studies. We use Breach [11] for formulating STL formulas and evaluating their STL Boolean semantics. Experiments were performed on an Intel Core i7-8750H CPU @ 2.20 GHz with 16 GB of RAM and Windows 10 operating system. Our resiliency framework has been implemented in MATLAB; our implementation along with our case studies can be found in a publicly-available library.[4]

---

[4] See https://github.com/hongkaichensbu/resiliency-specs.

4.1   UAV Package Delivery

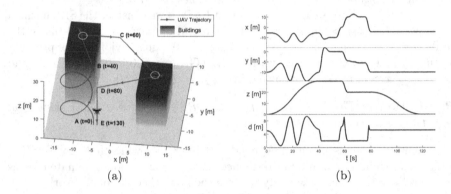

(a)   (b)

Fig. 3. (a) UAV trajectory and layout of buildings. (b) UAV coordinates and distance to closest building.

Our first case study involves package delivery via an unmanned aerial vehicle (UAV). We consider a quadrotor UAV model with a proportional–integral–derivative (PID) controller [21] and use $\mathbf{p} = (x, y, z)$ to denote the UAV's 3-D position vector. The UAV is tasked with dropping off packages on the rooftops of two adjacent buildings; a simulated trajectory of the UAV along with various points of interest along the trajectory are given in Fig. 3(a). As can be seen, the segment of the trajectory from A to B is spiral-like/unstable, and can be attributed to the disturbance caused by the load it is carrying (a disturbance that dissipates once the UAV reaches the building's rooftop). The coordinates of the UAV and its distance to the closest building are plotted over time in Fig. 3(b). The (discrete) trajectory is 130 s long, i.e., $T = 130$ s, with a time-step of $1/20$ s. We use the following STL formulas to specify the UAV's mission.

Height Regulation: the UAV should remain below $H_{max} = 120$ m [1].

$$\varphi_1 = \mathbf{G}_{[0,T]}\,\varphi_1', \quad \varphi_1' = (z \le H_{max})$$

Package Delivery: the UAV needs to hover at a delivery location for a specified period of time (delivery locations are closed $\mathcal{L}^2$-balls with radius $\epsilon = 1$ centered at C_1, C_2). The locations are set to $C_1 = (-10, 0, 30)$, $C_2 = (10, -5, 20)$, and $\|\cdot\|$ denotes the $\mathcal{L}^2$-norm.

$$\varphi_2 = \mathbf{F}_{[0,43]}\mathbf{G}_{[0,1]}\,\varphi_2', \quad \varphi_2' = (\|\mathbf{p} - C_1\| \le \epsilon)$$
$$\varphi_3 = \mathbf{F}_{[0,65]}\mathbf{G}_{[0,3]}\,\varphi_3', \quad \varphi_3' = (\|\mathbf{p} - C_2\| \le \epsilon)$$

Collision Avoidance: the UAV should maintain a minimum distance $d_{min} = 1.5$ m to the closest building. It is violated repeatedly in the spiral ascent from A to B.

$$\varphi_4 = \mathbf{G}_{[0,T]}\,\varphi_4', \quad \varphi_4' = (d \ge d_{min})$$

We compute the ReSV values of the above STL formulas when both φ_i and φ_i' are used as SRS atoms. In particular, in Table 1, we consider expressions of the form $R_{\alpha,\beta}(\varphi_i)$, i.e., where the temporal operators appear inside the SRS atoms, while in Table 2, nested φ_i' expressions are replaced by $R_{\alpha,\beta}(\varphi_i')$ expressions in φ_i, i.e., temporal operators appear outside the SRS atoms. Syntactically, this difference is subtle, but as we show, it is of significant importance semantically. We assume the UAV state is unchanged after the trajectory ends, when a longer trajectory is needed to determine satisfiability (see Remark 4). We choose $\alpha, \beta = 4$ for the SRS atoms so that we can illustrate repeated property violation and recovery.

Table 1. SRS expressions of the form $R_{\alpha,\beta}(\varphi_i)$ for UAV properties φ_i. All r-values are computed using trajectory ξ of Fig. 3(a) at time 0.

SRS formula	$r(\psi_i, \xi, 0)$	Exec. time (sec)
$\psi_1 = R_{4,4}(\varphi_1)$	$\{(4, 126)\}$	14.69
$\psi_2 = R_{4,4}(\varphi_2)$	$\{(0.1, 45.5)\}$	12.74
$\psi_3 = R_{4,4}(\varphi_3)$	$\{(-0.2, 65.05)\}$	12.53
$\psi_4 = R_{4,4}(\varphi_4)$	$\{(-73.3, 48.7)\}$	14.18

Table 2. Nested φ_i' expressions replaced by $R_{\alpha,\beta}(\varphi_i')$ expressions in UAV properties φ_i.

SRS formula	$r(\psi_i', \xi, 0)$	Corresponding SRS atoms	Exec. time (sec)
$\psi_1' = \mathbf{G}_{[0,T]} R_{4,4}(\varphi_1')$	$\{(4, -4)\}$	$r(R_{4,4}(\varphi_1'), \xi, 130)$	8.50
$\psi_2' = \mathbf{F}_{[0,43]} \mathbf{G}_{[0,1]} R_{4,4}(\varphi_2')$	$\{(3.95, -3.5), (4, -3.55)\}$	$r(R_{4,4}(\varphi_2'), \xi, 42.85),$ $r(R_{4,4}(\varphi_2'), \xi, 42.95)$	18.84
$\psi_3' = \mathbf{F}_{[0,65]} \mathbf{G}_{[0,3]} R_{4,4}(\varphi_3')$	$\{(3.95, -1.35), (4, -1.4), (-0.2, 3.05)\}$	$r(R_{4,4}(\varphi_3'), \xi, 61.5),$ $r(R_{4,4}(\varphi_3'), \xi, 61.6),$ $r(R_{4,4}(\varphi_3'), \xi, 65)$	26.70
$\psi_4' = \mathbf{G}_{[0,T]} R_{4,4}(\varphi_4')$	$\{(-0.25, 5.8), (4, -4)\}$	$r(R_{4,4}(\varphi_4'), \xi, 8.4),$ $r(R_{4,4}(\varphi_4'), \xi, 130)$	8.93

In Table 1, $r(\psi_1, \xi, 0) = \{(4, 126)\}$ reflects the UAV's resilience w.r.t. φ_1 (height regulation) as it holds in $[0, T]$, thus reaching its maximum *rec* and *dur*. Entry $r(\psi_3, \xi, 0) = \{(-0.2, 65.05)\}$ considers the resilience of φ_3: it is false at time 0 but becomes true at time 4.2, making recovery 0.2 s slower than $\alpha = 4$; φ_3 then remains true until time 73.25, resulting a durational period 65.05 s longer than $\beta = 4$.

Table 2 includes an extra column (the third one) showing the SRS atoms corresponding to each (*rec*, *dur*) pair in the formula's ReSV (second column). In the first row, the ReSV of ψ_1' is $r(\psi_1', \xi, 0) = \{(4, -4)\}$. Because of the outermost $\mathbf{G}_{[0,T]}$ operator in ψ_1', $(4, -4)$ represents the worst-case recovery episode (relative to the STL property φ_1') within the interval $[0, T]$, meaning that $(4, -4)$ is dominated by every other (rec, dur) pair in $[0, T]$. The third column tells us that such episode happens at time $t = 130$. The (rec, dur) values in entry $r(\psi'_3, \xi, 0) = \{(3.95, -1.35), (4, -1.4), (-0.2, 3.05)\}$ represent the best-case episodes (due to the outermost $\mathbf{F}$ operator) within $t \in [0, 65]$ of the ReSV of $\mathbf{G}_{[0,3]} R_{4,4}(\varphi'_3)$, which in turn, gives us the worst-case episodes (due to the inner $\mathbf{G}$ operator) of the ReSV of $R_{4,4}(\varphi'_3)$ within $[t, t + 3]$.

Even though there are some (relatively small) negative values in Table 2, overall, the results of Table 2 are consistent with those of Table 1, thereby reflecting the overall resiliency of the UAV package-delivery mission. Let us remark the difference between the results of Table 1 and 2, i.e., between the ReSVs of ψ_i and ψ'_i. The former are SRS atoms relative to a composite STL formula φ_i, and so their ReSVs are singleton sets representing the first recovery episode of φ_i. The latter are composite SRS formulas relative to an atomic STL formula φ'_i. As such, their ReSVs are obtained inductively following the structure of the SRS formulas and thus, they may include multiple non-dominated pairs.

We observe that execution times are largely affected by the size of the intervals in the temporal operators appearing in the SRS and STL formulas: computing ψ_2 and ψ_3 in Table 1 (ψ'_2 and ψ'_3 in Table 2) is more efficient than computing ψ_1 and ψ_4 (ψ'_1 and ψ'_4), even though the former expressions involve nested temporal operators. Indeed, the interval size directly affects both the number of subformula evaluations and the size of the ReSV set. Moreover, our ReSV algorithm uses an implementation of the *always* and *eventually* operators that makes them particularly efficient when applied to (atomic) subformulas that exhibit few recovery episodes (e.g., see the $\mathbf{G}_{[0,T]}$ operator in ψ'_1 in Table 2).

4.2   Multi-agent Flocking

We consider the problem of multi-agent flock formation and maintenance in the presence of external disturbances. We use the rule-based Reynolds flocking model (see Appendix E in [8]) involving boids $\mathcal{B} = \{1, \ldots, n\}$ in m-dimensional space. Boid i's position is $x_i \in \mathbb{R}^m$, $\mathbf{x} = [x_1, \ldots, x_n] \in \mathbb{R}^{m \cdot n}$ is a global configuration vector, and $\xi = [\mathbf{x}(1), \ldots, \mathbf{x}(k)] \in \mathbb{R}^{m \cdot n \cdot k}$ is a k-step trajectory.

We consider a 500-s simulation (trajectory) of a 30-boid flock with a time-step of 0.1 s in a 2-D plane; so, $T = 500$ s. We subject 20 of the boids to an intermittent uniformly random displacement [14] from $[0, M] \times [0, 2\pi]$, where $M = 20$ m and 2π are the maximum magnitude and direction of the displacement, respectively. The subset of 20 boids is chosen uniformly at random during the intervals $[100, 150]$, $[250, 300]$, and $[400, 450]$ in seconds. The simulation starts with the boids at random positions with random velocities, both sampled within some bounded intervals.

The relevant STL specifications for the flocking mission are the following.

Flock Formation: a cost function $J(\mathbf{x})$ consisting of a cohesion and a separation term determines whether the boids form a flock [19]:

$$J(\mathbf{x}) = \frac{1}{|\mathcal{B}| \cdot (|\mathcal{B}| - 1)} \cdot \sum_{i \in \mathcal{B}} \sum_{j \in \mathcal{B}, i < j} ||x_{ij}||^2 + \omega \cdot \sum_{(i,j) = \mathcal{E}(\mathbf{x})} \frac{1}{||x_{ij}||^2}$$

where $x_{ij} = x_i - x_j$, $\omega = 1/100$, and $\mathcal{E}(\mathbf{x})$ is the set of neighboring boid pairs within an interaction radius $r_c = 25$ m: $\mathcal{E}(\mathbf{x}) = \{(i,j) \in \mathcal{B}^2 \mid ||x_{ij}|| < r_c, i \neq j\}$. $J(\mathbf{x}) \leq \delta$, $\delta = 500$, implies that flock formation has been obtained.

$$\varphi_1 = \mathbf{G}_{[0,500]}\, \mathbf{F}_{[0,60]}\, \varphi_1', \quad \varphi_1' = (J(\mathbf{x}) \leq \delta)$$

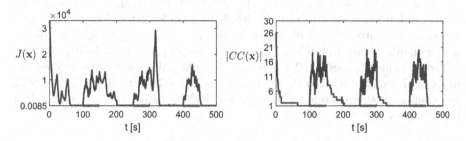

Fig. 4. $J(\mathbf{x})$ and $|CC(\mathbf{x})|$ for 30 boids. Red portions of x-axes indicate intervals of random displacement. (Color figure online)

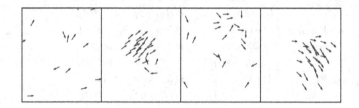

Fig. 5. Flock simulation snapshots at times 0, 75, 300, and 350 (left to right).

Table 3. SRS expressions of the form $R_{\alpha,\beta}(\varphi_i)$ for flocking properties φ_i. All r-values are computed using trajectory ξ of Fig. 4 at time 0.

SRS formula	$r(\psi_i, \xi, 0)$	Exec. time (sec)
$\psi_1 = R_{30,30}(\varphi_1)$	$\{(-239.4, 200.6)\}$	40.47
$\psi_2 = R_{30,30}(\varphi_2)$	$\{(-239.3, 200.7)\}$	39.75

Over the whole trajectory, the flock formation should always be obtained in a timely fashion. This is to be expected in the present of recurrent disturbances to the flock.

Connected Components: the number of connected components $|CC(\mathbf{x})|$ of the proximity net $\mathcal{G}(\mathbf{x}) = (\mathcal{B}, \mathcal{E}(\mathbf{x}))$ represents potential fragmentation of the flock. Ideally, $|CC(\mathbf{x})|$ should remain at 1 after flock formation.

$$\varphi_2 = \mathbf{G}_{[0,500]}\, \mathbf{F}_{[0,60]}\, \varphi_2', \quad \varphi_2' = (|CC(\mathbf{x})| = 1)$$

The functions $J(\mathbf{x})$ and $|CC(\mathbf{x})|$ are plotted in Fig. 4. Figure 5 shows flock formation at times 75 and 350 where $(J(\mathbf{x}),\ t) \models \varphi_1'$ and $(|CC(\mathbf{x})|,\ t) \models \varphi_2'$, and times 0 and 300 where $(J(\mathbf{x}),\ t) \not\models \varphi_1'$ and $(|CC(\mathbf{x})|,\ t) \not\models \varphi_2'$. Similar to Sect. 4.1, we consider two cases of SRS specifications. As in Sect. 4.1, we compute the ReSV values of φ_1, φ_2 in Table 3 and Table 4. We select time bounds that are consistent with the timescales of flock formation, i.e., $\alpha, \beta = 30$.

As shown in Table 3, $r(\psi_2, \xi, 0) = \{(-239.3, 200.7)\}$, meaning that φ_2 is false at time 0 but becomes true at time 269.3 (i.e., 239.3 s later than $\alpha = 30$) and remains true until the end of the trajectory (i.e., interval $[269.3, T]$ is 200.7 s longer than $\beta = 30$). In Table 4, $r(\psi_2', \xi, 0) = \{(-42.7, 17.2), (30, -30)\}$; i.e., the (rec, dur) pairs at times 130.2 and 500, representing the worst recovery episodes in $t \in [0, T]$, which are also the best episodes in the interval $[t, t + 60]$. Overall, our results show the resilience of Reynolds flocking model to repeated random disturbances.

Table 4. Nested φ_i' expressions replaced by $R_{\alpha,\beta}(\varphi_i')$ expressions in flocking properties φ_i.

SRS formula	$r(\psi_i', \xi, 0)$	Corresponding SRS atoms	Exec. time (sec)
$\psi_1' = \mathbf{G}_{[0,500]} (\mathbf{F}_{[0,60]}$ $R_{30,30}(\varphi_1'))$	$\{(-42.1,\ 17.8),$ $(-19,\ 13.4),$ $(-21.8,\ 15.3),$ $(30,\ -30)\}$	$r(R_{30,30}(\varphi_1'), \xi, 130.4),$ $r(R_{30,30}(\varphi_1'), \xi, 280.4),$ $r(R_{30,30}(\varphi_1'), \xi, 402.9),$ $r(R_{30,30}(\varphi_1'), \xi, 500)$	291.72
$\psi_2' = \mathbf{G}_{[0,500]} (\mathbf{F}_{[0,60]}$ $R_{30,30}(\varphi_2'))$	$\{(-42.7, 17.2),$ $(30,\ -30)\}$	$r(R_{30,30}(\varphi_2'), \xi, 130.2),$ $r(R_{30,30}(\varphi_2'), \xi, 500)$	279.54

5   Related Work

Resiliency has been studied in different system engineering contexts including computer hardware [16], communication [25], distributed systems [22], cyber-security [27], and model checking [24].

In the context of cyber-physical systems, the literature on resilience is diverse, both in the approach taken and terminology used [2,6,18,28]. Among the logic-based approaches, standard STL robustness provides a notion of the extent to which a signal can be perturbed in space before affecting property satisfaction, which is seen by some authors as a form of resilience [18]. STL time robustness [12, 23] is the equivalent notion when perturbations in time (forward or backward) are considered. There are similarities between (right) time robustness and our notion of recoverability, but the two semantics are fundamentally different as our ReSVs include a second dimension, durability. See Remark 5 for more details on this comparison. Aksaray et al. [2] propose a (time-) "shifting" version of STL and a resilient controller to maximize the robustness value of the shifted formula as fast as possible. This approach, however, only supports **GF**-formulas and does not provide a dedicated "shifting" semantics.

Control-theoretic characterizations of resiliency includes Bouvier et al. [6], which defines a resilience measure (optimized by the controller) based on the additional time it will take for a system to reach a target if under malfunctions. The control framework of Zhu et al. [28] defines a resilient system as one that can restore its state after extreme events caused by specific perturbation classes. In contrast, we answer the question "What is resilience in CPS?" from a temporal-logic perspective. Namely, we provide a syntax for CPS resilience using STL, and a corresponding quantitative semantics. Using our framework in optimal control is not the focus of the present work, but it is a natural continuation.

Another related line of work involves policy and parameter synthesis under multi-objective temporal-logic specifications [4,7,9,13]. Even though we similarly consider multiple requirements (namely recoverability and durability), there is an important difference: we use the satisfaction degrees of recoverability and durability to define the semantics of an STL-based logic, with the semantics of composite formulas derived via Pareto optimization. On the other hand, the above mentioned related work adopt, for each requirement, the usual (Boolean, probabilistic, or quantitative) semantics.

Finally, parametric STL [3,5] has, akin to our work, a set-based semantics. In this case, the semantics is given by the set of parameter evaluations p for which the resulting concrete formula (instantiated with p) is satisfied by the given signal. We remark that, in our approach, the specification is fixed, non-parametric, and the set-based semantics arises from the fact that our recoverability-durability pairs might not be directly comparable, i.e., mutually non-dominated.

6   Conclusion

In this paper, we presented a logic-based framework to reason about CPS resiliency. We define resiliency of an STL formula φ as the ability of the system to recover from violations of φ in a timely and durable manner. These requirements represent the atoms of our formally defined SRS logic, which allows to combine such resiliency statements using temporal and Boolean operators. We also introduced ReSV, the first multi-dimensional semantics for an STL-based logic. Under this semantics, an SRS formula is interpreted as a set of non-dominated (rec, dur) pairs, which respectively quantify how quickly the underlying system recovers from a property violation and for how long it satisfies the property thereafter. Importantly, we proved that our ReSV semantics is sound and complete w.r.t. the Boolean semantics of STL. We illustrated our new resiliency framework with two case studies: UAV package delivery and flock formation. Collectively, our results demonstrate the expressive power and flexibility of our framework in reasoning about resiliency in CPS.

In summary, the contribution of our work is not just establishing theoretical foundations of CPS resiliency but also providing a method to equip temporal logics with multi-dimensional semantics, an approach that in the future could be extended to support arbitrary multi-requirement specifications beyond resiliency.

Acknowledgments. We thank the anonymous reviewers for their valuable feedback and suggestions for improving the quality of this paper. Research supported in part by NSF CNS-1952096, CNS-1553273 (CAREER), OIA-2134840, OIA-2040599, CCF-1918225, and CPS-1446832.

References

1. Airspace 101 – Rules of the Sky, August 2021. https://www.faa.gov/uas/recreational_fliers/where_can_i_fly/airspace_101/
2. Aksaray, D.: Resilient satisfaction of persistent and safety specifications by autonomous systems. In: AIAA Scitech 2021 Forum, pp. 1124–1134, January 2021. https://doi.org/10.2514/6.2021-1124
3. Asarin, E., Donzé, A., Maler, O., Nickovic, D.: Parametric identification of temporal properties. In: Khurshid, S., Sen, K. (eds.) RV 2011. LNCS, vol. 7186, pp. 147–160. Springer, Heidelberg (2012). https://doi.org/10.1007/978-3-642-29860-8_12
4. Bakhirkin, A., Basset, N., Maler, O., Jarabo, J.-I.R.: ParetoLib: a Python library for parameter synthesis. In: André, É., Stoelinga, M. (eds.) FORMATS 2019. LNCS, vol. 11750, pp. 114–120. Springer, Cham (2019). https://doi.org/10.1007/978-3-030-29662-9_7
5. Bakhirkin, A., Ferrère, T., Maler, O.: Efficient parametric identification for STL. In: 21st International Conference on Hybrid Systems: Computation and Control, pp. 177–186 (2018)
6. Bouvier, J., Xu, K., Ornik, M.: Quantitative resilience of linear driftless systems. In: Proceedings of the Conference on Control and Its Applications, pp. 32–39. SIAM, July 2021. https://doi.org/10.1137/1.9781611976847
7. Calinescu, R., Češka, M., Gerasimou, S., Kwiatkowska, M., Paoletti, N.: Efficient synthesis of robust models for stochastic systems. J. Syst. Softw. **143**, 140–158 (2018). https://doi.org/10.1016/j.jss.2018.05.013
8. Chen, H., Lin, S., Smolka, S.A., Paoletti, N.: An STL-based formulation of resilience in cyber-physical systems (2022). https://doi.org/10.48550/ARXIV.2205.03961
9. Chen, T., Forejt, V., Kwiatkowska, M., Simaitis, A., Wiltsche, C.: On stochastic games with multiple objectives. In: Chatterjee, K., Sgall, J. (eds.) MFCS 2013. LNCS, vol. 8087, pp. 266–277. Springer, Heidelberg (2013). https://doi.org/10.1007/978-3-642-40313-2_25
10. Cook, B., Fisher, J., Krepska, E., Piterman, N.: Proving stabilization of biological systems. In: Jhala, R., Schmidt, D. (eds.) VMCAI 2011. LNCS, vol. 6538, pp. 134–149. Springer, Heidelberg (2011). https://doi.org/10.1007/978-3-642-18275-4_11
11. Donzé, A.: Breach, a toolbox for verification and parameter synthesis of hybrid systems. In: Touili, T., Cook, B., Jackson, P. (eds.) CAV 2010. LNCS, vol. 6174, pp. 167–170. Springer, Heidelberg (2010). https://doi.org/10.1007/978-3-642-14295-6_17
12. Donzé, A., Maler, O.: Robust satisfaction of temporal logic over real-valued signals. In: Chatterjee, K., Henzinger, T.A. (eds.) FORMATS 2010. LNCS, vol. 6246, pp. 92–106. Springer, Heidelberg (2010). https://doi.org/10.1007/978-3-642-15297-9_9
13. Etessami, K., Kwiatkowska, M., Vardi, M.Y., Yannakakis, M.: Multi-objective model checking of Markov decision processes. In: Grumberg, O., Huth, M. (eds.) TACAS 2007. LNCS, vol. 4424, pp. 50–65. Springer, Heidelberg (2007). https://doi.org/10.1007/978-3-540-71209-1_6

14. Grosu, R., Lukina, A., Smolka, S.A., Tiwari, A., Varadarajan, V., Wang, X.: V-formation via model predictive control. arXiv preprint arXiv:2002.08955 (2020)
15. Haghighi, I., Jones, A., Kong, Z., Bartocci, E., Gros, R., Belta, C.: SpaTeL: a novel spatial-temporal logic and its applications to networked systems. In: Proceedings of the 18th International Conference on Hybrid Systems: Computation and Control (HSCC 2015), pp. 189–198 (2015). https://doi.org/10.1145/2728606.2728633
16. Hari, S.K.S., Tsai, T., Stephenson, M., Keckler, S.W., Emer, J.: SASSIFI: an architecture-level fault injection tool for GPU application resilience evaluation. In: Proceedings of International Symposium on Performance Analysis of Systems and Software (ISPASS), pp. 249–258. IEEE, April 2017. https://doi.org/10.1109/ISPASS.2017.7975296
17. Maler, O., Nickovic, D.: Monitoring temporal properties of continuous signals. In: Lakhnech, Y., Yovine, S. (eds.) FORMATS/FTRTFT -2004. LNCS, vol. 3253, pp. 152–166. Springer, Heidelberg (2004). https://doi.org/10.1007/978-3-540-30206-3_12
18. Mehdipour, N.: Resilience for satisfaction of temporal logic specifications by dynamical systems. Ph.D. thesis, Boston University (2021). https://open.bu.edu/handle/2144/41871
19. Mehmood, U., et al.: Declarative vs rule-based control for flocking dynamics. In: Proceedings of the 33rd Annual ACM Symposium on Applied Computing, pp. 816–823, April 2018. https://doi.org/10.1145/3167132.3167222
20. Merriam-Webster Dictionary. https://www.merriam-webster.com/dictionary/resiliency
21. Michael, N., Mellinger, D., Lindsey, Q., Kumar, V.: The GRASP multiple micro-UAV testbed. IEEE Robot. Autom. Mag. 17(3), 56–65 (2010). https://doi.org/10.1109/MRA.2010.937855
22. Prokhorenko, V., Babar, M.A.: Architectural resilience in cloud, fog and edge systems: a survey. IEEE Access 8, 28078–28095 (2020). https://doi.org/10.1109/ACCESS.2020.2971007
23. Rodionova, A., Lindemann, L., Morari, M., Pappas, G.J.: Time-robust control for STL specifications. In: Proceedings of IEEE Conference on Decision and Control. IEEE, December 2021. https://doi.org/10.1109/CDC45484.2021.9683477
24. Selyunin, K., et al.: Runtime monitoring with recovery of the SENT communication protocol. In: Majumdar, R., Kunčak, V. (eds.) CAV 2017. LNCS, vol. 10426, pp. 336–355. Springer, Cham (2017). https://doi.org/10.1007/978-3-319-63387-9_17
25. Tan, S., Wu, Y., Xie, P., Guerrero, J.M., Vasquez, J.C., Abusorrah, A.: New challenges in the design of microgrid systems: communication networks, cyberattacks, and resilience. IEEE Electrification Mag. 8(4), 98–106 (2020). https://doi.org/10.1109/MELE.2020.3026496
26. Yaghoubi, S., Fainekos, G.: Worst-case satisfaction of STL specifications using feedforward neural network controllers: a lagrange multipliers approach. In: Proceedings of Information Theory and Applications Workshop, ITA, pp. 127:1–127:20. IEEE, February 2020. https://doi.org/10.1109/ITA50056.2020.9244969
27. Yuan, H., Xia, Y., Yang, H.: Resilient state estimation of cyber-physical system with multichannel transmission under DoS attack. IEEE Trans. Syst. Man Cybern. Syst. 51(11), 6926–6937 (2020). https://doi.org/10.1109/TSMC.2020.2964586
28. Zhu, Q., Başar, T.: Robust and resilient control design for cyber-physical systems with an application to power systems. In: Proceedings of IEEE Conference on Decision and Control and European Control Conference, pp. 4066–4071. IEEE, December 2011. https://doi.org/10.1109/CDC.2011.6161031

MITL Verification Under Timing Uncertainty

Daniel Selvaratnam[1], Michael Cantoni[1](✉), J. M. Davoren[1], and Iman Shames[2]

[1] Department of Electrical and Electronic Engineering, The University of Melbourne, Parkville, VIC 3010, Australia
cantoni@unimelb.edu.au
[2] CIICADA Lab, School of Engineering, Australian National University, Canberra, ACT 2600, Australia

Abstract. A Metric Interval Temporal Logic (MITL) verification algorithm is presented. It verifies continuous-time signals without relying on high frequency sampling. Instead, it is assumed that collections of over- and under-approximating intervals are available for the times at which the individual atomic propositions hold true for a given signal. These are combined inductively to generate corresponding over- and under-approximations for the specified MITL formula. The gap between the over- and under-approximations reflects timing uncertainty with respect to the signal being verified, thereby providing a quantitative measure of the conservativeness of the algorithm. The verification is exact when the over-approximations for the atomic propositions coincide with the under-approximations. Numerical examples are provided to illustrate.

Keywords: Runtime verification · Monitoring · Continuous-time · Dense-time · Path checking

1 Introduction

Metric Interval Temporal Logic (MITL), introduced in [1], is a logic for specifying behaviours of continuous-time signals. Given such a signal, the problem of interest is to test whether it satisfies a given MITL formula. Also known as *runtime verification* or *monitoring*, this has been called the *path checking* problem in [2,14]. Since the domain of a continuous-time signal is uncountably infinite, the design of a general MITL path checking algorithm is challenging. In practice, the times at which even well-behaved signals change value cannot be known with infinite precision. In various situations, it may still be possible to obtain upper and lower bounds on the times at which the individual atomic propositions switch between

---

The research for this paper received funding from the Australian Government through Trusted Autonomous Systems, a Defence Cooperative Research Centre funded through the Next Generation Technologies Fund.

S. Bogomolov and D. Parker (Eds.): FORMATS 2022, LNCS 13465, pp. 136–152, 2022.
https://doi.org/10.1007/978-3-031-15839-1_8

true and false. The verification of MITL formulas, given such bounds, is the topic of this paper. The proposed algorithm is intended for offline verification.

An algorithm for path checking continuous-time signals against MITL specifications is proposed in [10]. The algorithm operates directly on the time intervals over which the individual propositions are true. Exact knowledge of these intervals would suffice for a correct verification result. With such knowledge being unrealistic, the authors assume a sampling strategy, for the purpose of implementation, that is dense enough to capture every change over time to the set of atomic propositions true at each instant. Such a lossless sampling strategy remains impossible to guarantee in general. Our approach is to start instead with under- and over-approximations of those intervals, and combine them appropriately for the verification of compound formulas. For the purpose of analysis, we utilise the topological concepts of separation and connectedness. This formal approach enables us to present rigorous proofs, and to extend [10] in other directions as well. Specifically, [10] restricts all the atomic proposition intervals to be left-closed right-open, and all the operator timing bounds to be closed and bounded. We remove all of these restrictions, but for finiteness, still require the truth sets of the atomic propositions to be expressible as the union of a finite number of (possibly unbounded) intervals. Moreover, our procedure accommodates the *strict non-matching* until operator, which is more expressive [7] than the *non-strict matching* until adopted in [10]. For this reason, the strict non-matching until is taken as primitive in the standard semantics of MITL [1]. The developments herein make no modifications to those original semantics.

Other notable attempts to relax the lossless sampling assumption of [10] include [5] and [6]. The former relies on high-frequency sampling and spatial robustness margins in order to infer continuous-time satisfaction from discrete-time satisfaction. In addition, it requires a tightening of the sub-formulas at every level of the parse tree. The latter also relies on high-frequency sampling, and restricts attention to flat formulas, which do not have nested temporal operators. Interestingly, [6] also constructs over- and under-approximations to the truth, but in discrete-time. Our approach differs from [5,6] by not relying on high-frequency sampling. We also place no restrictions on, and make no modifications to, the original formula to be verified.

Instead of relaxing the lossless sampling assumption of [10], the approach in [14] ensures it by restricting the scope to continuous-time polynomial splines. Root isolation techniques from computer algebra are invoked to ensure that every change to the set of true atomic propositions is recorded. The formulas there are restricted to LTL without next, which is introduced as a fragment of MITL with only unbounded temporal operators. This paper can be viewed as a sequel to [14] that considers bounded temporal operators. The restricted setting in [14] yields a verification algorithm that always delivers a conclusive result. Due to the timing uncertainty accommodated here, some conservativeness is unavoidable: the outcome may be inconclusive. In view of this, our path checking algorithm quantifies how much the timing uncertainty in the atomic propositions may be amplified as it propagates through the parse tree of the formula. If the truth intervals for the atomic propositions are known exactly, then the algorithm also constructs the intervals for the formula exactly. More generally, the timing uncertainty associated with satisfying the formula relates to the gap between the over- and under-approximations produced by the algorithm. Although its precise nature is deferred to future work, we anticipate a relationship between this gap and the notions of temporal robustness in [3,9,13]. Such is of relevance to recent works [8,12], which aim to synthesize controllers that maximise temporal robustness.

Our approach relies on starting with over- and under-approximations to the truth sets of the atomic propositions. The following two scenarios provide examples of how such approximations may be generated. First, consider the verification of a continuous-time signal that passes through different state-space regions, each corresponding to an atomic proposition. In the polynomial setting of [14], root isolation algorithms provide samples on either side of every region transition, even though the transition points cannot be found exactly. This information translates directly to the over- and under-approximating time intervals assumed here. Second, suppose that the regions themselves are not known precisely, but outer and inner boundaries for them are known instead. Time spent within the outer boundaries correspond to over-approximations, and the inner-boundaries to under-approximations.

2   Preliminaries

2.1   Set Theory

The subset relation is denoted by $\subseteq$, and the strict subset relation by $\subsetneq$. Let $|A|$ be the cardinality of set A, and 2^A its power set. If $f : A \to B$, then let $f[X] \subseteq B$ denote the image of $X \subseteq A$, and $f^{-1}Y \subseteq A$ the preimage of $Y \subseteq B$. The operator $\bigcup$, when used without limits, takes the union of all the elements within a set of sets. It is then given binding precedence over all other set operations. Thus, $\bigcup \mathcal{P} := \bigcup_{B \in \mathcal{P}} B$, and $\bigcup \mathcal{P} \cap \bigcup \mathcal{Q} = (\bigcup \mathcal{P}) \cap (\bigcup \mathcal{Q})$, where the elements of $\mathcal{P}$ and $\mathcal{Q}$ are sets. For sequences of sets of sets, note that $\bigcup \mathcal{I}_k = \bigcup_{I \in \mathcal{I}_k} I \neq \bigcup_k \mathcal{I}_k$. Let $\mathbb{R}$ denote the real numbers, $\mathbb{Q}$ the rational numbers, $\mathbb{Z}$ the integers, and $\mathbb{N} := \{0, 1, ...\}$ the natural numbers. For $i, j \in \mathbb{Z}$, let $[i : j] := \{k \in \mathbb{Z} \mid i \leq k \leq j\}$. Analogous definitions apply for $[i : j), (i : j]$ and $(i : j)$.

2.2   Topology

We rely on the following facts from topology. Given a subset A of a topological space, let $\text{int}(A)$ denote its interior, and $\text{cl}(A)$ its closure. Recall that any subset of a topological space is itself a topological space when endowed with the subspace topology.

Proposition 1. *Let A, B be subsets of a topological space. If $A \subseteq B$, then $\text{cl}(A) \subseteq \text{cl}(B)$ and $\text{int}(A) \subseteq \text{int}(B)$.*

A topological space is *connected* iff it is not the union of two of its disjoint open subsets [11, §23]. Two subsets A, B are *separated* iff $A \cap \text{cl}(B) = B \cap \text{cl}(A) = \emptyset$.

Clearly, if A and B are separated, then they are disjoint, and furthermore, any $C \subseteq A$ and $D \subseteq B$ are also separated. The result below is from [4, Theorem 6.1.1].

Proposition 2. *Let A and B be non-empty subsets of a topological space. If A and B are separated, then $A \cup B$ is not connected.*

Proposition 3. *Let A and B be separated subsets of a topological space. Suppose $\emptyset \neq S \subseteq A \cup B$. If S is connected, then either $S \subseteq A$ or $S \subseteq B$, but not both.*

Proof. That $S \subseteq A$ or $S \subseteq B$ is established in [4, Corollary 6.1.8]. If $S \subseteq A \cap B$, then A and B intersect, which contradicts the assumption that they are separated. □

Proposition 4. *Let $A, B_1, ..., B_m$ be subsets of a topological space. If for every $i \in [1:m]$, A and B_i are separated, then A and $\bigcup_{i=1}^{m} B_i$ are separated.*

Proof. First observe that $\mathrm{cl}(A) \cap B_i = \emptyset$ for all $i \in [1:m]$, which implies $\mathrm{cl}(A) \cap \bigcup_{i=1}^{m} B_i = \emptyset$. It is also true that $A \cap \mathrm{cl}(B_i) = \emptyset$ for all $i \in [1:m]$, which implies $A \cap \mathrm{cl}\left(\bigcup_{i=1}^{m} B_i\right) = A \cap \bigcup_{i=1}^{m} \mathrm{cl}(B_i) = \emptyset$, because the finite union of closures is the closure of their union [4, Theorem 1.1.3]. □

In what follows, we work mostly with subsets of the real line $\mathbb{R}$, which is a connected topological space. Of particular interest are subsets of the non-negative reals. However, it must be noted that for any $A \subseteq [0, \infty)$, $\mathrm{int}(A)$ denotes the interior of A relative to $\mathbb{R}$, not $[0, \infty)$.

Definition 1. *An* interval *is a connected subset of the real line.*

An equivalent definition is that intervals are the convex subsets of the real line. An interval I is *degenerate* iff $|I| \leq 1$. Otherwise, it is *nondegenerate*. Let $\mathbb{I} := \{I \subseteq [0, \infty) \mid I \text{ is an interval}\}$, which is the set of non-negative real intervals, and

$$\mathbb{I}_{\mathbb{Q}} := \{I \in \mathbb{I} \setminus \{\emptyset\} \mid \sup I, \inf I \in \mathbb{Q} \cup \{\infty\}\},$$

the set of non-empty non-negative real intervals with rational endpoints.

Proposition 5. *For any interval I, $\mathrm{int}(\mathrm{cl}(I)) \subseteq I$.*

Proof. Taking the closure of an interval adds to it at most two points, which are its endpoints. The result remains an interval with the same endpoints. Taking the interior of that then simply removes the endpoints. No point is added by the closure that is not removed by the interior. □

3 Problem Formulation

3.1 Syntax and Semantics of MITL

We start with the syntax of MITL [1, Definition 2.3.1.1]. Note that while $\mathbb{I}$ is uncountable, $\mathbb{I}_{\mathbb{Q}}$ is countable—a necessary requirement for MITL to be a formal language.

Definition 2 (MITL). *Given a finite set of atomic propositions* G, φ *is an MITL formula over* G *iff it is generated by the grammar*

$$\varphi :: = \top \mid g \mid \neg\varphi \mid \varphi \wedge \varphi \mid \varphi\,\mathcal{U}_I\varphi,$$

where $g \in G$ *and* $I \in \mathbb{I}_\mathbb{Q}$ *must be non-degenerate. The set of MITL formulas over* G *is* $\mathfrak{F}(G)$.

The semantics of MITL in [1, Definition 2.3.2.1] is stated in terms of *timed state sequences* and *interval sequences*. Since we do not make use of such machinery explicitly, we provide a common restatement of the semantics instead, that is equivalent for signals of *finite variability*. Such signals cannot change values infinitely often within a finite time interval. Formally, a function $z : [0, \infty) \to A$ is of finite variability iff there exists an interval sequence [1, Definition 2.2.1] $I_1, I_2, \dots$ such that z is constant over I_i for every $i \in \mathbb{N}$.

Definition 3. *Let* $z : [0, \infty) \to 2^G$ *be a finite variability signal, with* G *a finite set of atomic propositions. The satisfaction relation* $\models$ *is defined inductively as follows: Given any* $t \geq 0$, *proposition* $g \in G$, *formulas* $\varphi_1, \varphi_2 \in \mathfrak{F}(G)$, *and non-degenerate* $I \in \mathbb{I}_\mathbb{Q}$,

$$(z, t) \models \top; \tag{1}$$
$$(z, t) \models g \iff g \in z(t); \tag{2}$$
$$(z, t) \models \neg\varphi_1 \iff (z, t) \not\models \varphi_1; \tag{3}$$
$$(z, t) \models \varphi_1 \wedge \varphi_2 \iff (z, t) \models \varphi_1 \text{ and } (z, t) \models \varphi_2; \tag{4}$$
$$(z, t) \models \varphi_1 \mathcal{U}_I \varphi_2 \iff$$
$$\exists t_2 \in I, \left((z, t + t_2) \models \varphi_2 \text{ and } \forall t_1 \in (0, t_2),\ (z, t + t_1) \models \varphi_1\right). \tag{5}$$

The variant of the until operator in Definition 3 is called the *strict non-matching until*. There are three other variants, corresponding to the other possible permutations of including or excluding the endpoints of $(0, t_2)$ in (5). All other variants can be expressed simply in terms of the strict non-matching until (see [7]), and it is therefore taken as primitive. It is now possible to formally state the problem of interest.

Problem 1. Given a finite set of atomic propositions G, formula $\varphi \in \mathfrak{F}(G)$, finite variability signal $z : [0, \infty) \to 2^G$, and time $t \in [0, \infty)$, determine whether $(z, t) \models \varphi$.

3.2 Truth Sets and Interval Queues

We are interested in tackling Problem 1 without precise knowledge of the times at which z changes value. To describe this scenario mathematically, we introduce the truth set of a formula.

Definition 4 (Truth set). *Given a finite set of atomic propositions* G, *and a finite-variability signal* $z : [0, \infty) \to 2^G$, *the truth set of* $\varphi \in \mathfrak{F}(G)$ *is given by*

$$T_z(\varphi) := \{t \in [0, \infty) \mid (z, t) \models \varphi\}.$$

By definition, $(z,t) \models \varphi$ if and only if $t \in T_z(\varphi)$. The obvious strategy for solving Problem 1 is to construct the truth set of a formula from the truth sets of the atomic propositions that appear in the formula. In general, truth sets may be quite complex, and they need not have a finite representation because z has an infinite duration. Let us initially restrict attention to problems where the truth sets of the atomic propositions can be written as the union of a finite set of non-empty separated intervals, which we call an interval queue. (Remark 2 later explains how this restriction can be relaxed.)

Definition 5 (Interval queue). *An* interval queue *is a finite set $\mathcal{I} \subseteq \mathbb{I} \setminus \{\emptyset\}$, such that for any $I, J \in \mathcal{I}$, $I \neq J \implies I$ and J are separated. Let $\mathfrak{Q}$ denote the set of interval queues.*

Thus, an interval queue is a finite set of non-empty non-negative separated real intervals. Note that separation here allows for 'isolated holes': $\{[0,1), (1,2]\}$ is an interval queue, for example. Although any interval queue is a finite set by definition, its elements may still be unbounded intervals. Also, note that $\emptyset$ is an interval queue, but $\{\emptyset\}$ is not. If we have interval queue representations for the truth sets of the atomic propositions, then Problem 1 reduces to the one below.

Problem 2. Let G be a finite set of atomic propositions, $z : [0, \infty) \to 2^{\mathsf{G}}$ a finite variability signal, and $\varphi \in \mathfrak{F}(\mathsf{G})$. Given $\mathcal{P} : \mathsf{G} \to \mathfrak{Q}$ such that $\forall \mathsf{g} \in \mathsf{G}$, $\bigcup \mathcal{P}(\mathsf{g}) = T_z(\mathsf{g})$, construct an interval queue $\mathcal{Q} \in \mathfrak{Q}$ such that $\bigcup \mathcal{Q} = T_z(\varphi)$.

Above, $\mathcal{P}$ assigns to each atomic proposition an interval queue representation of its truth set. To accommodate our lack of precise timing knowledge, we now introduce maps $\mathcal{P}^-$ and $\mathcal{P}^+$, that provide under- and over-approximating interval queues, respectively, for the truth set of every atomic proposition.

Problem 3. Let G be a finite set of atomic propositions, $z : [0, \infty) \to 2^{\mathsf{G}}$ a finite variability signal, and $\varphi \in \mathfrak{F}(\mathsf{G})$. Given $\mathcal{P}^- : \mathsf{G} \to \mathfrak{Q}$ and $\mathcal{P}^+ : \mathsf{G} \to \mathfrak{Q}$ such that

$$\forall \mathsf{g} \in \mathsf{G}, \ \bigcup \mathcal{P}^-(\mathsf{g}) \subseteq T_z(\mathsf{g}) \subseteq \bigcup \mathcal{P}^+(\mathsf{g}), \tag{6}$$

construct an under-approximating $\mathcal{Q}^- \in \mathfrak{Q}$ and over-approximating $\mathcal{Q}^+ \in \mathfrak{Q}$ such that

$$\bigcup \mathcal{Q}^- \subseteq T_z(\varphi) \subseteq \bigcup \mathcal{Q}^+.$$

An algorithm that solves Problem 3 is developed in Sect. 5 using foundations established in Sect. 4. In the special case that $\mathcal{P}^- = \mathcal{P}^+$ (i.e., the under- and over-approximations to the truth sets of the atomic propositions are equal), the algorithm solves Problem 2 exactly.

Remark 1 (Finite information horizons). In practice, information about the signal $z : [0, \infty) \to 2^{\mathsf{G}}$ may not be available infinitely far into the future. Suppose $z(t)$ is unknown for all $t > b$, where $b \geq 0$ represents the horizon of available information. To accommodate this, for every atomic proposition, the interval (b, ∞) must be contained in the over-approximation of its truth set, but not in the under-approximation. That is,

$$(b, \infty) \subseteq \bigcap_{\mathsf{g} \in \mathsf{G}} \left(\bigcup \mathcal{P}^+(\mathsf{g}) \setminus \bigcup \mathcal{P}^-(\mathsf{g}) \right).$$

Remark 2. Even for a finite variability signal $z : [0, \infty) \rightarrow 2^G$, the truth set $T_z(\mathbf{g})$ of atomic proposition $\mathbf{g} \in \mathbf{G}$ may not have an interval queue representation, because $\mathbf{g}$ may switch between true and false infinitely often over infinite time. Even so, it is always possible to construct interval queue under- and over-approximations for its truth set, by artificially imposing a finite information horizon $b \geq 0$, as described in Remark 1, but this time only requring $(b, \infty) \subseteq \bigcup \mathcal{P}^+(\mathbf{g}) \setminus \bigcup \mathcal{P}^-(\mathbf{g})$ to hold for the individual proposition $\mathbf{g}$. For example, if $T_z(\mathbf{g}) = \bigcup_{k=0}^{\infty} [k, k+\frac{1}{2}]$, choose $b \in \mathbb{N}$ positive, and set $\mathcal{P}^-(\mathbf{g}) = \{[k, k+\frac{1}{2}] \mid k < b\}$ and $\mathcal{P}^+(\mathbf{g}) := \mathcal{P}^-(\mathbf{g}) \cup \{[b, \infty)\}$. This effectively 'truncates' the truth set.

Remark 3 (Endpoint rationality). If an interval queue $\mathcal{Q} \subseteq \mathbb{I}_\mathbb{Q}$, then all of its elements have rational endpoints, and it admits a finite representation. The mathematical procedures that follow do not rely on endpoint rationality for their correctness, but it is of course vital for their algorithmic implementation. For simplicity then, results are stated for general interval queues, while noting alongside that all the necessary operations preserve endpoint rationality.

Remark 4 (Uniqueness). If an interval queue representation of a set exists, then it is unique. This fact follows from the separation of the individual intervals, but since the following results do not exploit uniqueness, it is not proved here.

4   Interval Queue Fundamentals

Our solution to Problem 3 features two key subroutines, which are discussed here. The first constructs an interval queue from a given finite set of (possibly overlapping) non-negative intervals, and the second an interval queue that complements another interval queue.

4.1   Construction Algorithm

Algorithm 1 simply merges any intervals that are adjacent or overlap. The set $\mathcal{J}$ maintains a collection of separated intervals. Every starting interval I_i is either added to $\mathcal{J}$ without modification, or merged with existing intervals in $\mathcal{J}$. Given a new candidate interval I_i, the set $\mathcal{W}$ in Line 4 selects both it and all intervals in $\mathcal{J}$ that are connected to it. In Line 5, these intervals are removed from $\mathcal{J}$, and replaced with their union, which is necessarily an interval.

Lemma 1. *For any finite set $\mathcal{I} \subseteq \mathbb{I}$, $\texttt{ConstructIQ}(\mathcal{I})$ is an interval queue such that $\bigcup \texttt{ConstructIQ}(\mathcal{I}) = \bigcup \mathcal{I}$. Moreover, $\mathcal{I} \subseteq \mathbb{I}_\mathbb{Q} \implies \texttt{ConstructIQ}(\mathcal{I}) \subseteq \mathbb{I}_\mathbb{Q}$.*

4.2   Complementation Algorithm

Given an interval queue $\mathcal{I} \in \mathfrak{Q}$, we now seek another interval queue $\mathcal{J} \in \mathfrak{Q}$ that complements it: $\bigcup \mathcal{J} = [0, \infty) \setminus \bigcup \mathcal{I}$. If $\mathcal{I} := \{(1, 2], (3, 4]\}$, then clearly its complement is $\mathcal{J} := \{[0, 1], (2, 3], (4, \infty)\}$. Although the intervals in $\mathcal{I}$ are all bounded left-open right-closed, the complementary queue $\mathcal{J}$ contains, in addition,

```
Input: I₁, ..., Iₘ ∈ 𝕀
Output: 𝒥 ∈ 𝔔 such that ⋃𝒥 = ⋃ᵢ₌₁ᵐ Iᵢ
1 Function ConstructIQ({I₁, ..., Iₘ}):
2     𝒥 := ∅
3     for i ∈ [1 : m] do
4         𝒲 := {J ∈ 𝒥 | Iᵢ ∪ J ∈ 𝕀} ∪ {Iᵢ}
5         𝒥 ← (𝒥 \ 𝒲) ∪ {⋃𝒲}
6     end
7     return 𝒥 \ {∅}
8 end
```

Algorithm 1: constructs an interval queue from a given finite set of non-negative intervals.

intervals that are closed, open, and unbounded. Given the possible types of endpoints, there are 6 different types of intervals that may arise. Considering each case in turn, and their pairwise combinations, threatens to be an excessively laborious task. To avoid this, we use notation that accommodates all of them within a unified framework, and allows our complementation algorithm to be stated succinctly. Given $A, B \subseteq [0, \infty)$, define

$$\overrightarrow{B} := \{t \geq 0 \mid \forall b \in B, \ t > b\} = \bigcap_{b \in B} (b, \infty) \tag{7}$$

$$\overleftarrow{A} := \{t \geq 0 \mid \forall a \in A, \ t < a\} = \bigcap_{a \in A} [0, a). \tag{8}$$

By the above definitions, $\overleftarrow{\emptyset} = \overrightarrow{\emptyset} = [0, \infty)$. If $A, B \neq \emptyset$, then $\overleftarrow{A}$ is an interval containing everything strictly to the right of A, and $\overrightarrow{B}$ is an interval containing everything strictly to the left of B. For example, given $0 < a < b$, $\overrightarrow{(a, b)} = [b, \infty)$, $\overleftarrow{(a, b)} = [0, a]$, $\overrightarrow{(a, b]} = (b, \infty)$, $\overleftarrow{[a, b)} = [0, a)$, $\overrightarrow{(a, \infty)} = \emptyset$, and $\overrightarrow{[0, b]} = \emptyset$.

Define the binary 'earlier-than' relation $\prec$ between non-empty subsets of $[0, \infty)$ as follows: $A \prec B$ iff $\forall a \in A, \forall b \in B, a < b$. That is, $A \prec B \iff B \subseteq \overleftarrow{A}$, for $A, B \neq \emptyset$. This relation is a strict partial order on $2^{[0,\infty)}$.

The complementation algorithm is presented in Algorithm 2. It yields separated outputs because the elements of the input interval queue lie strictly in-between them. Observe also that $\overrightarrow{(\cdot)}$ and $\overleftarrow{(\cdot)}$ preserve the endpoint rationality of intervals.

Lemma 2. *For any interval queue $\mathcal{I} \in \mathfrak{Q}$, ComplementIQ$(\mathcal{I}) \in \mathfrak{Q}$ is an interval queue such that $\bigcup$ComplementIQ$(\mathcal{I}) = [0, \infty) \setminus \bigcup \mathcal{I}$. Moreover, $\mathcal{I} \subseteq \mathbb{I}_\mathbb{Q} \implies$ ComplementIQ$(\mathcal{I}) \subseteq \mathbb{I}_\mathbb{Q}$.*

```
   Input: I ∈ 𝔔
   Output: J ∈ 𝔔 such that ⋃J = [0,∞) \ ⋃I
 1 Function ComplementIQ(I):
 2    if I = ∅ then
 3    |    return {[0,∞)}
 4    else
 5    |    Sort I = {I₁, ..., Iₘ} such that I₁ ≺ I₂ ... ≺ Iₘ
 6    |    J := {←I₁, →Iₘ}
 7    |    for k ∈ [1 : m) do
 8    |    |    J ← J ∪ {→Iₖ ∩ ←Iₖ₊₁}
 9    |    end
10    |    return J \ {∅}
11    end
12 end
```

Algorithm 2: constructs the complementary interval queue for a given interval queue.

5   Verification Procedure

The goal of this section is to construct maps $\mathcal{Q}^- : \mathfrak{F}(\mathsf{G}) \to \mathfrak{Q}$ and $\mathcal{Q}^+ : \mathfrak{F}(\mathsf{G}) \to \mathfrak{Q}$, such that, for any formula φ, $\mathcal{Q}^-(\varphi)$ is the under-approximation and $\mathcal{Q}^+(\varphi)$ the over-approximation that together solve Problem 3. Then if $t \in \bigcup \mathcal{Q}^-(\varphi)$, we can conclude that $(z, t) \models \varphi$, and $t \notin \bigcup \mathcal{Q}^+(\varphi)$ allows us to conclude that $(z, t) \not\models \varphi$.

5.1   Operators in the Interval Queue Domain

The MITL grammar in Definition 2 has three primitive operators: complementation; conjunction; and strict non-matching until. The semantics in Definition 3 can be re-expressed in terms of truth sets as follows:

$$T_z(\neg\varphi_1) = [0,\infty) \setminus T_z(\varphi_1); \tag{9}$$
$$T_z(\varphi_1 \wedge \varphi_2) = T_z(\varphi_1) \cap T_z(\varphi_2); \tag{10}$$
$$t \in T_z(\varphi_1 \mathcal{U}_I \varphi_2) \iff \exists t_2 \in I, \left(t + t_2 \in T_z(\varphi_2) \text{ and } (t, t+t_2) \subseteq T_z(\varphi_1)\right). \tag{11}$$

For each of these logical operators, corresponding operators in the interval queue domain can be defined to generate interval queues that preserve the above truth set relationships. First recall the Minkowski difference between sets $A, B \subseteq \mathbb{R}$ is as follows: $B \ominus A := \{b - a \mid b \in B, a \in A\}$.[1]

Definition 6. *The following operations are defined for any* $\mathcal{H}, \mathcal{I}, \mathcal{J} \in \mathfrak{Q}$:

---

[1] Cf. [10]: intersection with $[0,\infty)$ is redundant here, because of the intersection with $\mathrm{cl}(H) \subseteq [0,\infty)$ in (12).

6.1) $\sim\!\mathcal{I} := \texttt{ComplementIQ}(\mathcal{I});$

6.2) $\mathcal{I} \sqcap \mathcal{J} := \{I \cap J \mid I \in \mathcal{I}, J \in \mathcal{J}\} \setminus \{\emptyset\};$

6.3) *Given any* $I \in \mathbb{I}$, $\mathcal{H} \, \Box_I \, \mathcal{J} := \texttt{ConstructIQ}(\mathcal{Y})$, *where the set*

$$\mathcal{Y} := \left\{ \left((\text{cl}(H) \cap J) \ominus I\right) \cap \text{cl}(H) \mid H \in \mathcal{H}, J \in \mathcal{J} \right\}. \tag{12}$$

Remark 5. The simplicity of the $\sqcap$ operation in Definition 6 is one reason for choosing conjunction as primitive in Definition 2, rather than disjunction.

We now show that, if $\bigcup \mathcal{I} = T_z(\varphi_1)$ and $\bigcup \mathcal{J} = T_z(\varphi_2)$, given $\mathcal{I}, \mathcal{J} \in \mathfrak{Q}$ and $\varphi_1, \varphi_2 \in \mathfrak{F}(\mathsf{G})$, then $T_z(\neg\varphi_1) = \bigcup(\sim\!\mathcal{I})$, $T_z(\varphi_1 \wedge \varphi_2) = \bigcup(\mathcal{I} \sqcap \mathcal{J})$, $T_z(\varphi_1 \, \mathcal{U}_I \varphi_2) = \bigcup(\mathcal{I} \, \Box_I \, \mathcal{J})$, and $\sim\!\mathcal{I}, \mathcal{I} \sqcap \mathcal{J}, \mathcal{I} \, \Box_I \, \mathcal{J} \in \mathfrak{Q}$. Endpoint rationality is also preserved. The result for negation is a corollary of Lemma 2. Next we turn to conjunction.

Lemma 3. *If* $\mathcal{I}, \mathcal{J} \in \mathfrak{Q}$, *then* $\mathcal{I} \sqcap \mathcal{J} \in \mathfrak{Q}$ *and* $\bigcup(\mathcal{I} \sqcap \mathcal{J}) = \bigcup \mathcal{I} \cap \bigcup \mathcal{J}$. *Moreover,* $\mathcal{I}, \mathcal{J} \subseteq \mathbb{I}_\mathbb{Q} \implies \mathcal{I} \sqcap \mathcal{J} \subseteq \mathbb{I}_\mathbb{Q}$.

Proof. We first show that $\mathcal{I} \sqcap \mathcal{J}$ is an interval queue. The finiteness of $\mathcal{I} \sqcap \mathcal{J}$ follows from the finiteness of both $\mathcal{I}$ and $\mathcal{J}$. Also, $\emptyset \notin \mathcal{I} \sqcap \mathcal{J}$ by definition. We now establish separation. Since $I_1 \cap I_2 \in \mathbb{I}$ for any $I_1, I_2 \in \mathbb{I}$, it follows from Definition 6 that $\mathcal{I} \sqcap \mathcal{J} \subseteq \mathbb{I}$. Now let $U, V \in \mathcal{I} \sqcap \mathcal{J}$ and suppose that $U \neq V$. Then there exist $I_1, I_2 \in \mathcal{I}$ and $J_1, J_2 \in \mathcal{J}$ such that $U = I_1 \cap J_1$ and $V = I_2 \cap J_2$. Since the closure of a finite intersection is contained in the intersection of the closures [4, Exercise 1.1.A],

$$\text{cl}(U) \cap V = \text{cl}(I_1 \cap J_1) \cap I_2 \cap J_2 \subseteq \text{cl}(I_1) \cap \text{cl}(J_1) \cap I_2 \cap J_2, \tag{13}$$

$$U \cap \text{cl}(V) = I_1 \cap J_1 \cap \text{cl}(I_2 \cap J_2) \subseteq I_1 \cap J_1 \cap \text{cl}(I_2) \cap \text{cl}(J_2). \tag{14}$$

If both $I_1 = I_2$ and $J_1 = J_2$, then $U = V$, which contradicts the hypothesis that $U \neq V$. If $I_1 \neq I_2$, then they are separated because they are elements of an interval queue, and $\text{cl}(I_1) \cap I_2 = I_1 \cap \text{cl}(I_2) = \emptyset$, which implies $\text{cl}(U) \cap V = U \cap \text{cl}(V) = \emptyset$ in view of (13)–(14). Otherwise $J_1 \neq J_2$, which yields the same result. Thus U and V are separated. As such, $\mathcal{I} \sqcap \mathcal{J}$ is an interval queue.

Since $\mathcal{I}, \mathcal{J}$ are finite, we may assume $\mathcal{I} = \{I_1, ..., I_m\}$ and $\mathcal{J} = \{J_1, ..., J_n\}$ without loss of generality. Applying the distributive properties of set unions and intersections, $(\bigcup \mathcal{I}) \cap (\bigcup \mathcal{J}) = (\bigcup_{i=1}^m I_i) \cap \left(\bigcup_{j=1}^n J_j\right) = \bigcup_{j=1}^n \left((\bigcup_{i=1}^m I_i) \cap J_j\right) = \bigcup_{j=1}^n \bigcup_{i=1}^m (I_i \cap J_j) = \bigcup(\mathcal{I} \sqcap \mathcal{J})$. We conclude by noting that the intersection of two intervals with rational endpoints is an interval with rational endpoints. $\square$

The until operation is considerably more complicated than conjunction. The set $\mathcal{Y}$ in (12), which is inspired by [10, Section 3], may not be an interval queue. However, set intersections, closures, and Minkowski differences preserve convexity (which means that intervals remain intervals) and endpoint rationality. Non-negativity is also preserved, as noted in Footnote 1. Thus, $\mathcal{Y}$ is a finite set of non-negative intervals, and Algorithm 1 is required to ensure that $\mathcal{H} \, \Box_I \, \mathcal{J} \in \mathfrak{Q}$. Lemma 1 guarantees that

$$\bigcup(\mathcal{H} \, \Box_I \, \mathcal{J}) = \bigcup \mathcal{Y} = \bigcup_{H \in \mathcal{H}} \bigcup_{J \in \mathcal{J}} \left(\left((\text{cl}(H) \cap J) \ominus I\right) \cap \text{cl}(H)\right). \tag{15}$$

The lemma below is also of crucial importance to the until operation: if a non-empty interval is contained in the union of an interval queue, then it is fully contained within one of the intervals in that interval queue.

Lemma 4. *Suppose $S \in \mathbb{I}$ is non-empty, and $S \subseteq \bigcup \mathcal{I}$, with $\mathcal{I} \in \mathfrak{Q}$ an interval queue. Then there exists a unique $I \in \mathcal{I}$ such that $I \supseteq S$.*

Proof. Let $\mathcal{I} = \{I_1, \ldots, I_m\}$. Proposition 4 implies that I_1 and $\bigcup_{i=2}^m I_i$ are separated. Since $S \subseteq I_1 \cup \bigcup_{i=2}^m I_i$, Proposition 3 then implies that $S \subseteq I_1$ or $S \subseteq \bigcup_{i=2}^m I_i$, but not both. If the former, the result is proved. If the latter, then the same reasoning applied recursively yields the result. □

The next two Lemmas establish that if $\mathcal{H}$ and $\mathcal{J}$ are interval queue representations of the truth sets of formulas φ_1 and φ_2 respectively, then $\bigcup \mathcal{H} \, \square_I \, \mathcal{J}$ is the truth set of $\varphi_1 \mathcal{U}_I \varphi_2$.

Lemma 5. *Let $\mathcal{H}, \mathcal{J} \in \mathfrak{Q}$ be interval queues, G a finite set of atomic propositions, $I \in \mathbb{I}_\mathbb{Q}$ nondegenerate, $\varphi_1, \varphi_2 \in \mathfrak{F}(\mathsf{G})$, and $z : [0, \infty) \to 2^\mathsf{G}$ a signal of finite variability. If $T_z(\varphi_1) \subseteq \bigcup \mathcal{H}$ and $T_z(\varphi_2) \subseteq \bigcup \mathcal{J}$, then $T_z(\varphi_1 \mathcal{U}_I \varphi_2) \subseteq \bigcup(\mathcal{H} \, \square_I \, \mathcal{J})$.*

Proof. Suppose $t \in T_z(\varphi_1 \mathcal{U}_I \varphi_2)$. Then by (11), $\exists t_2 \in I$, $t + t_2 \in T_z(\varphi_2)$ and $(t, t + t_2) \subseteq T_z(\varphi_1)$. This in turn implies $\exists t_2 \in I$, $\exists J \in \mathcal{J}$, $t + t_2 \in J$ and $(t, t + t_2) \subseteq \bigcup \mathcal{H}$. Applying Lemma 4 then gives: $\exists t_2 \in I$, $\exists J \in \mathcal{J}$, $\exists H \in \mathcal{H}$, $t + t_2 \in J$ and $(t, t + t_2) \subseteq H$. As such, $[t, t + t_2] \subseteq \mathrm{cl}(H)$ by Proposition 1. In particular, $t \in \mathrm{cl}(H)$, and since $t + t_2 \in J$, we see that $\tau := t + t_2 \in \mathrm{cl}(H) \cap J$. Thus $t = \tau - t_2$, with $\tau \in \mathrm{cl}(H) \cap J$ and $t_2 \in I$, which implies $t \in (\mathrm{cl}(H) \cap J) \ominus I$, and therefore $t \in \Big((\mathrm{cl}(H) \cap J) \ominus I\Big) \cap \mathrm{cl}(H)$. Equation (15) then implies $t \subseteq \bigcup(\mathcal{H} \, \square_I \, \mathcal{J})$. □

Lemma 6. *Let $\mathcal{H}, \mathcal{J} \in \mathfrak{Q}$ be interval queues, G a finite set of atomic propositions, $I \in \mathbb{I}_\mathbb{Q}$ nondegenerate, $\varphi_1, \varphi_2 \in \mathfrak{F}(\mathsf{G})$, and $z : [0, \infty) \to 2^\mathsf{G}$ a signal of finite variability. If $T_z(\varphi_1) \supseteq \bigcup \mathcal{H}$ and $T_z(\varphi_2) \supseteq \bigcup \mathcal{J}$, then $T_z(\varphi_1 \mathcal{U}_I \varphi_2) \supseteq \bigcup(\mathcal{H} \, \square_I \, \mathcal{J})$.*

Proof. Suppose $t \in \bigcup(\mathcal{H} \, \square_I \, \mathcal{J})$. Then by (15), $\exists H \in \mathcal{H}$, $\exists J \in \mathcal{J}$, $t \in \Big((\mathrm{cl}(H) \cap J) \ominus I\Big) \cap \mathrm{cl}(H)$. It follows that $t \in \mathrm{cl}(H)$, and

$$\exists \tau \in \mathrm{cl}(H) \cap J, \ \exists t_2 \in I, \ t = \tau - t_2. \tag{16}$$

Since $t \in \mathrm{cl}(H)$ and $\tau = t + t_2 \in \mathrm{cl}(H)$ for the interval H, it follows that $[t, t + t_2] \subseteq \mathrm{cl}(H)$. So, by Proposition 1, $(t, t + t_2) = \mathrm{int}([t, t + t_2]) \subseteq \mathrm{int}(\mathrm{cl}(H))$, and by Proposition 5, $\mathrm{int}(\mathrm{cl}(H)) \subseteq H \subseteq T_z(\varphi_1)$. Thus, $(t, t + t_2) \subseteq T_z(\varphi_1)$, and $\tau = t + t_2 \in J \subseteq T_z(\varphi_2)$ by (16), where $t_2 \in I$. Finally, $t \in T_z(\varphi \mathcal{U}_I \varphi_2)$ then follows from (11). □

Corollary 1. *Under the hypotheses of Lemma 6, $\mathcal{H} \, \square_I \, \mathcal{J} \in \mathfrak{Q}$. Moreover, if $T_z(\varphi_1) = \bigcup \mathcal{H}$ and $T_z(\varphi_2) = \bigcup \mathcal{J}$, then $T_z(\varphi_1 \mathcal{U}_I \varphi_2) = \bigcup(\mathcal{H} \, \square_I \, \mathcal{J})$. Finally, $\mathcal{H}, \mathcal{J} \subseteq \mathbb{I}_\mathbb{Q} \implies \mathcal{H} \, \square_I \, \mathcal{J} \subseteq \mathbb{I}_\mathbb{Q}$.*

Proof. This follows directly from Lemmas 5 and 6, and the discussion immediately preceding Lemma 4. □

Remark 6. Corollary 1 extends the 'General Until' claim in [10, Section 3] in three directions. First, I needs neither be closed nor bounded. Second, the truth sets of the arguments need not be left-closed right-open. Finally, Corollary 1 holds for a strict non-matching until, which is more expressive [7] than the non-strict matching until of [10].

5.2   Constructing Under- and Over-Approximations

The maps $\mathcal{P}^-$ and $\mathcal{P}^+$ in Problem 3 provide, respectively, under-approximations and over-approximations to the truth sets of the atomic propositions. It is now shown how to combine them, using the operations in Definition 6, to obtain under- and over-approximations to the truth sets of any MITL formula, thereby solving Problem 3. Theorem 1 then states this result formally.

Definition 7. *Given the two maps $\mathcal{P}^-, \mathcal{P}^+ : \mathsf{G} \to \mathfrak{Q}$ in Problem 3, define $\mathcal{Q}^-, \mathcal{Q}^+ : \mathfrak{F}(\mathsf{G}) \to \mathfrak{Q}$ inductively as follows: for any $\varphi_1, \varphi_2 \in \mathfrak{F}(\mathsf{G})$,*

$$\mathcal{Q}^+(\top) = \{[0, \infty)\}, \qquad\qquad \mathcal{Q}^-(\top) = \{[0, \infty)\}, \qquad\qquad (17)$$
$$\mathcal{Q}^+(\mathsf{g}) = \mathcal{P}^+(\mathsf{g}), \qquad\qquad \mathcal{Q}^-(\mathsf{g}) = \mathcal{P}^-(\mathsf{g}), \qquad\qquad (18)$$
$$\mathcal{Q}^+(\neg\varphi_1) = {\sim}\mathcal{Q}^-(\varphi_1), \qquad\qquad \mathcal{Q}^-(\neg\varphi_1) = {\sim}\mathcal{Q}^+(\varphi_1), \qquad (19)$$
$$\mathcal{Q}^+(\varphi_1 \wedge \varphi_2) = \mathcal{Q}^+(\varphi_1) \sqcap \mathcal{Q}^+(\varphi_2), \quad \mathcal{Q}^-(\varphi_1 \wedge \varphi_2) = \mathcal{Q}^-(\varphi_1) \sqcap \mathcal{Q}^-(\varphi_2); \quad (20)$$

and finally for any non-degenerate $I \in \mathbb{I}_\mathbb{Q}$,

$$\mathcal{Q}^+(\varphi_1 \mathcal{U}_I \varphi_2) = \mathcal{Q}^+(\varphi_1) \mathbin{\boxdot_I} \mathcal{Q}^+(\varphi_2), \quad \mathcal{Q}^-(\varphi_1 \mathcal{U}_I \varphi_2) = \mathcal{Q}^-(\varphi_1) \mathbin{\boxdot_I} \mathcal{Q}^-(\varphi_2).$$
$$(21)$$

Theorem 1. *Under the hypotheses of Problem 3, the interval queues $\mathcal{Q}^+(\varphi) \in \mathfrak{Q}$ and $\mathcal{Q}^-(\varphi) \in \mathfrak{Q}$ constructed according to Definition 7 satisfy*

$$\bigcup \mathcal{Q}^-(\varphi) \subseteq T_z(\varphi) \subseteq \bigcup \mathcal{Q}^+(\varphi),$$

for any $\varphi \in \mathfrak{F}(\mathsf{G})$. Moreover, if both $\mathcal{P}^-(\mathsf{g}) \subseteq \mathbb{I}_\mathbb{Q}$ and $\mathcal{P}^+(\mathsf{g}) \subseteq \mathbb{I}_\mathbb{Q}$ for every $\mathsf{g} \in \mathsf{G}$, then for any $\varphi \in \mathfrak{F}(\mathsf{G})$, both $\mathcal{Q}^-(\varphi) \subseteq \mathbb{I}_\mathbb{Q}$ and $\mathcal{Q}^+(\varphi) \subseteq \mathbb{I}_\mathbb{Q}$. That is,

$$\bigcup_{\mathsf{g} \in \mathsf{G}} (\mathcal{P}^-(\mathsf{g}) \cup \mathcal{P}^+(\mathsf{g})) \subseteq \mathbb{I}_\mathbb{Q} \implies \bigcup_{\varphi \in \mathfrak{F}(\mathsf{G})} (\mathcal{Q}^-(\varphi) \cup \mathcal{Q}^+(\varphi)) \subseteq \mathbb{I}_\mathbb{Q}. \quad (22)$$

The proof of Theorem 1 is a straightforward application of all the preceding results, so it is deferred to Appendix A.

Corollary 2. *For any $\varphi \in \mathfrak{F}(\mathsf{G})$,*

$$t \in \bigcup \mathcal{Q}^-(\varphi) \implies (z, t) \models \varphi,$$
$$t \notin \bigcup \mathcal{Q}^+(\varphi) \implies (z, t) \not\models \varphi.$$

Thus, in order to test whether an MITL formula is satisfied (or not satisfied) at a given time, we need only look at whether the generated under- and over-approximations contain an interval containing that time.

Remark 7. The verification result is inconclusive for any $t \in \bigcup \mathcal{Q}^+(\varphi) \setminus \bigcup \mathcal{Q}^-(\varphi)$.

Our procedure also solves Problem 2 when the under- and over-approximations to the truth sets of the atomic propositions coincide.

Corollary 3. *If* $\mathcal{P}^- = \mathcal{P}^+$, *then* $\forall \varphi \in \mathfrak{F}(\mathsf{G})$, $\bigcup \mathcal{Q}^-(\varphi) = T_z(\varphi) = \bigcup \mathcal{Q}^+(\varphi)$. *That is,* $\mathcal{P}^- = \mathcal{P}^+ \implies \mathcal{Q}^- = \mathcal{Q}^+$.

5.3   Conservativeness

Corollary 2 establishes that our verification procedure is sound. However, due to the uncertainty in initial atomic proposition timing accommodated by Problem 3, it is necessarily conservative. For a given instance of the problem, the degree of conservativeness relates to the gap between under-approximation $\mathcal{Q}^-(\varphi)$ and over-approximation $\mathcal{Q}^+(\varphi)$, as noted in Remark 7. For example, one could use $\Delta := \lambda(\bigcup \mathcal{Q}^+(\varphi) \setminus \bigcup \mathcal{Q}^-(\varphi))$, where λ is the Lebesgue measure, to quantify conservativeness. The next section illustrates the growth of the gap through the parse tree of a formula by plotting Δ for each of its sub-formulas. A more comprehensive analysis of the gap, and its dependence on the complexity of the formula, is currently in progress. Also related to conservativeness is the notion of time robustness [3], which quantifies how robust the satisfaction of a formula is to shifts of the signal in time. The precise relationship between time robustness and the gap $\bigcup \mathcal{Q}^+(\varphi) \setminus \bigcup \mathcal{Q}^-(\varphi)$ is a topic of ongoing investigation.

6   Numerical Example

Here we consider a particular instance of Problem 3 involving two atomic propositions: $\mathsf{G} := \{g_1, g_2\}$. The corresponding truth sets are plotted in the first row of Fig. 1, together with their under- and over-approximations. The under-approximations are the interiors of the truth sets, and the over-approximations their closures, so initially $\Delta = 0$ for both g_1 and g_2 because their under- and over-approximations differ by only a finite number of points. In the next row of Fig. 1, we see the effect of two successive until operators is to increase Δ by 1 and then again by 2. Note that $\lozenge_I \psi := \top \mathcal{U}_I \psi$ is the *eventually* operator. In the third row, we see that this gap remains at 3, even for the validity $\varphi \vee \neg\varphi$, and the contradiction $\varphi \wedge \neg\varphi$.

Remark 8. For some formulas, the verification result can be known for all times simply by virtue of the structure of the formula. However, our procedure may still return an inconclusive result over a subset of times, due to the uncertainty at lower levels of the parse tree. For this reason, $\top$ is chosen as primitive in Definition 2, rather than defining $\top := \mathsf{g} \vee \neg\mathsf{g}$ in terms of some $\mathsf{g} \in \mathsf{G}$. Then, for contradictions, simply put $\bot := \neg\top$.

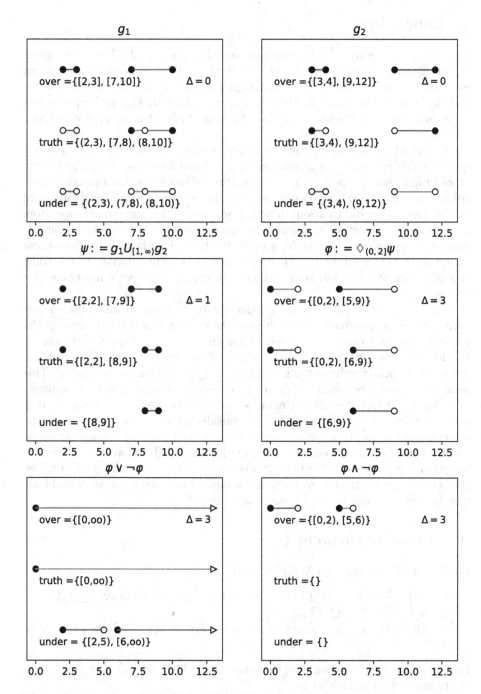

Fig. 1. Output of verification algorithm. The interval queues are written explicitly beneath each line. The measure of the gap between the over- and under-approximations is given by Δ.

7   Conclusion

Problem 2 is to verify a continuous-time signal against an MITL formula, given knowledge of the time intervals over which the individual atomic propositions are true. Problem 3 poses a more challenging version of this, in which only over- and under-approximations for those intervals are known. This paper presents a solution to Problem 3, which also solves Problem 2 when the intervals are known exactly.

To formulate and solve Problem 3, we introduce the notion of an interval queue, which is a finite set of non-empty separated intervals. Separation is the crucial topological property that our procedure relies on. Section 4 presents algorithms for constructing and complementing interval queues, which become core subroutines within our solution. In Sect. 5, we construct interval queue operators corresponding to each of the primitive logical operators: conjunction, complementation and strict non-matching until. We then show how to combine these operators to obtain interval queue over- and under-approximations to the truth sets of arbitrary MITL formulas. A numerical example in Sect. 6 illustrates this procedure.

The gap between the over- and under-approximations indicates the conservativeness of the approach. An analysis of the evolution of this gap through the parse tree of the formula is the topic of ongoing work; specifically, of the degree to which reducing the initial gap $\bigcup \mathcal{P}^+(g) \setminus \bigcup \mathcal{P}^-(g)$ for every atomic proposition $g \in G$, consequently reduces the gap $\bigcup \mathcal{Q}^+(\varphi) \setminus \bigcup \mathcal{Q}^-(\varphi)$ for any formula φ. This would help assess the benefits of spending more on computation or measurement, in order to improve the initial timing bounds for the atomic propositions. It is also of interest to address Remark 8, by considering how information about the structure of the formula can be exploited in order to reduce conservativeness. Finally, the relationships between the gap $\bigcup \mathcal{Q}^+(\varphi) \setminus \bigcup \mathcal{Q}^-(\varphi)$ and the notions of temporal robustness in [3,9,13] merit investigation. Recent works [8,12] consider the synthesis of controllers to maximise temporal robustness, so such problems may benefit from our interval queue-based analysis.

A   Proof of Theorem 1

We first show the result holds for $\varphi \in \{\top\} \cup G$.

- By (17), $\mathcal{Q}^-(\top) = \mathcal{Q}^+(\top) = \{[0,\infty)\} \in \mathfrak{Q}$, and therefore $\bigcup \mathcal{Q}^-(\top) = [0,\infty) = T_z(\top) = \bigcup \mathcal{Q}^+(\top)$.
- By (6), $\mathcal{Q}^-(g), \mathcal{Q}^+(g) \in \mathfrak{Q}$, and $\bigcup \mathcal{Q}^-(g) \subseteq T_z(g) \subseteq \bigcup \mathcal{Q}^+(g)$ for all $g \in G$ by (18).

For the remaining steps, suppose that that $\mathcal{Q}^-(\varphi_1), \mathcal{Q}^+(\varphi_1), \mathcal{Q}^-(\varphi_2), \mathcal{Q}^+(\varphi_2) \in \mathfrak{Q}$ are interval queues such that

$$\bigcup \mathcal{Q}^-(\varphi_1) \subseteq T_z(\varphi_1) \subseteq \bigcup \mathcal{Q}^+(\varphi_1), \tag{23}$$

$$\bigcup \mathcal{Q}^-(\varphi_2) \subseteq T_z(\varphi_2) \subseteq \bigcup \mathcal{Q}^+(\varphi_2). \tag{24}$$

- Lemma 2 implies $\mathcal{Q}^-(\neg\varphi_1) = \texttt{ComplementIQ}(\mathcal{Q}^+(\varphi_1)) \in \mathfrak{Q}$. If $t \in \bigcup\mathcal{Q}^-(\neg\varphi_1)$, then $t \notin \bigcup\mathcal{Q}^+(\varphi_1)$ by Lemma 2, and (23) then implies $t \notin T_z(\varphi_1)$. It follows that $(z,t) \not\models \varphi_1$, by which $(z,t) \models \neg\varphi_1$, and therefore $t \in T_z(\neg\varphi_1)$. Thus, $\bigcup\mathcal{Q}^-(\neg\varphi_1) \subseteq T_z(\neg\varphi_1)$.
- Lemma 2 implies $\mathcal{Q}^+(\neg\varphi_1) = \texttt{ComplementIQ}(\mathcal{Q}^-(\varphi_1)) \in \mathfrak{Q}$. If $t \in T_z(\neg\varphi_1)$, then $t \notin T_z(\varphi_1)$, and (23) then implies $t \notin \bigcup\mathcal{Q}^-(\varphi_1)$. Therefore $t \in [0,\infty) \setminus \bigcup\mathcal{Q}^-(\varphi_1) = \bigcup\mathcal{Q}^+(\neg\varphi_1)$ by Lemma 2. Thus, $T_z(\neg\varphi_1) \subseteq \bigcup\mathcal{Q}^+(\neg\varphi_1)$.
- Lemma 3 implies $\mathcal{Q}^-(\varphi_1 \wedge \varphi_2) = \mathcal{Q}^-(\varphi_1) \sqcap \mathcal{Q}^-(\varphi_2) \in \mathfrak{Q}$. Furthermore, (23) - (24) imply $\bigcup\mathcal{Q}^-(\varphi_1 \wedge \varphi_2) = \bigcup(\mathcal{Q}^-(\varphi_1) \sqcap \mathcal{Q}^-(\varphi_2)) = \bigcup\mathcal{Q}^-(\varphi_1) \cap \bigcup\mathcal{Q}^-(\varphi_2) \subseteq T_z(\varphi_1) \cap T_z(\varphi_2) = T_z(\varphi_1 \wedge \varphi_2)$.
- Similarly, $\mathcal{Q}^+(\varphi_1 \wedge \varphi_2) \in \mathfrak{Q}$, and $T_z(\varphi_1 \wedge \varphi_2) = T_z(\varphi_1) \cap T_z(\varphi_2) \subseteq \bigcup\mathcal{Q}^+(\varphi_1) \cap \bigcup\mathcal{Q}^+(\varphi_2) = \bigcup(\mathcal{Q}^+(\varphi_1) \sqcap \mathcal{Q}^+(\varphi_2)) = \bigcup\mathcal{Q}^+(\varphi_1 \wedge \varphi_2)$.
- Corollary 1 implies $\mathcal{Q}^-(\varphi_1\,\mathcal{U}_I\varphi_2) = \mathcal{Q}^-(\varphi_1)\boxdot_I\mathcal{Q}^-(\varphi_2) \in \mathfrak{Q}$ for any nondegenerate $I \in \mathbb{I}_\mathbb{Q}$, and $\bigcup\mathcal{Q}^-(\varphi_1\,\mathcal{U}_I\varphi_2) = \bigcup(\mathcal{Q}^-(\varphi_1) \boxdot_I \mathcal{Q}^-(\varphi_2)) \subseteq T_z(\varphi_1\,\mathcal{U}_I\varphi_2)$ by Lemma 6.
- Corollary 1 implies $\mathcal{Q}^+(\varphi_1\,\mathcal{U}_I\varphi_2) = \mathcal{Q}^+(\varphi_1)\boxdot_I\mathcal{Q}^+(\varphi_2) \in \mathfrak{Q}$ for any nondegenerate $I \in \mathbb{I}_\mathbb{Q}$, and $\bigcup\mathcal{Q}^+(\varphi_1\,\mathcal{U}_I\varphi_2) = \bigcup(\mathcal{Q}^+(\varphi_1) \boxdot_I \mathcal{Q}^-(\varphi_2)) \supseteq T_z(\varphi_1\,\mathcal{U}_I\varphi_2)$ by Lemma 5.

The result then follows by structural induction on the formula φ. Endpoint rationality is preserved (22) because all the individual operations preserve it. $\square$

References

1. Alur, R., Feder, T., Henzinger, T.A.: The benefits of relaxing punctuality. J. ACM **43**(1), 116–146 (1996). https://doi.org/10.1145/227595.227602
2. Basin, D., Bhatt, B.N., Traytel, D.: Optimal proofs for linear temporal logic on lasso words. In: Lahiri, S.K., Wang, C. (eds.) ATVA 2018. LNCS, vol. 11138, pp. 37–55. Springer, Cham (2018). https://doi.org/10.1007/978-3-030-01090-4_3
3. Donzé, A., Maler, O.: Robust satisfaction of temporal logic over real-valued signals. In: Chatterjee, K., Henzinger, T.A. (eds.) FORMATS 2010. LNCS, vol. 6246, pp. 92–106. Springer, Heidelberg (2010). https://doi.org/10.1007/978-3-642-15297-9_9
4. Engelking, R.: General Topology. Heldermann (1989)
5. Fainekos, G.E., Pappas, G.J.: Robustness of temporal logic specifications for continuous-time signals. Theoret. Comput. Sci. **410**(42), 4262–4291 (2009). https://doi.org/10.1016/j.tcs.2009.06.021
6. Furia, C.A., Rossi, M.: A theory of sampling for continuous-time metric temporal logic. ACM Trans. Comput. Logic **12**(1), 8:1–8:40 (2010). https://doi.org/10.1145/1838552.1838560
7. Furia, C.A., Rossi, M.: On the expressiveness of MTL variants over dense time. In: Raskin, J.-F., Thiagarajan, P.S. (eds.) Formal Modeling and Analysis of Timed Systems. LNCS, vol. 4763, pp. 163–178. Springer, Heidelberg (2007). https://doi.org/10.1007/978-3-540-75454-1_13
8. Lin, Z., Baras, J.S.: Optimization-based motion planning and runtime monitoring for robotic agent with space and time tolerances. IFAC-PapersOnLine **53**(2), 1874–1879 (2020). https://doi.org/10.1016/j.ifacol.2020.12.2606

9. Lindemann, L., Rodionova, A., Pappas, G.: Temporal robustness of stochastic signals. In: 25th ACM International Conference on Hybrid Systems: Computation and Control. pp. 1–11. HSCC 2022, Association for Computing Machinery, New York, NY, USA, May 2022. https://doi.org/10.1145/3501710.3519504

10. Maler, O., Nickovic, D.: Monitoring temporal properties of continuous signals. In: Lakhnech, Y., Yovine, S. (eds.) FORMATS/FTRTFT -2004. LNCS, vol. 3253, pp. 152–166. Springer, Heidelberg (2004). https://doi.org/10.1007/978-3-540-30206-3_12

11. Munkres, J.R.: Topology, 2nd edn. Prentice Hall Inc., Hoboken (2000)

12. Rodionova, A., Lindemann, L., Morari, M., Pappas, G.J.: Time-robust control for STL specifications. In: 2021 60th IEEE Conference on Decision and Control (CDC), pp. 572–579, December 2021. https://doi.org/10.1109/CDC45484.2021.9683477

13. Rodionova, A., Lindemann, L., Morari, M., Pappas, G.J.: Temporal Robustness of Temporal Logic Specifications: Analysis and Control Design, March 2022. arXiv:2203.15661

14. Selvaratnam, D., Cantoni, M., Davoren, J.M., Shames, I.: Sampling polynomial trajectories for LTL verification. Theoret. Comput. Sci. **897**, 135–163 (2022). https://doi.org/10.1016/j.tcs.2021.10.024

Classification of Driving Behaviors Using STL Formulas: A Comparative Study

Ruya Karagulle[1]($\boxtimes$), Nikos Aréchiga[2], Jonathan DeCastro[2], and Necmiye Ozay[1]

[1] University of Michigan, Ann Arbor, MI 48109, USA
{ruyakrgl,necmiye}@umich.edu
[2] Toyota Research Institute, Cambridge, MA, USA
{nikos.arechiga,jonathan.decastro}@tri.global

Abstract. In this paper, we conduct a preliminary comparative study of classification of longitudinal driving behavior using Signal Temporal Logic (STL) formulas. The goal of the classification problem is to distinguish between different driving styles or vehicles. The results can be used to design and test autonomous vehicle policies. We work on a real-life dataset, the Highway Drone Dataset (HighD). To solve this problem, our first approach starts with a formula template and reduces the classification problem to a Mixed-Integer Linear Program (MILP). Solving MILPs becomes computationally challenging with increasing number of variables and constraints. We propose two improvements to split the classification problem into smaller ones. We prove that these simpler problems are related to the original classification problem in a way that their feasibility imply that of the original. Finally, we compare our MILP formulation with an existing STL-based classification tool, LoTuS, in terms of accuracy and execution time.

Keywords: driving behavior · STL classification · formal methods

1 Introduction

A key factor in developing high-quality and robust policies for autonomous driving is strong understanding of the driving environment. An essential component to understanding this environment is high-quality prediction models of driving behaviors. In this paper, we compare methods to classify driving behaviors as exhibited in real-world data. We use the HighD dataset to work on naturalistic vehicle trajectories [13]. The dataset comprises 110500 vehicle tracks recorded on German highways. As our case study, we consider the task of distinguishing the longitudinal driving behavior of cars and trucks in this dataset.

Existing work in time series classification provides a variety of methods that can be used to classify behaviors. However, time-series classifiers such as Long Short-term Memory (LSTM) [11] or classification using Dynamic Time Warping [4] frequently lack interpretability. In the early stages of system development,

© Springer Nature Switzerland AG 2022
S. Bogomolov and D. Parker (Eds.): FORMATS 2022, LNCS 13465, pp. 153–162, 2022.
https://doi.org/10.1007/978-3-031-15839-1_9

human engineers are heavily involved in interacting with prediction models, as well as debugging erroneous conditions that may arise in either simulation or real-world testing. Engineers would greatly benefit from interpretable classification and prediction models, which would help them to better understand the root cause of failures as well as possible solutions. Temporal Logic (TL) [17] is extensively used to describe the behavior of cyber-physical systems [1,6–8]. The symbolic nature of temporal logic specifications make them a good candidate for interpretable classifiers. Moreover, they can be used for runtime decision-making.

Signal Temporal Logic (STL) [14] is a variant of temporal logic that can be used to reason about continuous, discrete, or even hybrid signals. In addition, several different quantitative semantics have been proposed for STL. The quantitative semantics can be used to compute the *robustness* metric, which is a measure of the degree of satisfaction of signals for a given STL formula and a signal trace. Robustness is a sound and non-smooth function [19].

TL formula inference problem tries to learn a TL formula from the data and it has been studied before in the literature [5,9,12,15]. [5,9,12] use another variant of STL called Parametric STL (PSTL) where numerical values of the formula are interpreted as unknown parameters. In [3], the authors approach the two-class classification problem as a statistical learning problem. Given the template formula, they explore the parameters using statistical model checking. The paper [12] defines a directed acyclic graph (DAG) of formula templates and searches over this graph, after proving the partial ordering of formulas. Their loss function is the number of misclassifications and the length of the formula (the number of linear predicates that appear in the formula). In [5], they propose a decision tree approach for both online and offline learning using STL formula. They incrementally update the binary tree linked to the STL formula decision and search for the smallest formula that can be constructed from a set of primitives. In this paper, we use their toolbox LoTuS for comparison. [15] solves a series of satisfiability problems in Boolean logic to obtain the smallest linear temporal logic formula possible.

Learning from formula templates can be used for car-truck classification as well. It is known that trucks tend to go slower than cars since they are heavier and tend to maintain a longer distance from lead vehicles since their deceleration rates are slower than cars. By considering this knowledge and taking inspiration from Adaptive Cruise Control (ACC) driving specifications [16], we develop an STL formula template. We recast the classification problem to an appropriate MILP problem in parameters of the STL formula template, and we optimize the robustness of the STL formula to find the optimal parameters. Since MILP problems can blow up in execution time with the number of variables and constraints, we propose two separation methods to improve execution time. The first separation is over the formula template and the second one is over the data. Although optimality is not preserved, we prove that the parameters found after improvements are also in the feasible domain for the original problem. We compare the MILP formulation with [5] and provide quantitative results for test error and for execution times. Limitations of both approaches are discussed.

2   Preliminaries

STL is defined with the syntax $\phi := \top \mid \pi \mid \neg\phi \mid \phi_1 \wedge \phi_2 \mid \phi_1 \mathcal{U}_I \phi_2$. The boolean true is $\top$, and π is a predicate of the form $f(s(t)) \leq \mu$ where $f : \mathbb{R}^n \to \mathbb{R}$, $\pi = \top$ when inequality holds. The logical not is $\neg$, and $\wedge$ is the conjunction operator. The temporal operator "Until" with the bounded interval I is shown as $\mathcal{U}_I$. Always $\square_I$, eventually $\Diamond_I$, disjunction $\vee$, are defined as $\phi_1 \vee \phi_2 = \neg(\neg\phi_1 \wedge \neg\phi_2)$, $\Diamond_I \phi = \top \mathcal{U}_I \phi$, and $\square_I \phi = \neg\Diamond_I \neg\phi$.

If a signal s satisfies a formula ϕ, it is shown as $s \models \phi$, and if it violates, it is shown as $s \not\models \phi$. Satisfaction rules are given by the qualitative semantics:

$$s(t) \models \pi \iff \pi$$
$$s(t) \models \neg\phi \iff \neg(s(t) \models \phi)$$
$$s(t) \models \phi_1 \wedge \phi_2 \iff ((s(t) \models \phi_1) \wedge (s(t) \models \phi_2))$$
$$s(t) \models \phi_1 \mathcal{U}_{[a,b]} \phi_2 \iff \exists t' \in [t+a, t+b] \text{ s.t. } (s(t') \models \phi_2) \wedge (\forall t'' \in [t,t'](s(t'') \models \phi_1))$$

In addition to their boolean semantics, STL formulas have a quantitative semantics, which quantify the degree to which a formula is satisfied or falsified. The quantitative semantics are defined with a metric called *robustness*. Given the signal and the formula, if the robustness metric is positive, then the signal satisfies the formula and vice versa. The robustness of the logical truth is $\rho(s, \top, t) = +\infty$ and the robustness of the predicate $\phi = f(s) \leq \mu$ is $\rho(s, \phi, t) = \mu - f(s(t))$. The robustness of a formula is defined recursively as follows:

$$\rho(s, \neg\phi, t) = -\rho(s, \phi, t)$$
$$\rho(s, \phi_1 \wedge \phi_2, t) = \min(\rho(s, \phi_1, t), \rho(s, \phi_2, t))$$
$$\rho(s, \phi_1 \mathcal{U}_{[a,b]} \phi_2, t) = \max_{t' \in [t+a, t+b]} (\min(\rho(s, \phi_2, t'), \min_{t'' \in [t,t']} \rho(s, \phi_1, t'')))$$

Robustness of derived operators can be found by re-writing the operator in terms of the primitive operators. In STL formulas, the predicate values μ and time intervals I are known. In [2], authors define another variant of STL, called Parametric Signal Temporal Logic (PSTL), where those values can be defined as parameters. A PSTL formula ϕ_μ will become an STL formula ϕ with a corresponding valuation of parameters $\boldsymbol{\mu}$, where $\boldsymbol{\mu}$ is the set of both scale and time parameters. With slight abuse of notation, we use φ_μ for corresponding valuation vector μ of parameters $\boldsymbol{\mu}$. We define an *STL formula template* as a PSTL formula with a set of unknown parameters.

3   Specifying Longitudinal Driving Behavior with STL

For the longitudinal driving scenario considered in this paper, the sample signal is two-dimensional, speed in $[km/h]$ and time headway in $[s]$, that is $s_i = \begin{bmatrix} v_i & w_i \end{bmatrix}^\top$, where $v_i \in \mathbb{R}^{T_i}$ and $w_i \in \mathbb{R}^{T_i}$ are the time series of speed and time headway values, respectively, with signal duration T_i. We want to find the formula that separates trucks from cars. From the intuition that trucks keep different speed and time headway than cars, we propose the following STL formula template:

$$\varphi = \Box\{\Box_{[0,\tau_1]}(w \geq w_\epsilon) \implies \Diamond_{[0,\tau_2]}(\Box(v \leq (1+\epsilon)v_{des}) \wedge \Box(v \geq (1-\epsilon)v_{des}) \vee w < w_\epsilon) \\ \wedge\Box_{[0,\tau_1]}(w < w_\epsilon) \implies \Diamond_{[0,\tau_2]}(\Box(w \leq (1+\epsilon)w_{des}) \wedge \Box(w \geq (1-\epsilon)w_{des}) \vee w \geq w_\epsilon)\}, \tag{1}$$

where w_ϵ is the time headway threshold, τ_1 is the cause time interval, τ_2 is the effect time interval, ϵ is the acceptance threshold for desired values, and v_{des} and w_{des} are desired speed and desired time headway, respectively. This formula comprises of two subformulas. The first subformula $\varphi_1 = \Box_{[0,\tau_1]}(w \geq w_\epsilon) \implies \Diamond_{[0,\tau_2]}(\Box(v \leq (1+\epsilon)v_{des} \wedge v \geq (1-\epsilon)v_{des}) \vee w > w_\epsilon)$ semantically represents that if there is no lead vehicle in close distance (time headway more than w_ϵ) for τ_1 seconds, the ego vehicle eventually reaches it desired speed v_{des} or lead vehicle happens to be in ego vehicle's close distance. This is similar to ACC set speed mode. The second subformula represents ACC time gap mode. $\varphi_2 = \Box_{[0,\tau_1]}(w < w_\epsilon) \implies \Diamond_{[0,\tau_2]}(\Box(w \leq (1+\epsilon)w_{des} \wedge w \geq (1-\epsilon)w_{des}) \vee w \geq w_\epsilon)$ means if there is a lead vehicle in front of the ego vehicle in time interval $[0,\tau_1]$, ego vehicle eventually reaches its desired time headway w_{des} in time interval $[0,\tau_2]$ or the time headway increases. Here in this formula, it is assumed that $w_\epsilon, \epsilon, \tau_1$ and τ_2 are known values. $\boldsymbol{\mu} = \boldsymbol{\mu_1} \cup \boldsymbol{\mu_2} = \{v_{des}, w_{des}\}$ are unknown parameters. Note that the formula can be seen as $\varphi_\mu = \Box(\varphi_{1,\mu_1} \wedge \varphi_{2,\mu_2})$.

4   Methods

Let $\mathcal{S} = \{(s_i, y_i)\}_{i=1}^N$ be the signal set. Let s_i be the ith sample signal, and $y_i \in \{0,1\}$ be its label. We assume there are two classes of signals that we wish to classify: Class 0 signals are denoted as $\mathcal{S}_0 := \{s_i \in \mathcal{S} : y_i = 0\}$, and class 1 signals are denoted as $\mathcal{S}_1 := \{s_i \in \mathcal{S} : y_i = 1\}$. The problem this paper addresses is to find an STL formula satisfied by class 0 signals and violated by class 1.

We can attempt to solve this problem by proposing a PSTL template and then solving an optimization problem over the formula parameters to maximize the robustness of the formula over class 0 while minimizing the robustness over class 1. This method can be useful when domain-specific knowledge allows proposing a suitable PSTL template, but specific parameters are unknown. Assuming that signal classes are separable with the formula above, the problem:

$$\begin{aligned} \max_{r,\mu} \quad & r \\ \text{s.t.} \quad & \rho(s_i, \varphi_\mu, 0) \geq r \quad \forall s_i \in \mathcal{S}_0 \\ & \rho(s_i, \varphi_\mu, 0) \leq -r \ \forall s_i \in \mathcal{S}_1 \\ & r \geq 0 \end{aligned} \tag{2}$$

returns the optimal parameter set. In particular, Problem (2) tries to find the parameter set that maximizes the margin r between two classes.

The classes might not be separable in reality, at least for two reasons. First, in real-life scenarios, it is likely to have outliers. Second, the formula template is heuristically selected. It is not guaranteed that experts are competent enough to separate the dataset with respect to the template or this separation may not be that obvious to human observation. Hence, we also consider a soft margin version of Problem (2):

$$\max_{r,\mu} r - \theta(\sum_i \zeta_i^+ + \sum_i \zeta_i^-)$$
$$\text{s.t.} \quad \rho(s_i, \varphi_\mu, 0) + \zeta_i^+ \geq r \ \forall s_i \in \mathcal{S}_0$$
$$\rho(s_i, \varphi_\mu, 0) - \zeta_i^- \leq -r \ \forall s_i \in \mathcal{S}_1 \tag{3}$$
$$r, \zeta_i^+, \zeta_i^- \geq 0,$$

where ζ_i^+ and ζ_i^- are slack variables, θ is a weight that penalizes the violation of margins. In this formulation, class 0 signals can have negative robustness and class 1 signals can have positive robustness.

Both problems (2) and (3) can be converted to MILP using standard encodings of robustness metrics [18]. The performance of a MILP depends on the number of variables and the number of constraints. Here, each signal adds new sets of variables and constraints. In addition, the number of constraints increases with increasing formula complexity, i.e., the number of operators in the formula. With large datasets and complex formulas such as HighD and the formula above, Problems (2) and (3) may not be solved in reasonable time. To address this issue, we propose two improvements and one formula template relaxation. First improvement uses the structure of the formula (1).

Proposition 1 (Formula Separation). *Given any PSTL formula of the form* $\varphi_\mu = \Box(\varphi_{1,\mu_1} \wedge \varphi_{2,\mu_2})$, *with* μ_1, μ_2 *disjoint, consider the following optimization problems:*

$$\max_{r_1,\mu_1} r_1$$
$$\text{s.t.} \quad \rho(s_i, \varphi_{1,\mu_1}, 0) \geq r_1 \ \forall s_i \in \mathcal{S}_0$$
$$\rho(s_i, \varphi_{1,\mu_1}, 0) \leq -r_1 \ \forall s_i \in \mathcal{S}_1$$
$$r_1 \geq 0, \tag{4}$$

$$\max_{r_2,\mu_2} r_2$$
$$\text{s.t.} \quad \rho(s_i, \varphi_{2,\mu_2}, 0) \geq r_2 \ \forall s_i \in \mathcal{S}_0$$
$$\rho(s_i, \varphi_{2,\mu_2}, 0) \leq -r_2 \ \forall s_i \in \mathcal{S}_1$$
$$r_2 \geq 0 \tag{5}$$

If Problems (4) and (5) are feasible, then Problem (2) is feasible. Specifically, if μ_1^*, μ_2^*, r_1^*, r_2^* *are the optimizers of Problem (4) and (5), then* $\tilde{\mu} = [\mu_1^* \ \mu_2^*]$ *and* $\tilde{r} = \min(r_1^*, r_2^*)$ *is a feasible solution for Problem (2).*

Proof of Proposition 1 can be found in [10]. Since the formula (1) satisfies the conditions in Proposition 1, we are able to halve the number of variables and number of constraints for each subproblem.

Next, we propose a relaxation of the formula template (1), inspired by [16]. Assuming that trucks move slower than cars, instead of using φ_{1,μ_1}, we can remove the upper bound and range acceptance threshold ϵ. The new formula becomes $\tilde{\varphi}_{1,\mu_1} = \Box_{[0,\tau_1]}(w \geq w_\epsilon) \implies \Diamond_{[0,\tau_2]}(\Box(v \leq \mu_1) \vee w < w_\epsilon)$. Note that this formula is to be satisfied by trucks. Therefore, trucks are set to class 0. Formula $\tilde{\varphi}_{1,\mu_1}$ tries to find limit speed that distinguishes two classes. Same approach can be applied for time headway. Since trucks are keeping longer time headways, we can remove the lower bound. Second subformula will be $\varphi_{2,\mu_2} = \Box_{[0,\tau_1]}(\Box w < w_\epsilon) \implies \Diamond_{[0,\tau_2]}(\Box(w \geq \mu_2) \vee w \geq w_\epsilon)$. Finally, we obtain

$$\tilde{\varphi}_\mu = \Box(\tilde{\varphi}_{1,\mu_1} \wedge \tilde{\varphi}_{2,\mu_2}). \tag{6}$$

Note that we can apply Proposition 1 to template (6). With the help of formula (6), we are able to discard two sets of constraints per each input. However, number of variables and constraints still depends on number of inputs and large input sets are still not solvable in reasonable time even with these improvements. Instead of solving the large input set as a whole, we can divide it into smaller chunks and handle them separately.

Proposition 2 (Data Separation). *Take one of the formulas $\tilde{\varphi}_{i,\mu_i}$, $i \in \{1,2\}$ from (6). Consider a dataset $\mathcal{S} = \mathcal{S}_0 \cup \mathcal{S}_1$, where $\mathcal{S}_0$ denotes trucks and $\mathcal{S}_1$ denotes cars. Partition $\mathcal{S}_0$ and $\mathcal{S}_1$ to form B batches $\{\mathcal{S}^i = (\mathcal{S}_0^i, \mathcal{S}_1^i)\}_{i=1}^B$. If Problem (4) solved for $\mathcal{S}$ is feasible, then Problem (4) is feasible for every batch $\mathcal{S}^i$. Conversely, let $\mu_{1,i}^*$ and r_i^* be the optimizers of Problem (4) solved for $\mathcal{S}^i$ for each i. Then, $\tilde{\mu}_1 = 1/B \sum_{i=1}^B \mu_{1,i}^*$ gives a feasible solution with $0 \leq \tilde{r} \leq \min_i(r_i^*)$ for Problem (4) for $\mathcal{S}$.*

Proof can be found in [10]. This proposition depends on class definitions, satisfaction rules posed in the problem setup, and formula template. Although we are losing optimality, we can still recover feasible STL formulas that are satisfied by class 0 and violated by class 1 signals. We use Proposition 2 for soft margin problem as well. Soft margin problem is not a feasibility problem, in fact every solution is feasible in that formulation. By dividing the dataset into smaller parts, we are finding optimal decision boundaries for each subproblem. Our intuition is by taking the mean of optimal parameters, we approach minimum error in total.

5   Experiments

HighD dataset consists of vehicle trajectory data from different highway sections. Since we are interested in longitudinal driving behavior, we discard vehicles that change lanes. Speed and time headway signals have different orders of magnitudes, effecting robustness differently. To avoid this, we normalize the data for training, and then denormalize to report the learned parameter values. Among all vehicles in the dataset, 79.24% of them of them are cars, the rest are trucks.

Initially, we conduct a baseline experiment. We use one of the well-known and interpretable classifiers, Support Vector Machines (SVM). The accuracy of SVM over HigD dataset is 80.59%. It is slightly more than assuming that all vehicles are cars. Therefore, it is clear that we need different approaches. Additional information for baseline experiment can be found in [10]. Next, we execute four different MILP instances: (M1) Soft margin MILP approach (Problem (3)) with formula template (1) without any improvement, (M2) using Proposition 1, (M3) Problem (3) with formula template (6) using only Proposition 1 and (M4) Problem (3) with formula template (6) using Proposition 1 and Proposition 2.

Known values of templates (1) and (6) are as follows: $w_\epsilon = 3$, $\tau_1 = 2$, $\tau_2 = 3$ and $\epsilon = 0.2$. We randomly partitioned data into batches of four inputs. MILP method does not require equal signal lengths but LoTuS needs equal signal lengths. In the first part of the experiments we compare only MILP instances with full data length. In the second part, for the sake of fair comparison with LoTuS, we truncate the data. There are two comparison metrics: test error and execution time. Training set is balanced with equal number of cars and trucks. However, the test set is not balanced. For all MILP instances, we use an off-the-shelf optimization solver, Gurobi. We set Gurobi's solving time limit to one hour per parameter and optimality gap to 5%. When time limit is reached, Gurobi returns its incumbent solution if there exists any. The optimality of the incumbent solution is not guaranteed. In tables below, "$\sim$" means that Gurobi cannot find a feasible solution within the time limit. For tests, a Macbook Pro with 2 GHz Quad-Core Intel Core i5 processors and 16 GB RAM is used.

Results for full length can be found in Table 1. The first column represents the number of training inputs. Methods (M1)–(M4) represent methods that are described in the beginning of this section. The minimum test error occurs when formula template (6) with MILP instance (M4) is trained with 2000 inputs, and
$$\tilde{\varphi} = \Box\{\Box_{[0,2]}(w \geq 3) \implies \Diamond_{[0,3]}(\Box(v \leq 98.95) \lor w < 3) \land \Box_{[0,2]}(w < 3) \implies \Diamond_{[0,3]}(\Box(w \geq 2.047) \lor w \geq 3)\}$$
is the STL formula. When shorter execution time is an important criterion, formula template (6) trained with 1000 inputs gives comparable results. The test error increases by 0.04% but execution times decreases almost 2.5 times. Optimal parameters for this instance are $\mu_{1000} = [97.13\ 1.99]$. Execution times between MILP methods decrease significantly with each improvement.

Table 1. Comparison among MILP methods with full time length

Inputs	(M1)		(M2)		(M3)		(M4)	
	Error	Time	Error	Time	Error	Time	Error	Time
	%	[s]	%	[s]	%	[s]	%	[s]
8	18.09	697	14.11	4011	14.29	11.71	13.18	3.057
20	25.07	7201	25.14	7201	12.87	119.7	13.19	4.991
40	$\sim$	$\sim$	$\sim$	$\sim$	13.87	725.3	13.37	31.24
200	$\sim$	$\sim$	$\sim$	$\sim$	15.02	7204	12.15	145.34
1000	$\sim$	$\sim$	$\sim$	$\sim$	43.95	7214	**11.35**	**675.6**
2000	$\sim$	$\sim$	$\sim$	$\sim$	79.83	7218	**11.31**	**1507**

Table 2 shows comparative results of each MILP instance with LoTuS on truncated data. When data is truncated, we lose information during truncation, and hence, test error increases. The minimum test error is obtained with LoTuS when trained with 200 inputs. The obtained formula is

$\varphi_{\text{LoTuS}_{2000}} = ((\Box_{[1e-06,0.5]}v < 90.4 \wedge (\Box_{[8.33,24]}v < 87.5 \vee (\Diamond_{[8.33,24]}v > 87.5 \wedge$
$\Diamond_{[15.3,24]}w > 1.74))) \vee (\Diamond_{[1e-06,0.5]}v > 90.4 \wedge (\Box_{[0.369,19.7]}v < 97.8 \wedge \Diamond_{[3.73,20]}w > 2.08))).$

Table 2. Comparison among MILP methods and LoTuS with truncated data

Inputs	(M3)		(M4)		LoTuS	
	Error %	Time [s]	Error %	Time [s]	Error %	Time [s]
8	16.88	3.011	17.37	1.894	17.00	7.098
20	16.76	10.80	21.86	5.607	16.22	5.319
40	13.17	152.5	16.89	10.20	15.15	9.749
200	14.03	7213	18.79	40.09	**13.69**	**15.51**
1000	30.06	7234	18.50	177.9	15.72	43.72
2000	79.83	7219	18.65	353.5	14.66	51.7

This formula is not as interpretable as the formula templates used in MILP. Besides, interpretability decreases as the number of inputs increases. E.g., the STL formula that LoTuS finds for eight inputs is $\Box_{[8.52,11.3]}v < 115$ whereas, for 2000 inputs is $\varphi_{\text{LoTuS}_{2000}}$. We can say that the test error is lower when using MILP with full length.

6   Discussion and Conclusions

In this paper, we considered STL-based classification of driving behaviors. First, we came up with an STL formula template and recast the classification problem with a template as a MILP. We observed MILP-based solutions suffer from computation complexity. We proposed two improvements to address the scalability issue. This approach was compared with the toolbox LoTuS in terms of accuracy and computation time. Both methods have some drawbacks. MILP approach requires domain knowledge to come up with a template and it cannot search for time parameters effectively. LoTuS has a set of primitives to search over (limited to eventually always and always eventually) and it connects them with disjunction or conjunction, not allowing further nesting. This restricts possible formula types that can be obtained. In addition, LoTuS loses interpretability as the training dataset grows. Further research is needed to find a better balance between scalability, interpretability, and accuracy on real datasets. For scalability, one can try satisfiability modulo convex optimization approaches, which have been shown to improve practical performance compared to MILP on some STL problems in recent years. For interpretability, using two different formula templates, one per class, might increase flexibility.

Acknowledgements. Toyota Research Institute provided funds to support this work.

References

1. Abbas, H., Hoxha, B., Fainekos, G., Ueda, K.: Robustness-guided temporal logic testing and verification for stochastic cyber-physical systems. In: 4th Annual IEEE International Conference on Cyber Technology in Automation, Control and Intelligent Systems, pp. 1–6. IEEE-CYBER 2014, October 2014. https://doi.org/10.1109/CYBER.2014.6917426

2. Asarin, E., Donzé, A., Maler, O., Nickovic, D.: Parametric identification of temporal properties. In: Khurshid, S., Sen, K. (eds.) RV 2011. LNCS, vol. 7186, pp. 147–160. Springer, Heidelberg (2012). https://doi.org/10.1007/978-3-642-29860-8_12

3. Bartocci, E., Bortolussi, L., Sanguinetti, G.: Data-driven statistical learning of temporal logic properties. In: Legay, A., Bozga, M. (eds.) FORMATS 2014. LNCS, vol. 8711, pp. 23–37. Springer, Cham (2014). https://doi.org/10.1007/978-3-319-10512-3_3

4. Berndt, D., Clifford, J.: Using dynamic time warping to find patterns in time series. In: Workshop on Knowledge Knowledge Discovery in Databases, vol. 398, pp. 359–370 (1994). http://www.aaai.org/Papers/Workshops/1994/WS-94-03/WS94-03-031.pdf

5. Bombara, G., Belta, C.: Offline and online learning of signal temporal logic formulae using decision trees. ACM Trans. Cyber-Phys. Syst. 5(3), 1–23 (2021). https://doi.org/10.1145/3433994

6. Chou, G., Ozay, N., Berenson, D.: Explaining multi-stage tasks by learning temporal logic formulas from suboptimal demonstrations. In: Proceedings of Robotics: Science and Systems. Corvalis, Oregon, USA, July 2020. https://doi.org/10.15607/RSS.2020.XVI.097

7. Fainekos, G.E., Girard, A., Kress-Gazit, H., Pappas, G.J.: Temporal logic motion planning for dynamic robots. Automatica 45(2), 343–352 (2009). https://doi.org/10.1016/j.automatica.2008.08.008, https://linkinghub.elsevier.com/retrieve/pii/S000510980800455X

8. Garg, K., Panagou, D.: Control-lyapunov and control-barrier functions based quadratic program for spatio-temporal specifications. In: 2019 IEEE 58th Conference on Decision and Control (CDC), pp. 1422–1429 (2019). https://doi.org/10.1109/CDC40024.2019.9029666

9. Jones, A., Kong, Z., Belta, C.: Anomaly detection in cyber-physical systems: a formal methods approach. In: Proceedings of the IEEE Conference on Decision and Control 2015-February (February), pp. 848–853 (2014). https://doi.org/10.1109/CDC.2014.7039487

10. Karagulle, R., Aréchiga, N., Decastro, J., Ozay, N.: Classification of driving behaviors using STL formulas: a comparative study (2022). https://doi.org/10.7302/4872, https://deepblue.lib.umich.edu/handle/2027.42/173041

11. Karim, F., Majumdar, S., Darabi, H., Chen, S.: LSTM Fully Convolutional Networks for Time Series Classification. IEEE Access 6, 1662–1669 (2017). https://doi.org/10.1109/ACCESS.2017.2779939

12. Kong, Z., Jones, A., Ayala, A.M., Gol, E.A., Belta, C.: Temporal logic inference for classification and prediction from data. In: HSCC 2014 - Proceedings of the 17th International Conference on Hybrid Systems: Computation and Control (Part of CPS Week), pp. 273–282 (2014). https://doi.org/10.1145/2562059.2562146, http://dx.doi.org/10.1145/2562059.2562146

13. Krajewski, R., Bock, J., Kloeker, L., Eckstein, L.: The highD dataset: a drone dataset of naturalistic vehicle trajectories on German highways for validation of highly automated driving systems. In: 2018 IEEE 21st International Conference on Intelligent Transportation Systems (ITSC) (2018). https://doi.org/10.1109/ITSC.2018.8569552

14. Maler, O., Nickovic, D.: Monitoring temporal properties of continuous signals. In: Lakhnech, Y., Yovine, S. (eds.) FORMATS/FTRTFT -2004. LNCS, vol. 3253, pp. 152–166. Springer, Heidelberg (2004). https://doi.org/10.1007/978-3-540-30206-3_12

15. Neider, D., Gavran, I.: Learning linear temporal properties. In: Proceedings of the 18th Conference on Formal Methods in Computer-Aided Design, FMCAD 2018, pp. 148–157, January 2019. https://doi.org/10.23919/FMCAD.2018.8603016

16. Nilsson, P., et al.: Correct-by-construction adaptive cruise control: two approaches. IEEE Trans. Control Syst. Technol. **24**(4), 1294–1307 (2016). https://doi.org/10.1109/TCST.2015.2501351

17. Pnueli, A.: The temporal logic of programs. In: Proceedings - Annual IEEE Symposium on Foundations of Computer Science, FOCS, vol. 1977-October, pp. 46–57. IEEE Computer Society (1977). https://doi.org/10.1109/sfcs.1977.32

18. Raman, V., Donzé, A., Maasoumy, M., Murray, R.M., Sangiovanni-Vincentelli, A., Seshia, S.A.: Model predictive control with signal temporal logic specifications. In: 53rd IEEE Conference on Decision and Control, pp. 81–87 (2014). https://doi.org/10.1109/CDC.2014.7039363

19. Varnai, P., Dimarogonas, D.V.: On robustness metrics for learning STL tasks. In: Proceedings of the American Control Conference 2020-July, pp. 5394–5399 (2020). https://doi.org/10.23919/ACC45564.2020.9147692

Timed Automata and Games

Timed Games with Bounded Window Parity Objectives

James C. A. Main[1]([✉]), Mickael Randour[1], and Jeremy Sproston[2]

[1] F.R.S.-FNRS & UMONS – Université de Mons, Mons, Belgium
james.main@umons.ac.be
[2] University of Turin, Turin, Italy

Abstract. The window mechanism, introduced by Chatterjee et al. [19] for mean-payoff and total-payoff objectives in two-player turn-based games on graphs, refines long-term objectives with time bounds. This mechanism has proven useful in a variety of settings [14,16], and most recently in timed systems [27].

In the timed setting, the so-called fixed timed window parity objectives have been studied. A fixed timed window parity objective is defined with respect to some time bound and requires that, at all times, we witness a time frame, i.e., a window, of size less than the fixed bound in which the smallest priority is even. In this work, we focus on the bounded timed window parity objective. Such an objective is satisfied if there exists some bound for which the fixed objective is satisfied. The satisfaction of bounded objectives is robust to modeling choices such as constants appearing in constraints, unlike fixed objectives, for which the choice of constants may affect the satisfaction for a given bound.

We show that verification of bounded timed window objectives in timed automata can be performed in polynomial space, and that timed games with these objectives can be solved in exponential time, even for multi-objective extensions. This matches the complexity classes of the fixed case. We also provide a comparison of the different variants of window parity objectives.

Keywords: window objectives · timed automata · timed games · parity games

1 Introduction

Real-Time Systems. Timed automata [4] are a means of modeling systems in which the passage of time is critical. A timed automaton is a finite automaton extended with a set of *real-valued* variables called *clocks*. All clocks of a timed automaton increase at the same rate and measure the elapse of time in a continuous fashion. Clocks constrain transitions in timed automata and can be reset on these transitions.

Mickael Randour is an F.R.S.-FNRS Research Associate and a member of the TRAIL institute. James C. A. Main is an F.R.S.-FNRS Research Fellow.

S. Bogomolov and D. Parker (Eds.): FORMATS 2022, LNCS 13465, pp. 165–182, 2022.
https://doi.org/10.1007/978-3-031-15839-1_10

Timed automata provide a formal setting for the verification of real-time systems [4,6]. When analyzing timed automata, we usually exclude some unrealistic behaviors. More precisely, we ignore *time-convergent paths*, i.e., infinite paths in which the total elapsed time is bounded. Even though timed automata induce uncountable transition systems, many properties can be checked using the *region abstraction*, a finite quotient of the transition system.

Timed automata can also be used to design correct-by-construction controllers for real-time systems. To this end, we model the interaction of the system and its uncontrollable environment as a timed automaton game [29], or more simply a *timed game*. A timed game is a two-player game played on a timed automaton by the system and its environment for an infinite number of rounds. At each round, both players propose a real-valued delay and an action, and the play progresses following the fastest move.

The notion of winning in a timed game must take time-convergence in account; following [1], we declare as winning the plays that are either *time-divergent and satisfy the objective of the player*, or that are *time-convergent and the player is not responsible for convergence*.

Parity Conditions. Parity conditions are a canonical way of specifying ω-regular conditions, such as safety and liveness. A parity objective is defined from a priority function, which assigns a non-negative integer to each location of a timed automaton. The *parity objective* requires that the smallest priority witnessed infinitely often is even.

The Window Mechanism. A parity objective requires that for all odd priorities seen infinitely often, there is some smaller even priority seen infinitely often. However, the parity objective does not enforce timing constraints; the parity objective can be satisfied despite there being arbitrarily large delays between odd priorities and smaller even priorities. Such behaviors may be undesirable, e.g., if odd priorities model requests in a system and even priorities model responses.

The window mechanism was introduced by Chatterjee et al. for mean-payoff games in graphs [19] and later applied to parity games in graphs [16] and mean-payoff and parity objectives in Markov decision processes [14]. It is a means of reinforcing the parity objective with *timing constraints*. A *direct fixed timed window parity objective* for some fixed time bound requires that at all times, we witness a *good window*, i.e., a time frame of size less than the fixed bound in which the smallest priority is even. In other words, this objective requires that the parity objective be locally satisfied at all times, where the notion of locality is fixed in the definition. This window parity objective and a prefix-independent variant requiring good windows from some point on were studied in [27].

The main focus of this article is another variant of timed window parity objectives called *direct bounded timed window parity objectives*, which extend the bounded window parity objectives of [16]. This objective is satisfied if and only if there exists some time bound for which the direct fixed objective is satisfied. While this objective also requires that the parity objective be locally satisfied at all times, the notion of locality is *not fixed a priori*. In particular, unlike the fixed objective, its satisfaction is robust to modeling choices such as the choice of constants constraining transitions, and depends only on the high-level behavior of the system being modeled. In addition to this direct objective, we also consider a prefix-independent variant, the *bounded timed window parity objective*, which requires that some suffix satisfies a direct bounded objective.

Contributions. We study conjunctions of (resp. direct) bounded timed window parity objectives in the setting of timed automata and of timed games. We show that checking that all time-divergent paths of a timed automaton satisfy a conjunction of (resp. direct) bounded timed window parity objectives can be done in PSPACE (Theorem 1). We also show that if all time-divergent paths of a timed automaton satisfy a (resp. direct) bounded timed window parity objective, then there exists a bound for which the corresponding fixed objective is satisfied.

In timed games, we show that in the direct case, the set of winning states can be computed in EXPTIME (Theorem 4) by means of a timed game with an ω-regular request-response objective [21,33]. We show that, assuming a global clock that cannot be reset, finite-memory strategies suffice to win, and if a winning strategy for a direct bounded objective exists, there exists a finite-memory winning strategy that is also winning for a direct fixed objective (Theorem 2). In the prefix-independent case, we provide a fixed-point algorithm to compute the set of winning states that runs in EXPTIME (Theorem 4). We infer from the correctness proof that, assuming a global clock, finite-memory strategies suffice for winning and if a winning strategy exists, then there exists a finite-memory winning strategy that is also winning for some fixed objective (Theorem 3).

We complement all membership results above with lower bounds and establish PSPACE-completeness for timed automata-related problems and EXPTIME-completeness for timed games-related problems.

Comparison. Window objectives strengthen classical objectives with timing constraints; they provide *conservative approximations* of these objectives (e.g., [14, 16,19]). The complexity of window objectives, comparatively to that of the related classical objective, depends on whether one considers a single-objective or multi-objective setting. In turn-based games on graphs, window objectives provide *polynomial-time* alternatives to the classical objectives [16,19] in the single-objective setting, despite, e.g., turn-based parity games on graphs not being known to be solvable in polynomial time (parity games were recently shown to be solvable in quasi-polynomial time [18]). On the other hand, in the multi-objective setting, the complexity is higher than that of the classical objectives; for instance, solving a turn-based game with a conjunction of fixed (resp. bounded) window parity objectives is EXPTIME-complete [16], whereas solving games with conjunctions of parity objectives is co-NP complete [22]. In the timed setting, we establish that solving timed games with conjunctions of bounded timed window parity objectives is EXPTIME-complete, i.e., dense time comes for free, similarly to the fixed case in timed games [27].

Timed games with classical parity objectives can be solved in exponential time [1,23], i.e., the complexity class of solving timed games with window parity objectives matches that of solving timed games with classical parity objectives. Timed games with parity objectives can be solved by means of a reduction to an untimed parity game played on a graph polynomial in the size of the region abstraction and the number of priorities [23]. However, most algorithms for games on graphs with parity objectives suffer from a blow-up in complexity due to the number of priorities. Timed window parity objectives provide an alternative to parity objectives that bypasses this blow-up; in particular, we show in this paper that *timed games with a single bounded timed window objective can be solved in time polynomial in the size of the region abstraction and the number of priorities.*

In timed games, we show that winning for a (resp. direct) bounded timed window parity objective is equivalent to winning for a (resp. direct) fixed timed window parity objective with some sufficiently large bound that depends on the number of priorities, number of objectives and the size of the region abstraction. Despite the fact that this bound can be directly computed (Theorems 2 and 3), solving timed games with (resp. direct) fixed timed window parity objectives for a certain bound takes time that is polynomial in the size of the region abstraction, the number of priorities and the *fixed bound*. This bound may be large; the algorithms we provide for timed games with (resp. direct) bounded timed window parity objectives avoid this additional contribution to the complexity.

Related Work. The window mechanism has seen numerous extensions in addition to the previously mentioned works, e.g., [5,7,10,13,17,25,32]. Window parity objectives, especially bounded variants, are closely related to the notion of finitary ω-regular games, e.g., [20], and the semantics of PROMPT-LTL [26]. The window mechanism can be used to ensure a certain form of (local) guarantee over paths; different techniques have been considered in stochastic models [9,12,15]. Timed automata have numerous extensions, e.g., hybrid systems (e.g., [11] and references therein) and probabilistic timed automata (e.g., [30]); the window mechanism could prove useful in these richer settings. Finally, we recall that game models provide a framework for the synthesis of correct-by-construction controllers [31].

Outline. Due to space constraints, we only present an overview of our work. Technical details and a comparison of the untimed and timed settings, and of fixed and bounded objectives can be found in the full version of this paper [28]. Section 2 presents all preliminary notions. Window objectives, relations between them and a useful property of bounded window objectives are presented in Sect. 3. The verification of bounded window objectives in timed automata is studied in Sect. 4. Section 5 presents algorithms for timed games with bounded window objectives.

2   Preliminaries

Timed Automata. We denote the set of non-negative real numbers by $\mathbb{R}_{\geq 0}$, and the set of non-negative integers by $\mathbb{N}$. Given some non-negative real number x, we write $\lfloor x \rfloor$ for the integral part of x and $\mathsf{frac}(x) = x - \lfloor x \rfloor$ for its fractional part. Given two sets A and B, we let 2^A denote the power set of A and A^B denote the set of functions $B \rightarrow A$.

A clock variable, or *clock*, is a real-valued variable. Let C be a set of clocks. A *clock constraint* over C is a conjunction of formulae of the form $x \sim c$ with $x \in C$, $c \in \mathbb{N}$, and $\sim \in \{\leq, \geq, >, <\}$. We write $x = c$ as shorthand for the clock constraint $x \geq c \wedge x \leq c$. Let $\Phi(C)$ denote the set of clock constraints over C.

We refer to functions $v \in \mathbb{R}_{\geq 0}^C$ as *clock valuations* over C. A clock valuation v over a set C of clocks satisfies a clock constraint of the form $x \sim c$ if $v(x) \sim c$ and v satisfies a conjunction $g \wedge h$ of two clock constraints g and h if it satisfies both g and h. Given a clock constraint g and clock valuation v, we write $v \models g$ if v satisfies g.

For a clock valuation v and $\delta \geq 0$, we let $v + \delta$ be the valuation defined by $(v + \delta)(x) = v(x) + \delta$ for all $x \in C$. For any valuation v and $D \subseteq C$, we define $\mathsf{reset}_D(v)$ to be the valuation agreeing with v for clocks in $C \setminus D$ and that assigns 0 to clocks in D. We denote by $\mathbf{0}^C$ the zero valuation, assigning 0 to all clocks in C.

A *timed automaton* (TA) is a tuple $(L, \ell_{\mathsf{init}}, C, \Sigma, I, E)$ where L is a finite set of *locations*, $\ell_{\mathsf{init}} \in L$ is an initial location, C a finite set of *clocks* containing a special clock γ which keeps track of the total time elapsed, Σ a finite set of actions, $I \colon L \rightarrow \Phi(C)$ an *invariant* assignment function and $E \subseteq L \times \Phi(C) \times \Sigma \times 2^{C \setminus \{\gamma\}} \times L$ a finite edge relation. We only consider deterministic timed automata, i.e., we assume that in any location ℓ, there are no two different outgoing edges $(\ell, g_1, a, D_1, \ell_1)$ and $(\ell, g_2, a, D_2, \ell_2)$ sharing the same action such that the conjunction $g_1 \wedge g_2$ is satisfiable. For an edge (ℓ, g, a, D, ℓ'), the clock constraint g is called the *guard* of the edge.

A TA $\mathcal{A} = (L, \ell_{\mathsf{init}}, C, \Sigma, I, E)$ gives rise to an uncountable transition system $\mathcal{T}(\mathcal{A}) = (S, s_{\mathsf{init}}, M, \rightarrow)$ with the state space $S = L \times \mathbb{R}_{\geq 0}^C$, the initial state $s_{\mathsf{init}} = (\ell_{\mathsf{init}}, \mathbf{0}^C)$, set of transition system actions $M = \mathbb{R}_{\geq 0} \times (\Sigma \cup \{\bot\})$ and the transition relation $\rightarrow \subseteq S \times M \times S$ defined as follows: for any action $a \in \Sigma$ and delay $\delta \geq 0$, we have that $((\ell, v), (\delta, a), (\ell', v')) \in \rightarrow$ if and only if there is some edge $(\ell, g, a, D, \ell') \in E$ such that $v + \delta \models g$, $v' = \mathsf{reset}_D(v + \delta)$, $v + \delta \models I(\ell)$ and $v' \models I(\ell')$; for any delay $\delta \geq 0$, $((\ell, v)(\delta, \bot), (\ell, v + \delta)) \in \rightarrow$ if $v + \delta \models I(\ell)$. Let us note that the satisfaction set of clock constraints is convex: it is described by a conjunction of inequalities. Whenever $v \models I(\ell)$, the above condition $v + \delta \models I(\ell)$ (the invariant holds after the delay) is equivalent to requiring $v + \delta' \models I(\ell)$ for all $0 \leq \delta' \leq \delta$ (the invariant holds at each intermediate time step).

A *move* is any pair in $\mathbb{R}_{\geq 0} \times (\Sigma \cup \{\bot\})$ (i.e., an action in the transition system). For any move $m = (\delta, a)$ and states $s, s' \in S$, we write $s \xrightarrow{m} s'$ or $s \xrightarrow{\delta, a} s'$ as shorthand for $(s, m, s') \in \rightarrow$. Moves of the form $(\delta, \bot)$ are called *delay moves*. For any move $m = (\delta, a)$, we let $\mathsf{delay}(m) = \delta$. We say a move m is enabled in a state s if there is some s' such that $s \xrightarrow{m} s'$. There is at most one successor per move in a state, as we do not allow two guards on edges labeled by the same action to be simultaneously satisfied.

A *path* in a TA $\mathcal{A}$ is a finite or infinite sequence $s_0 m_0 s_1 \ldots \in S(MS)^* \cup (SM)^\omega$ such that for all $j \in \mathbb{N}$, s_j is a state of $\mathcal{T}(\mathcal{A})$ and $s_j \xrightarrow{m_j} s_{j+1}$ is a transition in $\mathcal{T}(\mathcal{A})$. A path is *initial* if $s_0 = s_{\text{init}}$. For clarity, we write $s_0 \xrightarrow{m_0} s_1 \xrightarrow{m_1} \cdots$ instead of $s_0 m_0 s_1 m_1 \ldots$.

A state s is said to be *reachable from a state* s' if there exists a path from s' to s. Similarly, a set of states $T \subseteq S$ is said to be reachable from some state s' if there is a path from s' to a state in T. We say that a state is *reachable* if it is reachable from the initial state.

An infinite path $\pi = (\ell_0, v_0) \xrightarrow{m_0} (\ell_1, v_1) \xrightarrow{m_1} \cdots$ is *time-divergent* if the sequence $(v_j(\gamma))_{j \in \mathbb{N}}$ is not bounded from above. A path that is not time-divergent is called *time-convergent*; time-convergent paths are traditionally ignored in analysis of timed automata [3,4] as they model unrealistic behavior.

The transition system induced by a TA is infinite. Qualitative properties of TAs can nonetheless be analyzed using the region abstraction [4], a quotient of the transition system by an equivalence relation of finite index. Fix a TA $\mathcal{A} = (L, \ell_{\text{init}}, C, \Sigma, I, E)$. For each clock $x \in C$, let c_x denote the largest constant to which x is compared to in guards and invariants of $\mathcal{A}$.

We define an equivalence relation over clock valuations of C: we say that two clock valuations v and v' over C are *clock-equivalent* for $\mathcal{A}$, denoted by $v \equiv_{\mathcal{A}} v'$, if the following properties are satisfied: (i) for all clocks $x \in C$, $v(x) > c_x$ if and only if $v'(x) > c_x$; (ii) for all clocks $x \in \{z \in C \mid v(z) \leq c_z\}$, $\lfloor v(x) \rfloor = \lfloor v'(x) \rfloor$; (iii) for all clocks $x, y \in \{z \in C \mid v(z) \leq c_z\} \cup \{\gamma\}$, $v(x) \in \mathbb{N}$ if and only if $v'(x) \in \mathbb{N}$, and $\mathsf{frac}(v(x)) \leq \mathsf{frac}(v(y))$ if and only if $\mathsf{frac}(v'(x)) \leq \mathsf{frac}(v'(y))$. When $\mathcal{A}$ is clear from the context, we say that two valuations are clock-equivalent rather than clock-equivalent for $\mathcal{A}$.

An equivalence class for this relation is referred to as a *clock region*. We denote the equivalence class for $\equiv_{\mathcal{A}}$ of a clock valuation v as $[v]$. We let Reg denote the set of all clock regions. The number of clock regions is finite, and exponential in the number of clocks and the encoding of the constants c_x, $x \in C$. More precisely, we have the bound $|\mathsf{Reg}| \leq |C|! \cdot 2^{|C|} \cdot \prod_{x \in C}(2c_x + 1)$.

We extend the equivalence defined above to states as well. We say that two states $s = (\ell, v)$ and $s' = (\ell', v')$ are *state-equivalent*, denoted $s \equiv_{\mathcal{A}} s'$, whenever $\ell = \ell'$ and $v \equiv_{\mathcal{A}} v'$. An equivalence class for this relation is referred to as a *state region*. Given some state $s \in S$, we write $[s]$ for its equivalence class. We identify the set of state regions with the set $L \times \mathsf{Reg}$ and sometimes denote state regions as pairs $(\ell, R) \in L \times \mathsf{Reg}$ in the sequel. We assume familiarity with the region abstraction in the following (see the full paper [28] for details).

Priorities. A *priority function* is a function $p \colon L \to \{0, \ldots, \mathsf{D} - 1\}$ with $\mathsf{D} \leq |L| + 1$. We use priority functions to express parity objectives. A K-*dimensional priority function* is a function $p \colon L \to \{0, \ldots, \mathsf{D} - 1\}^{\mathsf{K}}$ which assigns vectors of priorities to locations. Given a K-dimensional priority function p and a dimension $k \in \{1, \ldots, \mathsf{K}\}$, we write p_k for the priority function given by p on dimension k.

Timed Games. We consider two player games played on TAs. We refer to the players as player 1 ($\mathcal{P}_1$) for the system and player 2 ($\mathcal{P}_2$) for the environment. We use the notion of timed automaton games of [1].

A *timed* (automaton) *game* (TG) is a tuple $\mathcal{G} = (\mathcal{A}, \Sigma_1, \Sigma_2)$ where $\mathcal{A} = (L, \ell_{\text{init}}, C, \Sigma, I, E)$ is a TA and (Σ_1, Σ_2) is a partition of Σ. We refer to actions in Σ_i as $\mathcal{P}_i$ actions for $i \in \{1, 2\}$.

Recall that a move is a pair $(\delta, a) \in \mathbb{R}_{\geq 0} \times (\Sigma \cup \{\bot\})$. Let S denote the set of states of $T(\mathcal{A})$. In each state $s = (\ell, v) \in S$, the moves available to $\mathcal{P}_1$ are the elements of the set $M_1(s) = \{(\delta, a) \in \mathbb{R}_{\geq 0} \times (\Sigma_1 \cup \{\bot\}) \mid \exists s', s \xrightarrow{\delta, a} s'\}$, i.e., moves with $\mathcal{P}_1$ actions and delay moves that are enabled in s. The set $M_2(s)$ is defined analogously with $\mathcal{P}_2$ actions. We write M_1 and M_2 for the set of all moves of $\mathcal{P}_1$ and $\mathcal{P}_2$ respectively.

At each state s along a play, both players simultaneously select a move $m^{(1)} \in M_1(s)$ and $m^{(2)} \in M_2(s)$. Intuitively, the fastest player gets to act and in case of a tie, the move is chosen non-deterministically. This is formalized by the *joint destination function* $\mathsf{JD} : S \times M_1 \times M_2 \to 2^S$, defined by $\mathsf{JD}(s, m^{(1)}, m^{(2)}) = \{s' \in S \mid s \xrightarrow{m^{(i)}} s', i \in \text{argmin}_{i=1,2}\, \mathsf{delay}(m^{(i)})\}$. For $m^{(1)} = (\delta^{(1)}, a^{(1)}) \in M_1$ and $m^{(2)} = (\delta^{(2)}, a^{(2)}) \in M_2$, we write $\mathsf{delay}(m^{(1)}, m^{(2)}) = \min\{\delta^{(1)}, \delta^{(2)}\}$ to denote the delay occurring when $\mathcal{P}_1$ and $\mathcal{P}_2$ play $m^{(1)}$ and $m^{(2)}$ respectively.

A play is defined similarly to an infinite path: a *play* is an infinite sequence of the form $s_0(m_0^{(1)}, m_0^{(2)})s_1(m_1^{(1)}, m_1^{(2)}) \ldots \in (S(M_1 \times M_2))^{\omega}$ where for all indices $j \in \mathbb{N}$, $m_j^{(i)} \in M_i(s_j)$ for $i \in \{1, 2\}$ and $s_{j+1} \in \mathsf{JD}(s_{j+1}, m_{j+1}^{(1)}, m_{j+1}^{(2)})$. A *history* is a finite prefix of a play ending in a state. A play or history $s_0(m_0^{(1)}, m_0^{(2)})s_1 \ldots$ is *initial* if $s_0 = s_{\text{init}}$. For any history $h = s_0(m_0^{(1)}, m_0^{(2)}) \ldots (m_{n-1}^{(1)}, m_{n-1}^{(2)})s_n$, we set $\mathsf{last}(h) = s_n$. For a play $\pi = s_0(m_0^{(1)}, m_0^{(2)})s_1 \ldots$, we write $\pi_{|n} = s_0(m_0^{(1)}, m_0^{(2)}) \ldots (m_{n-1}^{(1)}, m_{n-1}^{(2)})s_n$. Plays of $\mathcal{G}$ follow paths of $\mathcal{A}$. For a play, there may be several such paths: if at some point of the play both players use a move with the same delay and successor state, either move can label the transition in a matching path.

Similarly to paths, a play $\pi = (\ell_0, v_0)(m_0^{(1)}, m_0^{(2)}) \cdots$ is *time-divergent* if and only if $(v_j(\gamma))_{j \in \mathbb{N}}$ is not bounded from above. Otherwise, we say a play is *time-convergent*. We define the following sets: $\mathsf{Plays}(\mathcal{G})$ for the set of plays of $\mathcal{G}$; $\mathsf{Hist}(\mathcal{G})$ for the set of histories of $\mathcal{G}$; $\mathsf{Plays}_{\infty}(\mathcal{G})$ for the set of time-divergent plays of $\mathcal{G}$. We also write $\mathsf{Plays}(\mathcal{G}, s)$ to denote plays starting in state s of $T(\mathcal{A})$.

Strategies. A *strategy* for $\mathcal{P}_i$ is a function describing which move a player should use based on a history. Formally, a strategy for $\mathcal{P}_i$ is a function $\sigma_i : \mathsf{Hist}(\mathcal{G}) \to M_i$ such that for all $\pi \in \mathsf{Hist}(\mathcal{G})$, $\sigma_i(\pi) \in M_i(\mathsf{last}(\pi))$. This last condition requires that each move given by a strategy be enabled in the last state of a play.

A play or history $s_0(m_0^{(1)}, m_0^{(2)})s_1 \ldots$ is said to be consistent with a $\mathcal{P}_i$-strategy σ_i if for all indices j, $m_j^{(i)} = \sigma_i(\pi_{|j})$. Given a $\mathcal{P}_i$ strategy σ_i, we define $\mathsf{Outcome}_i(\sigma_i)$ (resp. $\mathsf{Outcome}_i(\sigma_i, s)$) to be the set of plays (resp. set of plays starting in state s) consistent with σ_i.

In general, strategies can exploit full knowledge of the past, and need not admit some finite representation. In the sequel, we focus on so-called *finite-memory region strategies*. A strategy is a finite-memory region strategy if it can be encoded by a finite Mealy machine, i.e., a deterministic automaton with outputs, that is well-behaved with respect to regions. Such a *Mealy machine* (for a strategy of $\mathcal{P}_1$) is a tuple $\mathcal{M} = (\mathfrak{M}, \mathsf{m}_{\mathsf{init}}, \alpha_{\mathsf{up}}, \alpha_{\mathsf{mov}})$ where $\mathfrak{M}$ is a finite set of states, $\mathsf{m}_{\mathsf{init}} \in \mathfrak{M}$ is an initial state, $\alpha_{\mathsf{up}} \colon \mathfrak{M} \times (L \times \mathsf{Reg}) \to \mathfrak{M}$ is the memory update function and $\alpha_{\mathsf{mov}} \colon \mathfrak{M} \times S \to M_1$ is the next-move function. We require that α_{mov} be such that for any memory state $\mathsf{m} \in \mathfrak{M}$ and any two state-equivalent states $s = (\ell, v)$, $s' = (\ell', v') \in S$, the moves $(\delta, a) = \alpha_{\mathsf{mov}}(\mathsf{m}, s)$ and $(\delta', a') = \alpha_{\mathsf{mov}}(\mathsf{m}, s')$ are such that $a = a'$, $[v + \delta] = [v' + \delta']$ and $\{[v + \delta_{\mathsf{mid}}] \mid 0 \le \delta_{\mathsf{mid}} \le \delta\} = \{[v' + \delta_{\mathsf{mid}}] \mid 0 \le \delta_{\mathsf{mid}} \le \delta'\}$.

Let $\mathcal{M} = (\mathfrak{M}, \mathsf{m}_{\mathsf{init}}, \alpha_{\mathsf{up}}, \alpha_{\mathsf{mov}})$ be a Mealy machine. We define the strategy induced by $\mathcal{M}$ as follows. Let ε denote the empty word. We first define the iterated update function $\alpha^*_{\mathsf{up}} \colon S^* \to \mathfrak{M}$ inductively as $\alpha^*_{\mathsf{up}}(\varepsilon) = \mathsf{m}_{\mathsf{init}}$ and for any $s_0 \ldots s_n \in S^*$, we let $\alpha^*_{\mathsf{up}}(s_0 \ldots s_n) = \alpha_{\mathsf{up}}(\alpha^*_{\mathsf{up}}(s_0 \ldots s_{n-1}), [s_n])$. The strategy σ induced by $\mathcal{M}$ is defined by $\sigma(h) = \alpha_{\mathsf{mov}}(\alpha^*_{\mathsf{up}}(s_0 \ldots s_{n-1}), s_n)$ for any history $h = s_0(m_0^{(1)}, m_0^{(2)}) \ldots (m_{n-1}^{(1)}, m_{n-1}^{(2)}) s_n \in \mathsf{Hist}(\mathcal{G})$. A strategy σ is a *finite-memory region strategy* if it is induced by a Mealy machine as described above.

Objectives. An objective represents the property we desire on paths of a TA or a goal of a player in a TG. Formally, we define an *objective* as a set $\Psi \subseteq S^\omega$ of infinite sequences of states. An objective Ψ is a *region objective* if given two sequences of states $s_0 s_1 \ldots, s'_0 s'_1 \ldots \in S^\omega$ such that for all $j \in \mathbb{N}$, $s_j \equiv_{\mathcal{A}} s'_j$, we have $s_0 s_1 \ldots \in \Psi$ if and only if $s'_0 s'_1 \ldots \in \Psi$. Intuitively, the satisfaction of a region objective depends only on the witnessed sequence of state regions.

An ω-regular region objective is a region objective recognized by some deterministic parity automaton. The window objectives we consider later on are derived from the parity objective, which is an ω-regular region objective. The *parity* objective for a one-dimensional priority function $p \colon L \to \{0, \ldots, \mathsf{D} - 1\}$ requires that the smallest priority seen infinitely often is even. Formally, we define $\mathsf{Parity}(p) = \{(\ell_0, v_0)(\ell_1, v_1) \ldots \in S^\omega \mid (\liminf_{n \to \infty} p(\ell_n)) \bmod 2 = 0\}$.

For the sake of brevity, given some path $\pi = s_0 m_0 s_1 \ldots$ of a TA or a play of a TG $\pi = s_0(m_0^{(1)}, m_0^{(2)}) s_1 \ldots$ and an objective $\Psi \subseteq S^\omega$, we write $\pi \in \Psi$ to mean that the sequence of states $s_0 s_1 \ldots$ underlying π is in Ψ, and say that π satisfies the objective Ψ.

Winning Conditions. In games, we distinguish objectives and *winning conditions*. We adopt the definition of [1]. Let Ψ be an objective. It is desirable to have victory be achieved in a physically meaningful way: for example, it is unrealistic to have an undesirable location be avoided by stopping time. This motivates a restriction to time-divergent plays. However, this requires $\mathcal{P}_1$ to force the divergence of plays, which is not reasonable, as $\mathcal{P}_2$ can stall using delays with zero time units. Thus we also declare winning time-convergent plays where $\mathcal{P}_1$ is *blameless*. Let $\mathsf{Blameless}_1$ denote the set of $\mathcal{P}_1$-blameless plays, which we define as follows.

Let $\pi = s_0(m_0^{(1)}, m_0^{(2)}) s_1 \ldots$ be a play or a history. We say $\mathcal{P}_1$ is *not responsible* (or not to be blamed) for the transition at step k in π if either $\delta_k^{(2)} < \delta_k^{(1)}$ ($\mathcal{P}_2$ is faster) or $\delta_k^{(1)} = \delta_k^{(2)}$ and $s_k \xrightarrow{\delta_k^{(1)}, a_k^{(1)}} s_{k+1}$ does not hold in $\mathcal{T}(\mathcal{A})$ ($\mathcal{P}_2$'s move was selected and did not have the same target state as $\mathcal{P}_1$'s) where $m_k^{(i)} = (\delta_k^{(i)}, a_k^{(i)})$ for $i \in \{1, 2\}$. The set $\mathsf{Blameless}_1$ is formally defined as the set of infinite plays π such that there is some j such that for all $k \geq j$, $\mathcal{P}_1$ is not responsible for the transition at step k in π.

Given an objective Ψ, we set the winning condition $\mathsf{WC}_1(\Psi)$ for $\mathcal{P}_1$ to be the set of plays $\mathsf{WC}_1(\Psi) = (\mathsf{Plays}(\mathcal{G}, \Psi) \cap \mathsf{Plays}_\infty(\mathcal{G})) \cup (\mathsf{Blameless}_1 \setminus \mathsf{Plays}_\infty(\mathcal{G}))$, where $\mathsf{Plays}(\mathcal{G}, \Psi) = \{\pi \in \mathsf{Plays}(\mathcal{G}) \mid \pi \in \Psi\}$. Winning conditions for $\mathcal{P}_2$ are defined by exchanging the roles of the players in the former definition.

A *winning strategy* for $\mathcal{P}_i$ for an objective Ψ from a state s_0 is a strategy σ_i such that $\mathsf{Outcome}_i(\sigma_i, s_0) \subseteq \mathsf{WC}_i(\Psi)$. We say that a state is winning for $\mathcal{P}_1$ for an objective Ψ if $\mathcal{P}_1$ has a winning strategy from this state.

Given a TG with an ω-regular region objective given as a deterministic parity automaton, the set of winning states can be computed in exponential time and finite-memory region strategies suffices for winning [1, 2].

Decision Problems. We consider two different problems for an objective Ψ. The first is the *verification problem* for Ψ, which asks given a TA whether all *time-divergent initial* paths satisfy the objective. Second is the *realizability problem* for Ψ, which asks whether in a TG, $\mathcal{P}_1$ has a winning strategy from the initial state.

3   Bounded Window Objectives

The main focus of this paper is a variant of timed window parity objectives called *bounded timed window parity objectives*. These are defined from the *fixed timed window parity objectives* studied in [27], where these fixed objectives are referred to as timed window parity objectives. We first define the different timed window parity objectives, then present the relationships between the different variants and the original parity objective. Finally, we state a technical result used to obtain simple witnesses to the violation of a bounded window objective. Technical details are presented in the full version of this paper [28].

For this entire section, we fix a TG $\mathcal{G} = (\mathcal{A}, \Sigma_1, \Sigma_2)$ where $\mathcal{A} = (L, \ell_{\mathsf{init}}, C, \Sigma_1 \cup \Sigma_2, I, E)$ and a one-dimensional priority function $p \colon L \to \{0, \ldots, \mathsf{D} - 1\}$.

Fixed Objectives. Fixed window objectives depend on a fixed time bound $\lambda \in \mathbb{N}$. The first building block for the definition of window objectives is the notion of good window. A good window for the bound λ is intuitively a time interval of length strictly less than λ for which the smallest priority of the locations visited in the interval is even. We define the *timed good window (parity) objective* as the set of sequences of states that have a good window at their start. Formally, we define $\mathsf{TGW}(p, \lambda) = \{(\ell_0, v_0)(\ell_1, v_1) \ldots \in S^\omega \mid \exists n \in \mathbb{N}, \min_{0 \leq j \leq n} p(\ell_j) \bmod 2 = 0 \text{ and } v_n(\gamma) - v_0(\gamma) < \lambda\}$.

The *direct fixed timed window (parity) objective* for the bound λ, denoted by $\mathsf{DFTW}(p, \lambda)$, requires that the timed good window objective is satisfied by all suffixes of a sequence. Formally, we define $\mathsf{DFTW}(p, \lambda)$ as the set $\{s_0 s_1 \ldots \in S^\omega \mid \forall n \in \mathbb{N}, s_n s_{n+1} \ldots \in \mathsf{TGW}(p, \lambda)\}$.

Unlike the parity objective, $\mathsf{DFTW}(p, \lambda)$ is not prefix-independent. Therefore, a prefix-independent variant of the direct fixed timed window objective, the *fixed timed window (parity) objective* $\mathsf{FTW}(p, \lambda)$, was also studied in [27]. Formally, we define $\mathsf{FTW}(p, \lambda) = \{s_0 s_1 \ldots \in S^\omega \mid \exists n \in \mathbb{N}, s_n s_{n+1} \ldots \in \mathsf{DFTW}(p, \lambda)\}$.

Bounded Objectives. A sequence of states satisfies the (resp. direct) bounded timed window objective if there exists a time bound λ for which the sequence satisfies the (resp. direct) fixed timed window objective. Unlike the fixed case, this bound depends on the sequence of states, and need not be uniform, e.g., among all sequences of states induced by time-divergent paths of a TA or among all sequences of states induced by time-divergent outcomes of a strategy in a TG.

We formally define the *(resp. direct) bounded timed window (parity) objective* $\mathsf{BTW}(p)$ (resp. $\mathsf{DBTW}(p)$) as the set $\mathsf{BTW}(p) = \{s_0 s_1 \ldots \in S^\omega \mid \exists \lambda \in \mathbb{N}, s_0 s_1 \ldots \in \mathsf{FTW}(p, \lambda)\}$ (resp. $\mathsf{DBTW}(p) = \{s_0 s_1 \ldots \in S^\omega \mid \exists \lambda \in \mathbb{N}, s_0 s_1 \ldots \in \mathsf{DFTW}(p, \lambda)\}$). The objective $\mathsf{BTW}(p)$ is a prefix-independent variant of $\mathsf{DBTW}(p)$.

In the sequel, to distinguish the prefix-independent variants from direct objectives, we may refer to the fixed timed window or bounded timed window objectives as *indirect objectives*.

Multi-objective Extensions. In addition to the direct and indirect bounded objectives, we will also study some of their multi-objective extensions. More precisely, we assume for these definitions that p is a multi-dimensional priority function, i.e., $p \colon L \to \{0, \ldots, \mathsf{D} - 1\}^\mathsf{K}$, and define a multi-dimensional objective as the conjunction of the objectives derived from the component functions $p_1, \ldots, p_\mathsf{K}$.

Multi-dimensional extensions are referred to as generalized objectives. In the fixed case, for a bound $\lambda \in \mathbb{N}$, we define the *generalized (resp. direct) fixed timed window objective* as $\mathsf{GFTW}(p, \lambda) = \bigcap_{1 \leq k \leq \mathsf{K}} \mathsf{FTW}(p_k, \lambda)$ (resp. as $\mathsf{GDFTW}(p, \lambda) = \bigcap_{1 \leq k \leq \mathsf{K}} \mathsf{DFTW}(p_k, \lambda)$). In the bounded case, we define the *generalized (resp. direct) bounded timed window objective* as $\mathsf{GBTW}(p) = \bigcap_{1 \leq k \leq \mathsf{K}} \mathsf{BTW}(p_k)$ (resp. as $\mathsf{GDBTW}(p) = \bigcap_{1 \leq k \leq \mathsf{K}} \mathsf{DBTW}(p_k)$).

Relationships Between Objectives. Inclusions are induced by the fact that a direct objective is more restrictive than its prefix-independent counterpart, and similarly, by the fact that a fixed objective is more restrictive than its bounded counterpart. Parity objectives, on the other hand, are less restrictive than any of the timed window objectives, as they require no time-related aspect to hold.

Lemma 1. *The following inclusions hold for any* $\lambda \in \mathbb{N}$:

- $\mathsf{DFTW}(p, \lambda) \subseteq \mathsf{FTW}(p, \lambda) \subseteq \mathsf{BTW}(p) \subseteq \mathsf{Parity}(p)$ *and*
- $\mathsf{DFTW}(p, \lambda) \subseteq \mathsf{DBTW}(p) \subseteq \mathsf{BTW}(p) \subseteq \mathsf{Parity}(p)$.

In general, timed window parity objectives are a strict strengthening of parity objectives. Consider the TA $\mathcal{B}$ depicted in Fig. 1 and let $p_\mathcal{B}$ denote its priority function. It is easy to see that all time-divergent paths satisfy the parity objective: if the TA remains in location ℓ_1 after some point, letting time diverge, the only priority seen infinitely often is 2; if location ℓ_2 is visited infinitely often, the smallest priority seen infinitely often is 0.

However, there is a time-divergent initial path of $\mathcal{B}$ that does not satisfy $\mathsf{BTW}(p_\mathcal{B})$, i.e., a path that satisfies the parity objective but no timed window parity objective. Initialize n to 0. We consider the sequence of states induced by the path obtained by sequentially using the moves $(0, a)$ in location ℓ_0, (n, a) in location ℓ_1 and $(0, a)$ in location ℓ_2, increasing n and then repeating the procedure. This sequence does not satisfy $\mathsf{BTW}(p)$. At each step of the construction of the path, a delay of n takes place between priority 1 in ℓ_0 and priority 0 in ℓ_2. No matter the suffix of the sequence of states and the bound λ, the objective $\mathsf{DFTW}(p_\mathcal{B}, \lambda)$ cannot be satisfied, therefore the objective $\mathsf{BTW}(p_\mathcal{B})$ is not satisfied.

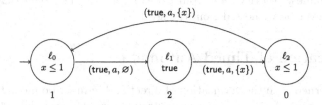

Fig. 1. Timed automaton $\mathcal{B}$. Edges are labeled with triples guard-action-resets. Priorities are beneath locations. The incoming arrow with no origin indicates the initial location.

Simplifying Paths Violating Window Objectives. We provide a technical result used for the verification and realizability of bounded timed window objectives. This result states that, if for some large enough λ, there is no good window in some path or play, then there must be some repeated state up to state-equivalence. This result follows from the finite index of state equivalence.

To abstract whether we consider paths or plays, we state the result in terms of sequences of states. For technical convenience and without loss of generality, we require that delays are bounded in the sequence of states. We say that for any sequence of states $(\ell_0, v_0)(\ell_1, v_1) \ldots \in S^\omega$, the delays are bounded by $B \in \mathbb{N}$ if $v_{n+1}(\gamma) - v_n(\gamma) \leq B$ for all $n \in \mathbb{N}$. We also extend this terminology to paths and plays via their induced sequence of states.

In the context of TGs, we will seek to apply the result to construct an outcome of a given finite-memory region strategy violating a window objective. A *deterministic finite automaton* (DFA) over state regions is a tuple $(\mathfrak{M}, \mathsf{m}_{\mathsf{init}}, \alpha_{\mathsf{up}})$ where $\mathfrak{M}$ is a finite set of states, $\mathsf{m}_{\mathsf{init}} \in \mathfrak{M}$ and $\alpha_{\mathsf{up}} \colon \mathfrak{M} \times (L \times \mathsf{Reg}) \to \mathfrak{M}$. Given a Mealy machine $\mathcal{M} = (\mathfrak{M}, \mathsf{m}_{\mathsf{init}}, \alpha_{\mathsf{up}}, \alpha_{\mathsf{mov}})$ encoding a finite-memory region strategy, we refer to $(\mathfrak{M}, \mathsf{m}_{\mathsf{init}}, \alpha_{\mathsf{up}})$ as the DFA underlying $\mathcal{M}$. To exploit the result in TGs, we require that we can find a cycle in the product of the region abstraction of $\mathcal{A}$ and a DFA underlying a Mealy machine within the first λ time units of the sequence of states.

Lemma 2. *Let* $(\mathfrak{M}, \mathfrak{m}_{\mathsf{init}}, \alpha_{\mathsf{up}})$ *be a DFA. Let* $\pi = s_0 s_1 s_2 \ldots \in S^\omega$ *be a sequence of states induced by some time-divergent path or play in which delays are bounded by* 1*, and* $\mathfrak{m}_0 \mathfrak{m}_1 \mathfrak{m}_2 \ldots \in \mathfrak{M}^\omega$ *be the sequence inductively defined by* $\mathfrak{m}_0 = \mathfrak{m}_{\mathsf{init}}$ *and* $\mathfrak{m}_{k+1} = \alpha_{\mathsf{up}}(\mathfrak{m}_k, [s_k])$*. Let* $\lambda = 2 \cdot |L| \cdot |\mathsf{Reg}| \cdot |\mathfrak{M}| + 3$*. If* $\pi \notin \mathsf{TGW}(p, \lambda)$*, then there exist some indices* $i < j$ *such that* $([s_i], \mathfrak{m}_i) = ([s_j], \mathfrak{m}_j)$*, the global clock* γ *passes some integer bound between indices* i *and* j*, and strictly less than* λ *time units elapse before reaching* s_j *from* s_0*.*

The main interest of the lemma is to construct witness paths or plays that violate the direct bounded timed window objective. By following the sequence of states up to index i and then looping in the cycle formed by the sequence of states from i to index j (modulo clock-equivalence), one obtains a time-divergent path (the global clock passes infinitely many integer bounds) along which, at all steps, the smallest priority seen from the start is odd, i.e., such that no good window can ever be witnessed from the start.

4   Verification of Timed Automata

We are concerned with the verification of direct and indirect bounded timed window objectives in TAs. Due to space constraints, we only provide and comment on our main result. The full presentation can be found in the full paper [28]. We fix a TA $\mathcal{A} = (L, \ell_{\mathsf{init}}, C, \Sigma, I, E)$ and a priority function $p \colon L \to \{0, \ldots, \mathsf{D} - 1\}$.

Theorem 1. *The verification problem for generalized direct and indirect bounded timed window objectives is* PSPACE*-complete. Furthermore, all time-divergent paths satisfy* $\mathsf{BTW}(p)$ *(resp.* $\mathsf{DBTW}(p)$*) if and only if all time-divergent paths satisfy* $\mathsf{FTW}(p, 2 \cdot |L| \cdot |\mathsf{Reg}| + 3)$ *(resp.* $\mathsf{DFTW}(p, 2 \cdot |L| \cdot |\mathsf{Reg}| + 3)$*).*

Proof (sketch). Lemma 2 (with a trivial, one-state DFA) states that, from any time-divergent path violating $\mathsf{TGW}(p, 2 \cdot |L| \cdot |\mathsf{Reg}| + 3)$, one can derive a time-divergent path along which the smallest priority seen in all prefixes is odd at all steps. The form of such a path is simple; it first follows a finite path before following a cycle in the region abstraction.

For the direct bounded objective, this provides an immediate criterion to verify whether all time-divergent paths satisfy the objective. A straightforward adaptation of the classical algorithm for reachability in timed automata that ensures that priorities are odd at all times can be used to effectively perform verification in polynomial space, i.e., by guessing a reachable state from which there is a suitable path eventually following a cycle.

In the indirect case, this approach does not suffice, e.g., it may be the case that the smallest priority in the eventual cycle is even, in which case by prefix-independence of the objective, the indirect objective is satisfied. Let π be a time-divergent path violating the bounded timed window objective. It follows that there are infinitely many suffixes of π violating $\mathsf{TGW}(p, 2 \cdot |L| \cdot |\mathsf{Reg}| + 3)$. The finite index of state equivalence ensures that one can find a state s in π from which this timed good window objective is violated in π and such that

$[s]$ is reachable from the cycle obtained by applying Lemma 2 to the suffix of π starting in s. Verification can be done similarly to the direct case, with an additional check to ensure that the guessed state is reachable from the cycle.

A by-product of the reliance on Lemma 2 is that all time-divergent paths satisfy the (resp. direct) bounded timed window objective if and only if they all satisfy $\mathsf{FTW}(p, 2 \cdot |L| \cdot |\mathsf{Reg}| + 3)$ (resp. $\mathsf{DFTW}(p, 2 \cdot |L| \cdot |\mathsf{Reg}| + 3)$).

For the multi-dimensional case, an algorithm checking satisfaction one dimension at a time has a complexity in $\mathsf{P}^{\mathsf{PSPACE}} = \mathsf{PSPACE}$ [8]. Hardness can be proven by adapting techniques used to establish hardness in the fixed case [27]. □

5 Solving Timed Games

This section presents algorithms for timed games with bounded window objectives. We first present the direct case, then the indirect case, and close the section by commenting on the complexity of the algorithms. Due to space constraints, we provide an overview of our results and algorithms; full details can be found in the full paper [28]. For this entire section, we fix a TG $\mathcal{G} = (\mathcal{A}, \Sigma_1, \Sigma_2)$ with $\mathcal{A} = (L, \ell_{\mathsf{init}}, C, \Sigma_1 \cup \Sigma_2, I, E)$ and a multi-dimensional priority function $p \colon L \to \{0, \ldots, \mathsf{D} - 1\}^{\mathsf{K}}$.

Direct Bounded Timed Window Objectives. Timed games with generalized direct bounded timed window objectives can be solved by a reduction to timed games with the ω-regular *request-response* objective [21,33]. The request-response objective is defined from pairs of sets of state regions $\mathcal{R} = ((\mathsf{Rq}_j, \mathsf{Rp}_j))_{j=1}^r$. It requires that whenever some region in a set Rq_j is visited, then a region in the set Rp_j must be visited later. Formally, we define the request-response objective for $\mathcal{R} = ((\mathsf{Rq}_j, \mathsf{Rp}_j))_{j=1}^r$ as $\mathsf{RR}(\mathcal{R}) = \{s_0 s_1 \ldots \in S^\omega \mid \forall j \leq r, \forall n, \exists n' \geq n, [s_n] \in \mathsf{Rq}_j \implies [s_{n'}] \in \mathsf{Rp}_j\}$.

Request-response objectives can be used to encode that there are good windows on all dimensions at all times. To achieve this, we encode odd priorities on some dimension as requests and smaller even priorities on the same dimension as responses. Assume that this request-response objective is satisfied by a play. Any odd priority on a dimension is followed by a smaller even priority on the same dimension. By induction, we can choose this response smaller than all other priorities appearing on this dimension between this request and its response. Intuitively, if the response is greater than some odd priority appearing between the request and response, we can consider a response to this smaller odd priority. We eventually witness a good window, because there are finitely many priorities.

Formally, if p is a one-dimensional priority function, we define $\mathcal{R}(p)$ as the family of request-response pairs that contains for each odd priority $j \in \{0, 1, \ldots, \mathsf{D} - 1\}$, the pair $(\mathsf{Rq}_j, \mathsf{Rp}_j)$ where $\mathsf{Rq}_j = p^{-1}(j) \times \mathsf{Reg}$ and $\mathsf{Rp}_j = \{\ell \in L \mid p(\ell) \leq j \wedge p(\ell) \bmod 2 = 0\} \times \mathsf{Reg}$. If p is K-dimensional, we let $\mathcal{R}(p)$ be the family $\mathcal{R}(p) = \bigcup_{1 \leq i \leq \mathsf{K}} \mathcal{R}(p_i)$. The objective of interest is $\mathsf{RR}(\mathcal{R}(p))$. A similar construction is used for direct bounded objectives in games in graphs [16].

Theorem 2. *Let* $\lambda = 8 \cdot |L| \cdot |\mathsf{Reg}| \cdot (\lfloor \frac{D}{2} \rfloor + 1)^{\mathsf{K}} \cdot \mathsf{K} + 3$. *The sets of winning states for the objectives* $\mathsf{GDFTW}(p, \lambda)$, $\mathsf{GDBTW}(p)$ *and* $\mathsf{RR}(\mathcal{R}(p))$ *coincide. Furthermore, there exists a finite-memory region strategy that is winning for all three objectives from any state in these sets.*

Proof (sketch). The main technical hurdle consists in showing that the existence of a winning strategy for the objective $\mathsf{RR}(\mathcal{R}(p))$ is equivalent to the existence of a winning strategy ensuring bounded delays between requests and responses, so that we obtain a bound on the size of good windows. Finite-memory region strategies suffice to win for request-response objectives in TGs. We can use Lemma 2 to show that, if a winning finite-memory region strategy does not ensure bounded delays between requests and responses, then there must be an outcome of this strategy along which some request goes unanswered. We can construct an outcome that eventually follows a cycle in the product of the region abstraction and the Mealy machine inducing the strategy and such that, on some dimension, some odd priority is never followed by a smaller even priority. It follows that such strategies must be winning for the direct bounded timed window objective. Furthermore, they are also winning for the direct fixed window objective for the bound of Lemma 2, as this lemma used to reach the contradiction.   □

Indirect Bounded Timed Window Objectives. We now show that the set of winning states for a TG with a bounded timed window objective can be computed by a fixed-point algorithm. Our procedure is summarized in Algorithm 1, where we assume a sub-routine SolveRR for solving TGs with request-response objectives.

The main ideas are the following. In the first iteration, the algorithm computes the winning set W^1 for the direct bounded timed window objective, hence a subset of the winning set for the bounded timed window objective. Prefix-independence of the bounded objective ensures that any play that reaches W^1 can be extended into a winning play by $\mathcal{P}_1$. Therefore, we change our requests and responses so that visiting W^1 clears all requests.

In later iterations, we show inductively that $\mathcal{P}_1$ has a winning strategy. In the set W^k computed in iteration k, $\mathcal{P}_1$ has a winning strategy for the bounded objective that consists in conforming to a winning strategy ensuring bounded delays between requests and responses for the request-response objective from which W^k was computed as long as W^{k-1} is not visited, and switches to a winning strategy in W^{k-1} if W^{k-1} is visited. A time-divergent outcome of this strategy satisfies the direct bounded objective if W^{k-1} is never visited, and otherwise its suffix starting from the first state in W^{k-1} satisfies the bounded objective by induction. Therefore, this strategy is winning for the bounded objective. Similarly to the direct case, this strategy is even winning for a fixed timed window objective.

Algorithm 1: Computing the set of winning states for BTW(p)

Data: A TG $\mathcal{G} = (\mathcal{A}, \Sigma_1, \Sigma_2)$, a multi-dimensional priority function p over $\mathcal{A}$.

$k \leftarrow 0;\ W^0 \leftarrow \emptyset;\ \mathcal{R} \leftarrow \mathcal{R}(p);$

repeat

    $k \leftarrow k+1;\ W^k \leftarrow \mathsf{SolveRR}(\mathcal{G}, \mathcal{R});$

    for (Rq, Rp) $\in \mathcal{R}$ **do**

        Rq $\leftarrow$ Rq $\setminus \{[s] \in L \times \mathsf{Reg} \mid [s] \subseteq W^k\};$

        Rp $\leftarrow$ Rp $\cup \{[s] \in L \times \mathsf{Reg} \mid [s] \subseteq W^k\};$

until $W^k \setminus W^{k-1} = \emptyset;$

return $W^k;$

Finite-memory region strategies suffice for winning: one can use a Mealy machine that keeps track of the smallest k such that W^k was visited, and encodes for each k a winning finite-memory strategy ensuring bounded delays between requests and responses for the objective from which W^k was computed.

In addition to the above, on the complement of the set W returned by Algorithm 1, $\mathcal{P}_1$ has no winning strategy. Intuitively, for all strategies of $\mathcal{P}_1$, there is an outcome that stabilizes in $S \setminus W$, and such that a request goes unanswered, i.e., some odd priority is never followed by a smaller even priority. We can exploit this to construct an outcome in which requests go unanswered for increasingly greater amounts of time, because $S \setminus W$ is a set from which $\mathcal{P}_1$ has no winning strategy for the last request-response objective in the loop of Algorithm 1, hence we can always extend any outcome so that a request goes unanswered for an arbitrary amount of time.

Algorithm 1 computes a sequence of sets that is non-decreasing; at each step the considered objective is less constraining. Because winning sets for ω-regular region objectives are unions of regions, it follows that the algorithm terminates.

The arguments sketched above for the correctness of Algorithm 1 yield the following theorem.

Theorem 3. *Let* $\lambda = 8 \cdot |L| \cdot |\mathsf{Reg}| \cdot (\lfloor \frac{D}{2} \rfloor + 1)^K \cdot K + 3$. *The sets of winning states for the objectives* GFTW(p, λ) *and* GBTW(p) *coincide. Furthermore, there exists a finite-memory region strategy that is winning for both objectives from any state in these sets of winning states.*

Complexity. The algorithms described in the two previous sections run in exponential time. For the direct case, we solve a request-response TG with $\lfloor \frac{D}{2} \rfloor \cdot K$ request-response pairs, which can be solved in exponential time [1,2,33]. In the indirect case, we solve, in the worst case, as many request-response games as there are state regions. We still obtain an EXPTIME algorithm because the exponential terms from the complexity of solving the TGs with request-response objectives and from the number of state regions are multiplied rather than stacked. Lower bounds can be established by adapting techniques used in the fixed case [27]. We obtain the following result.

Theorem 4. *The realizability problem for generalized direct and indirect bounded timed window objectives is* **EXPTIME**-*complete.*

References

1. de Alfaro, L., Faella, M., Henzinger, T.A., Majumdar, R., Stoelinga, M.: The element of surprise in timed games. In: Amadio, R., Lugiez, D. (eds.) CONCUR 2003. LNCS, vol. 2761, pp. 144–158. Springer, Heidelberg (2003). https://doi.org/10.1007/978-3-540-45187-7_9
2. de Alfaro, L., Henzinger, T.A., Majumdar, R.: Symbolic algorithms for infinite-state games. In: Larsen, K.G., Nielsen, M. (eds.) CONCUR 2001. LNCS, vol. 2154, pp. 536–550. Springer, Heidelberg (2001). https://doi.org/10.1007/3-540-44685-0_36
3. Alur, R., Courcoubetis, C., Dill, D.L.: Model-checking in dense real-time. Inf. Comput. **104**(1), 2–34 (1993). https://doi.org/10.1006/inco.1993.1024
4. Alur, R., Dill, D.L.: A theory of timed automata. Theor. Comput. Sci. **126**(2), 183–235 (1994). https://doi.org/10.1016/0304-3975(94)90010-8
5. Baier, C.: Reasoning about cost-utility constraints in probabilistic models. In: Bojańczyk, M., Lasota, S., Potapov, I. (eds.) RP 2015. LNCS, vol. 9328, pp. 1–6. Springer, Cham (2015). https://doi.org/10.1007/978-3-319-24537-9_1
6. Baier, C., Katoen, J.: Principles of Model Checking. MIT Press, Cambridge (2008)
7. Baier, C., Klein, J., Klüppelholz, S., Wunderlich, S.: Weight monitoring with linear temporal logic: complexity and decidability. In: Henzinger, T.A., Miller, D. (eds.) Joint Meeting of the Twenty-Third EACSL Annual Conference on Computer Science Logic (CSL) and the Twenty-Ninth Annual ACM/IEEE Symposium on Logic in Computer Science (LICS), CSL-LICS 2014, Vienna, Austria, 14–18 July 2014, pp. 11:1–11:10. ACM (2014). https://doi.org/10.1145/2603088.2603162. http://dl.acm.org/citation.cfm?id=2603088
8. Baker, T.P., Gill, J., Solovay, R.: Relativizations of the P =? NP question. SIAM J. Comput. **4**(4), 431–442 (1975). https://doi.org/10.1137/0204037
9. Berthon, R., Randour, M., Raskin, J.: Threshold constraints with guarantees for parity objectives in Markov decision processes. In: Chatzigiannakis, I., Indyk, P., Kuhn, F., Muscholl, A. (eds.) 44th International Colloquium on Automata, Languages, and Programming, ICALP 2017, 10–14 July 2017, Warsaw, Poland. LIPIcs, vol. 80, pp. 121:1–121:15. Schloss Dagstuhl - Leibniz-Zentrum fuer Informatik (2017). https://doi.org/10.4230/LIPIcs.ICALP.2017.121. http://www.dagstuhl.de/dagpub/978-3-95977-041-5
10. Bordais, B., Guha, S., Raskin, J.: Expected window mean-payoff. In: Chattopadhyay, A., Gastin, P. (eds.) 39th IARCS Annual Conference on Foundations of Software Technology and Theoretical Computer Science, FSTTCS 2019, 11–13 December 2019, Bombay, India. LIPIcs, vol. 150, pp. 32:1–32:15. Schloss Dagstuhl - Leibniz-Zentrum für Informatik (2019). https://doi.org/10.4230/LIPIcs.FSTTCS.2019.32
11. Bouyer, P., Brihaye, T., Randour, M., Rivière, C., Vandenhove, P.: Decisiveness of stochastic systems and its application to hybrid models. In: Raskin, J., Bresolin, D. (eds.) Proceedings 11th International Symposium on Games, Automata, Logics, and Formal Verification, GandALF 2020, Brussels, Belgium, 21–22 September 2020. EPTCS, vol. 326, pp. 149–165 (2020). https://doi.org/10.4204/EPTCS.326.10

12. Brázdil, T., Chatterjee, K., Forejt, V., Kucera, A.: Trading performance for stability in Markov decision processes. J. Comput. Syst. Sci. **84**, 144–170 (2017). https://doi.org/10.1016/j.jcss.2016.09.009
13. Brázdil, T., Forejt, V., Kucera, A., Novotný, P.: Stability in graphs and games. In: Desharnais and Jagadeesan [24], pp. 10:1–10:14. https://doi.org/10.4230/LIPIcs.CONCUR.2016.10. http://www.dagstuhl.de/dagpub/978-3-95977-017-0
14. Brihaye, T., Delgrange, F., Oualhadj, Y., Randour, M.: Life is random, time is not: Markov decision processes with window objectives. Log. Methods Comput. Sci. **16**(4) (2020). https://lmcs.episciences.org/6975
15. Bruyère, V., Filiot, E., Randour, M., Raskin, J.: Meet your expectations with guarantees: beyond worst-case synthesis in quantitative games. Inf. Comput. **254**, 259–295 (2017). https://doi.org/10.1016/j.ic.2016.10.011
16. Bruyère, V., Hautem, Q., Randour, M.: Window parity games: an alternative approach toward parity games with time bounds. In: Cantone, D., Delzanno, G. (eds.) Proceedings of the Seventh International Symposium on Games, Automata, Logics and Formal Verification, GandALF 2016, Catania, Italy, 14–16 September 2016. EPTCS, vol. 226, pp. 135–148 (2016). https://doi.org/10.4204/EPTCS.226.10
17. Bruyère, V., Hautem, Q., Raskin, J.: On the complexity of heterogeneous multidimensional games. In: Desharnais and Jagadeesan [24], pp. 11:1–11:15. https://doi.org/10.4230/LIPIcs.CONCUR.2016.11. http://www.dagstuhl.de/dagpub/978-3-95977-017-0
18. Calude, C.S., Jain, S., Khoussainov, B., Li, W., Stephan, F.: Deciding parity games in quasipolynomial time. In: Hatami, H., McKenzie, P., King, V. (eds.) Proceedings of the 49th Annual ACM SIGACT Symposium on Theory of Computing, STOC 2017, Montreal, QC, Canada, 19–23 June 2017, pp. 252–263. ACM (2017). https://doi.org/10.1145/3055399.3055409
19. Chatterjee, K., Doyen, L., Randour, M., Raskin, J.: Looking at mean-payoff and total-payoff through windows. Inf. Comput. **242**, 25–52 (2015). https://doi.org/10.1016/j.ic.2015.03.010
20. Chatterjee, K., Henzinger, T.A., Horn, F.: Finitary winning in omega-regular games. ACM Trans. Comput. Log. **11**(1), 1:1–1:27 (2009). https://doi.org/10.1145/1614431.1614432
21. Chatterjee, K., Henzinger, T.A., Horn, F.: The complexity of request-response games. In: Dediu, A.-H., Inenaga, S., Martín-Vide, C. (eds.) LATA 2011. LNCS, vol. 6638, pp. 227–237. Springer, Heidelberg (2011). https://doi.org/10.1007/978-3-642-21254-3_17
22. Chatterjee, K., Henzinger, T.A., Piterman, N.: Generalized parity games. In: Seidl, H. (ed.) FoSSaCS 2007. LNCS, vol. 4423, pp. 153–167. Springer, Heidelberg (2007). https://doi.org/10.1007/978-3-540-71389-0_12
23. Chatterjee, K., Henzinger, T.A., Prabhu, V.S.: Timed parity games: complexity and robustness. Log. Methods Comput. Sci. **7**(4) (2011). https://doi.org/10.2168/LMCS-7(4:8)2011
24. Desharnais, J., Jagadeesan, R. (eds.): 27th International Conference on Concurrency Theory, CONCUR 2016, 23–26 August 2016, Québec City, Canada. LIPIcs, vol. 59. Schloss Dagstuhl - Leibniz-Zentrum fuer Informatik (2016). http://www.dagstuhl.de/dagpub/978-3-95977-017-0
25. Hunter, P., Pérez, G.A., Raskin, J.-F.: Looking at mean payoff through foggy windows. Acta Informatica **55**(8), 627–647 (2017). https://doi.org/10.1007/s00236-017-0304-7

26. Kupferman, O., Piterman, N., Vardi, M.Y.: From liveness to promptness. Formal Methods Syst. Des. **34**(2), 83–103 (2009). https://doi.org/10.1007/s10703-009-0067-z

27. Main, J.C.A., Randour, M., Sproston, J.: Time flies when looking out of the window: timed games with window parity objectives. In: Haddad, S., Varacca, D. (eds.) 32nd International Conference on Concurrency Theory, CONCUR 2021, 24–27 August 2021, Virtual Conference. LIPIcs, vol. 203, pp. 25:1–25:16. Schloss Dagstuhl - Leibniz-Zentrum für Informatik (2021). https://doi.org/10.4230/LIPIcs.CONCUR.2021.25

28. Main, J.C.A., Randour, M., Sproston, J.: Timed games with bounded window parity objectives. CoRR abs/2205.04197 (2022). https://doi.org/10.48550/arXiv.2205.04197

29. Maler, O., Pnueli, A., Sifakis, J.: On the synthesis of discrete controllers for timed systems. In: Mayr, E.W., Puech, C. (eds.) STACS 1995. LNCS, vol. 900, pp. 229–242. Springer, Heidelberg (1995). https://doi.org/10.1007/3-540-59042-0_76

30. Norman, G., Parker, D., Sproston, J.: Model checking for probabilistic timed automata. Formal Methods Syst. Des. **43**(2), 164–190 (2013). https://doi.org/10.1007/s10703-012-0177-x

31. Randour, M.: Automated synthesis of reliable and efficient systems through game theory: a case study. In: Gilbert, T., Kirkilionis, M., Nicolis, G. (eds.) ECCS 2012, pp. 731–738. Springer, Cham (2013). https://doi.org/10.1007/978-3-319-00395-5_90

32. Roux, S.L., Pauly, A., Randour, M.: Extending finite-memory determinacy by Boolean combination of winning conditions. In: Ganguly, S., Pandya, P.K. (eds.) 38th IARCS Annual Conference on Foundations of Software Technology and Theoretical Computer Science, FSTTCS 2018, 11–13 December 2018, Ahmedabad, India. LIPIcs, vol. 122, pp. 38:1–38:20. Schloss Dagstuhl - Leibniz-Zentrum fuer Informatik (2018). https://doi.org/10.4230/LIPIcs.FSTTCS.2018.38. http://www.dagstuhl.de/dagpub/978-3-95977-093-4

33. Wallmeier, N., Hütten, P., Thomas, W.: Symbolic synthesis of finite-state controllers for request-response specifications. In: Ibarra, O.H., Dang, Z. (eds.) CIAA 2003. LNCS, vol. 2759, pp. 11–22. Springer, Heidelberg (2003). https://doi.org/10.1007/3-540-45089-0_3

Non-blind Strategies in Timed Network Congestion Games

Aline Goeminne, Nicolas Markey$^{(\boxtimes)}$, and Ocan Sankur

Univ Rennes, Inria, CNRS, IRISA, Rennes, France
{aline.goeminne,nicolas.markey,ocan.sankur}@irisa.fr

Abstract. Network congestion games are a convenient model for reasoning about routing problems in a network: agents have to move from a source to a target vertex while avoiding congestion, measured as a cost depending on the number of players using the same link. Network congestion games have been extensively studied over the last 40 years, while their extension with timing constraints were considered more recently.

Most of the results on network congestion games consider *blind* strategies: they are static, and do not adapt to the strategies selected by the other players. We extend the recent results of [Bertrand *et al.*, Dynamic network congestion games. FSTTCS'20] to timed network congestion games, in which the availability of the edges depend on (discrete) time. We prove that computing Nash equilibria satisfying some constraint on the total cost (and in particular, computing the best and worst Nash equilibria), and computing the social optimum, can be achieved in exponential space. The social optimum can be computed in polynomial space if all players have the same source and target.

1 Introduction

Network congestion games allow one to model situations in which agents compete for resources such as routes or bandwidth [21], e.g. in communication networks [2,20]. In these games, the objective of each agent is to go from a source to a target vertex, traversing a number of edges that represent resources. The cost incurred by the player for the use of each resource is a function of the *load*, that is, the number of agents using the same resource. One of the fundamental notions studied in these games is that of *Nash equilibria* which is used to model stable situations. A strategy profile is a Nash equilibrium if none of the players can reduce their cost by unilaterally changing their strategy.

It is well-known that these games can be *inefficient* in the sense that there are Nash equilibria whose social cost (*i.e.*, the sum of the agents' costs) is bounded away from the optimum that can be achieved by arbitrary profiles (that may not be Nash equilibria). Research has been focused on proving bounds on this inefficiency, formalized by the *price of anarchy (PoA)* [15]. A tight bound of $\frac{5}{2}$

This work was partially funded by ANR project Ticktac (ANR-18-CE40-0015). A full version of this paper is available as [11].

S. Bogomolov and D. Parker (Eds.): FORMATS 2022, LNCS 13465, pp. 183–199, 2022.
https://doi.org/10.1007/978-3-031-15839-1_11

on the price of anarchy was given in [7,10]. The *price of stability (PoS)* is dual to PoA: it is the ratio between the cost of the best Nash equilibrium and the social cost, and was introduced in [4]. Bounds on PoA and PoS have been studied for restricted classes of graphs or types of cost functions [18].

Timed Network Games. Extensions of these games with real-time constraints have been considered. In the setting of [12], each edge is traversed with a fixed duration, independent of its load, while the cost is still a function of the load at the traversal time. The model thus has *time-dependent* costs since the load depends on the times at which players traverse a given edge. The existence of Nash equilibria is proven by reduction to [21]. The work in [5] propose another real-time extension, in which transitions are instantaneous, and can only be taken during some intervals of time. Time elapses in vertices, which incurs a cost that is proportional to the load and the delay. In those works, time is continuous; *boundary strategies* are strategies that take transitions at dates that are boundaries of the constraining intervals. It is shown that *boundary Nash equilibria* always exist, but need not capture optimal Nash equilibria. The prices of anarchy and stability are shown to be bounded by $5/2$ and $1 + \sqrt{3}/3$, respectively, and computing *some* Nash equilibrium is PLS-complete. This study was further extended to richer timing constraints (involving clocks) in [6].

Non-blind Strategies. In all the works mentioned above, the considered strategies are *blind*: each player chooses a path to follow at the beginning of the game, and cannot adapt their behaviors to their observations during the game. *Non-blind* strategies which allow players to choose their next moves depending on the whole history were studied in [8]. The advantage of non-blind players it that these allow one to obtain Nash equilibria that have a lower social cost than with blind profiles. Thus, in general, the price of anarchy is lower with non-blind strategies. In [8], the existence of Nash equilibria was established for these strategies, and an algorithm was given to decide the existence of Nash equilibria satisfying given constraints on the costs of the players.

Our Contributions. We pursue the study of the real-time extensions of network congestion games by considering non-blind strategies. We consider timed network congestion games similar to [5] (albeit with a discrete-time semantics), in which the edges in the network are guarded by a time interval which defines the time points at which the edges can be traversed. Moreover, each vertex is endowed with a cost function depending on the load, and the players incur a cost for each time unit spent on the vertex. We consider both the *symmetric* case in which all players source and target vertex pairs are identical, and the *asymmetric* case where these pairs vary. We formally define the semantics of our setting with non-blind strategies, show how to compute the social optimum in PSPACE in the symmetric case and in EXPSPACE in the asymmetric case. Moreover, we give an algorithm to decide the existence of Nash equilibria satisfying a given set of cost constraints in EXPSPACE, for both the symmetric and asymmetric cases. We can then compute the prices of anarchy and of stability in EXPSPACE.

Related Works. The existence of Nash equilibria in all atomic congestion games is proven using potential games. The notion of potential was generalized by Monderer and Shapley [17] who showed how to iteratively use best-response computation to obtain a Nash equilibrium. We refer the interested reader to [22] for an introduction and main results on the subject.

Timing constraints are also considered in [16,19] where travel times also depend on the load. Other works focus on flow models with a timing aspect [9,14].

2   Preliminaries

2.1   Timed Network Congestion Game

Timed Network. A *timed network* $\mathcal{A}$ is a tuple $(V, E, \mathsf{wgt}, \mathsf{guard})$ where V is a set of vertices, $E \subseteq V \times V$ is a set of edges, $\mathsf{wgt} \colon V \to (\mathbb{N}_{>0} \to \mathbb{N}_{>0})$ associates with each vertex a non-decreasing weight function, and $\mathsf{guard} \colon E \to \mathcal{P}(\mathbb{N})$ associates with each edge the dates at which that edge is available. We require in the sequel that for all $e \in E$, $\mathsf{guard}(e)$ is a finite union of disjoint intervals with bounds in $\mathbb{N} \cup \{+\infty\}$. A guard $\mathsf{guard}(e)$ is said to be satisfied at date d if $d \in \mathsf{guard}(e)$.

A *trajectory* in a timed network $\mathcal{A} = (V, E, \mathsf{wgt}, \mathsf{guard})$ is a (finite or infinite) sequence $(v_j, d_j)_{0 \le j \le l}$ such that for all $0 \le j < l$, $(v_j, v_{j+1}) \in E$ and $d_{j+1} \in \mathsf{guard}(v_j, v_{j+1})$. We write $\mathsf{Traj}_{\mathcal{A}}(v, d, v')$ for the set of trajectories with $v_0 = v$, $d_0 = d$, and $v_l = v'$, possibly omitting to mention $\mathcal{A}$ when no ambiguity arises.

Timed Network Game. A *timed network congestion game* (a.k.a. *timed network game*, or TNG for short) is a model to represent and reason about the congestion caused by the simultaneous use of some resources by several users.

Definition 1. *A timed network game $\mathcal{N}$ is a tuple $(n, \mathcal{A}, (src_i, tgt_i)_{1 \le i \le n})$ where*

- *n is the number of players (in binary). We write $[\![n]\!]$ for the set of players;*
- *$\mathcal{A} = (V, E, \mathsf{wgt}, \mathsf{guard})$ is a timed network;*
- *for each $1 \le i \le n$, the pair $(src_i, tgt_i) \in V^2$ is the objective of Player i.*

Symmetric TNGs are TNGs in which all players have the same objective $(\mathsf{src}, \mathsf{tgt})$, i.e., $\mathsf{src}_i = \mathsf{src}$ and $\mathsf{tgt}_i = \mathsf{tgt}$ for all $i \in [\![n]\!]$.

Remark 1. Several encodings can be used for the description of $(\mathsf{src}_i, \mathsf{tgt}_i)_{1 \le i \le n}$, which may impact the size of the input: for symmetric TNGs, the players' objectives would naturally be given as a single pair $(\mathsf{src}, \mathsf{tgt})$. For the asymmetric case, the players' objectives could be given explicitly as a list of $(\mathsf{src}, \mathsf{tgt})$-pairs (the size is then linear in n and logarithmic in $|V|$), or as a function $V^2 \to \mathbb{N}$ (size quadratic in $|V|$ and logarithmic in n). Usually, the number of players is large (and can be seen as a parameter), and the size of the input is at least linear in $|V|$, so that the latter representation is preferred.   ◁

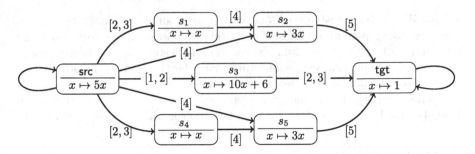

Fig. 1. Example of a timed network game

A *configuration* of a TNG $\mathcal{N}$ is a mapping $c\colon \llbracket n \rrbracket \to V$ that maps each player to some vertex. We write Conf for the set of all configurations of $\mathcal{N}$. There are two particular configurations: the *initial configuration* init, in which all players are in their source vertices, *i.e.*, init: $i \mapsto src_i$; and the final configuration final in which all players are in their target vertices, *i.e.*, final: $i \mapsto tgt_i$. A timed configuration of $\mathcal{N}$ is a pair (c,d) where c is a configuration and $d \in \mathbb{N}$ is the current time. We write TConf for the set of all timed configurations of $\mathcal{N}$, and st for the starting timed configuration $(init, 0)$.

Remark 2. We assume in the sequel that for each $0 \le i \le n$, there is a trajectory from $(src_i, 0)$ to the target vertex tgt_i; this can be checked in polynomial time by exploring $\mathcal{N}$. We also require that for each vertex $v \in V$ and each date d, there exist a vertex v' and a time $d' > d$ such that $(v, v') \in E$ and $d' \in guard(v, v')$. ◁

Example 1. Figure 1 represents a timed network $\mathcal{A}$ (that we will use throughout this section to illustrate our formalism). The guards label the corresponding edges with two conventions: guards of the form $[d, d]$ for $d \in \mathbb{N}$ are denoted by $[d]$ and edges without label have $[0, +\infty)$ as a guard, *e.g.*, $guard(src, s_4) = [2, 3]$ and $guard(src, src) = [0 + \infty)$.

The weight function wgt is defined inside the corresponding vertex, *e.g.*, wgt(src): $x \mapsto 5x$ and wgt(tgt): $x \mapsto 1$. As explained in the sequel, this function indicates the cost of spending one time unit in each vertex, depending on the number of players. For instance, if two players spend one time unit in src, they both pay 10. Notice that to comply with Remark 2, extra edges with guard $[6, +\infty)$ are added from each vertex s_k $(1 \le k \le 5)$ to an additional sink vertex (omitted in the figure for clarity). ◁

Concurrent Game Associated with a Timed Network Game. Consider a TNG $\mathcal{N} = (n, \mathcal{A}, (src_i, tgt_i)_{1 \le i \le n})$, with $\mathcal{A} = (V, E, wgt, guard)$. The semantics runs intuitively as follows: a timed configuration represents the positions of the players in the network at a given date. At each round, each player selects the transition they want to take in $\mathcal{A}$, together with the date at which they want to take it. All players selecting the earliest date will follow the edges they selected, giving rise to a new timed configuration, from where the next round will take place.

We express this semantics as an n-player infinite-state weighted concurrent game $\mathcal{G} = (\mathsf{States}, \mathsf{Act}, (\mathsf{Allow}_i)_{1 \leq i \leq n}, \mathsf{Upd}, (\mathsf{cost}_i)_{1 \leq i \leq n})$ [3]. The set States of states of $\mathcal{G}$ is the set TConf of timed configurations. The set Act of actions is the set $\{(v, d) \mid v \in V, d \in \mathbb{N}_{\geq 0}\}$. Functions Allow_i return the set of allowed actions for Player i from each configuration: for a timed configuration (c, d), we have $(v, d') \in \mathsf{Allow}_i(c, d)$ whenever $d' > d$ and $(c(i), v) \in E$ and $d' \in \mathsf{guard}(c(i), v)$. Notice that by Remark 2, $\mathsf{Allow}_i(c, d)$ is never empty. An *action vector* in $\mathcal{G}$ is a vector $\vec{a} = (a_i)_{1 \leq i \leq n}$ of actions, one for each player. We write Mov for the set of action vectors. An action vector $\vec{a}$ is valid from state (c, d) if for all $1 \leq i \leq n$, action $a_i \in \mathsf{Allow}_i(c, d)$. We write $\mathsf{Valid}(c, d)$ for the set of valid action vectors from state (c, d).

From a state (c, d), a valid action vector $\vec{a} = (v_i, d_i)_{1 \leq i \leq n}$ leads to a new state (c', d') where $d' = \min\{d_i \mid 1 \leq i \leq n\}$ and for all $1 \leq i \leq n$, $c'(i) = v_i$ if $d_i = d'$, and $c'(i) = c(i)$ otherwise. This is encoded in the update function Upd by letting $\mathsf{Upd}((c, d), \vec{a}) = (c', d')$. This models the fact that the players proposing the shortest delay apply their action once this shortest delay has elapsed. We write $\mathsf{Select}(\vec{a}) = \{1 \leq i \leq n \mid \forall 1 \leq j \leq n. \ d_i \leq d_j\}$.

We let $\mathsf{Trans} = \{(s, \vec{a}, s') \in \mathsf{States} \times \mathsf{Mov} \times \mathsf{States} \mid \vec{a} \in \mathsf{Valid}(s), \mathsf{Upd}(s, \vec{a}) = s'\}$ be the set of *transitions* of $\mathcal{G}$. We write G for the graph structure $(\mathsf{States}, \mathsf{Trans})$.

The delays elapsed in the vertices of $\mathcal{N}$ come with a cost for each player, computed as follows: given a configuration c, we write $\mathsf{load}_c \colon V \to \mathbb{N}$ for the load of each vertex of the timed network, i.e., the number of players sitting in that vertex: $\mathsf{load}_c(v) = \#\{1 \leq i \leq n \mid c(i) = v\}$. For each $1 \leq i \leq n$, the cost for Player i of taking a transition $t = ((c, d), \vec{a}, (c', d'))$, moving from timed configuration (c, d) to timed configuration (c', d'), then is $\mathsf{cost}_i(t) = (d' - d) \cdot \mathsf{wgt}(c(i))(\mathsf{load}_c(c(i)))$: it is proportional to the time elapsed and to the load of the vertex where Player i is waiting. Notice that it does not depend on $\vec{a}$ (nor on c').

Remark 3. With our definition, players remain in the game even after they have reached their targets. This may be undesirable in some situations. One way of avoiding this is to add another limitation on the availability of transitions to players: transitions would be allowed only to some players, and in particular, from their target states, players would only be allowed to go to a sink state. All our results can be adapted to this setting. ◁

Example 2. We illustrate those different notions on a two-player symmetric timed network game $\mathcal{N} = (2, \mathcal{A}, (\mathsf{src}, \mathsf{tgt}))$, where $\mathcal{A}$ is the timed network of Example 1.

Let $(c, d) = ((\mathsf{src}, s_1), 2)$ be the timed configuration in TConf, with $c(1) = \mathsf{src}$, $c(2) = s_1$ and $d = 2$. From this timed configuration, the set of allowed actions for Player 1 is $\mathsf{Allow}_1(c, d) = \{(s_1, 3), (s_4, 3), (s_2, 4), (s_5, 4), (\mathsf{src}, d) \mid d \geq 3\}$. If we consider the valid action vector $\vec{a} = ((s_1, 3), (s_2, 4))$, then $\mathsf{Upd}((c, d), \vec{a}) = (c', d')$ with $c' = (s_1, s_1)$ and $d' = 3$. Indeed even if both players choose their actions simultaneously, we have $\mathsf{Select}(\vec{a}) = \{1\}$, and Player 1 is the only player who moves at time 3. Moreover, writing $t = ((c, d), \vec{a}, (c', d'))$, we have $\text{cost}_1(t) = 5$, because $\text{load}_{(c,d)}(\text{src}) = 1$. Finally, let us consider another example of cost computation: let $(c, d) = ((s_3, s_3), 1)$ and $(c', d') = ((\text{tgt}, \text{tgt}), 3)$, and $\vec{a} = ((\text{tgt}, 3), (\text{tgt}, 3))$; we have that $\text{cost}_1((c, d), \vec{a}, (c', d')) = 2 \cdot (10 \cdot 2 + 6) = 52$.   ◁

Plays and Histories. A play $\rho = (s_k, \vec{a}_k, s'_k)_{k \in \mathbb{N}} \in \text{Trans}^\omega$ in $\mathcal{G}$ (also called play in $\mathcal{N}$) is an infinite sequence of transitions such that for all $k \in \mathbb{N}$, $s'_k = s_{k+1}$. We denote by Plays the set of plays of $\mathcal{G}$. We denote by Plays(s) the set of plays that start in state $s \in \text{States}$, i.e. $\text{Plays}(s) = \{(s_k, \vec{a}_k, s'_k)_{k \geq 0} \in \text{Plays} \mid s_0 = s\}$.

A history is a finite prefix of a play. We denote the set of histories by Hist, and the subset of histories starting in a given state s by Hist(s).

Given a play $\rho = (s_k, \vec{a}_k, s'_k)_{k \geq 0} \in \text{Plays}$ and an integer $j \in \mathbb{N}$, we write ρ_j for the timed configuration s_j, $\rho_{\geq j}$ for the suffix $(s_{j+k}, \vec{a}_{j+k}, s'_{j+k})_{k \geq 0} \in \text{Plays}(s_j)$, and $\rho_{<j}$ for the history $(s_k, \vec{a}_k, s'_k)_{k<j} \in \text{Hist}(s_0)$. For a history $h = (s_k, \vec{a}_k, s'_k)_{0 \leq k < j}$ in Hist(s_0), we write $\text{last}(h) = s'_{j-1}$ when $j > 0$ (we may also write it as s_j when no ambiguity arises), and $\text{last}(h) = s_0$ otherwise.

Cost Functions. For each player $i \in [\![n]\!]$, we define a cost function $\text{cost}_i \colon \text{Plays} \to \mathbb{N} \cup \{+\infty\}$ such that for all $\rho = (s_k, \vec{a}_k, s'_k)_{k \in \mathbb{N}} \in \text{Plays}$,

$$\text{cost}_i(\rho) = \begin{cases} +\infty & \text{if } s_k(i) \neq \text{tgt}_i \text{ for all } k \in \mathbb{N} \\ \sum_{k=0}^{\ell-1} \text{cost}_i(s_k, \vec{a}_k, s'_k) & \text{if } \ell \text{ is the least index such that } s_\ell(i) = \text{tgt}_i \end{cases}$$

This function is extended to histories in the natural way. For all $\rho \in \text{Plays} \cup \text{Hist}$, the vector $\text{cost}(\rho) = (\text{cost}_i(\rho))_{1 \leq i \leq n}$ is the *cost profile* of ρ.

Strategies. Given a concurrent game $\mathcal{G}$, a state s in $\mathcal{G}$, and $1 \leq i \leq n$, a *strategy* for Player i from s is a function $\sigma_i \colon \text{Hist}(s) \to \text{Act}$ such that $\sigma_i(h) \in \text{Allow}_i(\text{last}(h))$ for all $h \in \text{Hist}(s)$. We denote by $\Sigma_i(s)$ the set of strategies of Player i from s (we may omit to mention s when it is the initial timed configuration st). Given a state s, a subset $I \subseteq [\![n]\!]$ of players, and strategies $(\sigma_i)_{i \in I}$ from s for those players, a play $\rho = (s_k, \vec{a}_k, s'_k)_{k \in \mathbb{N}}$ from s is consistent with $(\sigma_i)_{i \in I}$ if for all $k \in \mathbb{N}$ and all $i \in I$, it holds $\vec{a}_{k,i} = \sigma_i(\rho_{<k})$.

A *strategy profile* $\sigma = (\sigma_i)_{1 \leq i \leq n}$ from s is a tuple of strategies from s, one for each player. We write $\Sigma(s)$ for the set of strategy profiles from s. Given a strategy profile σ from s, there is a unique play ρ from s that is *consistent* with that strategy profile. This play is denoted by $\langle \sigma \rangle_s$ and is called the *outcome* of the strategy profile σ from s.

Given a strategy profile σ from s, a player $i \in [\![n]\!]$ and a strategy σ'_i from s for Player i, we write (σ_{-i}, σ'_i) for the strategy profile $(\tau_j)_{1 \leq j \leq n}$ for which $\tau_j = \sigma_j$ when $j \neq i$ and $\tau_i = \sigma'_i$. Given a player $1 \leq i \leq n$ and a strategy σ_i from s for Player i, for all $h \in \text{Hist}(s)$, we denote by $\sigma_{i \upharpoonright h}$ the strategy of Player i from $\text{last}(h)$ such that $\sigma_{i \upharpoonright h} \colon h' \in \text{Hist}(\text{last}(h)) \mapsto \sigma_i(hh')$. This is extended to strategy profiles in the natural way.

Blind Strategies. An important class of strategies is the class of *blind strategies*. Intuitively, a blind strategy follows a single trajectory, without looking at how the other players are moving. In order to define blind strategies, we first introduce a notion of *projection* of plays on the actions of each player.

For any play $\rho = (s_k, \vec{a}_k, s'_k)_{k \in \mathbb{N}}$ from st and any $1 \le i \le n$, writing $\vec{a}_k = (v_{k,i}, d_{k,i})_{1 \le i \le n}$ for all $k \in \mathbb{N}$, we define $\mu_i \colon \mathbb{N} \mapsto \mathbb{N} \cup \{+\infty\}$ inductively as $\mu_i(0) = -1$ and, for all j for which $\mu_i(j) < +\infty$,

$$\mu_i(j+1) = \inf\{k > \mu_i(j) \mid d_{k,i} = \min\{d_{k,l} \mid 1 \le l \le n\}\}.$$

In other terms, μ_i returns the indices where Player i proposed a minimal delay, and thus could move to the vertex they proposed. The trajectory of Player i along ρ, denoted with $\mathsf{traj}_i(\rho)$, is then defined as the trajectory $(v_{\mu_i(j),i}, d_{\mu_i(j),i})_{j \ge 0}$, with the convention that $(v_{-1,i}, d_{-1,i}) = (\mathsf{src}_i, 0)$. Notice that this trajectory could be finite. Functions traj_i are extended to histories in the natural way.

Definition 2. *A strategy σ_i for Player i is* blind *if, for any two histories h and h' such that $\mathsf{traj}_i(h) = \mathsf{traj}_i(h')$, it holds $\sigma_i(h) = \sigma_i(h')$.*

As the next lemma suggests, playing a blind strategy amounts to following a fixed trajectory in the timed network, independently of the actions of the other players.

Lemma 3. *Let $i \in [\![n]\!]$ be a player and σ_i be a strategy of Player i from some state s_0. If σ_i is blind, then for all strategies σ_{-i} and σ'_{-i} from s_0, we have*

$$\mathsf{traj}_i(\langle \sigma_{-i}, \sigma_i \rangle s_0) = \mathsf{traj}_i(\langle \sigma'_{-i}, \sigma_i \rangle s_0).$$

In view of this lemma, any blind strategy σ_i for Player i from some state s_0 can be associated with a *trajectory*, denoted with $\langle \sigma_i \rangle_{s_0}$, and defined as $\langle \sigma_i \rangle_{s_0} = \mathsf{traj}_i(\langle \sigma_{-i}, \sigma_i \rangle s_0)$ (for any $\sigma_{-i} \in \Sigma_{-i}(s_0)$.) Conversely, for any trajectory π from (v_0, d_0), any player $i \in [\![n]\!]$, and any timed configuration $s_0 = (c, d_0)$ with $c(i) = v_0$, there exists a blind strategy σ_i for Player i from s_0 whose associated trajectory is π.

A play $\rho = (s_k, \vec{a}_k, s'_k)_{k \in \mathbb{N}}$ from the initial timed configuration st is said *winning* for Player i if there exists $k \in \mathbb{N}$ such that $s_k = (c_k, d_k)$ with $c_k(i) = \mathsf{tgt}_i$. A strategy σ_i for Player i from st is winning if any play consistent with that strategy is winning for Player i. For each $1 \le i \le n$, as we assumed $\mathsf{Traj}(\mathsf{src}_i, 0, \mathsf{tgt}_i) \ne \varnothing$, we get that there exists a winning (blind) strategy σ_i for Player i.

Example 3. We consider the two-player symmetric TNG described in Example 2. The infinite sequence of transitions ρ: $((\mathsf{src}, \mathsf{src}), 0) \xrightarrow{\left[\begin{smallmatrix} (s_1, 2) \\ (s_2, 4) \end{smallmatrix}\right]} ((s_1, \mathsf{src}), 2)$ $\xrightarrow{\left[\begin{smallmatrix} (s_2, 4) \\ (s_2, 4) \end{smallmatrix}\right]} ((s_2, s_2), 4) \left(\xrightarrow{\left[\begin{smallmatrix} (\mathsf{tgt}, 5+k) \\ (\mathsf{tgt}, 5+k) \end{smallmatrix}\right]} ((\mathsf{tgt}, \mathsf{tgt}), 5+k) \right)_{k \ge 0}$ is a play in $\mathcal{N}$ such that $\mathsf{cost}_1(\rho) = 2 \cdot (5 \cdot 2) + 2 \cdot (1 \cdot 1) + 1 \cdot (3 \cdot 2) = 28$ and $\mathsf{cost}_2(\rho) = 2 \cdot (5 \cdot 2) + 2 \cdot (5 \cdot 1) + 1 \cdot (3 \cdot 2) = 36$.

Let us now consider two trajectories $\pi_1\colon (\mathsf{src},0)(s_1,2)(s_2,4)(\mathsf{tgt},5+k)_{k\geq 0}$ and $\pi_2\colon (\mathsf{src},0)(s_2,4)(\mathsf{tgt},5+k)_{k\geq 0}$ together with σ_1, a blind strategy of Player 1, and σ_2, a blind strategy of Player 2, such that $\langle\sigma_1\rangle_{\mathsf{st}} = \pi_1$ and $\langle\sigma_2\rangle_{\mathsf{st}} = \pi_2$. The outcome of the strategy profile (σ_1,σ_2) from st is ρ, i.e., $\langle\sigma_1,\sigma_2\rangle_{\mathsf{st}} = \rho$.   ◁

Social Optima and Nash Equilibria. Let $\mathcal{G}$ be a concurrent game. The *social welfare* of a play ρ in $\mathcal{G}$ is the sum of the costs of the players along ρ: $\mathrm{SW}(\rho) = \sum_{1\leq i\leq n}\mathsf{cost}_i(\rho)$. The social welfare of a strategy profile is the social welfare of its outcome.

A strategy profile σ from the starting configuration st is a social optimum (SO) whenever $\mathrm{SW}(\langle\sigma\rangle_{\mathsf{st}}) = \inf_{\sigma'\in\Sigma(\mathsf{st})}\mathrm{SW}(\langle\sigma'\rangle_{\mathsf{st}})$. When no ambiguity arises, social optimum may also refer to the social welfare of socially-optimal strategy profiles. Notice that since we consider discrete time, this value is an integer, and a strategy profile realizing the social optimum always exists.

A strategy profile σ from st is a *Nash equilibrium* (NE) if for all $1\leq i\leq n$, for all strategies $\sigma_i'\in\Sigma_i(\mathsf{st})$ of Player i, $\mathsf{cost}_i(\langle\sigma\rangle_{\mathsf{st}})\leq\mathsf{cost}_i(\langle\sigma_{-i},\sigma_i'\rangle_{\mathsf{st}})$: for all $1\leq i\leq n$, the strategy σ_i of Player i is (one of) the best strategies against the strategies σ_{-i} of the other players.

Example 4. We show an example of a Nash equilibrium from st in the two-player symmetric TNG described in Example 2. The strategy of Player 1, denoted by σ_1, is given by a blind strategy associated with the trajectory $\pi_1 = (\mathsf{src},0)(s_3,1)(\mathsf{tgt},2+k)_{k\geq 0}$. The strategy of Player 2, denoted by σ_2, is a more involved. The first action of Player 2 from the timed configuration st is $(\mathsf{src},1)$, then at time 1 they observe if Player 1 has complied with their strategy, i.e., if Player 1 is in s_3. If so, Player 2 moves to s_4 at time 2, to s_5 at time 4, and ends in tgt at time 5; otherwise, they wait in src in order to observe the exact deviation of Player 1, and punish them adequately, by moving from src to s_5 at time 4 if Player 1 is in s_4 or to s_2 otherwise, and ending in tgt at time 5. The outcome $\langle\sigma_1,\sigma_2\rangle_{\mathsf{st}}$ of this strategy profile from st is:

$$\rho\colon \mathsf{st} \xrightarrow{\begin{bmatrix}(s_3,1)\\(\mathsf{src},1)\end{bmatrix}} ((s_3,\mathsf{src}),1) \xrightarrow{\begin{bmatrix}(\mathsf{tgt},2)\\(s_4,2)\end{bmatrix}} ((\mathsf{tgt},s_4),2) \xrightarrow{\begin{bmatrix}(\mathsf{tgt},3)\\(s_5,4)\end{bmatrix}} ((\mathsf{tgt},s_4),3)$$

$$\xrightarrow{\begin{bmatrix}(\mathsf{tgt},4)\\(s_5,4)\end{bmatrix}} ((\mathsf{tgt},s_5),4) \left(\xrightarrow{\begin{bmatrix}(\mathsf{tgt},5+k)\\(\mathsf{tgt},5+k)\end{bmatrix}} ((\mathsf{tgt},\mathsf{tgt}),5+k)\right)_{k\geq 0}.$$

We have that $\mathrm{Cost}_1(\rho) = 26$ and $\mathsf{cost}_2(\rho) = 20$. In particular, the social welfare of ρ is $\mathrm{SW}(\rho) = 46$.

We can prove that (σ_1,σ_2) is a Nash equilibrium. We only explain here the interest of the threat of punishment of Player 2 by considering the deviating strategy σ_1' of Player 1 such that he moves from src to s_1 at time 2, to s_2 at time 4 and ends in tgt at time 5. The outcome $\langle\sigma_1',\sigma_2\rangle_{\mathsf{st}}$ of this new strategy profile from st is

$$\rho': \mathsf{st} \xrightarrow{\begin{bmatrix} (s_1,2) \\ (\mathsf{src},1) \end{bmatrix}} ((\mathsf{src},\mathsf{src}),1) \xrightarrow{\begin{bmatrix} (s_1,2) \\ (\mathsf{src},2) \end{bmatrix}} ((s_1,\mathsf{src}),2) \xrightarrow{\begin{bmatrix} (s_2,4) \\ (s_2,4) \end{bmatrix}}$$

$$((s_2,s_2),4)\left(\xrightarrow{\begin{bmatrix} (\mathsf{tgt},5+k) \\ (\mathsf{tgt},5+k) \end{bmatrix}} ((\mathsf{tgt},\mathsf{tgt}),5+k) \right)_{k \geq 0}.$$

The new cost of Player 1 is $\mathsf{cost}_1(\rho') = 28$ proving that σ_1' is not a provitable deviation for Player 1 w.r.t. (σ_1,σ_2).

Remark that if Player 2 does not apply this punishment and moves to s_4 at time 2 whatever the behavior of Player 1, playing the deviating strategy σ_1' would be a profitable deviation for Player 1.   ◁

2.2   Studied Problems

Given a timed network game $\mathcal{N}$, the price of anarchy of $\mathcal{N}$, denoted by $\mathrm{PoA}_{\mathcal{N}}$, is the ratio between the worst social welfare of a Nash equilibrium and the social optimum. Similarly, the *price of stability* of $\mathcal{N}$, denoted by $\mathrm{PoS}_{\mathcal{N}}$, is the ratio between the best social welfare of a Nash equilibrium and the social optimum. Those values measure the impact of playing selfishly. In this paper, we address the following three problems:

Problem 1 (Constrained social welfare). Given a timed network game $\mathcal{N}$ and a threshold $x \in \mathbb{N}$, is the social optimum in $\mathcal{N}$ less than or equal to x?

Problem 2 (Constrained existence of a Nash equilibrium). Given a timed network game $\mathcal{N}$ with n players and a family of linear constraints $(\phi_q)_q$ over n variables, does there exist a Nash equilibrium σ from st such that all constraints $\phi_q(\mathsf{cost}(\langle\sigma\rangle_{\mathsf{st}}))$ are satisfied?

Problem 3 (Constrained price of anarchy and stability). Given a timed network game $\mathcal{N}$ and a threshold $x \in \mathbb{N}$, is the price of anarchy (resp. of stability) in $\mathcal{N}$ less than or equal to x?

Theorem 4. *The constrained-social-welfare problem is in* PSPACE *in the symmetric case, and in* EXPSPACE *in the asymmetric setting. The constrained existence of a Nash equilibrium and constrained price of anarchy and stability are in* EXPSPACE *in both the symmetric and asymmetric cases.*

3   Existence and Computation of Nash Equilibria

We first notice that, similarly to the untimed case [8], there are more Nash equilibria in non-blind strategies than when restricting to blind strategies:

Proposition 5. *There exists a timed network game $\mathcal{N}$ that admits a Nash equilibrium σ from* st*, and whose all blind Nash equilibria τ from* st *are such that* $\mathrm{SW}(\langle\sigma\rangle_{st}) < \mathrm{SW}(\langle\tau\rangle_{st})$.

In this section, we transform the infinite concurrent game associated with a timed network congestion game into a finite one, preserving the set of costs of Nash equilibria. We use this finite game to solve the constrained-Nash-equilibrium problem, and then explain how to compute witnessing Nash equilibria.

3.1   Transformation into an Equivalent Finite Concurrent Game

Let $\mathcal{N} = (n, \mathcal{A}, (\mathsf{src}_i, \mathsf{tgt}_i)_{1 \leq i \leq n})$ be a timed network game, and M be the largest integer appearing in the guards of $\mathcal{A}$. In our assumption of Remark 2 that, for all $1 \leq i \leq n$, there must exist a trajectory $(v_j, d_j)_{j \in \mathbb{N}}$ from $(\mathsf{src}_i, 0)$ to $(\mathsf{tgt}_i, \delta_i)$ for some date δ_i, we can additionally require that $\delta_i \leq M + |V|$. Indeed, consider such a winning trajectory with minimal δ_i: then either $\delta_i \leq M$, or for some j_0, $d_{j_0-1} < M$ and $d_{j_0} \geq M$. Since M is the maximal constant appearing in the guard of $\mathcal{A}$, we can then modify the dates after d_{j_0} so that $d_{j_0} = M$ and $d_{j_0+k} = M + k$, while still satisfying the guards.

Let $\kappa = \max_{v \in V} \mathsf{wgt}(v)(n)$ be the maximum cost per time unit that may occur in the game. With the arguments above, all players can always ensure a cost of at most $K = \kappa \cdot (M + |V|)$. Since each time unit costs at least one cost unit, $\kappa \cdot (M + |V|)$ is also a bound on the maximum time within which any player must have reached their target vertex in any Nash equilibrium: if this were not the case, then that player would have a profitable deviation. It follows:

Lemma 6. *Let* $\rho = (s_k, \vec{a}_k, s'_k)_{k \geq 0}$ *be a play in* $\mathcal{G}$. *For all* $1 \leq i \leq n$, *if* $\mathsf{cost}_i(\rho)$ *is finite, then there exists a position* $k^* \leq \mathsf{cost}_i(\rho)$ *such that* $s_{k^*} = (c_{k^*}, d_{k^*})$ *with* $c_{k^*}(i) = \mathsf{tgt}_i$ *and* $d_{k^*} \leq \mathsf{cost}_i(\rho)$.

This applies to the particular case where ρ *is the outcome of a Nash equilibrium, since in this case, for all* $1 \leq i \leq n$, $\mathsf{cost}_i(\rho)$ *is finite, and bounded by* K.

Definition of the Finite Concurrent Game. From the lemma above, when looking for Nash equilibrium, we can unfold the concurrent game $\mathcal{G}$ into a tree (actually, a directed acyclic graph) and prune all subtrees at depth K. Formally:

Definition 7. *Let* $\mathcal{N}$ *be a timed network game, and* $K = \kappa \cdot (M + |V|)$. *With this timed network game, we associate the (finite) concurrent game* $\mathcal{G}^F = (States^F, Act^F, (Allow_i^F)_{1 \leq i \leq n}, Upd^F, (cost_i^F)_{1 \leq i \leq n})$ *defined as follows:*

- *$States^F = \{(c, d) \in TConf \mid 0 \leq d \leq K + 1\}$ is the set of time-bounded timed configurations;*
- *$Act^F = \{(v, d) \in Act \mid d \leq K + 1\} \cup \{(\bot, K + 1)\}$ is the finite set of actions;*
- *for any $1 \leq i \leq n$ and any state $(c, d) \in States^F$ with $d < K$, we have action $(v, d') \in Allow_i^F(c, d)$ if, and only if, $d < d' \leq K + 1$ and $(c(i), v) \in E$ and $d' \in guard(c(i), v)$. For states (c, d) with $d \geq K$, we have $Allow_i^F(c, d) = \{(\bot, K + 1)\}$. We write Mov^F for the set of action vectors. An action vector $\vec{a} = (a_i)_{1 \leq i \leq n}$ is in $Valid^F(c, d)$ if each a_i is in $Allow_i^F(c, d)$;*
- *for a state $s = (c, d)$ and a valid action vector $\vec{a} = (v_i, d'_i)_{1 \leq i \leq n}$, writing $m = \min\{d'_i \mid 1 \leq i \leq n\}$, we have $Upd^F(s, \vec{a}) = (c, K + 1)$ if $m = K + 1$, and $Upd^F(s, \vec{a}) = Upd(s, \vec{a})$ otherwise;*
- *in the same way as for (infinite) concurrent games, we let $Trans^F = \{(s, \vec{a}, s') \in States^F \times Mov^F \times States^F \mid \vec{a} \in Valid^F(s) \text{ and } s' = Upd^F(s, \vec{a})\}$ be the set of transitions of $\mathcal{G}^F$. Cost functions $cost_i^F$ are defined on $Trans^F$ in the same way as for $\mathcal{G}$: we set $cost_i^F((c, d), \vec{a}, (c', d'))$ as $(d' - d) \cdot wgt(c(i))(load_c(c(i)))$ if $d' \leq K$, and as 0 otherwise.*

Notice that States^F has size doubly-exponential in the size of the input, since the number of players is given in binary. We write $\mathcal{G}^F$ for the graph $(\mathsf{States}^F, \mathsf{Trans}^F)$. Plays, histories, costs and strategies are defined as for infinite concurrent games.

Remark 4. By construction of $\mathcal{G}^F$, any play $\rho = (s_k, \vec{a}_k, s'_k)_{k \geq 0}$ in $\mathcal{G}^F$ ends in a self-loop on some configuration $(c, K+1)$, where the only valid action vector $\vec{a}$ is such that $a_i = (\bot, K+1)$ for all $1 \leq i \leq n$. The prefix of ρ before entering this loop corresponds to a prefix of a play ρ' in $\mathcal{G}$, with the difference that some actions (with $d > K$) in $\mathcal{G}$ may not be available in $\mathcal{G}^F$, but can be modified by setting $d = K+1$. As a consequence, Lemma 6 also holds for plays in $\mathcal{G}^F$.

Also, since the set of actions is finite, and that there is a single available action in the terminal self-loop, there is a finite number of strategies in $\mathcal{G}^F$. ◁

We now establish a correspondence between the Nash equilibria of $\mathcal{G}^F$ and $\mathcal{G}$:

Theorem 8. *Let $\mathcal{N}$ be a timed network game and let $\mathcal{G}$ and $\mathcal{G}^F$ be its associated infinite and finite concurrent games. Let $x \in (\mathbb{N} \cup \{+\infty\})^n$. Then there exists a Nash equilibrium σ in $\mathcal{G}$ with $\mathsf{cost}(\langle \sigma \rangle_{\mathsf{st}}) = x$ if, and only if, there exists a Nash equilibrium τ in $\mathcal{G}^F$ with $\mathsf{cost}^F(\langle \tau \rangle_{\mathsf{st}}) = x$.*

We prove this result by establishing simulation relations between $\mathcal{G}$ and $\mathcal{G}^F$, satisfying special properties for Proposition 9 below to apply. We let $\sim_{\mathrm{BT}} \subseteq \mathsf{States} \times \mathsf{States}^F$ such that, for any $s_1 = (c_1, d_1) \in \mathsf{States}$ and for any $s_2 = (c_2, d_2) \in \mathsf{States}^F$, $s_1 \sim_{\mathrm{BT}} s_2$ if, and only if, either *(i)* $d_1 = d_2 < K$ and $c_1 = c_2$, or *(ii)* $d_1 > K$ and $d_2 > K$.

We then use this relation (and its inverse) in the following generic proposition in order to prove the correspondence between the Nash equilibria in $\mathcal{G}$ and $\mathcal{G}^F$:

Proposition 9. *Let $\mathcal{G} = (\mathsf{States}, \mathsf{Act}, (\mathsf{Allow}_i)_{1 \leq i \leq n}, \mathsf{Upd}, (\mathsf{cost}_i)_{1 \leq i \leq n})$ and $\mathcal{G}' = (\mathsf{States}', \mathsf{Act}', (\mathsf{Allow}'_i)_{1 \leq i \leq n}, \mathsf{Upd}', (\mathsf{cost}'_i)_{1 \leq i \leq n})$ be two n-player concurrent games, $s_0 \in \mathsf{States}$ and $s'_0 \in \mathsf{States}'$, and $\lhd \subseteq \mathsf{States} \times \mathsf{States}'$ be a relation such that*

1. *$s_0 \lhd s'_0$;*
2. *there exists $\lambda \in \mathbb{N}$ such that for any NE σ in $\mathcal{G}$ from s_0, for any $1 \leq i \leq n$, it holds $\mathsf{cost}_i(\langle \sigma \rangle_{s_0}) \leq \lambda$;*
3. *for all plays $\rho \in \mathsf{Plays}_{\mathcal{G}}$ and $\rho' \in \mathsf{Plays}_{\mathcal{G}'}$ such that $\rho \lhd \rho'$ (i.e., $\rho_j \lhd \rho'_j$ for all $j \in \mathbb{N}$), all $1 \leq i \leq n$, if $\mathsf{cost}_i(\rho) \leq \lambda$ or $\mathsf{cost}'_i(\rho') \leq \lambda$, then $\mathsf{cost}_i(\rho) = \mathsf{cost}'_i(\rho')$;*
4. *For all $s \in \mathsf{States}$, for all $\vec{a} \in \mathsf{Valid}(s)$, for all $s' \in \mathsf{States}'$, if $s \lhd s'$, then there exists $\vec{a}' \in \mathsf{Valid}'(s')$ such that:*
   (a) *$\mathsf{Upd}(s, \vec{a}) \lhd \mathsf{Upd}'(s', \vec{a}')$;*
   (b) *for all $1 \leq i \leq n$, for all $b'_i \in \mathsf{Allow}'_i(s')$, there exists $b_i \in \mathsf{Allow}_i(s)$ such that*
   $$\mathsf{Upd}(s, (a_{-i}, b_i)) \lhd \mathsf{Upd}'(s', (a'_{-i}, b'_i)).$$

Then for any Nash equilibrium σ in $\mathcal{G}$ from s_0, there exists a Nash equilibrium σ' in $\mathcal{G}'$ from s'_0 such that $\mathsf{cost}(\langle \sigma \rangle_{s_0}) = \mathsf{cost}'(\langle \sigma' \rangle_{s'_0})$.

3.2   Existence of Nash Equilibria

Theorem 10. *Let $\mathcal{N}$ be a timed network game and let $\mathcal{G}$ be its associated concurrent game. There exists a Nash equilibrium σ from* st *in $\mathcal{G}$.*

We prove this result using a *potential function* Ψ [17]; a potential function is a function that assigns a non-negative real value to each strategy profile, and decreases when the profile is *improved* (in a sense that we explain below). Since those improvements are performed among a finite set of strategy profiles, this entails convergence of the sequence of improvements.

An *improvement* consists in changing the strategy of one of the players by a better strategy for that player (if any), in the sense that their individual cost descreases. Because the game admits a potential function over finitely many strategies, this *best-response dynamics* must converge in finitely many steps, and the limit is a strategy profile where no single player can improve their strategy, *i.e.*, a Nash equilibrium.

We prove that timed network games admit a potential function when considering winning blind strategies; hence there exists Nash equilibria for that set of strategies. We then prove that a Nash equilibrium in this restricted setting remains a Nash equilibrium w.r.t. the set of all strategies.

For all $1 \leq i \leq n$, there are a finite number of strategies of Player i in $\mathcal{G}^F$. It follows that the set of winning blind strategies of Player i is also finite; we let

$$\Sigma_i^{WB} = \{\sigma_i \mid \sigma_i \text{ is a winning blind strategy of Player } i\}.$$

Let $\Sigma^{WB} = \Sigma_1^{WB} \times \ldots \times \Sigma_n^{WB}$; Σ^{WB} is a finite set of strategy profiles. We consider a restriction of $\mathcal{G}^F$ in which for all $1 \leq i \leq n$, Player i is only allowed to play a strategy in Σ_i^{WB}. A Σ^{WB}-Nash equilibrium then is a strategy profile in Σ^{WB} such that for all $1 \leq i \leq n$, Player i has no profitable deviation *in* Σ_i^{WB}. The next proposition implies that $\mathcal{G}^F$ always admits Σ^{WB}-Nash equilibria [17].

Proposition 11. *Let $\mathcal{N}$ be a timed network game and let $\mathcal{G}^F$ be its associated finite concurrent game and Σ^{WB} be the set of winning blind strategy profiles. The game $\mathcal{G}^F$ restricted to strategy profiles in Σ^{WB} has a potential function.*

Moreover each Σ^{WB}-Nash equilibrium corresponds to a Nash equilibrium with the same cost profile (Proposition 12). Notice that the converse result fails to hold, as proved in Proposition 5.

Proposition 12. *Let $\mathcal{N}$ be a timed network game. Let $\mathcal{G}^F$ be its associated finite concurrent game, and Σ^{WB} the set of winning blind strategy profiles. If there exists a Σ^{WB}-Nash equilibrium σ in $\mathcal{G}^F$ from* st, *then there exists a Nash equilibrium τ from* st *in $\mathcal{G}^F$ with the same costs for all players.*

3.3   Computation of Nash Equilibria

Characterization of Outcomes of Nash Equilibria. In this section, we develop an algorithm for deciding (and computing) the existence of a Nash equilibrium

satisfying a given constraint on the costs of the outcome. We do this by computing the maximal punishment that a coalition can inflict to a deviating player.
This value can be computed using classical techniques in a two-player zero-sum
concurrent game: from a timed configuration $s = (c, d)$, this value is defined as

$$\underline{\mathrm{Val}}_i(s) = \sup_{\sigma_{-i} \in \Sigma_{-i}(s)} \inf_{\sigma_i \in \Sigma_i(s)} \mathrm{cost}_i(\langle \sigma_{-i}, \sigma_i \rangle_s).$$

For all histories $h = (s_k, \vec{a}_k, s_k')_{0 \le k < \ell}$ in $\mathrm{Hist}_{\mathcal{G}^F}(s)$, we let $\mathrm{Visit}(h)$ be the
set of players who visit their target vertex along h. Formally, for the empty
history from $s = (c, d)$, we let $\mathrm{Visit}(h) = \{1 \le i \le n \mid c(i) = \mathsf{tgt}_i\}$. If $h =
(s_k, \vec{a}_k, s_k')_{0 \le k < \ell}$ is non-empty, writing $s_k = (c_k, d_k)$ for all $0 \le k \le \ell$, we have
$\mathrm{Visit}(h) = \{1 \le i \le n \mid \exists 1 \le k \le \ell.\ c_k(i) = \mathsf{tgt}_i\}$.

The following theorem is a characterization of outcomes of Nash equilibria.
Similar characterizations were proven in [8] for (untimed) network congestion
games, and in [1,13] for generic concurrent games:

Theorem 13. *Let $\mathcal{N}$ be a timed network congestion game and $\mathcal{G}^F$ be its asso-
ciated finite concurrent game. A play $\rho = (s_k, \vec{a}_k, s_k')_{k \in \mathbb{N}} \in \mathrm{Plays}_{\mathcal{G}^F}(\mathsf{st})$ is the
outcome of a Nash equilibrium from st in $\mathcal{G}^F$ if, and only if,*

$$\forall 1 \le i \le n.\ \forall k \in \mathbb{N}.\ \forall b_i \in \mathsf{Allow}_i^F(s_k).\ i \notin \mathrm{Visit}(\rho_{<k}) \implies$$
$$\mathrm{cost}_i^F(\rho_{\ge k}) \le \underline{\mathrm{Val}}_i(s') + \mathrm{cost}_i^F(s_k, (\vec{a}_{k,-i}, b_i), s') \quad (1)$$

where $s' = \mathsf{Upd}^F(s_k, (\vec{a}_{k,-i}, b_i))$.

The values $\underline{\mathrm{Val}}_i(s)$ can be computed by transforming the finite game $\mathcal{G}^F$ into
a two-player game, since the deviating player competes against the coalition of
all the other players. In this transformation, we do not need to keep track of
the position of all the other players individually, since their aim now only is to
maximize the cost for the deviating player. This two-player game thus has size
exponential, and each $\underline{\mathrm{Val}}_i(s)$ can be computed in exponential time. Then:

Proposition 14. *Problem 2 can be decided in EXPSPACE, both for the symmetric and for the asymmetric cases.*

Proof. Let $\mathcal{N}$ be a timed network game and $(\phi_q)_q$ be a set of linear constraints.
We prove that we can decide in exponential space the existence of a Nash equi-
librium σ in $\mathcal{G}^F$ such that $\mathrm{cost}^F(\langle \sigma \rangle_{\mathsf{st}})$ satisfies all linear constraints $(\phi_q)_q$. By
Theorem 8, this entails the same result in $\mathcal{G}$.

As already argued, each play ρ in $\mathcal{G}^F$ ends up in a loop after at most K steps.
Our algorithm will guess such a play until the loop; the play can be stored in
exponential space. The algorithm will then check that it is a valid play, that Eq. 1
holds at each step (which requires to compute $\underline{\mathrm{Val}}$), compute the costs paid by the
players until they reach their targets, and check that the cost constraints $(\phi_q)_q$
are satisfied.

This algorithm uses pseudo-polynomial space, as it has to store a polynomial
quantity of data for each player. Notice that the algorithm would not store all
$\underline{\mathrm{Val}}$ values as the number of values would be doubly-exponential; instead, it will
re-compute those values on-demand. □

Remark 5. Our definition of plays and histories include the action vectors at each step, which implies that strategies observe the actions of all players and can base their decisions on that information. In our setting, however, it is possible to identify one of the deviating players based only on the configurations; in particular, if a single player deviates, they can be identified and punished. As a consequence, our results still hold in the setting where strategies may only depend on the sequence of timed configurations.   ◁

4   Social Optimality and Prices of Anarchy and Stability

In this section, given a timed network game $\mathcal{N}$, we study the social optimum $SO_{\mathcal{N}}$. In order to obtain the best social welfare, the players aim at minimizing the sum of their costs whatever their selfish interrest. Thus we want to find a play from st in the concurrent game $\mathcal{G}$ such that the sum of the costs of all the players is as small as possible. We also consider the price of stability $PoS_{\mathcal{N}}$ (resp. of anarchy $PoA_{\mathcal{N}}$) to know how far is the social optimum from the best (resp. worst) social welfare of a Nash equilibrium from st in $\mathcal{N}$.

Before studying the social optimum and the prices of anarchy and stability, we explain how to solve the constrained-social-welfare problem both in asymmetric and symmetric timed network games. First notice that the following lemma is a consequence of Lemma 6:

Lemma 15. *For all plays $\rho \in \mathrm{Plays}_{\mathcal{G}}(st)$ such that $SW(\rho)$ is finite, for all $i \in [\![n]\!]$, there exists $k_i \leq SW(\rho)$ such that $\rho_{k_i} = (c_{k_i}, d_{k_i})$ with (i) $c_{k_i}(i) = tgt_i$ and (ii) $d_{k_i} \leq SW(\rho)$.*

4.1   Constrained-Social-Welfare Problem: Asymmetric Case

First of all, let us assume that the players' objectives are asymmetric. In this setting, Problem 1 can be solved by non-deterministically guessing a (finite) play in $\mathcal{G}$ step-by-step: Lemma 15 gives a polynomial bound on the size of the configurations to be guessed; keeping track of the set of players who reached their targets requires exponential space. By Savitch's theorem, we get:

Proposition 16. *The constrained-social-welfare problem (Problem 1) can be decided in EXPSPACE if the players' objectives are asymmetric.*

4.2   Constrained-Social-Welfare Problem: Symmetric Case

For symmetric TNGs, the objectives of the players are identical: there exist src and tgt in V such that $src_i = src$ and $tgt_i = tgt$ for all $1 \leq i \leq n$.

We could of course reuse the algorithm we developed for the asymmetric case, resulting in an EXPSPACE algorithm. Nevertheless, we can refine this approach by considering a weighted graph in which we only take into account *abstract timed configurations*. An abstract timed configuration $\tilde{c}$ is a tuple $(P_A, P_W, d) \in$

$[0, n]^V \times [0, n]^V \times \mathbb{N}$ where (i) P_A maps each vertex to the number of *active players* (players who have not visited the target vertex yet) in that vertex; (ii) P_W maps each vertex to the number of *winning players* (players who have already visited their target set) in that vertex and (iii) d is the current time.

Abstract timed configurations store enough information to compute the social welfare of a play in symmetric TNGs and give rise to a weighted graph $\mathcal{W} = (A, B, \tilde{w})$. The set A is the set of abstract timed configurations, $B \subseteq A \times A$ is the set of edges such that there exists an edge $(\tilde{c}_1, \tilde{c}_2) \in B$ between two abstract timed configurations $\tilde{c}_1$ and $\tilde{c}_2$ if there exists a valid action for each player regarding their position given by $\tilde{c}_1$ such that updating P_A, P_B and the current time w.r.t. this action vector leads to the abstract configuration $\tilde{c}_2$. The weight function $\tilde{w} \colon B \to \mathbb{N}$ represents the sum of the costs of active players for an edge. Notice that the winning players are taken into account to compute the cost of an active player since their presence in a vertex influences the load in that vertex.

A path p in $\mathcal{W}$ is a finite sequence of abstract timed configurations consistent with the graph structure (A, B), starting from the initial vertex $(\tilde{\mathsf{st}}; \{0\}^V; 0)$ (assuming src $\neq$ tgt) with $\tilde{\mathsf{st}} \colon V \to [0, n] : v \mapsto \#\{1 \le i \le n \mid \mathrm{init}(i) = v\}$. The cost of a path p in $\mathcal{W}$ is either the sum of the weights $\tilde{w}(a_1, a_2)$ along the path until visiting a final vertex (where $P_A(v) = 0$ for all $v \in V$), or $+\infty$ if no such vertices appear along p. Clearly enough, the abstract weighted graph encodes the trajectories of $\mathcal{N}$ in the following sense:

Lemma 17. *Let $\mathcal{N}$ be a timed network game and $\mathcal{W}$ be its associated abstract weighted graph. For all $c \in \mathbb{N}$, there exists a play $\rho \in \mathrm{Plays}_\mathcal{G}(\mathsf{st})$ such that $\mathrm{SW}(\rho) = c$ if, and only if, there exists a path p in $\mathcal{W}$ with cost c.*

The constrained-social-welfare problem for symmetric objectives can then be solved by non-deterministically guessing the successive vertices of a path p in $\mathcal{W}$, step-by-step. The constraint c gives a bound on the length of the path, so that the algorithm runs in polynomial space.

Proposition 18. *The constrained-social-welfare problem (Problem 1) can be decided in PSPACE if the players' objectives are symmetric.*

4.3 Social Optimum and Prices of Anarchy and Stability

Optimum Social. We now explain how we can compute the exact social optimum: noticing that the social optimum can be bounded by $n \cdot K$, it can be computed by performing a binary search, iteratively applying the algorithm above. Computing the social optimum can thus be performed in polynomial space in the symmetric case, and exponential space in the asymmetric case.

Prices of Anarchy and Stability. The constrained-price-of-anarchy (resp. stability) problem can now be solved using our algorithms for solving the constrained-social-welfare and constrained-Nash-equilibrium problems: thanks to the pseudo-polynomial bound $n \cdot K$ on the social welfare of the social optimum and on the social welfare of any Nash equilibrium, and the fact that those values are integers, we can perform binary searches for the exact social welfare of the social optimum and for the worst (resp. best) social welfare of a Nash equilibrium. This only requires a polynomial number of iterations, so that the whole algorithm runs in exponential space.

References

1. Almagor, S., Alur, R., Bansal, S.: Equilibria in quantitative concurrent games (2018)
2. Altman, E., Kumar, A., Hayel, Y.: A potential game approach for uplink resource allocation in a multichannel wireless access network. In: Proceedings of the Fourth International ICST Conference on Performance Evaluation Methodologies and Tools, pp. 1–9 (2009)
3. Alur, R., Henzinger, T.A., Kupferman, O.: Alternating-time temporal logic. J. ACM **49**(5), 672–713 (2002). https://doi.org/10.1145/585265.585270
4. Anshelevich, E., Dasgupta, A., Kleinberg, J., Tardos, É., Wexler, T., Roughgarden, T.: The price of stability for network design with fair cost allocation. In: Proceedings of the 45th Annual Symposium on Foundations of Computer Science (FOCS 2004), pp. 295–304. IEEE Computer Society Press, October 2004. https://doi.org/10.1109/FOCS.2004.68
5. Avni, G., Guha, S., Kupferman, O.: Timed network games. In: Larsen, K.G., Bodlaender, H.L., Raskin, J.F. (eds.) Proceedings of the 42nd International Symposium on Mathematical Foundations of Computer Science (MFCS 2017). Leibniz International Proceedings in Informatics, vol. 84, pp. 37:1–37:16. Leibniz-Zentrum für Informatik, August 2017. https://doi.org/10.4230/LIPIcs.MFCS.2017.37
6. Avni, G., Guha, S., Kupferman, O.: Timed network games with clocks. In: Potapov, I., Spirakis, P.G., Worrell, J. (eds.) Proceedings of the 43rd International Symposium on Mathematical Foundations of Computer Science (MFCS 2018). Leibniz International Proceedings in Informatics, vol. 117, pp. 23:1–23:18. Leibniz-Zentrum für Informatik (Aug 2018). https://doi.org/10.4230/LIPIcs.MFCS.2018.23
7. Awerbuch, B., Azar, Y., Epstein, A.: The price of routing unsplittable flow. In: Proceedings of the Thirty-Seventh Annual ACM Symposium on Theory of Computing, STOC 2005, pp. 57–66. Association for Computing Machinery, New York (2005). https://doi.org/10.1145/1060590.1060599
8. Bertrand, N., Markey, N., Sadhukhan, S., Sankur, O.: Dynamic network congestion games. In: Saxena, N., Simon, S. (eds.) FSTTCS 2020. LIPIcs, vol. 182, pp. 40:1–40:16. Schloss Dagstuhl - Leibniz-Zentrum für Informatik (2020)
9. Bhaskar, U., Fleischer, L., Anshelevich, E.: A stackelberg strategy for routing flow over time. Games Econ. Behav. **92**, 232–247 (2015). https://doi.org/10.1016/j.geb.2013.09.004
10. Christodoulou, G., Koutsoupias, E.: The price of anarchy of finite congestion games. In: Proceedings of the Thirty-Seventh Annual ACM Symposium on Theory of Computing, STOC 2005, pp. 67–73. Association for Computing Machinery, New York (2005). https://doi.org/10.1145/1060590.1060600
11. Goeminne, A., Markey, N., Sankur, O.: Non-blind strategies in timed network congestion games. Technical report (2022). arXiv:2207.01537
12. Hoefer, M., Mirrokni, V.S., Röglin, H., Teng, S.H.: Competitive routing over time. Theoret. Comput. Sci. **412**(39), 5420–5432 (2011). https://doi.org/10.1016/j.tcs.2011.05.055

13. Klimoš, M., Larsen, K.G., Štefaňák, F., Thaarup, J.: Nash equilibria in concurrent priced games. In: Dediu, A.H., Martín-Vide, C. (eds.) Language and Automata Theory and Applications, pp. 363–376. Springer, Heidelberg (2012)
14. Koch, R., Skutella, M.: Nash equilibria and the price of anarchy for flows over time. Theory Comput. Syst. **49**(1), 71–97 (2011). https://doi.org/10.1007/s00224-010-9299-y
15. Koutsoupias, E., Papadimitriou, C.: Worst-case equilibria. Comput. Sci. Rev. **3**(2), 65–69 (2009). https://doi.org/10.1016/j.cosrev.2009.04.003, https://www.sciencedirect.com/science/article/pii/S1574013709000203
16. Koutsoupias, E., Papakonstantinopoulou, K.: Contention issues in congestion games. In: Czumaj, A., Mehlhorn, K., Pitts, A., Wattenhofer, R. (eds.) ICALP 2012. LNCS, vol. 7392, pp. 623–635. Springer, Heidelberg (2012). https://doi.org/10.1007/978-3-642-31585-5_55
17. Monderer, D., Shapley, L.S.: Potential games. Games Econ. Behav. **14**(1), 124–143 (1996). https://doi.org/10.1006/game.1996.0044
18. Nisan, N., Roughgarden, T., Tardos, E., Vazirani, V.V.: Algorithmic Game Theory. Cambridge University Press, New York (2007)
19. Penn, M., Polukarov, M., Tennenholtz, M.: Random order congestion games. Math. Oper. Res. **34**(3), 706–725 (2009). https://doi.org/10.1287/moor.1090.0394
20. Qiu, L., Yang, R., Zhang, Y., Shenker, S.: On selfish routing in internet-like environments. IEEE Trans. Comput. **14**(4), 725–738 (2006). https://doi.org/10.1109/TNET.2006.880179
21. Rosenthal, R.W.: The network equilibrium problem in integers. Networks **3**, 53–59 (1973)
22. Roughgarden, T.: Routing games. In: Nisan, N., Roughgarden, T., Tardos, É., Vazirani, V.V. (eds.) Algorithmic Game Theory, chap. 18, pp. 461–486. Cambridge University Press (2007)

Efficient Convex Zone Merging
in Parametric Timed Automata

Étienne André[1], Dylan Marinho[1]([✉]), Laure Petrucci[2],
and Jaco van de Pol[3]

[1] Université de Lorraine, CNRS, Inria, LORIA, 54000 Nancy, France
dylan.marinho@loria.fr
[2] LIPN, CNRS UMR 7030, Université Sorbonne Paris Nord, Villetaneuse, France
[3] Aarhus University, Aarhus, Denmark

Abstract. Parametric timed automata are a powerful formalism for reasoning on concurrent real-time systems with unknown or uncertain timing constants. Reducing their state space is a significant way to reduce the inherently large analysis times. We present here different merging reduction techniques based on convex union of constraints (parametric zones), allowing to decrease the number of states while preserving the correctness of verification and synthesis results. We perform extensive experiments, and identify the best heuristics in practice, bringing a significant decrease in the computation time on a benchmarks library.

1 Introduction

Parametric timed automata (PTAs) [2] are a powerful extension of timed automata (TAs) [1] with timing parameters, allowing to reason on concurrent real-time systems with unknown or uncertain timing constants. PTAs go beyond the expressiveness of the classical model checking problem of TAs (with a binary "yes"/"no" answer), and can address *parameter synthesis*, i.e. the exhibition of valuations for these timing parameters s.t. a given property holds. A common problem (addressed here) is that of *reachability synthesis*: "synthesize parameter valuations such that a given location is reachable".

PTAs are an inherently expressive but hard formalism, in the sense that most decision problems are undecidable (see e.g. [3] for a survey), while verification and parameter synthesis are subject to the infamous state space explosion in practice. Reducing the state space, built on-the-fly when performing parameter synthesis, is a significant way to reduce the sometimes large computation times.

The symbolic semantics of TAs is often represented as *zones*, i.e. linear constraints over the clocks with a special form. In [22], a convex zone merging technique is presented for UPPAAL, that preserves reachability properties. This merging technique was extended to PTAs in [7], and applied to the symbolic semantics of PTAs in the form of parametric zones, i.e. linear constraints over the clocks and the parameters, obeying to a special form [30]. In [7], the analysis

This work is partially supported by the ANR-NRF French-Singaporean research program ProMiS (ANR-19-CE25-0015) and CNRS-INS2I project TrAVAIL.

S. Bogomolov and D. Parker (Eds.): FORMATS 2022, LNCS 13465, pp. 200–218, 2022.
https://doi.org/10.1007/978-3-031-15839-1_12

is only performed in the framework of the "inverse method" (IM, also called "trace preservation synthesis" [8]); no other properties are considered.

Contributions. We propose here different merging techniques for PTAs, with the goal to reduce the state space size and/or the analysis time. We implement our techniques in IMITATOR [4], and we perform extensive experiments on a standard benchmarks set [10]. It turns out that these various heuristics have very different outcomes in terms of size of the state space and analysis speed. We then identify the best heuristics in practice, allowing to significantly decrease the number of states and the computation time, while preserving the correctness of the parameter synthesis for the whole class of reachability properties. The two main differences with [7] are *i*) the definition of merging for reachability synthesis (and not only for IM), and *ii*) the systematic investigation of new heuristics, leading to a largely increased efficiency w.r.t. the original merging of [7].

Related Work. As said above, merging was first proposed for TAs in [22], and then extended to the "inverse method" for PTAs in [7]. In [17], Ben Salah *et al.* show that it is safe to perform the convex merging of various constraints, when they are the result of an interleaving. The exploration is done in a BFS (breadth-first search) manner, and states are merged at each depth level.

Beyond merging, various heuristics were proposed to efficiently reduce the state space of TAs. Extrapolation and abstractions were proposed in [1, 16, 27, 28] for TAs, and then extended to PTAs in [9, 18]. Exploration orders were discussed in [29] and then in [11] for PTAs. The efficiency of model checking liveness properties for TAs is discussed notably in [25, 26]. Zone inclusion (subsumption) for liveness checking is discussed for TAs in [32] and for PTAs in [5]. Inclusion/subsumption is a special case of merging. The other mentioned techniques are orthogonal to the merging technique, and they can be combined.

In addition, computing efficiently exact or over-approximated successors of "zones" in the larger class of *hybrid automata* (HAs) [23] is an active field of research (e.g. [19–21, 34]). Beyond the target formalism (PTAs instead of HAs), a main difference is that we are concerned here exclusively with an *exact* analysis.

2   Preliminaries

We assume a set $\mathbb{X} = \{x_1, \ldots, x_H\}$ of *clocks*, i.e. real-valued variables that evolve over time at the same rate. A *clock valuation* is a function $\mu : \mathbb{X} \to \mathbb{R}_{\geq 0}$. The clock valuation $\mathbf{0}$ assigns 0 to all clocks. Given a delay $d \in \mathbb{R}_{\geq 0}$, $\mu + d$ denotes the valuation $(\mu + d)(x) = \mu(x) + d$, for $x \in \mathbb{X}$. Given $R \subseteq \mathbb{X}$, we define the *reset* of valuation μ by $[\mu]_R(x) = 0$ if $x \in R$, and $[\mu]_R(x) = \mu(x)$, otherwise.

We assume a set $\mathbb{P} = \{p_1, \ldots, p_M\}$ of *parameters*, i.e. unknown constants. A linear term is of the form $\sum_{1 \leq i \leq H} \alpha_i x_i + \sum_{1 \leq j \leq M} \beta_j p_j + d$, with $\alpha_i, \beta_j, d \in \mathbb{Z}$. A *constraint* $\mathbf{C}$ (i.e. a convex polyhedron) over $\mathbb{X} \cup \mathbb{P}$ is a conjunction of inequalities of the form $lt \bowtie 0$, where lt is a linear term and $\bowtie \in \{<, \leq, =, \geq, >\}$. A *parameter valuation* v is a function $v : \mathbb{P} \to \mathbb{Q}_{\geq 0}$. Given a parameter valuation v, $v(\mathbf{C})$

denotes the constraint over $\mathbb{X}$ obtained by replacing each parameter p in $\mathbf{C}$ with $v(p)$. Likewise, given a clock valuation μ, $\mu(v(\mathbf{C}))$ denotes the expression obtained by replacing each clock x in $v(\mathbf{C})$ with $\mu(x)$. We write $\mu \models v(\mathbf{C})$ if $\mu(v(\mathbf{C}))$ evaluates to true. We say that $\mathbf{C}$ is *satisfiable* if $\exists \mu, v$ s.t. $\mu \models v(\mathbf{C})$.

Definition 1 (PTA [2]). *A PTA $\mathcal{A}$ is a tuple $\mathcal{A} = (\Sigma, L, \ell_0, \mathbb{X}, \mathbb{P}, I, E)$, where: i) Σ is a finite set of actions, ii) L is a finite set of locations, iii) $\ell_0 \in L$ is the initial location, iv) $\mathbb{X}$ is a finite set of clocks, v) $\mathbb{P}$ is a finite set of parameters, vi) I is the invariant, assigning to every $\ell \in L$ a constraint $I(\ell)$, vii) E is a finite set of edges $e = (\ell, g, a, R, \ell')$ where $\ell, \ell' \in L$ are the source and target locations, $a \in \Sigma$, $R \subseteq \mathbb{X}$ are the clocks to be reset, and the guard g is a constraint.*

Given a parameter valuation v, $v(\mathcal{A})$ denotes the non-parametric TA [1], where all occurrences of any parameter p_i have been replaced by $v(p_i)$.

Definition 2 (Concrete semantics). *Given PTA $\mathcal{A} = (\Sigma, L, \ell_0, \mathbb{X}, \mathbb{P}, I, E)$, and a parameter valuation v, the concrete semantics of $v(\mathcal{A})$ is given by the timed transition system (TTS) [1,24] $T_{v(\mathcal{A})} = (S, s_0, \overset{e}{\mapsto} \cup \overset{d}{\mapsto})$, with*

- *$S = \{(\ell, \mu) \in L \times \mathbb{R}_{\geq 0}^H \mid \mu \models v(I(\ell))\}$, initial state $s_0 = (\ell_0, \mathbf{0})$,*
- *discrete transitions: $(\ell, \mu) \overset{e}{\mapsto} (\ell', \mu')$, if $(\ell, \mu), (\ell', \mu') \in S$, and there exists $e = (\ell, g, a, R, \ell') \in E$, such that $\mu' = [\mu]_R$, and $\mu \models v(g)$.*
- *delay transitions: $(\ell, \mu) \overset{d}{\mapsto} (\ell, \mu + d)$ for $d \in \mathbb{R}_{\geq 0}$, if $\forall d' \in [0, d], (\ell, \mu + d') \in S$.*

We write $(\ell, \mu) \overset{(d,e)}{\longrightarrow} (\ell', \mu')$ for a combined step: $\exists \mu'' : (\ell, \mu) \overset{d}{\mapsto} (\ell, \mu'') \overset{e}{\mapsto} (\ell', \mu')$.

Given a TA $v(\mathcal{A})$ with concrete semantics $T_{v(\mathcal{A})} = (S, s_0, \rightarrow)$, we refer to the states of $T_{v(\mathcal{A})}$ as the *concrete states* of $v(\mathcal{A})$. A *run* of $v(\mathcal{A})$ is a (finite or infinite) alternating sequence of concrete states of $v(\mathcal{A})$ and pairs of delay and discrete transitions starting from the initial state s_0 of the form $s_0, (d_0, e_0), s_1, \cdots$ with $i = 0, 1, \ldots$, $e_i \in E$, $d_i \in \mathbb{R}_{\geq 0}$ and $s_i \overset{(d_i, e_i)}{\longrightarrow} s_{i+1}$.

Given a state $s = (\ell, \mu)$, we say that s is reachable in $v(\mathcal{A})$ if s appears in a run of $v(\mathcal{A})$. By extension, we say that ℓ is reachable in $v(\mathcal{A})$.

Symbolic Semantics. We recall the symbolic semantics of PTAs [6,30,31]. Define the *time elapsing* of $\mathbf{C}$, denoted by $\mathbf{C}^{\nearrow}$, as the constraint over $\mathbb{X}$ and $\mathbb{P}$ obtained by delaying all clocks in $\mathbf{C}$ by an arbitrary amount of time. That is, $\mu' \models v(\mathbf{C}^{\nearrow})$ if $\exists \mu : \mathbb{X} \rightarrow \mathbb{R}_{\geq 0}, \exists d \in \mathbb{R}_{\geq 0}$ s.t. $\mu \models v(\mathbf{C}) \wedge \mu' = \mu + d$. Given $R \subseteq \mathbb{X}$, define the *reset* of $\mathbf{C}$, denoted by $[\mathbf{C}]_R$, as the constraint obtained from $\mathbf{C}$ by resetting the clocks in R to 0, keeping other clocks unchanged. That is,

$$\mu' \models v([\mathbf{C}]_R) \text{ if } \exists \mu : \mathbb{X} \rightarrow \mathbb{R}_{\geq 0} \text{ s.t. } \mu \models v(\mathbf{C}) \wedge \forall x \in \mathbb{X} \begin{cases} \mu'(x) = 0 & \text{if } x \in R \\ \mu'(x) = \mu(x) & \text{otherwise.} \end{cases}$$

We denote by $\mathbf{C}\!\downarrow_{\mathbb{P}}$ the projection of $\mathbf{C}$ onto $\mathbb{P}$, i.e. obtained by eliminating the variables not in $\mathbb{P}$ (e.g. using Fourier-Motzkin). The application of one of these operations (time elapsing, reset, projection) to a constraint yields a constraint; existential quantification can be handled, e.g. by adding variables and subsequently eliminating them using, e.g. Fourier-Motzkin.

A symbolic state is a pair $(\ell, \mathbf{C})$ where $\ell \in L$ is a location, and $\mathbf{C}$ its associated constraint over $\mathbb{X} \cup \mathbb{P}$ called *parametric zone*.

Definition 3 (Symbolic semantics). *Given a PTA* $\mathcal{A} = (\Sigma, L, \ell_0, \mathbb{X}, \mathbb{P}, I, E)$, *the symbolic semantics of* $\mathcal{A}$ *is the labelled transition system called* parametric zone graph $\mathbf{PZG} = (E, \mathbf{S}, \mathbf{s}_0, \Rightarrow)$, *with*

- $\mathbf{S} = \{(\ell, \mathbf{C}) \mid \mathbf{C} \subseteq I(\ell)\}$, $\mathbf{s}_0 = (\ell_0, (\bigwedge_{1 \leq i \leq H} x_i = 0)^{\nearrow} \wedge I(\ell_0))$, *and*
- $((\ell, \mathbf{C}), e, (\ell', \mathbf{C}')) \in \Rightarrow$ *if* $e = (\ell, g, a, R, \ell') \in E$ *and* $\mathbf{C}' = ([(\mathbf{C} \wedge g)]_R \wedge I(\ell'))^{\nearrow} \wedge I(\ell')$ *with* $\mathbf{C}'$ *satisfiable.*

That is, in the parametric zone graph, nodes are symbolic states, and arcs are labeled by *edges* of the original PTA. Given a symbolic state $\mathbf{s}$ reachable in $\mathbf{PZG}$, we define $\mathsf{SuccE}(\mathbf{s})$, successors with edges, by $\{(e, \mathbf{s}') \mid (\mathbf{s}, e, \mathbf{s}') \in \Rightarrow\}$. We also write $\mathbf{s} \Rightarrow \mathbf{s}'$ to denote that for some e, $(\mathbf{s}, e, \mathbf{s}') \in \Rightarrow$. Given $\mathbf{t} = (\mathbf{s}, e, \mathbf{s}') \in \Rightarrow$, $\mathbf{t}.source$ denotes $\mathbf{s}$ while $\mathbf{t}.target$ denotes $\mathbf{s}'$. Given $\mathbf{s} = (\ell, \mathbf{C})$, $\mathbf{s}.constr$ denotes $\mathbf{C}$ while $\mathbf{s}.loc$ denotes ℓ. Note that we usually use bold font to denote anything symbolic, i.e. (sets of) symbolic states, and constraints.

A well-known result [30] is that, given a PTA $\mathcal{A}$ and a reachable symbolic state $(\ell, \mathbf{C})$, if a parameter valuation v belongs to the projection onto the parameters of $\mathbf{C}$ (i.e. $v \in \mathbf{C}{\downarrow}_\mathbb{P}$), then ℓ is reachable in the TA $v(\mathcal{A})$.

The *(symbolic) state space* of a PTA is its parametric zone graph. This structure is in general infinite, due to the intrinsic undecidability of most decision problems for PTAs. However, for semi-algorithms for parameter synthesis (without a guarantee of termination), it is of utmost importance to *reduce* the size of this state space, so as to perform synthesis more efficiently.

3 Efficient State Merging in Parametric Timed Automata

3.1 Merging Algorithm

We recall the notion of merging from [7]. Two states are *mergeable* if 1) they share the same location, and 2) the union of their constraints is convex.

Definition 4 (Merging [7]). *Two symbolic states* $\mathbf{s}_1 = (\ell_1, \mathbf{C}_1)$, $\mathbf{s}_2 = (\ell_2, \mathbf{C}_2)$ *are* mergeable, *denoted by the predicate* is_mergeable$(\mathbf{s}_1, \mathbf{s}_2)$, *if* $\ell_1 = \ell_2$ *and* $\mathbf{C}_1 \cup \mathbf{C}_2$ *is convex. In that case, we define their* merging *as* $(\ell_1, \mathbf{C}_1 \cup \mathbf{C}_2)$.

Merging is a generalisation of inclusion abstraction (also known as subsumption). Note that if $\mathbf{s}_2$ includes $\mathbf{s}_1$, i.e. $\mathbf{C}_1 \subseteq \mathbf{C}_2$, then $\mathbf{C}_1 \cup \mathbf{C}_2 = \mathbf{C}_2$ is convex, so the states can be merged, and the result will be $\mathbf{s}_2$.

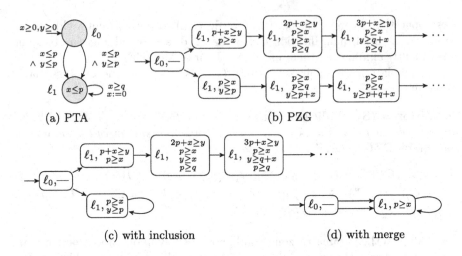

Fig. 1. Example with infinite PZG that becomes finite by merging

Example 1. We display examples of 2-dimensional zones in Fig. 2c. (These box-shaped parametric zones are fictitious and displayed for the purpose of illustration; similar zones, sometimes using "diagonal" edges, can be obtained from actual PTAs.) Zone C_1 can be merged with C_4; C_2 can also be merged with C_4. The result of these two merging operations is shown in Fig. 2g. These two new zones can also be merged together, leading to the zone in Fig. 2h.

Example 2. Let us now consider the PTA in Fig. 1a, with two clocks (x and y) and two parameters (p and q). Both clocks and parameters are initially bound to be non-negative (clocks initially different from 0 can be simulated using an appropriate gadget, omitted here).

The PZG of this PTA is shown in Fig. 1b. It features two separate infinite executions which depend on the first chosen transition. In the upper branch, the first state with location ℓ_1 has constraint $p + x \geq y$ (which can read $y - x \leq p$) since, although we have $y \leq p$ when taking the transition from ℓ_0, time can then elapse in ℓ_1—but only up to p time units, due to invariant $x \leq p$. Then coefficients on p (i.e. $2p$ then $3p$, etc.) start to appear from the second state with location ℓ_1 due to the self-loop on ℓ_1 that resets x.

Inclusion reduces one of these two symbolic executions, which exhibits decreasing zones, as in Fig. 1c. Even using inclusion, the PZG remains infinite.

Finally, Fig. 1d displays the graph obtained with the *merging* approach: the two states obtained after taking a single transition can be merged. Here, the PZG with merging becomes finite, which illustrates the importance of merging.

Algorithm 1 constructs the state space for a given PTA $\mathcal{A}$ by breadth-first search (BFS) from the initial state s_0. It computes the set of reachable states **Visited** by repeatedly adding the next layer of successor states $\mathbf{Q}_{new}$ (line 6), maintaining the transitions (line 7). Note that each iteration (line 9) calls a

---

Algorithm 1: BFS by layer layerBFS($\mathcal{A}$)

```
/* Building PZG = (E, Visited, s₀, ⇒)                              */
```
1 **Visited** ← {s₀} ; **Queue** ← {s₀} ; ⇒ ← ∅
2 **while Queue** ≠ ∅ **do**
3 | $\mathbf{Q}_{new}$ ← ∅
4 | **foreach s ∈ Queue do**
5 | | **foreach** $(e, \mathbf{s}')$ ∈ SuccE(s) **do**
6 | | | $\mathbf{Q}_{new}$ ← $\mathbf{Q}_{new}$ ∪ ({s'} \ **Visited**)
7 | | | ⇒ ← ⇒ ∪ {(s, e, s')}
8 | **Visited** ← **Visited** ∪ $\mathbf{Q}_{new}$
9 | **Visited, Queue** ← $mergeSets($**PZG, Visited,** $\mathbf{Q}_{new})$

Algorithm 2: Heuristics to merge states within Q and/or V

| Visited | Queue | Ordered |

---

1 **Function** $mergeSets($**PZG**, $V, Q)$
2 | **foreach s ∈ Q do**
3 | | $mergeOneState($**s, PZG**, $Q)$
   | | $mergeOneState($**s, PZG**, $V)$
4 | **return** (V, Q)

---

merging function $mergeSets$ (given in Algorithm 2), which may reduce both **Visited** and **Queue**. This call to the merging function is the crux of our approach.

Algorithm 1 can be extended, depending on the analysis or parameter synthesis problem. For instance, an invariant property can be checked for each reachable symbolic state and terminate as soon as the property is violated. For reachability synthesis, one may accumulate all solutions as a set of constraints that lead to a state satisfying a property (this algorithm, EFsynth, was formalized in e.g. [31]).

Then, Algorithm 2 "simply" calls recursively the $mergeOneState$ function (given in Algorithm 3) on each state of **Queue**, using additional arguments **PZG** and **Visited** and/or **Queue**. The heuristics to select arguments for calls to $mergeOneState$ will be discussed later. Note that $mergeOneState$ modifies its arguments, notably **PZG** (in the implementation, we use a call by reference).

Algorithm 3 attempts at merging a state **s** while looking for candidate states in **SiblingCandidates**. We first look for the *siblings* of **s** (states with same location) within **SiblingCandidates** (line 3). We use a function $getSiblings(($$\ell, \mathbf{C}), \mathbf{S})$ that returns the siblings, as in $\{(\ell', \mathbf{C}') \in \mathbf{S} \mid \ell = \ell'\}$. If the union of the constraints is convex (line 5), state **s** becomes the result of merging **s** with the candidate **y** (line 6). The candidate **y** is deleted (line 11), as well as all transitions leading to or coming from it (lines 8 to 10). We finally modify the initial state $\mathbf{s}_0$ of **PZG**, in case it was merged (line 12).

Algorithm 3: Merging a state with an update of the statespace $\mathbf{PZG} = (E, \mathbf{S}, \mathbf{s}_0, \Rightarrow)$ on-the-fly. The variant with restart after a merge is indicated as in Restart

---

```
1   Function mergeOneState(s, PZG, SiblingCandidates)
2   │   isMerged ← false
3   │   Candidates ← getSiblings(s, SiblingCandidates)
4   │   foreach y ∈ Candidates do
        │   /* Mergeability test                                              */
5       │   if is_mergeable(s, y) then
6       │   │   s.constr ← s.constr ∪ y.constr
7       │   │   isMerged ← true
            │   /* Update transition targets and source                       */
8       │   │   foreach t ∈ ⇒ do
9       │   │   │   if t.target = y then t.target ← s ;
10      │   │   └   if t.source = y then t.source ← s ;
            │   /* Delete y                                                    */
11      │   │   S ← S \ {y}
            │   /* Handle initial state                                       */
12      │   └   if s_0 = y then s_0 ← s ;
13  │   └   if isMerged then mergeOneState(s, PZG, SiblingCandidates) ;
```

3.2   Heuristics for Merging

We now introduce and discuss several heuristics for merging states, leading to various options in the merging algorithm. There is no provably best option that is guaranteed to be superior over all other possible options. We will perform extensive experiments in Sect. 4 to find out what works well on a number of benchmarks. The two main driving forces to select between these options are: 1) a maximal reduction of the state space; and 2) a minimisation of the computation time. Although usually smaller state spaces tend to require less computation time, this is not always the case: Sometimes one might need extra effort to check if states can be merged, in order to perform even more reduction. Subsequent computations might profit from the smaller state space, but if one is checking properties on-the-fly, the extra effort might not be justifiable. The discussion on the options will be guided by some questions. A question that we have not investigated is if it is advantageous to merge triples of states.

The subsequent Example 3 will show that different choices can indeed lead to state spaces of different size. Note that, even when we fix the answers to the questions, the result is still non-deterministic, since the result of merging depends on the *order* in which we would consider the siblings.

Question 1: What to merge with what? Assume that we are computing the next level of reachable states in a BFS process (Algorithm 1). Assuming that the states in **Visited** have been properly merged, we clearly still need to merge the new states in **s** ∈ **Queue**. What to merge them with? Do we only compare **s** with other states in the **Queue**? Or also with **Visited**? If we merge with **Visited** states, the final state space could become smaller. On the other hand, since time was spent to compute those states already, is it worth looking at them? The different strategies considered merge a new state with its siblings:

- only in the queue (`Queue`), or
- in all visited states (`Visited`) (including the queue), or
- first in the queue and, after that, in the visited list (`Ordered`).

These different possibilities are pictured by different colours in Algorithm 2.

Question 2: Restart after a merge? The next question is what to do if we find that **s** could be merged with some **s'** into the (larger) $\mathbf{s}_m$? We have already searched through some set Q' of states before we found **s'**. Those states in Q' could not be merged with **s**. However, it could be possible that a state in $\mathbf{s}'' \in Q'$ can be merged with $\mathbf{s}_m$. So should we *restart* the search (and lose some time to find more reduction), or should we just resume the search, and only find merge candidates for $\mathbf{s}_m$ in the remaining states that we have not yet considered? So, if a state can be merged with one of its siblings, should we restart or not restart the search through all candidate siblings?

Question 3: When to update the statespace? Assume that we find a successful merge of a state **s** ∈ **Queue** with some other state **s'** ∈ **Visited**, leading to a larger state $\mathbf{s}_m$. How do we now modify the already computed part of the state space? We replace **s'** by $\mathbf{s}_m$, redirecting all transitions going to **s'** to $\mathbf{s}_m$. This could make the successors of **s'** unreachable, so we could also redirect transitions from **s'** to transitions from $\mathbf{s}_m$. Alternatively, we could just remove the successors of **s'**. This is valid, since we will still compute all successors of $\mathbf{s}_m$ in the next level. Similar considerations apply to all states reachable from successors of **s'**.

These approaches can have unforeseen effects: First of all, if we remove successor states, they cannot act anymore as merge candidates, thus potentially blocking future merges. Second, removing transitions may change the "shortest path" to reachable states, leading to wrong answers for depth-bounded and shortest-path searches. Third, not removing states leads to a larger state space than necessary. Finally, doing a full reachability analysis is linear in the size of the state space generated so far (but does not involve any polyhedra computations).

So one question is how often we should update the computed part of the state space? The options we considered are to do "garbage collection" after:

- each merge with each sibling, or
- having processed the whole candidate list of a state, or
- having processed all states in a complete level.

Question 4: How to update the statespace? The "garbage collection" can be implemented in two ways: If we can merge a state, we update the statespace:

- reconstruct: with a copy of the reachable part of the statespace, or
- on-the-fly: deleting the merged state and updating its transitions *in situ.*

Deleting states on-the-fly is cheaper than running a separate algorithm to mark and copy the reachable part of the state space. However, note that when updating transitions on-the-fly, some unnecessary successor states may stay in the state space. These unnecessary states and transitions lead to a waste of memory. On the other hand, they might still be useful as merge candidates for future merges.

Example 3. Recall that Fig. 2 presents a fictitious example summarising the effect of the options discussed in this section. The parametric zone graph (with five states) is shown in Fig. 2a, the corresponding projections of the zones on the parameters in Fig. 2c and the legend for the different colours in Fig. 2b. All states have the same location, hence may be candidates for merging. Two states (s_0 and s_1) are in the visited set, while two are in the queue (s_2 and s_3), and the last one, s_4, is currently being handled.

Let us first consider that the merge is only done with states in the queue. Then s_4 is merged with s_2 and no merge with s_3 can occur. This leads to the zones depicted in Fig. 2d.

Let us now consider that the merge is done with all visited states. Then the following execution becomes possible: State s_4 could be first merged with s_1, leading to the zones in Fig. 2e. Now, if the restart option is used, this newly computed zone could be merged with s_0, leading to the zones in Fig. 2f. Note that we cannot merge the result with s_2 anymore.

Finally, let us consider the case where we merge with the queue first and then with visited. State s_4 is then merged with s_2, as in Fig. 2d. Then no merge with s_3 nor with s_0 can be performed, but a merge with s_1 is possible, leading to Fig. 2g. If furthermore the state space is updated immediately after a merge, the new state (instead of s_4) is merged with s_1, leading to Fig. 2h.

3.3 Preservation of Properties

Proposition 1. *Given a PTA $\mathcal{A}$, let* **PZG** *and* **PZG'** *be the parametric zone graph before and after merging. Then* **PZG'** *simulates* **PZG**.

Proof (sketch). Consider the relation $s \sqsubseteq s'$ if and only if $s.loc = s'.loc$ and $s.constr \subseteq s'.constr$. It is well-known [33] that this forms a simulation relation, i.e. if $s \sqsubseteq s'$ and $s \Rightarrow s_0$, then for some s'_0, we have $s_0 \sqsubseteq s'_0$ and $s' \Rightarrow s'_0$.

Note that while merging, we repeatedly replace a state $(\ell, \mathbf{C})$ by a state $(\ell, \mathbf{C} \cup \mathbf{C}')$, in which case $(\ell, \mathbf{C}) \sqsubseteq (\ell, \mathbf{C} \cup \mathbf{C}')$. So indeed, merged states can simulate the behaviour of all original states that were merged.

Corollary 1. *Given a PTA $\mathcal{A}$, let* **PZG** *and* **PZG'** *be the parametric zone graph before and after merging. Let φ be a property in $\forall CTL^*$ with atomic propositions defined in terms of state locations only. Then* **PZG'** $\vDash \varphi$ *implies* **PZG** $\vDash \varphi$.

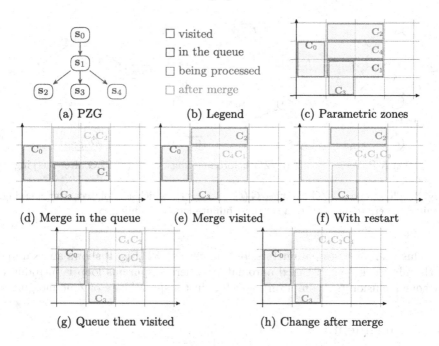

(a) PZG   (b) Legend   (c) Parametric zones

(d) Merge in the queue   (e) Merge visited   (f) With restart

(g) Queue then visited   (h) Change after merge

Fig. 2. Illustration of the merging options

Proof (sketch). All universal properties (in ∀CTL*) are preserved by simulation [13, Thm 7.76]. In this case, the simulation ⊑ also implies that related states have the same locations, so they satisfy the same atomic properties.

The next proposition shows that we do not add arbitrary new behaviour. Although merging can add behaviour, it cannot add unreachable locations and, more precisely, the set of locations reachable for each parameter valuation remains unchanged. This guarantees that merging preserves reachability synthesis. (A version of this result was shown in a different context in [7, Thm. 1]).

Proposition 2 (preservation of reachability properties). *Given a PTA $\mathcal{A}$, let* **PZG**′ *be the parametric zone graph after merging. Let ℓ be a location, let v be a parameter valuation.*
*ℓ is reachable in $v(\mathcal{A})$ iff $\exists(\ell, \mathbf{C}') \in$ **PZG**′ such that $v \in \mathbf{C}'\!\downarrow_{\mathbb{P}}$.*

Note that path properties in **PZG** are not always preserved in **PZG**′, as the following example shows. Also, liveness properties in **PZG** (such as "every path visits location ℓ infinitely often") are not necessarily preserved in **PZG**′.

Example 4. Figure 3b shows the parametric zone graph of the PTA in Fig. 3a. The maximal paths are $\ell_0, \ell_1, \ell_3, \ell_4$ and $\ell_0, \ell_1, \ell_3, \ell_2$ (for $p \leq 1$) and ℓ_0, ℓ_2, ℓ_3 (for $p > 1$). All maximal paths satisfy the LTL property $\mathbf{G}(\ell_2 \rightarrow \mathbf{G}\,\neg\ell_4)$ ("no ℓ_4 after an ℓ_2"). Also, there is no loop (infinite run) containing ℓ_2. However, the result after merging in Fig. 3c introduces the spurious path $\ell_0, \ell_2, \ell_3, \ell_4$, violating the first property. It also introduces a spurious loop $\ell_0, (\ell_2, \ell_3)^\omega$, around ℓ_2.

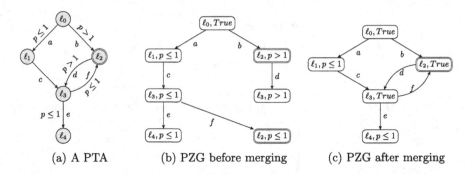

(a) A PTA   (b) PZG before merging   (c) PZG after merging

Fig. 3. The original PZG satisfies $\mathbf{G}\,(\ell_2 \rightarrow \mathbf{G}\,\neg\ell_4)$, which is violated after merging. Similarly, merging introduces a spurious infinite loop containing ℓ_2.

This example uses parameters, but no clocks. [32, Fig. 4] shows an example with only clocks (i.e. a timed automaton) where a spurious loop is introduced by zone inclusion (subsumption), which is just a special case of zone merging.

4   Experiments

We evaluate here the effect of the merging heuristics on reachability synthesis. The synthesis algorithm explores the PZG to find all valid parameter valuations.

We implemented all our heuristics in the IMITATOR parametric timed model checker [4]. The parametric zones in the symbolic states are encoded using polyhedra. All operations on polyhedra, and notably the mergeability test, are performed using the Parma Polyhedra Library [12]. We also reimplemented and compared with the original merging technique of IMITATOR 2.12, which was an upgrade of the merging technique (in IMITATOR 2.6.1) of [7].

4.1   Dataset and Experimental Environment

We use the full set of models with reachability properties from the IMITATOR benchmark library [10]. The library is made of a set of *benchmarks*. Each benchmark may have different *models* and each model comes with one or more *properties*. For example, Gear comes with ten models, of different sizes, named Gear-1000 to Gear-10000; each of them may have one or more properties.

Our dataset comprises 124 pairs made of a model and a reachability property (i.e. 124 possible executions of IMITATOR). We set a timeout of 120 s; only 102 executions terminate within this time bound for at least one of the merging heuristics. For 42 of these executions, at least one of the heuristics performs at least one successful merge. Full statistics on our dataset are given in Table 1.

Table 1. Size of our dataset

	# benchmarks	# models	# properties
Whole reachability dataset	49	84	124
Where at least one execution ends within 120 s	35	68	102
Where at least one merge is performed	24	35	42

Experiments were run on an Intel Xeon Gold 5220 (Cascade Lake-SP, 2.20 GHz, 1 CPU/node, 18 cores/CPU) with 96 GiB running Linux Ubuntu 20.[1]

4.2 Description of the Experiments

We compare each combination of the heuristics proposed in Sect. 3.2. We reference each merge heuristic as a combination of three or four letters:

1. R or O: the state-space is updated by reconstruction (R) or on-the-fly (O);
2. V,Q or O: the selected candidates are Visited (V), Queue (Q) or Ordered (O);
3. M or C: state-space is updated for each merge (M) or after all candidates (C);
4. r: the restart option is enabled (nothing otherwise).

These algorithms are compared according to: *i*) the total computation time needed for a property; and *ii*) the size of the generated state space.

Our results are obtained over the 102 executions of the dataset for which at least one algorithm ends before reaching the 120 s timeout. We do not use any penalty on executions that do not end: their execution time is set to the timeout (120 s) in the subsequent analyses. The metrics tagged by "(merge)" in Table 2 are computed over the 42 executions where some states can be merged, while the "(no merge)" only consider the 60 executions where no merge can be made.

We present in Table 2 some of the experimental results obtained for the different merge heuristics that allow the best reduction of computation time or in the state-space size. The results for all the heuristics are presented in Appendix A. In order to allow a good visualization of the results, the best result in each cell is given in **bold**, while the level of green denotes the "quality" of the value in each cell (white is worst, and 100 % green is best).

The different lines tabulate the following information: *i*) the number of wins over the computation time, i.e. the number of executions for which the current heuristics gives the smallest execution time; *ii*) the average time (in s) over all executions; *iii*) the average time (in s), excluding executions where no states can be merged for any heuristics; *iv*) the average time (in s) for only the executions where no states can be merged for any heuristics; *v*) the median time (in s) over all executions; *vi*) the normalized time average, compared to the Nomerge results, i.e. the ratio between the heuristic execution time and the Nomerge one; *vii*) the normalized time average, excluding executions where no states can be merged for

---

[1] We used IMITATOR 3.3-beta-2 "Cheese Caramel au beurre salé". Sources, binaries, models, raw results and full experiments tables are available at 10.5281/zenodo. 6806915.

Table 2. Partial results comparing merge heuristics over 102 models

		Nomerge	M2.12	RVMr	OQM
Time	# wins	24	20	22	**42**
	Avg (s)	10.0	5.47	4.56	**3.77**
	Avg (merge) (s)	18.8	7.83	5.57	**3.63**
	Avg (no merge) (s)	3.83	**3.82**	3.85	3.88
	Median (s)	1.39	1.2	1.14	**1.12**
	Norm. avg	1.0	0.91	0.91	**0.87**
	Norm. avg (merge)	1.0	0.75	0.74	**0.64**
	Norm. avg (no merge)	**1.0**	1.02	1.03	1.03
States	# wins	0	19	**37**	16
	Avg	11443.08	11096.54	**11064.37**	11120.79
	Avg (merge)	1512.02	670.43	**592.31**	729.33
	Median	2389.5	703.5	**604.5**	905.0
	Norm. avg	1.0	0.86	**0.84**	0.88

any heuristics; *viii*) the normalized time average, for only the executions where no states can be merged for any heuristics; *ix*) the number of wins over the size of the state space (i.e. the total number of symbolic states after merging); *x*) the average size of the state space over all models; *xi*) the average size of the state space over all models, excluding the executions where no states can be merged; *xii*) the median size of the state space over all models; *xiii*) the normalized size average, compared to the Nomerge results.

The reason to give both an average time (resp. number of states) and a normalized time (resp. number of states) is because both metrics complement each other: the weight of the large models has a higher influence in the average (which can be seen as unfair, as a few models have a large influence), while all models have equal influence in the normalized average (which can also be seen as unfair, as very small models have the same influence as very large models).

In Table 2 (and in Appendix A), we notice that the best (i.e. smallest) times are obtained when the merging is performed on the queue and when the update is done after a performed merge, even though doing it with a reconstruction of the state space after each step loses time compared to the Otf heuristic. Moreover, restarting when a merge is performed does not seem to bring any gain in time. Thus, with respect to time, when the winner is OQM (i.e. merging when the candidates are taken from the Queue, when the update is done on-the-fly after each merge without any restart), which minimizes both the time when a merge is possible, but also when considering models where no merge can be performed. Moreover, this heuristic gives the smaller times for the executions where no merge can be done.

Concerning the state space size, the winner is RVMr (i.e. merging when the candidates are taken from the Visited states, updating the state space by a reconstruction after each merge, and with a restart if a merge can be performed). This performs more checks to identify states for merging (comparing with all the visited, not only those in the queue), thus reducing the state space even more.

Note that the methods Nomerge and M2.12 are almost always the losers (i.e. slowest and largest state space), except for the heuristic where the update of the state-space is performed after the list of candidates.

Concerning our new heuristics, we note that OQM decreases the average computation time to 69 % when compared to the previous merging heuristic (M2.12 [7]), and even to only 46 % (i.e. a division by a factor >2) compared with M2.12 on the subset of models for which at least one merge can be done. Compared to disabling merging (Nomerge), our new heuristic OQM decreases to 38 % on the whole benchmark set, and even to 19 % (i.e. a division by a factor > 5) on the subset of models for which at least one merge can be done. This leads us to consider the new combination of merging only in the queue and with an on-the-fly update after each merge and without restart (heuristic OQM) as the default merging heuristic in IMITATOR. For use cases that require a minimal state space, the new combination RVMr is the recommended option. Note that this version is still faster on average (83 %) than the previous heuristic (M2.12), and more than twice as fast (46 %) as not merging at all (Nomerge).

5   Conclusion

In this paper, we investigated the importance of the merging operations in reachability synthesis using parametric timed automata. We investigated different combinations of options. The chosen heuristic (OQM, when the candidates are taken from the Queue, when the update is done on-the-fly after each merge without any restart) brings a decrease to 38 % of the average computation time for our entire benchmarks library compared to the absence of merging. Compared to the previous merging heuristic from [7], the gain of our new heuristic is a decrease to 69 % of the average computation time—meaning that our new heuristic decreases the computation time by 31 % compared to the former heuristic from [7]. In other words, despite the cost of the mergeability test, the overall gain is large and shows the importance of the merge operation for parameter synthesis. We also provide a heuristic for use cases where a minimal state space is important, for instance for a follow-up analysis. Even though this is not the fastest heuristic, it is still faster than not merging at all, and faster than the old merging heuristic [7]. Our experiments show the high importance of carefully choosing the merging heuristics. Our heuristics preserve the correctness of parameter synthesis for reachability properties.

Future Work. We noted that pruning merged states away ("garbage collection") can prevent future merges. Another option would be to keep such states in a collection of "potential mergers". These extra states could be useful as "glue" to merge a number of other states, that otherwise could not be merged, into one superstate—but at the cost of more memory. Another option could be to merge more than two states in one go. These options remain to be investigated.

It is well-known that less heuristics can be used for *liveness* properties than for reachability properties. Investigating whether *some* merging can still be used for liveness synthesis (i.e. the synthesis of parameter valuations for which some location is infinitely often reachable) is an interesting future work.

Another, more theoretical question is to define and compute the "best possible merge". Currently, the result of merging is not canonical, since it depends on the exploration order and the order of searching for siblings. We have not found a candidate definition that minimizes the state space and provides natural, canonical merge representatives.

Finally, investigating the recent PPLite [14, 15] instead of PPL for polyhedra computation is on our agenda.

Acknowledgements. We thank Benjamin Loillier for helping us testing our artifact. Experiments presented in this paper were carried out using the Grid'5000 testbed, supported by a scientific interest group hosted by Inria and including CNRS, RENATER and several universities as well as other organizations (see https://www.grid5000.fr).

A   Results for All Heuristics on the Full Benchmark

With Restarting

	Metric	Nomerge	M2.12	RVMr	RVCr	RQMr	RQCr	RDMr	RDCr	OVMr	OVCr	OQMr	OQCr	ODMr	ODCr
States	# wins	20	17	15	2	10	3	5	3	9	4	8	8	8	4
	Avg (s)	10.0	5.47	4.56	46.7	3.84	43.53	4.69	49.05	5.58	5.7	**3.79**	3.81	5.54	5.63
	Avg (merge) (s)	18.8	7.83	5.57	17.8	3.83	10.1	5.86	18.69	8.0	8.32	**3.66**	3.7	7.89	8.14
	Avg (no merge) (s)	**3.83**	3.85	3.85	66.93	3.85	66.93	3.88	70.29	3.89	3.87	3.88	3.88	3.89	3.87
	Median (s)	1.39	1.2	1.14	4.85	**0.87**	2.98	1.19	6.49	1.15	1.15	1.11	1.12	1.17	1.17
	Nrm. avg	1.0	0.91	0.91	9.06	1.14	8.91	0.92	10.34	0.92	0.92	0.88	0.88	0.92	0.93
	Nrm. avg (merge)	1.0	0.91	0.74	1.74	0.66	1.4	0.76	1.86	0.75	0.76	0.66	**0.65**	0.77	0.78
	Nrm. avg (no-mrg)	1.0	1.02	1.03	14.27	14.27	14.25	1.03	16.38	1.03	1.03	1.04	1.03	1.03	1.04
Time	# wins	19	19	**32**	29	15	15	29	30	20	20	16	16	20	20
	Avg	11445.61	11096.54	**11064.37**	11106.09	11120.34	11120.55	11066.85	11105.73	11089.5	11089.5	11118.73	11118.73	11087.77	11087.77
	Avg (merge)	1518.17	670.43	**592.31**	693.62	728.24	728.74	598.33	692.74	653.33	653.33	724.31	724.31	649.14	649.14
	Median	2389.5	703.5	**604.5**	607.0	905.0	905.0	**604.5**	607.0	701.0	701.0	905.0	905.0	701.0	701.0
	Nrm. avg	1.0	0.86	**0.84**	0.85	0.88	0.88	**0.84**	0.85	0.86	0.86	0.88	0.88	0.86	0.85

No Restarting

	Metric	Nomerge	M2.12	RVM	RVC	RQM	RQC	RDM	RDC	OVM	OVC	OQM	OQC	ODM	ODC
States	# wins	20	17	11	4	8	3	4	2	6	6	6	6	8	8
	Avg (s)	10.0	5.47	4.56	46.48	3.85	43.31	4.65	48.92	5.09	5.19	**3.77**	3.78	5.16	5.25
	Avg (merge) (s)	18.8	7.83	5.58	17.19	3.86	9.57	5.74	18.41	6.8	7.07	**3.63**	3.64	7.0	7.24
	Avg (no merge) (s)	**3.83**	3.85	**3.85**	66.97	3.85	66.94	3.89	70.28	3.89	3.88	3.88	3.88	3.88	3.87
	Median (s)	1.39	1.2	1.14	4.34	1.14	2.82	1.17	5.4	1.13	**1.12**	1.12	1.12	1.13	1.15
	Nrm. avg	1.0	0.9	9.04	9.04	0.88	8.91	0.92	10.33	0.9	0.91	**0.87**	0.87	0.92	0.92
	Nrm. avg (merge)	1.0	0.75	0.74	1.69	0.65	1.38	0.76	1.83	0.72	0.74	**0.64**	0.65	0.74	0.76
	Nrm. avg (no-mrg)	1.0	1.02	14.28	14.28	1.04	14.27	1.03	16.38	1.03	1.03	1.03	1.03	1.03	1.04
Time	# wins	0	19	26	15	15	15	29	**32**	19	19	15	15	19	19
	Avg	11445.61	11096.54	11073.57	11105.33	11123.2	11122.24	**11068.0**	11105.41	11096.89	11096.89	11120.79	11120.79	11090.01	11090.01
	Avg (merge)	1518.17	670.43	614.64	691.79	735.17	732.83	**601.12**	691.98	671.29	671.29	729.33	729.33	654.57	654.57
	Median	2389.5	636.5	583.0	905.0	905.0	905.0	**604.5**	**577.0**	706.5	706.5	905.0	905.0	701.0	701.0
	Nrm. avg	1.0	**0.84**	0.85	0.88	0.88	0.88	**0.84**	0.85	0.86	0.86	0.88	0.88	0.86	0.86

216   É. André et al.

References

1. Alur, R., Dill, D.L.: A theory of timed automata. Theor. Comput. Sci. **126**(2), 183–235 (1994). https://doi.org/10.1016/0304-3975(94)90010-8
2. Alur, R., Henzinger, T.A., Vardi, M.Y.: Parametric real-time reasoning. In: Kosaraju, S.R., Johnson, D.S., Aggarwal, A. (eds.) STOC, pp. 592–601. ACM, New York (1993). https://doi.org/10.1145/167088.167242
3. André, É.: What's decidable about parametric timed automata? Int. J. Softw. Tools Technol. Transfer **21**(2), 203–219 (2017). https://doi.org/10.1007/s10009-017-0467-0
4. André, É.: IMITATOR 3: synthesis of timing parameters beyond decidability. In: Silva, A., Leino, K.R.M. (eds.) CAV 2021. LNCS, vol. 12759, pp. 552–565. Springer, Cham (2021). https://doi.org/10.1007/978-3-030-81685-8_26
5. André, É., Arias, J., Petrucci, L., Pol, J.: Iterative bounded synthesis for efficient cycle detection in parametric timed automata. In: Groote, J.F., Larsen, K.G. (eds.) TACAS 2021. LNCS, vol. 12651, pp. 311–329. Springer, Cham (2021). https://doi.org/10.1007/978-3-030-72016-2_17
6. André, É., Chatain, T., Encrenaz, E., Fribourg, L.: An inverse method for parametric timed automata. Int. J. Found. Comput. Sci. **20**(5), 819–836 (2009). https://doi.org/10.1142/S0129054109006905
7. André, É., Fribourg, L., Soulat, R.: Merge and conquer: state merging in parametric timed automata. In: Van Hung, D., Ogawa, M. (eds.) ATVA 2013. LNCS, vol. 8172, pp. 381–396. Springer, Cham (2013). https://doi.org/10.1007/978-3-319-02444-8_27
8. André, É., Lime, D., Markey, N.: Language preservation problems in parametric timed automata. Log. Methods Comput. Sci. **16**(1) (2020). https://doi.org/10.23638/LMCS-16(1:5)2020
9. André, É., Lime, D., Roux, O.H.: Integer-complete synthesis for bounded parametric timed automata. In: Bojańczyk, M., Lasota, S., Potapov, I. (eds.) RP 2015. LNCS, vol. 9328, pp. 7–19. Springer, Cham (2015). https://doi.org/10.1007/978-3-319-24537-9_2
10. André, É., Marinho, D., van de Pol, J.: A benchmarks library for extended parametric timed automata. In: Loulergue, F., Wotawa, F. (eds.) TAP 2021. LNCS, vol. 12740, pp. 39–50. Springer, Cham (2021). https://doi.org/10.1007/978-3-030-79379-1_3
11. André, É., Nguyen, H.G., Petrucci, L.: Efficient parameter synthesis using optimized state exploration strategies. In: Hu, Z., Bai, G. (eds.) ICECCS, pp. 1–10. IEEE (2017). https://doi.org/10.1109/ICECCS.2017.28
12. Bagnara, R., Hill, P.M., Zaffanella, E.: The Parma Polyhedra Library: toward a complete set of numerical abstractions for the analysis and verification of hardware and software systems. Sci. Comput. Program. **72**(1–2), 3–21 (2008). https://doi.org/10.1016/j.scico.2007.08.001
13. Baier, C., Katoen, J.P.: Principles of Model Checking. MIT Press, Cambridge (2008)
14. Becchi, A., Zaffanella, E.: An efficient abstract domain for not necessarily closed polyhedra. In: Podelski, A. (ed.) SAS 2018. LNCS, vol. 11002, pp. 146–165. Springer, Cham (2018). https://doi.org/10.1007/978-3-319-99725-4_11
15. Becchi, A., Zaffanella, E.: PPLite: zero-overhead encoding of NNC polyhedra. Inf. Comput. **275**, 1–36 (2020). https://doi.org/10.1016/j.ic.2020.104620

16. Behrmann, G., Bouyer, P., Larsen, K.G., Pelánek, R.: Lower and upper bounds in zone-based abstractions of timed automata. Int. J. Softw. Tools Technol. Transfer **8**(3), 204–215 (2006). https://doi.org/10.1007/s10009-005-0190-0

17. Ben Salah, R., Bozga, M., Maler, O.: On interleaving in timed automata. In: Baier, C., Hermanns, H. (eds.) CONCUR 2006. LNCS, vol. 4137, pp. 465–476. Springer, Heidelberg (2006). https://doi.org/10.1007/11817949_31

18. Bezděk, P., Beneš, N., Barnat, J., Černá, I.: LTL parameter synthesis of parametric timed automata. In: De Nicola, R., Kühn, E. (eds.) SEFM 2016. LNCS, vol. 9763, pp. 172–187. Springer, Cham (2016). https://doi.org/10.1007/978-3-319-41591-8_12

19. Bogomolov, S., Forets, M., Frehse, G., Potomkin, K., Schilling, C.: Reachability analysis of linear hybrid systems via block decomposition. IEEE Trans. Comput. Aided Des. Integr. Circ. Syst. **39**(11), 4018–4029 (2020). https://doi.org/10.1109/TCAD.2020.3012859

20. Chen, X., Ábrahám, E., Frehse, G.: Efficient bounded reachability computation for rectangular automata. In: Delzanno, G., Potapov, I. (eds.) RP 2011. LNCS, vol. 6945, pp. 139–152. Springer, Heidelberg (2011). https://doi.org/10.1007/978-3-642-24288-5_13

21. Chen, X., Sankaranarayanan, S., Ábrahám, E.: Under-approximate flowpipes for non-linear continuous systems. In: FMCAD, pp. 59–66. IEEE (2014). https://doi.org/10.1109/FMCAD.2014.6987596

22. David, A.: Merging DBMs efficiently. In: NWPT, pp. 54–56. DIKU, University of Copenhagen (2005)

23. Henzinger, T.A.: The theory of hybrid automata. In: Vardi, M.Y., Clarke, E.M. (eds.) LiCS, pp. 278–292. IEEE Computer Society (1996). https://doi.org/10.1109/LICS.1996.561342

24. Henzinger, T.A., Manna, Z., Pnueli, A.: Temporal proof methodologies for real-time systems. In: Wise, D.S. (ed.) POPL, pp. 353–366. ACM Press (1991). https://doi.org/10.1145/99583.99629

25. Herbreteau, F., Srivathsan, B., Tran, T.T., Walukiewicz, I.: Why liveness for timed automata is hard, and what we can do about it. ACM Trans. Comput. Log. **21**(3), 17:1–17:28 (2020). https://doi.org/10.1145/3372310

26. Herbreteau, F., Srivathsan, B., Walukiewicz, I.: Efficient emptiness check for timed Büchi automata. Formal Methods Syst. Des. **40**(2), 122–146 (2012). https://doi.org/10.1007/s10703-011-0133-1

27. Herbreteau, F., Srivathsan, B., Walukiewicz, I.: Lazy abstractions for timed automata. In: Sharygina, N., Veith, H. (eds.) CAV 2013. LNCS, vol. 8044, pp. 990–1005. Springer, Heidelberg (2013). https://doi.org/10.1007/978-3-642-39799-8_71

28. Herbreteau, F., Srivathsan, B., Walukiewicz, I.: Better abstractions for timed automata. Inf. Comput. **251**, 67–90 (2016). https://doi.org/10.1016/j.ic.2016.07.004

29. Herbreteau, F., Tran, T.-T.: Improving search order for reachability testing in timed automata. In: Sankaranarayanan, S., Vicario, E. (eds.) FORMATS 2015. LNCS, vol. 9268, pp. 124–139. Springer, Cham (2015). https://doi.org/10.1007/978-3-319-22975-1_9

30. Hune, T., Romijn, J., Stoelinga, M., Vaandrager, F.W.: Linear parametric model checking of timed automata. J. Log. Algebraic Program. **52–53**, 183–220 (2002). https://doi.org/10.1016/S1567-8326(02)00037-1

31. Jovanović, A., Lime, D., Roux, O.H.: Integer parameter synthesis for real-time systems. IEEE Trans. Softw. Eng. **41**(5), 445–461 (2015). https://doi.org/10.1109/TSE.2014.2357445

32. Laarman, A., Olesen, M.C., Dalsgaard, A.E., Larsen, K.G., van de Pol, J.: Multi-core emptiness checking of timed Büchi automata using inclusion abstraction. In: Sharygina, N., Veith, H. (eds.) CAV 2013. LNCS, vol. 8044, pp. 968–983. Springer, Heidelberg (2013). https://doi.org/10.1007/978-3-642-39799-8_69

33. Nguyen, H.G., Petrucci, L., Van de Pol, J.: Layered and collecting NDFS with subsumption for parametric timed automata. In: Lin, A.W., Sun, J. (eds.) ICECCS, pp. 1–9. IEEE Computer Society, December 2018. https://doi.org/10.1109/ICECCS2018.2018.00009

34. Schupp, S., Nellen, J., Ábrahám, E.: Divide and conquer: variable set separation in hybrid systems reachability analysis. In: Wiklicky, H., de Vink, E.P. (eds.) QAPL@ETAPS. Electronic Proceedings in Theoretical Computer Science, vol. 250, pp. 1–14 (2017). https://doi.org/10.4204/EPTCS.250.1

Neural Networks

Neural Network Repair with Reachability Analysis

Xiaodong Yang[1]([✉]), Tom Yamaguchi[2], Hoang-Dung Tran[3], Bardh Hoxha[2], Taylor T. Johnson[1]([✉]), and Danil Prokhorov[2]

[1] Vanderbilt University, Nashville, TN, USA
sheldon.uestc@gmail.com, taylor.johnson@gmail.com
[2] TRINA, Toyota NA R&D, Ann Arbor, MI, USA
[3] University of Nebraska, Lincoln, NE, USA

Abstract. Safety is a critical concern for the next generation of autonomy that is likely to rely heavily on deep neural networks for perception and control. This paper proposes a method to repair unsafe ReLU DNNs in safety-critical systems using reachability analysis. Our repair method uses reachability analysis to calculate the unsafe reachable domain of a DNN, and then uses a novel loss function to construct its distance to the safe domain during the retraining process. Since subtle changes of the DNN parameters can cause unexpected performance degradation, we also present a minimal repair approach where the DNN deviation is minimized. Furthermore, we explore applications of our method to repair DNN agents in deep reinforcement learning (DRL) with seamless integration with learning algorithms. Our method is evaluated on the ACAS Xu benchmark and a rocket lander system against the state-of-the-art method ART. Experimental results show that our repair approach can generate provably safe DNNs on multiple safety specifications with negligible performance degradation, even in the absence of training data (Code is available online at https://github.com/Shaddadi/veritex.git).

Keywords: Neural network repair · reachability analysis

1 Introduction

Although deep neural networks (DNNs) have been successful in many areas, their trustworthiness remains a primary issue preventing widespread use. Recently, many techniques for analyzing behaviors of DNNs have been presented [6, 9, 14, 19]. Given a DNN, these works present post-training verification methods that generate a safety certificate over input-output specifications. One challenge that remains is the repair problem, where given a DNN with erroneous behaviors, an automatic process repairs the network with respect to the specification.

Existing works that improve the safety and robustness of DNNs can be classified into two main categories. The first category relies on singular adversarial inputs to make specialized modifications on neural weights that likely cause misbehavior. In [13], the paper presents a technique named *Arachne*. There, given a

© Springer Nature Switzerland AG 2022
S. Bogomolov and D. Parker (Eds.): FORMATS 2022, LNCS 13465, pp. 221–236, 2022.
https://doi.org/10.1007/978-3-031-15839-1_13

set of finite adversarial inputs, with the guidance of a fitness function, *Arachne* searches and subsequently modifies neural weights that are likely related to these undesired behaviors. In [2], the paper proposes a DNN verification-based method that modifies undesirable behavior of DNNs by manipulating neural weights of the output layer. The correctness of the repaired DNN is then proved with a verification technique. In [15], the repair approach first localizes the potential faulty DNN parameter at an intermediate layer or the last layer, and then conducts a small modification using constraint solving. In [11], the method poses the repair problem as a mixed-integer quadratic program to adjust the parameter of a single layer, such that undesired behaviors can be reduced and meanwhile the change in DNNs is minimized. However, these methods only enhance the robustness of DNNs, meaning that provably safe DNNs cannot be generated. In addition, the modification of weights based on individual adversarial examples may not capture the impact on the whole performance of the network.

The second category is based on adversarial training, such as [3,10]. However, these methods do not provide guarantees regarding the safety of the DNN. To solve this issue, some works incorporate reachability analysis in this process, such that they can train a model that is provably safe on a norm-bounded domain [8,12,17]. Given a norm-bounded input range, these approaches over approximate the output reachable domain of DNNs with a convex region. Then they minimize the worst-case loss over these regions, which aims to migrate all unsafe outputs to the desired domain. The primary issue of these approaches is that the approximation error accumulates during computation. For large input domains or complex DNNs, their approximated domain can be so conservative that a low-fidelity worst-case loss may result in significant accuracy degradation. We confirm this issue through experiments in comparison with ART [8].

In this paper, we propose a repair method for ReLU DNNs based on exact reachability analysis. Compared to over-approximation approaches, the exact analysis enables us to precisely compute the unsafe reachable domain of a DNN and its distance to the safe domain. In the repair process, this distance is constructed with a loss function for minimization. Additionally, by combining it with another objective function that minimizes the change of the DNN parameters, a minimal-repaired DNN can be learned, which aims to preserve the performance. Experiments indicate that our method can successfully repair unsafe DNNs on multiple safety specifications with negligible impact on performance.

2   Deep Neural Network Repair

This section provides definitions and problem statements for DNN repair, and a brief overview of reachability analysis for DNNs. The problem is also extended to repair DNN agents in deep reinforcement learning.

2.1   Provably Safe DNNs

Let $f_\theta : \mathcal{X} \to \mathcal{Y}$ where $\mathcal{X} \subseteq \mathbb{R}^{|\mathbf{x}|}$ and $\mathcal{Y} \subseteq \mathbb{R}^{|\mathbf{y}|}$ denote the input and output space of a DNN with the parameter set θ, where given an input $\mathbf{x} \in \mathcal{X}$, it produces an output $\mathbf{y} = f_\theta(\mathbf{x}) \in \mathcal{Y}$. The safety problem of DNNs with reachability analysis on safety properties is formally defined as follows.

Definition 1 (Safety Property). *A safety property $\mathcal{P}$ of a DNN f_θ specifies a bounded input domain $\mathcal{I} \subseteq \mathcal{X}$ and a corresponding undesired output domain $\mathcal{U} \subseteq \mathcal{Y}$. The domain $\mathcal{I}$ refers to an interval with the lower bound $\underline{x}$ and the upper bound $\overline{x}$. The domain $\mathcal{U}$ refers to either a convex domain $Ay + b \leq 0$ or a non-convex domain consisting of multiple such convex domains.*

Definition 2 (DNN Reachable Domain). *Given an input domain $\mathcal{I} \subseteq \mathcal{X}$ to a DNN f_θ, its output reachable domain will be a subspace $\mathcal{O} \subseteq \mathcal{Y}$ where $\forall \mathbf{x} \in \mathcal{I}$, its output $\mathbf{y} = f_\theta(\mathbf{x})$ and $\mathbf{y} \in \mathcal{O}$. The domain $\mathcal{O}$ is exact if it only contains the output of $\mathbf{x} \in \mathcal{I}$. Otherwise, it is over approximated. It is formulated as $\mathcal{O} = \mathbb{N}(\mathcal{I})$.*

Definition 3 (DNN Safety Verification). *A DNN f_θ is safe on a safety property $\mathcal{P}$ that specifies an input domain $\mathcal{I}$ and an output unsafe domain $\mathcal{U}$, or $f_\theta \models \mathcal{P}$, if the exact output reachable domain $\mathcal{O} = \mathbb{N}(\mathcal{I})$ satisfies that $\mathcal{O} \cap \mathcal{U} = \emptyset$. Otherwise, it is unsafe, or $f_\theta \not\models \mathcal{P}$.*

Given a set of safety properties $\{\mathcal{P}\}_{i=1}^n$ and a candidate DNN f_θ, we define the DNN Repair problem as the problem of repairing the DNN to generate a new DNN f'_θ such that all the properties are satisfied, as defined in Problem 1. While repairing DNNs, it is also extremely important to preserve the parameter θ of the candidate DNN to the most extent because a subtle deviation on the parameter can lead to a high impact on the original performance and even introduce unexpected unsafe behaviors. These changes can be difficult to identify due to the black-box nature of DNNs. Therefore, our work also considers the minimal repair, which is formally defined in Problem 2.

Problem 1 (DNN Repair). Given a DNN candidate f_θ and a set of safety properties $\{\mathcal{P}\}_{i=1}^n$, at least one of which is violated, the repair problem is to train a new parameter set θ' based on θ, such that $f_{\theta'}$ satisfies all the safety properties, $f_{\theta'} \models \{\mathcal{P}\}_{i=1}^n$.

Problem 2 (Minimal DNN Repair). Given a DNN candidate f_θ and a set of safety properties $\{\mathcal{P}\}_{i=1}^n$, at least one of which is violated, the minimal repair problem is to train a new parameter set θ' based on θ, such that $f_{\theta'}$ satisfies all the safety properties, $f_{\theta'} \models \{\mathcal{P}\}_{i=1}^n$ while minimizing the L-distance $\|\theta' - \theta\|_L$.

For DNN classifier, we use classification accuracy on finite test data to analyze the performance of a repaired DNN $f_{\theta'}$ with respect to its original DNN f_θ. While for DNN regressor, we use the prediction error on test data. The parameter deviation $\|\theta' - \theta\|_L$ is used to evaluate the DNN change caused by the repair. Additionally, we also analyze the impact of the DNN deviation on the reachability of a DNN. Here, reachability indicates the reachable domain on safety properties. As reachability characterizes the behaviors of a DNN, a desired repair method should preserve its reachability. In the repair of DNN agents in DRL, the DNN performance is set to the averaged rewards on a certain number of episode tests.

2.2 DNN Agent Repair for Deep Reinforcement Learning

In Deep Reinforcement Learning (DRL), an agent is replaced with a DNN controller. The inputs to the DNN are states or observations, and their outputs correspond to agent actions. Similarly, a *property* $\mathcal{P}$ for the DNN agent defines a scenario where it specifies an input state space $\mathcal{I}$ containing all possible inputs, and also a domain $\mathcal{U}$ of undesired output actions. Different from regular DNN learning that uses existing training data, DRL learns through trial and error from their own experience collected from interactions with the environment. How to utilize the unsafe state domain computed with the reachability analysis to repair unsafe behaviors of the agent remains a problem. This problem is formally defined as follows:

Problem 3 (DNN Agent Repair). Given a DNN agent candidate f_θ and a set of safety properties $\{\mathcal{P}\}_{i=1}^n$, at least one of which is violated. The repair problem is to learn a DNN f'_θ through trial and error from the experience in the interactive environment, such that $f'_\theta \models \{\mathcal{P}\}_{i=1}^n$ while maximizing the reward.

2.3 Computation of Exact Unsafe Domain of ReLU DNNs

The exact unsafe reachable domain of a DNN is defined with respect to input-output safety properties. This domain is computed not only for safety verification but also for retraining purposes. The problem of computing the unsafe domain is known to be an NP-complete problem [5]. In this paper, the computation of the unsafe domain is based on [18]. In the following, we provide a brief overview of the algorithm.

Given a DNN f_θ and a safety property $\mathcal{P}$ that specifies an input domain $\mathcal{I}$ and an unsafe output domain $\mathcal{U}$, the reachability analysis algorithm computes a set of output reachable sets $\mathcal{S}_k$, the union of which is the exact output reachable domain $\mathcal{O} = \bigcup_{k=1}^m \mathcal{S}_k$. Here, a set $\mathcal{S}_k$ refers to a convex set. The computation is denoted as $\mathcal{O} = \mathbb{N}(\mathcal{I})$. This process is illustrated in Fig. 1. For each $\mathcal{S}_k$, we compute its overlap $\mathcal{S}_u^{[k]}$ with the specified unsafe output domain $\mathcal{U}$, and then apply a backtracking algorithm to compute its corresponding unsafe input subspace $\mathcal{E}_u^{[k]}$ which is also a convex set. The union of $\mathcal{S}_u^{[k]}$ is the exact unsafe output reachable domain $\mathcal{O}_u = \bigcup_{k=1}^m \mathcal{S}_u^{[k]}$ and the union of $\mathcal{E}_u^{[k]}$ is the exact unsafe input space $\mathcal{I}_u = \bigcup_{k=1}^m \mathcal{E}_u^{[k]}$. The backtracking process is denoted as $\mathcal{I}_u = \mathbb{B}(\mathcal{O}_u)$ in Fig. 1.

In the reachability analysis method described above, the set representation for $\mathcal{E}_u$ and $\mathcal{S}_u$ includes their vertices. These vertices of all $\mathcal{E}_u$s and $\mathcal{S}_u$s distribute over the entire unsafe input domain $\mathcal{I}_u$ and unsafe output reachable domain $\mathcal{O}_u$, respectively. In addition, $\mathcal{E}_u$ is actually a subset of a *linear region* of the DNN and the *linear region* is a maximal convex subset of the input domain to the DNN, over which the DNN is linear. Therefore, $\mathcal{S}_u$ and $\mathcal{E}_u$ have an affine mapping relation, and so do their vertices. Overall, these vertices can be utilized to approximate the distance between unsafe domains and safe domains in Eq. 3 for the repair process.

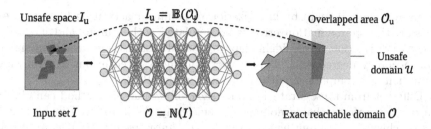

Fig. 1. Computation of the unsafe input-output reachable domain $\mathcal{I}_u \times \mathcal{O}_u$.

3 Framework for DNN Repair

3.1 Formulation of Loss Function for Problems 1 & 2

We treat *Problem* 1 for DNN repair as a single-objective optimization problem where we seek to minimize the distance between the reachable unsafe domain and the known safe domain. For *Problem* 2, which defines the minimal DNN repair problem, we would also like to minimize the change in DNN parameters such that the repaired network does not falsify the specifications and its behavior is as close as possible to the original network.

Loss Function for DNN Repair. We define a distance between the unsafe domain and the safe domain through the parameter set θ. By minimizing this distance, the unsafe domain can be gradually eliminated. The loss function can be formulated as:

$$\mathcal{L}_u(\theta) = \sum_{i=1}^{n} dist(\mathcal{O}_u(\mathcal{I}^{[i]}, \mathcal{U}^{[i]}, \theta), \overline{\mathcal{U}^{[i]}}) \tag{1}$$

where $\mathcal{I}^{[i]}$ and $\mathcal{U}^{[i]}$ are the input domain and output unsafe domain specified by the property $\mathcal{P}_i$, the function *dist* computes the distance between the identified unsafe reachable domain $\mathcal{O}_u$ and the safe domain $\overline{\mathcal{U}}$. This distance is designed to be the minimum distance of each $\mathbf{y} \in \mathcal{O}_u$ to the safe domain $\overline{\mathcal{U}}$, such that the modification of unsafe behaviors can be minimal. This minimum l-norm distance of $\mathbf{y} \in \mathcal{O}_u$ to the safe domain can be formulated as $\min_{\hat{\mathbf{y}} \in \overline{\mathcal{U}}} \|\mathbf{y}(\mathbf{x}, \theta) - \hat{\mathbf{y}}\|_l$.

The common strategy of related works which aim to repair or improve the safety of DNNs with reachability analysis [8,12,17] is by considering the largest distance which is formulated as

$$dist : \quad \max_{\mathbf{y} \in \mathcal{O}_u} \min_{\hat{\mathbf{y}} \in \overline{\mathcal{U}}} \|\mathbf{y}(\mathbf{x}, \theta) - \hat{\mathbf{y}}\|_l. \tag{2}$$

However, the issues are twofold with this approach. First, it is unknown whether the unsafe domain $\mathcal{O}_u$ is convex or concave, which makes it significantly challenging to convert the computation of the exact largest distance to an LP problem. Secondly, Their solutions are based on the over-approximation of the output unsafe reachable domain by linearization of nonlinear activation functions. As a result, the approximation error is accumulated with neurons and it can be so conservative that a low-fidelity approximated distance may result in significant accuracy degradation. This remark is demonstrated in our experimental evaluation and comparison with the related work ART [8].

Different from these strategies, our reachability analysis method can obtain the exact unsafe reachable domain $\mathcal{O}_u$ efficiently. As introduced in Sect. 2.3, this is achieved by computing the exact unsafe *linear regions* $\{\mathcal{E}_u\}_{k=1}^m$ and their output reachable domains $\{\mathcal{S}_u\}_{k=1}^m$, where $\mathcal{S}_u^{[k]} = \mathrm{N}(\mathcal{E}_u^{[k]})$ and $\mathcal{O}_u = \bigcup_{k=1}^m \mathcal{S}_u^{[k]}$. The vertices of each pair of domains $\mathcal{E}_u^{[k]} \times \mathcal{S}_u^{[k]}$ can be denoted as $V_k : x \times y$. The $y \in \mathcal{O}_u$ having the largest distance in Eq. 2 is also included in $\bigcup_{k=1}^m V_k$ which contains all the vertices of $\mathcal{O}_u$. Here, instead of identifying the $\mathbf{y}$, we choose to apply all the vertices to Eq. 1. This enables us to avoid searching the $\mathbf{y}$ in $\bigcup_{k=1}^m V_k$, which significantly reduces computation time. More importantly, since these vertices are distributed over the entire $\mathcal{O}_u$, they encode more geometrical information of this domain and hence are more representative than a single point $\mathbf{y}$ which only captures its largest distance to the safe domain $\overline{\mathcal{U}}$. Therefore, we substitute the *dist* function in Eq. 1 with a more general formulation:

$$dist : \quad \sum_{k=1}^{m} \sum_{j=1}^{|V_k|} \min_{\hat{\mathbf{y}} \in \overline{\mathcal{U}}} \|\mathbf{y}_j(\mathbf{x}_j, \theta) - \hat{\mathbf{y}}\|_l \tag{3}$$

where $|V_k|$ denotes the vertices set's cardinality.

In the following, we present our approach of approximating the closest safe $\hat{\mathbf{y}}$ to the unsafe $\mathbf{y}$. Recall that the unsafe domain $\mathcal{U}$ defined in the safety property is either a convex set formulated as $A\mathbf{x} + b \leq 0$ or a non-convex domain consisting of multiple such convex sets. Therefore, the problem of finding $\hat{\mathbf{y}}$ can be encoded as an LP problem of finding a $\hat{\mathbf{y}}$ on the boundaries of $\mathcal{U}$ such that the distance between $\hat{\mathbf{y}}$ and the interior $\mathbf{y}$ is minimal, where the optimal $\hat{\mathbf{y}}$ is located on one of its boundaries along its normal vector from $\mathbf{y}$. Let the vector from $\mathbf{y}$ to $\hat{\mathbf{y}}$ along the normal vector be denoted as $\Delta\mathbf{y}$. Then, the problem of finding $\hat{\mathbf{y}}$ can be formulated as

$$\hat{\mathbf{y}} = \mathbf{y} + (1 + \alpha)\Delta\mathbf{y}, \quad \min_{\hat{\mathbf{y}} \notin \mathcal{U}} \|\mathbf{y} - \hat{\mathbf{y}}\| \tag{4}$$

where α is a very small positive scalar to divert $\hat{\mathbf{y}}$ from the boundary of $\mathcal{U}$ into the safe domain.

Loss Function for the Minimal DNN Repair. The minimal repair problem is posed as a multi-objective optimization problem. In addition to the optimization for the repair problem explained previously, the minimal change of the DNN parameter θ is also considered in the problem formulation. For the minimization of the change, one simple and promising approach is to apply the training data in the retraining process of repair. Let the training input-output data be

---

Algorithm 1. DNN Repair

Input: $\mathcal{N}$, $\{\mathcal{P}\}_{i=1}^{m}$, $(\mathbf{x}, \mathbf{y})_{training}$ ▷ an unsafe DNN, safety properties, training data
Output: $\mathcal{N}'$ ▷ an safe DNN satisfying all its safety properties.
1: **procedure** $\mathcal{N}' = $ REPAIR$(\mathcal{N})$
2:　　$\mathcal{N}' \leftarrow \mathcal{N}$
3:　　**while** $\mathcal{N}'$ is not safe on $\{\mathcal{P}\}_{i=1}^{m}$ **do**
4:　　　$\mathcal{D}_{unsafe} = $ reachAnalysis$(\mathcal{N}, \{\mathcal{P}\}_{i=1}^{m})$ ▷ compute unsafe data domains
5:　　　$\mathcal{L}_u = $ Dist$(\mathcal{D}_{unsafe})$ ▷ approximate the distance using Eq. 3.
6:　　　$\mathcal{L}_c = $ Loss$((\mathbf{x}, \mathbf{y})_{training})$ ▷ compute loss on the training data in Eq. 5
7:　　　$\mathcal{N}' = $ Update$(\mathcal{N}', \mathcal{L}_u, \mathcal{L}_c)$ ▷ learn through the loss function in Eq. 6

---

denoted as $\mathcal{X} \times \mathcal{T}$, then the function for measuring parameter change can be formulated as

$$\mathcal{L}_c(\theta) = \sum_{i=1}^{N} \|\mathbf{y}_i(\mathbf{x}_i, \theta) - \mathbf{t}_i\|_l \tag{5}$$

where $(\mathbf{x}, \mathbf{t}) \in \mathcal{X} \times \mathcal{T}$. Here, we combine the function $\mathcal{L}_u$ for repair in Eq. 3 and the function $\mathcal{L}_c$ in Eq. 5 into one composite loss function using the weighted sum, and the minimal repair process can be formulated as

$$\underset{\theta}{\text{minimize}} \left(\alpha \cdot \mathcal{L}_u(\theta) + \beta \cdot \mathcal{L}_c(\theta) \right) \tag{6}$$

where $\alpha, \beta \in [0, 1]$ and $\alpha + \beta = 1$. The configuration $\alpha = 1$, $\beta = 0$ indicates only the repair process, while $\alpha = 0$, $\beta = 1$ indicates the process does not include the repair but only the minimization of the parameter change.

The process of the DNN repair is described in Algorithm 1. Given an unsafe DNN candidate, in each iteration, its unsafe domain over safety properties are first computed. With the unsafe domain, the distance in Eq. 3 is then computed. Finally, together with the loss value on the training data, the total loss value in Eq. 6 is computed and used to updated the DNN parameters. The algorithm terminates when the DNN is verified safe or the maximum number of iterations is reached.

3.2 Repair for Deep Reinforcement Learning

DRL is a machine learning technique where a DNN agent learns in an interactive environment from its own experience. Our method aims to repair an agent which violates its safety properties while performance is maintained as defined in Problem 3. In each *time step* of DRL, the agent computes the action and the next state based on the current state. A reward is assigned to the state transition. This transition is denoted as a *tuple* $\langle s, a, r, s' \rangle$ where s is the current state, a is the action, s' is the next state, and r is the reward. Then, this tuple together with previous experience is used to update the agent. The sequence of *time steps* from the beginning with an initial state to the end of the task is called an *episode*. The DRL algorithm in this work considers one of the most popular algorithms, the deep deterministic policy gradients algorithm (DDPG) [7] and is utilized on the rocket-lander benchmark[1] inspired by the lunar lander [1].

Our repair method for DRL is demonstrated in Fig. 2. Given an unsafe agent candidate in Fig. 2(a), our reachability analysis method computes the unsafe state domain that leads to an unsafe action by the agent. The vertices of unsafe *linear regions* are selected as representative unsafe states for the unsafe domain. Instead of minimizing its distance to the closest safe state as proposed for the regular repair, we run one *episode* with the unsafe state as an initial state as shown in Fig. 2(b). In this process, a penalty r is applied to the unsafe action observed in the learning process, from which safety can be more naturally learned. The penalty r is normally set to the least reward in the old experience, where the *old experience* refers to the experience from learning the original unsafe agent. In the repair process, the *tuple* in each *time step* will be stored into a global buffer for previous experience, which is named *new experiences*. For training, a set of *tuples* will be randomly selected from both experiences. The process in Fig. 2(a) will be repeated until the agent becomes safe. The process is also described in Algorithm 2.

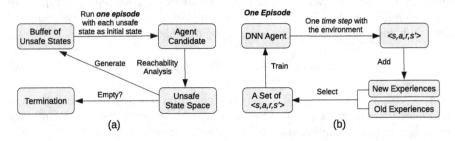

Fig. 2. Repair framework for deep reinforcement learning. In the loop (a), given an agent, its unsafe state space is first computed with our reachability analysis method. Then, *episodes* in (b) are run with unsafe states as initial states to update the agent, where the occurrence of unsafe states will be penalized.

4   Experiments and Evaluation

In this section, we evaluate our repair methods with two benchmarks. One is the DNN controllers for the Airborne Collision System X Unmanned (ACAS Xu) [4]. Our repair method in Sect. 3.1 is evaluated against the work ART [8]. We also study the different performance between our non-minimal repair method in Eq. 1 and our minimal repair in Eq. 5. To measure the impact of repair algorithms on DNNs, besides the accuracy on finite test data, we also analyze the changes of the DNN's reachability. The other benchmark is a set of DNN agents for a rocket lander system based on the lunar lander [1]. With this benchmark, we explore our repair method proposed in Sect. 3.2 to repair unsafe DNN agents for DRL. The hardware for all experiments is Intel Core i9-10900K CPU @3.7 GHz×, 10-core Processor, 128 GB Memory, 64-bit Ubuntu 18.04.

---

[1] https://github.com/arex18/rocket-lander.

Algorithm 2. Repair for Deep Reinforcement Learning

Input: $\mathcal{N}$, E, $\{\mathcal{P}\}_{i=1}^{m}$ ▷ an unsafe DNN agent, its old experience, safety properties

Output: $\mathcal{N}'$ ▷ a safe agent satisfying all its safety properties

1: **procedure** $\mathcal{N}' = \mathrm{REPAIR}(\mathcal{N})$
2:     $\mathcal{N}' \leftarrow \mathcal{N}$
3:     **while** $\mathcal{N}'$ is not safe on $\{\mathcal{P}\}_{i=1}^{m}$ **do**
4:         $\mathcal{D}_{unsafe} = \mathrm{reachAnalysis}(\mathcal{N}, \{\mathcal{P}\}_{i=1}^{m})$ ▷ compute unsafe state domains
5:         $S_{unsafe} = \mathrm{Vertices}(\mathcal{D}_{unsafe})$ ▷ representative unsafe states
6:         **for** s in S_{unsafe} **do**
7:             $\mathcal{N}' = \mathrm{Episode}(\mathcal{N}', s, E)$ ▷ one episode learning

---

4.1   Repair of ACAS Xu Neural Network Controllers

The ACAS Xu DNN controllers consist of an array of 45 fully-connected ReLU DNNs. They are used to approximate a large lookup table that converts sensor measurements into maneuver advisories in an airborne collision avoidance system, such that they can significantly reduce the massive memory usage and also the lookup time. All DNNs have the same architecture which includes 5 inputs, 5 outputs and 6 hidden layers with each containing 50 ReLU neurons. The 5 inputs correspond to the sensor measurement of the relative dynamics between the own ship and one intruder. The 5 outputs are prediction scores for 5 advisory actions. There are 10 safety properties defined, and each neural network is supposed to satisfy a subset of them.

Among these 45 network controllers, there are 35 unsafe networks violating at least one of the safety properties. Some works [5,8] report there are 36 unsafe networks due to numerical rounding issues [16]. Since the original dataset is not publicly available, we uniformly sample a set of 10k training data and 5k test data from the state space of DNNs, the same strategy as ART [8]. To repair these unsafe networks, our minimal repair and ART [8] require these datasets while our non-minimal repair approach does not.

The parameter configurations for the retraining process of a DNN in our repair are as follows. For non-minimal repair, the learning rate $lr = 0.001$. The learning rate for our non-minimal repair normally needs to be small, because the retraining of the DNN is only guided by the modification of unsafe behaviors and a large value may also greatly affect other safe behaviors. For the minimal repair, which is a multi-objective optimization problem, a set of configurations are applied to estimate the optimal performance. Here, the learning rate lr and the value (α, β) in Eq. 6 are set as below. There are 6 different settings for the minimal repair of each unsafe network. The optimal result is selected for performance comparison. The loss functions in Eq. 1 and 5 are computed with the Euclidean norm. As introduced, each iteration of our repair consists of the reachability analysis and epochs of retraining. Here, we empirically set the maximum iteration to 100 and the number of epochs to 200 for all our repair methods. For ART [8], their default settings are applied for the comparison.

	Learning Rate (lr)	(α, β)
Non-minimal Repair	0.001	-
Minimal Repair	{0.01, 0.001}	{(0.2,0.8),(0.5, 0.5),(0.8,0.2)}

Success and Accuracy. The experimental results are shown in Table 1. Table 1 describes the repair successes and the accuracy of repaired networks. Recall that the test data are sampled from the original network, therefore, the accuracy of the original network on these data is 100%. As shown, in terms of success, our non-minimal repair and minimal repair methods both successfully repair all 35 unsafe networks. ART can repair 33 networks. While ART with refinement which computes tighter approximation than ART can repair all of the networks. In terms of accuracy, our repaired networks exhibit a higher accuracy than ART and some of our repaired networks even have 100% accuracy, indicating less performance degradation. We hypothesize that the difference of performance in ART, as discussed in Sect. 1 is primarily due to the use of over-approximation methods for the unsafe domains of DNNs. They may be so conservative that the estimated distance in Eq. 1 is inaccurate, resulting in performance degradation. It can be also noticed that with the refinement in ART which computes a tighter approximation of domains, the number of repair successes and their accuracy increase. Overall, with the exact reachability analysis, our methods can outperform ART in terms of accuracy.

Table 1. Repair of ACAS Xu neural network controllers.

Methods	Repair Successes	Min Accu.	Mean Accu.	Max Accu.
Art	33/35	88.74%	94.87%	99.92%
Art-refinement	35/35	90.38%	96.23%	99.92%
Our Non-minimal Repair	**35/35**	**98.66%**	**99.74%**	**100.0%**
Our Minimal Repair	**35/35**	**99.38%**	**99.83%**	**100.0%**

For our non-minimal repair and minimal repair methods, we can notice that the accuracy difference of their repaired networks in Table 1 is trivial. Recall that our minimal repair can have the Pareto optimality issue in its multi-objective optimization in Eq. 6, while our non-minimal repair does not. It means that in the minimal repair, the minimization of the DNN deviation may impede the optimization for repair. By contrast, our non-minimal repair can consistently repair all networks with one parameter setting and meanwhile maintain the high accuracy without the usage of training data.

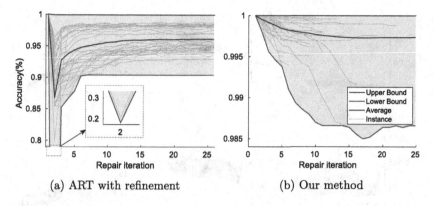

(a) ART with refinement   (b) Our method

Fig. 3. Accuracy evolution of models with respect to the number of repair iterations. All models before the repair are unsafe on at least one safety property. All repairs successfully generate safe models in the end.

DNN Deviation After Repair. Additionally, the accuracy evolution of networks under repair is also demonstrated in Fig. 3. It includes ART with refinement (a) and our non-minimal repair method (b). We can notice that at the beginning of ART, the accuracy of the repaired DNN will first drop quickly and in some instances, it even drops below 20%. Then, the accuracy gradually converges to a higher value. We speculate that at the beginning of the repair, ART mainly generates a safe model with a large modification of the original network and then, train this safe network with the training data to improve the accuracy.

We also analyze the impact of repair on the reachability of DNNs. The reachability refers to the output reachable domain of DNNs on the input domains $\mathcal{I}$ of their safety properties. Here, we consider the network N_{21} which includes safety properties 1, 2, 3, 4. It violates Property 2 whose unsafe output domain is that $\mathbf{y}_1$ is the maximum. The output reachable domain of N_{21} has 5 dimensions, and it is projected on two dimensions for visualization.

The output reachable domains of N_{21} on Properties 1 & 2, projected on $(\mathbf{y}_1, \mathbf{y}_3)$ and $(\mathbf{y}_1, \mathbf{y}_5)$, are shown in Fig. 4. (a) represents the reachable domain of the original unsafe N_{21}. (b) and (c) represents the reachable domain of repaired N_{21} by our method and ART, respectively. The blue area represents the safe reachable domain, and the red area represents the unsafe reachable domain. We can notice that the unsafe domain is successfully eliminated by our method and ART. We can also notice that compared to ART, our method barely changes the reachable domain. With respect to the original reachable domain, our reachable domain on $(\mathbf{y}_1, \mathbf{y}_5)$ exhibits a more obvious change than the one on $(\mathbf{y}_1, \mathbf{y}_3)$. This is because in the majority of safety violations, $\mathbf{y}_5$ is the second-largest output, next to $\mathbf{y}_1$. Therefore, our repair modifies $\mathbf{y}_5$ the most to eliminate the unsafe domain, which avoids large changes on other dimensions.

In addition, the reachability on Properties 3 & 4, projected on $(\mathbf{y}_1, \mathbf{y}_5)$, is also shown in Fig. 5. Similarly, we can notice that the impact of our repair method

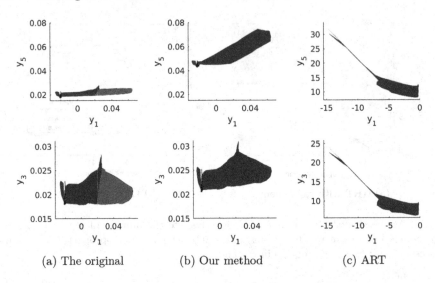

(a) The original   (b) Our method   (c) ART

Fig. 4. Reachability of repaired network N_{21} on Properties 1 & 2, projected on dimensions $(\mathbf{y}_1, \mathbf{y}_5)$ and $(\mathbf{y}_1, \mathbf{y}_3)$. It shows the output reachable domains of the original network and its repaired networks. The red area represents the unsafe reachable domain, while the blue area represents the safe domain. (Color figure online)

on the reachability of N_{21} is negligible, but ART changes the entire reachable domain. It can justify that a slight deviation on the DNN parameter may cause a tremendous change in its behaviors. It also shows that our DNN repair on one property hardly affects the DNN performance on other properties.

Table 2. Running time (**sec**) of our repair method and ART

Methods	**Regular Cases** (33 Nets)			**Hard Cases** (2 Nets)	
	Min	Mean Time	Max	Time (N_{19})	Time (N_{29})
Art	66.5	71.4	100.3	**65.6**	**71.5**
Art-refinement	85.4	89.2	90.1	84.6	90.4
Our Method	7.4	**65.5**	230.1	7173.2	3634.9

The running time of our repair method and ART is shown in Table 2. Here, we divide the repair of all 35 networks into regular cases and hard cases in terms of the volume of input domain of their safety properties. Normally, a larger input domain requires more computation for reachability analysis. The regular cases include all 33 networks whose safety properties specify small input domains. While the hard cases include the 2 networks N_{19} and N_{29} whose safety properties 7 and 8 specify large input domains. It can be noticed that our method is faster than ART in the regular cases but slower in the hard cases. That is

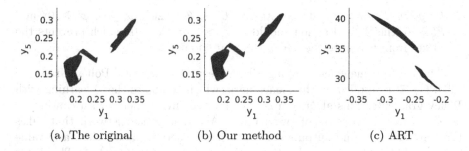

(a) The original   (b) Our method   (c) ART

Fig. 5. Reachability of repaired network N_{21} on Properties 3 & 4, on which the original network is safe. The domain is projected on dimensions $(\mathbf{y}_1, \mathbf{y}_5)$. We observe that due to the over approximation, ART repairs the network needlessly and changes the reachable set of the network.

because that unlike the over-approximation method utilized by ART, the exact reachability analysis of networks is an NP-complete problem [5]. When handling hard cases, it becomes less efficient. Despite this undesired efficiency in the hard cases, the exact analysis enables our method to repair all networks with much less performance degradation than ART.

4.2 Rocket Lander Benchmark

The rocket lander benchmark[2] is based on the lunar lander [1]. It is a vertical rocket landing model simulating SpaceX's Falcon 9 first stage rocket. Unlike the lunar lander whose action space is discrete, its action space is continuous, which commonly exists in the practical applications. Besides the rocket, a barge is also included on the sea which moves horizontally, and its dynamics are monitored. The rocket includes one main engine thruster at the bottom with an actuated joint and also two other side nitrogen thrusters attached to the sides of the top by unactuated joints. The main engine has a power F_E ranging in $[0,1]$ and its angle relative to the rocket body is φ. The power F_S of the side thrusters ranges in $[-1, 1]$, where -1 indicates that the right thruster has full throttle and the left thruster is turned off, while 1 indicates the opposite. The rocket landing starts in certain height. Its goal is to land on the center of the barge without falling or crashing by controlling its velocity and lateral angle θ through the thrusters.

There are three actions, the main engine thruster F_E, its angle φ and the side nitrogen thrusters F_S. The observation contains the position x and y of the rocket relative to the barge, the velocity v_x and v_y of the rocket, its lateral angle θ, its angular velocity ω, and also last action advisory. It can be denoted as $[x, y, v_x, v_y, \theta, \omega, F'_E, \varphi', F'_S]$. Two safety properties are defined as below.

1. *Property 1*: for the state constraints $-20° \leq \theta \leq -6°$, $\omega < 0$, $\varphi' \leq 0°$ and $F'_S \leq 0$, the desired action should be $\varphi < 0$ or $F_S < 0$, which prevents the rocket from tilting to the right in this state domain.

---

[2] https://github.com/arex18/rocket-lander.git.

2. *Property 2*: for the state constraints $6° \leq \theta \leq 20°$, $\omega \geq 0$, $\varphi' \geq 0°$ and $F_S' \geq 0$, the desired action should be $\varphi > 0$ or $F_S > 0$, which prevents the rocket from tilting to the left in this state domain.

The reinforcement learning algorithm Deep Deterministic Policy Gradients (DDPG) [7] is applied on this benchmark, which combines the Q-learning with Policy gradients. This algorithm is used for the environments with continuous action spaces. It consists of two models: Actor, a policy network that takes the state as input and outputs exact continuous actions, and Critic, a Q-value network that takes state and action as input and outputs Q-values. The Actor is our target agent controller. Here, among well-trained agents with DDPG, we first identify unsafe agents that violate these properties. Then, we apply our method to repair these agents. The Actor is designed with 9 inputs for state, 5 hidden layers with each containing 20 ReLU neurons, 3 outputs with subsequent *tanh* function.

Three unsafe agent controllers are learned. For the repair process, the learning rate for Actor and Critic is set to 10^{-4} and 10^{-3} respectively. The old experience from the learning process and the new experience from the current repair process are randomly selected for the learning, as shown in Fig. 2(b). A penalty reward is added for any wrong actions generated from input states. Its value is set to the lowest reward in the old experience. The change of performance is evaluated by $\mathbf{R} = (r' - r)/r$ where r' and r are the averaged reward of the repaired agent and the original agent tested on 1000 *episodes*.

Table 3. Repair of unsafe agents for the rocket lander. **ID** is the index of each repair. **R** denotes the performance change ratio of the repaired agent compared to the original unsafe agent. **Iter** denotes the number of iterations for repair. **Time** (*sec*) denotes the running time for one repair with our method.

ID	Agent 1			Agent 2			Agent 3		
	R	Iter	Time	R	Iter	Time	R	Iter	Time
1	+0.063	3	332.7	+0.048	3	635.7	+0.053	2	446.1
2	+0.088	3	302.0	+0.012	6	1308.4	+0.085	3	1451.6
3	+0.079	3	447.9	-0.084	4	812.9	-0.033	3	2417.1
4	+0.078	3	884.2	+0.025	3	620.3	+0.073	2	1395.3
5	+0.085	3	754.3	-0.001	4	813.5	-0.165	5	2632.9

For each unsafe agent, we conduct repair 5 times with each repair aiming to obtain a safe agent. There are totally 15 instances. The experimental results are shown in Table 3, which describe the performance change ratio **R**, the iterations of repair and the total time. We note that our framework can successfully repair the 3 agents in all 15 instances. In most cases, the performance of the repaired agent is slightly improved. The performance degradation in other instances is also trivial. The repair process takes 2–6 iterations for all instances with the running time ranging from 332.7 s to 2632.9 s. The evolution of the reachability of repaired network is also shown in Fig. 6. It shows that our repair only slightly affects the reachable domain of the agent.

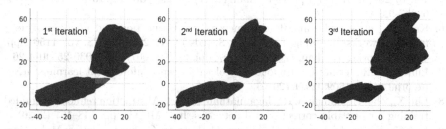

Fig. 6. The evolution of the output reachable domain on Property 1&2 in the repair of Agent 1 on ID 1. The domain is projected on $(\mathbf{y}_2, \mathbf{y}_3)$. The blue area represents the exact output reachable domain while the red area represents the unsafe reachable domain. (Color figure online)

5   Conclusion and Future Work

We have presented methods to repair unsafe DNN controllers for autonomous systems. our method can be utilized to repair unsafe DNNs, even without training data. It can also be integrated into existing reinforcement algorithms to synthesize safe DNN controllers. Our experimental results on two practical benchmarks have shown that our method can successfully obtain a provably safe DNN while maintaining its accuracy and performance.

Acknowledgements. The material presented in this paper is based upon work supported by the National Science Foundation (NSF) through grant numbers 1910017 and 2028001, the Defense Advanced Research Projects Agency (DARPA) under contract number FA8750-18-C-0089, and the Air Force Office of Scientific Research (AFOSR) under contract number FA9550-22-1-0019. Any opinions, findings, and conclusions or recommendations expressed in this paper are those of the authors and do not necessarily reflect the views of AFOSR, DARPA, or NSF.

References

1. Brockman, G., et al.: Openai gym. arXiv preprint arXiv:1606.01540 (2016)
2. Goldberger, B., Katz, G., Adi, Y., Keshet, J.: Minimal modifications of deep neural networks using verification. In: LPAR, vol. 2020, p. 23 (2020)
3. Goodfellow, I.J., Shlens, J., Szegedy, C.: Explaining and harnessing adversarial examples. arXiv preprint arXiv:1412.6572 (2014)
4. Julian, K.D., Lopez, J., Brush, J.S., Owen, M.P., Kochenderfer, M.J.: Policy compression for aircraft collision avoidance systems. In: 2016 IEEE/AIAA 35th Digital Avionics Systems Conference (DASC), pp. 1–10. IEEE (2016)

5. Katz, G., Barrett, C., Dill, D.L., Julian, K., Kochenderfer, M.J.: Reluplex: an efficient SMT solver for verifying deep neural networks. In: Majumdar, R., Kunčak, V. (eds.) Reluplex: an efficient smt solver for verifying deep neural networks. LNCS, vol. 10426, pp. 97–117. Springer, Cham (2017). https://doi.org/10.1007/978-3-319-63387-9_5
6. Katz, G., et al.: The marabou framework for verification and analysis of deep neural networks. In: Dillig, I., Tasiran, S. (eds.) CAV 2019. LNCS, vol. 11561, pp. 443–452. Springer, Cham (2019). https://doi.org/10.1007/978-3-030-25540-4_26
7. Lillicrap, T.P., et al.: Continuous control with deep reinforcement learning. arXiv preprint arXiv:1509.02971 (2015)
8. Lin, X., Zhu, H., Samanta, R., Jagannathan, S.: Art: Abstraction refinement-guided training for provably correct neural networks. In: FMCAD, pp. 148–157 (2020)
9. Liu, C., Arnon, T., Lazarus, C., Strong, C., Barrett, C., Kochenderfer, M.J.: Algorithms for verifying deep neural networks. arXiv preprint arXiv:1903.06758 (2019)
10. Madry, A., Makelov, A., Schmidt, L., Tsipras, D., Vladu, A.: Towards deep learning models resistant to adversarial attacks. arXiv preprint arXiv:1706.06083 (2017)
11. Majd, K., Zhou, S., Amor, H.B., Fainekos, G., Sankaranarayanan, S.: Local repair of neural networks using optimization. arXiv preprint arXiv:2109.14041 (2021)
12. Mirman, M., Gehr, T., Vechev, M.: Differentiable abstract interpretation for provably robust neural networks. In: International Conference on Machine Learning, pp. 3578–3586 (2018)
13. Sohn, J., Kang, S., Yoo, S.: Search based repair of deep neural networks. arXiv preprint arXiv:1912.12463 (2019)
14. Tran, H.-D., et al.: NNV: the neural network verification tool for deep neural networks and learning-enabled cyber-physical systems. In: Lahiri, S.K., Wang, C. (eds.) CAV 2020. LNCS, vol. 12224, pp. 3–17. Springer, Cham (2020). https://doi.org/10.1007/978-3-030-53288-8_1
15. Usman, M., Gopinath, D., Sun, Y., Noller, Y., Pasareanu, C.: NNrepair: constraint-based repair of neural network classifiers. arXiv preprint arXiv:2103.12535 (2021)
16. Wang, S., Pei, K., Whitehouse, J., Yang, J., Jana, S.: Formal security analysis of neural networks using symbolic intervals. In: 27th {USENIX} Security Symposium ({USENIX} Security 2018), pp. 1599–1614 (2018)
17. Wong, E., Kolter, Z.: Provable defenses against adversarial examples via the convex outer adversarial polytope. In: International Conference on Machine Learning, pp. 5286–5295. PMLR (2018)
18. Yang, X., Johnson, T.T., Tran, H.D., Yamaguchi, T., Hoxha, B., Prokhorov, D.: Reachability analysis of deep RELU neural networks using facet-vertex incidence. In: Proceedings of the 24th International Conference on Hybrid Systems: Computation and Control. HSCC 2021, Association for Computing Machinery, New York, NY, USA (2021). https://doi.org/10.1145/3447928.3456650
19. Yang, X., Yamaguchi, T., Tran, H.D., Hoxha, B., Johnson, T.T., Prokhorov, D.: Reachability analysis of convolutional neural networks. arXiv preprint arXiv:2106.12074 (2021)

On Neural Network Equivalence Checking Using SMT Solvers

Charis Eleftheriadis[1], Nikolaos Kekatos[1], Panagiotis Katsaros[1(✉)],
and Stavros Tripakis[1,2]

[1] School of Informatics, Aristotle University of Thessaloniki, Thessaloniki, Greece
{celefther,nkekatos,katsaros}@csd.auth.gr
[2] Khoury College of Computer Sciences, Northeastern University, Boston, USA
stavros@northeastern.edu

Abstract. Two pretrained neural networks are deemed (approximately) equivalent if they yield similar outputs for the same inputs. Equivalence checking of neural networks is of great importance, due to its utility in replacing learning-enabled components with (approximately) equivalent ones, when there is need to fulfill additional requirements or to address security threats, as is the case when using knowledge distillation, adversarial training, etc. In this paper, we present a method to solve various strict and approximate equivalence checking problems for neural networks, by reducing them to SMT satisfiability checking problems. This work explores the utility and limitations of the neural network equivalence checking framework, and proposes avenues for future research and improvements toward more scalable and practically applicable solutions. We present experimental results, for diverse types of neural network models (classifiers and regression networks) and equivalence criteria, towards a general and application-independent equivalence checking approach.

Keywords: Neural network · Equivalence checking · Verification · SMT

1 Introduction

Equivalence checking is the problem of checking whether two given artifacts (e.g. digital circuits, programs, etc.) are equivalent in some sense. Equivalence checking is standard practice in the domain of hardware design and the EDA industry [27,31,33,38]. There, digital circuits are subject to successive transformations for optimization and other purposes, and it is important to ensure that each successive design preserves the functionality of (i.e., is functionally equivalent to) the original.

In this paper, we are interested in the problem of equivalence checking for neural networks (NNs). For two pretrained NNs of different architectures, or of the same architecture with different parameters, the problem is to check whether they yield similar outputs for the same inputs. Contrary to equivalence checking for digital circuits, where strict functional equivalence is typically desired, *similar outputs* does not necessarily mean *identical* outputs in the case of NNs. As we shall see, the exact definition

© Springer Nature Switzerland AG 2022
S. Bogomolov and D. Parker (Eds.): FORMATS 2022, LNCS 13465, pp. 237–257, 2022.
https://doi.org/10.1007/978-3-031-15839-1_14

of equivalence depends on the application and NNs at hand (e.g. classifier, regression, etc.). Therefore, we consider both strict and approximate equivalences in this paper.

The equivalence checking problem for NNs is not only fundamental, intellectually interesting, and challenging. It is also motivated by a series of concerns similar to those motivating equivalence checking in the EDA industry, as well as recent developments in machine learning technology. The objective is to ensure that the smaller network is in some sense equivalent or approximately equivalent to the original one. Specifically, one application area is *neural network compression* [8]. Different compression techniques exist, e.g. *knowledge distillation, pruning, quantization, tensor decomposition*; see surveys in [8, 26, 29]. *Knowledge distillation* [15] is the process of transferring knowledge from a large neural network to a smaller one that may be appropriate for deployment on a device with limited computational resources. Another related application area includes the techniques widely known under the term *regularization* [21], which aim to lower the complexity of NNs in order to achieve better performance. In other cases, NNs used in systems with learning-enabled components [9] may have to be updated for a number of reasons [30]; for example, security concerns such as the need to withstand data perturbations (e.g. adversarial examples), or possibly incomplete coverage of the neural network's input domain. In the context of NN verification, several *abstraction* methods are often employed, for instance in order to reduce the complexity of the verification problem, e.g. see [3]. In all the aforementioned cases, the original and resulting NNs need to be functionally comparable in some way. A number of cases where equivalence checking for neural networks arise are also discussed in [19, 28].

This paper presents the first, to our knowledge, systematic study of the equivalence checking problem for NNs, using a *Satisfiability Modulo Theory* (SMT) [5] approach. We define several formal notions of (approximate) equivalence for NNs, present encodings of the corresponding NN equivalence checking problems into satisfiability checking problems, and describe experimental results on examples of varying complexity.

In particular, the contributions of this paper are the following:

– We define several formal equivalence checking problems for neural networks based on various strict and approximate equivalence criteria that may each be appropriate for different neural network applications.
– We reduce the equivalence checking problem to a logical satisfiability problem using an SMT-based encoding. The approach is sound and complete in the sense that the two given NNs are equivalent iff the resulting SMT formula is unsatisfiable.
– We present a prototype implementation and experimental results including (i) sanity checks of our SMT-based encoding, and (ii) checks showing the equivalence and non-equivalence, as well as checking the scalability of SMT solvers for three diverse neural network applications covering the cases of classifiers (including the well-known MNIST dataset), as well as regression models.

The rest of this paper is organized as follows. Section 2 provides a formal definition of NN models. Section 3 presents diverse equivalence criteria for the wide range of common NN applications and formally defines the equivalence checking problem. Section 4 presents our SMT-based encoding for reducing equivalence checking to a logical satisfiability problem. Section 5 includes the experimental results. In Sect. 6, we review the related work and in Sect. 7 we provide our concluding remarks.

2 Preliminaries: Neural Networks

2.1 Notation

The set of real numbers is denoted by $\mathbb{R}$. The set of natural numbers is denoted by $\mathbb{N}$. Given some $x \in \mathbb{R}^n$ and some $i \in \{1, ..., n\}$, $x(i)$ denotes the i-th element of x.

2.2 Neural Networks

In general, a neural network (NN) can be defined as a function:

$$f : I \to O \tag{1}$$

where $I \subseteq \mathbb{R}^n$ is some input domain with n *features* and $O \subseteq \mathbb{R}^m$ an output domain.

For a NN image classifier, we typically have $I = [0, 255]^n \subseteq \mathbb{N}^n$ and a labeling function $L : \mathbb{R}^m \to \mathbb{N}$ that maps each $y \in O$ to some label $l \in \mathbb{N}$. For NNs solving regression problems, we have $I \subseteq \mathbb{R}^n$ and no labeling function.

The above definition of NNs is purely semantic. Concretely, a NN consists of layers of *nodes* (neurons), including one *hidden layer* (H) or more, beyond the layers of input (I) and output (O) nodes. Nodes denote a combination of affine value transformation with an *activation function*, which is typically piecewise linear or nonlinear. Value transformations are *weighted* based on how nodes of different layers are connected, whereas an extra term called *bias* is added per node. Weights (W) and biases (b) for all nodes are the NN's *parameters* and their values are determined via *training*.

Since every layer is multidimensional we use vectors and/or matrices to represent all involved operations. Let $\mathbf{x} \in \mathbb{R}^{1 \times n}$ be the matrix denoting some $x \in I$. For a hidden layer with r nodes, $\mathbf{H}^{1 \times r}$ represents the output of this hidden layer. Assuming that the hidden and output layers are fully connected, we denote with $\mathbf{W}^{(1)} \in \mathbb{R}^{n \times r}$ the hidden layer weights and with $\mathbf{b}^{(1)} \in \mathbb{R}^{1 \times r}$ the biases associated with its nodes. Similarly, the output layer weights are denoted by $\mathbf{W}^{(2)} \in \mathbb{R}^{r \times m}$, where m refers to the number of output layer nodes, and $\mathbf{b}^{(2)} \in \mathbb{R}^{1 \times m}$ denotes the corresponding biases. Then, the output $y = f(x)$ of the NN is given by $\mathbf{y} \in \mathbb{R}^m$ where $\mathbf{y}$ is computed as:

$$\mathbf{H} = \alpha(\mathbf{x}\,\mathbf{W}^{(1)} + \mathbf{b}^{(1)}) \tag{2}$$

$$\mathbf{y} = \alpha'(\mathbf{H}\,\mathbf{W}^{(2)} + \mathbf{b}^{(2)}) \tag{3}$$

where $\alpha(\cdot), \alpha'(\cdot)$ are the *activation functions* (e.g. sigmoid, hyperbolic tangent, etc.) applied to the vectors of the hidden and output layers element-wise. A common activation function is the Rectified Linear Unit (ReLU), which is defined, for $\chi \in \mathbb{R}$, as:

$$ReLU(\chi) = \begin{cases} \chi, & \text{if } \chi \geq 0 \\ 0, & \text{otherwise} \end{cases} \tag{4}$$

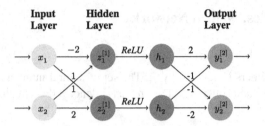

Fig. 1. Feedforward NN with an input layer of 2 inputs (x_1, x_2), an output layer with 2 outputs (y_1, y_2) and no activation function, and 1 hidden layer with 2 neurons and a ReLU activation function. The values on transitions refer to the *weights* and the superscript values to the biases.

Another example is the *hard tanh* function [10] (used in the experiments of Sect. 5) that typically serves as the output layer activation function of NNs trained for regression. For $\chi \in \mathbb{R}$, *hardtanh* is defined as:

$$HardTanh(\chi) = \begin{cases} 1, & \text{if } \chi > 1 \\ -1, & \text{if } \chi < -1 \\ \chi, & \text{otherwise} \end{cases} \tag{5}$$

Multiple Hidden Layers: The NN definition provided above is easily generalised to multiple hidden layers $H, H', H'', \cdots$. We consider that weights and biases for all layers and nodes are fixed, since we focus on equivalence checking of NNs *after* training.

Example 1. Consider a simple feedforward NN with two inputs, two outputs, and one hidden layer with two nodes (Fig. 1). The selection of the weights and biases is done randomly, the activation function of the hidden layer is ReLU and there is no activation function for the output layer. For this example, Eq. (2) takes the form:

$$\begin{bmatrix} x_1 & x_2 \end{bmatrix} \cdot \begin{bmatrix} W_{11} & W_{12} \\ W_{21} & W_{22} \end{bmatrix} + \begin{bmatrix} b_1^{(1)} & b_2^{(1)} \end{bmatrix} = \begin{bmatrix} x_1 & x_2 \end{bmatrix} \cdot \begin{bmatrix} -2 & 1 \\ 1 & 2 \end{bmatrix} + \begin{bmatrix} 1 & 1 \end{bmatrix}$$

$$= \begin{bmatrix} -2 \cdot x_1 + x_2 + 1 & x_1 + 2 \cdot x_2 + 1 \end{bmatrix}$$

Denote the result of the affine transformation of the NN's hidden layer by:

$$\begin{bmatrix} z_1 & z_2 \end{bmatrix} = \begin{bmatrix} -2 \cdot x_1 + x_2 + 1 & x_1 + 2 \cdot x_2 + 1 \end{bmatrix} \quad \text{and}$$

$$\mathbf{H} = \begin{bmatrix} h_1 & h_2 \end{bmatrix} = \begin{bmatrix} ReLU(z_1) & ReLU(z_2) \end{bmatrix}$$

The output $\mathbf{y}$ of the NN from Eq. (3) is:

$$\mathbf{y} = \begin{bmatrix} h_1 & h_2 \end{bmatrix} \cdot \begin{bmatrix} 2 & -1 \\ -1 & -2 \end{bmatrix} + \begin{bmatrix} b_1^{(2)} & b_2^{(2)} \end{bmatrix} = \begin{bmatrix} 2 \cdot h_1 - h_2 + 2 & -h_1 - 2 \cdot h_2 + 2 \end{bmatrix}$$

3   Strict and Approximate Equivalences for Neural Networks

In this section, we present various equivalence relations for NNs and we formulate the equivalence checking problem. Similar equivalence notions appeared recently in [19, 28].

3.1 Strict Neural Network Equivalence

Strict NN equivalence is essentially functional equivalence:

Definition 1 (Strict NN Equivalence). *For two neural networks $f : I \to O$ and $f' : I \to O$, we say that they are strictly equivalent, denoted $f \equiv f'$, if and only if:*

$$\forall x \in I, f(x) = f'(x) \tag{6}$$

Strict NN equivalence is a true equivalence relation, i.e., it is reflexive ($f \equiv f$ for any f), symmetric ($f \equiv f'$ iff $f' \equiv f$), and transitive ($f \equiv f'$ and $f' \equiv f''$ implies $f \equiv f''$).

However, strict NN equivalence can be a very restrictive requirement. For example, if we have two classifiers we may want to consider them equivalent if they *always* select the same top output class, even if the remaining output classes are not ordered in the same way. This motivates us to consider the following *approximate* notions of equivalence. These approximate "equivalences" need not be true equivalences, i.e., they may not satisfy the transitivity property (although they are always reflexive and symmetric).

3.2 Approximate Neural Network Equivalences Based on L_p Norms

As usual, we assume that $O \subseteq \mathbb{R}^m$. Let $\|y\|_p = norm_p(y)$ denoting the L_p-norm of vector $y \in O$, for $norm_p : O \to \mathbb{R}$ with $p = 1, 2, \infty$. For two vectors $y, y' \in O$, if $p = 1$ we obtain the Manhattan norm, $L_1(y, y') = \|y - y'\|_1 = \sum_{i=1}^{m}|y(i) - y'(i)|$, which measures the sum of differences between the two vectors. For $p = 2$, we refer to the Euclidean distance $L_2(y, y') = \|y - y'\|_2 = (\sum_{i=1}^{m}|y(i) - y'(i)|^2)^{\frac{1}{2}}$. Finally, for $p = \infty$, the L_∞ distance measures the maximum change to any coordinate:

$$L_\infty(y, y') = \| y - y' \|_\infty = \max(|y(1) - y'(1)|, \ldots, |y(m) - y'(m)|). \tag{7}$$

Then, we define the following notion of approximate equivalence:

Definition 2 ((p, ϵ)-approximate equivalence). *Consider two neural networks $f : I \to O$ and $f' : I \to O$, $norm_p : O \to \mathbb{R}$, and some $\epsilon > 0$. We say that f and f' are (p, ϵ)-approximately equivalent, denoted $f \sim_{p,\epsilon} f'$, if and only if:*

$$\forall x \in I, \quad \|f(x) - f'(x)\|_p < \epsilon \tag{8}$$

It can be seen that the relation $\sim_{p,\epsilon}$ is reflexive and symmetric.

3.3 Approximate Neural Network Equivalences Based on Order of Outputs

NN classifiers work essentially by computing output values and then mapping them to specific classes. Two such networks may be considered equivalent, if they always produce the same order of outputs, even though the output values might not be the same. For example, consider two classifiers f and f' over three possible output classes. Suppose that, for a given input, f produces $(0.3, 0.5, 0.2)$ and f' produces $(0.25, 0.6, 0.15)$. We may then consider that for this input the outputs of f and f' are equivalent, since they have the same order, namely, $2, 1, 3$ (assuming vector indices start at 1). If this happens for all inputs, we may want to consider f and f' (approximately) equivalent.

To capture the above notion of approximate equivalence, we introduce the function:

$$\texttt{argsort}_m : \mathbb{R}^m \to \mathcal{Z}_m, \text{ for } m \in \mathbb{N}$$

where $\mathcal{Z}_m \subseteq \{1, 2, 3, \ldots, m\}^m$ is the set of permutations of indices of the m elements. For a given $s \in \mathbb{R}^m$, $\texttt{argsort}_m(s)$ returns the permutation that sorts s in decreasing order. Thus, $\texttt{argsort}_3(0.3, 0.5, 0.2) = \texttt{argsort}_3(0.25, 0.6, 0.15) = (2, 1, 3)$. If two vector values are equal, $\texttt{argsort}$ orders them from lower to higher index. This ensures determinism of the $\texttt{argsort}$ function, e.g., $\texttt{argsort}_3(0.3, 0.4, 0.3) = (2, 1, 3)$.

Definition 3 (Top-k $\texttt{argsort}$ equivalence). *Suppose $O \subseteq \mathbb{R}^m$. Consider two neural networks $f : I \to O$ and $f' : I \to O$, and some $k \in \{1, ..., m\}$. We say that f and f' are top-k $\texttt{argsort}$ equivalent, denoted $f \approx_k f'$, if and only if*

$$\forall x \in I, \forall i \in \{1, ..., k\}, \left(\texttt{argsort}_m \big(f(x) \big) \right)(i) = \left(\texttt{argsort}_m \big(f'(x) \big) \right)(i) \quad (9)$$

Top-k $\texttt{argsort}$ equivalence requires the first k indices of the $\texttt{argsort}$ of the outputs of f and f' to be equal. It is a true equivalence (reflexive, symmetric, and transitive).

A special case of top-k $\texttt{argsort}$ equivalence is when $k = 1$. We call this $\texttt{argmax}$ *equivalence*, with reference to the $\texttt{argmax}$ function that returns the index of the maximum value of a vector, e.g., $\texttt{argmax}(0.3, 0.5, 0.2) = \texttt{argmax}(0.25, 0.6, 0.15) = 2$.

Definition 4 ($\texttt{argmax}$ equivalence). *Consider the same setting as in Definition 3. We say that f and f' are $\texttt{argmax}$ equivalent iff $f \approx_1 f'$.*

3.4   Hybrid L_p–$\texttt{argsort}$ Equivalences

Approximate NN equivalences based on L_p norms may not respect the order of outputs, e.g., with $\epsilon = 1$, the output vectors $(1, 2)$ and $(2, 1)$ may be considered equivalent, even though the order is reversed. On the other hand, $\texttt{argsort}$ and $\texttt{argmax}$ based equivalences respect the order of outputs but may allow too large differences to be acceptable: the output vectors $(90, 7, 3)$ and $(40, 35, 25)$ both have the same order of outputs, but if the numbers are interpreted as confidence levels, we may not wish to consider them equivalent, due to the large discrepancy between the respective confidence values.

This discussion motivates the need for an equivalence, called *hybrid $L_p - \texttt{argsort}$ equivalence*, which considers *both* the order of outputs and their differences in value.

Definition 5 (Hybrid top-k $\texttt{argsort}$ equivalence). *Suppose $O \subseteq \mathbb{R}^m$. Consider two neural networks $f : I \to O$ and $f' : I \to O$, and some $k \in \{1, ..., m\}$. Consider also $norm_p : O \to \mathbb{R}$, and some $\epsilon > 0$. We say that f and f' are (p, ϵ)-approximately and top-k $\texttt{argsort}$ equivalent iff $f \sim_{p,\epsilon} f'$ and $f \approx_k f'$, i.e., they are both (p, ϵ)-approximately equivalent and top-k $\texttt{argsort}$ equivalent.*

Specializing to $k = 1$ yields the following hybrid equivalence:

Definition 6 (Hybrid `argmax` equivalence). *Consider the same setting as in Definition 6. We say that f and f' are (p, ϵ)-approximately and* `argmax` *equivalent iff $f \sim_{p,\epsilon} f'$ and $f \approx_1 f'$.*

Definition 5 could be generalized further to involve different norms for each i-th element of the output vector, as well as a different bound ϵ_i for each $i \in \{1, ..., m\}$. We refrain from presenting such a generalization explicitly here, for the sake of simplicity.

3.5 The Neural Network Equivalence Checking Problem

Definition 7 (NN equivalence checking problem). *Given two (trained) neural networks f and f', and given a certain NN equivalence relation $\simeq \in \{\equiv, \sim_{p,\epsilon}, \approx_k\}$, and parameters p, ϵ, k as required, the* neural network equivalence checking problem *(NNECP) is to check whether $f \simeq f'$.*

3.6 Discussion of Application Domains for the Above Equivalence Relations

Strict equivalence is a true equivalence relation, but it might be impractical for realistic networks and numerical errors. Approximate equivalences can find several applications. For example, (p, ϵ)-equivalence can be used for multi-output learning problems [40]; specifically for i) regression problems where the goal is to simultaneously predict multiple real-valued output variables [6], and ii) classification tasks to ensure that the NN output values associated with every label are close to each other with respect to some L_p-norm. Approximate equivalences based on the order of outputs can be useful for classification. Top-1 accuracy is an established evaluation metric. For problems with hundreds of classes, e.g. ImageNet [11], it is common practice to present the top-5 accuracy along with top-1 accuracy when benchmarking. Top-k accuracy captures if any of the top k highest values of the output prediction vector is assigned the correct label. As such, it could be interesting to check if two NNs are equivalent using the top-k `argsort` equivalence. This equivalence could be important for Hierarchical Multi-label Classification [37], a classification task where the classes are hierarchically structured and each example may belong to more than one class simultaneously [7].

4 Neural Network Equivalence Checking Using SMT Solvers

Our approach to solving the NNECP is to reduce it to a logical *satisfiability* problem. The basic idea is the following. Suppose we want to check whether $f \simeq f'$, for two NNs $f : I \to O$ and $f' : I \to O$ and a given NN equivalence relation $\simeq$. We proceed as follows: (1) encode f into an SMT formula ϕ; (2) encode f' into an SMT formula ϕ'; (3) encode the equivalence relation $f \simeq f'$ into an SMT formula Φ such that $f \simeq f'$ iff Φ is unsatisfiable; (4) check, using an SMT solver, whether Φ is satisfiable: if not, then $f \simeq f'$; if Φ is satisfiable, then f and f' are not equivalent, and the SMT solver might provide a *counterexample*, i.e., an input violating the equivalence of f and f'.

This idea is based on the fact that the negation of $f \simeq f'$ can be encoded as a formula which asserts that there is $x \in I$ and $y, y' \in O$, such that $y = f(x), y' = f'(x)$,

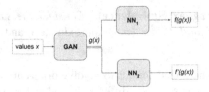

Fig. 2. Complete Neural Network Scheme for GAN generated inputs

with y and y' not satisfying the equivalence conditions imposed by $\simeq$. For example, for the case of strict NN equivalence, checking whether $f \equiv f'$ amounts to checking:

$$\neg \Big(\exists x \in I, y \in O, y' \in O, \ \ y = f(x) \wedge y' = f'(x) \wedge y \neq y' \Big)$$

This in turn amounts to checking that: $y = f(x) \wedge y' = f'(x) \wedge y \neq y'$ is unsatisfiable. In this case, we have $\phi := y = f(x)$, $\phi' := y' = f'(x)$, and $\Phi := \phi \wedge \phi' \wedge y \neq y'$.

We proceed to provide the details of building ϕ and ϕ' for given NNs, as well as Φ for the NN equivalence relations defined earlier. We note that although we present the SMT encoding of a single NN, our method is general and allows the two NNs to have different internal architectures (e.g., number and type of hidden layers, etc.).

4.1   Encoding Neural Networks as SMT Formulas

Input Variables. From Eq. (2), the input of a NN f is a vector $\mathbf{x} = [x_1, ..., x_n] \in \mathbb{R}^{1 \times n}$. The SMT formula ϕ encoding f will have n *input variables*, denoted as $x_1, ..., x_n$.

Encoding Input Bounds. Sometimes, the inputs are constrained to belong in a certain region. For example, we might assume that the input lies between given lower and upper bounds. In such cases, we can add input constraints as follows:

$$\bigwedge_{j=1}^{n} l_j \leq x_j \leq u_j \tag{10}$$

with $l_j, u_j \in \mathbb{R}$ denoting the lower and upper bounds for the domain of input x_j.

Encoding Other Input Constraints. Often, we may only care about inputs that are "meaningful", e.g. if we want to preserve equivalence only for "reasonable" photos of human faces, or "reasonable" pictures of handwritten digits. Encoding such input constraints can be difficult. After all, if we had a precise way to encode such "meaningfulness" as a formal mathematical constraint, we may not need NNs in the first place.

One way to address this fundamental problem is by using *generative NNs* [14]. The idea is depicted in Fig. 2. The output of the generative network g is fed into f and f' that we wish to test for equivalence. The generative network g models the input constraints, e.g. the output of g may be pictures of human faces. Let N denote the complete network consisting of the connection of all three g, f, f', plus the equivalence constraints. We encode N as an SMT constraint and check for satisfiability. An example to satisfiability is an input x of g such that $f(g(x))$ and $f'(g(x))$ differ in the sense of the given equivalence relation. Then, $g(x)$ provides a counterexample to the equivalence of f and f'. Moreover, $g(x)$ has been generated by g, therefore it belongs by definition to the set of input constraints modeled by g (e.g., $g(x)$ is a picture of a human face).

Internal Variables. For each hidden layer, we associate the *internal variables* z_i for the affine transformation, and the internal variables h_i for the activation function.

Constraints Encoding the Affine Transformations. Consider a single hidden layer of f with r nodes. Then, from the affine transformation of Eq. (2), we derive the constraints:

$$\bigwedge_{j=1}^{r} \left(z_j = \sum_{k=1}^{n} x_k W_{kj}^{(1)} + b_j^{(1)} \right) \tag{11}$$

Constraints Encoding the ReLU Activation Function. If the activation function is $ReLU$, then its effect is encoded with the following constraints:

$$\bigwedge_{j=1}^{r} (z_j \geq 0 \wedge h_j = z_j) \vee (z_j < 0 \wedge h_j = 0) \tag{12}$$

Constraints Encoding the Hard *tanh* Activation Function. If the activation function is the hard *tanh*, then its effect is encoded with the following constraints:

$$\bigwedge_{j=1}^{r} (z_j \geq 1 \wedge h_j = 1) \vee (z_j \leq -1 \wedge h_j = -1) \vee (-1 < z_j < 1 \wedge z_j = h_j) \tag{13}$$

Other Activation Functions. The constraints described so far include atoms of the linear real arithmetic theory [20] that most SMT-solvers can check for satisfiability through decision procedures of various degrees of efficiency. Encoding other activation functions, like $Tanh$, $Sigmoid$, and $Softmax$, can be problematic as they include nonlinear and exponential terms that most SAT/SMT cannot handle. A workaround is to opt for "hard" versions of these activation functions, as it is done in [1,10]. In [24], $Softmax$ is replaced by a piecewise linear function called $Sparsemax$.

Multiple Hidden Layers and Output Layer. The constraints Eq. (11–13) are generalized to multiple hidden layers, say $H, H', \ldots$ (with $r, r', \ldots$ nodes, respectively).

The NN encoding is completed with the constraints for the output layer that are derived, for $\mathbf{y} \in \mathbb{R}^m$ from Eq. (3), as previously.

Example 2 (cont. of example 1*).* We assume that there are input constraints, i.e. $0 \leq x_1 \leq 1$ and $0 \leq x_2 \leq 1$ and we derive the SMT constraints for the NN of Fig. 1. For the affine transformation, we obtain $z_1 = -2 \cdot x_1 + x_2 + 1$ and $z_2 = x_1 + 2 \cdot x_2 + 1$. For the activation functions, we add the constraints $\{(z_1 \geq 0 \wedge h_1 = z_1) \vee (z_1 < 0 \wedge h_1 = 0)\}$, encoding $h_1 = ReLU(z_1) = \max(0, z_1)$ and $\{(z_2 \geq 0 \wedge h_2 = z_2) \vee (z_2 < 0 \wedge h_2 = 0)\}$, for $h_2 = ReLU(z_2) = \max(0, z_2)$. Finally, we add the output constraints $y_1 = 2 \cdot h_1 - h_2 + 2$ and $y_2 = -h_1 - 2 \cdot h_2 + 2$. The resulting SMT formula is

$$\phi := \big\{ 0 \leq x_1 \leq 1 \wedge 0 \leq x_2 \leq 1 \wedge z_1 = -2x_1 + x_2 + 1 \wedge \big((z_1 \geq 0 \wedge h_1 = z_1) \vee$$
$$(z_1 < 0 \wedge h_1 = 0) \big) \wedge z_2 = x_1 + 2x_2 + 1 \wedge \big((z_2 \geq 0 \wedge h_2 = z_2) \vee (z_2 < 0$$
$$\wedge h_2 = 0) \big) \wedge y_1 = 2 \cdot h_1 - h_2 + 2 \wedge y_2 = -h_1 - 2 \cdot h_2 + 2 \big\}$$

4.2 Encoding of the Equivalence Relation

As mentioned at the beginning of this section, to check the equivalence of two NNs f and f', we need to generate, first, their encodings ϕ and ϕ' (Sect. 4.1), and then, the encoding of the (negation of the) equivalence relation. The latter encoding is described next. We assume that f and f' have the same number of outputs m, and we let $\mathbf{y} = (y_1, ..., y_m)$ and $\mathbf{y}' = (y_1', ..., y_m')$ denote their respective output variables.

Strict Equivalence Checking. Strict equivalence (c.f., Definition 1) requires that $\mathbf{y} = \mathbf{y}'$. To reduce this verification problem to a satisfiability problem, we encode the negation of the above constraint, more specifically:

$$\bigvee_{i=1}^{m} y_i \neq y_i' \tag{14}$$

(p, ϵ)-Approximate Equivalence Checking. (p, ϵ)-approximate equivalence (c.f., Definition 2) requires that $\|\mathbf{y} - \mathbf{y}'\|_{\mathbf{p}} < \epsilon$. Again, we encode the negation:

– for $p = 1$,

$$\sum_{i=1}^{m} |y_i - y_i'| \geq \epsilon \tag{15}$$

– for $p = 2$, it would be expected to be

$$\left(\sum_{i=1}^{m} |y_i - y_i'|^2 \right)^{\frac{1}{2}} \geq \epsilon$$

which involves the square-root function that yields an *undecidable* constraint. Instead, our encoding takes the form,

$$u = \sum_{i=1}^{m} |y_i - y_i'|^2 \wedge u = v \cdot v \wedge v \geq 0 \wedge v \geq \epsilon \tag{16}$$

– and for $p = \infty$,

$$\bigvee_{i=1}^{m} |y_i - y_i'| \geq \epsilon \tag{17}$$

argmax Equivalence Checking. This equivalence type (c.f., Definition 4) requires that $\text{argmax}(y) = \text{argmax}(y')$. Again, we wish to encode the negation, i.e., $\text{argmax}(y) \neq \text{argmax}(y')$. This can be done by introducing the macro $\text{argmaxis}(y, i, m)$ which represents the constraint $\text{argmax}(y) = i$, assuming the vector y has length m. Then, $\text{argmax}(y) \neq \text{argmax}(y')$ can be encoded by adding the constraints below:

$$\bigvee_{\substack{i,i' \in \{1,\dots,m\} \\ i \neq i'}} \text{argmaxis}(y, i, m) \wedge \text{argmaxis}(y', i', m) \tag{18}$$

where argmaxis is defined as follows:

$$\text{argmaxis}(y, i, m) := \Big(\bigwedge_{j=1}^{i-1} y_i > y_j \Big) \wedge \Big(\bigwedge_{j=i+1}^{m} y_i \geq y_j \Big) \tag{19}$$

For example, for $m = 2$, we have:

$$\text{argmaxis}(y, 1, 2) = y_1 \geq y_2 \quad \text{argmaxis}(y', 1, 2) = y_1' \geq y_2'$$
$$\text{argmaxis}(y, 2, 2) = y_2 > y_1 \quad \text{argmaxis}(y', 2, 2) = y_2' > y_1'$$

and the overall constraint encoding $\text{argmax}(y) \neq \text{argmax}(y')$ becomes:

$$(y_1 \geq y_2 \wedge y_2' > y_1') \vee (y_2 > y_1 \wedge y_1' \geq y_2')$$

Example 3 (cont. example 2). For the NN f, we have obtained the formula ϕ. Now assume that there is a second NN f' that has the same number of inputs and outputs as f. We define as y' the outputs of f' and the constraints are SMT encoded via ϕ'. The complete SMT formula Φ for the different equivalence relations is:

$$\Phi_{strict} := \{\phi \wedge \phi' \wedge \bigvee_{i=1}^{m} y_i \neq y_i'\}$$

$$\Phi_{(1,\epsilon)-\text{approx}} := \{\phi \wedge \phi' \wedge \sum_{i=1}^{m} |y_i - y_i'| \geq \epsilon\}$$

$$\Phi_{(2,\epsilon)-\text{approx}} := \{\phi \wedge \phi' \wedge u = \sum_{i=1}^{m} |y_i - y_i'|^2 \wedge u = v \cdot v \wedge v \geq 0 \wedge v \geq \epsilon\}$$

$$\Phi_{(\infty,\epsilon)-\text{approx}} := \{\phi \wedge \phi' \wedge \bigvee_{i=1}^{m} |y_i - y_i'| \geq \epsilon\}$$

$$\Phi_{argmax} := \{\phi \wedge \phi' \wedge \bigvee_{\substack{i,i' \in \{1,\dots,m\} \\ i \neq i'}} \text{argmaxis}(y, i, m) \wedge \text{argmaxis}(y', i', m)\}$$

Algorithm 1 introduces an implementation in the Z3 SMT solver[1] for `argmax`, which in our experiments showed better scalability behaviour when compared with the straightforward implementation of the aforementioned encoding for `argmax`.

Algorithm 1: Pseudo-code of `argmax` implementation in Z3

Require: Vector y of length m
Ensure: $argmax(y)$
  $y_{max} \leftarrow y(m)$
  $i_{max} \leftarrow m$
  for $i = m - 1$ **to** $i = 1$ **step** -1 **do**
    if $y(i) > y_{max}$ **then**
      $y_{max} \leftarrow y(i)$
    end if
    if $y(i) = y_{max}$ **then**
      $i_{max} \leftarrow i$
    end if
  end for
  return i_{max}

Hybrid Equivalence Checking. The encoding of the hybrid equivalence relations in Sect. 3.4 consists of combining the corresponding constraints of the (p, ϵ)-approximate equivalence and the `argsort`/`argmax` equivalence with a logical conjunction.

4.3 Optimizing the Encoding

The encoding presented so far is not optimal in the sense that it uses more SMT variables than strictly necessary. Many internal variables can be eliminated and replaced by their corresponding expressions in terms of other variables. In particular, the z_i variables encoding the affine transformations (as in Eq. 11) and the h_i variables for encoding the activation function can be easily eliminated.

5 Experimental Results

In this section, we report the results of experiments on verifying the equivalence of two NNs. We have used the SMT solver Z3 to check the satisfiability of all constraints that encode NN equivalence. The experiments were conducted on a laptop with a 4-core 2.8 GHz processor and 12 GB RAM. Our problems concern with NNs of different sizes, for checking their equivalence, with respect to the equivalence relations of Sect. 3. We focus on two main categories of supervised learning problems, i) classification (two case studies), and ii) regression (one case study). The source code of the implementation of the NNECP for the equivalence encoding of Sect. 4 is provided online[2].

---

[1] https://z3prover.github.io/api/html/.
[2] https://github.com/hariselef/NNequiv_Experiments.

Bit-Vec Case Study – Classification: A bit vector (Bit-Vec) is a sequence of bits. We consider that the inputs of our NN classifier are 10-bit vectors and the targets (labels) are either True (1) or False (0). The models we check for equivalence are Feed-Forward Multi-Layer Perceptrons and we focus on two architectures. In the first case, there is a single hidden layer, while in the second, there are two hidden layers; NNs have the same number of nodes per layer. We experimented with 8 different models per architecture and for each model we increased step-wise the number of nodes per layer. NNs have been trained with the objective to "learn" that for a vector with 3 or more consecutive 1s, the output label is True and the output label is False otherwise.

MNIST Case Study – Classification: The second use case is the popular *MNIST* dataset on image classification. MNIST contains 70,000 grayscale images, from which 60,000 are for training and the rest for testing the models' performance. The size of images is 28×28 (pixels), and every pixel value is a real in the range $[0, 1]$. We experimented with the same two architectures used for the Bit-Vec NNs and 5 models for each of them.

Automotive Control – Regression: For the regression case study, the goal is to use NNs that approximate the behaviour of a Model Predictive Controller, which has been designed for an automotive lane keeping assist system. The dataset contains 10,000 instances with six features representing different system characteristics obtained using sensors, along with the resulting steering angle that the car should follow (target). More details for the case study that we have reproduced can be found in Mathworks website[3].

5.1 Sanity Checks

The main goals of this set of experiments are: i) to ensure that our prototype implementation for equivalence checking does not have any bugs (sanity checks) and ii) to conduct a scalability analysis of the computational demands for NNs of increasing complexity when they are checked for equivalence, with the criteria of Sect. 3.

To this end, we verified the equivalence of two identical NNs, for two different architectures, both for the BitVec case study and the MNIST. The results are shown in Tables 1, 2 for the BitVec case study and in Tables 3, 4 for the MNIST. We report the number of nodes per hidden layer, the number of trainable parameters and the total number of variables in the formula generated for the SMT solver. For the BitVec experiments and for each equivalence relation, tables show the average time in seconds over 10 runs for the SMT solver to verify the equivalence of the identical NNs (standard deviation in all cases was less than 3%). For the MNIST experiments, we report the same results, but all sanity checks were conducted only once, since these experiments took more time to complete. In all cases, the SMT solver returned *UNSAT*, which correctly indicates that the two NNs are equivalent, as expected.

---

[3] https://www.mathworks.com/help/reinforcement-learning/ug/imitate-mpc-control
ler-for-lane-keeping-assist.html.

Table 1. Sanity check for the BitVec case study - 1st Architecture; all equivalences are true, i.e. all SMT formulas are *UNSAT*; the values in columns 4–8 show the computational time in seconds.

# nodes per layer	# params	# SMT variables	Strict Equiv.	L_1 Equiv.	L_2 Equiv.	L_∞ Equiv.	Argmax Equiv.
10	132	498	0.06	0.07	0.06	0.07	0.06
20	262	978	0.1	0.1	0.09	0.1	0.1
35	457	1698	0.17	0.17	0.14	0.17	0.17
50	652	2418	0.23	0.24	0.21	0.24	0.23
100	1302	4818	0.44	0.45	0.40	0.45	0.45
150	1952	7218	0.61	0.63	0.57	0.62	0.65
200	2602	9618	0.84	0.85	0.75	0.85	0.84
300	3902	14418	1.23	1.25	1.1	1.25	1.25

Table 2. Sanity check for the BitVec case study - 2nd Architecture; all equivalences are true, i.e. all SMT formulas are *UNSAT*; the values in columns 4–8 show the computational time in seconds.

# nodes per layer	# params	# SMT variables	Strict Equiv.	L_1 Equiv.	L_2 Equiv.	L_∞ Equiv.	Argmax Equiv.
5	97	378	0.04	0.04	0.04	0.04	0.04
10	242	938	0.1	0.09	0.08	0.09	0.1
15	437	1698	0.15	0.15	0.14	0.16	0.15
20	682	2658	0.24	0.24	0.20	0.23	0.23
30	1322	5178	0.4	0.39	0.37	0.39	0.42
40	2162	8498	0.62	0.62	0.58	0.63	0.63
50	3202	12618	0.87	0.91	0.85	0.88	0.92
60	4442	17538	1.17	1.2	1.21	1.16	1.23

Table 3. Sanity check for the MNIST case study - 1st Architecture; all equivalences are true, i.e. all SMT formulas are *UNSAT*; the values in columns 4–8 show the computational time in seconds.

# nodes per layer	# params	# SMT variables	Strict Equiv.	L_1 Equiv.	L_2 Equiv.	L_∞ Equiv.	Argmax Equiv.
10	7960	32424	2.5	2.53	2.2	2.63	2.67
30	23860	95624	7.52	7.73	6.3	7.63	7.5
50	39760	158824	12.2	12.4	10.4	12.8	12.4
100	79510	316824	24.5	24.3	21.9	25	24.6
200	159010	632824	48.4	55.1	44.8	48.8	48.2
300	238510	948824	74	74	74	62.4	73
500	397510	1580824	121	124	110	128	119
750	596260	2370824	182	193	167	203	182
1000	795010	3160824	241	247	220	257	256
1300	1033510	4108824	314	336	283	331	321
1700	1351510	5372824	420	434	394	435	437
2000	1590010	6320824	467	512	483	492	508

Table 4. Sanity check for the MNIST case study - 2nd Architecture; all equivalences are true, i.e. all SMT formulas are *UNSAT*; the values in columns 4–8 show the computational time in seconds.

# nodes per layer	# params	# SMT variables	Strict Equiv.	L_1 Equiv.	L_2 Equiv.	L_∞ Equiv.	Argmax Equiv.
10	8070	32864	2.7	2.7	2.3	2.54	2.57
30	24790	99344	7.55	7.86	6.7	7.5	7.5
50	42310	169024	13.2	12.9	11.0	13.7	12.9
100	89610	357224	26.5	27.5	24.9	26	27.7
200	199210	793624	58.7	62.2	50.6	61.6	64.4
300	328810	1310024	99	100	90	99	101
500	648010	2582824	194	194	167	192	192
750	1159510	4623824	334	340	298	354	349
1000	1796010	7164824	524	530	514	523	560
1300	2724810	10874024	797	779	784	836	857
1700	4243210	16939624	1225	1161	1359	1237	1223
2000	5592010	22328824	1435	1530	2837	1549	1581

5.2 Equivalence Checking

In the second set of experiments, we perform equivalence checking between NNs of different architectures. The solver will return *UNSAT* if the NNs are equivalent or *SAT* if they are not. This allows us to gain insight into the efficiency and the scalability bounds of the proposed encoding for both possible outcomes. We expect that when the two NNs are not equivalent (*SAT*) the solver is quite likely to return a counterexample shortly. A time limit of 10 min was set for the solver to respond and when this did not happen the end result was recorded as a "timeout".

Experiments with NN Classifiers. A series of experiments focused on the equivalence checking for NN classifiers, i.e. those trained for the BitVec and MNIST case studies. The pairs of NNs that were compared consist of the two NN architectures that were also used for the sanity checks (Sect. 5.1). Thus, the first pair of NNs includes the NN referred in the first line of Table 1 and the NN referred in the first line of Table 2, and so on. For the BitVec equivalence checking experiments, Table 5 summarizes the obtained results, for all equivalence relations apart from the $(2, \epsilon)$-approximate equivalence, which takes much more time than the set time limit and the results for two pairs of NNs are shown separately in Table 7. For each pair of NNs in Tables 5 and 7, the answer of the SMT solver is reported (*SAT* or *UNSAT*) along with the time that it took to respond. For the ϵ-approximate equivalences, we also note the ϵ values, for which the NN equivalence was checked. The reason for using relatively big values for ϵ is that the NNs do not have a nonlinear activation function in the output layer, e.g. sigmoid, and there was no way to guarantee that the outputs would scale in the same value ranges. The term **MME**, in some cells of the tables, stands for Maximum Memory Exceeded and is the reason for which the solver fails to respond, when not having reached the time limit of 10 min. Table 6 (and Table 7 for $(2, \epsilon)$-approximate equivalence) report the corresponding results, for the MNIST case study.

When the outcome of equivalence checking is *SAT*, the solver returns a counterexample (NN input) that violates the equivalence relation. If the input space is finite, it may be possible to obtain all counterexamples, as in the BitVec case study, for which we found two counterexamples of `argmax` equivalence for the NNs of the pair *model_1_4* vs *model_2_4*. The NN predictions for all possible inputs were then tested and it was confirmed that the two counterexamples are the only ones that violate `argmax` equivalence. Beyond seeing them as an extra sanity check, the counterexamples of equivalence checking may be useful, toward improving the NN robustness. However, we have not yet developed a systematic way to utilize them for this purpose. For most applications, as is the case in MNIST, it may not be feasible to obtain all possible counterexamples, due to the size of their input space. Moreover, often there is no easy way to limit the counterexample search to only "meaningful" inputs. This is the case in the MNIST case study, where the most common counterexample in the equivalence checking

Table 5. Equivalence checking for the BitVec case study

Model Pairs	# SMT variables			Strict Equiv.	$L_1 > 5$	$L_\infty > 10$	Argmax Equiv.
	Input	*Internal*	*Output*				
model_1_1 vs model_2_1	10	424	4	SAT/0.042 s	UNSAT/35 s	UNSAT/48 s	SAT/0.23 s
model_1_2 vs model_2_2	10	944	4	SAT/0.075 s	SAT/0.20 s	UNSAT/157 s	SAT/0.4 s
model_1_3 vs model_2_3	10	1630	4	SAT/0.124 s	UNSAT/385 s	UNSAT/531 s	UNSAT/182 s
model_1_4 vs model_2_4	10	2524	4	SAT/0.19 s	SAT/245 s	Timeout	SAT/86 s
model_1_5 vs model_2_5	10	4984	4	SAT/0.35 s	Timeout	MME/509 s	SAT/240 s
model_1_6 vs model_2_6	10	7844	4	SAT/0.5 s	Timeout	MME/568 s	SAT/450 s
model_1_7 vs model_2_7	10	11104	4	SAT/0.75 s	Timeout	MME/588 s	Timeout
model_1_8 vs model_2_8	10	15964	4	SAT/1.13 s	Timeout	Timeout	Timeout

Table 6. Equivalence checking for the MNIST case study

Model Pairs	# SMT variables			Strict Equiv.	$L_1 > 5$	$L_\infty > 10$	Argmax Equiv.
	Input	*Internal*	*Output*				
mnist_1_1 vs mnist_2_1	784	31840	20	SAT/2.1 s	SAT/44 s	SAT/42 s	SAT/41 s
mnist_1_2 vs mnist_2_2	784	96680	20	SAT/6.2 s	SAT/16 s	SAT/17 s	SAT/17 s
mnist_1_3 vs mnist_2_3	784	163120	20	SAT/10.3 s	SAT/28 s	SAT/28 s	MME/230 s
mnist_1_4 vs mnist_2_4	784	336220	20	SAT/21 s	SAT/56 s	SAT/ 57 s	SAT/54 s
mnist_1_5 vs mnist_2_5	784	712420	20	SAT/45 s	SAT/120 s	SAT/120 s	SAT/118 s

Table 7. Equivalence checking on BitVec and MNIST under L_2 ϵ-approximate equivalence

Model Pairs	# SMT variables			$L_2 > 1$	$L_2 > 10$
	Input	*Internal*	*Output*		
model_1_1 vs model_2_1	10	424	4	SAT/35 s	UNSAT/1494 s
model_1_2 vs model_2_2	10	944	4	SAT/105 s	UNSAT/2793 s
mnist_1_1 vs mnist_2_1	784	31840	20	MME/15436 s	-

experiments was an input vector filled with the value 0.5, which corresponds to a grayscale image whose pixels have all the same color, i.e. it is not a digit.

Experiments with Regression NNs. In another case study, we focused on NNs that serve as controllers in lane keeping assistant systems. Table 8 presents the details for the features and the outputs of the regression NNs for this case, as well as the valid value ranges. The pairs of NNs that were checked for equivalence consist of different versions of the same NN, produced through varying the number of epochs, for which the model was trained before being verified. We experimented with three versions of the NN controller trained for 30, 35 and 40 epochs. The `argmax` equivalence is meaningless, since there is only one output variable. Additionally, for the same reason, the results in Table 9 refer only to the $(1, \epsilon)$-approximate equivalence, since the various L_p norms are indistinguishable, when they are applied to scalar values.

Experiments with Weight Perturbations. Table 10 reports the results of a set of experiments with a NN for MNIST, in which we have randomly altered the values of some weights before checking the equivalence with the original NN. In this way, since it is very likely to have a pair of equivalent NNs, the solver is forced to search for almost all possible inputs before reaching the UNSAT result. We observe that when having altered two weights (out of 7960) the solver reaches the 10 min timeout.

Table 8. Regression Problem Input Characteristics – Constraints

Type/Parameter	Answer/Value	Remarks
output/target	$[-1.04, 1.04]$	steering angle $[-60, 60]$
input range x_1	$[-2,2]$	v_x (m/s)
input range x_2	$[-1.04, 1.04]$	rad/s
input range x_3	$[-1,1]$	m
input range x_4	$[-0.8, 0.8]$	rad
input range x_5	$[-1.04, 1.04]$	u_0 (steering angle)
input range x_6	$[-0.01, 0.01]$	ρ

Table 9. Equivalence checking for the Regression NNs

Model Pairs	# SMT variables			Strict Equivalence	$L_1 > 0.5$
	Input	Internal	Output		
MPC_30 vs MPC_35	6	17912	2	SAT/1.95 s	Timeout
MPC_30 vs MPC_40	6	17912	2	SAT/1.97 s	Timeout
MPC_35 vs MPC_40	6	17912	2	SAT/1.98 s	Timeout

Table 10. Equivalence checking with weight perturbations on the MNIST case study

Model	# SMT variables			# weight changes	Value range	$L_1 > 5$	$L_\infty > 10$	Argmax Equiv.
	Input	*Internal*	*Output*					
mnist_1_1	784	31840	20	1	1e−1 - 1e−6	UNSAT/30 s	UNSAT/30 s	Timeout
mnist_1_1	784	31840	20	2	1e−1 - 1e−6	Timeout	Timeout	Timeout

6   Related Work

Verification of NNs for various kinds of properties, such as safety, reachability, robustness, is of fast-growing interest, due to the many, often critical applications, in which NNs are employed. The authors of [23] present several algorithms for verifying NNs and classify them into three categories: reachability-based, optimization-based, and search-based. Typically, SMT-based approaches belong to the latter category. Two comprehensive surveys that include the verification of NNs using SMT solvers are given in [22] and [16]. An extensive survey of methods for the verification and validation of systems with learning enabled-components, not only NNs, is given in [39]. The equivalence checking problem for NNs is different from other verification problems for NNs: (a) in robustness verification, the goal is to check whether the output of a NN remains stable despite perturbations of its input; (b) for input-output verification of a NN, the goal is to check whether for a given range of input values, the output of the NN belongs in a given range of output values.

Other works on the equivalence of NNs are [28] and [19,35]. [28] only considers the case of strict equivalence where the outputs of the two networks must be identical for all inputs. We also define notions of approximate equivalence, as we believe strict equivalence is often too strong a requirement. [28] is also based on a SAT/SMT based encoding of the equivalence checking problem, but the overall approach is applicable only to a specific category of NNs, the so-called binarized NNs [2,17] that are not widely used in many different real-life applications. Approximate NN equivalence checking is also studied in [19,35], but their approach is based on mixed-integer linear programming (MILP) instead of SMT encoding. [19] applies the solution only to restricted regions of the input space, within a radius around the training data, whereas [35] introduces an abstraction-based solution. None of these works allows checking of hybrid equivalence.

The work in [30] focuses on the relationship between two NNs, e.g. whether a modified version of a NN produces outputs within some bounds relative to the original network. A "differential verification" technique is proposed consisting of a forward interval analysis through the network's layers, followed by a backward pass, which iteratively refines the approximation, until having verified the property of interest. Differential verification is related to equivalence checking, but it is actually a different problem.

In [32], the authors adopt abstractions of the input domain using zonotopes and polyhedra, along with an MILP solver for verifying properties of NNs. An SMT-based verification method for a single NN is also presented in [18], whose applicability is limited only to NNs with ReLU activation functions. Finally, an interesting symbolic representation targeting only piecewise linear NNs is the one presented in [34].

7 Conclusions

In this work, we examined a series of formal equivalence checking problems for NNs, with respect to equivalence relations that can be suitable for various applications and verification requirements. We provided an SMT-based verification approach, as well as a prototype implementation and experimental results.

In our future research plans, we aim to explore whether the equivalence checking problem can be encoded in existing verification tools for NNs (e.g. Reluplex [18], ERAN [32], $\alpha-\beta$ Crown [36,41,42], VNN competition [4]) through the parallel composition of the two networks that are to be compared. An interesting prospect is to extend our approach towards finding the smallest ϵ, for which two NNs become equivalent.

As additional research priorities, we also intend to explore the scalability margins of alternative solution encodings, including the optimized version of the current encoding (as described in Sect. 4.3) and to compare them with the MILP encoding in [19]. Lastly, it may be also worth exploring the effectiveness of techniques applied to similar problems from other fields, like for example the equivalence checking of digital circuits [12,13,25]. In this context, we may need to rely on novel ideas toward the layer-by-layer checking of equivalence between two NNs.

Acknowledgment. This project has received funding from the European Union's Horizon 2020 research and innovation programme under grant agreement No 956123.

References

1. Albarghouthi, A.: Introduction to neural network verification. Found. Trends® Program. Lang. **7**(1–2), 1–157 (2021)
2. Amir, G., Wu, H., Barrett, C., Katz, G.: An SMT-based approach for verifying binarized neural networks. In: TACAS 2021. LNCS, vol. 12652, pp. 203–222. Springer, Cham (2021). https://doi.org/10.1007/978-3-030-72013-1_11
3. Ashok, P., Hashemi, V., Křetínský, J., Mohr, S.: DeepAbstract: neural network abstraction for accelerating verification. In: Hung, D.V., Sokolsky, O. (eds.) ATVA 2020. LNCS, vol. 12302, pp. 92–107. Springer, Cham (2020). https://doi.org/10.1007/978-3-030-59152-6_5
4. Bak, S., Liu, C., Johnson, T.: The second international verification of neural networks competition (VNN-COMP 2021): summary and results (2021)
5. Barrett, C.W., Sebastiani, R., Seshia, S.A., Tinelli, C.: Satisfiability modulo theories. In: Biere, A., Heule, M., van Maaren, H., Walsh, T. (eds.) Handbook of Satisfiability, vol. 185, pp. 825–885. IOS Press, Amsterdam (2009)
6. Borchani, H., Varando, G., Bielza, C., Larrañaga, P.: A survey on multi-output regression. Wiley Int. Rev. Data Min. Knowl. Disc. **5**(5), 216–233 (2015)
7. Cerri, R., Barros, R.C., de Carvalho, A.C.P.L.F.: Hierarchical multi-label classification using local neural networks. J. Comput. Syst. Sci. **80**(1), 39–56 (2014)
8. Cheng, Y., Wang, D., Zhou, P., Zhang, T.: A survey of model compression and acceleration for deep neural networks. arXiv preprint arXiv:1710.09282 (2017)
9. Christakis, M., et al.: Automated safety verification of programs invoking neural networks. In: Silva, A., Leino, K.R.M. (eds.) CAV 2021. LNCS, vol. 12759, pp. 201–224. Springer, Cham (2021). https://doi.org/10.1007/978-3-030-81685-8_9

10. Collobert, R.: Large scale machine learning. PhD thesis, Université Paris VI (2004)
11. Deng, J., Dong, W., Socher, R., Li, L.-J., Li, K., Fei-Fei, L.: Imagenet: a large-scale hierarchical image database. In: 2009 IEEE Conference on Computer Vision and Pattern Recognition, pp. 248–255 (2009)
12. Disch, S., Scholl, C.: Combinational equivalence checking using incremental sat solving, output ordering, and resets. In: 2007 Asia and South Pacific Design Automation Conference, pp. 938–943 (2007)
13. Goldberg, E.I., Prasad, M.R., Brayton, R.K.: Using SAT for combinational equivalence checking. In: Proceedings Design, Automation and Test in Europe. Conference and Exhibition 2001, pp. 114–121 (2001)
14. Goodfellow, I., et al.: Generative adversarial nets. In: Ghahramani, Z., Welling, M., Cortes, C., Lawrence, N., Weinberger, K.Q. (eds.) Advances in Neural Information Processing Systems, vol. 27. Curran Associates Inc., Red Hook (2014)
15. Hinton, G., Vinyals, O., Dean, J.: Distilling the knowledge in a neural network. In: NIPS Deep Learning and Representation Learning Workshop (2015)
16. Huang, X., et al.: A survey of safety and trustworthiness of deep neural networks: verification, testing, adversarial attack and defence, and interpretability. Comput. Sci. Rev. **37**, 100270 (2020)
17. Hubara, I., Courbariaux, M., Soudry, D., El-Yaniv, R., Bengio, Y.: Binarized neural networks. In: Lee, D., Sugiyama, M., Luxburg, U., Guyon, I., Garnett, R. (eds.) Advances in Neural Information Processing Systems, vol. 29. Curran Associates Inc., Red Hook (2016)
18. Katz, G., Barrett, C., Dill, D.L., Julian, K., Kochenderfer, M.J.: Reluplex: an efficient SMT solver for verifying deep neural networks. In: Majumdar, R., Kunčak, V. (eds.) CAV 2017. LNCS, vol. 10426, pp. 97–117. Springer, Cham (2017). https://doi.org/10.1007/978-3-319-63387-9_5
19. Kleine Büning, M., Kern, P., Sinz, C.: Verifying equivalence properties of neural networks with ReLU activation functions. In: Simonis, H. (ed.) CP 2020. LNCS, vol. 12333, pp. 868–884. Springer, Cham (2020). https://doi.org/10.1007/978-3-030-58475-7_50
20. Kroening, D., Strichman, O.: Decision Procedures: An Algorithmic Point of View, 1st edn. Springer, Heidelberg (2008). https://doi.org/10.1007/978-3-540-74105-3
21. Kukacka, J., Golkov, V., Cremers, D.: Regularization for deep learning: a taxonomy. arXiv, abs/1710.10686 (2017)
22. Leofante, F., Narodytska, N., Pulina, L., Tacchella, A.: Automated verification of neural networks: advances, challenges and perspectives (2018)
23. Liu, C., Arnon, T., Lazarus, C., Strong, C., Barrett, C., Kochenderfer, M.J.: Algorithms for verifying deep neural networks. Found. Trends® Optim. **4**(3–4), 244–404 (2021)
24. Martins, A., Astudillo, R.: From softmax to sparsemax: a sparse model of attention and multi-label classification. In: International Conference on Machine Learning, pp. 1614–1623. PMLR (2016)
25. Mishchenko, A., Chatterjee, S., Brayton, R., Een, N.: Improvements to combinational equivalence checking. In: Proceedings of the 2006 IEEE/ACM International Conference on Computer-Aided Design, ICCAD 2006, pp. 836–843. Association for Computing Machinery, New York (2006)
26. Mishra, R., Gupta, H.P., Dutta, T.: A survey on deep neural network compression: challenges, overview, and solutions. arXiv preprint arXiv:2010.03954 (2020)
27. Molitor, P., Mohnke, J., Becker, B., Scholl, C.: Equivalence Checking of Digital Circuits. Springer, New York (2004). https://doi.org/10.1007/b105298
28. Narodytska, N., Kasiviswanathan, S., Ryzhyk, L., Sagiv, M., Walsh, T.: Verifying properties of binarized deep neural networks. In: Proceedings of the AAAI Conference on Artificial Intelligence (2018)

29. Neill, J.O.: An overview of neural network compression. arXiv preprint arXiv:2006.03669 (2020)
30. Paulsen, B., Wang, J., Wang, C.: Reludiff: differential verification of deep neural networks. In: Proceedings of the ACM/IEEE 42nd International Conference on Software Engineering, pp. 714–726 (2020)
31. Rülling, W.: Formal verification. In: Jansen, D. (ed.) The Electronic Design Automation Handbook, pp. 329–338. Springer, Boston (2003). https://doi.org/10.1007/978-0-387-73543-6_14
32. Singh, G., Gehr, T., Püschel, M., Vechev, M.: An abstract domain for certifying neural networks. Proc. ACM Program. Lang. 3(POPL), 1–30 (2019)
33. Somenzi, F., Kuehlmann, A.: Equivalence checking. In: Lavagno, L., Martin, G.E., Scheffer, L.K., Markov, I.L. (eds.) Electronic Design Automation For Integrated Circuits Handbook, vol. 2. CRC Press, Boca Raton (2016)
34. Sotoudeh, M., Thakur, A.V.: A symbolic neural network representation and its application to understanding, verifying, and patching networks. CoRR, abs/1908.06223 (2019)
35. Teuber, S., Büning, M.K., Kern, P., Sinz, C.: Geometric path enumeration for equivalence verification of neural networks. In: 2021 IEEE 33rd International Conference on Tools with Artificial Intelligence (ICTAI), pp. 200–208. IEEE (2021)
36. Wang, S., et al.: Beta-CROWN: efficient bound propagation with per-neuron split constraints for complete and incomplete neural network verification. In: Advances in Neural Information Processing Systems, vol. 34 (2021)
37. Wehrmann, J., Cerri, R., Barros, R.: Hierarchical multi-label classification networks. In: Dy, J., Krause, A. (eds.) Proceedings of the 35th International Conference on Machine Learning. Proceedings of Machine Learning Research, vol. 80, pp. 5075–5084. PMLR (2018)
38. Wen, H.P.C., Wang, L.C., Cheng, K.T.T.: Functional verification. In: Wang, L.-T., Chang, Y.-W., Cheng, K.-T.T. (eds.) Electronic Design Automation, pp. 513–573. Morgan Kaufmann, Boston (2009)
39. Xiang, W., et al.: Verification for machine learning, autonomy, and neural networks survey. arXiv preprint arXiv:1810.01989 (2018)
40. Xu, D., Shi, Y., Tsang, I.W., Ong, Y.-S., Gong, C., Shen, X.: Survey on multi-output learning. IEEE Trans. Neural Netw. Learn. Syst. 31(7), 2409–2429 (2019)
41. Xu, K., et al.: Fast and complete: enabling complete neural network verification with rapid and massively parallel incomplete verifiers. In: International Conference on Learning Representations (2021)
42. Zhang, H., Weng, T.-W., Chen, P.-Y., Hsieh, C.-J., Daniel, L.: Efficient neural network robustness certification with general activation functions. In: Advances in Neural Information Processing Systems, vol. 31 (2018)

Reachability Analysis of a General Class of Neural Ordinary Differential Equations

Diego Manzanas Lopez[✉], Patrick Musau, Nathaniel P. Hamilton, and Taylor T. Johnson

Vanderbilt University, Nashville, TN 37212, USA
{diego.manzanas.lopez,taylor.johnson}@vanderbilt.edu

Abstract. Continuous deep learning models, referred to as Neural Ordinary Differential Equations (Neural ODEs), have received considerable attention over the last several years. Despite their burgeoning impact, there is a lack of formal analysis techniques for these systems. In this paper, we consider a general class of neural ODEs with varying architectures and layers, and introduce a novel reachability framework that allows for the formal analysis of their behavior. The methods developed for the reachability analysis of neural ODEs are implemented in a new tool called NNVODE. Specifically, our work extends an existing neural network verification tool to support neural ODEs. We demonstrate the capabilities and efficacy of our methods through the analysis of a set of benchmarks that include neural ODEs used for classification, and in control and dynamical systems, including an evaluation of the efficacy and capabilities of our approach with respect to existing software tools within the continuous-time systems reachability literature, when it is possible to do so.

1 Introduction

Neural Ordinary Differential Equations (ODEs) were first introduced in 2018, as a radical new neural network design that boasted better memory efficiency, and an ability to deal with irregularly sampled data [21]. The idea behind this family of deep learning models is that instead of specifying a discrete sequence of hidden layers, we instead parameterize the derivative of the hidden states using a neural network [8]. The output of the network can then be computed using a differential equation solver [8]. This work has spurred a whole range of follow-up work, and since 2018 several variants have been proposed, such as augmented neural ODEs (ANODEs) and their ensuing variants [11,16,39]. These variants provide a more expressive formalism by augmenting the state space of neural ODEs to allow for the flow of state trajectories to cross. This crossing, prohibited in the original framework, allows for the learning of more complex functions that were prohibited by the original neural ODE formulation [11].

Due to the potential that neural networks boast in revolutionizing the development of intelligent systems in numerous domains, the last several years have witnessed a significant amount of work towards the formal analysis of these

S. Bogomolov and D. Parker (Eds.): FORMATS 2022, LNCS 13465, pp. 258–277, 2022.
https://doi.org/10.1007/978-3-031-15839-1_15

models. The first set of approaches that were developed considered the formal verification of neural networks (NN), using a variety of techniques including reachability methods [3,40,46,47], and SAT techniques [13,29,30]. Thereafter, many researchers proposed novel formal method approaches for neural network control systems (NNCS), where the majority of methods utilized a combination of NN and hybrid system verification techniques [6,14,22,23,26,44]. Building on this work, a natural outgrowth is extending these approaches to analyze and verify neural ODEs, and some recent studies have considered the analysis of formal properties of neural ODEs. One such study aims to improve the understanding of the inner operation of these networks by analyzing and experimenting with multiple neural ODE architectures on different benchmarks [36]. Some studies have considered analyses of the robustness of neural ODEs such as [7] and [48], which evaluate the robustness of image classification neural ODEs and compare the efficacy of this class of network against other more traditional image classifier architectures. The first reachability technique targeted for neural ODEs presented a theoretical regime for verifying neural ODEs using Stochastic Lagrangian Reachability (SLR) [19]. This method is an abstraction-based technique that computes confidence intervals for the calculated reachable set with probabilistic guarantees. In a follow-up work, these methods were improved and implemented in a tool called Gotube [20], which is able to compute reach sets for longer time horizons than most state-of-the-art reachability tools. However, these methods only provide stochastic bounds on the reach sets, so there are no formal guarantees on the derived results.

To the best of our knowledge, this paper presents the first deterministic verification framework for a general class of neural ODEs with multiple continuous-time and discrete-time layers. In this work, we present our verification framework NNVODE that makes use of deterministic reachability approaches for the analysis of neural ODEs. Our methods are evaluated on a set of benchmarks with different architectures and conditions in the area of dynamical systems, control systems, and image classification. We also compare our results against three state-of-the-art verification tools when possible. In summary, the contributions of this paper are:

– We introduce a general class of neural ODEs that allows for the combination of multiple continuous-time and discrete-time layers.
– We develop NNVODE, an extension of NNV [46], to formally analyze a general class of neural ODEs using sound and deterministic reachable methods.
– We run an extensive evaluation on a collection of benchmarks within the context of time-series analysis, control systems, and image classification. We compare the results to Flow*, GoTube, and JuliaReach for neural ODE architectures where this is possible.

2   Background and Problem Formulation

Neural ODEs emerged as a continuous-depth variant of neural networks becoming a special case of ordinary differential equations (ODEs), where the derivatives are defined by a neural network, and can be expressed as:

$$\dot{z} = g(z), \qquad z(t_0) = z_0, \tag{1}$$

where the dynamics of the function $g : \mathbb{R}^j \to \mathbb{R}^p$ are represented as a neural network, and initial state $z_0 \in \mathbb{R}^j$, where j corresponds to the dimensionality of the states z. A *neural network* (NN) is defined to be a collection of consecutively connected $\mathcal{NN}$-Layers as described in Definition 1.

Definition 1 ($\mathcal{NN}$-Layer). *A $\mathcal{NN}$-Layer is a function $h\colon \mathbb{R}^j \to \mathbb{R}^p$, with input $x \in \mathbb{R}^j$, output $y \in \mathbb{R}^p$ defined as follows*

$$y = h(x) \tag{2}$$

where the function h is determined by parameters θ, typically defined as a tuple $\theta = \langle \sigma, \mathbf{W}, \mathbf{b} \rangle$ for fully-connected layers, where $\mathbf{W} \in \mathbb{R}^{j \times p}, \mathbf{b} \in \mathbb{R}^p$, and activation function $\sigma\colon \mathbb{R}^j \to \mathbb{R}^p$, thus the fully-connected $\mathcal{NN}$-Layer is described as

$$y = h(x) = \sigma(\mathbf{W}(x) + \mathbf{b}). \tag{3}$$

However, for other layers such as convolutional-type $\mathcal{NN}$-Layers, θ may include parameters like the filter size, padding, or dilation factor and the function h in (3) may not necessarily apply. For a formal definition and description of the reachability analysis for each of these layers that are integrated within NNVODE, we refer the reader to Section 4 of [43]. For the Neural ODEs (NODEs), we assume that g is Lipschitz continuous, which guarantees that the solution of $\dot{z} = g(z)$ exists. This assumption allows us to model g with m layers of continuously differentiable activation functions σ_k for $k \in \{1, 2, ..., m\}$ such as sigmoid, tanh, and exponential activation functions. Described in (1) is the notion of a NODE as introduced in [8] and an example is illustrated in Fig. 1.

Definition 2 (NODE). *A **NODE** is a function $\dot{z} = g(z)$ with m fully-connected $\mathcal{NN}$-Layers, and it is defined as follows*

$$\dot{z} = g(z) = h_m(h_{m-1}(...h_1(z))), \tag{4}$$

where $g : \mathbb{R}^j \to \mathbb{R}^p$, $\sigma_k : \mathbb{R}^{j_k} \to \mathbb{R}^{p_k}$, $\mathbf{W}_k \in \mathbb{R}^{j_k \times p_k}$, and $\mathbf{b}_k \in \mathbb{R}^{p_k}$. For each layer $k = \{1, 2, ..., m\}$, we describe the function h_k as in (3).

2.1 General Neural ODE

The general class of neural ODEs (GNODEs) considered in this work is more complex than previously analyzed neural ODEs as it may be comprised of two types of layer: NODEs and $\mathcal{NN}$-Layers. We introduce a more general framework where multiple NODEs can make up part of the overall architecture along with other $\mathcal{NN}$-Layers, as described in Definition 3. This is the reachability problem subject of evaluation in this work.

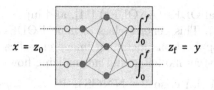

Fig. 1. Illustration of an example of NODE with m = 2 hidden layers, 2 inputs and 2 outputs, as defined in (1) and (4), and Definition 2.

Definition 3 (GNODE). *A **GNODE** $\mathcal{F}$ is any sequence of consecutively connected N layers $\mathcal{L}_k$ for $k \in \{1, \ldots N\}$ with N_O NODEs and N_D NN-Layers, that meets the conditions $1 \leq N_O \leq N$, $0 \leq N_D < N$, and $N_D + N_O = N$.*

With the above definition, we formulate a theorem for the restricted class of neural ODEs (NODE) that we use to compare our methods against existing techniques.

Observation 1 (Special case 1: NODE). *Let $\mathcal{F}$ be a GNODE with N layers. If $N = 1$, $N_O = 1$ and $N_D = 0$, then $\mathcal{F}$ is equivalent to an ODE whose continuous-time dynamics are defined as a neural network, and we refer to it as a **NODE** (as in Definition 2).*

In Fig. 2, an example of a GNODE is shown, which has 1 input (x), 1 output (y), $N_O = 2$ NODEs, and $N_D = 5$ NN-Layers, with its 5 numbered segments described as: 1) The first segment has a NN-Layer, with one hidden layer of 2 neurons and an output layer of 2 neurons, 2) a NODE with one hidden layer of 3 neurons and an output layer of 2 neurons, 3) NN-Layer with 3 hidden layers of 4,1, and 2 neurons respectively, and an output layer of 2 neurons, 4) NODE with a hidden layer of 3 neurons and output layer of 2 neurons, and 5) NN-Layer with a hidden layer of 4 neurons and output layer with 1 neurons.

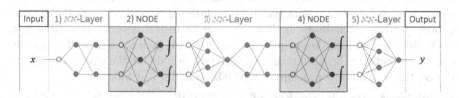

Fig. 2. Example of a GNODE. The filled circles represent weighted neurons in each layer, non-filled neurons represent the inputs of each layer-type segment, shown for visualization purposes.

Given this GNODE architecture, we are capable of encoding the originally proposed neural ODE [8], as well as several of its model improvements including higher-order neural ODEs like the second-order neural ODE (SONODE)

[39], augmented neural ODEs (ANODEs) [11], and input-layer augmented neural ODEs (ILNODEs). This general class of neural ODEs from Definition 3 is applicable to many applications including image classification, time series prediction, dynamical system modeling and normalizing flows.

Observation 2 (Special case 2 - NNCS). *We can consider the NNCS as a special case of the GNODE, as the NNCS models also consist of NN-Layers and NODE, under the assumption that the plant is described as an NODE. NNCS in the general architecture have NN-Layers followed by an ODE or NODE, which connects back to the NN-Layers in a feedback loop manner for cp control steps. Thus, by unrolling the NNCS cp times, we consecutively connect the NN-Layers with the NODE, creating a GNODE.*

2.2   NODE: Applications

There are two application modes of a NODE, model reduction and dynamical systems. On one hand, we can use it as a substitute for multiple similar layers to reduce the depth and overall size of a model [8]. In this context, we treat the NODE as an input-output mapping function, and set the integration time t_f to a fixed number during training, which will be then used during simulation or reachability. Typically, this value is set to 1. On the other hand, we can make use of NODEs to capture the behavior of time-series data or dynamical systems. In this sense, t_f is not fixed, and it will be determined by the user/application. In summary, we can use NODEs for: 1) time-series or dynamical system modeling, and 2) model reduction. For time-series, t_f is variable, user or application dependent. For model reduction, t_f is a parameter of the model fixed before training. Only the output value at time $= t_f$ is used, while for the time-series models, we are interested in the interval $[0, t_f]$.

2.3   Reachability Analysis

The main focus of this manuscript is to introduce a framework for the reachability analysis of GNODEs. This framework combines set representations and methods from Neural Network (NN), Convolutional Neural Network (CNN) and hybrid systems reachability analysis. Similar to neural network reachability in NNV [46], we consider the set propagation through each layer as well as the set conversion between layers for all reachability methods for the supported layers. Hence, the reachability problem of GNODE is defined as follows:

Definition 4 (Reachable Set of a GNODE). *Let $\mathcal{F}\colon \mathbb{R}^j \to \mathbb{R}^p$ be a **GNODE** with N layers. The output reachable set $\mathcal{R}_N$ of a **GNODE** with input set $\mathcal{R}_0$ is defined as:*

$$\mathcal{R}_1 \triangleq \{y_1 \mid y_1 = f_1(y_0),\ y_0 \in \mathcal{R}_0\},$$
$$\mathcal{R}_2 \triangleq \{y_2 \mid y_2 = f_2(y_1),\ y_1 \in \mathcal{R}_1\},$$

$$\vdots \tag{5}$$

$$\mathcal{R}_N \triangleq \{y_N \mid y_N = f_N(y_{N-1}),\ y_{N-1} \in \mathcal{R}_{N-1}\},$$

where $f_i: \mathbb{R}^{j_i} \to \mathbb{R}^{p_i}$ is the function f of layer i, where f is either a NODE (g) or a NN-Layer (h).

The proposed solution to this problem is sound and incomplete, in other words, an over-approximation of the reachable set. This means that, given a set of inputs, we compute an output set of which, given any point in the input set, we simulate the GNODE and the output point is always contained within the reachable output set (sound). However, it is incomplete because the opposite is not true; there may be points in the output reachable set that cannot be traced back to be within the bounds of the input set.

Definition 5 (Soundness). *Let $\mathcal{F}: \mathbb{R}^j \to \mathbb{R}^p$ be a GNODE with an input set $\mathcal{R}_0$ and output reachable set $\mathcal{R}_f$. The computed $\mathcal{R}_f$ given $\mathcal{F}$ and $\mathcal{R}_0$ is **sound** iff $\forall x \in \mathcal{R}_0, | \ y = \mathcal{F}(x), y \in \mathcal{R}_f$.*

Definition 6 (Completeness). *Let $\mathcal{F}: \mathbb{R}^j \to \mathbb{R}^p$ be a GNODE with an input set $\mathcal{R}_0$ and output reachable set $\mathcal{R}_f$. The computed $\mathcal{R}_f$ given $\mathcal{F}$ and $\mathcal{R}_0$ is **complete** iff $\forall x \in \mathcal{R}_0, \exists y = \mathcal{F}(x) \ | \ y \in \mathcal{R}_f$ and $\forall y \in \mathcal{R}_f, \exists x \in \mathcal{R}_0 \ | \ y = \mathcal{F}(x)$.*

Definition 7 (Reachable set of a NN-Layer). *Let $h: \mathbb{R}^j \to \mathbb{R}^p$ be a NN − Layer as described in Definition 1. The reachable set $\mathcal{R}_h$, with input $\mathcal{X} \subset \mathbb{R}^n$ is defined as*

$$\mathcal{R}_h = \{y \mid y = h(x), x \in \mathcal{X}\}.$$

Definition 7 applies to any discrete-time layer that is part of a GNODE, including, but not limited to the following supported NN − *Layers* supported in NNVODE: fully-connected layers with ReLU, tanh, sigmoid and leaky-ReLU activation functions, and convolutional-type layers such as batch normalization, 2-D convolutional, and max-pooling.

The reachability analysis of NODEs is akin to the general reachability problem for any continuous-time system modeled by an ODE. If we represent the NODE as a single layer i of a GNODE with continuous dynamics described by (1), and assume that for a given initial state $z_0 \in \mathbb{R}^{j_i}$, the system admits a unique trajectory defined on $\mathbb{R}_0^+$, described by $\zeta(., z(t_0))$, then the reachable set of the given NODE can be characterized by Definition 8.

Definition 8 (Reachable set of a NODE). *Let g be a **NODE** with solution $\zeta(t; z_0)$ to (1) for initial state z_0. The reachable set, $\mathcal{R}_g$ at $t = t_F$, $\mathcal{R}_g(t_F)$, with initial set $\mathcal{R}_0 \subset \mathbb{R}^n$ at time $t = t_0$ is defined as*

$$\mathcal{R}_g(t_F) = \{\zeta(t; z_0) \in \mathbb{R}^n \mid z_0 \in \mathcal{R}_0, t \in [0, t_f]\}.$$

We also describe the reachable set for a time interval $[t_0, t_f]$ as follows

$$\mathcal{R}_g([t_0, t_f]) := \bigcup_{t \in [t_0, t_f]} \mathcal{R}_g(t)$$

Now that we have outlined the general reachability problem of a NODE, whether we compute a single reachable set for the NODE at $t = t_F$, or over an interval $t \in [t_0, t_F]$ (computed by *get_ time()*), depends on how the neural ODE was trained and the specific application of its use. However, the core computation remains the same. This is outlined in Algorithm 1.

Algorithm 1. Reachability analysis of a GNODE.
___
Input: $\mathcal{F}, \mathcal{R}_0$ // GNODE, input set
Output: $\mathcal{R}_f$ // output reachable set
 1: **procedure** $\mathcal{R}_f$ = REACH$(\mathcal{F}, \mathcal{R}_0)$
 2:      N = $\mathcal{F}$.layers // number of layers
 3:      **for** $i = 1 : N$ **do** // loop through every layer
 4:          $\mathcal{L}_i = \mathcal{F}$.layer(i)
 5:          **if** $\mathcal{L}_i$ *is* NODE **then** // check layer type
 6:              $\mathbf{t}_i = $ get_time$(\mathcal{L}_i)$ // get integration time bounds of layer i
 7:              $\mathcal{R}_i = $ reach$_{NODE}(\mathcal{L}_i, \mathcal{R}_{i-1}, \mathbf{t}_i)$ // reach set of layer i, Definition 8
 8:          **else**
 9:              $\mathcal{R}_i = $ reach$_{NN}(\mathcal{L}_i, \mathcal{R}_{i-1})$ // reach set of layer i, Definition 7
10:      $\mathcal{R}_f = \mathcal{R}_N$ // output reachable set
___

2.4 Reachability Methods

In the previous sections, we defined the reachable set of a GNODE using a layer-by-layer approach. However, the computation of these reachable sets is defined by the reachability methods and set representations utilized in their construction. For instance, the same operations are not utilized to compute the reachable set for a fully-connected layer with a hyperbolic tangent activation function as with a fully convolutional layer. In the following section, we describe the set of methods in the NNVODE tool available to the community to compute the reachable set of each specific layer.

We begin with the NODE approaches, where we make a distinction based on the underlying dynamics. If the NODE is nonlinear, we make use of zonotope and polynomial-zonotope based methods that are implemented and available in CORA [1,2]. If the NODE is purely linear, then we utilize the star set-based methods introduced in [5], which are more scalable than other zonotope-based methods and possess soundness guarantees as well.

For the NN-Layers, there are several methods available, including zonotope-based and star-set based methods. However, we limited our implementation only using star sets to handle these layers, as this representation was demonstrated to be more computationally efficient and to enable tighter over-approximations of the derived reachable sets than zonotope methods [45]. Additionally, in using star set methods, we allow for the use of both approximate methods (*approx-star*) and exact methods (*exact-star*). A summary of these methods and supported layers is depicted in Table 1, and for a complete description of the reachability methods utilized in our work, we refer the reader to [46] and the manual[1,2].

Implementation. One of the key aspects of the verification of GNODEs is the proper encoding of the NODEs within reachability schemes. Depending on the software that is used, this process may vary and require distinct steps. As an example, some tools, like NNVODE, are simpler and allow for matrix multiplications

___
[1] NNV manual: https://github.com/verivital/nnv/blob/master/docs/manual.pdf.
[2] CORA manual: https://tumcps.github.io/CORA/data/Cora2021Manual.pdf.

Table 1. Layers supported in NNVODE and reachability sets and methods available.

	Layer Type – Set Rep. (method name)
NODE	Linear – Star-set ("direct") [5]
NODE	Nonlinear – Zonotope, Polynomial Zonotope * [1,2]
NN-Layer	FC: linear, ReLU – Star-set ("approx-star", "exact-star") [45]
NN-Layer	FC: leakyReLU, tanh, sigmoid, satlin – Star-set ("approx-star") [46]
NN-Layer	Conv2D – ImageStar ("approx-star", "exact-star") [46]
NN-Layer	BatchNorm – ImageStar ("approx-star", "exact-star") [46]
NN-Layer	MaxPooling2D – ImageStar ("approx-star", "exact-star") [46]
NN-Layer	AvgPooling2D – ImageStar ("approx-star", "exact-star") [46]

*We support several methods available using Zonotope and PolyZonotopes, which includes user-defined fixed reachability parameters ("ZonoF", "PolyF") as well as adaptive reachability methods ("ZonoA" and "PolyA"), which require no prior knowledge on reach methods or systems to verify to produce relevant results.

within the definition of equations. However, for tools like Flow*, the set of steps required to properly encode this problem are more complex as it requires a definition for each individual equation of the state derivative. Thus, a more general conversion is needed, illustrated in the extended version [34].

3 Evaluation

Having described the details of our reachability definitions, algorithm, and implementation, we now present the experimental evaluation of our proposed work. We begin by presenting, a method and tool comparison analysis against GoTube[3] [20], Flow*[4] [9] and JuliaReach[5] [6]. Then, we present a case study of an Adaptive Cruise Control system, and conclude with an evaluation of the scalability of our techniques using a random set of architectures for dynamical system applications as well as a set of classification models for MNIST. The GNODE architectures for each benchmark can be found in the extended version. To facilitate the reproducibility of our experiments, we set a timeout of 2 h (7200 s) for each reach set computation[6]. All our experiments were conducted on a desktop with the following configuration: Intel Core i7-7700 CPU @ 3.6 GHz 8 core Processor, 64 GB Memory, and 64-bit Ubuntu 16.04.3 LTS OS.

3.1 Method and Tool Comparison

We have implemented several methods within NNVODE, and the first evaluation consists of comparing the available methods for nonlinear NODEs, fixed-step zonotope and polynomial zonotopes (zono-F, poly-F) and adaptive zonotope

---

[3] GoTube can be found at https://github.com/DatenVorsprung/GoTube.
[4] Flowstar version 2.1.0 is available at https://flowstar.org/.
[5] JuliaReach can be found at https://juliareach.github.io/.
[6] NNV Release: https://zenodo.org/record/6840545#.YtGlrzfMKUk.

and polynomial zonotope (zono-A, poly-A) based methods [1]. For all other
$\mathcal{NN}$-Layers in the GNODEs, we use the star-set over-approximate methods. We
considered multiple models, all inspired by the ILNODE representation that was
introduced by Massaroli. They consist of a set of models with a varying number
of augmented dimensions. All these models are instances of the GNODE class
presented in Definition 3, which present an architecture of the form $\mathcal{NN}$-Layers +
NODE + $\mathcal{NN}$-Layers. In this context, we were concerned with how the methods
scale with respect to the number of dimensions of each model.

Table 2. Computation time of the reachability analysis of the Damped Oscillator
benchmark. Results are shown in seconds with up to one decimal place.

Aug. Dims	Zono-F	Zono-A	Poly-F	Poly-A
0	**34.0**	574.5	201.7	654.0
1	**146.4**	4205.0	1573.9	3440.9
2	**441.0**	–	–	–

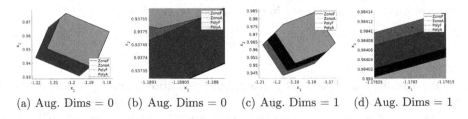

(a) Aug. Dims = 0   (b) Aug. Dims = 0   (c) Aug. Dims = 1   (d) Aug. Dims = 1

Fig. 3. Reach sets comparison of the Damped Oscillator benchmark of the model with
0 and 1 augmented dimensions. Plots (a) and (c) show the reachable set at $t = 1$ s,
and plots b) and d) show the zoomed-in reach sets to observe the minor size differences
between the four methods: ZonoA, **ZonoF**, **PolyF** and PolyA. (Color figure online)

In Table 2, we observe that the Zono-F method is the fastest across all models,
while the adaptive methods are the slowest. Moreover, only Zono-F is able to
complete the reach set computation for all three models, while the other methods
time out. In terms of the size of the computed reach sets, we compare the last
reach set obtained in Fig. 3. In the subplots Fig. 3(b) and 3(d) we see the zoomed
in reach sets, and observe that the Poly-A method computes the smallest over-
approximate reach set across both experiments. Based on these results, in all
subsequent experiments, we use the *zono-F* method for nonlinear NODEs, the
direct method for linear NODEs, and the over-approximate star-set methods for
all the $\mathcal{NN}$-Layers.

The next part of our evaluation consists of comparing NNVODE's methods for NODEs to those of Flow* [9], Gotube [20] and JuliaReach [6] across a
collection of benchmarks that include a linear and nonlinear 2-dimensional spiral [8], a Fixed-Point Attractor (FPA) [38] and a controlled cartpole [18]. The

computation reachability results are displayed in Table 3 with the intention to characterize major differences between tools, i.e., to show some tools are 10× to 20× faster than others for some benchmarks. It is worth noting, that we are not experts on every tool that we considered. Thus it may be possible to optimize the reachable set computation for each benchmark with depending on the tool. However, we did not do so. Instead, we attempted around 3 to 5 different parameter combinations for each benchmark, and used the best results we could obtain when comparing against the other tools. The details can be found in the extended version [34]. The first three rows correspond to the linear spiral 2D model, and the subsequent three rows to the nonlinear one. The first set of observations that can be made in this context is that Flow* times out on all problems involving nonlinear neural ODEs, and that GoTube cannot obtain a solution to the reachability problem for the linear model. In terms of computation time, the results vary. Flow* is the fastest for the linear Spiral 2D model, regardless of the size of the initial set. In general, JuliaReach and NNVODE are much faster than GoTube, with JuliaReach being the fastest tool across the board. Additionally, there is not a significant difference between NNVODE and JuliaReach in the treatment of the nonlinear spiral model and FPA models. However, JuliaReach is an order of magnitude faster than NNVODE and two orders of magnitude faster than GoTube on the cartpole benchmark. In Fig. 4 we display a subset of the reachability results from Table 3 where we observe that JuliaReach is able to compute smaller over-approximations of the reachable set on all the benchmarks except for the linear spiral model. Notably, in most cases, GoTube computes the largest over-approximation, and this effect grows far more significantly than the other tools when the complexity of the model increases. This can be observed in Figs. 4(d) and 4(h).

Table 3. Results of the reachability analysis of the NODE benchmarks. All results are shown in seconds. TH stands for Time Horizon and δ_μ to the input uncertainty.

Name	TH (s)	δ_μ	Flow*	GoTube	JuliaReach	NNVODE (ours)
Spiral$_{L_1}$	10	0.01	**4.0**	–	10.2	8.0
Spiral$_{L_2}$	10	0.05	**3.7**	–	7.2	7.4
Spiral$_{L_3}$	10	0.1	**3.7**	–	7.2	7.3
Spiral$_{NL_1}$	10	0.01	–	106.4	58.9	**47.4**
Spiral$_{NL_2}$	10	0.05	–	106.7	**41.7**	46.2
Spiral$_{NL_3}$	10	0.1	–	106.5	**41.9**	46.2
FPA$_1$	0.5	0.01	-	13.6	1.9	**1.3**
FPA$_2$	2.5	0.01	-	42.4	**5.6**	6.6
FPA$_3$	10.0	0.01	-	140.2	28.4	**7.5**
Cartpole$_1$	0.1	1e-4	-	183.0	**3.2**	67.9
Cartpole$_2$	1.0	1e-4	-	1590.9	**13.8**	404.3
Cartpole$_3$	2.0	1e-4	-	3065.7	**35.5**	834.7

3.2 Case Study: Adaptive Cruise Control (ACC)

This case study was selected to evaluate an original NNCS benchmark used in all the AINNCS ARCH-Competitions [27,28,35,46] against NNCS with NODEs as dynamical plants learned from simulation data using 3rd order NODEs [39]. We demonstrate the verification of the ACC with different GNODEs learned as the plant model of the ACC and compare against the original benchmark, while using the same NN controller across all three models. The details of the original ACC NNCS benchmark can be found in [46], and the architectures of the third order neural ODEs can be found in the extended version [34].

We considered all three models using the same initial conditions and present the results in Fig. 5. The reachable sets obtained from all three plants are largely

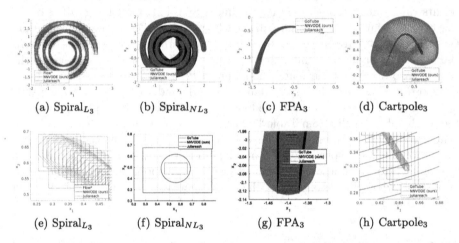

(a) Spiral$_{L3}$ (b) Spiral$_{NL3}$ (c) FPA$_3$ (d) Cartpole$_3$

(e) Spiral$_{L3}$ (f) Spiral$_{NL3}$ (g) FPA$_3$ (h) Cartpole$_3$

Fig. 4. NODE reach set comparisons. The top 4 figures ([a, d]) show the complete reachable sets of each benchmark, while the bottom 4 correspond to the zoomed-in reach sets (e, g) and to the zoomed-in figure of the last reach set (f, h). The figures show the computed reach sets of GoTube, **NNVODE**, **JuliaReach** and Flow*. (Color figure online)

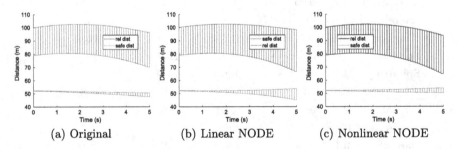

(a) Original (b) Linear NODE (c) Nonlinear NODE

Fig. 5. Adaptive Cruise Control comparison. In red we display the relative distance of the original plant, in blue the linear NODE, in **black** the nonlinear NODE, and in magenta, the safe distance. (Color figure online)

similar, and we can guarantee that all the models are safe since the intersection between the safe distance and the relative distance is empty. When we consider the size of the reachable sets, one can see that the original model returns the smallest reach set, whereas the linear model boasts the largest one. In all, the biggest difference between the plant dynamics is the computation time. Here, the linear 3rd order NODE boasts the fastest computation time of 0.86 s, whereas the original plant takes 14.9 s, and the nonlinear 3rd order NODE takes 998.7 s.

3.3 Classification NODEs

Our second set of experiments considered performing a robustness analysis for a set of MNIST classification models with only fully-connected $\mathcal{NN}$-Layers and other 3 models with convolutional layers as well. There is one linear NODE in each model, and we vary the number of parameters and states across all of them to study the scalability of our methods. We evaluate the robustness of these models under an L_∞ adversarial perturbation of $\epsilon = \{0.05, 1, 2\}$ over all the pixels, and $\epsilon = \{2.55, 12.75, 25.5\}$ over a subset of pixels (80).[7] The complete evaluation of this benchmark consists of a robustness analysis using 50 randomly sampled images for each attack. We compare the number of images the neural ODEs are robust to, as well as the total computation time to run the reachability analysis for each model in Table 4.

Definition 9 (Robustness). *Given a classification-based GNODE $\mathcal{F}(z)$, input $z \in \mathbb{R}^j$, perturbation parameter $\epsilon \in \mathbb{R}$ and an input set Z_p containing z_p such that $Z_p = \{z : \|z - z_p\| \leq \epsilon\}$ that represents the set of all possible perturbations of z. The neural ODE is locally **robust** at z if it classifies all the perturbed inputs z_p to the same label as z, i.e., the system is **robust** if $\mathcal{F}(z_p) = \mathcal{F}(z)$ for all $z_p \in Z_p$.*

Table 4. Robustness analysis of MNIST classification GNODEs under L_∞ adversarial perturbations. The accuracy and robustness results are described as percentage values between 0 and 1, and the time computation corresponds to the average time to compute the reachable set per image. Columns 3–8 corresponds to $\epsilon = \{0.5, 1, 2\}$ over all pixels in the image, columns 9–14 corresponds to $\epsilon = \{2.55, 12.75, 25.5\}$ attack over a subset of pixels (80) n each image.

| | | ℓ_∞ | | | | | | $\ell_{\infty \ (80)}$ | | | | | |
| | | 0.5 | | 1 | | 2 | | 2.55 | | 12.75 | | 25.5 | |
Name	Acc.	Rob.	T(s)	Rob.	T(s)	Rob.	T(s)	Rob.	T(s)	Rob.	T(s)	Rob.	T(s)
FNODE$_S$	0.9695	1	0.0836	0.98	0.1062	0.98	0.1186	1	0.0192	0.98	0.0193	0.98	0.0295
FNODE$_M$	0.9772	1	0.0948	1	0.1177	0.98	0.2111	1	0.0189	1	0.0225	0.98	0.0396
FNODE$_L$	0.9757	1	0.1078	1	0.1674	0.96	0.5049	1	0.0187	1	0.0314	0.96	0.0709
CNODE$_S$	0.9706	0.98	13.95	0.96	15.82	0.86	17.58	0.98	1.943	0.94	3.121	0.78	4.459
CNODE$_M$	0.9811	1	176.5	1	193.8	1	293.8	1	21.45	1	83.28	1	182.0
CNODE$_L$	0.9602	1	1064	1	1089	1	1736	1	234.6	1	522.7	1	779.3

---

[7] Adversarial perturbations are applied before normalization, pixel values $z_p \in [0, 255]$.

Finally, we performed a scalability study using a set of random GNODE architectures with multiple NODEs. Here, we focus on the nonlinear methods for both the NN-Layers and the NODEs and evaluate how our methods scale with the number of neurons, inputs, outputs and dimensions in the NODE. The main challenge of these benchmarks is the presence of multiple NODEs within the GNODE. There are a total of 6 GNODEs (XS, S, M, L, XL, and XXL), all with the same number of layers. However, we increase the number of inputs, outputs, and parameters across all the layers of the GNODEs. Here, XS corresponds to the smallest model and XXL to the largest. A description of these architectures can be found in the extended version [34].

Several trends can be observed from Table 5. The first is that in general, smaller models have smaller reach set computation times, with two notable exceptions: the first run with XS and the last experiment with XL. Furthermore, one can observe that the largest difference in the reach set computation times comes from increasing the number of states in the NODEs, which are $\{2, 3, 4, 4, 5, 5\}$ for both NODEs in every model in $\{$XS, S, M, L, XL, and XXL$\}$ respectively, while increasing the input and output dimensions ($\{1, 2, 2, 3, 3, 4\}$ respectively) does not affect the reachability computation as much. This is because of the complexity of nonlinear ODE reachability as state dimensions increase, while for $NN - Layers$, increasing the size of the inputs or neurons by 1 or a few units does not affect the reachability computation as much.

Table 5. Computation time of the reachability analysis of the randomly generated GNODEs. Results are shown in seconds.

	XS	S	M	L	XL	XXL
$\delta_\mu = 0.01$	57.0	16.2	59.3	61.8	168.3	223.9
$\delta_\mu = 0.02$	3.4	11.4	42.2	41.0	262.4	115.4
$\delta_\mu = 0.04$	3.1	10.3	37.6	72.9	1226.3	243.6

4 Related Work

Analysis of Neural ODEs. To the best of our knowledge, this is the first empirical study of the formal verification of neural ODEs as presented in the general neural ODE (GNODE) class. Some other works have analyzed neural ODEs, but are limited to a more restricted class of neural ODEs with only purely continuous-time models. We refer to these models in this paper as NODEs. The most comparable work is a theoretical inquiry of the neural ODE verification problem using Stochastic Lagrangian Reachability (SLR) [19], which was later extended and implemented in a stochastic reachability analysis tool called GoTube [20]. The SLR method is an abstraction-based technique that is able to compute a tight over-approximation of the set of reachable states, and provide stochastic guarantees in the form of confidence intervals for the derived reachable set. Beyond reachability analysis, there have also been several works investigating the robustness of neural ODEs. In [7], the robustness of neural ODE image classifiers is empirically evaluated against residual networks, which are a standard deep learning model for image classification tasks. Their analysis demonstrates that neural ODEs are more robust to input perturbations than residual networks. In a similar work, a robustness comparison of neural ODEs and standard CNNs was performed [48]. Their work considers two standard adversarial attacks, Gaussian noise and FGSM [17], and their analysis illustrate that neural ODEs are more robust to adversarial perturbations. In terms of the analysis of GNODEs, to the best of our knowledge, no comparable work as been done, although for specific models where all the $\mathcal{NN}$-Layers of a GNODE have fully-connected layers with continuous differentiable activation functions like sigmoid or tanh, it may be possible to compare our methods to other tools (with minor modifications) like Verisig [23,26] or JuliaReach [6]. However, that would restrict the more general class of neural ODEs (GNODEs) that we evaluate in this manuscript.

Verification of Neural Networks and Dynamical Systems. The considered GNODEs are a combination of dynamical systems equations (ODEs) modeled using neural networks, and neural networks. When these subjects are treated in isolation, one finds that there are numerous studies that consider the verification of dynamical systems, and correspondingly there are numerous works that deal with the neural network verification problem. With respect to the former, the hybrid systems community has considered the verification of dynamical systems for decades and developed tools such as SpaceEx [15], Flow* [9], CORA [1], and JuliaReach [6] that deal with the reachability problem for discrete-time, continuous-time or even hybrid dynamics. A more comprehensive list of tools can be found in the following paper [10]. Within the realm of neural networks, the last several years have witnessed numerous promising verification methods proposed towards reasoning about the correctness of their behavior. Some representative tools include Reluplex [29], Marabou [30], ReluVal [47], NNV [46] and ERAN [42]. The tools have drawn inspiration from a wide range of techniques including optimization, search, and reachability analysis [33]. A discussion of these approaches, along with pedagogical implementations of existing methods, can be found in the following paper [33]. Building on the advancements of these fields, as a natural progression, frameworks that consider the reachability problem involving neural networks and dynamical systems have also emerged. Problems within the space are typically referred to as Neural Network Control Systems (NNCS), and some representative tools include NNV [46], Verisig [23,26], and ReachNN* [14,22]. These tools have demonstrated their capabilities and efficiency in several works including the verification of an adaptive cruise control (ACC) [46], an automated emergency breaking system [44], and autonomous racing cars [24,25] among others, as well as participated in the yearly challenges of NNCS verification [27,28,35]. These studies and their respective frameworks are very closely related to the work contained herein. In a sense, they deal with a restricted GNODE architecture, since their analysis combines the basic operations of neural network and dynamical system reachability in a feedback-loop manner. However, this restricted architecture would only consist of a fully-connected neural network followed by a NODE. In Table 6, we present a **comparison to verification tools** that can support one or more of the following verification problems: the analysis of continuous-time models with linear, nonlinear or hybrid dynamics (ODE), neural networks (NN), neural network control systems (NNCS), neural ODEs (NODE) and GNODEs as presented in Fig. 2.

Table 6. Summary of related verification tools. A ✓ means that the tool supports verification of this class, a ○ means that it may be supported it, but some minor changes may be needed, a − means it does not support it, and a ⊙ means that some small changes have been made to the tool for comparison and the tools has been used to verify at least one example on this class.

Tool	ODE[a]	NODE[b]	NN[c]	NNCS	GNODE
CORA [1]	✓	⊙	−	−	−
ERAN [42]	−	−	✓	−	−
Flow* [9]	✓	⊙	−	−	−
GoTube [20]	✓	✓	−	−	−
JuliaReach [6]	✓	⊙	✓	✓	−
Marabou [30]	−	−	✓	−	−
nnenum [3]	−	−	✓	−	−
ReachNN [14,22]	✓	○	✓	✓	−
Reluplex [29]	−	−	✓	−	−
ReluVal [47]	−	−	✓	−	−
Sherlock [12]	✓	○	✓	✓	−
SpaceEx [15]	✓	○	−	−	−
Verisig [23,26]	✓	○	✓	✓	−
NNV [46]	✓	⊙	✓	✓	−
NNVODE (ours)	✓	✓	✓	✓	✓

[a]ODE verification is considered to be supported for any tool than can verify at least one of linear or nonlinear continuous-time ODEs. [b]NODE is a specific type of ODE, so in theory any tool that supports ODE verification may be able to support NODE. However, these tools are optimized for NODE and in practice may not be able to verify most of these models as seen on our comparison with Flow*. [c]We include in this category any tool that supports one or more verification methods for fully-connected, convolutional or pooling layers.

5   Conclusion and Future Work

We have presented a verification framework to compute the reachable sets of a general class of neural ODEs (GNODE) that no other existing methods are able to solve. We have demonstrated through a comprehensive set of experiments the capabilities of our methods on dynamical systems, control systems and classification tasks, as well as the comparison to state-of-the-art reachability analysis tools for continuous-time dynamical systems (NODE). One of the main challenges we faced was the scalability of the nonlinear ODE reachability analysis as the dimension complexity of the models increased, as observed in the cartpole and damped oscillator examples. Possible improvements include integrating other methods into our framework such as [32], which improves the current nonlinear reachability analysis via an improved hybridization technique that reduces the sizes of the linearization domains, and therefore reduces over-approximation error. Another approach would be to make use of the Koopman Operator linearization prior to analysis in order to compute the reach sets of the linear system, which are easier and faster to compute as observed from the experiments conducted using the two-dimensional spiral benchmark [4]. In terms of models and architectures, latent neural ODEs [41] and some of its proposed variations such as controlled neural DEs [31] and neural rough DEs [37] have demonstrated great success in the area of time-series prediction, improving the performance of NODEs, ANODEs and other deep learning models such as RNNs or LSTMs in time-series tasks. The main idea behind these models is to learn a *latent* space from the input of the neural ODE from which to sample and predict future values. In the future, we will analyze these models in detail and explore the addition of verification techniques that can formally analyze their behavior.

Acknowledgements. The material presented in this paper is based upon work supported by the National Science Foundation (NSF) through grant numbers 1910017 and 2028001, the Defense Advanced Research Projects Agency (DARPA) under contract number FA8750-18-C-0089, and the Air Force Office of Scientific Research (AFOSR) under contract number FA9550-22-1-0019. Any opinions, findings, and conclusions or recommendations expressed in this paper are those of the authors and do not necessarily reflect the views of AFOSR, DARPA, or NSF.

References

1. Althoff, M.: An introduction to CORA 2015. In: Proceedings of the Workshop on Applied Verification for Continuous and Hybrid Systems (2015)
2. Althoff, M.: Reachability analysis of nonlinear systems using conservative polynomialization and non-convex sets. In: Proceedings of the 16th International Conference on Hybrid Systems: Computation and Control, HSCC 2013, pp. 173–182. Association for Computing Machinery, New York (2013). https://doi.org/10.1145/2461328.2461358
3. Bak, S.: nnenum: verification of ReLU neural networks with optimized abstraction refinement. In: Dutle, A., Moscato, M.M., Titolo, L., Muñoz, C.A., Perez, I. (eds.) NFM 2021. LNCS, vol. 12673, pp. 19–36. Springer, Cham (2021). https://doi.org/10.1007/978-3-030-76384-8_2
4. Bak, S., Bogomolov, S., Duggirala, P.S., Gerlach, A.R., Potomkin, K.: Reachability of black-box nonlinear systems after Koopman operator linearization. In: Jungers, R.M., Ozay, N., Abate, A. (eds.) 7th IFAC Conference on Analysis and Design of Hybrid Systems, ADHS 2021, Brussels, Belgium, 7–9 July 2021 (2021). IFAC-PapersOnLine **54**, 253–258. Elsevier. https://doi.org/10.1016/j.ifacol.2021.08.507

5. Bak, S., Duggirala, P.S.: Simulation-equivalent reachability of large linear systems with inputs. In: Majumdar, R., Kunčak, V. (eds.) CAV 2017. LNCS, vol. 10426, pp. 401–420. Springer, Cham (2017). https://doi.org/10.1007/978-3-319-63387-9_20

6. Bogomolov, S., Forets, M., Frehse, G., Potomkin, K., Schilling, C.: JuliaReach: a toolbox for set-based reachability. In: Proceedings of the 22nd ACM International Conference on Hybrid Systems: Computation and Control, pp. 39–44 (2019)

7. Carrara, F., Caldelli, R., Falchi, F., Amato, G.: On the robustness to adversarial examples of neural ode image classifiers. In: 2019 IEEE International Workshop on Information Forensics and Security (WIFS), pp. 1–6 (2019). https://doi.org/10.1109/WIFS47025.2019.9035109

8. Chen, R.T.Q., Rubanova, Y., Bettencourt, J., Duvenaud, D.: Neural ordinary differential equations. In: Advances in Neural Information Processing Systems (2018)

9. Chen, X., Ábrahám, E., Sankaranarayanan, S.: Flow*: an analyzer for non-linear hybrid systems. In: Sharygina, N., Veith, H. (eds.) CAV 2013. LNCS, vol. 8044, pp. 258–263. Springer, Heidelberg (2013). https://doi.org/10.1007/978-3-642-39799-8_18

10. Doyen, L., Frehse, G., Pappas, G.J., Platzer, A.: Verification of hybrid systems. In: Clarke, E., Henzinger, T., Veith, H., Bloem, R. (eds.) Handbook of Model Checking, pp. 1047–1110. Springer, Cham (2018). https://doi.org/10.1007/978-3-319-10575-8_30

11. Dupont, E., Doucet, A., Teh, Y.W.: Augmented neural ODEs. In: Wallach, H., Larochelle, H., Beygelzimer, A., d'Alché-Buc, F., Fox, E., Garnett, R. (eds.) Advances in Neural Information Processing Systems, vol. 32. Curran Associates, Inc. (2019)

12. Dutta, S., Chen, X., Sankaranarayanan, S.: Reachability analysis for neural feedback systems using regressive polynomial rule inference. In: Proceedings of the 22nd ACM International Conference on Hybrid Systems: Computation and Control, HSCC 2019, pp. 157–168. ACM, New York (2019). https://doi.org/10.1145/3302504.3311807

13. Ehlers, R.: Formal verification of piece-wise linear feed-forward neural networks. In: D'Souza, D., Narayan Kumar, K. (eds.) ATVA 2017. LNCS, vol. 10482, pp. 269–286. Springer, Cham (2017). https://doi.org/10.1007/978-3-319-68167-2_19. https://doi.org/10/gh25vg

14. Fan, J., Huang, C., Chen, X., Li, W., Zhu, Q.: ReachNN*: a tool for reachability analysis of neural-network controlled systems. In: Hung, D.V., Sokolsky, O. (eds.) ATVA 2020. LNCS, vol. 12302, pp. 537–542. Springer, Cham (2020). https://doi.org/10.1007/978-3-030-59152-6_30

15. Frehse, G., et al.: SpaceEx: scalable verification of hybrid systems. In: Gopalakrishnan, G., Qadeer, S. (eds.) CAV 2011. LNCS, vol. 6806, pp. 379–395. Springer, Heidelberg (2011). https://doi.org/10.1007/978-3-642-22110-1_30

16. Gholaminejad, A., Keutzer, K., Biros, G.: ANODE: unconditionally accurate memory-efficient gradients for neural ODEs. In: Proceedings of the Twenty-Eighth International Joint Conference on Artificial Intelligence, IJCAI-2019, pp. 730–736. International Joint Conferences on Artificial Intelligence Organization, July 2019. https://doi.org/10.24963/ijcai.2019/103

17. Goodfellow, I., Shlens, J., Szegedy, C.: Explaining and harnessing adversarial examples. In: International Conference on Learning Representations (2015)

18. Gruenbacher, S., Cyranka, J., Lechner, M., Islam, M.A., Smolka, S.A., Grosu, R.: Lagrangian reachtubes: the next generation (2020)

19. Gruenbacher, S., Hasani, R.M., Lechner, M., Cyranka, J., Smolka, S.A., Grosu, R.: On the verification of neural ODEs with stochastic guarantees. In: AAAI (2021)

20. Gruenbacher, S., et al.: GoTube: scalable stochastic verification of continuous-depth models. In: Proceedings of the AAAI Conference on Artificial Intelligence, pp. 6755–6764 (2022)

21. Hao, K.: A radical new neural network design could overcome big challenges in AI, April 2020. https://www.technologyreview.com/2018/12/12/1739/a-radical-new-neural-network-design-could-overcome-big-challenges-in-ai/

22. Huang, C., Fan, J., Li, W., Chen, X., Zhu, Q.: ReachNN: reachability analysis of neural-network controlled systems. ACM Trans. Embed. Comput. Syst. **18**(5s), 1–22 (2019)

23. Ivanov, R., Carpenter, T., Weimer, J., Alur, R., Pappas, G., Lee, I.: Verisig 2.0: verification of neural network controllers using Taylor model preconditioning. In: Silva, A., Leino, K.R.M. (eds.) CAV 2021. LNCS, vol. 12759, pp. 249–262. Springer, Cham (2021). https://doi.org/10.1007/978-3-030-81685-8_11

24. Ivanov, R., Carpenter, T.J., Weimer, J., Alur, R., Pappas, G.J., Lee, I.: Case study: verifying the safety of an autonomous racing car with a neural network controller. Association for Computing Machinery, New York (2020)

25. Ivanov, R., Jothimurugan, K., Hsu, S., Vaidya, S., Alur, R., Bastani, O.: Compositional learning and verification of neural network controllers. ACM Trans. Embed. Comput. Syst. **20**(5s), 1–26 (2021). https://doi.org/10.1145/3477023

26. Ivanov, R., Weimer, J., Alur, R., Pappas, G.J., Lee, I.: Verisig: verifying safety properties of hybrid systems with neural network controllers. In: Proceedings of the 22nd ACM International Conference on Hybrid Systems: Computation and Control, HSCC 2019, pp. 169–178. ACM, New York (2019). https://doi.org/10.1145/3302504.3311806

27. Johnson, T.T., et al.: ARCH-COMP21 category report: artificial intelligence and neural network control systems (AINNCS) for continuous and hybrid systems plants. In: Frehse, G., Althoff, M. (eds.) 8th International Workshop on Applied Verification of Continuous and Hybrid Systems (ARCH 2021). EPiC Series in Computing, vol. 80, pp. 90–119. EasyChair (2021). https://doi.org/10.29007/kfk9

28. Johnson, T.T., et al.: ARCH-COMP20 category report: artificial intelligence and neural network control systems (AINNCS) for continuous and hybrid systems plants. In: Frehse, G., Althoff, M. (eds.) ARCH 2020. 7th International Workshop on Applied Verification of Continuous and Hybrid Systems (ARCH 2020). EPiC Series in Computing, vol. 74, pp. 107–139. EasyChair (2020). https://doi.org/10.29007/9xgv

29. Katz, G., Barrett, C., Dill, D.L., Julian, K., Kochenderfer, M.J.: Reluplex: an efficient SMT solver for verifying deep neural networks. In: Majumdar, R., Kunčak, V. (eds.) CAV 2017. LNCS, vol. 10426, pp. 97–117. Springer, Cham (2017). https://doi.org/10.1007/978-3-319-63387-9_5

30. Katz, G., et al.: The marabou framework for verification and analysis of deep neural networks. In: Dillig, I., Tasiran, S. (eds.) CAV 2019. LNCS, vol. 11561, pp. 443–452. Springer, Cham (2019). https://doi.org/10.1007/978-3-030-25540-4_26

31. Kidger, P., Morrill, J., Foster, J., Lyons, T.: Neural controlled differential equations for irregular time series. In: Advances in Neural Information Processing Systems (2020)

32. Li, D., Bak, S., Bogomolov, S.: Reachability analysis of nonlinear systems using hybridization and dynamics scaling. In: Bertrand, N., Jansen, N. (eds.) FORMATS 2020. LNCS, vol. 12288, pp. 265–282. Springer, Cham (2020). https://doi.org/10.1007/978-3-030-57628-8_16

33. Liu, C., Arnon, T., Lazarus, C., Strong, C., Barrett, C., Kochenderfer, M.J.: Algorithms for verifying deep neural networks. Found. Trends Optim. **4**(3–4), 244–404 (2021). https://doi.org/10.1561/2400000035

34. Lopez, D.M., Musau, P., Hamilton, N., Johnson, T.T.: Reachability analysis of a general class of neural ordinary differential equations (2022). https://doi.org/10.48550/ARXIV.2207.06531

35. Manzanas Lopez, D., et al.: ARCH-COMP19 category report: artificial intelligence and neural network control systems (AINNCS) for continuous and hybrid systems plants. In: Frehse, G., Althoff, M. (eds.) ARCH 2019. 6th International Workshop on Applied Verification of Continuous and Hybrid Systems. EPiC Series in Computing, vol. 61, pp. 103–119. EasyChair, April 2019. https://doi.org/10.29007/rgv8

36. Massaroli, S., Poli, M., Park, J., Yamashita, A., Asama, H.: Dissecting neural ODEs. In: Larochelle, H., Ranzato, M., Hadsell, R., Balcan, M.F., Lin, H. (eds.) Advances in Neural Information Processing Systems, vol. 33, pp. 3952–3963. Curran Associates, Inc. (2020)

37. Morrill, J., Salvi, C., Kidger, P., Foster, J., Lyons, T.: Neural rough differential equations for long time series (2021)

38. Musau, P., Johnson, T.T.: Continuous-time recurrent neural networks (CTRNNs) (benchmark proposal). In: 5th Applied Verification for Continuous and Hybrid Systems Workshop (ARCH), Oxford, UK, July 2018. https://doi.org/10.29007/6czp

39. Norcliffe, A., Bodnar, C., Day, B., Simidjievski, N., Lió, P.: On second order behaviour in augmented neural ODEs. In: Larochelle, H., Ranzato, M., Hadsell, R., Balcan, M.F., Lin, H. (eds.) Advances in Neural Information Processing Systems, vol. 33, pp. 5911–5921. Curran Associates, Inc. (2020)

40. Ruan, W., Huang, X., Kwiatkowska, M.: Reachability analysis of deep neural networks with provable guarantees. In: The 27th International Joint Conference on Artificial Intelligence (IJCAI 2018) (2018)

41. Rubanova, Y., Chen, R.T.Q., Duvenaud, D.K.: Latent ordinary differential equations for irregularly-sampled time series. In: Wallach, H., Larochelle, H., Beygelzimer, A., d'Alché-Buc, F., Fox, E., Garnett, R. (eds.) Advances in Neural Information Processing Systems, vol. 32. Curran Associates, Inc. (2019)

42. Singh, G., Gehr, T., Mirman, M., Püschel, M., Vechev, M.: Fast and effective robustness certification. In: Proceedings of the 32nd International Conference on Neural Information Processing Systems, NIPS 2018, Red Hook, NY, USA, pp. 10825–10836. Curran Associates Inc. (2018)

43. Tran, H.-D., Bak, S., Xiang, W., Johnson, T.T.: Verification of deep convolutional neural networks using ImageStars. In: Lahiri, S.K., Wang, C. (eds.) CAV 2020. LNCS, vol. 12224, pp. 18–42. Springer, Cham (2020). https://doi.org/10.1007/978-3-030-53288-8_2

44. Tran, H.D., Cei, F., Lopez, D.M., Johnson, T.T., Koutsoukos, X.: Safety verification of cyber-physical systems with reinforcement learning control. In: ACM SIGBED International Conference on Embedded Software (EMSOFT 2019). ACM, October 2019

45. Tran, H.-D., et al.: Star-based reachability analysis of deep neural networks. In: ter Beek, M.H., McIver, A., Oliveira, J.N. (eds.) FM 2019. LNCS, vol. 11800, pp. 670–686. Springer, Cham (2019). https://doi.org/10.1007/978-3-030-30942-8_39

46. Tran, H.-D., et al.: NNV: the neural network verification tool for deep neural networks and learning-enabled cyber-physical systems. In: Lahiri, S.K., Wang, C. (eds.) CAV 2020. LNCS, vol. 12224, pp. 3–17. Springer, Cham (2020). https://doi.org/10.1007/978-3-030-53288-8_1

47. Wang, S., Pei, K., Whitehouse, J., Yang, J., Jana, S.: Formal security analysis of neural networks using symbolic intervals. In: 27th USENIX Security Symposium (USENIX Security 2018), pp. 1599–1614 (2018)
48. Yan, H., Du, J., Tan, V.Y.F., Feng, J.: On robustness of neural ordinary differential equations (2020)

Reinforcement Learning

Robust Event-Driven Interactions in Cooperative Multi-agent Learning

Daniel Jarne Ornia$^{(\boxtimes)}$ and Manuel Mazo Jr.

Delft Center for Systems and Control, Delft University of Technology,
2628 CD Delft, The Netherlands
d.jarneornia@tudelft.nl

Abstract. We present an approach to safely reduce the communication required between agents in a Multi-Agent Reinforcement Learning system by exploiting the inherent robustness of the underlying Markov Decision Process. We compute robustness certificate functions (off-line), that give agents a conservative indication of how far their state measurements can deviate before they need to update other agents in the system with new measurements. This results in fully distributed decision functions, enabling agents to decide when it is necessary to communicate state variables. We derive bounds on the optimality of the resulting systems in terms of the discounted sum of rewards obtained, and show these bounds are a function of the design parameters. Additionally, we extend the results for the case where the robustness surrogate functions are learned from data, and present experimental results demonstrating a significant reduction in communication events between agents.

Keywords: Multi-Agent Systems · Event-Triggered Communication · Reinforcement Learning

1 Introduction

In the last two decades we have seen a surge of learning-based techniques applied to the field of multi agent game theory, enabling the solution of larger and more complex problems, both model based and model free [3,13,24]. Lately, with the wide adoption of Deep Learning techniques for compact representations of value functions and policies in model-free problems [17,23,34], the field of Multi-Agent Reinforcement Learning (MARL) has seen an explosion in the applications of such algorithms to solve real-world problems [20]. However, this has naturally led to a trend where both the amount of data handled in such data driven approaches and the complexity of the targeted problems grow exponentially. In a MARL setting where communication between agents is required, this may inevitably lead to restrictive requirements in the frequency and reliability of the communication to and from each agents (as it was already pointed out in [25]).

This work was partially supported by the ERC Starting Grant SENTIENT #755953.

S. Bogomolov and D. Parker (Eds.): FORMATS 2022, LNCS 13465, pp. 281–297, 2022.
https://doi.org/10.1007/978-3-031-15839-1_16

The effect of asynchronous communication in dynamic programming problems was studied already in [2]. In particular, one of the first examples of how communication affects learning and policy performance in MARL is found in [32], where the author investigates the impact of agents sharing different combinations of state variable subsets or Q values. After that, there have been multiple examples of work studying different types of communication in MARL and what problems arise from it [1,16,28,30]. In this line, in [37] actor coordination minimization is addressed and in [10,15] authors allow agents to choose a communication action and receive a reward when this improves the policies of other agents. In [6] multi agent policy gradient methods are proposed with convergence guarantees where agents communicate gradients based on some trigger conditions, and in [19] agents are allowed to communicate a simplified form of the parameters that determine their value function.

We focus particularly in a *centralised training - decentralised execution*, where agents must communicate state measurements to other agents in order to execute the distributed policies. Such a problem represents most real applications of MARL systems: It is convenient to train such systems in a simulator, in order to centrally learn all agents' value functions and policies. But if the policies are to be executed in a live (real) setting, agents will have access to different sets of state variables that need to be communicated with each-other. In this case, having non-reliable communication leads to severe disruptions in the robustness of the distributed policies' performance. The authors in [18] demonstrated experimentally how very small adversarial disruptions in state variable communications leads to a collapse of the performance of general collaborative MARL systems. In this regard, [7] proposes learning an "adviser" model to fall back on when agents have too much uncertainty in their state measurements, and more recently in [14] the authors enable agents to run simulated copies of the environment to compensate for a disruption in the communication of state variables, and in [36] agents are trained using adversarial algorithms to achieve more robust policies. This lack of robustness in communicative multi-agent learning presents difficulties when trying to design efficient systems where the goal is to communicate less often.

With this goal in mind, we can look into event triggered control (ETC) as a strategy to reduce communication [22,31] in a networked system by trading off communication for robustness against state measurement deviations. This has been applied before in linear multi-agent systems [8] and non-linear systems [9,38]. In [33] and [26] ideas on how to use ETC on model-free linear and non-linear systems were explored. Additionally in other learning problems such as [29], where authors show how event triggered rules can be applied to learn model parameters more efficiently, and in [12] by applying a similar principle to demonstrate how ETC can be used to compute stochastic gradient descent steps in a decentralised event-based manner.

1.1 Main Contribution

We consider in this work a general cooperative MARL scenario where agents have learned distributed policies that must be executed in an on-line scenario, and that depend on other agent's measurements. We propose a constructive approach to synthesise communication strategies that minimise the amount of communication required and guarantee a minimum performance of the MARL system in terms of cumulative reward when compared to an optimal policy. We construct so-called *robustness surrogate* functions, which quantify the robustness of the system to disturbances in agent state variable measurements, allowing for less communication in more robust state regions. Additionally, we consider the case where these surrogate functions are learned through the *scenario approach* [4,5], and show how the guarantees are adapted for learned approximated functions.

2 Preliminaries

2.1 Notation

We use calligraphic letters for sets and regular letters for functions $f : \mathbb{R}^m \to \mathbb{R}^n$. We say a function $f : \mathbb{R}_+ \to \mathbb{R}_+$ is $f \in \mathcal{K}_\infty$ if it is continuous, monotonically increasing and $f(0) = 0$, $\lim_{a\to\infty} f(a) = \infty$. We use $\mathcal{F}$ as the σ-algebra of events in a probability space, and P as a probability measure $P : \mathcal{F} \to [0,1]$. We use $E[\cdot]$ and $\mathrm{Var}[\cdot]$ for the expected value and the variance of a random variable. We use $\| \cdot \|_\infty$ as the sup-norm, $| \cdot |$ as the absolute value or the cardinality, and $\langle v, u \rangle$ as the inner product between two vectors. We say a random process X_n converges to a random variable X *almost surely* (a.s.) as $t \to \infty$ if it does so with probability one for any event $\omega \in \mathcal{F}$. For a conditional expectation, we write $E[X|Y] \equiv E_Y[X]$.

2.2 MDPs and Multi-agent MDPs

We first present the single agent MDP formulation.

Definition 1 *[Markov Decision Process]. A Markov Decision Process (MDP) is a tuple $(\mathcal{X}, \mathcal{U}, P, r)$ where $\mathcal{X}$ is a set of states, $\mathcal{U}$ is a set of actions, $P : \mathcal{U} \to \mathbb{P}^{|\mathcal{X}| \times |\mathcal{X}|}$ is a probability measure of the transitions between states and $r : \mathcal{X} \times \mathcal{U} \times \mathcal{X} \to \mathbb{R}$ is a reward function, such that $r(\mathbf{x}, u, \mathbf{x}')$ is the reward obtained when action u is performed at state $\mathbf{x}$ and leads to state $\mathbf{x}'$.*

In general, an agent has a policy $\pi : \mathcal{X} \to \mathbb{P}(\mathcal{U})$, that maps the states to a probability vector determining the chance of executing each action. We can extend the MDP framework to the case where multiple agents take simultaneous actions on an MDP. For the state transition probabilities we write in-distinctively $P_{\mathbf{xx}'}(u) \equiv P(\mathbf{x}, \mathbf{x}', u)$, and for the reward obtained in two consecutive states $\mathbf{x}_t, \mathbf{x}_{t+1}$ we will write $r_t \equiv r(\mathbf{x}_t, u_t, \mathbf{x}_{t+1})$.

Definition 2 *[Collaborative Multi-Agent MDP]. A Collaborative Multi-Agent Markov Decision Process (c-MMDP) is a tuple* $(\mathcal{N}, \mathcal{X}, \mathcal{U}^n, P, r)$ *where* $\mathcal{N}$ *is a set of n agents,* $\mathcal{X}$ *is a cartesian product of metric state spaces* $\mathcal{X} = \prod_{i \in \mathcal{N}} \mathcal{X}_i$, $\mathcal{U}^n = \prod_{i \in \mathcal{N}} \mathcal{U}_i$ *is a joint set of actions,* $P : \mathcal{U}^n \to \mathbb{P}^{\mathcal{X} \times \mathcal{X}}$ *is a probability measure of the transitions between states and* $r : \mathcal{X} \times \mathcal{U}^n \times \mathcal{X} \to \mathbb{R}$ *is a reward function.*

Assumption 1. *We assume that each agent i has access to a set* $\mathcal{X}_i \subset \mathcal{X}$, *such that the observed state for agent i is* $\mathbf{x}(i) \in \mathcal{X}_i$. *That is, the global state at time t is* $\mathbf{x}_t = (\mathbf{x}_t(1) \ \mathbf{x}_t(2) \ ... \mathbf{x}_t(n))^T$. *Furthermore, we assume that the space* $\mathcal{X}$ *accepts a sup-norm* $\| \cdot \|_\infty$.

In the c-MMDP case, we can use $U \in \mathcal{U}^n$ to represent a specific joint action $U := \{U(1), U(2), ..., U(n)\}$, and $\Pi := \{\pi_1, \pi_2, ..., \pi_n\}$ to represent the joint policies of all agents such that $\Pi : \mathcal{X} \to \mathcal{U}^n$. We assume in this work that agents have a common reward function, determined by the joint action. That is, even if agents do not have knowledge of the actions performed by others, the reward they observe still depends on everyone's joint action. Additionally, we assume in the c-MMDP framework that the control of the agents is fully distributed, with each agent having its own (deterministic) policy π_i that maps the global state to the individual action, i.e. $\pi_i : \mathcal{X} \to \mathcal{U}_i$. We define the optimal policy in an MDP as the policy π^* that maximises the expected discounted reward sum $E[\sum_{t=1}^\infty \gamma^t r_t | \pi, \mathbf{x}_0] \ \forall \mathbf{x}_0 \in \mathcal{X}$ over an infinite horizon, for a given discount $\gamma \in (0, 1)$. The optimal joint (or *centralised*) policy in a c-MMDP is the joint policy Π^* that maximises the discounted reward sum in the "centrally controlled" MDP, and this policy can be decomposed in a set of agent-specific optimal policies $\Pi^* = \{\pi_1^*, \pi_2^*, ..., \pi_n^*\}$.

Remark 1. Assumption 1 is satisfied in most MARL problems where the underlying MDP represents some real physical system (*e.g.* robots interacting in a space, autonomous vehicles sharing roads, dynamical systems where the state variables are metric...). In the case where $\mathcal{X}$ is an abstract discrete set, we can still assign a trivial bijective map $I : \mathcal{X} \to \mathbb{N}$ and compute distances on the mapped states $\|\mathbf{x}_1 - \mathbf{x}_2\|_\infty \equiv \|I(\mathbf{x}_1) - I(\mathbf{x}_2)\|_\infty$. However, we may expect the methods proposed in this work to have worse results when the states are artificially numbered, since the map I may have no relation with the transition probabilities (we come back to this further in the work).

2.3   Value Functions and Q-Learning in c-MMDPs

Consider a c-MMDP, and let a value function under a joint policy Π, V^Π : $\mathcal{X} \to \mathbb{R}$ be $V^\Pi(\mathbf{x}) = \sum_{\mathbf{x}'} P_{\mathbf{x}\mathbf{x}'}(\Pi(\mathbf{x}))(r(\mathbf{x}, \Pi(\mathbf{x}), \mathbf{x}') + \gamma V^\Pi(\mathbf{x}'))$. There exists an optimal value function V^* for a centralised controller in a c-MMDP that solves the Bellman equation:

$$V^*(\mathbf{x}) := \max_U \sum_{\mathbf{x}'} P_{\mathbf{x}\mathbf{x}'}(U)(r(\mathbf{x}, U, \mathbf{x}') + \gamma V^*(\mathbf{x}')).$$

Now consider so-called Q functions $Q : \mathcal{X} \times \mathcal{U}^n \to \mathbb{R}$ on the centrally controlled c-MMDP [35], such that the optimal Q function satisfies

$$Q^*(\mathbf{x}, U) := \sum_{\mathbf{x}'} P_{\mathbf{xx}'}(U)(r(\mathbf{x}, U, \mathbf{x}') + \gamma \max_{U'} Q^*(\mathbf{x}', U')),$$

and the optimal centralised policy is given by $U^* := \pi^*(\mathbf{x}) = \mathrm{argmax}_U Q^*(\mathbf{x}, U)$. Additionally, $\max_U Q^*(\mathbf{x}, U) = V^*(\mathbf{x}) = E[\sum_{t=1}^{\infty} \gamma^t r(\mathbf{x}, \Pi^*(\mathbf{x}), \mathbf{x}') | \mathbf{x}_0]$.

3   Information Sharing Between Collaborative Agents: Problem Formulation

Consider now the case of a c-MMDP where each agent has learned a distributed policy $\pi_i : \mathcal{X} \to \mathcal{U}_i$. We are interested in the scenario where the state variable $\mathbf{x}_t \in \mathcal{X}$ at time t is composed by a set of joint observations from all agents, and these observations need to be communicated to other agents for them to compute their policies.

Assumption 2. *Agents have a set of optimal policies Π^* available for executing on-line and a global optimal function Q^* (learned as a result of e.g. a multi-agent actor critic algorithm [20]).*

Consider the case where at a given time t, a subset of agents $\hat{\mathcal{N}}_t \subseteq \mathcal{N}$ does not share their state measurements with other agents. Let t_i be the last time agent i transmitted its measurement. We define $\hat{\mathbf{x}}_t \in \mathcal{X}$ as

$$\hat{\mathbf{x}}_t := (\mathbf{x}_{t_1}(1), \mathbf{x}_{t_2}(2), ..., \mathbf{x}_{t_n}(n)). \tag{1}$$

That is, $\hat{\mathbf{x}}_t$ is the last known state corresponding to the collection of agent states last transmitted, at time t. Then, the problem considered in this work is as follows.

Problem 1. *Consider a c-MMDP with a set of optimal shared state policies Π^*. Synthesise strategies that minimise the communication events between agents and construct distributed policies $\hat{\Pi}$ that keep the expected reward within some bounds of the optimal rewards, these bounds being a function of design parameters.*

4   Efficient Communication Strategies

To solve the problem of minimizing communication, we can first consider a scenario where agents can request state measurements from other agents. Consider a c-MMDP where agents have optimal policies Π^*. If agents are allowed to request state observations from other agents at their discretion, a possible algorithm to reduce the communication when agents execute their optimal policies is to use sets of neighbouring states $\mathcal{D} : \mathcal{X} \to 2^{\mathcal{X}}$ such that $\mathcal{D}(\mathbf{x}) = \{\mathbf{x}' : \|\mathbf{x} - \mathbf{x}'\| \leq d\}$ for some maximum distance d. Agents could compute such sets for each point

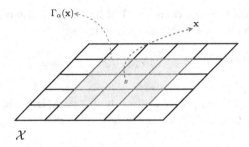

Fig. 1. Robustness surrogate representation.

in space, and request information from others only if the optimal action changes for any state $\mathbf{x}' \in \mathcal{D}(\mathbf{x})$. This approach, however, is not practical on a large scale multi agent system. First, it requires agents to request information, which could already be considered a communication event and therefore not always desirable. Additionally, computing the sets "on the fly" has a complexity of $\mathcal{O}(|\mathcal{X}|^2)$ in the worst case, and it has to be executed at every time-step by all agents. We therefore propose an approach to reduce communication in a MARL system where agents do not need to request information, but instead send messages (or not) to other agents based on some triggering rule.

4.1   Event-Driven Interactions

To construct an efficient communication strategy based on a distributed triggering approach, let us first define a few useful concepts. In order to allow agents to decide when is it necessary to transmit their own state measurements, we define the *robustness indicator* $\Gamma : \mathcal{X} \to \mathbb{R}_{\geq 0}$ as follows.

Definition 3. *For a c-MMDP with optimal global* $Q^* : \mathcal{X} \times \mathcal{U}^n \to \mathbb{R}$, *we define the robustness surrogate* $\Gamma_\alpha : \mathcal{X} \to \mathbb{R}_{\geq 0}$ *with sensitivity parameter* $\alpha \in \mathbb{R}_{\geq 0}$ *as:*

$$\Gamma_\alpha(\mathbf{x}) := \max\{d \,|\, \forall \mathbf{x}' : \|\mathbf{x}' - \mathbf{x}\|_\infty \leq d \Rightarrow$$
$$\Rightarrow Q^*(\mathbf{x}', \Pi^*(\mathbf{x})) \geq V^*(\mathbf{x}') - \alpha\}.$$

The function Γ_α gives a maximum distance (in the sup-norm) such that for any state $\mathbf{x}'$ which is Γ_α close to $\mathbf{x}$ guarantees the action $\Pi^*(\mathbf{x})$ has a Q value which is α close to the optimal value in $\mathbf{x}'$. A representation can be seen in Fig. 1. Computing the function Γ_α in practice may be challenging, and we cover this in detail in following sections.

Proposition 1. *Consider a c-MMDP communicating and acting according to Algorithm 1. Let* $\hat{\mathbf{x}}_t^i$ *be the last known joint state stored by agent* i *at time* t, *and* $\mathbf{x}_t$ *be the true state at time* t. *Then, it holds:*

$$\hat{\mathbf{x}}_t^i = \hat{\mathbf{x}}_t \ \forall i \in \mathcal{N}, \tag{2}$$

$$\|\hat{\mathbf{x}}_t - \mathbf{x}_t\|_\infty \leq \Gamma_\alpha(\hat{\mathbf{x}}_t) \ \forall t. \tag{3}$$

Algorithm 1. Self-Triggered state sharing

Initialise $\mathcal{N}$ agents at $\mathbf{x}_0$;
Initialise last-known state vector $\hat{\mathbf{x}}_0 = \mathbf{x}_0$, $i \in \mathcal{N}$
$t = 0$,
while $t < t_{max}$ **do**
    for $i \in \mathcal{N}$ **do**
        if $\|\mathbf{x}_t(i) - \hat{\mathbf{x}}_{t-1}(i)\|_\infty > \Gamma_\alpha(\hat{\mathbf{x}}_{t-1})$ **then**
            $\hat{\mathbf{x}}_t(i) \leftarrow \mathbf{x}_t(i)$
            Send updated $\hat{\mathbf{x}}_t(i)$ to all $\mathcal{N}_{-i}$;
        end if
        Execute action $\hat{U}_i^* = \pi_i^*(\hat{\mathbf{x}})$;
    end for
    $t + +$;
end while

Proof. Properties (2) and (3) hold by construction. First, all agents update their own $\hat{\mathbf{x}}_t^i$ based on the received communication, therefore all have the same last-known state. Second, whenever the condition $\|\mathbf{x}_t(i) - \hat{\mathbf{x}}_{t-1}(i)\|_\infty > \Gamma_\alpha(\hat{\mathbf{x}})$ is violated, agent i transmits the new state measurement to others, and $\hat{\mathbf{x}}_t$ is updated. Therefore $\|\mathbf{x}_t - \hat{\mathbf{x}}_t\|_\infty > \Gamma_\alpha(\hat{\mathbf{x}}_t)$ holds for all times. $\square$

Now let us use $\hat{r}_t = r(\mathbf{x}_t, \Pi^*(\hat{\mathbf{x}}_t), \mathbf{x}_{t+1})$ as the reward obtained when using the delayed state $\hat{\mathbf{x}}_t$ as input for the optimal policies. We then present the following result.

Theorem 1. *Consider a c-MMDP and let agents apply Algorithm 1 to update the delayed state vector $\hat{\mathbf{x}}_t$. Then it holds $\forall \mathbf{x}_0 \in \mathcal{X}$:*

$$E_{\mathbf{x}_0}[\sum_{t=0}^{\infty} \gamma^t r(\mathbf{x}_t, \Pi^*(\hat{\mathbf{x}}_t), \mathbf{x}_{t+1})] \geq V^*(\mathbf{x}_0) - \alpha \frac{\gamma}{1 - \gamma}.$$

Proof. From Proposition 1, $\|\mathbf{x}_t - \hat{\mathbf{x}}_t\|_\infty \leq \Gamma_\alpha(\hat{\mathbf{x}}_t) \,\forall t$, and recalling the expression for the optimal Q values:

$$Q^*(\mathbf{x}_t, \Pi^*(\hat{\mathbf{x}}_t)) = E_{\mathbf{x}_t}[\hat{r}_t + \gamma V^*(\mathbf{x}_{t+1})] \geq V^*(\mathbf{x}_t) - \alpha. \tag{4}$$

Now let $\hat{V}(\mathbf{x}_0) := E_{\mathbf{x}_0}[\sum_{t=0}^{\infty} \gamma^t \hat{r}_t]$ be the value of the policy obtained from executing the actions $\Pi^*(\hat{\mathbf{x}}_t)$. Then:

$$\begin{aligned} E_{\mathbf{x}_0}[\sum_{t=0}^{\infty} \gamma^t \hat{r}_t] &= E_{\mathbf{x}_0}[\hat{r}_0 + \gamma V^{\hat{\Pi}}(\mathbf{x}_1)] \\ &= E_{\mathbf{x}_0}[\hat{r}_0 + \gamma \hat{V}(\mathbf{x}_1) + \gamma V^*(\mathbf{x}_1) - \gamma V^*(\mathbf{x}_1)] \\ &= E_{\mathbf{x}_0}[\hat{r}_0 + \gamma V^*(\mathbf{x}_1)] + \gamma E_{\mathbf{x}_0}[\hat{V}(\mathbf{x}_1) - V^*(\mathbf{x}_1)]. \end{aligned} \tag{5}$$

Then, substituting (4) in (5):

$$E_{\mathbf{x}_0}[\sum_{t=0}^{\infty} \gamma^t \hat{r}_t] \geq V^*(\mathbf{x}_0) - \alpha + \gamma E_{\mathbf{x}_0}[\hat{V}(\mathbf{x}_1) - V^*(\mathbf{x}_1)]. \tag{6}$$

Now, observe we can apply the same principle as in (5) for the last term in (6),

$$
\begin{aligned}
\hat{V}(\mathbf{x}_1) - V^*(\mathbf{x}_1) &= E_{\mathbf{x}_1}[\hat{r}_1 + \gamma \hat{V}(\mathbf{x}_2)] - V^*(\mathbf{x}_1) \\
&= Q^*(\mathbf{x}_1, \Pi^*(\hat{\mathbf{x}}_1)) + \gamma E_{\mathbf{x}_1}[\hat{V}(\mathbf{x}_2) - V^*(\mathbf{x}_2)] - V^*(\mathbf{x}_1) \\
&\geq V^*(\mathbf{x}_1) - \alpha - V^*(\mathbf{x}_1) + \gamma E_{\mathbf{x}_1}[\hat{V}(\mathbf{x}_2) - V^*(\mathbf{x}_2)] \\
&= -\alpha + \gamma E_{\mathbf{x}_1}[\hat{V}(\mathbf{x}_2) - V^*(\mathbf{x}_2)].
\end{aligned}
\tag{7}
$$

Substituting (7) in (6):

$$
E_{\mathbf{x}_0}\Big[\sum_{t=0}^{\infty} \gamma^t \hat{r}_t\Big] \geq V^*(\mathbf{x}_0) - \alpha - \gamma\alpha + \gamma^2 E_{\mathbf{x}_0}[E_{\mathbf{x}_1}[\hat{V}(\mathbf{x}_2) - V^*(\mathbf{x}_2)]].
\tag{8}
$$

Now it is clear that, applying (7) recursively:

$$
E_{\mathbf{x}_0}\Big[\sum_{t=0}^{\infty} \gamma^t \hat{r}_t\Big] \geq V^*(\mathbf{x}_0) - \alpha
$$
$$
- \gamma\alpha + \gamma^2 E_{\mathbf{x}_0}[E_{\mathbf{x}_1}[\hat{V}(\mathbf{x}_2) - V^*(\mathbf{x}_2)]] \geq V^*(\mathbf{x}_0) - \alpha \sum_{k=0}^{\infty} \gamma^k.
\tag{9}
$$

Substituting $\sum_{k=0}^{\infty} \gamma^k = \frac{\gamma}{1-\gamma}$ in (9):

$$
E_{\mathbf{x}_0}\Big[\sum_{t=0}^{\infty} \gamma^t \hat{r}_t\Big] \geq V^*(\mathbf{x}_0) - \alpha \frac{\gamma}{1-\gamma}.
$$

$\square$

5   Robustness Surrogate and Its Computation

The computation of the robustness surrogate Γ_α may not be straight forward. When the state-space of the c-MMDP is metric, we can construct sets of neighbouring states for a given $\mathbf{x}$. Algorithm 2 produces an exact computation of the robustness surrogate Γ_α for a given c-MMDP and point $\mathbf{x}$. Observe, in the worst case, Algorithm 2 has a complexity of $O(|\mathcal{X}|)$ to compute the function $\Gamma_\alpha(\mathbf{x})$ for a single point $\mathbf{x}$. If this needs to be computed across the entire state-space, it explodes to an operation of worst case complexity $O(|\mathcal{X}|^2)$. In order to compute such functions more efficiently while retaining probabilistic guarantees, we can make use of the Scenario Approach for regression problems [5].

5.1   Learning the Robustness Surrogate with the Scenario Approach

The data driven computation of the function Γ_α can be proposed in the terms of the following optimization program. Assume we only have access to a uniformly sampled set $\mathcal{X}_S \subset \mathcal{X}$ of size $|\mathcal{X}_S| = S$. Let $\hat{\Gamma}_\alpha^\theta$ be an approximation of the

---

Algorithm 2. Computation of Robustness Indicator

Initialise $\mathbf{x}$.
Initialise $d = 1$.
Done = *False*
while Not Done **do**
    Compute Set $\mathcal{X}^d := \{\mathbf{x}' : \|\mathbf{x} - \mathbf{x}'\| = d\}$;
    if $\exists \mathbf{x}' \in \mathcal{X}^d : Q^*(\mathbf{x}', \Pi^*(\mathbf{x})) \leq V^*(\mathbf{x}') - \alpha$ **then**
        Done = *True*
    else $d ++$
    end if
end while
$\Gamma_\alpha(\mathbf{x}) = d - 1$

---

real robustness surrogate parametrised by θ. To apply the scenario approach optimization, we need $\hat{\Gamma}_\alpha^\theta$ to be convex with respect to θ. For this we can use a Support Vector Regression (SVR) model, and embed the state vector in a higher dimensional space trough a feature non-linear map $\phi(\cdot)$ such that $\phi(\mathbf{x})$ is a feature vector, and we use the kernel $k(\mathbf{x}_1, \mathbf{x}_2) = \langle \phi(\mathbf{x}_1), \phi(\mathbf{x}_2) \rangle$. Let us consider sampled pairs $\{(\mathbf{x}_s, y_s)\}_S$, with $y_s = \Gamma_\alpha(\mathbf{x}_s)$ computed through Algorithm 2. Then, we propose solving the following optimization problem with parameters $\tau, \rho > 0$:

$$\min_{\substack{\theta \in \mathcal{X}, \kappa \geq 0, b \in \mathbb{R}, \\ \xi_i \geq 0, i = 1, 2, \ldots, S}} \left(\kappa + \tau \|\theta\|^2 \right) + \rho \sum_{i=1}^{S} \xi_i, \tag{10}$$

$$s.t. \quad |y_i - k(\theta, \mathbf{x}_i) - b| - \kappa \leq \xi_i, \quad i = 1, \ldots, S.$$

The solution to the optimization problem (10) yields a trade-off between how many points are outside the *prediction tube* $|y - k(\theta^*, \mathbf{x}_i) - b^*| < \kappa^*$ and how large the tube is (the value of κ^*). Additionally, the parameter ρ enables us to tune how much we want to penalise sample points being out of the prediction tube. Now take $(\theta^*, \kappa^*, b^*, \xi_i^*)$ as the solution to the optimization problem (10). Then, the learned robustness surrogate function will be:

$$\hat{\Gamma}_\alpha^{\theta^*} := k(\theta^*, \mathbf{x}_i) + b^*.$$

From Theorem 3 [5], it then holds for a sample of points $\mathcal{X}_S$ and a number of outliers $s^* := |\{(\mathbf{x}, y) \in \mathcal{X}_S : |y - k(\theta^*, \mathbf{x}) - b^*| > \kappa^*\}|$:

$$\Pr^S \left\{ \underline{\epsilon}(s^*) \leq \Pr \left\{ \mathbf{x} : \left| \Gamma_\alpha(\mathbf{x}) - \hat{\Gamma}_\alpha^{\theta^*}(\mathbf{x}) \right| > \kappa^* \right\} \leq \bar{\epsilon}(s^*) \right\} \geq 1 - \beta \tag{11}$$

where $\underline{\epsilon}(s^*) := \max\{0, 1 - \bar{t}(s^*)\}$, $\bar{\epsilon}(s^*) := 1 - \underline{t}(s^*)$, and $\bar{t}(s^*), \underline{t}(s^*)$ are the solutions to the polynomial

$$\binom{S}{s^*} t^{S-s^*} - \frac{\beta}{2S} \sum_{i=k}^{S-1} \binom{i}{s^*} t^{i-k} - \frac{\beta}{6S} \sum_{i=S+1}^{4S} \binom{i}{s^*} t^{i-s^*} = 0.$$

Now observe, in our case we would like $\Gamma_\alpha(\mathbf{x}) \geq \hat{\Gamma}_\alpha^{\theta^*}(\mathbf{x})$ to make sure we are never over-estimating the robustness values. Then, with probability larger than $1 - \beta$:

$$\bar{\epsilon}(s^*) \geq \Pr\left\{\mathbf{x} : \left|\Gamma_\alpha(\mathbf{x}) - \hat{\Gamma}_\alpha^{\theta^*}(\mathbf{x})\right| > \kappa^*\right\} \geq \Pr\left\{\mathbf{x} : \Gamma_\alpha(\mathbf{x}) - \hat{\Gamma}_\alpha^{\theta^*}(\mathbf{x}) < -\kappa^*\right\}$$

$$= \Pr\left\{\mathbf{x} : \Gamma_\alpha(\mathbf{x}) < \hat{\Gamma}_\alpha^{\theta^*}(\mathbf{x}) - \kappa^*\right\}.$$

$$(12)$$

Therefore, taking $\|\mathbf{x}_t(i) - \hat{\mathbf{x}}_{t-1}(i)\|_\infty > \hat{\Gamma}_\alpha^{\theta^*}(\hat{\mathbf{x}}_{t-1}) - \kappa^*$ as the condition to transmit state measurements for each agent, we know that the probability of using an over-estimation of the true value $\Gamma_\alpha(\mathbf{x}_t)$ is at most $\bar{\epsilon}(s^*)$ with confidence $1 - \beta$.

Then, let $\{\hat{U}_t\}$ be the sequence of joint actions taken by the system. The probability of U_t violating the condition $Q^*(\mathbf{x}_t, U_t) \geq V^*(\mathbf{x}_t) - \alpha$ for any $\mathbf{x}_t \in \mathcal{X}$ is at most $\bar{\epsilon}(s^*)$. Then, we can extend the results from Theorem 1 for the case where we use a SVR approximation as a robustness surrogate. Define the worst possible suboptimality gap $\iota := \max_{\mathbf{x}, U} |V^*(\mathbf{x}) - Q^*(\mathbf{x}, U)|$.

Corollary 1. *Let $\hat{\Gamma}_\alpha^{\theta^*}$ obtained from (10) from collection of samples $\mathcal{X}_S$. Then, a c-MMDP communicating according to Algorithm 1 using as trigger condition $\|\mathbf{x}_t(i) - \hat{\mathbf{x}}_{t-1}(i)\|_\infty > \hat{\Gamma}_\alpha^{\theta^*}(\hat{\mathbf{x}}_{t-1}) - \kappa^*$ yields, with probability higher than $1 - \beta$:*

$$E_{\mathbf{x}_0}\left[\sum_{t=0}^{\infty} \gamma^t \hat{r}_t\right] \geq V^*(\mathbf{x}_0) - \delta,$$

with $\delta := (\alpha + \bar{\epsilon}(s^*)(\iota - \alpha))\frac{\gamma}{1-\gamma}$.

Proof. Take expression (12), and consider the action sequence executed by the c-MMDP to be $\{\hat{U}_t\}_{t=0}^{\infty}$. We can bound the total expectation of the sum of rewards by considering $\{\hat{U}_t\}_{t=0}^{\infty}$ to be a sequence of random variables that produce $Q^*(\mathbf{x}_t, \hat{U}_t) \geq V^*(\mathbf{x}_t) - \alpha$ with probability $1 - \bar{\epsilon}(s^*)$, and $Q^*(\mathbf{x}_t, \hat{U}_t) \geq V^*(\mathbf{x}_t) - \iota$ with probability $\bar{\epsilon}(s^*)$. Then,

$$E_{\mathbf{x}_0}\left[\sum_{t=0}^{\infty} \gamma^t \hat{r}_t\right] = E\left[E_{\mathbf{x}_0}\left[\sum_{t=0}^{\infty} \gamma^t \hat{r}_t | \{\hat{U}_t\}\right]\right] = E[E_{\mathbf{x}_0}[\hat{r}_0 + \gamma \hat{V}(\mathbf{x}_1)|\{\hat{U}_t\}]] \qquad (13)$$

$$= E[E_{\mathbf{x}_0}[\hat{r}_0 + \gamma V^*(\mathbf{x}_1)|\{\hat{U}_t\}] + \gamma E_{\mathbf{x}_0}[\hat{V}(\mathbf{x}_1) - V^*(\mathbf{x}_1)|\{\hat{U}_t\}]].$$

Observe now, for the first term in (13):

$$E[E_{\mathbf{x}_0}[\hat{r}_0 + \gamma V^*(\mathbf{x}_1)|\{\hat{U}_t\}]] \geq (1 - \bar{\epsilon}(s^*))(V^*(\mathbf{x}_0) - \alpha)$$
$$+ \bar{\epsilon}(s^*)(V^*(\mathbf{x}_0) - \iota) = V^*(\mathbf{x}_0) - \alpha - \bar{\epsilon}(s^*)(\iota - \alpha). \qquad (14)$$

Take the second term in (13), and $\forall \mathbf{x}_1 \in \mathcal{X}$ given actions $\{\hat{U}_t\}$ it holds:

$$E[\hat{V}(\mathbf{x}_1) - V^*(\mathbf{x}_1)|\{\hat{U}_t\}] \geq E[\hat{r}_1 + \gamma V^*(\mathbf{x}_2) + \gamma(\hat{V}(\mathbf{x}_2)) - V^*(\mathbf{x}_2))$$
$$- V^*(\mathbf{x}_1)|\{\hat{U}_t\}] \geq -\alpha - \bar{\epsilon}(s^*)(\iota - \alpha) + \gamma E[\hat{V}(\mathbf{x}_2) - V^*(\mathbf{x}_2)].$$

Therefore, we can write

$$
\begin{aligned}
\gamma E[E_{\mathbf{x}_0}[\hat{V}(\mathbf{x}_1) - V^*(\mathbf{x}_1)|\{\hat{U}_t\}]] &= \gamma E_{\mathbf{x}_0}[E[\hat{V}(\mathbf{x}_1) - V^*(\mathbf{x}_1)|\{\hat{U}_t\}]] \\
&\geq \gamma\left(-\alpha - \bar{\epsilon}(s^*)(\iota - \alpha) + \gamma E_{\mathbf{x}_0}[E[\hat{V}(\mathbf{x}_2) - V^*(\mathbf{x}_2)]]\right)
\end{aligned}
\tag{15}
$$

At last, substituting (14) and (15) in (13):

$$
E_{\mathbf{x}_0}[\sum_{t=0}^{\infty} \gamma^t \hat{r}_t] \geq V^*(\mathbf{x}_0) - (\alpha + \bar{\epsilon}(s^*)(\iota - \alpha))\frac{\gamma}{1-\gamma}.
\tag{16}
$$

□

We can interpret the results of Corollary 1 in the following way. When using the exact function Γ_α, the sequence of actions produced ensures that, at all times, an action is picked such that the expected sum of rewards is always larger than some bound close to the optimal. When using the approximated $\hat{\Gamma}_\alpha^{\theta^*}$, however, we obtain from the scenario approach a maximum probability of a real point not satisfying the design condition: $\|\mathbf{x} - \mathbf{x}'\| \leq \hat{\Gamma}_\alpha^{\theta^*} - \kappa^* \wedge Q^*(\mathbf{x}', \Pi^*(\mathbf{x})) < V^*(\mathbf{x}') - \alpha$. When this happens during the execution of the c-MMDP policies it means that the agents are using delayed state information for which they do not have guarantees of performance, and the one-step-ahead value function can deviate by the worst sub-optimality gap ι.

6 Experiments

We set out now to quantify experimentally the impact of Algorithm 1 on the performance and communication requirements of a benchmark c-MMDP system. First of all, it is worth mentioning that the comparison of the proposed algorithm with existing work is not possible since, to the best of our knowledge, no previous work has dealt with the problem of reducing communication when executing learned policies in a c-MMDP system. For this reason, the results are presented such that the performance of different scenarios (in terms of different Γ_α functions) is compared with the performance of an optimal policy with continuous communication.

6.1 Benchmark: Collaborative Particle-Tag

We evaluate the proposed solution in a typical particle tag problem (or predator-prey) [20]. We consider a simple form of the problem with 2 predators and 1 prey. The environment is a 10×10 arena with discrete states, and the predators have the actions $\mathcal{U}_i = \{up, down, left, right, wait\}$ available at each time step and can only move one position at a time. The environment has no obstacles, and the prey can move to any of the 8 adjacent states after each time step. The predators get a reward of 1 when, being in adjacent states to the prey, *both* choose to move into the prey's position (tagging the prey). They get a reward of -1 when they move

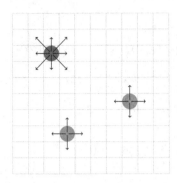

Fig. 2. Particle Tag, Predators in orange, Prey in blue. (Color figure online)

into the same position (colliding), and a reward of 0 in all other situations. A representation of the environment is presented in Fig. 2. The global state is then a vector $\mathbf{x}_t \in \{0, 1, 2, ..., 9\}^6$, concatenating the x, y position of both predators and prey. For the communication problem, we assume each agent is only able to measure its own position and the prey's. Therefore, in order to use a joint state based policy $\pi_i : \{0, 1, 2, ..., 9\}^6 \to \mathcal{U}$, at each time-step predators are required to send its own position measurement to each other.

6.2   Computation of Robustness Surrogates

With the described framework, we first compute the optimal Q^* function using a fully cooperative vanilla Q-learning algorithm [3], by considering the joint state and action space, such that $Q : \{0, 1, 2, ..., 9\}^6 \times \mathcal{U}^2 \to \mathbb{R}$. The function was computed using $\gamma = 0.97$. We then take the joint optimal policy as $\Pi^*(\mathbf{x}) = \text{argmax}_U Q^*(\mathbf{x}, U)$, and load in each predator the corresponding projection π_i^*. To evaluate the trade-off between expected rewards and communication events, we compute the function $\hat{\Gamma}_\alpha$ by solving an SVR problem as described in (10) for different values of sensitivity α. Then, the triggering condition for agents to communicate their measurements is $\|\mathbf{x}_t(i) - \hat{\mathbf{x}}_{t-1}(i)\|_\infty > \hat{\Gamma}_\alpha^{\theta^*}(\mathbf{x}) - \kappa^*$.

The hyper-parameters for the learning of the SVR models are picked through heuristics, using a sample of size $S = 10^4$ to obtain reasonable values of mis-predicted samples s^* and regression mean-squared error scores. Note that $S = \frac{1}{100}|\mathcal{X}|$. To estimate the values $\bar{\epsilon}(s^*)$, a coefficient of $\beta = 10^{-3}$ was taken, and the values were computed using the code in [11]. For more details on the computation of ρ-SVR models (or μ–SVR) [27] see the project code[1]. For more details on the computation

Figure 3 shows a representation of the obtained SVR models for different values of α, plotted over a 2D embedding of a subset of state points using a t-SNE [21] embedding. It can be seen how for larger α values, more "robust" regions appear, and with higher values of Γ_α. This illustrates how, when increasing the sensitivity, the obtained approximated $\hat{\Gamma}_\alpha^{\theta^*}$ take higher values almost everywhere in the state space, and form clusters of highly robust points.

---

[1] https://github.com/danieljarne/Event-Driven-MARL.

Fig. 3. Obtained $\hat{\Gamma}_\alpha^{\theta*}$ models on a 2D embedding.

6.3 Results

The results are presented in Table 1. We simulated in each case 1000 independent runs of 100 particle tag games, and computed the cumulative reward, number of communication events and average length of games. For the experiments, $\hat{E}[\cdot]$ is the expected value approximation (mean) of the cumulative reward over the 1000 trajectories, and in every entry we indicate the standard deviation of the samples (after $\pm$). We use $\mathcal{T}_\alpha$ as the generated trajectories (games) for a corresponding parameter α, $h(\mathcal{T}_\alpha)$ as the total sum of communication events per game for a collection of games, and $\bar{g} := \sum_{g \in \mathcal{T}_\alpha} \frac{|g|}{|\mathcal{T}_\alpha|}$ as the average length of a game measured over the collected $\mathcal{T}_\alpha$. For the obtained Q^* function, the worst optimality gap is computed to be $\iota = 1.57$.

Table 1. Simulation results

α	$\hat{E}[\sum_{t=0}^{\infty} \gamma^t r]$	$\bar{g}$	$h(\mathcal{T}_\alpha)$	$\frac{h(\mathcal{T}_\alpha)}{\bar{g}}$	$\bar{\epsilon}(s^*)$	δ
0	2.72 ± 0.50	10.72 ± 0.44	21.49 ± 0.89	2.00	-	-
0.4	2.72 ± 0.53	10.77 ± 0.44	19.13 ± 0.87	1.78	0.079	16.33
0.5	1.62 ± 0.92	12.45 ± 0.58	16.75 ± 0.85	1.35	0.148	22.39
0.6	0.99 ± 1.09	13.71 ± 0.71	14.49 ± 0.87	1.06	0.205	26.61
0.7	0.93 ± 1.08	13.74 ± 0.69	14.09 ± 0.85	1.03	0.117	26.85
0.8	0.74 ± 1.10	14.65 ± 0.80	14.11 ± 0.87	0.96	0.075	28.10
0.9	0.64 ± 1.08	14.82 ± 0.83	14.33 ± 0.88	0.96	0.097	31.69

Let us remark the difference between the 4th and 5th column in Table 1. The metric $h(\mathcal{T}_\alpha)$ is a direct measure of amount of messages for a given value of α. However, note that we are simulating a fixed number of games, and the average number of steps per game increases with α: the lack of communication causes the agents to take longer to solve the game. For this reason we add the metric $h(\mathcal{T}_\alpha)/\bar{g}$, which is a measure of total amount of messages sent versus amount of simulation steps for a fixed α (i.e. total amount of steps where a message *could* be sent). Broadly speaking, $h(\mathcal{T}_\alpha)$ compares raw amount of information shared to solve a fixed amount of games, and $h(\mathcal{T}_\alpha)/\bar{g}$ compares amount of messages per time-step (information transmission rate). Note at last that there are two collaborative players in the game, therefore a continuous communication scheme would yield $h(\mathcal{T}_\alpha)/\bar{g} = 2$.

From the experimental results we can get an qualitative image of the trade-off between communication and performance. Larger α values yield a decrease in expected cumulative reward, and a decrease in state measurements shared between agents. Note finally that in the given c-MMDP problem, the minimum reward every time step is $\min r(\mathbf{x}_t, U, \mathbf{x}_{t+1}) = -1$, therefore a lower bound for the cumulative reward is $E[\sum_{t=0}^{\infty} \gamma^t r] \geq -1\frac{\gamma}{1-\gamma} = -32.333$. Then, the performance (even for the case with $\alpha = 0.9$ remains relatively close to the optimum computed with continuous communication.

At last, let us comment on the general trend observed regarding the values of α. Recall the bound obtained in Corollary 1, and observe that for $\alpha = 0.5 \Rightarrow \delta = 22.39$. On average, $\hat{E}[V^*(\mathbf{x}_0)] \approx 2.72$ when initialising $\mathbf{x}_0$ at random (as seen on Table 1). This yields a quite conservative bound of $\hat{E}[V^*(\mathbf{x}_0)] - \delta = -19.67$ on the expected sum of rewards, while the communication events are reduced by around 22% due to the conservative computation of Γ_α. One first source of conservativeness is in Algorithm 1. When computing the exact value $\Gamma_\alpha(\mathbf{x}) = d$, it requires every point $\mathbf{x}' : \|\mathbf{x} - \mathbf{x}'\|_\infty \leq d$ to satisfy the condition in Definition 3. The number of states to be checked grows exponentially with d, and many of those states may not even be reachable from $\mathbf{x}$ by following the MDP transitions. Therefore we are effectively introducing conservativeness in cases where probably, for many points $\mathbf{x}$, we could obtain much larger values $\Gamma_\alpha(\mathbf{x})$ if we could check the transitions in the MDP. Another source of conservativeness comes from the SVR learning process and in particular, the values of κ^*. Since the states are discretised, $\|\mathbf{x}_t(i) - \hat{\mathbf{x}}_{t-1}(i)\|_\infty \in \{0, 1, 2, 3, ..., 10\}$. Therefore, the triggering condition is effectively constrained to $\|\mathbf{x}_t(i) - \hat{\mathbf{x}}_{t-1}(i)\|_\infty > \lfloor \hat{\Gamma}_\alpha^{\hat{\theta}^*}(\mathbf{x}) - \kappa^* \rfloor$, which makes it very prone to under-estimate even further the true values of $\Gamma_\alpha(\mathbf{x})$. Additionally, for most SVR models we obtained predictions $\hat{\Gamma}_\alpha^{\hat{\theta}^*}(\mathbf{x}) - \kappa^*$ that are extremely close to the real value, so small deviations in κ^* can have a significant impact in the number of communications that are triggered "unnecessarily".

7   Discussion

We have presented an approach to reduce the communication required in a collaborative reinforcement learning system when executing optimal policies in real time, while guaranteeing the discounted sum of rewards to stay within some bounds that can be adjusted through the parameters α and $\bar{\epsilon}(s^*)$ (this last one indirectly controlled by the learning of data driven approximations $\hat{\Gamma}_\alpha^{\theta^*}$). The guarantees were first derived for the case where we have access to *exact* robustness surrogates Γ_α, and extended to allow for surrogate functions learned through a *scenario approach* based SVR optimization. In the proposed experiments for a 2-player particle tag game the total communication was reduced between 10%–44% and the communication rate by 12%–52%, while keeping the expected reward sum $\hat{E}[\sum_{t=0}^{\infty} \gamma^t r] \in [0.68, 2.76]$. The conclusion to draw from this is that, in general, agents are able to solve the c-MMDP problem with delayed state information introduced through robustness surrogate triggers, resulting in a significant reduction in communication requirements. When extending these methods to larger number of agents, the main bottleneck is the computation of Γ_α. For many c-MMDPs the SVR representation may still be an efficient approach to compute them, but otherwise more efficient approaches (perhaps decentralised) could be devised.

The computation of the values $\Gamma_\alpha(\mathbf{x})$ and the learning of the SVR models for $\hat{\Gamma}_\alpha^{\theta^*}(\mathbf{x})$ introduced significant conservativeness with respect to the theoretical bounds. A possible improvement for future work could be to compute the true values $\Gamma_\alpha(\mathbf{x})$ through a Monte-Carlo based approach by sampling MDP trajectories. This would yield a much more accurate representation of how "far" agents can deviate without communicating, and the guarantees could be modified to include the possibility that the values $\Gamma_\alpha(\mathbf{x})$ are correct up to a certain probability. At last, we can come back now to the statements in Remark 1. It is now evident how having a certain physical structure in the MDP (*i.e.* transition probabilities being larger for states closer in space) would help mitigate the conservativeness. An MDP with large transition jumps with respect to the sup-norm will result in more conservative and less meaningful robustness surrogates.

Other problems that branch out of this work are the implications of learning robustness surrogate functions. These functions could be used to modify the agent policies, to sacrifice performance in favour of robustness versus communication faults or attacks. Finally, it would be insightful to compare the approaches presented in this work with ideas in the line of [10], where we can incorporate the communication as a binary action (to communicate or not) into the learning algorithm, to optimise simultaneously with the sum of rewards.

Acknowledgements. The authors want to thank Gabriel Gleizer, Giannis Delimpaltadakis and Andrea Peruffo for the useful and insightful discussions related to this work.

References

1. Ackley, D.H., Littman, M.L.: Altruism in the evolution of communication. In: Artificial Life IV, Cambridge, MA, pp. 40–48 (1994)
2. Bertsekas, D.: Distributed dynamic programming. IEEE Trans. Autom. Control **27**(3), 610–616 (1982)

3. Busoniu, L., Babuska, R., De Schutter, B.: A comprehensive survey of multiagent reinforcement learning. IEEE Trans. Syst. Man Cybern. Part C (Appl. Rev.) **38**(2), 156–172 (2008)
4. Calafiore, G.C., Campi, M.C.: The scenario approach to robust control design. IEEE Trans. Autom. Control **51**(5), 742–753 (2006)
5. Campi, M.C., Garatti, S.: Scenario optimization with relaxation: a new tool for design and application to machine learning problems. In: 2020 59th IEEE Conference on Decision and Control (CDC), pp. 2463–2468. IEEE (2020)
6. Chen, T., Zhang, K., Giannakis, G.B., Basar, T.: Communication-efficient distributed reinforcement learning. arXiv preprint arXiv:1812.03239 (2018)
7. Da Silva, F.L., Hernandez-Leal, P., Kartal, B., Taylor, M.E.: Uncertainty-aware action advising for deep reinforcement learning agents. In: Proceedings of the AAAI Conference on Artificial Intelligence, vol. 34, pp. 5792–5799 (2020)
8. Dimarogonas, D.V., Frazzoli, E., Johansson, K.H.: Distributed event-triggered control for multi-agent systems. IEEE Trans. Autom. Control **57**(5), 1291–1297 (2012). https://doi.org/10.1109/TAC.2011.2174666
9. Elvis Tsang, K.F., Johansson, K.H.: Distributed event-triggered learning-based control for nonlinear multi-agent systems. In: 2021 60th IEEE Conference on Decision and Control (CDC), pp. 3399–3405 (2021). https://doi.org/10.1109/CDC45484.2021.9683215
10. Foerster, J.N., Assael, Y.M., De Freitas, N., Whiteson, S.: Learning to communicate with deep multi-agent reinforcement learning. arXiv preprint arXiv:1605.06676 (2016)
11. Garatti, S., Campi, M.C.: Risk and complexity in scenario optimization. Math. Program. **191**, 243–279 (2019). https://doi.org/10.1007/s10107-019-01446-4
12. George, J., Gurram, P.: Distributed stochastic gradient descent with event-triggered communication. In: Proceedings of the AAAI Conference on Artificial Intelligence, vol. 34, pp. 7169–7178 (2020)
13. Hu, J., Wellman, M.P., et al.: Multiagent reinforcement learning: theoretical framework and an algorithm. In: ICML, vol. 98, pp. 242–250. Citeseer (1998)
14. Karabag, M.O., Neary, C., Topcu, U.: Planning not to talk: multiagent systems that are robust to communication loss (2022)
15. Kim, D., et al.: Learning to schedule communication in multi-agent reinforcement learning. arXiv preprint arXiv:1902.01554 (2019)
16. Kok, J.R., Vlassis, N.: Sparse cooperative Q-learning. In: Proceedings of the Twenty-First International Conference on Machine Learning, p. 61 (2004)
17. Lillicrap, T.P., et al.: Continuous control with deep reinforcement learning. arXiv preprint arXiv:1509.02971 (2015)
18. Lin, J., Dzeparoska, K., Zhang, S.Q., Leon-Garcia, A., Papernot, N.: On the robustness of cooperative multi-agent reinforcement learning. In: 2020 IEEE Security and Privacy Workshops (SPW), pp. 62–68. IEEE (2020)
19. Lin, Y., et al.: A communication-efficient multi-agent actor-critic algorithm for distributed reinforcement learning. In: 2019 IEEE 58th Conference on Decision and Control (CDC), pp. 5562–5567. IEEE (2019)
20. Lowe, R., Wu, Y., Tamar, A., Harb, J., Abbeel, P., Mordatch, I.: Multi-agent actor-critic for mixed cooperative-competitive environments. arXiv preprint arXiv:1706.02275 (2017)
21. Van der Maaten, L., Hinton, G.: Visualizing data using t-SNE. J. Mach. Learn. Res. **9**(11), 2579–2605 (2008)

22. Mazo, M., Tabuada, P.: On event-triggered and self-triggered control over sensor/actuator networks. In: 2008 47th IEEE Conference on Decision and Control, pp. 435–440. IEEE (2008)
23. Mnih, V., et al.: Playing Atari with deep reinforcement learning. arXiv preprint arXiv:1312.5602 (2013)
24. Nowé, A., Vrancx, P., De Hauwere, Y.M.: Game theory and multi-agent reinforcement learning. In: Wiering, M., van Otterlo, M. (eds.) Reinforcement Learning. ALO, vol. 12, pp. 441–470. Springer, Heidelberg (2012). https://doi.org/10.1007/978-3-642-27645-3_14
25. Panait, L., Luke, S.: Cooperative multi-agent learning: the state of the art. Auton. Agent. Multi-Agent Syst. 11(3), 387–434 (2005). https://doi.org/10.1007/s10458-005-2631-2
26. Sahoo, A., Xu, H., Jagannathan, S.: Neural network-based event-triggered state feedback control of nonlinear continuous-time systems. IEEE Trans. Neural Netw. Learn. Syst. 27(3), 497–509 (2015)
27. Schölkopf, B., Bartlett, P., Smola, A., Williamson, R.C.: Shrinking the tube: a new support vector regression algorithm. In: Advances in Neural Information Processing Systems, vol. 11 (1998)
28. Sen, S., Sekaran, M., Hale, J., et al.: Learning to coordinate without sharing information. In: AAAI, vol. 94, pp. 426–431 (1994)
29. Solowjow, F., Trimpe, S.: Event-triggered learning. Automatica 117, 109009 (2020)
30. Szer, D., Charpillet, F.: Improving coordination with communication in multi-agent reinforcement learning. In: 16th IEEE International Conference on Tools with Artificial Intelligence, pp. 436–440. IEEE (2004)
31. Tabuada, P.: Event-triggered real-time scheduling of stabilizing control tasks. IEEE Trans. Autom. Control 52(9), 1680–1685 (2007)
32. Tan, M.: Multi-agent reinforcement learning: independent vs. cooperative agents. In: Proceedings of the Tenth International Conference on Machine Learning, pp. 330–337 (1993)
33. Vamvoudakis, K.G., Ferraz, H.: Model-free event-triggered control algorithm for continuous-time linear systems with optimal performance. Automatica 87, 412–420 (2018)
34. Van Hasselt, H., Guez, A., Silver, D.: Deep reinforcement learning with double Q-learning. In: Proceedings of the AAAI Conference on Artificial Intelligence, vol. 30 (2016)
35. Watkins, C.J., Dayan, P.: Q-learning. Mach. Learn. 8(3–4), 279–292 (1992). https://doi.org/10.1007/BF00992698
36. Xue, W., Qiu, W., An, B., Rabinovich, Z., Obraztsova, S., Yeo, C.K.: Mis-spoke or mis-lead: achieving robustness in multi-agent communicative reinforcement learning. arXiv preprint arXiv:2108.03803 (2021)
37. Zhang, C., Lesser, V.: Coordinating multi-agent reinforcement learning with limited communication. In: Proceedings of the 2013 International Conference on Autonomous Agents and Multi-Agent Systems, pp. 1101–1108 (2013)
38. Zhong, X., Ni, Z., He, H., Xu, X., Zhao, D.: Event-triggered reinforcement learning approach for unknown nonlinear continuous-time system. In: 2014 International Joint Conference on Neural Networks (IJCNN), pp. 3677–3684. IEEE (2014)

Learning that Grid-Convenience Does Not Hurt Resilience in the Presence of Uncertainty

Mathis Niehage$^{(\boxtimes)}$ ⓘ and Anne Remke ⓘ

University of Münster, Einsteinstr. 62, 48149 Münster, Germany
{mathis.niehage,anne.remke}@uni-muenster.de

Abstract. *Grid-convenience* is often seen as conflicting with other measures of interest, such as *self-use* or *resilience*. We adopt a Hybrid Petri net model (HPnG) of a smart home with local power generation, local storage and different battery management strategies in the presence of power outages. Applying Q-learning allows us to derive schedulers with an optimal loading percentages for the battery. We show that (near-)optimal schedulers can be synthesized for accurate predictions, which achieve grid-convenience without decreasing resilience and self-use. Introducing uncertainty to the predictions of solar production shows that a good balance can be maintained between such measures, when allowing the system to adapt the loading percentage during the day.

Keywords: Stochastic hybrid model · resilience · case study

1 Introduction

Resilience in the energy sector is defined as the ability of a power system to withstand initial shock, rapidly recover from disruptions and apply measures to mitigate the impact of similar events in the future [5]. With the increasing amount of decentralized solar production and local storage, peak feed-in rates pose a threat to the stable operation of the power grid. Hence, such peaks should be avoided, e.g. by so-called grid-convenient schedulers, which charge local storage more evenly over the day. However, in the presence of grid failures, resilient schedulers need to ensure that local storage contains sufficient back-up energy to satisfy the local demand in case of a power outage.

Different (dis)charging strategies for a smart home with local storage have been evaluated in [11,12] for simulated production and consumption profiles and a linear battery model. Accurate predictions of production and demand at individual households have a huge potential to better balance the energy load, as they can feed into data-driven control strategies for local storage [24]. However, uncertainty in predictions can lead to less resilient system states. A mismatch between forecast and realization can e.g., lead to insufficient energy in storage, which results in less resilient systems in case of a power outage.

© Springer Nature Switzerland AG 2022
S. Bogomolov and D. Parker (Eds.): FORMATS 2022, LNCS 13465, pp. 298–306, 2022.
https://doi.org/10.1007/978-3-031-15839-1_17

This paper applies a machine learning approach to obtain resilient and grid-convenient schedulers for batteries in smart homes. In practice, this technique has the potential to improve control of local storage by automatically updating the amount of renewable energy that is fed into the battery.

We use the Hybrid Petri net model from [11], which models the control of local storage in a smart home. The model includes two power sources, i.e. the local power generation as well as the power grid and explicitly incorporates the battery and any losses that occur due to charging and discharging the battery. Furthermore, power outages with a randomly distributed duration may occur, during which the current charge of the battery is used to power the house. Recently, we proposed Q-learning to compute optimal schedulers within a discrete-event simulation (DES) [16]. This probabilistic approach applies discretization of the continuous state-space of the model under study and then finds a near-optimal scheduler, which maximizes a specific property, defined in stochastic time logic (STL). We apply these findings to the above mentioned model to obtain schedulers which maximize *grid-convenience*, while ensuring resilience. In a second step, the model is statistically simulated [20] to analyze the impact of uncertainty on the resilience of the resulting system.

This paper learns schedulers with respect to grid-convenience, self-use and resilience. While [11] was able to identify optimal schedulers through a state-space exploration, this paper applies Q-learning to automatically and efficiently identify appropriate schedulers. Furthermore, we are able to show that the learned parameters strive a good balance between different measures of interest.

Related Work. Resilience on local energy systems only recently became a topic of investigation [5,15]. Methods from data science and machine learning have been used to predict energy production [7] and energy demand, e.g., via Deep Learning [2]. However, the adverse effect which imprecise predictions may have on the resilience of the power grid is usually not considered. Reinforcement learning was used on MDPs (e.g. [10]), to deal with stochastic behavior [1,9], or with linear-time logic specifications (e.g. [1,8,22]). Deep reinforcement learning is used in [25] on a MDP, which models a smart home, to minimize the energy cost while holding a comfortable temperature range. Applying machine learning on (infinite-state) stochastic hybrid systems in continuous time requires discretization, as e.g., formalized in [13]. Learning for stochastic hybrid systems is considered from a formal perspective in a discrete-time setting in [14]. An abstraction of the continuous state-space is used for learning, providing guarantees on the error of the final result. More generally, an overview on challenges related to learning is presented in [4].

Outline. Section 2 describes the case study in more detail, Sect. 3 repeats the methodology and Sect. 4 presents and discusses the learned results. Section 5 concludes the paper and hints to further work.

2 Case Study

We adopt the *Extended Battery Model* (EBM), illustrated in Fig. 1a (c.f. [11]), by including the *Random Occurrence of Disasters* (ROOD). Thus our model allows multiple random grid failures and repair times with a random duration.

Similar to [6,11], we use the standard demand profile E1a, from EDSN [3] for the Dutch market with a yearly demand of 3 kWh and a granularity of 15 min. The production profile for the PV-installation is obtained from the internet tool PVWatts by the National Renewable Energy Laboratory for a sunny day in summer [18], as shown in Fig. 1b.

Battery management controls (dis)charging according to a predefined strategy. This paper solely considers *greedy* discharging which drains the battery when the demand is greater than the production. Charging follows the *Delayed Loading* strategy, which performed best concerning grid-convenience in [6,11]. This strategy only stores a certain amount, i.e. the loading percentage, of the produced solar energy in the battery and forwards the rest to the grid. This ensures that the feed-in energy is distributed more evenly over the day and keeps the gradient of the feed-in rate lower. A scheduler determines the loading percentage forwarded to the battery. [11] precomputes the scheduler via a design-space exploration if the production- and demand-profiles are known and the scheduler only chooses one loading percentage during the day. As, we aim to learn near-optimal schedulers, a nondeterministic choice between different loading percentages is included into the model, possibly multiple times during a day.

Measures of interest are expressed in STL [21]. Since we always serve the local demand before charging the battery or feeding into the grid, self-use simplifies to reaching a state where the battery is full once a day:

$$\Phi_{selfuse} = tt\ U^{[0,24]}(SoC = batteryCapacity). \tag{1}$$

We define resilience as the ability to cope with multiple grid failures without reaching a state where no power is available over the considered time t_{max}:

$$\Phi_{res} = \neg(tt\ U^{[0,t_{max}]}(battery_{empty} \wedge \neg grid_{on})). \tag{2}$$

Grid-convenience aims at minimizing the difference between two successive feed-in rates into the grid. Note that, STL only allows the comparison of continuous values to a constant, hence grid-convenience cannot be expressed in STL. The maximum gradient between two subsequent decisions at times t_1 and t_2 is

$$G_{(t_1,t_2)} = \max_{t\in[t_1,t_2]} grad(t),\ \text{with}\ grad(t) = |feed_{in}(t) - feed_{in}(t + \epsilon)|. \tag{3}$$

3 Methodology

Applying the approach presented in [16], a discretized representation with a finite state space $\mathcal{S}$ and action space $\mathcal{A}$ of the Hybrid Petri net model, presented

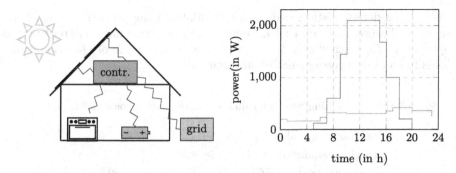

(a) Model of a smart home with battery, (b) Estimated production (blue) and de-
connected to the power grid.   mand (orange) for a sunny day in summer.

Fig. 1. Case study: Extended battery model

in [11], is generated. The function $Q\colon \mathcal{S} \times \mathcal{A} \to \mathbb{R}$ then learns the optimal action-
value function based on the reward assigned to that action in a specific state.
Discretization is used for learning the Q-function, while the evaluation of a STL
property Φ is done on the continuous model via statistical model checking, which
returns an estimate of the probability that Φ holds. We rely on the implementation of the Q-learning approach in the statistical model checker HYPEG [19],
which support Hybrid Petri nets with general transitions.

A predefined number of *training runs* is performed to update the Q-function
for the state-action pairs just observed. Initially, the Q-function is arbitrary for
all $(s, a) \in \mathcal{S} \times \mathcal{A}$. For each training run the state $s \in \mathcal{S}$ is set to its initial
value, potentially chosen from a set. Afterwards the system is simulated until a
terminal state is reached, which here always corresponds to reaching the time
bound. At each state $s \in \mathcal{S}$ that requires a decision, an available action $a \in \mathcal{A}$ is
selected which leads to a state s'. Additionally, a reward $R\colon \mathcal{S} \to \mathbb{R}$ is defined
as a function of s'. We compose the reward of the satisfaction of a STL formula
and the maximum gradient between s and s'. $Q(s, a)$ is then updated as:

$$Q(s, a) = Q(s, a) + \alpha \left(R(s') + \gamma \max_{\tilde{a}} Q(s', \tilde{a}) - Q(s, a) \right). \tag{4}$$

The current value $Q(s, a)$ increases with the learning rate $\alpha \in [0, 1]$ times the sum
of the reward and the potential reward from state s', which in turn is discounted
by $\gamma \in [0, 1]$, minus the current value of the learning function. The open interval
of gamma is relaxed to the closed range due to episodic learning. The potential
reward is determined as the maximum value of Q over all possible actions.

Q-learning can use different *policies* to choose an action during the training
process. For example, the ϵ-greedy policy chooses the action which results in the
maximum value of Q with probability $1 - \epsilon$ and an arbitrary action otherwise
[23]. Thus, every action will be sampled infinitely often assuming an infinite
number of episodes, which ensures the convergence to the optimal action-value
function. Then taking the action with the maximum value at a given state grants

the optimal deterministic scheduler after infinitely many runs [23]. It has been shown in Theorem 3.6 [16] that a vanishing discretization has no impact on the optimality of the scheduler. Together with the convergence of Q-learning, this leads to an overall convergence of our approach.

Table 1. Training results for different optimization goals and t_{max}.

optimization goal	$R_{(0,24)}$	$\Phi_{selfuse}$	$R_{(0,24)} \wedge \Phi_{selfuse}$
charging parameter	25%	$\geq 30\%$	30%
max gradient	567.0	[580.0,1794.0]	580.0
max battery SoC	2540.4	3000.0	3000.0
training time	3.6 s	3.1 s	2.7 s
simulation time	0.5 s	0.6 s	0.5 s
simulation runs	1000	1000	1000

4   Results

In the following we show, that our learning approach is able to identify optimal schedulers. First, we reproduce results from [11] using the model without grid failures. We consider delayed loading (after 9 a.m.), where the scheduler chooses a loading percentage once, i.e., before loading is initiated.

To allow automated learning, loading percentages have been discretized to bins of 5%, resulting in the action set $\{0, 5, 10, \ldots, 100\}$. Table 1 shows the training results for different optimization goals, i.e., minimizing the feed-in gradient (c.f. Eq. 3) or maximizing self-use, i.e., the probability that $\Phi_{selfuse}$ holds. We also investigate a combination of grid-convenience and self-use. The reward function depends on the optimization goal, i.e. for a goal formulated in STL, a positive reward is distributed if that formula is satisfied. For the goal grid-convenience Eq. 3 defines the reward. In case the goal combines both, the reward function weights both inputs. Learning was based on 5000 training runs with a learning rate decreasing from $\alpha = 0.1$, a discount factor 1 and ϵ-greedy parameter 0.15. When minimizing the gradient, the learned optimal scheduler chooses as charging percentage 25%, which is not sufficient to completely charge the battery, as indicated by a maximum battery state-of-charge (SoC) of 2540.4.

When maximizing the battery SoC all charging percentages $\geq 30\%$ achieve a full battery and are hence rated equally when training is performed long enough. The maximum gradient which occurs for the defined parameter setting, equals $G_{(0,24)}$ (c.f. Eq. 3). It increases with the charging percentage and ranges from 580 for 30% charging to 1794.0 for 100% (c.f. Table 1). When training for a combination of grid-convenience and self-use, the scheduler learned 30% as optimal parameter, which results in a fully charged battery and a maximum gradient

Table 2. Training results for maximizing $\Phi_{selfuse}$ and minimizing $\sum G_{(t_i, t_i + \Delta_t)}$ for $t_i \in \{x | x = i \cdot \Delta_t \leq 48, i \in \mathbb{N}_0\}$ and $\Delta_t \in \{1, 6, 24\}$ and $t_{max} = 48$.

decisions	every 24 h	every 6 h	every 1 h
max gradient	580.0	655.2	897.0
avg gradient	324.0	288.6	278.3
max bat. SoC	3000.0	3000.0	3000.0
train time	142.2 s	695.7 s	2548.2 s
train runs	100 000	500 000	1 000 000
sim. time	1.5 s	1.5 s	2.5 s
sim. runs	1000	1000	1000

of 580. Training and simulation times are similar for the different charging percentages. The predefined minimum number of simulation runs of 1000 achieves the required precision, as the model does not contain stochasticity, yet.

The optimal loading percentage chosen in [11] is 31% is not contained in our action set, due to the chosen discretization. Instead, we obtain 30% as optimal charging parameter. While it is possible to recompute the results by changing the discretization, we focus on learning reasonable schedulers. Our discretization currently results in 21 loading percentages as opposed to only 4 in [11].

Multiple Decisions. We now extend the model, such that the scheduler may adapt the charging percentage during the day, and optimize towards a combination of grid-convenience and self-use. Delayed loading (after 9 a.m.) with loading percentages between 0% to 100% and step-size of 5% forms the action set of the scheduler. We extend the time horizon to 48 h, so that the second day starts with a different initial battery SoC. Table 2 shows results when adapting the charging parameter every 24, 6 or 1 h. Actions are taken only if charging is possible. The number of training runs increases with the number of actions, the training parameters remain equal to Table 1. In all cases the maximum battery SoC is reached and hence, probability 1 is estimated for self-use.

The maximum gradient in Table 2 corresponds to the largest observed maximum gradient, i.e. for 24 h $\max\{G_{(0,24)}, G_{(24,48)}\}$. The average gradient is computed over all gradients occurring between discrete events with time greater zero. While the average gradient decreases with more decisions, the maximum gradient increases. The reason lies in the reward structure, where the influence of a single maximum gradient decreases with the number of decisions. Hence, the system learns to accept few large gradients, to minimize the average gradient.

Training times increase considerably with the number of decisions, as the action set becomes larger. Simulation times only increase slightly and the number of simulation runs equals the minimum required number in all cases since the model does not contain uncertainty, yet.

Uncertainty is introduced in the form of random grid failures and repairs. The former follows an *Exponential* [0.025] distribution and the latter is *Uniform*[2, 5]. We allow the scheduler to adapt the charging percentage every hour considering a step-size of 5% over 48 h. Training is performed on the adapted model using the predicted production profiles without uncertainties. Since the impact of grid failures and uncertainties becomes more relevant when less solar production is available, we reduce production (and its prediction) to 75%.

We investigate the impact of inaccurate predictions on resilience, by introducing a realization of the production which follows a folded normal distribution. For every hour, the prediction is used as mean and the impact of different standard deviations {0, 10, 20}% w.r.t. that mean is investigated.

Table 3 shows the results for maximizing Φ_{res} and for optimizing the combination of resilience and grid-convenience. For both optimization goals we perform 2.5 million training runs on the model without uncertain productions and use the learned schedulers for statistical model checking models with {0, 10, 20}% deviation. In contrast to the previously evaluated model versions, the 99% confidence level and the interval width 0.02 become relevant in the model with grid failures and uncertain predictions, as indicated by the required number of simulation runs to achieve this precision. Simulation times increase slightly when uncertainty is introduced to the prediction. Furthermore, we indicate in Table 3 the average of the maximum gradient and the average gradient computed over the statistically different simulation runs.

Table 3. Results for charging optimized w.r.t. Φ_{res} and grid-convenience on the model including grid failures and repairs. Realizations of production are evaluated with a standard deviation of {0, 10, 20}% of the production mean.

deviation	0%		10%		20%	
optim. goal	Φ_{res}	$\Phi_{res} \wedge$ $\sum G_{(t_1,t_2)}$	Φ_{res}	$\Phi_{res} \wedge$ $\sum G_{(t_1,t_2)}$	Φ_{res}	$\Phi_{res} \wedge$ $\sum G_{(t_1,t_2)}$
mean p	0.792	0.789	0.799	0.793	0.799	0.792
avg max gradient	1171.8	758.8	1189.6	1085.0	1294.1	1214.2
avg avg gradient	227.2	171.9	299.6	267.2	324.4	303.8
avg max battery SoC	3000.0	3000.0	3000.0	3000.0	3000.0	3000.0
train time	8765.4 s	8885.5 s	n.a.	n.a.	n.a.	n.a.
sim. time	37.0 s	39.9 s	42.5 s	44.9 s	41.4 s	44.4 s
sim. runs	10 953	11 068	10 655	10 908	10 659	10 951

The estimated mean probabilities of Φ_{res} for the production mean of 75% all lie within each others confidence intervals. Hence, we state that Q-learning is able to maintain a high resilience, even in the presence of a high probability of grid failures and uncertain production. However, to achieve this level of resilience, the gradients increase with more uncertainty in the production. The largest average maximum gradient in Table 3 occurs when maximizing resilience and production is 20% uncertain. A higher degree of uncertainty also leads to smaller differences between the results for the two optimization goals. This indicates that the maximum gradients occur more often in case the predictions are less accurate, hence forming a larger percentage of the average gradient.

The SoC reaches 3000 for all considered scenarios, i.e. selfuse is maintained even though not optimized for, as resilience benefits from a full battery.

5 Reproducibility and Conclusions

We have shown that Q-learning can be used to learn loading percentages for local storage which achieve grid-convenience, without decreasing self-use. Even when considering random grid failures and inaccurate predictions, the learned parameters are able to maintain a good balance between resilience and grid-convenience. The results have been obtained on a Intel Core i5-8250U (4 × 1.6–3.4 GHz) system with 16 GB memory and the artifact is available at [17]. Future work will replace the linear battery model by the more realistic kinetic battery model and evaluate the applicability of Q-learning in real time to control local storage using data-driven charging strategies.

References

1. Cai, M., Peng, H., Li, Z., Kan, Z.: Learning-based probabilistic LTL motion planning with environment and motion uncertainties. IEEE Trans. Autom. Control **66**(5), 2386–2392 (2021)
2. del Real, A.J., Dorado, F., Durán, J.: Energy demand forecasting using deep learning: applications for the French grid. Energies **13**(9), 2242 (2020)
3. EDSN: EDSN demand profiles. http://www.edsn.nl/verbruiksprofielen/
4. Fulton, N., Hunt, N., Hoang, N., Das, S.: Formal verification of end-to-end learning in cyber-physical systems: progress and challenges. arXiv:2006.09181 (2020)
5. Gasser, P., et al.: A review on resilience assessment of energy systems. Sustain. Resilient Infrastruct. **6**(5), 1–27 (2019)
6. Ghasemieh, H., Haverkort, B.R., Jongerden, M.R., Remke, A.: Energy resilience modelling for smart houses. In: Proceedings of the 45th Annual IEEE/IFIP International Conference on Dependable Systems and Networks (DSN 2015), pp. 275–286 (2015)
7. Gieseke, F., Igel, C.: Training big random forests with little resources. In: 24th ACM SIGKDD International Conference on Knowledge Discovery & Data Mining, KDD 2018, pp. 1445–1454. ACM (2018)
8. Hahn, E.M., Perez, M., Schewe, S., Somenzi, F., Trivedi, A., Wojtczak, D.: Faithful and effective reward schemes for model-free reinforcement learning of omega-regular objectives. In: Hung, D.V., Sokolsky, O. (eds.) ATVA 2020. LNCS, vol. 12302, pp. 108–124. Springer, Cham (2020). https://doi.org/10.1007/978-3-030-59152-6_6
9. Hasanbeig, M., Kantaros, Y., Abate, A., Kroening, D., Pappas, G.J., Lee, I.: Reinforcement learning for temporal logic control synthesis with probabilistic satisfaction guarantees. In: IEEE Conference on Decision and Control (CDC), pp. 5338–5343. IEEE, Nice, France (2019)

10. Hasanbeig, M., Abate, A., Kroening, D.: Cautious reinforcement learning with logical constraints. In: Proceedings of the 19th International Conference on Autonomous Agents and Multiagent Systems, AAMAS 2020, Auckland, New Zealand, 9–13 May 2020, pp. 483–491. International Foundation for Autonomous Agents and Multiagent Systems (2020)

11. Huels, J., Remke, A.: Energy storage in smart homes: grid-convenience versus self-use and survivability. In: 24th IEEE International Symposium on Modeling, Analysis and Simulation of Computer and Telecommunication Systems, MASCOTS 2016, London, United Kingdom, 19–21 September 2016, pp. 385–390 (2016)

12. Jongerden, M., Hüls, J., Remke, A., Haverkort, B.R.: Does your domestic photovoltaic energy system survive grid outages? Energies **9**(9), 736:1–736:17 (2016)

13. Junges, S., Jansen, N., Katoen, J.-P., Topcu, U., Zhang, R., Hayhoe, M.: Model checking for safe navigation among humans. In: McIver, A., Horvath, A. (eds.) QEST 2018. LNCS, vol. 11024, pp. 207–222. Springer, Cham (2018). https://doi.org/10.1007/978-3-319-99154-2_13

14. Lavaei, A., Somenzi, F., Soudjani, S., Trivedi, A., Zamani, M.: Formal controller synthesis for continuous-space MDPs via model-free reinforcement learning. In: 2020 ACM/IEEE 11th International Conference on Cyber-Physical Systems (ICCPS), pp. 98–107. IEEE, Sydney, Australia (2020)

15. Mola, M., Feofilovs, M., Romagnoli, F.: Energy resilience: research trends at urban, municipal and country levels. Energy Procedia **147**, 104–113 (2018)

16. Niehage, M., Hartmanns, A., Remke, A.: Learning optimal decisions for stochastic hybrid systems. In: 19th ACM-IEEE International Conference on Formal Methods and Models for System Design, MEMOCODE 2021. ACM (2021)

17. Niehage, M., Remke, A.: Learning that grid-convenience does not hurt resilience in the presence of uncertainty (artifact) (2022). https://doi.org/10.5281/zenodo.6840881

18. NREL: PVWatts. http://pvwatts.nrel.gov/index.php

19. Pilch, C., Edenfeld, F., Remke, A.: HYPEG: statistical model checking for hybrid petri nets: tool paper. In: EAI International Conference on Performance Evaluation Methodologies and Tools (VALUETOOLS), pp. 186–191. ACM Press (2017)

20. Pilch, C., Remke, A.: Statistical model checking for hybrid petri nets with multiple general transitions. In: 2017 47th IEEE/IFIP International Conference on Dependable Systems & Networks, DSN, pp. 475–486. IEEE (2017)

21. Pilch, C., Remke, A.: Statistical model checking for hybrid petri nets with multiple general transitions. In: Annual IEEE/IFIP International Conference on Dependable Systems and Networks (DSN), pp. 475–486. IEEE (2017)

22. Sadigh, D., Kim, E.S., Coogan, S., Sastry, S.S., Seshia, S.A.: A learning based approach to control synthesis of Markov decision processes for linear temporal logic specifications. In: IEEE Conference on Decision and Control, pp. 1091–1096. IEEE (2014)

23. Sutton, R.S., Barto, A.G.: Reinforcement Learning: An Introduction. Adaptive Computation and Machine Learning Series, 2nd edn. The MIT Press, Cambridge (2018)

24. Tagawa, Y., et al.: Day-ahead scheduling for supply-demand-storage balancing - model predictive generation with interval prediction of photovoltaics. In: 2015 European Control Conference (ECC), pp. 247–252 (2015)

25. Yu, L., et al.: Deep reinforcement learning for smart home energy management. IEEE Internet Things J. **7**(4), 2751–2762 (2020)

Author Index

André, Étienne 200
Aréchiga, Nikos 153
Asarin, Eugene 65

Bouyer, Patricia 16

Cantoni, Michael 136
Chen, Hongkai 117

Davoren, J. M. 136
DeCastro, Jonathan 153
Degorre, Aldric 65
Desu, Surya Sai Teja 98

Eleftheriadis, Charis 237

Gastin, Paul 16
Goeminne, Aline 183
Grosen, Thomas Møller 43

Hamilton, Nathaniel P. 258
Herbreteau, Frédéric 16
Hoxha, Bardh 221

Jacobo Inclán, Bernardo 65
Jarne Ornia, Daniel 281
Johnson, Taylor T. 221, 258

Karagulle, Ruya 153
Katsaros, Panagiotis 237
Kauffman, Sean 43
Kekatos, Nikolaos 237

Larsen, Kim Guldstrand 43
Lin, Shan 117
Liu, Jun 80
Luca, Florian 3

Main, James C. A. 165
Manzanas Lopez, Diego 258
Marinho, Dylan 200
Markey, Nicolas 183
Mazo Jr., Manuel 281
Meng, Yiming 80
Musau, Patrick 258

Niehage, Mathis 298

Ouaknine, Joël 3
Ozay, Necmiye 153

Paoletti, Nicola 117
Petrucci, Laure 200
Prokhorov, Danil 221

Randour, Mickael 165
Rao, M. V. Panduranga 98
Remke, Anne 298

Sankur, Ocan 16, 183
Selvaratnam, Daniel 136
Shames, Iman 136
Smolka, Scott A. 117
Sproston, Jeremy 165
Srivastava, Anubhav 98
Srivathsan, B. 16

Tran, Hoang-Dung 221
Tripakis, Stavros 237

van de Pol, Jaco 200

Worrell, James 3

Yamaguchi, Tom 221
Yang, Xiaodong 221

Zimmermann, Martin 43

Printed in the United States
by Baker & Taylor Publisher Services